KIRIUM FORMULA ONE
MULTIFUNCTIONAL DIGITAL CHRONOGRAPH

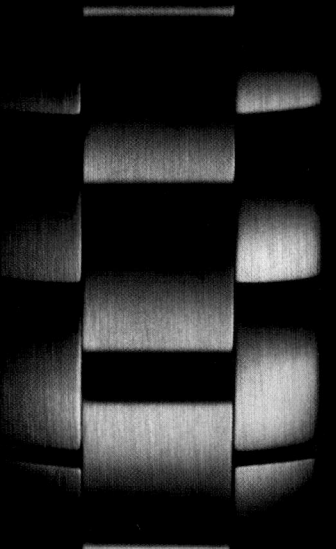

www.tagheuer.com

THE ORIGINAL ANNUAL OF THE WORLD'S FINEST WRISTWATCHES®

First published in the United States of America in 2002 by

Tourbillon International, LLC.
11 West 25th Street, 8th floor
New York, NY 10010
Tel: +1 (212) 627-7732 - Telefax +1 (212) 627-9093
Website: www.watches2002.com

CHAIRMAN
Joseph Zerbib

CHIEF EXECUTIVE OFFICER & PUBLISHER
Caroline Childers

EDITORIAL DIRECTOR
Maurizio Zinelli

ITALIAN EDITOR
Renata Pescatori

U.S. EDITOR
Roberta Naas

In association with **RIZZOLI** INTERNATIONAL PUBLICATIONS INC.

300 Park Avenue South
New York, NY 10010
John Brancati, VICE PRESIDENT & GENERAL MANAGER, RIZZOLI BOOKSTORES

Distributed all over the world by: Rizzoli International, St. Martin's Press

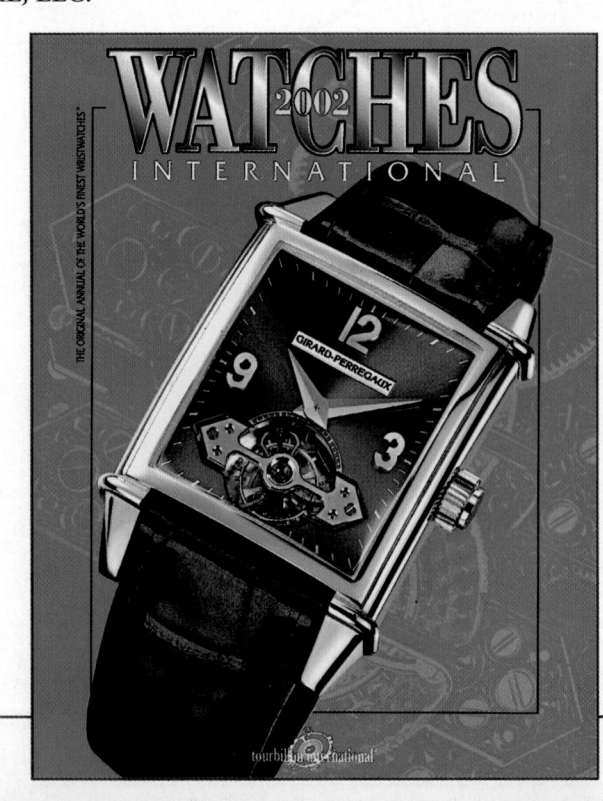

What is even more golden than silence?

Master Grande Memovox

Our master-watchmakers, such as Eric Coudray, head of our workshop "Horlogerie Perpétuelle", relish in reaching beyond the frontiers of fine horology. They have now achieved the technical feat of combining the two functions of perpetual calendar and alarm into a single, exceptional movement of 349 parts. A tribute to time in all its dimensions, the timepiece displays the year, month, date, day, phase of the moon and the twenty-four hour cycle. The crystalline sound of the alarm is created by a tiny hammer striking a coil... and by craftsmen skilled in the secrets of metallurgy. The Master Grande Memovox thus adds a new chapter to Jaeger-LeCoultre's history of technical innovation. And its pure note, in harmony with its elegant lines, will make your next appointment music to your ears.

JAEGER-LeCOULTRE

Facts

520. It sounds like the name of a BMW sedan or perhaps the code name of a future AIRBUS wide-body aircraft born to shatter all previous passenger-capacity records. Not at all. It's the total number of pages in this third issue of *Watches International 2002*. And with regard to records, this annual will probably set up a couple of them:

- Bigger: A massive increase in page quantity (+74.5 %) in only two years; we started with just 298 pages in April 2000!

- Better: *Watches International 2002* is filled with the highest number of prestigious models ever to be featured in an international publication exclusively devoted to wristwatches and to their lovers. This edition also includes Group Profiles, new and exclusive to *Watches International 2002*. Like for anyone who competes for a better performance, these numbers are a physiological phenomenon for *Watches International 2002*.

In our case, our rising success is due to the never-ending amount of information and industry news made available to us by watchmakers and researchers; and also, naturally, due to the growing interest this annual has generated all around the world since its first introduction.

Maurizio Zinelli
Editorial Director

A Time for Thanks

With the 2002 issue of *Watches International*, my team and myself begin a season of gratitude and thanks, and dedicate this publication in remembrance of the unspeakable events of September 11, 2001.

Because of the personal concerns and support from you, dear watchmakers, companies, associates and readers around the world, I am fortunate enough to continue to be inspired by the life around me. Producing *Watches International 2002* has been one of the most enlightening experiences of my life as a publisher.

Upon publication of this annual, made possible by you, I am very happy to have the opportunity to continue your generosity by donating a portion of this book's proceeds to U.S. crisis foundations and to several charities worldwide.

I thank each of you for your patience, your trust and continued support. With all good wishes of peace and freedom to you, your families and the ones you love.

Caroline Childers
Publisher & CEO

de GRISOGONO®
GENEVE

INSTRUMENTO
DOPPIO
by de GRISOGONO

Be late. Time is a luxury.

Concord Watch Company, SA
35 Rue de Nidau
CH 2501 Bienne, Switzerland
41 32 329 3400
concord-watch.com

CONCORD.

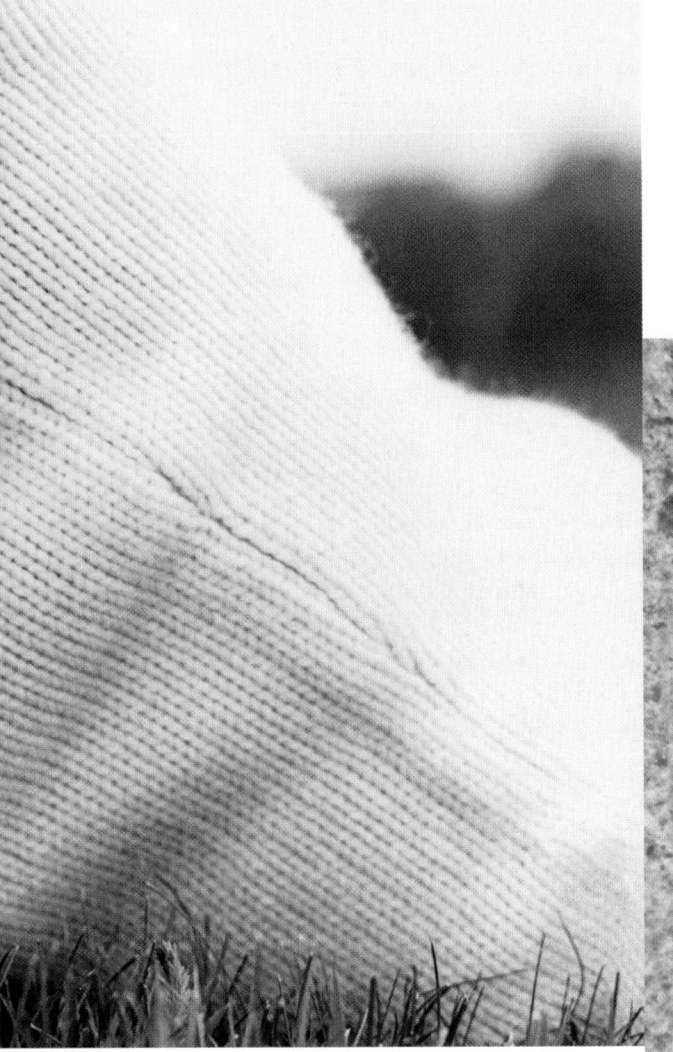

The Concord La Scala™ Chronograph
in stainless steel with diamonds
and pastel alligator strap.

THE ORIGINAL ANNUAL OF THE WORLD'S FINEST WRISTWATCHES ®

TOURBILLON INTERNATIONAL, LLC.
HEAD OFFICE, ADMINISTRATION, ADVERTISING SALES
11 West 25th Street, 8th Floor, New York, NY 10010
T: +1 (212) 627-7732   Fax: +1 (212) 627-9093

EDITORIAL DIVISION, SUBSCRIPTIONS & ORDERS
Via Pietro Maestri 3, 00191 Rome, Italy
E-mail: tourbillon@tourbillon.it
T: +39 (06) 3294-976   Fax: +39 (06) 3294-977

CHAIRMAN   Joseph Zerbib

CHIEF EXECUTIVE OFFICER & PUBLISHER
Caroline Childers   E-mail: cchilders@bway.net

EDITORIAL DIRECTOR
Maurizio Zinelli   E-mail: zinelli@tourbillon.it

ITALIAN EDITOR
Renata Pescatori   E-mail: pescatori@tourbillon.it

U.S. EDITOR   Roberta Naas

MANAGING EDITOR   Elizabeth Kindt

ASSOCIATE EDITORS
Kurt R. Schmidt, Caroline Ruiz, Claire Eisner

CONTRIBUTING EDITORS
Ruth Katz, Dominique Fléchon, Léa Franciosi, Barbara Notarangelo,
Verena Fisher, Maurizio M. Alessi, Donatella Aragozzini,
Maria Teresa Steri, Gabriele Marconi, Alessandro Lodolini,
Daniele Conti, Antonia Fabiano, Francesca di Pasquale

TRANSLATIONS   Igino Schraffl

ART DIRECTOR   Mutsumi Hyuga

COVER BY   Franca Vitali

PRE-PRESS & COLOR TECHNICIAN   Andrea D'Autilia

PHOTOGRAPHERS
Corinto Marianelli, Studio Sergio Bortolotti,
Igor Perchuk of Image Source Productions
PHOTOGRAPHIC ARCHIVES, PROPERTY OF EDITORIALE TOURBILLON SRL
AND BW PUBLISHING ASSOCIATES, INC.

WEBMASTER
Dimitri Darseyne   E-mail: impakt42@yahoo.com

DISTRIBUTION
Rizzoli International Publications
Antonio Polito, CEO
John Brancati, Vice President & General Manager
Rizzoli Bookstores; St. Martin's Press

ACCOUNTING
Maria Aprile, The Videre Group LLP

WEB DISTRIBUTION   www.amazon.com

SUBSCRIPTIONS DEPARTMENT   Massimo Centrone

Editorial

the evolution of time

Man's insatiable desire to measure and track time is as old as man himself. Etchings on cave walls reflect the sun and moon, days and nights. Natural progression led to measuring time with water urns, sundials, candles and, eventually, mechanical devices.

Throughout the second millennium, the evolution of time-keeping took flight. Man progressed from large tower clocks of the 11th and 12th centuries, to the table clocks of the 14th and 15th centuries. Pocket clocks reigned supreme in the 16th and 17th centuries, and pocket watches, fobs and decorative timepieces emerged strong in the 18th and 19th centuries. By the 20th century, wrist-watches caught on, and the race ensued to develop new technology and advancements. Records for the smallest, thinnest and most complicated watches were set—primarily with the Swiss leading the way. Technical inventions and design innovations were regularly unveiled.

Today, the selection of fine timepieces on the market runs the gamut from sports watches to classically elegant venues; from bejeweled masterpieces to the most complex and complicated watchmaking inventions. Ingenuity regularly reveals itself in the form of art and design, of traditional craftsmanship blended with modernity.

Watches International 2002 is pleased to present an insight into the world's finest watch brands and their newest creations. For the second year in a row, I have been personally and intimately involved in the creation of this annual catalog. I have chronicled the pasts of these illustrious brands, discussed current direction with their top executives, and inventoried their most recent unveilings.

Within the pages of this book are all types of timepieces: complex and complicated watches from the finest Manufactures (which create their own movements and parts); haute joaillerie watches; elegant classics for men and women; professional sports watches and instruments of time and measurement; designer watches; watches from European jewelry houses that have incorporated timepieces into their domain with exquisite elegance.

This year, we presented an historical review of each of the brands profiled in an effort to relate the brand's age, tradition and watchmaking philosophy. Because this is an annual publication, we focused primarily on the newest additions to each brand's collections.

Additionally—unique to an annual publication—we have created a compendium of the premier luxury groups. Each of the Gucci, LVMH, Movado, Richemont, and Swatch Groups is featured individually. These various articles outline each Group's origin, its growth, its acquisitions (as of press time of this catalog), an insight into the brands of the Group, and a peek at the Group's future tendencies. With these overviews, it is our goal to provide a more comprehensive view of the world of fine watchmaking. Enjoy.

Roberta Naas

OPERA TWO

CARILLON "WESTMINSTER "MINUTE REPEATER,
PERPETUAL CALENDAR AND TOURBILLON WITH THREE GOLD BRIDGES

GP
GIRARD-PERREGAUX

F.P.JOURNE
Invenit et Fecit

The Latin expression, -Invenit et Fecit- chosen by F.P. Journe guarantees
that each calibre of his timepieces collection has been invented and made in
his workshops. For those seeking the authentic watchmaking of a new age.

Sonnerie souveraine – unique pièce –

Tourbillon Souverain

Chronomètre à Résonance

Collection Souveraine

*The Souveraine collection is made up of exceptional
mechanical watches. They result from technical horological challenges driven beyond established limits, in
an ultimate tribute to chronometry.
Their innovative features assert them as world firsts.*

Distribution: Montres Journe SA, Genève

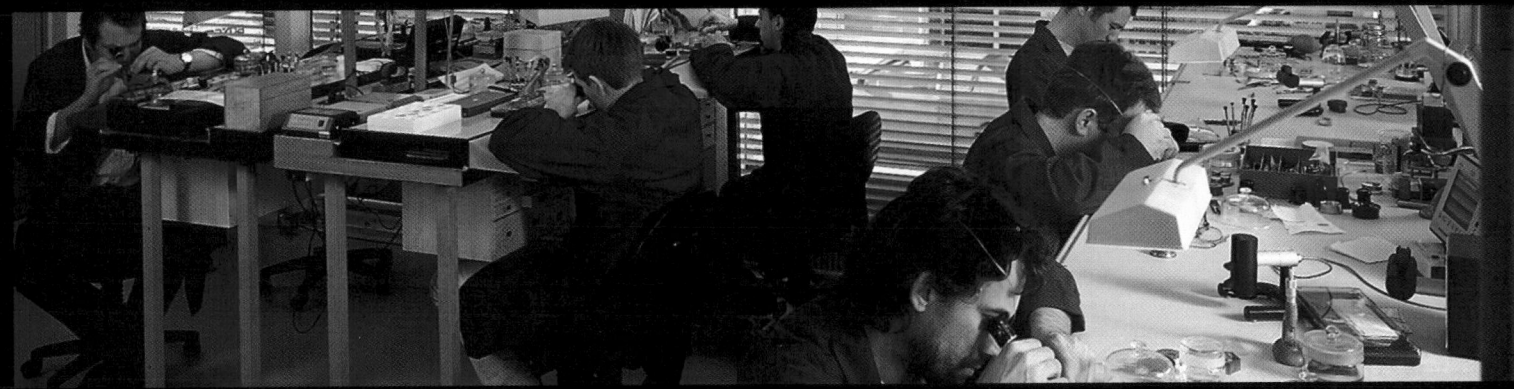

In keeping with his creative vision, François-Paul Journe's workshops are open, welcoming and full of light. A place where he and his team are crafting a new, exclusive generation of watches embodying the spirit of authenticity and innovation.

Cases in platinum. 18 carat gold faces with dials in silver.

Octa Réserve de Marche

Octa Chronographe

Collection Octa

The Octa collection is developed around one of the most sophisticated inventions by F.P. Journe; a self-winding calibre designed to incorporate the most varied complications without modifying its size. Offering authentic chronometer levels of performance, it is endowed with the perfect blend of strength, functions and efficiency.

www.fpjourne.com

F.P. Journe–Invenit et Fecit–

"There is nothing new to invent in mechanical horology. There is no point in trying, because a mechanical watch can never be as accurate as quartz."

This was the credo that launched the revival of mechanical watches in the 1980s and 1990s. With nothing to be invented, the great watch brands concentrated on perfecting traditional watchmaking, reviving a golden past of tourbillons and complications, of period styling and decorative techniques.

Tradition has served the brands well in the watch boom of the past 12 years, but art without invention must surely become decadent. Traditional watchmaking needs a revolution before it degenerates into gadgetry.

A quiet revolution is being plotted in the Geneva workshops of 45-year-old François-Paul Journe, a French chronometer-maker and horologist determined to get traditional watchmaking back on the path of progress.

As a horological purist, Journe focuses his research on the original purpose of watchmaking, which is to measure time as exactly and as reliably as possible. He won't surrender to electronics and he signs each watch "Invenit et Fecit," which means he invented and made it.

Journe started watchmaking school at the age of 14. His graduation piece, a tourbillon pocket watch, revealed his talent to an elite group of collectors for whom he made special timepieces to order. In academic circles he became known as an expert restorer of some of the world's most important historical clocks and watches. He moved to Geneva in 1996, developing complications for the major Swiss brands.

Watchmaking's best-kept secret was let out in 1999 when Journe unveiled a wristwatch that brought him to public attention. Its revolutionary movement generated an extra-mechanical force and harnessed it to jump the limits of mechanical precision. The concept exploits resonance to keep twin balances synchronized at a constant frequency. The revolutionary aspect of the resonance watch is that the twin balances are self-correcting when disturbed by violent motion or shocks on the wrist.

Since then, Journe's workshops have maintained the flow of invention with new compensation devices and original watch constructions,

F.P. JOURNE
Invenit et Fecit

Or 22 Carats

F.P. JOURNE Invenit et Fecit

while their pro-
duction of some 700
watches a year struggles to satisfy a
growing cult following. For the sophisticated enthusi-
ast he makes the only wristwatch with a remontoir device, designed to
release a constant force to the escapement. This "cruise control" mechanism keeps the balance at a rock-steady rate despite the declining power of the mainspring. Journe has made a tourbillon for this watch because its compact construction leaves enough room for the constant-
force mechanism.

Journe's watches have the sober, practical look of finely made scientific instruments and a
minimalism worthy of Abraham-Louis Breguet. The stylistic originality is reflected in the movements, which are entirely of his own construction. The free-sprung chronometer balance is
Journe's own design, as is the large date display, retrograde indication, chronograph and annual
calendar. All of these mechanisms are integrated within Journe's latest development—the Octa
automatic caliber with five days of power-reserve. This original multi-function construction swal-
lows complications without altering its dimensions.

While other watch manufacturers might take years and spend millions of dollars to develop
a new watch movement, Journe finds the task relatively easy. He attributes this to a highly developed spatial imagination. He can construct in his mind the four dimensions of a watch movement, seeking the most elegant mechanical solution.

What more is there to invent and can mechanical watches rival quartz? Journe is currently
attacking the main bastion of the traditional watch—the Swiss lever escapement, based on a design that has ticked in watches for more than two centuries.

He believes that he can devise a new constant-force, oil-free escapement that will perform
even better than his resonance watch and bring the day closer when mechanical watches will turn
the tables and make quartz obsolete.

Summary

EBEL

INTRODUCING
CLASSIC WAVE

MEMBRE DE L'ASSOCIATION INTERPROFESSIONNELLE DE LA HAUTE HORLOGERIE

Website Directory

Alain Silberstein:
www.a-silberstein.fr

Alfex:
www.alfex.ch

Antoine Preziuso:
www.antoine-preziuso.com

Audemars Piguet: www.audemarspiguet.com

Baume & Mercier:
www.baume-et-mercier.com

Bédat & Cº:
www.bedat.com

Bell & Ross:
www.bellross.com

Beretta:
www.berettawatches.com

Bertolucci:
www.bertolucci-watches.com

Blancpain:
www.blancpain.com

Boucheron:
www.boucheron.com

Breguet:
www.breguet.com

Breitling:
www.breitling.com

Bvlgari:
www.bulgari.com

Cartier:
www.cartier.com

Certina:
www.certina.com

Chanel:
www.chanel.com

Charriol:
www.philippe-charriol.com

Chopard:
www.chopardgeneve.com

Christian Dior:
www.dior.com

Chronoswiss:
www.chronoswiss.de

Clerc:
www.clercwatches.com

Concord:
www.concord.ch

Corum:
www.corum.ch

Daniel JeanRichard:
www.danieljeanrichard.ch

Daniel Mink:
www.danielmink.com

David Yurman:
www.davidyurman.com

de Grisogono:
www.degrisogono.com

Dubey & Schaldenbrand:
www.dubeywatch.com

Ebel:
www.ebel.com

Eberhard:
www.eberhard-co-watches.ch

Eterna:
www.eterna.ch

F.P. Journe:
www.fpjourne.com

Festina:
www.festina.com

Fortis:
www.fortiswatches.com

Franck Muller:
www.franckmuller.com

Fred:
www.fred-paris.com

Frédérique Constant:
www.frederique-constant.com

Gevril:
www.gevril.ch

Girard-Perregaux:
www.girard-perregaux.ch

Glashütte Original:
www.glashuette.de

Gucci:
www.gucci.com

Harry Winston:
www.harry-winston.com

Hublot:
www.hublot.com

Ikepod:
www.ikepod.com

IWC:
www.iwc.ch

Jaeger-LeCoultre:
www.jaeger-lecoultre.com

Jean d'Eve:
www.jeandeve.ch

Jean-Mairet & Gillman:
www.jmgwatches.com

L.Leroy:
www.l-leroy.com

Leschot:
www.leschot.com

Locman:
www.locman.com

Longines:
www.longines.com

Mauboussin:
www.mauboussin.com

Maurice Lacroix: www.mauricelacroix.com

Mellerio Dits Meller:
www.mellerio.fr

Michel Jordi:
www.micheljordi.com

Minerva:
www.minervawatches.com

Montblanc:
www.montblanc.com

Movado:
www.movado.com

Officine Panerai: www.panerai.com

Omega:
www.omegawatches.com

Oris:
www.oris-watch.com

Parmigiani Fleurier:
www.parmigiani.com

Patek Philippe:
www.patekphilippe.com

Paul Picot:
www.paulpicot.ch

Perrelet:
www.perrelet.com

Piaget:
www.piaget.com

Pierre Balmain:
www.balmainwatches.com

Poiray:
www.french-horology.com/poiray

Porsche Design: www.porsche-design.com

Quinting:
www.quinting-watches.com

Rado:
www.rado.com

Raymond Weil:
www.raymond-weil.com

Repossi:
www.repossi.mc

Revue Thommen:
www.revue-thommen.ch

Roger Dubuis:
www.roger-dubuis.com

Rolex:
www.rolex.com

Scatola del Tempo:
www.scatoladeltempo.com

Swatch:
www.swatch.com

TAG Heuer:
www.tagheuer.com

Tissot:
www.tissot.ch

Tudor:
www.tudorwatch.com

Ulysse Nardin:
www.ulysse-nardin.com

Universal:
www.universal.ch

Vacheron Constantin:
www.vacheron-constantin.com

Van der Bauwede:
www.vdb.ch

Vincent Calabrese:
www.vincent-calabrese.ch

Zannetti:
E-mail: zannettiwatches@yahoo.it

Zenith:
www.zenith-watches.com

RELATED SITES

Tourbillon International:
www.watches-2002.com

Association Interprofessionnelle de la Haute Horlogerie: www.aihh.com

Fédération de l'Industrie Horlogére Suisse:
www.fhs.ch

Salon Mondial de l'Horlogère:
www.baselshow.com

Auctions:
www.christies.com
www.sothebys.com

Museums:
www.thewatchmuseum.com
www.uhrenmuseum.ch

DeLaneau

Le Joaillier de la montre

Known as The Jeweller of Watches and recognised for its exceptional creativity, Delaneau insists on an irreproachable craftsmanship, from the inside out to the subtlest details of its watches. The one-of-a-kind or small series are all the more exclusive in that they are crafted by the finest artisans of Swiss tradition and set with gems of the highest quality. The combination of a very special style and craft as well as their Creative Director Cristina Thévenaz, is what defines Delaneau's unique personality.

TOP LEFT

Cristina Thévenaz,
Creative Director.

FACING PAGE

The famous Marlène
of the collection
"Les Capricieuses"

ACKNOWLEDGEMENTS

This book could not have been produced without the assistance and kindness of the many people who generously shared with us their knowledge and experience of the watchmaking industry.

We wish to thank Ms. Annette Bamert from A. Lange & Söhne Germany; Mr. François Henry Benhamias from Audemars Piguet USA; Mr. Olivier Bacher, Mr. Georges-Henri Meylan from Audemars Piguet Switzerland; Mr. Jacques-Philippe Auriol from Baume & Mercier Switzerland; Ms. Peggy Azrak, Ms. Simone Bédat, Mr. Christian Bédat from Bedat & C° Geneva; Ms. Robin Davis from the Townsend Group for Bedat & C° New York; Mr. Mirko Bertolucci, Mr. Jean Paul Gaillard, Mr. Arnaud Cymerman from Bertolucci Switzerland; Ms. Helena Nichols, Mr. Paul Wood from Boucheron USA; Mr. Tomasso Galli, Ms. Murielle Blanchard, Ms. Sophie Brun, Ms. Claudine Sablier from Boucheron Paris; Ms. Marie Bodmann, Ms. Kimberly Grogan from Breitling USA; Ms. Valérie Burgat, Mr. Theodore Schneider from Breitling Switzerland; Mr. Simon Critchell from Cartier New York; Mr. Franco Cologni, Ms. Véronique Sacuto from Cartier International Paris; Mr. Cédric Johner, Ms. Christine Johner from Cédric Johner S.A. Switzerland; Mr. Camille Berthet, Mr. Jean-Louis Merandet, Ms. Léa Franciosi from Charles Oudin Paris; Ms. Kari Allen, Mr. Jack D. Zemer, Ms. Sandy Zemer from Charriol USA; Mr. David Savidan from Chaumet USA; Mr. Thierry Fritsch, Mr. Lionel Giraud, Ms. Evelyne Menager, Ms. Blandine Castaigne, Ms. Sandrine Atamaniuk from Chaumet Paris;

**FROM TOP TO BOTTOM
LEFT TO RIGHT**

Georges-Henri Meylan
Christian Bédat
Mirko Bertolucci
Jean Paul Gaillard
Cédric Johner
Camille Berthet
Thierry Fritsch

BERTOLUCCI

ONE DAY OR ANOTHER

www.bertolucci-watches.com

TRUELY EXCEPTIONAL WATCHMAKING:
A TONNEAU-SHAPED MOVEMENT WITH
MORE THAN A WEEK OF INDEPENDENCE.
THE PARMIGIANI 8-DAY IONICA

RESTORING COLLECTORS' TIMEPIECES. HANDCRAFTING NEW ONES.

For further information please contact:
Parmigiani Mesure et Art du Temps SA
Rue de l'Hôpital 33, CH 2114 Fleurier, Switzerland
T: (41) 32 862 66 30 • F (41) 32 862 66 31
www.parmigiani.com

Michel Parmigiani: *The Prince of Restoration*

*B*orn in 1950 and raised in Fleurier—the same Swiss-mountain town in which he and his wife live with their three children—Michel Parmigiani became firmly rooted in his cultural timekeeping-heritage at an early age and soon flourished as a world-renown clockmaker and restorer.

Upon graduating from Fleurier's watchmaking school, Parmigiani began his illustrious career as a watch repairer for Marcel JeanRichard, a local descendent of another highly celebrated master of watches. At age 25, Parmigiani established his own company, Parmigiani Mesure et Art du Temps (PMAT), which focused on the restoration of historic timepieces and the manufacture of specially commissioned mechanisms for other watch companies.

Perhaps Parmigiani's most noted restoration was that of a legendary Breguet table clock originally crafted in 1820. Until Michel Parmigiani came across it, this timepiece had been long-regarded by industry experts as "beyond repair." After 1,600 hours of painstaking labor, Parmigiani had beautifully restored the clock to its former eminence. Later, this exquisite piece would draw in over a million dollars at an auction in Geneva.

His love of timekeeping and his determination for perfection led Parmigiani to create his own timepieces. He started his own brand, Parmigiani Fleurier, just eight years ago. Today, while timepiece restoration is still an important part of his art, Michel Parmigiani enjoys working on his own creations. Parmigiani Fleurier is an outstanding collection of 60 timepieces created specifically for people demanding the ultimate in quality craftsmanship as well as technical and artistic mastery.

ACKNOWLEDGEMENTS

**FROM TOP TO BOTTOM
LEFT TO RIGHT**

Caroline Gruosi-Scheufele
Karl-Friedrich Scheufele
Thierry Chaunu
Nathalie Clerc
Gérald Clerc
Efraim Grinberg
Mitchell Caplan

Ms. Susan Nicholas from Chaumet/LVMH Watches and Jewelry USA; Ms. Sandra Hedqvist from CIA Communications; Ms. Caroline Gruosi-Scheufele, Mr. Karl-Friedrich Scheufele, Ms. Annick Benoit-Godet from Chopard Geneva; Mr. Thierry Chaunu from Chopard New York; Mr. Stephen Butler, Mr. John Keil, Ms. Christine Sullivan from Chronoswiss USA; Ms. Josefine Müller, Mr. Gerd-Rudiger Lang from Chronoswiss Germany; Ms. Nathalie Clerc, Mr. Gérald Clerc from Clerc New York; Mr. Gedalio "Gerry" Grinberg, Mr. Efraim Grinberg, Ms. Mary Leach, Mr. Steve Jager, Ms. Alix Mendes, Ms. Kerry Mezzina, Ms. Barbara Binner, Ms. Jeanne Massaro, Ms. Diana Moran from Movado Group USA for Concord; Mr. Ronald R. Jackson from Daniel JeanRichard USA; Mr. Bernard Fleury, Ms. Sylvie Rumo, Dr. Luigi Macaluso from Daniel JeanRichard Switzerland; Mr. Mitchell Caplan from Daniel Mink USA;

CEDRIC JOHNER
GENÈVE

Tourbillon Abyss 5380/4 N° 1
Guilloché "petit panier"
Manufacturé dans nos ateliers de Vandoeuvres

V.J.W
60-62 Rue François 1ᵉʳ

75008 PARIS
Tél. +33 1 42 25 15 41
Fax + 33 1 42 25 23 35

YAFRIRO
Paragon, #01-27
290 Orchard Road
SINGAPORE 238859
Tél. +65 / 734 61 61 / 738 61 61
Fax +65 / 735 61 61
E-Mail: yafriro@singnet.com.sg

AVAKIAN GENEVA
Hotel Noga Hilton
19, quai du Mont-Blanc
1201 Genève / Switzerland
Tél. +42 21 / 716 15 20
Fax +42 21 / 741 02 10
E-mail: info@avakian.com

AVAKIAN LONDON
Hotel Hyatt Carlon Tower
2, Cadogan Place
London SW1X9PY United Kingdom
Tél. +44 20 / 07235 13 23
Fax +44 20 / 07235 27 21
E-mail: info@avakian.co.uk

CEDRIC JOHNER S.A.
28, rte de Pressy 1253 Vandoeuvres Geneva/Switzerland Tél. +41-22 750 82 13 Fax +41-22 750 82 14
E-mail: cedric.johner@span.ch

ACKNOWLEDGEMENTS

Mr. David Yurman, Ms. Sybil Yurman, Mr. Gabriel Gima, Mr. Josh Reed, Ms. Julie Luchs from David Yurman New York; Ms. Corinne Celeyron, Ms. Michelle Reichenbach, Mr. Fawaz Gruosi from de Grisogono Geneva; Ms. Cristina Thévenaz from DeLaneau Switzerland; Ms. Robin Davis from the Townsend Group for DeLaneau USA; Mrs. Cinette Robert, Ms. Léa Franciosi from Dubey & Schaldenbrand Switzerland; Ms. Céline Bertin, Ms. Miriam Di Ninni, Mr. Guillaume Brochard, Mr. Xavier Gauderlot from Ebel Switzerland; Mr. Dennis Phillips from Ebel USA; Ms. Missy Farren from Farren Communications; Mr. Franck Muller from Franck Muller Switzerland; Mr. François-Paul Journe, Ms. Natalia Signoroni from François-Paul Journe Switzerland; Mr. Peter Stas from Frédérique Constant Switzerland;

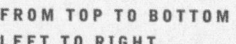

**FROM TOP TO BOTTOM
LEFT TO RIGHT**

David and Sybil Yurman
Fawaz Gruosi
Cristina Thévenaz
Cinette Robert
Guilaume Brochard
Xavier Gauderlot
François-Paul Journe

LOCMAN

Introducing the 2002 Diamond Aluminum Total Pavé

from $3,390 to $3,690

For further information please contact Locman Italy + 39 (0565) 979003 or Locman U.S.A. +1 (213) 6228776

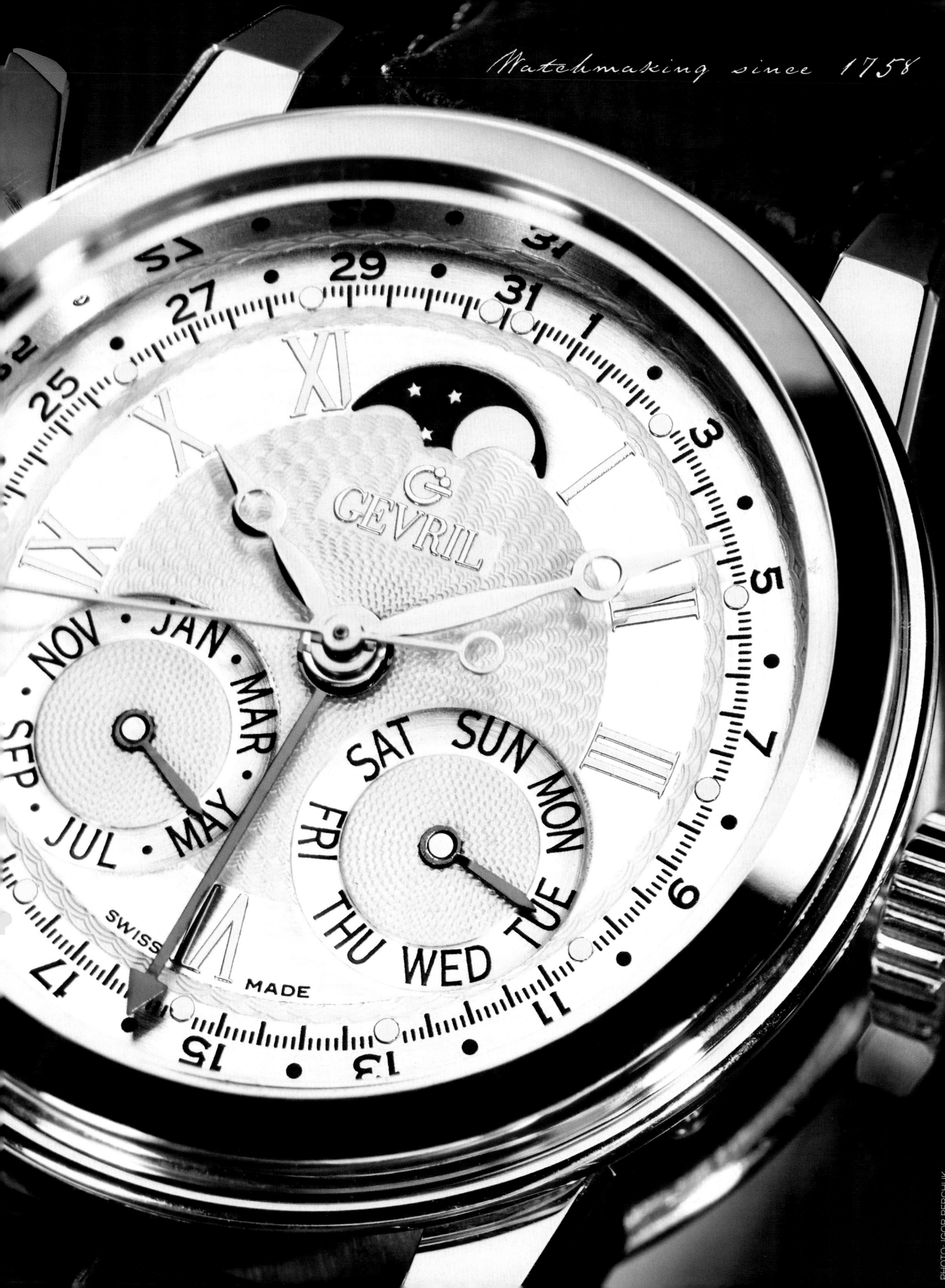

Watchmaking since 1758
GEVRIL
NOV JAN MAR MAY JUL SEP
SAT SUN MON TUE WED THU FRI
SWISS
MADE
PHOTO: IGOR PERCHUK

ACKNOWLEDGEMENTS

Mr. Pasquale Gangi, Mr. René Schmidlin, Ms. Irina Navarro, Ms. Aurélie Simone from Gangi International Switzerland; Mr. Samuel Friedmann, Ms. Monica Friedmann from Gevril USA; Mr. Igor Perchuk from Image Source Productions, Ms. Robin Davis from the Townsend Group, Mr. Mark Weisz for Gevril USA; Ms. Anne Biéler, Ms. Aline Ischer, Ms. Hannie Kyriacos, Mr. Dennis Schnegg, Ms. Sylvie Rumo, Dr. Luigi Macaluso from Girard-Perregaux, Jacqueline Briggen Switzerland; Mr. Ronald R. Jackson from Girard-Perregaux USA; Mr. Tomasso Galli, Mr. Massimo Machi, Ms. Jennifer Dudley, Mr. Tom Ford from Gucci Italy; Mr. Guillaume de Seynes, Mr. Vincent Moesch from La Montre Hermès Switzerland; Ms. Véronique Chaignat, Ms. Brigitte Makhzani, Mr. Carlo Crocco from MDM Hublot Switzerland; Mr. Ed Suhyda from Hublot USA; Ms. Robin Davis from the Townsend Group USA for Hublot; Mr. Oliver Ike from Ikepod Switzerland; Ms. Jacqueline Rose, Mr. Marc Bernhardt, Ms. Nicola Wehrli, from International Watch Company;

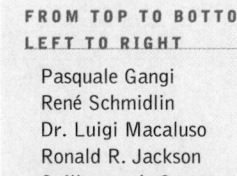

**FROM TOP TO BOTTOM
LEFT TO RIGHT**

Pasquale Gangi
René Schmidlin
Dr. Luigi Macaluso
Ronald R. Jackson
Guillaume de Seynes
Carlo Crocco
Oliver Ike

"Each of my watches is a thought. That's why each one has a different face."

The faces of my watches are as individual as the people who wear them. Allow your gaze to wander slowly across these two pages. At the foot of this page, you'll meet our unconventional "Delphis," whose dial features three different ways of displaying the time. And our "Opus," a timepiece for people with a penchant for peering into the depths of things. On the opposite page, you'll find the "Lunar," a watch for all those who love to live their lives in harmony with the phases of the moon. Global Villagers will no doubt appreciate our "Tora," which shows the time of day (or night) in your home time zone and can also display the current time in any other location elsewhere on our big-small planet. You'll find more about "moon faces," watches for frequent flyers, and all our other models in my book *Signs of the Times*, which is yours for the asking. Incidentally, if my hands weren't firmly grasping the wheel of the roadster at the top of the opposite page, you could see which wristwatch I've taken along for the ride.

Which one would you have chosen?

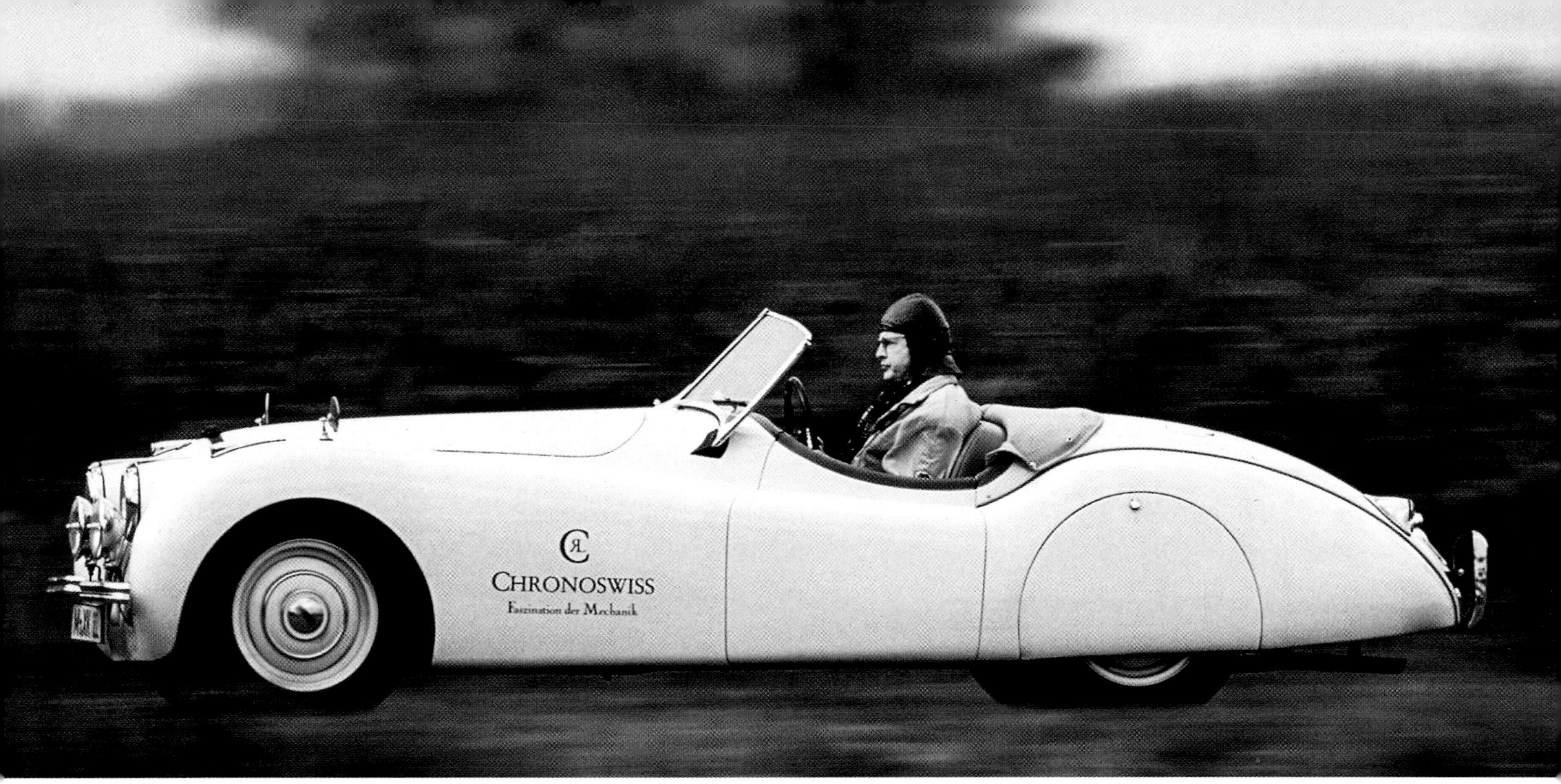
CHRONOSWISS
Faszination der Mechanik

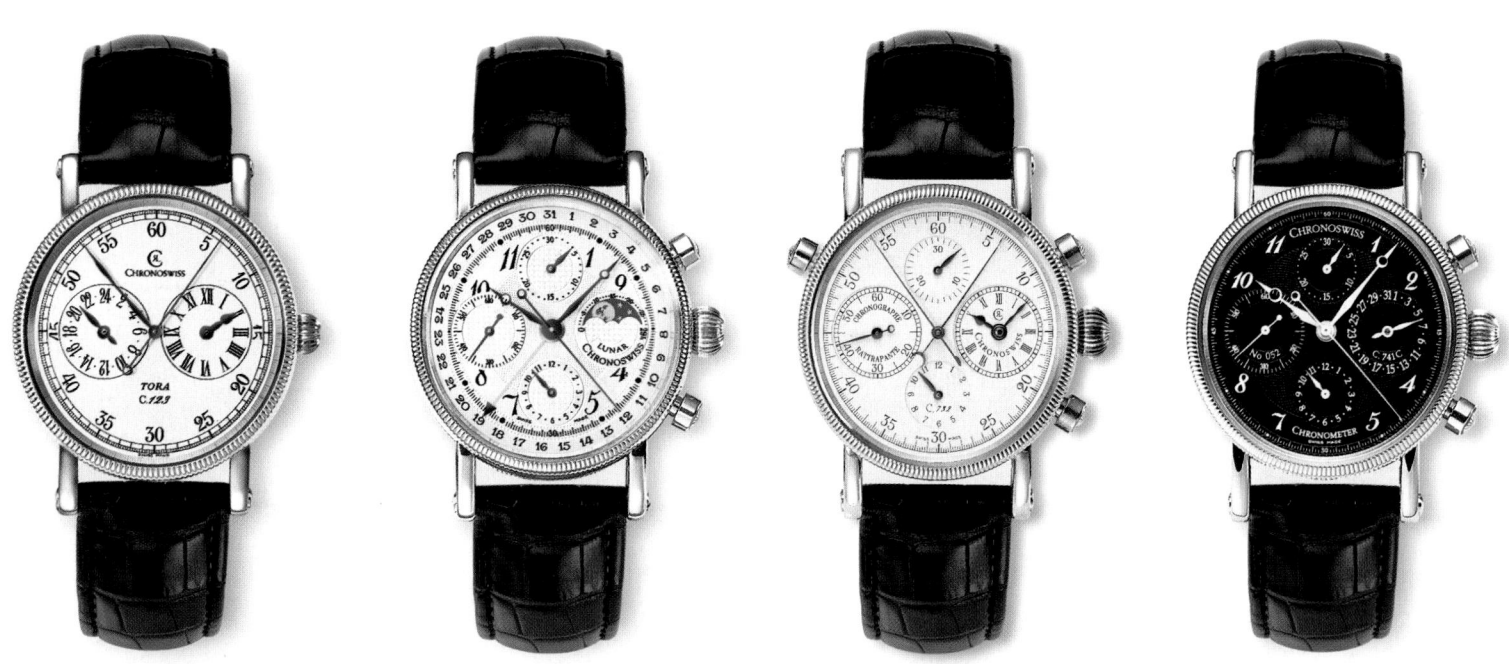

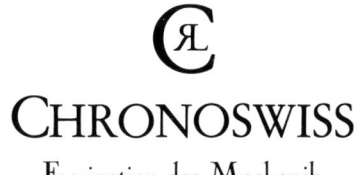

ACKNOWLEDGEMENTS

FROM TOP TO BOTTOM
LEFT TO RIGHT

John-Henry Belmont
Riccardo Guadalupe
Walter von Känel
Jean-Bernard Maeder
Michael Parmigiani
Henry Stern
Philippe Pascal

Ms Sandrine-Lise Taboada, Ms. Corinne Paget-Blanc, Ms. Simone Prévalet, Ms. Mathilde Michel, Ms. Lydie Clement, Mr. John-Henry Belmont from Jaeger-LeCoultre Switzerland; Mr. Ronald Wolfgang from Jaeger-LeCoultre New York; Mr. Riccardo Guadalupe from Leonard Switzerland; Ms. Elizabeth Torovin, Mr. Ben Feighenbaum from Locman USA; Ms. Linda Miller for Locman USA; Mr. Marco Mantavoni from Locman Italy; Mr. Walter von Känel from Longines Switzerland; Ms. Simonetta Ruggeri, Ms. Candace Gillen, Mr. John Argento from Luxury Timepieces International Switzerland; Mr. Philippe Pascal, Mr. Albert Bensoussan from LVMH Watch and Jewelry Paris; Mr. Richard Mille from Montres Mille Switzerland; Mr. Gedalio "Gerry" Grinberg, Mr. Efraim Grinberg, Ms. Mary Leach, Mr. Steve Jager, Ms. Alix Mendes, Ms. Kerry Mezzina, Ms. Barbara Binner, Ms. Jeanne Massaro, Ms. Diana Moran from Movado Group USA; Mr. Jean-Bernard Maeder, Ms. Sylvie Humbert-Droz, Mr. Michel Parmigiani from Parmigiani Fleurier Switzerland; Mr. Donald R. Loke from Parmigiani Fleurier USA; Ms. Tania Edwards from Patek Philippe New York; Mr. Christian Cini, Mr. Mario Boiocchi from Paul Picot Switzerland; Mr. Leopold Philippe Metzger, Ms. Beatrice Vuille-Willemetz, Ms. Sharon Mizrahi from Piaget Switzerland;

RICHARD

MILLE

ACKNOWLEDGEMENTS

Ms. Sandra Hedqvist from CIA Communications for Piaget Switzerland; Ms. Nathalie Hocq-Choay, Ms. Christine Albasini from Poiray France; "Mr. Pascal Berclaz, Mr. Oscar J. Gonzalez, from Quinting Switzerland; Mr. Alberto Repossi, Mr. Marc Corven, Mr. Stephane Mordo, Ms. Christel Kadian from Repossi Paris; Ms. Dorothy Henriot from Richemont International UK; Mr. Franco Cologni, Mr. Dominique Fléchon, from Richemont Paris; Ms. Sandra Hedqvist from CIA Communications for Richemont Switzerland; Mr. Antonio Polito, Mr. John Brancati, Ms. Sheilah Ledwidge from Rizzoli International; Mr. Carlos Dias from Roger DuBuis Switzerland; Mr. William Sullivan from Rolex New York; Ms. Dominique Tadion from Rolex Switzerland; Mr. Franco Cologni, Dr. Luigi Macaluso, Mr. Sebastien Ratto from Assouline Paris; Ms. Barbara Colarieti from Scatola del Tempo Italy; Ms. Anne Biéler from SIHH Genéve; Mr. Nicolas G. Hayek, Ms. Valerie Bastardoz from Swatch Group Switzerland; Mr. Giorgio Sarné, Mr. Thierry Huron, Ms. Sandrine Segato from Tag Heuer Switzerland; Ms. Susan Nicholas from Tag Heuer/LVMH Watches and Jewelry USA; Ms. Salma Ahmad from TBWA Paris; Mr. Pierre Halimi Lacharlotte, Mr. Franck Dubarry, Ms. Yvette Erviti from TechnoMarine USA;

**FROM TOP TO BOTTOM
LEFT TO RIGHT**

Nathalie Hocq-Choay
Pascal Berclaz
Alberto Repossi
Dominique Fléchon
G. Nicolas Hayek
Frank Dubarry
Mario Boiocchi

ACKNOWLEDGEMENTS

My dear friends and associates Ms. Renata Pescatori, Mr. Maurizio Zinelli, Mr. Andrea D'Autilia, Mr. Massimo Centrone from Editoriale Tourbillon Italy; Ms. Roberta Naas, Ms. Elizabeth Kindt, Ms. Mutsumi Hyuga, Mr. Kurt R. Schmidt, Ms. Ruth Katz, Caroline Riuz, from Tourbillon International New York; Mr. Igino Schraffl from the Editoriale Tourbillon , Italy; Ms. Anne Bieler, Ms. Magdalena Rakowski from SIHH Geneva, Mrs. Sandra Hedqvist from Media Edge, Mr. Patrick Ketterer from Vacheron Constantin Switzerland; Mr. Giovanni Mattera from Versace USA; Ms. Donatella Versace from Versace Italy; Ms. Yael Baranes from Assouline Paris; Mr. Riccardo Zannetti, Ms. Claudia Zerbe from Zannetti Italy; Ms. Claudia Zerbe from Zannetti Rome; Mr. Michael Fankhauser from Zenith USA; Mr. Thierry Nataf, Cécile Levallois from Zenith International Switzerland; We would also like to extend our special thanks to The Frenchway Travel, who makes the impossible travel possible; And our most heartfelt thanks are extended to Mr. Joseph Zerbib, a tireless source of strength who supported us every step of the way and without whom *Watches International 2002* would not be possible.

FROM TOP TO BOTTOM LEFT TO RIGHT

Andrea D'Autilia
Mutsumi Hyuga
Elizabeth Kindt
Thierry Nataf
Caroline Ruiz
Giovanni Mattera
Donatella Versace
Thierry Huron

GUCCI GROUP

Gucci Group N.V., one of the world's leading multi-brand luxury goods companies, has experienced tremendous changes in the last few years. A new era in Gucci history began with the appointments of Domenico De Sole as Chief Executive Officer and Tom Ford as Creative Director of Gucci Group. The De Sole-Ford team has successfully transformed Gucci's business and style, subsequently reinventing the company from the mono-brand Gucci to a multi-brand group with several outstanding luxury brands. The Group designs, produces and distributes high-quality personal luxury goods, including ready-to-wear, accessories and timepieces.

GUCCI

One essential aspect in the implementation of the De Sole-Ford strategy at Gucci was to regain complete control over the brand's production and distribution in every product category. The acquisition of the watch business in 1997 from its long time licensee Severin Montres Ltd was one of the cornerstones of the plan.

Like many Gucci products, the watch designs are intended to be streamlined versions of classic shapes—beautiful objects consistent with the overall Gucci image. Gucci timepieces are modern, functional and made of the finest watchmaking materials. Luxurious elements, including precious stones and an increased number of gold pieces, have been added to today's current collection.

BOUCHERON

In May 2000, Gucci Group acquired Boucheron International S.A., the renowned jewelry-, watch-, and perfume maker. Founded in France in 1858, Boucheron has a long-established heritage as an international luxury jeweler and watchmaker. In 1893, Boucheron was the first jeweler to open a shop in the prestigious Place Vendôme, the world's capital for haute joaillerie. The company has built upon its reputation for high quality and exclusivity by expanding into luxury fragrances with a product range strongly identified with its jewelry creations. Each Boucheron timepiece and jewelry creation is a work of art inspired by passion and translated into reality with painstaking attention to detail. Boucheron is aggressively pursuing the expansion of its retail markets outside of France by opening directly operated stores in key luxury goods markets such as London, Tokyo, San Francisco, New York and Milan.

ABOVE
Boucheron

TOP RIGHT
Boucheron

BOTTOM RIGHT
Boucheron

BEDAT & C°

At the end of 2000, Gucci Group acquired BEDAT & C°, a young Swiss watch making company based in Geneva. Founded in 1996 by Christian and Simone Bédat, the company is built on the family's many years of experience in the Swiss watch industry. BEDAT & C°'s products are the perfect combinations of precision watchmaking coupled with quality, elegance and exclusivity. Basic models are priced in the $4,000-$5,000 range, while more exclusive pieces are priced as high as $30,000. Initially introduced into the Swiss market in 1997, the BEDAT line of products has experienced steady growth since its U.S. launch in September 1998.

BEDAT & C° was introduced in Italy and Japan in 2001 and plans are underway for launches in Germany and France for 2002.

YVES SAINT LAURENT

Yves Saint Laurent had a defining influence on 20th century fashion. Part of the Gucci Group since 1999, the re-launching of the brand is now underway. Under the auspices of Creative Director Tom Ford, Yves Saint Laurent plans to introduce its first new watch line in 2002, which will reflect the sexy yet mysterious image of the brand.

zuppinger geneva

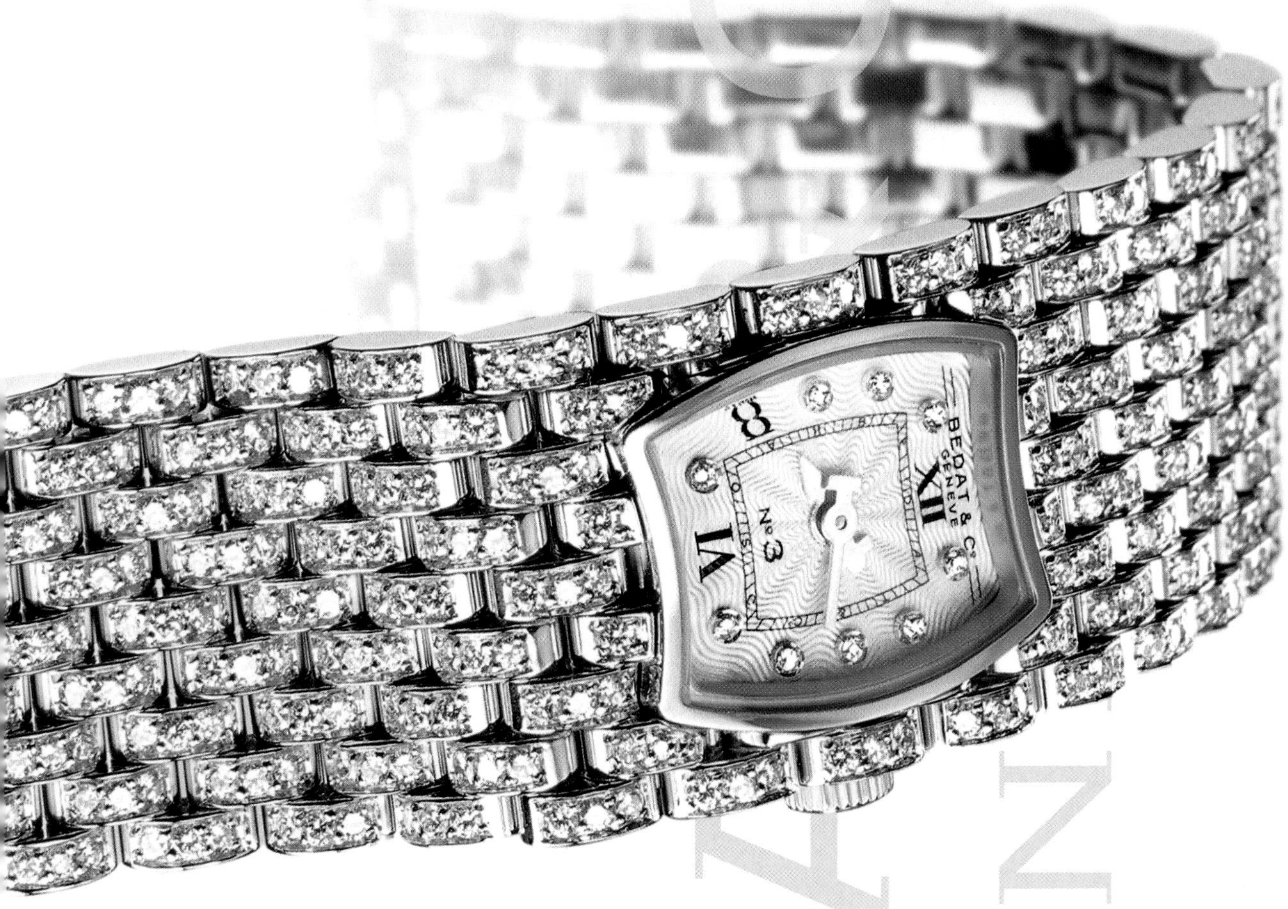

BEDAT & C° N°3
BRACELET WATCH. STEEL SET WITH DIAMONDS.

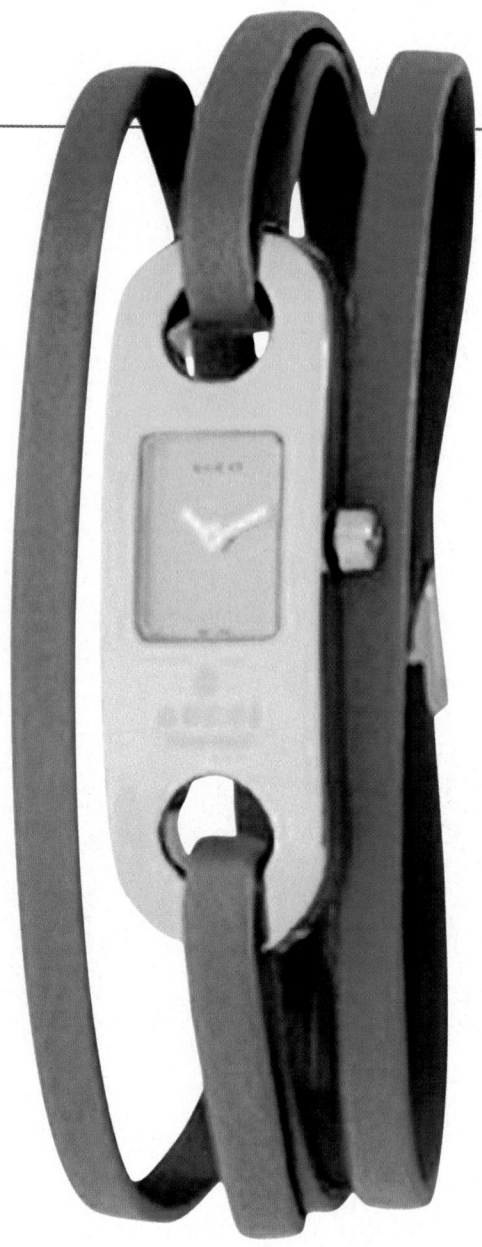

luxury timepieces design

In March 2001, the Group purchased the design studio and production facilities of Swiss watch designer Dino Modolo thus enhancing Gucci Group's own capabilities in the manufacture of timepieces.

For over 20 years, Dino Modolo's design studio (now known as Luxury Timepieces Design) has been designing timepieces for some of the leading brands in the high-end luxury timepiece market and his name is synonymous with high-quality watch design and production. The company specializes in manufacturing time-piece components, in particular bracelets and cases in precious metals, and has outstanding knowledge of the manufacture of jewelry watch-es. Today, LTD is involved in the design and production of all Gucci Group timepiece brands.

In 2000, Gucci Group's timepieces revenues reached US$239 million, representing an impor-tant 11% of the Group's total revenues of US$2,258 million.

Through the Gucci, Boucheron, BEDAT & C° and Yves Saint Laurent brands, the Group has built a solid and credible position in today's luxury watch business. With outstanding creative talent, industry know-how, strong management and financial resources, Gucci Group is well positioned to continue its role as a leader within this rapidly expanding industry.

TOP

Gucci

GUCCI

LVMH GROUP

a Passion for Creativity

A symbol of a discerning lifestyle and all its refinements, LVMH embodies elegance and creativity in a myriad of facets: Wines and Spirits, Fashion and Leather Goods, Perfumes and Cosmetics, Watches and Jewelry, and Selective Retailing. Our Group's culture is built on both the passion of the people, who are our greatest strength, and on our founding values.

INNOVATION, THE ANTITHESIS OF ORDINARY

Because creativity means constantly surprising, it is our job to innovate, invent and give substance to the dream of an elegant lifestyle. New blood is the source of innovation. We attract top young designers by giving them the chance to blossom and hone their talents - thus, perpetually renewing the creative magic and setting the pace of the ongoing renaissance.

An unremitting quest for excellence. Not just doing things well, but excelling and always surprising. The luxury market demands both the best of time-honored craftsmanship and cutting edge technology. Its passion is never quenched and perfection is its obsession. The love of beauty accepts no compromise.

BEAUTY ALONE IS NOT ENOUGH

LVMH is a unique union of highly creative young brands and legendary names in the luxury market. Our role is to spur them to constantly reinvent themselves, because behind each brand, is an unflinching demand for originality and quality.

OBJECTS OF DESIRE

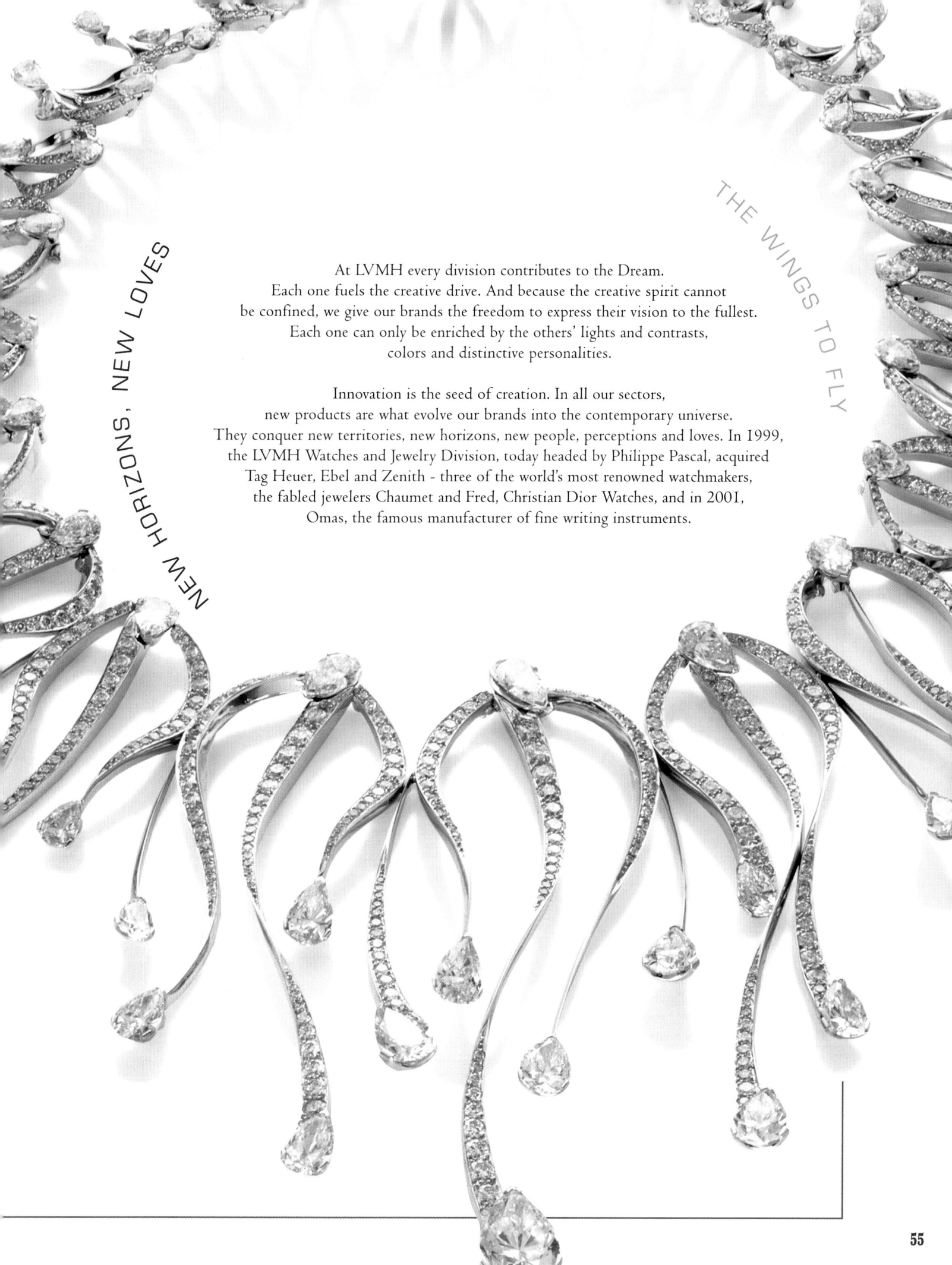

NEW HORIZONS, NEW LOVES

At LVMH every division contributes to the Dream.
Each one fuels the creative drive. And because the creative spirit cannot
be confined, we give our brands the freedom to express their vision to the fullest.
Each one can only be enriched by the others' lights and contrasts,
colors and distinctive personalities.

Innovation is the seed of creation. In all our sectors,
new products are what evolve our brands into the contemporary universe.
They conquer new territories, new horizons, new people, perceptions and loves. In 1999,
the LVMH Watches and Jewelry Division, today headed by Philippe Pascal, acquired
Tag Heuer, Ebel and Zenith - three of the world's most renowned watchmakers,
the fabled jewelers Chaumet and Fred, Christian Dior Watches, and in 2001,
Omas, the famous manufacturer of fine writing instruments.

LUXURY WITH SPLIT-SECOND TIMING

the brands

With the creation of a constellation dedicated to timepieces and jewelry, LVMH has inaugurated a new selective acquisition policy focused on strong brands that complement the strength of existing member companies. Tag Heuer, Ebel, Zenith, Chaumet, Fred, Christian Dior Watches and Omas are prestigious names that are redefining the times and design in their own inimitable style.

Tag Heuer

Founded in the heart of Switzerland, Tag Heuer is an international benchmark in the watchmaking industry, with models that combine avant-garde technology and timeless design. Strength, originality and elegance are the attributes of a brand that has firmly withstood the test of time - as exemplified by the watches in the 2000 Exclusive Collection, the purest distillation of the sporting spirit, and by the brand new Kirium Formula One. Re-editions of its more classic models anchored in a proud tradition — such as the Carerra, the Monaco and the 1930's automatic chronograph, the Monza — perpetuate Tag Heuer's pioneering spirit.

Ebel

Founded in La-Chaux-de-Fonds, Switzerland, in 1911, Ebel watches rapidly acquired a reputation for originality and technical ingenuity. Ebel is once again in the forefront of originality with the Classic Wave, an updated version of the legendary Sport Classic, as well as with its flagship lines, the Beluga and the 1911. Ebel remains true to the inimitable style that has madeit so successful – a style that is in turn paradoxical, timeless, classic, bold and creative.

Zenith

The face and heart of time

Since its foundation in 1865, Zenith is one of the very few firms to fully integrate the design and manufacture of its mechanical movements. Today, Zenith is the only Swiss watchmaker to produce a complete range of factory-made movements and three exceptional mechanical movements, including the legendary El Primero chronograph. Classic designs and the extreme mechanical precision of its watches have won Zenith more awards than any other watchmaker in the world, making it one of the most highly prized names among connoisseurs.

TRENDSETTING TIME

Christian Dior
Advancing time with style

A star firmly fixed in the galaxy of Haute Couture, the House of Christian Dior has always dazzled with its unique style and taste for extravagance. The company's watches are exclusive creations designed by the Christian Dior Couture Studio, brilliantly reflecting the bold spirit of the house. With its acidulated colors and upbeat design - inspired by streetwear and the techno scene - Chris 47 is a symbol of the times and embodies the essence of the Christian Dior style.

Chaumet

Chaumet has held a special place at the pinnacle of Parisian Haute Joaillerie for more than two centuries. Perpetuating the company's pioneering tradition, åthe Class One led the new wave of pairing diamonds with steel instead of gold. The famous "Anneau de Chaumet" combines noble materials with fluid curves that flatter the woman who wears it. The "Liens de Chaumet" collection evokes the beating of a loving heart and expresses the deepest emotions in yellow, pink or white gold.

THE SUMMIT OF ADORNMENT

THE FLOWER OF LUXURY

Fred

The prestige jewelry and
watches created by Fred combine contemporary style with
the Haute Joaillerie tradition
of perfection. A new environment, an original showcase for
Fred's ultra-sensual creations,
has been inaugurated in the new
stores in Paris and will gradually
be introduced to the company's
other stores. The brilliant launch of
the "Ruban" and "Success" lines
ushers in an ambitious policy in terms
of both design and strategy.

Omas

Refinement in a gesture

In its 75-year history, Omas, the small workshop of Armando Simoni in Bologna, Italy,
has reached the peak of the luxury writing instrument industry, thanks to its use of
exceptional materials, unrivaled design, outstanding ergonomics and sophisticated
technology. Its legendary Arte Italiana, 360 and Ogiva lines are highly prized by
collectors and by all those who cultivate the fine art of writing throughout the world.
With the introduction of new models and special re-editions, Omas will continue to
delight its loyal fans and attract admiring new collectors.

MOVADO GROUP INC.

an historical perspective

The making of Movado Group Inc. is perhaps one of the most interesting stories of all of the watchmaking groups. With roots dating back only about 40 years, this renowned company is primarily the result of one man's efforts and foresightedness.

After Castro's takeover of Cuba, Gedalio "Gerry" Grinberg—today Chairman of the Board of Movado Group Inc.—relocated to America to pursue his dreams. In Cuba, Grinberg had been the exclusive distributor of Omega and Piaget timepieces. When he arrived in America in 1960 at the young age of 29, the ambitious Grinberg established a U.S. distributorship for the Piaget brand and soon moved from Miami, Florida to New York. An entrepreneur with a vision, Grinberg methodically set about building his business. It was Grinberg's ultimate goal to develop the luxury watch market in America.

The 1960s were filled with growth and wide acceptance for Piaget in America thanks to Grinberg's keen focus in the positioning and marketing of the brand. Grinberg quickly became recognized for his successes with Piaget and, in 1967, he acquired the distributorship for the prestigious Corum watch line. In 1970, Grinberg's company—then called North American Watch Corporation—purchased Concord Watch Company.

Firmly entrenched in the luxury watch world, Grinberg spent the next decade building each of the brands according to its own niche. Then, in a 1983 landmark move, he acquired the Movado watch brand. His acquisition of this small Swiss watchmaking firm was the beginning of a new era for his company.

Through his sophisticated marketing techniques and smart associations with the performing and cultural arts, Grinberg transformed the Movado brand into an international success within a matter of years. Grinberg positioned Movado as a principal benefactor of the American Ballet Theatre, and later created a collection of timepieces based on the works of different artists from around the world.

In 1990, Grinberg's son Efraim, who had joined the company in 1980, was appointed president of North American Watch Corporation. Two years later, in 1992, the company launched Esquire—a value-oriented line that was geared for a younger market segment.

Around the same time, Gerry Grinberg made a conscious decision to take his company public. Beginning in 1993, North American Watch Corporation was officially traded under the symbol "MOVA" on the NASDAQ National Market. Extensive growth was imminent. To better reflect the growing international scope of its business, North American Watch Corporation changed its name to Movado Group Inc. in 1996.

In typical Grinberg style, Movado Group continued to focus on growth and expansion—always seeking new opportunities. In 1998, through an exclusive licensing agreement with Coach, the esteemed maker of fine leathergoods, Movado Group unveiled Coach Watch.

TOP

On May 21, 2001, Movado Group began trading on the New York Stock Exchange under the symbol "MOV." Pictured, left to right: Rick Coté, chief operating officer for Movado Group; Dick Grasso, chairman of the Exchange; Efraim Grinberg, chief executive officer of Movado Group; Gedalio "Gerry" Grinberg, chairman of Movado Group; Sonia Grinberg; William R. Johnston, president of the Exchange.

BOTTOM

Proud of its 15-year association with American Ballet Theatre, Movado continues its benefactor support.

Movado salutes American Ballet Theatre's World Premiere of *Weren't We Fools?*

current organization

In 2001, Movado Group launched the Tommy Hilfiger Watches collection, which was the result of another brilliant licensing agreement. With this addition, Movado Group now encompasses five distinct watch brands that also include Movado, Concord, Coach Watch and ESQ. In 1999 and 2000 respectively, Movado Group discontinued its North American distribution rights for the Piaget and Corum brands in order to focus its efforts on its core brands. Nonetheless, Movado Group's extensive collections address a multitude of lifestyles and maintain the luxury niche positioning.

For each of its brands, the company continues to pursue applicable cultural associations and sponsorships. Similarly, Gerry Grinberg's lifelong passion for the arts continues to translate into the marketing and positioning of Movado Group as a whole. In 1999, through Grinberg's private support as well as a corporate sponsorship by Movado Group, an 18-foot-tall sculptured bronze clock tower designed by architect Philip Johnson was installed in Dante Park in front of Lincoln Center in New York City. This tribute to time and the arts further represents Movado Group's commitment to cultural support.

In true Grinberg tradition, marketing and advertising remain key on the road to further growth for each of the company's brands. On the heels of Concord's dramatic and successful "be late" advertising campaign, the Movado brand unveiled a striking new campaign in 2001. Depicting filmstrips of famous Movado personalities and naturally featuring Movado watches, "the art of time" ad campaign evokes a sense of elegance and performance. Similarly, both ESQ and Coach Watch received updated advertising that focuses more intently on lifestyle for more targeted appeal.

Additionally, Movado Group has expanded its retail business so that today there are 10 Movado Boutiques in the U.S., equipped not just with Movado watches and fine jewelry, but also with tabletop, home décor and gift items. Current plans call for the opening of two-to-five new Movado stores each year for the next five years in key metropolitan markets.

On May 21, 2001, Movado Group Inc. began trading on the New York Stock Exchange under the symbol "MOV." According to Efraim Grinberg, the listing on the NYSE is a milestone for the company, enabling the business to become more global and to achieve better visibility around the world.

future perspective

With its listing on the New York Stock Exchange and its accomplished executive management team focused on accelerating growth, Movado Group is positioned to realize its short- and long-term goals. It remains committed to its licensing partners and to fulfilling luxury and niche lifestyles with timepieces of the highest quality.

TOP LEFT

Movado's "the art of time" ad campaign.

ABOVE

Movado's exclusive Radius jewelry collection.

BOTTOM RIGHT

The new Movado flagship store was opened in the SoHo section of New York City in November 2001.

THIS PAGE
TOP

The Concord La Scala Steel Diamond chronograph is offered in a choice of soleil dials and pastel alligator straps.

FACING PAGE
LEFT

Movado Elliptica features a unique, comma-shaped case.

TOP RIGHT

Movado Elliptica, on stainless steel bracelet or black alligator strap, is an innovative update of a popular Movado watch style from the early 20th century.

CONCORD
Acquired in 1970

This luxury watch manufacturer was founded nearly 100 years ago in Bienne, Switzerland, on the principles of watchmaking tradition and haute couture styling. The brand was purchased by Grinberg and incorporated into North American Watch Corporation in 1970.

In 1979, in a record-setting move, Concord unveiled the quartz-powered Delirium—the thinnest watch in the world. Soon afterwards, the brand broke its own record by creating an even slimmer (1mm-wide) watch and setting a world record that has remained unchallenged.

The brand made a new foray into the world of luxury sport watches in 1980 with the Mariner collection—an elegantly thin, water-resistant style, a version of which remains in the Concord line today. Six years later, the Saratoga series of elegant sport watches made its debut. Another shining success, Saratoga also continues to be an important collection for Concord.

Under the ownership of Movado Group, Concord has regularly unveiled masterpieces of technology and style. Among them: stunning, one-of-a-kind, high-jeweled timepieces, the technically advanced Impresario collection, and the classically modern La Scala Steel series.

Today Concord is worn on the wrists of celebrities and enjoys international attention for its varied collections, cutting-edge designs and impressive lifestyle-driven timepieces.

MOVADO
Acquired in 1983

Founded in La Chaux-de-Fonds in 1881, Movado is perhaps best known and most internationally recognized for its strikingly modern Museum Watch, unveiled just about 65 years after the birth of the brand.

Focusing on technological excellence and forward-thinking design, Movado has accumulated nearly 100 patents since its inception. One of its early innovations was the Polyplan—an elongated watchcase that followed the curves of the wrist and housed a patented "form" movement constructed inside the curved case. Unveiled in 1912, the Polyplan was ahead of its time in terms of design and its unusual shape garnered it much attention.

Indeed, throughout the first quarter of the 20th century, Movado was regularly on the cutting-edge of design—pioneering innovative styles decade after decade. In 1961, Movado introduced the now-famous Museum Watch. Designed by American artist Nathan George Horwitt in 1947, the dial of this watch was completely devoid of markings except for a single dot at 12 o'clock that symbolized the sun at high noon. The watch dial was considered a pure way to conceptualize time and has since become a part of the permanent collections of more than 20 museums around the world, including the Museum of Modern Art in New York City. Today, the Museum Watch has evolved into an entire range of styles, including a bracelet series called Esperanza and a rectangular collection called Eliro.

In the mid 1980s, shortly after his purchase of Movado, Grinberg reinforced the brand's association with the fine arts by becoming a long-standing supporter of the performing arts. In 1986, the brand became a principal benefactor of American Ballet Theatre—a position it continues to date. Movado is also affiliated with Miami City Ballet and Lincoln Center. Other cultural involvements and sponsorships ensued.

In 1988, Grinberg launched the Movado Artists' Series, a collection of limited-edition watches designed by established international artists. First among the artists commissioned by Movado Group was Andy Warhol, whose Times/5 watch was a bracelet of five self-contained cases, each featuring a different cityscape of New York. Other artists commissioned by Movado Group include Yaacov Agam, Max Bill and Romero Britto. The Artists' Series timepieces have become true collectors' items.

In the 1990s, Movado boutiques began opening and the brand began designing other products such as jewelry, eyewear and accessories. In 2001, Movado unveiled a striking new advertising campaign called "the art of time." Each ad features one of three important personalities (dancer Irina Dvorovenko, tennis champ Pete Sampras, jazz legend Wynton Marsalis) who personify grace, movement and exceptional performance—attributes inherent in Movado timepieces.

Also in 2001, in tribute to its legendary past and its ability to interpret time as design, Movado unveiled the Elliptica. Artfully blending past, present and future, the sensually curved Elliptica is a futuristic rendition of the Polyplan. With its ergonomic shape and graceful elegance, Elliptica's profile emulates a comma. Innovatively curved and contoured, Elliptica allows nothing to interfere with its harmony and balance: the crown is masterfully placed at 12 o'clock so that it flows in the direction of the strap and doesn't impede the smoothness of the watch's side.

Indeed, the unique product creations regularly unveiled by the Movado brand leave one anxiously awaiting the next launch—perhaps exactly the way Grinberg planned it.

ESQ
Launched by Movado Group in 1992

First introduced to the world as Esquire, the name of this value-oriented line was shortened to ESQ in 1995. This collection of sport and fashion watches is characterized by bold styling and is geared for those with active lifestyles.

Designed for a youthful, free-spirited consumer, ESQ offers a range of timepieces crafted in steel and offering strong, attention-grabbing detail. The line includes 200-meter water-resistant diver-style watches, high-performance chronographs, and sleek, fashion-forward timepieces.

COACH WATCH
Launched in 1998 as the result of an exclusive licensing agreement

Coach Watch is the product of a close and successful collaboration between Movado Group and Coach, America's largest leathergoods manufacturer. The collection is based on the hallmarks of Coach's design philosophy of understated elegance and meticulous craftsmanship—traits that come naturally to Movado Group.

First unveiled in the spring of 1998, the Coach Watch collection has evolved into a complete series of fashion-forward, classically modern timepieces for men and women. All Coach watches are distinguished by details that are in keeping with Coach's classic heritage. In 2001, Coach Watch unveiled the tonneau-shaped Coach Morgan in celebration of the 60th anniversary of Coach leathergoods. The watch is crafted in a limited edition of just 40 18-karat gold pieces.

Also in 2001, as it does annually, Coach Watch produced a special-edition "Metropolitan in Pink" rectangular-shaped watch that is sold only during the month of October (designated Breast Cancer Awareness month). Created in two sizes, the watch is accented with a lizard strap of sorbet-pink—the color that has come to symbolize the efforts made to fight this disease. Coach Watch donates 100 percent of the profits from "Metropolitan in Pink" sales to the Susan G. Komen Breast Cancer Foundation.

TOP

ESQ's diver-style 9900 SLX.

LEFT

The limited-edition, 18-karat yellow- or white-gold Coach Morgan was created in honor of Coach's 60th anniversary.

TOMMY HILFIGER WATCHES
Launched in 2001 as the result of an exclusive licensing agreement

Manufactured and distributed by Movado Group through an exclusive licensing agreement, Tommy Hilfiger Watches embody the casual to sporty, classic to nautical spirit of the brand that is its namesake.

The collection includes chronograph models, multi-function sports pieces and analog-digital versions. Conceptualized by Hilfiger, the watches are designed to reflect the classic American style for which his sportswear is known. Additionally, they had to be affordable, fresh and fun. All watches are water resistant to 99 feet and are designed to reflect a variety of lifestyles. Currently, there are five different watch collections. Many watches feature the Tommy Hilfiger red, white and blue flag logo on the dial.

THE RICHEMONT GROUP

an historical perspective

The rise to success for this steller Swiss luxury goods group would not have been possible without the commitment its astute leaders have continuously demonstrated to preserving the heritage, integrity and originality of each of its brands.

The roots of the Richemont Group, as it is known today, date back 30 years and intermingle with the growth of its premier brand, Cartier. In 1972, shortly before the last of the fourth generation of Cartiers stepped down, a group of investors—led by visionaries Joseph Kanoui, Robert Hocq and Alain Dominique Perrin—took control of Cartier Paris. Within two years, they completed the full acquisition of Cartier—purchasing first Cartier London and then Cartier New York. It was the goal of these men to carry on the legend that was Cartier.

Dedicated to preserving the heritage and innovation that had made Cartier a tremendous success, these leaders unveiled new collections and products throughout the ensuing decades that nourished the brand's tradition and fed its future. Under the vigilant and foresighted eye of Perrin, Cartier International soared to new heights by expanding its expertise and opening its own Swiss watchmaking facility.

In 1988, Cartier purchased the Piaget & Baume & Mercier brands. It was the first of many acquisitions. Also in 1988, the Richemont Group was formed as a holding and investment company for the various luxury products. Around this time, Richemont acquired a percentage of Philip Morris's interest in Rothmans International—under whose umbrella the prestigious Alfred Dunhill brand fell. Richemont's dossier was now rich with jewelry, watches, leathergoods, accessories and tobacco.

To separate the Richemont Group's tobacco interests from its specialized luxury goods brands, in 1993 the firm created a subsidiary called the Vendôme Luxury Group. Expansion was on the horizon. In 1996, the Vendôme Luxury Group purchased the legendary Vacheron Constantin, and a year later it acquired Officine Panerai. In 1998, Richemont bought out the minority shareholders of the Vendôme Luxury Group and took 100 percent control of its luxury goods interests.

Over the next two years, the company went on to purchase three more brands (Jaeger-LeCoultre, IWC, and A. Lange & Söhne) and the controlling percentage of renowned jeweler, Van Cleef & Arpels.

TOP

Jaeger-LeCoultre's Manufacture in Le Sentier.

LEFT CENTER

Piaget's all new Manufacture in Geneva.

current organization

From its earnest start with one brand, the Richemont Group has prevailed in its acquisition endeavors: today 18 luxury brands reside under its umbrella. Of those 18 brands, 11 are watch and jewelry related. This clearly places Richemont as one of the world's leading luxury goods groups.

The Group's astute leaders have recruited a top-notch team of executives committed to taking these brands to the next level in terms of product development and ingenuity. Yet—consistent with Richemont's original intentions—each brand remains true to its own heritage, exclusivity and identity.

Jewelry and watches comprise the majority of Richemont's luxury products. Key jewelry houses include Cartier and Van Cleef & Arpels. The specialized watch brands owned by Richemont include Piaget, Jaeger-LeCoultre, Vacheron Constantin, IWC, A. Lange & Söhne and Officine Panerai and Baume & Mercier.

Additionally, Dunhill, Montblanc and Cartier create timepieces as well as writing instruments. Richemont also owns Montegrappa—another leader in the writing instrument field. Among its other luxury brands are Lancel and Old England (leathergoods), Hackett (men's clothing), Chloé (women's clothing), and Purdy (guns, clothing, accessories). The Group continues to hold and add to its investments in the tobacco industry.

future perspective

The 2000 acquisition of IWC, Jaeger-LeCoultre and A. Lange & Söhne was instrumental in shaping the company's future positioning as a leader of luxury timepieces. The three companies had an industrial strength in all aspects of watch manufacture—a prized asset that complements Richemont's growing competency in this area.

A major force in today's luxury market, The Richemont Group is managed with a view toward the long-term development of these successful international brands. Richemont's aim is to maintain the highest respect for and to protect the integrity of each brand. Each brand will retain its own life, past, roots and originality and from this will draw inspiration for its contemporary spirit.

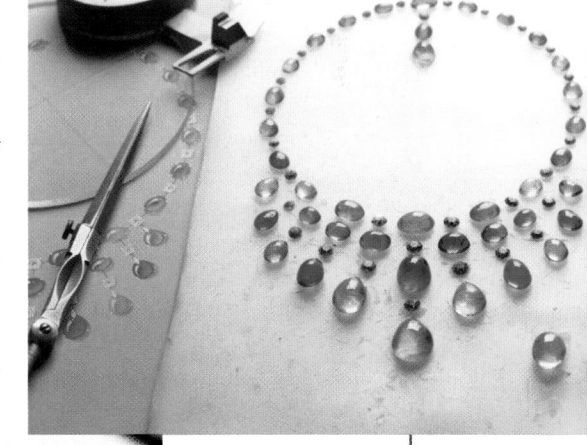

Borrowing a phrase from John Ruskin for the cover of its 2001 Annual Report, Richemont richly sums up its abilities and on-going intentions: "When love and skill work together, expect a masterpiece."

CARTIER

Fully acquired between 1972 and 1974

Founded in Paris in 1847, Cartier is a brand rich with history, innovation and success. Renowned as the king of jewelers and the jeweler of kings, Cartier has long provided the world's leaders with bejeweled master-pieces. For a century and a half, Cartier has established trends with its originality and has defined the bound-aries of craftsmanship for others to follow.

Famed for its collection of panthers and grand animals, for its Russian-inspired Tutti-frutti collection and for its majestic high-jeweled creations, Cartier has also set the pace for watch fashions. From the Santos (1904) to the Bagnoir (1912) to the Tank (1919) to the Pasha (1932), Cartier was regularly hailed for its creativity. Today, the brand continues to build on its foundations—unveiling haute joaillerie and timepieces that embody elegance and exude sophistication.

PIAGET

Acquired in 1988

This illustrious brand was founded in 1874 by 19-year-old Georges-Édouard Piaget, who was intent on creating elegant watches that would smack of technical excel-lence. Decade after decade, generation after generation, Piaget continued in this vein.

Throughout the 20th century, the brand regularly unveiled marvels of techni-cal advancement or aesthetic achievement. From its ultra-slim watches to the famed Piaget Polo to the coveted Protocole, Piaget has been praised for its innovation. Today, the brand continues to launch new generations of these fine collections and to unveil new high-jeweled or complex masteries.

TOP
Cartier

BOTTOM
Piaget

BAUME & MERCIER

Acquired in 1988

Called the Baumes Frères Company when it was founded in 1830, the brand officially became Baume et Mercier when it was registered in 1918 by William Baume and Paul Mercier. Committed to creating fine, fashionable timepieces, Baume & Mercier has regularly unveiled stylish men's and ladies' watches that offer self-expression and individuality.

The brand's key collections today include the Linea (a sleek women's watch that has been a best-seller since its introduction in 1987) and the CapeLand (a masculine sports watch line that was unveiled in the early 1990s and continues to gain appeal with new chronograph and chronometer versions).

ALFRED DUNHILL

The first percentages were acquired around 1989

A brand whose history is rooted in old England, Alfred Dunhill started out as a maker of saddles and horse haberdashery. As the times progressed, so did Dunhill. The brand was quick to adapt its skills when automobiles arrived on the scene and immediately began equipping cars with luxuries such as leather trunks and leather steering wheel covers. Dunhill created riding clothes, hoods and goggles for drivers and placed its first watch on the dashboard in 1903.

In 1998, The Richemont Group completed the acquisition of the remaining percentages of the brand. Today, Alfred Dunhill creates men's and women's luxury clothing with distinctive style. Additionally, the brand is adept at creating scintillating lighters, writing instruments, watches and accessories.

TOP RIGHT
Baume & Mercier

CENTER
Alfred Dunhill

BOTTOM RIGHT
Montblanc

MONTBLANC

The first percentages were acquired around 1989

Known for its style, quality and craftsmanship, Montblanc has long been hailed as a leader in the field of prestige writing instruments. The company has branched out into the development of leather-goods and watches that complement its writing instrument collections. The premier watch line is the Meisterstück collection, which includes such creative timepieces as the limited-edition Skeleton Star Watch 333. This mechanical watch houses a finely skeletonized movement that depicts the signature Montblanc star in the center. Additionally, there is a complete collection of Meisterstück Sports watches.

VACHERON CONSTANTIN
Acquired in 1996

This venerable brand is the keeper of an uninterrupted watchmaking tradition stretching back nearly 250 years. What's more, Vacheron Constantin has unveiled invention and innovation since its inception in 1755. A leader in creating complex timepieces and jeweled masterpieces, Vacheron Constantin has bedecked kings and queens, czars and czarinas.

Even today, the brand caters to those with refined taste and style. It draws on its aesthetic and technical heritage to create new interpretations for our times. Its distinctive timepieces for men and women are meticulously hand crafted and selectively limited in production.

OFFICINE PANERAI
Acquired in 1997

Founded in Florence in 1860 by Guido Panerai, this Italian company has a history rich in providing technically advanced professional dive and sports watches. Panerai has been the official supplier to the Royal Italian Navy since 1938.

Today, the brand continues to create timekeeping instruments geared for professional use. Its successful Radiomir and Luminor lines combine technical innovation with bold design.

VAN CLEEF & ARPELS
Acquired controlling interests in 1999

This renowned jewelry house was founded in 1906 by Louis, Julien and Charles Arpels. The three brothers, joined by Alfred Van Cleef, wisely situated the brand in Paris's prestigious Place Vendôme and set about creating a legacy of creativity, invention and perfection. The first to develop the famed "invisible setting" (a technique of placing gemstones next to each other in such a way that no metal is visible to the eye), Van Cleef & Arpels regularly unveiled regal creations of rubies, emeralds, sapphires and diamonds.

Today, this heritage is enriched by innovative design mixed with an infusion of classic elegance. Using its secret setting techniques to create objects of art, Van Cleef & Arpels offers jewelry and jeweled watches that convey a sense of refinement and richness.

THIS PAGE

TOP LEFT

Vacheron Constantin

LEFT CENTER

Officine Panerai

BELOW

Van Cleef & Arpels

FACING PAGE

TOP CENTER

IWC

LEFT

Jaeger-LeCoultre

BOTTOM RIGHT

A. Lange & Söhne

IWC
Acquired in 2000

Since 1868, IWC has been creating technically and aesthetically advanced timepieces in its workshops in Schaffhausen, Switzerland. Founded by an American (Florentine Ariosto Jones), the history of this brand is rich with technological advancements and inventions. In the early 1930s, IWC mastered the negative effects that gravity has on watches worn by pilots. The brand unveiled the Mark IX—a pilot's watch with an inner case of soft iron that rendered the watch antimagnetic. This watch has since achieved an almost cult-like status with connoisseurs and aficionados. Similarly, the famed oversized Portuguieser, the elegantly complex DaVinci, and the record-breaking Il Destriero Scafusia (arguably one of the most complicated wristwatches in the world) have also achieved cult status.

Today, IWC continues production of these renowned lines and also regularly unveils strategic new products that revolve around its professional GST sports line, its classic complications, or its historical commemoratives.

JAEGER-LeCOULTRE
Acquired in 2000

First founded in 1833 by Antoine LeCoultre, the company created watches based on the principles of technical advancement and prowess. The pioneering spirit of LeCoultre prevailed time and again, earning the brand accolades and awards. By 1890, LeCoultre & Co was already producing a range of 125 different movements. In 1903, the LeCoultres joined forces with Parisian clockmaker Edmond Jaeger and the Jaeger-LeCoultre brand emerged.

A unique watchmaking house, Jaeger-LeCoultre has earned hundreds of patents and conquered new fields of design. From the tiny rectangular wristwatches it produced during the art deco era to the caliber 101 (the smallest mechanical watch movement ever made) to the famed Reverso, Jaeger-LeCoultre has deftly demonstrated its commitment to watchmaking excellence.

A. LANGE & SÖHNE
Acquired in 2000

Lange Uhren GmbH, with the brand name A. Lange & Söhne, was founded immediately after the reunification of Germany in 1990. The brand launched its first collection of mechanical watches to the world in 1994. Focusing on technical originality, classical elegance and traditional design, A. Lange & Söhne watches are produced in Lange's state-of-the-art workshops in Germany. They offer sophisticated complications such as split-seconds chronograph, oversized date display, and perpetual calendar functions.

THE SWATCH GROUP

an historical perspective

The essential roots of what is today known as The Swatch Group actually date as far back as 1930. In that year, an amalgamation of the Omega and Tissot watch brands was formed. Called SSIH, the corporation planned not only to sell Omega and Tissot watches, but also to purchase and distribute other brands in a range of price points and to acquire companies that produced high-quality movements. Over the years, SSIH gradually established a strong leadership position as a Swiss watch manufacturer and supplier.

In 1931, another group—called ASUAG—was formed. Its intention was also to improve and develop the Swiss watch industry. Naturally, it expanded through the purchasing of companies that produced movements and through the acquisition of other watch brands. For decades, SSIH and ASUAG co-existed as two of the major players in the Swiss watch industry.

In the mid-to-late 1970s, after repeated crises within the Swiss watch industry, the two firms found themselves in trouble. With the onset of the quartz watch production from Japan, Switzerland was rapidly losing its foothold as the world leader in watchmaking. Facing liquidation of both ASUAG and SSIH, and recognizing the probable ensuing death of Swiss watchmaking, government officials called upon a solutions expert to assess the industry's chances of survival and to develop a strategy for the future of its two largest companies.

The expert who was called in was Nicolas G. Hayek, then CEO of Hayek Engineering and today Chairman of the Board and Chief Executive Officer of The Swatch Group. In his report referred to as the Hayek Study, he indicated several measures that should be implemented to ensure survival. The two most famous recommendations were the merging of ASUAG and SSIH into one firm called SMH, and the launching of a low-priced, high-tech watch called Swatch. In 1983, these measures were implemented, along with the take-over of the majority of shares through the Hayek Pool. In 1995, Hayek was named CEO of the SMH Swiss Corporation for Microelectronics and Watchmaking Industries Ltd.

current organization

SMH—as it was commonly called—was renamed The Swatch Group Ltd in 1998. It remains headquartered in Biel, Switzerland, and has grown to become the world's largest manufacturer of finished watches.

The Group is active in the manufacture of finished watches, as well as movements and components (via ETA and other companies). In fact, the Group produces practically all of the components necessary to equip its 17 different watch brands. Additionally, the Group's various subsidiary companies supply movements and components to the Swiss watch industry at large, as well as to some manufacturers outside of Switzerland.

TOP

Nicolas G. Hayek, Chairman of the Board and Chief Executive Officer of The Swatch Group.

BOTTOM

This Longines pocket watch was created in 1867.

In addition to the creation of finished watches and components, research and development of state-of-the-art technologies play a major role in the Group's activities. Microelectronics and micromechanics represent another important part of its operations. The Swatch Group delivers high-tech components to other sectors such as the computer field, the medical arena, the automotive industry and the telecommunications sector. In 1998, the Smart car—developed through a joint venture between The Swatch Group and Daimler-Benz—was introduced to Europe.

Naturally, The Swatch Group is particularly active in sports timing, and measures the time at various Olympic Games and for a myriad of international sporting events. In 2001, Rado was intimately involved in the French Open, and Omega continued its sailing sponsorships. Also in 2001, The Swatch Group and the International Olympic Committee came to an agreement: The Swatch Group will be exclusively responsible for the timekeeping, data display and data processing at the Summer Olympic Games in 2004 and 2008, and the Winter Games in 2006 and 2010.

future perspective

With its own Swatch products, such as SwatchAccess (wireless access control) and SwatchTalk (a wristwatch telephone), The Swatch Group is entering the telecommunications business where it can utilize its experience in micromechanics and microelectronics.

The Swatch Group also is entering the accessories and jewelry arena via collections introduced under the wings of certain brands. Swatch has unveiled a trendy line of fashion jewelry called Bijoux. Breguet offers an exclusive selection of high-end jewelry and Omega will be unveiling its collection sometime this year.

Nonetheless, the principal focus of The Swatch Group will remain the watch industry. New and innovative watches are continuously being added to the range of products in the various brands. Additionally, the Group will continue to seek new sponsorships, involvements and spokespersons for its brands.

the brands

The Swatch Group offers watches in all price and market categories. Some of the current brands were already under the auspices of the SSIH and ASUAG groups when they merged, others were developed under the vigilant eye of The Swatch Group and others have since been purchased.

In the luxury segment of the market are Breguet, Blancpain, Omega, Glashütte, Jaquet-Droz and Lèon Hatot. In the upper-priced range are Rado and Longines. Falling in the mid-priced market are Tissot, Hamilton, cK Watch, Certina, Mido and Pierre Balmain. Swatch and Flik Flak are in the basic, lower-priced market. The Swatch Group also has a brand called Endura, which produces private-label watches in all price categories depending upon the client needs.

LUXURY BRANDS

Breguet

Acquired by The Swatch Group in September 1999

Breguet is a brand synonymous with luxury and Swiss watchmaking heritage. Founded in 1775 by the famed Abraham-Louis Breguet, the brand has always embodied the spirit of tradition. Dubbed the "father of watchmaking," Breguet was guided by an inventive spirit and a passion for perfection that drove him to create some of the most technically excellent timepieces in history. His mastery of complicated watchmaking yielded numerous inventions, including the legendary tourbillon escapement. In 2000, Breguet celebrated its 225th anniversary.

Today, under the direction of The Swatch Group, Breguet continues to produce luxury timepieces of the highest caliber. In fact, in 2001, Breguet celebrated the 200th anniversary of the tourbillon and created several anniversary and limited-edition tourbillon watches in honor of its founding father.

Blancpain

Acquired by The Swatch Group in 2000

This luxury brand's roots date back to 1735 when Jehan-Jacques Blancpain began creating timepieces in his home village in Villeret. He focused on crafting his own components and complex watches.

Today, Blancpain continues to produce technical masterpieces based on the theories and practices of traditional watchmaking. In 1988, Blancpain unveiled a collection that proved its mastery of six of the most complex feats of watchmaking: the ultra-slim watch, the moonphase date calendar watch, the split-seconds chronograph, the perpetual calendar, the tourbillon, and the minute repeater. In 1991, Blancpain unveiled its famed "1735" complicated watch. Six years in the making, the platinum watch houses 740 parts that offer numerous functions. Blancpain timepieces are all mechanical—created in platinum, 18-karat gold or steel.

Omega

Existed under the original auspices of SSIH

Founded in 1848 by Louis Brandt, Omega was a brand dedicated to precision timekeeping from the very beginning. Focusing on the creation of new and innovative movements, Omega's reputation for perfection has earned the brand international respect decade after decade. In 1932, Omega was the first "Official Timekeeper" at the Los Angeles Olympic Games.

In 1969, the Omega Speedmaster became NASA qualified. That same year Omega was the first watch on the moon: a Speedmaster Professional was strapped to the wrist of Buzz Aldrin as he

BOTTOM

Omega

stepped onto the moon's surface. A year later, the ultimate precision of the Speedmaster enabled the astronauts aboard Apollo 13 to successfully time their reentry into the Earth's atmosphere when the spaceship's equipment malfunctioned. To this day, Omega remains actively involved in the space program.

Today, Omega's wide variety of coveted timepieces include the internationally recognized Speedmaster, Seamaster and Constellation collections, as well as a series of complicated watches, high-jeweled masterpieces and watches housing the Co-axial escapement movement launched by Omega in 2000.

Glashütte

Acquired by The Swatch Group in October 2000

This elegant watch line traces its roots to the Saxony region of Germany where watchmaking had begun in the 1800s. Watchmaking was, however, thwarted by World War II bombings, after which the city of Glashütte was under the control of the East German government. The brands of the region were all merged into one company. Following the German reunification in 1990, the dream of the return of German watchmaking became a possibility again. In 1994, the Glashütte Original brand was established. With a loyalty to traditional values, the brand creates complex mechanical timepieces.

Jaquet-Droz

Acquired by The Swatch Group in 2000

This luxury brand dates back to 1758 when Pierre Jaquet-Droz opened his watchmaking shop in La Chaux-de-Fonds. The timepieces from the brand today are created in select numbers and house mechanical movements.

Lèon Hatot

Acquired by The Swatch Group in 1999

Devoted exclusively to women, this brand was founded as a jewelry collection first and then extended into watches. The concept of mobility is key, and the watch line features 18-karat gold and diamond pieces with covers that lift or move to reveal the watch dial.

Elegance is an attitude

Longines

Existed under the original auspices of ASUAG

Watchmaker since 1832, this distinct brand has its workshops in Saint Imier, Switzerland. In 1896, Longines was the timekeeper for the first modern Olympics Games in Athens. The brand played a major role in the development of automatic watches and, in 1912, used the world's first automatic timing in sports for Federal Gymnastics in Switzerland.

In 1931 Longines completed the plans designed by Charles Lindbergh for an aviation watch. Called the Hour Angle watch, the timepiece is still part of Longine's Lindbergh Spirit collection. Other Longines collections, produced with either automatic or quartz movements, include the DolceVita and Conquest lines. The year 2001 marked the production of Longines's 30 millionth watch.

Rado

Existed under the auspices of ASUAG

Founded in 1917 by the Schlup brothers as a supplier of watch movements, Rado did not appear as a finished watch brand until 40 years later in 1957. In 1962, the brand introduced the DiaStar, dubbed the world's first scratchproof watch. Rado's timepieces continue to be on the cutting-edge in terms of both materials and designs. Ceramic and other high-tech materials are regularly used in its creations.

MID-PRICED BRANDS

Tissot

Existed under the original auspices of SSIH

Founded in 1853, Tissot's workshops are in Le Locle. In 1971, the brand introduced the world's first plastic watch movement and, in the early 1980s, Tissot unveiled the first Rock Watch—made of stone from the Swiss Alps. In 1999, the brand introduced the T-Touch—the world's first tactile watch whose functions are activated by touching the watch crystal. Today Tissot continues to offer high-style technical timepieces.

Hamilton
Existed under the auspices of SSIH

A brand with American roots, Hamilton Watch Company was founded in 1892. The brand began supplying watches to the U.S. armed forces in 1914 to assist in the war efforts. During World War II, Hamilton ceased the majority of its production and sales of watches to consumers so it could fill the U.S. military's demand for chronographs.

In 1957, Hamilton introduced the world's first electric watch using a battery. Called Ventura, it was worn by Elvis Presley in the movie Blue Hawaii in 1961. In 1970, Hamilton introduced the world's first digital watch. Today, Hamilton continues to introduce not just new collections, but timepieces based on its archives, as well.

cK Watch
Founded in 1997 by The Swatch Group

This avant-garde brand regularly unveils creative, sleek designs that are always on the cutting-edge of fashion.

Certina
Acquired by The Swatch Group in 1983

This brand offers sporty chic watches crafted primarily in steel.

Mido
Existed under the auspices of The Swatch Group

This mid-priced brand is primarily a sports watch line with an elegant twist.

Pierre Balmain

The Swatch Group acquired the exclusive license to produce Pierre Balmain watches in 1987. In 1995, The Swatch Group gained the exclusive right to market and distribute these watches worldwide.

An exclusive, high-fashion jewelry line, Pierre Balmain was founded in Paris as a haute couture line in 1945. The watch brand is naturally feminine and fashion-forward.

BASIC-LEVEL BRANDS
Swatch
Developed and introduced under the umbrella of the SMH Group in 1982

Swatch was Switzerland's response to the Japanese quartz watch explosion. The watch consisted of just 51 components and was fashioned in plastic. Wildly popular, this high-tech brand was the start of an all-new watch category—fashion timepieces. It garnered an international following and has since become a coveted collectible. Year after year, Swatch has broken the mold—unveiling a plethora of decadent, free-spirited collections.

Flik Flak Developed and introduced under the umbrella of the SMH Group in 1987

Flik Flak was designed as an instrument to teach children how to tell time. It continues to be a fun brand that entices youngsters to learn.

the Frenchway travel

we do it ... with passion

**thanks to our clients for believing in the
frenchway travel for seventeen years**

AZZEDINE ALAIA • ALLEGRA MAGAZINE • AMICA MAGAZINE
• ART DEPARTMENT • ART PARTNER • ART PRODUC-
TION • ENRIQUE BADULESCU • STEPHEN BALD-
WIN • BRADLEY CURRY MANAGEMENT • BRIAN
HOWARD PROD • BW PUBLICATIONS • CALYPSO •
CARLYN CERF • JUDY CASEY • CITY MODELS • COM-
PANY MODELS • ELYSE CONNOLLY • COSMOPOLI-
TAN (GERMANY) • PATRICK DEMARCHELIER • DNA
MODELS • ELLE (GERMANY) • ELLE (ITALY) • FINAN-
CO • FRAME • FRANCOIS HALARD • STEPHEN GAN
• HAMID BECHERI • HARPER'S BAZAAR • MARC HIS-
PARD • IZAK • RITA JAEGER • VERNON JOLLY •
CHRISTOPHE JOUANY • KARIN MODELS • TCHEKY
KARYO • JEAN GABRIEL KAUSS • LA PAC • DAVID
LACHAPELLE • LAZARD FRERES • LE BOOK • CHRIST-
IAN LOUBOUTIN • MADISON MODELS • MARIE CLAIRE
(FRANCE) • MARILYN MODELS • MEGA MODELS • JU-
LIAN MEIJER PRODUCTIONS • LAURA MERCIER • MOD-
EL TEAM • NEXT MANAGEMENT • SERGE NORMANT •
NOVA MODELS • OPRAH MAGAZINE • PAULINE
AGENCY • RESERVOIR PROD • SATOSHI SAIKUSA
• JULIAN SCHNABEL • SCOR INSURANCE • PEGGY SIRO-
TA • VINCENT PEREZ • MIRA SORVINO • STREETERS
SUCCESS TAPESTRY • THE AGENCY • MARIO
TESTINO • VAN KASPER & CO • ANTOINE VERGLAS •
VISION MODELS • VISIONNAIRE • VIVA MODELS •
VOGUE (FRANCE) • DIANE VON FURSTENBERG • WHY
NOT • WOMEN MODELS • CAROLINE CHILDERS

11 west 25 street 8th Floor • NEW YORK • N.Y. 10010

Tel: 212 243 35 00 FAX: 212 243 35 35.

WWW. FrenchwayTravel.com

A TIMEPIECE IS BORN

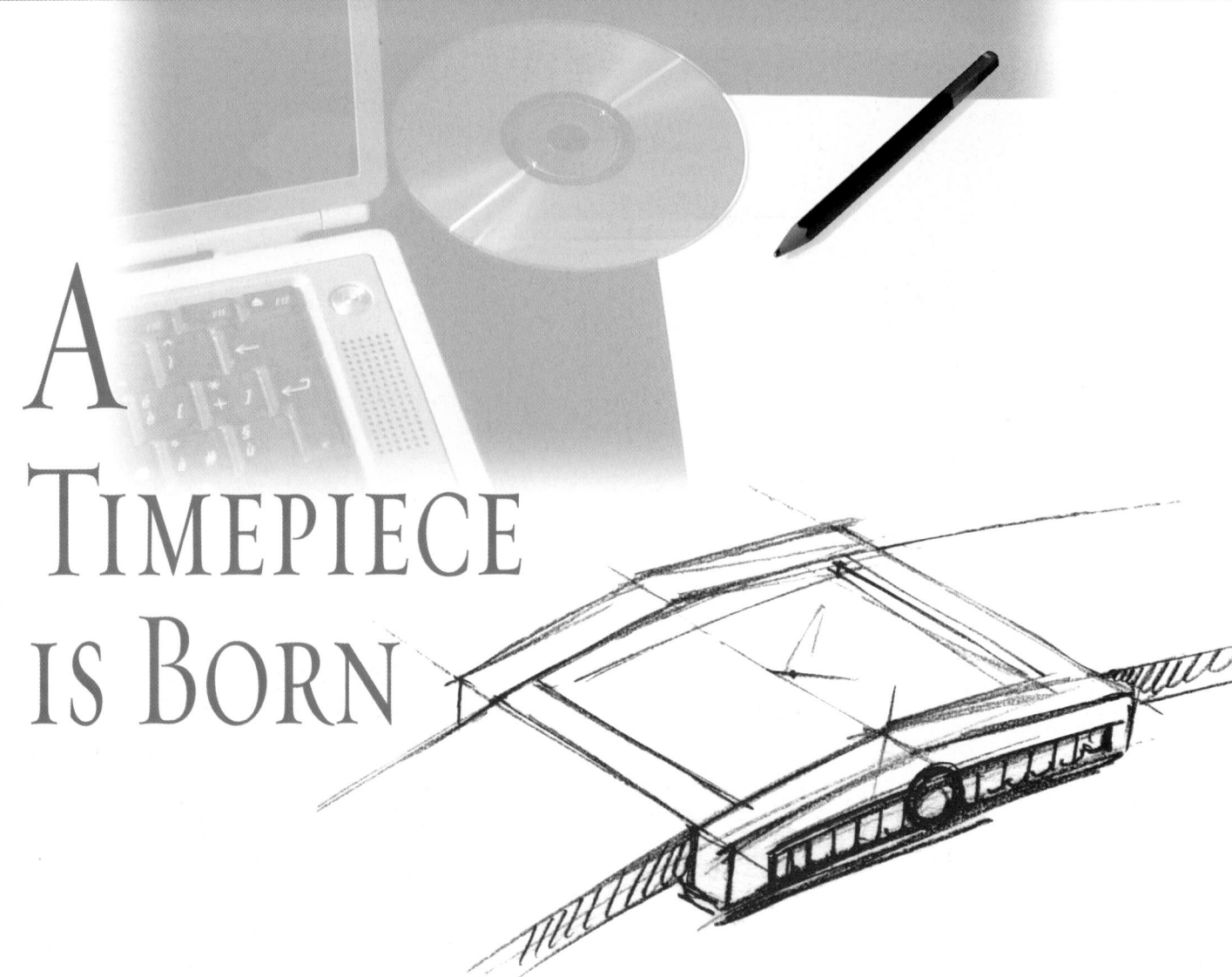

*B*ehind every product that comes into the market there is an accurate work of design investigation, in which differently trained and skilled professional contribute. Anyway, the starting point is always the designer's intuition. We asked Stefano Ricci, a Roman architect who has been working for many years in this sector with very prestigious firms, to accompany us on a trip into creativity.

It happens to see a watch in the window of a jeweler's shop near one's home or on the wrist of a beloved friend or perhaps also in a television spot, and instinctively to think of its beauty.

The reason can hardly be explained, and often we are not aware of what occurs, but what appears as beautiful and becomes an object of desire is the result of a well balanced mix of aesthetic qualities, manufacturing technique, innovation and image, and very little is left to hazard.

Such a team work needs the contribution of several competences: first of all design, but also marketing, production techniques, psychology of image.

The designer's job description is not at all easy to define. His or hers is an extremely multi-faceted activity - consisting mainly of research, communication and exchange, reflection and brainstorming - all of which must be translated into terms easily understood by both business partners and the customers who use or wear the final products.

Many architects choose design as their field, and their university background leaves an evident mark on them, so that they are led to envisage the design of a watch or lamp by the same method by which they would plan a reinforced concrete pillar.

Minute-Repeater 4888/4

Architecture as a Passion

For a designer, architecture is an almost inexhaustible source of inspiration motives which are translated, interpreted and worked out again to generate new shapes, each of which having its own character. One of the models our talk partner likes best is the Pantheon that Stendhal defined the most beautiful trace of Roman antiquity because it suffered so little that it appears us as it appeared to the Roman. Stefano Ricci, who was ever since attracted by the fascination emanating from the Pantheon, shares this point of view. From the architectural standpoint the Pantheon, a mysterious monument that fascinates and seduces visitors inviting them to meditate about power, the order in the world and the destiny of religions, can be defined as an attempt to let three different constructive conceptions coexist: the Greek — evident in the pronaos with pediment and its sixteen Corinthian columns, the Roman of the Imperial period — represented by the solidity of the central body in the shape of a cylindrical drum, and the Etruscan of the cupola. The architect stresses the importance of the reading of the architectural reference, considered as a whole or in all of its details and that can generate each time objects completely different from each other from the aesthetic point of view, but consequently maintaining the expressive values of the original archetype.

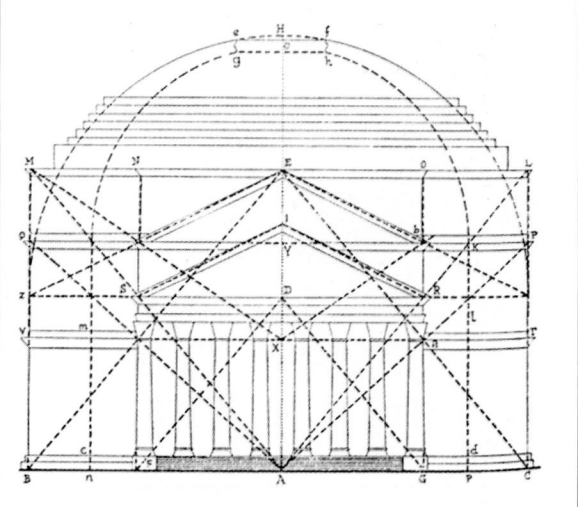

The Project

One of the themes inspired by the Pantheon, already produced and marketed, is the "Aria" wristwatch signed by Stefano Ricci for Christofle.

The first step on the creative path of this watch was the Cahier des Charges, a collage ordered from the architect Henri Bouilhet, then in charge of the product development at Christofle's, and made of journal and catalogue cuts showing watch details and comments on the reasons for which he liked or disliked such details or to what extent they corresponded to Christofle's philosophy.

This was very helpful and is a procedure that may be suggested to orderers. It is like a briefing by images, allowing to center the firm's objectives without wasting too much time and avoiding the risk of plagiarism.

On the basis of these data, the designer makes a series of sketches by hand. These are discussed and selected together with the orderer.

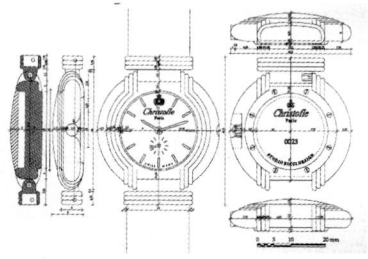

Christofle's choice fell just on the model inspired by the Pantheon and defined the commemorative product for the two-hundredth anniversary of the foundation of the French House. This means that the reference to one of the symbols of the glory of the Roman Empire, that is said to have been conceived like an enormous sundial, was deemed particularly suitable to match the firm's objectives.

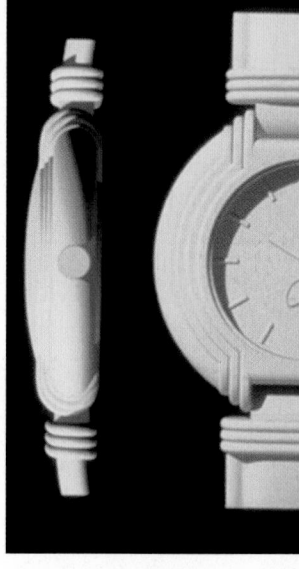

(Photograph of Christofle's watch)ase as many times as necessary to indicate the hour by finger contact.

Noblesse du détail

TECHNICUM

Split-second chronograph with power reserve and complete calendar.

Hand guilloché silver dial and solid 18ct gold rotor behind sapphire crystals. Water-resistant to 50 m.

Certified "Chronometer" by C.O.S.C. Also available in yellow, rose and white gold.

Paul Picot

Artisan - Horloger - Suisse

Paul Picot S.A. - 2340 Le Noirmont - Switzerland - Tel. **4132 953 15 31 - Fax **4132 953 10 15 - www.paulpicot.ch - E-mail: paulpicot@bluewin.ch

Design as a Profession

Every designer has his own working method, suggested by both his academic educational background and the individual talent in particular techniques. In this case, the project is divided into several stages: the first is the creative one, when work is done by hand and much time is devoted to documentation and discussion. On the contrary, during the second stage, aided by computer science, at first a general proportioning of the object is carried out, of course taking into account the technical prerequisites imposed by the movement to be housed and

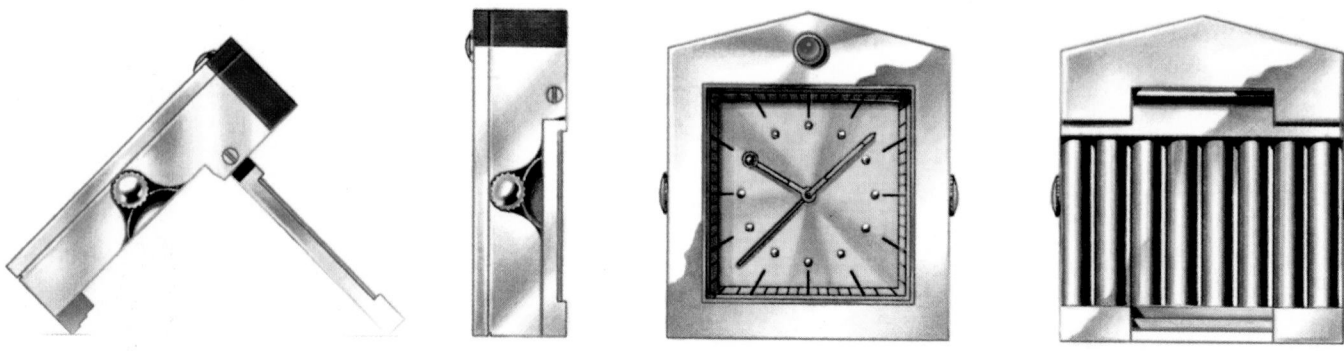

the "accessories" that have to fix it on the future owner's wrist. Subsequently, the "realizational" details of case, strap or bracelet and clasps are studied. Then, by having recourse to the tridimensional "rendering" technique, it is also possible to assign materials to volumes and to obtain a realistic image of the finished product, before proceeding to the realization of a prototype. This can be made by a craftsman, by using traditional techniques, or directly by means of computer-controlled machine tools, in plastic resin or brass, at a considerably lower cost.

In the latter case, which is certainly the more up-dated one, the designer can directly supervise

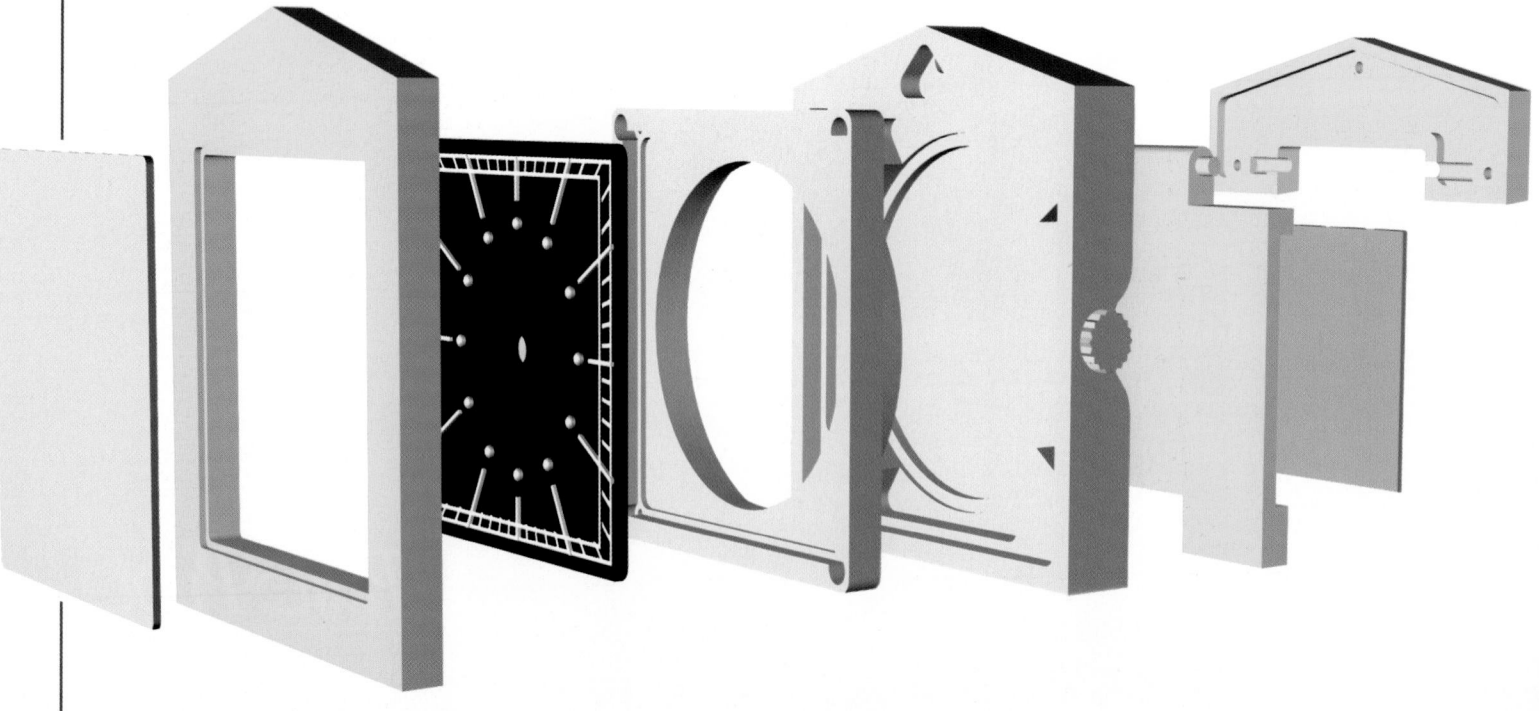

art Paolo Gobbi - ppgobbi@tin.it

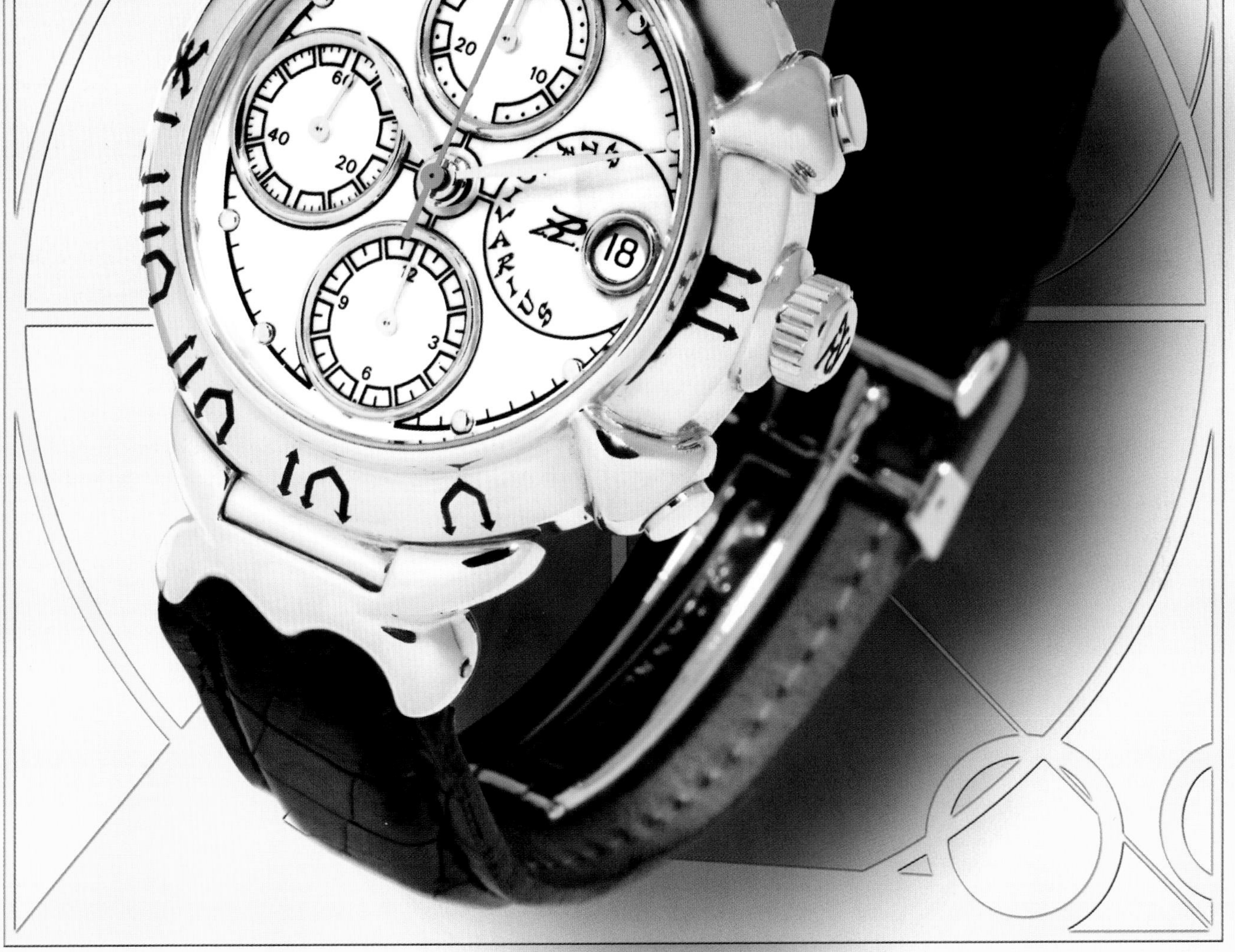

STRADIVARIUS, automatic chronograph, yellow Gold

ZANNETTI
handmade watches

the product's aesthetic definition and engineering in all its components, with the advantage of considerably shortening the time elapsing between the initial project choice and the actual start of the production process. In fact, all the stages are tested in advance, thus ensuring the actual feasibility of the final product, since it is possible to up-date the required working tolerances and accuracy of assembly in real time.

In some cases the designer is also asked to deal with packaging and the conception of the coordination of the display in sellers' windows.

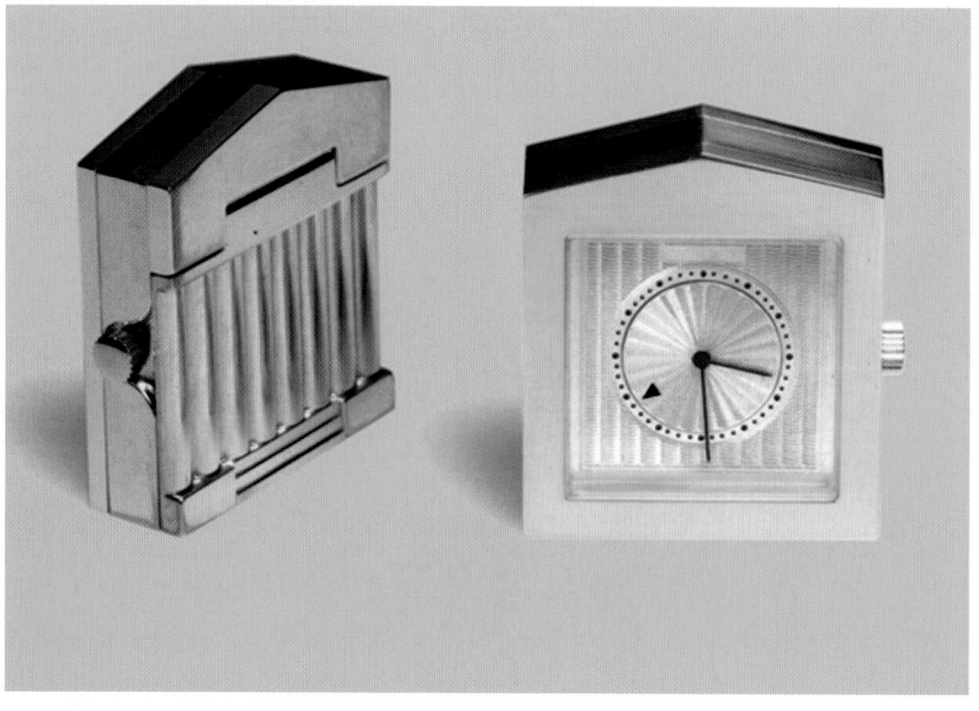

TOP

Plexiglass prototype showed unassembled. It helps also to define in advance tolerances for easy assembly.

LEFT

This travel alarm clock in two color gold and steel version. It's now ready to be personalized with name and logo of the customer.

Development of Collections

Once the product is set up, the next step is usually the production of a first series used for marketing tests and to set up all of the aspects of the production economy.

If the market response is positive, the most logical further step is to develop the inspiring concept in a horizontal sense.

Today it is very important for business firms to conceive product families with a few signs which can generate a vast assortment. This helps the firms to definitely affirm their identities in the market.

Ricci, starting from the concept inspired by the Pantheon, created many products for the most different brands and product classes, such as a paper-knife, a whiskey bottle

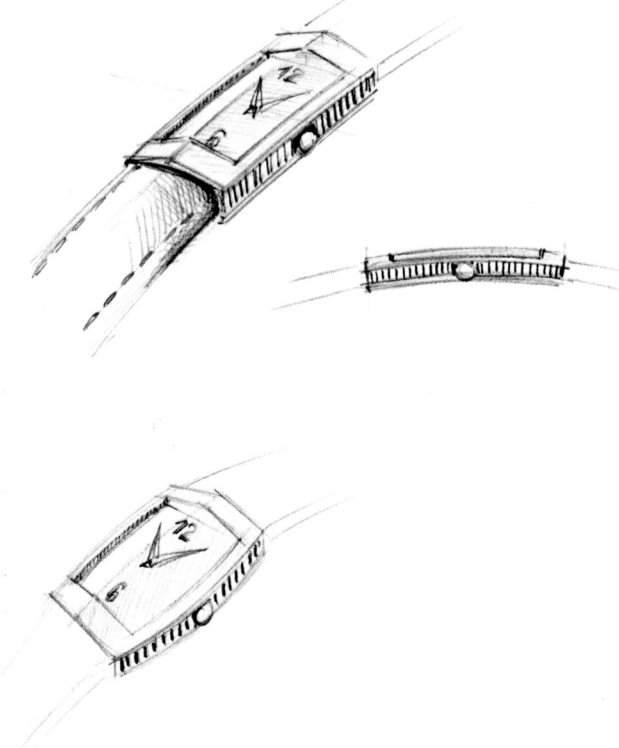

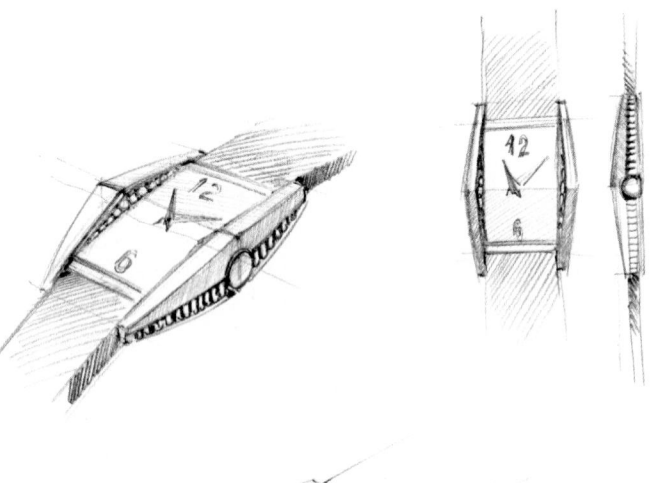

and a key-ring. As an example, we have shown in the previous pages, the travel clock called "Arch'Time" in preview: this project was not yet implemented in the series production stage. Arch'Time was conceived to be realized according to a modular production concept with all the (easy-to-realize) sub-components assembled in a mechanical way, with the aim to generate a complex final whole. Therefore, a numerous series of variants as far as the use of materials and the final intrinsic value are concerned. The same concept can be applied to wristwatches and eventually to a complete line of accessories, including cuff-links, key-rings, paper-weights, frames etc.

Antonia Fabiani

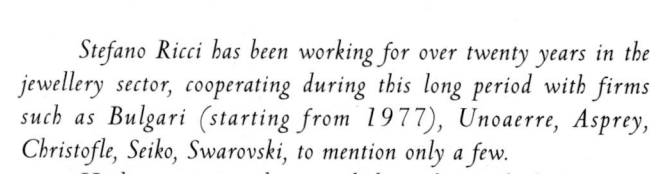

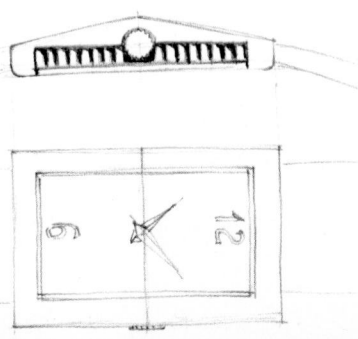

Stefano Ricci has been working for over twenty years in the jewellery sector, cooperating during this long period with firms such as Bulgari (starting from 1977), Unoaerre, Asprey, Christofle, Seiko, Swarovski, to mention only a few.

He has ever since been worked together with the respective marketing and production services of the firms. He considers himself a designer, and not an artist, i.e. he believes in organized creativity. He likes dreaming, as every creative person does, but considers that expressing oneself at best within a project scope under production and market rules is also a stimulating exercise.

VERSACE

VERSACE SA, VIA CANTONALE - CH - 6928 MANNO • TEL. +41 91 610 87 00 - FAX +41 91 610 86 31

THE ART OF TRADITIONAL WATCHMAKING AT THE *Salon International de la Haute Horlogerie* GENEVA 2001

Since people began keeping time, master watchmakers have tried to complete the mechanisms of simple watches—which at the first introduction were driven by only an hour hand—by adding more hands in an effort to give additional time data. The fruits of their efforts, watches with additional hands, were called "complicated." For centuries—thanks to these exceptional pieces — research, science and knowledge have advanced so far that, with the advent of different technologies, man was no longer restricted simply to measuring time, but was able to calculate it.

During the 1980s, complicated watches played an essential role in the return of traditional watches, and not just to the result of a passing fashion. Today, like miniaturized worlds that generally show only their exterior features, complication watches fascinate those who consider watches not as mere time-measuring tools, but rather as works of art, piths of culture, results of skills and creativity, universes of matchless expression by Master Watchmakers.

Since the 16th century, watchmaking has been intricately developed in Geneva—thanks initially to Huguenot refugees who brought with them skills and capital. The town's reputation as famed watchmakers extraordinaire grew and complicated watchmaking reached the Jura valleys where the majority of the most complex movements were produced for Geneva watchmakers.

Geneva, having become the acknowledged capital of high-quality horology, was chosen in 1991 as the most suitable place to hold the Salon International de la Haute Horlogerie, a private event specializing in the field of highest quality and precious watches. The Salon—assuring a perfect osmosis between place and objects, manufacture and artists, tradition and innovation—also began hosting topical shows in 1995 that depict the deep roots that nourish the contemporary art of watchmaking.

In 2001 the organizers of the Salon asked Dominique Fléchon, the manager responsible for topical shows, to gather the masterpieces of Master Watchmakers under the topic "The Universe of Complication Watches." Following the traditions of past events such as "Master Watchmaker, Culture, Profession, Art" (2000) and "Genevan Haute Horlogerie" (1999), the timepieces were displayed in the context of the times in which they were created and used, thus illustrating their adaptations to life's changing demands from yesterday and today.

The Genevan Musée de l'Horlogerie et de l'Emaillerie offered its premises to house the show and the Comité International de la Haute Horlogerie accepted so that the great public could discover it during the 2001 Spring and Summer seasons.

WHEN "COMPLICATION" IS SYNONYMOUS WITH "FUNCTION"

In current language, the word "complication" often carries a negative connotation. In watchmaking, however, its definition is reversed by the skills of Master Watchmakers who, because of their creativity and know-how, are able to place several functions in the limited space of a pocket watch (yesterday) or wristwatch (today), making complicated watches symbols of the great realizations of mankind. In other words, a complication watch is a mechanical watch featuring more functions than hour, minute and second indications, independent of its winding mode—automatic or mechanical—and the thickness of its case. According to tradition, tourbillon devices and automatic-winding systems are considered complications of the truest kind. Furthermore, some connoisseurs extend traditional watch complications (moonphase calendar, split-second chronograph, perpetual calendar, tourbillon, minute repeater) to design-related complications (ultra-thin movement, simple chronograph) or realization-related complications (skeletonized or miniaturized movement). Disregarding definition discrepancies, today's complications are not signs of mere whimsical fashions, but rather a rediscovery of watchmaking art. They played an essential role in the revival of traditional watches in the 1980s and have since fascinated those who love beautiful watches.

TIME READING

All time-related data of complications, including hour, minute and second data, are displayed in different timepieces by means affecting three of the five human senses: sight, sound and touch.

Sight

The "language" of hands is generally based on a code originated by watchmakers at the end of the 13th century.

Until 1700, only one hand turned on a dial showing the hours. It was then that minute and second hands first began to appear. At a glance, one could perceive not only the present hour, but the time elapsed and the time left until the hour changes. Their understanding is universal, for it descends from writings and languages. Some hands suddenly fly back to their starting points as soon as they have completed a rotation. They are often dedicated to particular functions and may be chosen according to aesthetic criteria.

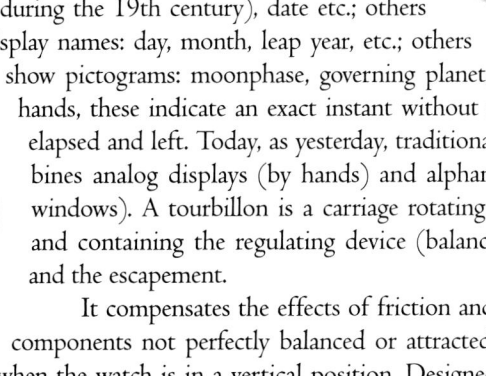

The alphanumeric display adopted since the 16th century for astronomic watches, is characterized by discs moving behind windows. The display shows figures: minute and hour (developed during the 19th century), date etc.; others display names: day, month, leap year, etc.; others show pictograms: moonphase, governing planet, etc. Different from hands, these indicate an exact instant without referring to the time elapsed and left. Today, as yesterday, traditional watchmaking combines analog displays (by hands) and alphanumeric displays (by windows). A tourbillon is a carriage rotating around its own axis and containing the regulating device (balance wheel and spring) and the escapement.

It compensates the effects of friction and those originated by components not perfectly balanced or attracted by the earth's mass when the watch is in a vertical position. Designed by Abraham-Louis

Bréguet, it can be provided with any usual type of escapement. Since its production by highly skilled watchmakers, today the tourbillon with an anchor escapement is mounted in wristwatches and often drives the second hand. When atomic time was unknown, the tourbillon found its preferential place in observation chronometers. The counting of its tick-tock, especially during astronomic measuring, was associated with an acoustic function.

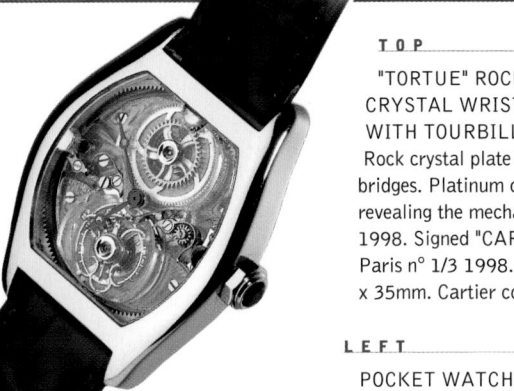

Sound

In watchmaking, "alarm" was originated by the tradition of watchmen who rang the bells of public and religious buildings, striking the number of hours to inform citizens of the time.

Watches were still in their infancy when the production of alarm clocks started, as evidenced in letters dating back to the end of the 15th century. Starting from the 16th century, some watches were provided with an alarm function based on a "sonnerie au passage" device. Thanks to this acoustic feature, hours were represented by the corresponding number of strokes to one or more bells. These were replaced with timbres—circular blades tuned like music instruments—at the end of the 18th century.

Also during the 18th century, this kind of sonnerie progressively was replaced with the quarter repeater movements that were invented in 1675 by the English watchmakers Edward "Barlow" Booth, Daniel Quare and Thomas Tompion. They were also replaced later with minute repeaters, first developed by Thomas Mudge in 1750.

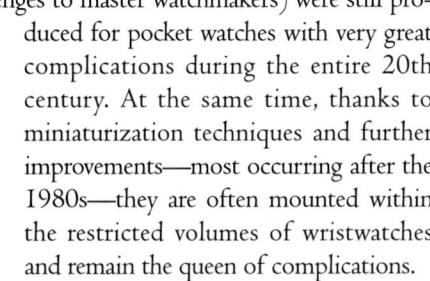

In a watch, a repeater is a complication that, by pushing down a pusher or pulling a bolt, loads the sonnerie mechanism that "repeats" the hour on request. At quarters it indicates the hours and quarters elapsed; at five minutes: hours and five-minute units elapsed; at minutes: hours, quarters and minutes of present time.

Repeater watches, which were very popular when electric light did not yet exist, went out of fashion with the introduction of safety matches invented by von Schrotter in 1845. These matches allowed candles to be lit safely and later petrol and gas lamps.

Nonetheless, minute repeaters (one of the major challenges to master watchmakers) were still produced for pocket watches with very great complications during the entire 20th century. At the same time, thanks to miniaturization techniques and further improvements—most occurring after the 1980s—they are often mounted within the restricted volumes of wristwatches and remain the queen of complications.

Pre-adjustable alarm clocks are used to calculate times on a 24-hour basis and are appreciated by travelers who wish to be awakened at a specific time. Acoustic counters are designed for short-

*All strike the number of hours on a low timbre

QUARTER REPEATER	(Daniel QUARE, 1687)	• two strokes (a low sound, a high sound) at each elapsed quarter
HALF-QUARTER REPEATER	(Daniel QUARE, 1695)	• as the quarter repeater, plus one stroke (high sound) when the half of the nextquarter of an hour has passed
FIVE-MINUTE REPEATER	(Samuel Watson 1710)	• a stroke at 5 minutes, 2 at 10, 3 at 15...11 at 55 on a high sound • other system (a high sound) at each elapsed quarter plus one stroke (high sound) each 5 minutes after the quarter: 2 strokes (a low sound timbre)
MINUTE REPEATER	(Thomas MUDGE, 1750)	• Two strokes (a low sound, a high sound) at each elapsed quarter, then one stroke (high sound) at each minute after the quarter
GRANDE SONNERIE WATCH		• Striking the hours and the quarters by repeating the hours at each quarter and, by request, repeating hours, quarters and minutes.
PETITE SONNERIE WATCH		• Striking the hours and the quarters without repeating the hours at each quarter and, by request, repeating hours, quarters and minutes.
REPEATER WATCHES WITH CARILLON		• Quarters are struck on two or four timbres or with additional, differently pitched tones, thus allowing the wearer to hear melodies; that of Big Ben is the best known.

er time intervals and can be used by scientists for countdown purposes, by musicians as metronomes, or by clock-watchers for reminders of appointments, events, etc.

Touch

For many centuries, looking at one's watch in society was contrary to customs and good manners. To respect the rules of proper social etiquette, watchmakers developed pocket watches without crystals, whose single hand turned on a dial with twelve hour-bumps. Because the bump at 12:00 was larger than the other eleven, it was easy to determine by sense of touch the time of day. Many of these watches were double-faced and provided a normal dial on the reverse side.

Some repeater mechanisms of the 18th century were also designed with tactful etiquette in mind and were provided with a touch system allowing a small point to pop out of the case as many times as necessary to indicate the hour by finger contact.

ASTRONOMICAL

At a time when the minute hand was still unknown, Renaissance watches showed hours, date, day of the week and corresponding planet, month and its duration, phase and age of the moon, as well as the zodiacal signs. These watches seemed to be the successors of the big astronomic clocks of the 14th and 15th centuries, which had been developed from the former mechanical astrolabes and calendars. Many of these functions could be found in clocks such as the Astrarium built around 1380 by De Dondi; in the mechanical astrolabe offered to the Emperor Frederic II in 1232; in the four astronomic clocks built in China about the year 1000 AD; and in the two anaphoric clocks created between the first and third century AD, found respectively in Gand (France) and Salzburg (Austria).

The so-called astronomic watches that were particularly popular in Europe and the Middle East until the end of the 17th century were designed for lovers of physical and occult sciences. At that time, people were fascinated with astronomy and astrology. The latter, which is not related to time measuring at all, tries to determine possible influences of stars on man and nature. To meet the requests of those who are interested in these matters, watchmakers provided their mechanisms with zodiacal indications.

Ancient cultures identified the zodiac as the zones of the celestial sphere that extend by 8.5 degrees on both sides of the ecliptic, i.e. the plane of the earth's trajectory. The first begins at the vernal

TOP

"CAPELAND" WRISTWATCH WITH TWO TIME ZONES AND ALARM.
Self-winding movement. Steel case revealing the mechanism. 2000. Dial signed "BAUME & MERCIER Genève Alarm." Dim: diameter 39mm. Baume & Mercier.

CENTER

QUARTER-REPEATER POCKET WATCH FUNCTIONING À TOC (6:00), À TACT (8:00) AND BY MEANS OF A BELL
(in the back of the case). Verge escapement movement signed "François PERRET-JEANNERET à Paris." Yellow-gold case. Circa 1780. Dim: diameter 52mm. Musée international d'horlogerie. La Chaux-de-Fonds.

equinox, when the sun rises at the spring equinox as it passes from the southern hemisphere into the northern hemisphere. When they were adopted some 3,000 years ago, these signs were named after the corresponding constellations, the first of which was Aries. Today the vernal equinox is in the middle of the Pisces constellation, 41 degrees from its origin. This shift is due to the precession of equinoxes, a conic movement made by the earth in 25,800 years and perturbed by vertical oscillations having a periodical duration of 18.6 years.

When men began to live in civilized societies, they tried to understand the movements of stars that regulated the seasons so they could plan religious festivals (rather than to measure time in structured daily units, which no one saw a need for yet). Earth and the moon offered a universal solution.

It takes the earth 24 hours to rotate on its axis thus this movement determines the length of a day. At the same time, its yearly rotation around the sun defines the year. As the earth's axis shows an inclination with respect to its trajectory plane around the sun, the earth's southern and northern hemispheres do not always have equal exposure to the sun's rays over the course of a year and it is the amount of sun-exposure which determines the seasons.

The time interval between two new moons lasts about 29.5 days and suggests the division of the year into twelve months. Depending on the position of the moon with respect to the earth, its illuminated face is totally visible (full moon), partially visible (quarter moon), or not visible at all (new moon).

Calendar watches

These main astronomic movements were configured to mechanical processes to obtain all, or a part of, the simple full-calendar functions. This includes the date; the number corresponding to the day of the month; the name of the day of the week; the month (manually driven); the moonphases (new and full moon and the first and last quarters); and the moon's age (number of days elapsed since the last new moon). As months with less than thirty-one days and, hence, leap years, are left out of consideration, it is necessary to correct the date manually five times a year.

Some simpler watches do not perform all of the full-calendar functions. Therefore they are called "simple calendar watches." Other, more complex types group these data according to an annual calendar that automatically takes into account the length of months, but not leap years. For this reason they need to be corrected once a year on the first of March.

The so-called leap years are due to the difference between the tropical or astronomic year, whose duration is equal to 365.2421897 days, and the calendar year that can contain only a whole number of days (365 or 366). Either way, the calendar that man puts to practical use will be shorter or longer than the astronomic year. A calendar will make allowances for this discrepancy because, in the long run, it must correspond to the four seasons of the astronomic year.

In 46 B.C., Julius Caesar, on the basis of his astronomer's data, fixed the duration of a basic year at 365.25 days. In the Julian calendar, three consecutive years were to be followed by a leap year of 366 days. However, while Julius Caesar's formula was very close to being accurate, the real tropical year is actually

CALENDAR WATCHES

SIMPLE FULL CALENDAR
These watches include the date, the number corresponding to the day of the month, the name of the day of the week, the month (manually driven), the moon's age (from 1 to 29½ days old) and the moonphases. As months with less than thirty-one days and leap years are left out of consideration, it is necessary to correct the date manually five times a year.

SIMPLE CALENDAR
This displays one or several simple full-calendar functions.

ANNUAL CALENDAR, FULL OR SIMPLE
This automatically takes into account the months of 30 and 31 days and needs to be corrected once a year, in February.

PERPETUAL CALENDAR
Simple or full, this watch automatically takes into account the months of 30 and 31 days and leap years. Generally, it needs to be corrected only in non-bissextile years of century change. The next corrections shall be done in 2100 and 2200.

LUNATIONS
Thanks to the most-adopted mechanical solutions, a manual retardation of one day must be performed every 2 years, 7 months, 22 days on a standard mechanism based on 29 days, 12 hours or a manual advancement of one day every 122 years, 1 month, 14 days for an astronomic lunation-mechanism based on 29 days, 12 hours, 45 minutes.

365 days, 5 hours and 48 minutes and 46 seconds—11 minutes and 14 seconds slower than Caesar's astronomer, Sosigenes, had calculated.

1,628 years after its implementation, this tiny miscalculation had caused the Julian Calendar to fall a full 10 days behind the seasons. Pope Gregory XIII corrected this default in 1582 by ordering Friday, October 15th to follow Thursday, October 4th. By eliminating those 10 days in 1582's calendar, he adjusted the seasonal discrepancy. To avoid the problem in the future, he kept the leap year in the calendar once every four years, but determined that leap years shall not be in affect in the century-years that are not divisible by 400. For this reason, 2000 was a leap year and 2400 will be, but 2100, 2200, 2300, 2500 will be common years. Thus the Gregorian calendar, in use today, was born.

A Gregorian year exceeds the astronomic year by 0.0003 days, i.e. three days every 10,000 years. On the other hand, it does not include the lengthening of the year due to the moon's progressive move away from the earth, which slows the latter's movement by 0.60 second every century. These two phenomena require periodical adjustments.

At the end of the 13th century, watchmakers developed the perpetual calendar that automatically considers months of 30 and 31 days and leap years. Generally, it does not integrate the non-bissextile years of century change and it is necessary to correct it on such dates. The next interventions of this kind will be due in 2100 and 2200.

The first wristwatches with perpetual calendars appeared in 1925. From then on, the dial displaying 48 months, corresponding to a cycle of three common years and a leap year, stemming from pocket watches, was mostly replaced with the easier to read 12-month dial, where the years are visible through a window.

Some exceptional watches display the number of the week, the thousandth or the function of the ecclesiastical calendar whose most important function is to automatically determine Easter Day. Some very rare watches display the Jewish calendar.

Astronomical watches

The indication of the equation of time—the difference between mean and true solar time at a given moment — had been determined by sundials and used for a long time to set watches, pendulum and other clocks correctly. Today, the equation of time relies on the master watchmakers' skills to accurately reproduce heavenly mechanics.

A true solar day is the time elapsed between two true noons. True noon, i.e. midday, is the moment when the sun reaches its highest point (zenith in tropical regions) and crosses the meridian plane of a place. The elliptic shape of the terrestrial orbit causes the duration of a true solar day to be irregular and therefore this is not a valid unit.

For this reason, classical watches indicate the duration of the 86,400 seconds of a mean solar day by averaging all of the true solar days in a year.

Equation of time equals: +14 minutes and 22 seconds on February 11 and −16 minutes and 23 seconds on November 4. It is zero on April 16, June 15, September 2 and December 26. Such variations are mechanically reproduced by means of a cam which has a specific shape and rotates on its own axis in one year; and a feeler which transmits the information to a differently

TOP RIGHT UPPER
"MALTE" WRISTWATCH WITH CHRONOGRAPH AND PERPETUAL CALENDAR Platinum "officer" case with transparent back. 2000. Dial signed "VACHERON CONSTANTIN GENÈVE." Dim: diameter 39mm. Vacheron Constantin.

TOP RIGHT LOWER
"SYMPATHIE" WRIST-CHRONOGRAPH WITH BI-RETROGRADE PERPETUAL CALENDAR Date and days displayed by retrograde hands, moonphases by aperture, other functions including the week displayed by hands. Movement hallmarked with the "Poinçon de Genève." White-gold case revealing the mechanism. Adjustable gold back. 2000. Dial signed "ROGER DUBUIS Horloger Genevois Biretrographe Perpetual Calendar Bulletin d'Observatoir." Dim: diameter 43mm. Roger Dubuis S.A.

BOTTOM
POCKET WATCH MOVEMENT Displays mean time and true time by means of separate hands. Ring showing months with days, age and phases of the moon, power-reserve indicator. Self-winding ("perpetual") system. 1992. Dim : movement diameter 53mm. Parmigiani Mesure et Art du Temps and Bréguet.

colored or differently shaped second minute-hand, coaxial with the normal hour and minute hands. Sometimes, the equation of time is displayed on a subdial, swept by a hand on both sides of a zero point.

Such exceptional masterworks of knowledge, technique and skill are sometimes completed by the master watchmakers who add further functions: sidereal time; sunrise and sunset hours; sun declination; movements of planets; astrolabe; node line allowing for eclipse forecasts; heaven map; or ephemeris (solstices, equinoxes, seasons). Many of these functions are only valid for a specific place. Today the display of these data is merely amazing, but in the past it was very useful. Such features included the equation of time used to keep watches accurate, sunrise and sunset hours for travelling or setting combat times, and node lines to forecast and explain darkness due to lunar eclipses.

COMPLICATIONS DEFINED USEFUL AND RELATED TO EVERYDAY LIFE

Epochs preferred one or several functions according to their respective needs: sunrise and sunset hours when nighttime made travelling impossible; equation of time when watches were set according to sundials; minute repeaters before there was electric light. Today, in addition to calendar watches and alarm clocks, further complications that correspond to the needs of our time are very useful, especially to travelers, businessmen and sportsmen.

The chronograph function (chronoscope)

Progresses made in astronomy, physics, chemistry, medicine, and ballistics were accompanied by those made in watchmaking and vice-versa. The measuring of seconds and their fractions is also a very old practice. After the second hand had been mounted in pocket watches, watchmakers tried to develop a device to stop it. The solution adopted by Romilly in 1754 simply consisted of stopping the movement's work. In 1776, Jean Moise Pouzait submitted to the Société des Art of Geneva a writing wherein he described the principle of a watch with a dead independent second-hand.

Driven by an autonomous wheelwork, the second hand can be released and stopped as one wishes, without disturbing the functioning of hour and minute mechanisms. However, this system, very similar to the "lightning" second caliber, which divides a second into four or five fractions did not allow setting the second hand back to zero.

On March 9, 1822, in Paris Nicholas Mathieu Rieussec was granted a five-year patent for a "timekeeper or run-through way counter" called "second chronograph" indicating the fifths of a second. At that time, the expression "chronograph" was perfectly chosen because the hand left an ink dot on the dial at the beginning and the end of each measurement. Current language has preserved this word despite the fact that present-day hands leave no traces of ink, for which reason the expression "chronoscope" would be more suitable.

In 1822 Frédérick Louis Fatton transformed Rieussec's inven-

TOP LEFT

WATCH WITH SIMPLE CALENDAR AND EQUATION OF TIME
Movement with fusee and chain; cylinder escapement. Silver case. Circa 1830. Dial signed COURVOISIER & COMPE. N° 47311." Dim: diameter 60mm. Musée International d'Horlogerie. La Chaux-de-Fonds.

TOP

JULES AUDEMARS SUNRISE AND SUNSET— EQUATION OF TIME— PERPETUAL CALENDAR WRISTWATCH
Self-winding. Astronomical moon, accurate for 122 years, culmination of the sun. Each watch has cams for sunrise and sunset, and a bezel corresponding to a specific city. White-gold case. 2000. Dial signed "AUDEMARS PIGUET Automatic." Dim: diameter 39mm. AP Audemars Piguet.

CENTER

REGULATOR POCKET WATCH WITH INDEPENDENT SECOND-HAND
Hours at 12:00, center minute hand, seconds at 4:00, independent second-hand at 8:00. Silver case. 1850. Anonymous dial. Dim: diameter 54mm. Vacheron et Constantin private collection.

BOTTOM

"MALTE" DUAL TIME REGULATOR WRISTWATCH
Hours at 12:00, center minute hand, date and seconds at 6:00, 24-hour dual time at 9:00, adjusted using a push-piece at 10:00. Self-winding. Certified chronometer. Yellow-gold "officer" case with transparent back. 2000. Dial signed "VACHERON CONSTANTIN GENÈVE RÉGULATEUR CHRONOMETER AUTOMATIC DUAL TIME." Dim: diameter 38.5mm. Vacheron Constantin.

tion into a fixed-dial pocket chronograph for Abraham-Louis Bréguet. The split-second feature was a further improvement that allowed simultaneous measurement of two or more events beginning—but not ending—at the same time. Two or more hands are mounted on top of each other. Once a hand is stopped for a time-reading and then released again, it runs after the other hand that continued its run. This system was further improved by Louis Frédéric Perrelt and his son with their patent dated March 11, 1828, and definitely established in 1832 and 1838 by Joseph Taddeus Winnerl with his split-second chronograph, whose second hands were driven

by means of heart-shaped cams. However astonishing, these chronographs reached total satisfaction only by Adolphe Nicole's English (1844) and French (1862) patents concerning a triple starting-stopping-zeroing system. These essential inventions are still used in traditional watchmaking.

After several further improvements in 1909 and 1910, some wristwatch models were patented. While the first ones, with or without minute totalizer, were provided with only one pusher integrated into the crown, Breitling patented some "two-stroke" systems (i.e. provided with two pushers) in 1933.

These allow wearers to add subsequent measures by stopping the chronograph and counter hands and then letting them start again, without setting them back to zero.

In order to replace the column wheel, which was very fragile and expensive, a cam device was developed in 1937 to assure the control of different levers. During the same year, Mido presented the first waterproof chronoscope and in 1938 an hour totalizer was added to the thirty-minute counter. Full calendars were added to chronoscope features in 1943. In 1969, the first automatic-winding chronograph was marketed.

Chronoscopes can be used in a variety of fields: science, astronomy, industrial manufacture, communications, armed forces, medicine, motor-cars, aviation, navy, sports. These watches became most popular in the latter fields.

To meet different needs, a vast series of models was designed with tachometers, telemeters, asthmometers, pulsometers, flow-measuring devices, and were suitable for sports such as boxing, soccer, boat races etc.

World-time and multiple time-zone features

Modern life involves much mobility and permanent international contacts. However, since the middle of the 18th century, travelers around the world often need to compare local time to their home country time.

Before the earth was divided into time zones—a measure introduced and eventually adopted by each country between

1884 and 1911—everyone used local time, related to their respective longitudes.

Prior to that time, 74 different local times—more or less regulated by regions—existed in North America, which now has just five. Europe originally had about 30, and now has three zones.

Later, watchmakers developed timepieces called "captain's" watches, displaying the local time of the place of departure on the main dial and featuring a second dial to indicate the time of the traveler's current location.

Other watches now display the local time of many towns around the world; in this case the main hands indicate the current local time. The names of representative towns for each time zone are written on the bezel, on the concentric ring around the dial, or in the dial center—all of which are mobile. It is sufficient to match a town name with the hour hand to immediately know the time of the different towns indicated.

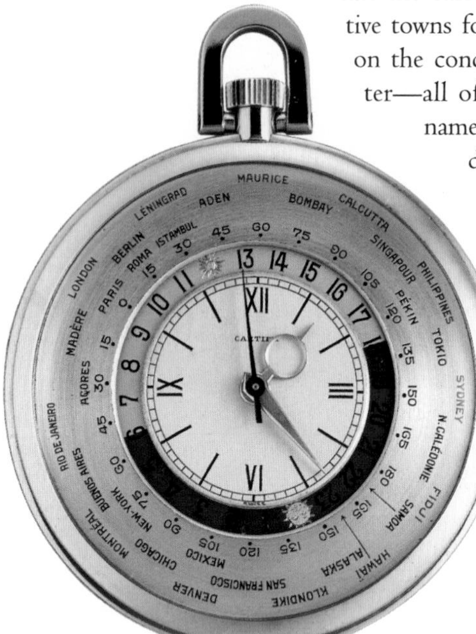

Although the design and use of world-time watches are simple, multiple time-zone watches are often more popular thanks to their easy readability assured by adding specific dials or a complementary hour hand. The minute indication remains unchanged, as only the hours differ between time zones.

In order to avoid confusion between daytime and nighttime, often a "day and night hour" function is added.

There are numerous multiple time-zone versions. The same is true for watches used for sporting or other particular purposes.

TOP LEFT

POCKET WATCH WITH THREE DIALS
Can be used to display three time zones. Platinum case engraved with the initials "HDG." Circa 1928. Dial signed "CARTIER France." Dim: diameter 46mm. Cartier collection.

TOP

WRISTWATCH WITH TWO MOVEMENTS
Can be used to display two time zones. Yellow-gold case and bracelet. 1974. Onyx and coral dial, signed "PIAGET." Dim: 3.5 x 3.1mm. Piaget collection.

CENTER

POCKET WATCH WITH UNIVERSAL DAY AND NIGHTTIME
Yellow-gold case engraved with the initials "KHL." 1940. New York. Dial signed "CARTIER." Dim: diameter 45mm. Cartier collection.

BOTTOM LEFT

DIVER'S WRISTWATCH WITH UNDERWATER ALARM
Dial featuring a rotating disc displaying decompression stops and times through an aperture. An alarm sounds to indicate surfacing time. Steel case. Circa 1961. Dial signed "VULCAIN." Case inscribed "VULCAIN CRICKET NAUTICAL 30 ATM." Musée International d'Horlogerie. La Chaux-de-Fonds.

Sporting or other specific activity features

Boat-race watches are equipped with countdown devices corresponding to different boat positions before the start of the race. In the diving field, watchmakers developed features to indicate decompression levels and the duration of stoppage times.

Some watches are equipped with alarm devices to announce the need to ascend. Tide-gauge watches—useful to fishermen and boat-racers although their data are only approximate—indicate high and low tides at a given latitude.

During the 25 hours and 60 minutes of each lunar day, high and low tides follow one another twice. By the law of mass attraction, the moon mass attracts every mass, causing the tides of oceans and, to a lesser extent, those of seas and lakes. The same is true for the sun. In fact, when the sun, moon and earth are in conjunction, the action of the first adds to that of the second and spring tides—the sum of the tides that the moon and sun would generate separately—occur. In the opposite case, tides are weaker. They reach their minimum level during the first and last moon quarters, when the centers of the sun, moon and earth form a right angle in space.

Some tide gauges, apart from the display of tide hours, indicate tide coefficients. They must be adjusted by users according to the respective latitude of the location and mostly on the basis of official tide yearbooks. An orientation feature allows determining North without using traditional compasses. The northern direction is indicated by a special hand rotating on the 24-hour dial while the hour hand is turned toward the sun. The fly-back feature, suitable for measuring at high speeds and appreciated by pilots, is a mechanical function linked with the chronograph complication. Pressing a pusher once allows the chronograph hand to go back to zero and immediately start again, thus avoiding the normal three manipulations: hand-stop, zero setback, and new release of the second hand.

The power-reserve indication feature

The power-reserve indicator shows, by a hand or through a window, the working time left before the spring needs winding again. Automatic-winding devices allow winding of the main spring by the oscillations of a mass freely rotating around its axis and driven by the movements of the arm.

With similar movements, the indicator adjusts itself inasmuch as winding is the result of the number of gestures and their amplitude.

It is also highly appreciated with manual-winding movements, which have a greater autonomy of between 36 and 48 hours.

EXTRA-COMPLICATED WATCHES

Extra-complicated watches represent the field preferred by master watchmakers to give their talents and skills free play.

The refinement of its expression must not be evaluated on the basis of the greatest number of complications incorporated, but rather according to the art of arranging the different mechanisms, the compatibility of functions, and the harmonious mastery of the piece.

A highly complicated (H.C.) piece may consist of an automatic-winding movement driving a minute-totalizer chronograph and a twelve-month perpetual calendar.

A very highly complicated (T.H.C.) piece has a basic minute repeater completed by a chronograph, a perpetual calendar, or a three-hammer sonnerie. Finally, very, very highly complicated (T.T.H.C.) watches have a grande sonnerie, a petite sonnerie, a mute feature and a minute repeater, completed by at least two complications such as a perpetual calendar, a split-second chronograph, and possibly a tourbillon escapement or a tourbillon release-spring escapement.

The watch called "Marie Antoinette," produced in 1802, is considered the model of great-complication watches. It includes an automatic-winding device, a power-reserve indicator, an independent second counter, a jumping-hour hand, a minute repeater, a perpetual calendar with retrograde day indication, an equation of time, and a thermometer, which is not a typical timepiece feature.

After this magical watch, others were produced, especially in the Joux Valley (in the Swiss Jura). Some of these left an ineffaceable trace in the history of watchmaking, such as Universelle (1870) and Royale (1873) by Louis Audemars; Merveilleuse (1878) by A. LeCoultre-Piguet; Leroy 01 (1904) by Charles Piguet, Audemars Piguet (1915); Graves (1932), Caliber 89 (1989), and Star Caliber 2000, all three by Patek Philippe; and the Great Complications of the 1930s by Vacheron Constantin.

Wristwatches with great complications as well as ultra-thin and automatic-winding movements accompanied the revival of traditional watchmaking after the breakthrough of quartz movements. Such complications boosted the popularity of mechanical watches once again, making them strong factors against electronic modules. Numerous creations, unique pieces or very limited series marked the history of watchmaking. Among these are: DaVinci by IWC (1985), a wrist chronograph with full thousandth and programmed over 500 years; Astrolabium Galileo Galilei (1985), Planetarium Copernicus (1989) and Tellurium Johannes Kepler (1992), a trilogy by Dr. Ludwig Oechslin for Ulysse Nardin.

The model 1735 by Blancpain (1991) includes the following features: perpetual calendar; split-second chronograph; tourbillon device; and minute repeater. Also in 1991, Bréguet presented an automatic wristwatch with perpetual calendar and equation of time. Two years later, Philippe Dufour designed the first wristwatch provided with a grande sonnerie.

More recently, in 2000, Roger Dubuis produced a watch with minute repeater and bi-retrograde perpetual calendar. For the first time in the world, on the occasion of the new millennium, Audemars Piguet unveiled a Jules Audemars watch with sunrise and sunset times, equation of time, and perpetual calendar whose execution is personalized according to the latitude and longitude of 14 important cities.

This enumeration does not pretend to be exhaustive and numerous masterworks are under way. As the development and use of complications mirror the way of life of an epoch, undoubtedly new functions devoted to sporting, traveling and calendars will be invented.

Dominique Fléchon

The author expresses his sincere gratitude to the Comité International de la Haute Horlogerie for providing the resources and photographs necessary to complete this piece. © CIHH

Would You Park a Ferrari on the Street?

Single-watch boxes are more than a convenience - they help watches last longer and run more accurately.

Then surely you don't drop your fine watches into a drawer.

Serious watch enthusiasts the world over use Scatola del Tempo boxes. With compartments for bracelet or strap watches and rotors to keep automatic watches fully wound–they're the ideal place for fine watch collections.

Choose from more than two dozen Italian handcrafted leather-and-silk collector boxes.

SCATOLA del TEMPO ®

The World's Finest Time Keepers.

S.C.S. & Co. - Via dei Mille, 17 - I-23891 Barzanò - ITALY - Tel. +39 (039) 9211481 - Fax +39 (039) 958970 • www.scatoladeltempo.com

Distributors: ITALY, Roberto Cella, Via Carlo Osma 2, I-20151 Milano - Tel. +39 (02) 3085705 - Fax +39 (02) 33402 73 • SWITZERLAND, Techno Temps, CH-1521 Curtilles - Tel. +41 (21) 9069681 - Fax +41 (21) 9069682 • GERMANY-AUSTRIA, Unkhoff Uhren Vertrieb, Niederoesbern 156, D-58708 Menden, Germany - Tel. +49 (23) 732237 - Fax +49 (23) 7310374 • SPAIN, Pamies, Plaza Llibertat 11, E-43201 Reus - Tel. +34 (97) 7127082 - Fax +34 (97) 7772808 • PORTUGAL, Carlos, Rua Alvaro Casteloes 88, P-2900 Setubal - Tel. +351 (2) 65529700 - Fax +351 (2) 65529706 • BELGIUM, G-M Lens Imexport, Schupstraat 13/15, B-2818 Antwerp - Tel. +32 (32) 321074 - Fax +32 (32) 315399 • U.S.A., Chronoswiss USA Luxury Products, 112 South Country Road, NY 11713 Bellport - Tel. +1 (631) 7761135 - Fax +1 (631) 7761136 • MEXICO, Grupo Mondi S.A., Av. Popocatepetl 204, 03340 Mexico D.F. - Tel. +525 6884165 - Fax +525 6882589 • ARGENTINA, Zanotti, Av. Alvear 1850, 1129 Capital Federal, Buenos Aires - Tel. +541 (14) 8053211 - Fax +541 (14) 8053213 • JAPAN, Asai & Co., 1-34-8 Ohsu Nakaku, 460 Nagoja - Tel. +81 (52) 2311972 -Fax +81 (52) 2311962 • HONG-KONG, Wonderful Grand Ltd., Room 2302-2303, Fu Fai Commercial Center, No. 27 Hillier Street - Tel. +852 (2) 8041182 -Fax +852 (2) 8663581

Introduction

The following pages pay homage to the fine watch-making houses, their heritages and the craft they have passed on from generation to generation. The timepieces built by the watchmakers of these brands—true masters of their profession—are among the most prestigious.

The newest timepieces on the market from these companies offer a wealth of choices for watch lovers internationally. From cutting-edge styling to sports precision to technological advancements, the watches featured in this catalog represent a commitment to advancement and achievement.

In an effort to offer as much information as possible to the knowledge-hungry reader, we have devoted a good deal of space to editorial profiles of the brands. Each profile in this catalog offers insight into the brand, its history, its guiding philosophies and its newest collections.

Where possible, in these profiles, we have provided extremely detailed information on the new models. For the companies that were abundantly prolific in their unveilings in 2001, we have outlined the highlights. Arranged alphabetically by brand for ease of use, the technical descriptions of the new watches give preferential treatment to the mechanical watch—the forefather, backbone and future legacy of the Swiss watchmaking tradition.

Photography

In the technical description sections of each watch brand, *Watches International 2002* and the staff of Tourbillon International paid exacting attention to detail when photographing the watches. Each timepiece was placed on the same background, and each photograph was taken from the same angle under the same lighting to assure unbiased presentation and consistency. We have even maintained the proportions between one watch and another. This approach enables readers to make their own comparisons between different models.

Technical description

Each technical description is thorough—offering all of the information needed to evaluate and compare the timepieces. In every case, we provide the movement information and functions of the watch, and list the aesthetic details, including case size, diameter and height, dial base and finish, and bracelet descriptions. Additionally, where other models or versions are available, we have so noted.

For watch movements that have been built upon a base caliber, we have indicated the base caliber wherever possible. In these instances, we attempt to indicate the difference between the caliber and the execution mounted on the watch shown therein—differences that are technical-functional rather than those that are based on decoration and further hand-finishing.

Again, for ease of use, the section marked "indications" gives the reader a complete description of the dial readouts and displays.

We are confident that the information provided in this annual will give you many hours of enjoyable reading and that the catalog will be an invaluable reference in the coming year.

A MINUTE IN TIME IS AS IMPORTANT
AS 24 HOURS IN WOMAN'S LIFE.

BERTOLUCCI
ONE DAY OR ANOTHER

MANUFACTURE
DE MONTRES
NEUCHÂTEL
SUISSE

www.bertolucci-watches.com

A. LANGE & SÖHNE

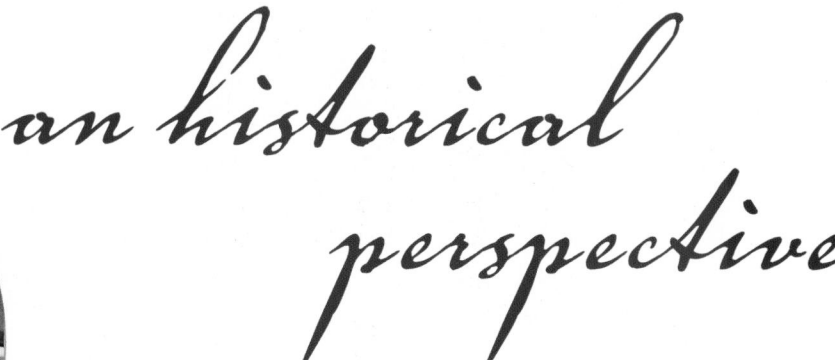

an historical perspective

*J*ust a dozen short years ago, an historical wrong may finally have been righted. In 1990, with the technical, financial, and otherwise supportive help of IWC, A. Lange & Söhne— German watchmaker extraordinaire— reopened its doors. Not only was a great name revived, but a new sense of glory and awe swept through the city of Glashütte.

Once housed in this famed Saxony city, Lange had been a revered and profitable watch firm. Founded in 1845 by Ferdinand Adolph Lange, the brand had been committed to creating the finest precision German timepieces. For 100 years A. Lange was a stellar success—bringing recognition to the Dresden region and its watchmakers.

World War II bombings and political unrest put an end to the brand's significance and lifeblood. Bombs destroyed the workshops in 1945, and the brand was further plundered three years later when A. Lange & Söhne was expropriated by the socialist regime. Ordered to the uranium mines, fourth-generation Walter Lange fled to the west. Then, in 1989, when the East-West conflict ended and the Berlin Wall fell, bringing down the communist regime in East Germany, Walter Lange thought that at long last his dream of reestablishing the family brand and grand tradition might be within his grasp.

Thanks to a close partnership with IWC, Lange returned to Glashütte and set up state-of-the-art workshops in the city of its birth. Reforming the link with Saxony's great watchmaking heritage and with his family's past, Lange hired many descendants of former employees—whose knowledge had been passed on from generation to generation despite the war.

The first A. Lange & Söhne watches swept back onto the world stage in 1994— with immediate international recognition. Once again these fine mechanical timepieces had joined the ranks of the most sought-after quality products of German origin. To safeguard the financial situation of his company, Walter Lange had entrusted it to the LMH (Les Manufactures Horlogeres) watch group—owner of IWC and Jaeger-LeCoultre. In 2001, LMH was sold to the prestigious Richemont Group—offering Lange new opportunities.

Today, Lange is one of the very few watch brands that creates its own movements. A true Manufacture, the brand is poised—under Richemont's umbrella and Walter Lange's personal interest—to carry its superior horological accomplishments to even higher heights.

THIS PAGE

TOP LEFT

Ferdinand Adolph Lange, founder of A. Lange & Söhne.

TOP RIGHT

Walter Lange relaunched the brand in 1990.

BOTTOM

An inside view of the Langematik Perpetual movement.

FACING PAGE

The Langematik Perpetual calendar watch in platinum made its world debut this past year. It features the Sax-o-Mat movement and zero-reset function.

A. LANGE & SÖHNE

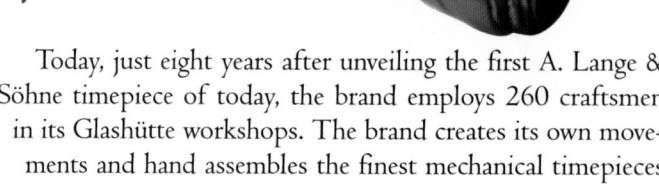

unveiling masterpieces

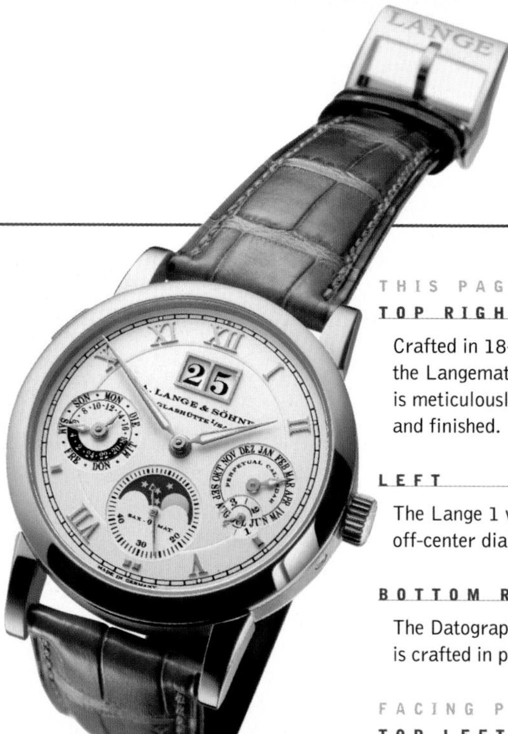

Today, just eight years after unveiling the first A. Lange & Söhne timepiece of today, the brand employs 260 craftsmen in its Glashütte workshops. The brand creates its own movements and hand assembles the finest mechanical timepieces to the tune of just a few thousand watches annually.

All Lange watches share several important characteristic features that help define the new standard. Housed in either platinum or 18-karat gold, Lange watches feature screw-on casebacks, sapphire crystals and sealed pushpieces. Additionally, a host of haute horlogerie accomplishments rests within the hallowed Lange cases.

Created only in small numbers, the Lange collection consists of several important models, including: the Lange I (an exclusive design with off-center main dial, small seconds hand and outsized date); Arkade (mechanical gemset watch for women); Lange Saxonia (identified by its oversized date); 1815 and 1815 Up and Down (commemorating the year in which founding father of the firm, Adolph Lange, was born); Langematik with Sax-o-Mat caliber (automatic movement with integrated patented outsized date and the unique time-setting mechanism "zero-reset"); Datograph (extraordinary flyback chronograph); Lange-Tourbillon—the ultimate watchmaking accomplishment.

Indeed, since its rebirth, the brand has focused clearly on creating only the finest timepieces with the utmost technical prowess. Remaining faithful to this commitment, Lange unveils the Langematik Perpetual.

THIS PAGE

TOP RIGHT

Crafted in 18-karat gold, the Langematik Perpetual is meticulously hand crafted and finished.

LEFT

The Lange 1 with elegant off-center dial.

BOTTOM RIGHT

The Datograph chronograph is crafted in platinum.

FACING PAGE

TOP LEFT

Watchmaking in all its glory at Lange's state-of-the-art Glashütte workshops.

TOP CENTER

The Lange 1 Tourbillon houses one of watchmaking's finest feats.

TOP RIGHT

The 1815 Up and Down pays homage to the year in which Lange's founding father was born.

BOTTOM RIGHT

The Arkade is Lange's premiere timepiece for women.

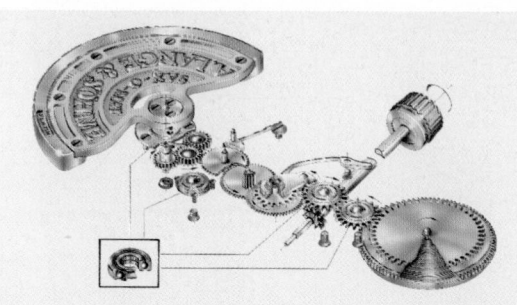

CHRONOLOGY

1830s Ferdinand Adolph Lange serves apprenticeship with Johann Christian Friedrich Gutkaes and attends Dresden's technical college.

1842 Lange weds Gutkaes's daughter, Charlotte, and becomes a partner in the Gutkaes manufactory.

1845 Lange founds Saxony's fine-watch industry in Glashütte with 15 apprentices and a loan from the state; He adopts the metric system and develops his own measuring instruments.

1863 Lange produces a pocket watch with chronograph stop-work and mechanism under the dial.

1884 Lange introduces the three-quarter-plate caliber, a distinguishing feature of Glashütte watchmaking.

1866 Adolph Lange develops an astronomical watch indicating the date, day, month and moonphase.

1868 Son Richard becomes joint owner of the family business, now renamed "A. Lange & Söhne" (& Sons).

1869 Adolph Lange is elected to Saxon state parliament.

1874 Lange introduces the smallest lever watch with seconds for ladies. The movement diameter is only 25mm.

1895 The company is connected directly to Berlin's observatory for the true time; Produces navigational timepieces for several of the world's naval forces and merchant fleets; Glashütte erects a memorial to honor Adolph Lange, who served as mayor for 18 years.

1898 In Constantinople, Kaiser William presents Sultan Abdul Hamit II with a richly decorated A. Lange & Söhne pocket watch featuring an enamel miniature of the Kaiser.

1900 Emil Lange represents A. Lange & Söhne on the international jury at the Paris Universal Exhibition and is made a knight of the French Legion of Honour in 1902.

1908 A Lange Grande Complication repeating clock-watch in a "Louis XV à goutte" case sells for 4930 gold marks — the price of two houses.

1945 Russian bombers destroy Lange's main workshops.

1948 East Germany's communist regime seizes the Lange company; Fourth-generation Walter Lange is forced into West Germany.

1951 Lange is one of seven nationalized Glashütte companies whose names and trademarks cease to exist.

1989 Collapse of both the communist regime and the Berlin Wall dividing Germany.

1990 Germany is reunified; Walter Lange founds "Lange Uhren GmbH" of Glashütte, registering the company in Dresden and the traditional trademark of A. Lange & Söhne worldwide.

1994 In Dresden and Glashütte, the first Lange watches of the new era are presented; Distribution is limited to 15 retail outlets in German-speaking countries.

1995 Walter Lange is made freeman of Glashütte. The Lange 1 is voted Watch of the Year by the readers of *Armbanduhren International*.

1997 Completion of the Sax-o-Mat; The Lange 1 and the Langematik win various awards in Europe.

1998 The Lange Watchmaking School opens in Glashütte; Walter Lange is awarded the Order of Merit of the Free State of Saxony; Lange is the first top watch brand to advertise on German-speaking television with a 30-second spot; Walter Lange is the first chairman of House of the Watch Glashütte; A. Lange & Söhne is voted Best New Brand (Italy).

1999 A moonphase display computed for 1,000 years is integrated into the 1815 Moonphase that pays tribute to Emil Lange's 150th birthday; Distribution expands through Europe to Asia and the United Arab Emirates.

2000 The company reacquires its original headquarters; Lange marks the 10th anniversary of reestablishment by opening a permanent in-house exhibition displaying its accomplishments.

This supreme perpetual calendar watch with outsized date utilizes both a main pushpiece for all day-by-day calendar-related functions and three smaller pushpieces for individual correction. The sophisticated and advanced Sax-o-Mat self-winding bi-directional rotor powers the exclusive timepiece. The watch features the brand's remarkable automatic zero-reset mechanism and an additional 24-hour display with day/night indicator.

As with all Lange watches, this elegant timepiece is created only in platinum or in gold. Its superb dial is striking in its clarity, despite the numerous indications it offers. The Lange patented outsized date is at 12:00. A subsidiary dial at 9:00 displays the day of week, night/day indicator and 24-hour display. At 6:00, a golden moon enters a subdial with such a high degree of precision that it requires a correction of one day every 122 years. (This correction can be easily performed with a separate pushpiece recessed into the case). This 6:00 subdial also offers the small seconds and the zero-reset function. When the crown is pulled out to set the time, the movement stops and the seconds hand instantly jumps to the 12:00 position—an incredibly precise technological achievement. Finally, at 3:00, the subdial offers the 12 months in annual cycle, as well as the four-year leap-year cycle.

The main pushpiece at 10:00 allows all five indications (date, day, month, leap-year and moonphase display) to be collectively advanced in steps of one day. Regardless of the momentary setting of the calendar mechanism, the hands can be turned forward or backward without affecting any of the indications. This watch, along with Lange's other creative ventures in timekeeping, attests to the brand's commitment to technical perfection.

A. LANGE & SÖHNE

L 921.4 CALIBER SAX-O-MAT

L 921.2 caliber base (without big date thickness 3.80 mm). Automatic movement, autonomy 46 h, 21 kt off-center rotor con with screwed-on platinum segment, mounted on ball bearing. **Functions:** hour, minute, small second, zero-reset, patented big date (with fast correction).
Shape: round. **Diameter:** 30.4 mm. **Thickness:** 5.55 mm. **Jewels:** 45. **Balance:** with compensation screws, with two arms, in Glucydur. **Frequency:** 21,600 vibrations/hour. **Balance spring:** flat, Nivarox 1, with micrometer regulation and swan-neck regulator spring. **Shock-absorbing system:** Kif.
Note: alpaca pillar-plate decorated with circular graining; alpaca bridges decorated by the "Glashütte polishing" process and beveled; escape wheel with endstone set in gold, setting locked by a polished steel plate; hand-engraved balance bridge.

Small photograph (right): dial side of the L 921.4 version with big date display, patented device allowing big digit display for easy data reading. Its working is concisely described under L 911.4 caliber. Among the other features of this movement the following are worthwhile noting: the valuable winding device and the zero-resetting of the continuing second hand during hour settings.

L 922.1 CALIBER SAX-O-MAT

By using the 921.2 caliber as a base and adding a calendar module, taking automatically into account the different lengths of months, Lange was able to enrich its catalogue by the Langematik Perpetual model. Thus, the complete movement has 43 jewels and is 5.4 millimeters thick. These values are extraordinarily lower than those of the movement with only the integrated big date feature (left). An original characteristic of this module is represented by the possibility of adjusting the single calendar displays independently by three classic correctors or of making them advance together by one click (1 day) by pressing down once the special pusher positioned at 10 o'clock. This possibility permits to select the quickest mode of calendar adjustment in cases in which the movement has been left stopped for a few days or some months: in the first case it is recommended to act simultaneously by using the pusher, in the second case it will be better to perform individual and separate adjustments through the correctors. The module's working, as far as the other technical features are concerned, is similar to that of many other pieces of high horology.

Lange, when realizing its automatic movement, introduced really unique and original technical sophistication, such as the use of four ball bearings to reduce driving friction during the transmission of motion from the rotor to the barrel or the zero-reset system, that exploits the typical elements of chronograph movements to zero and stop the small second hand as long as the crown is extracted.

MOTION TRANSMISSION SYSTEM

The sketch below shows the complex gear train connecting rotor and barrel. The rotor (realized in gold, personalized and provided with a screwed-on platinum segment) is mounted on two bearings, one of which is a ball bearing used to reduce friction and the other is equipped with a jewel to regulate its accurate centering. It is linked first with an inverter (it can be recognized by its two toothed wheels with jewels inside); this element keeps the gear rotation way always unidirectional in spite of the two-way rotor oscillations. The rotor mass and transmission ra-

tios with the barrel have been calculated in such a way as to achieve a higher performance with respect to the average, so that even the slightest arm movement corresponds to a tangible winding action. The final part of the gear train connects the winding shaft with the barrel to transmit the motion from the crown (for manual winding, when the watch has not been used for a certain period and is, therefore, completely discharged).

ZERO-RESET SYSTEM

Thanks to this device, it is possible to proceed to an accurate adjustment of hours, minutes and seconds during the precise synchronization of the watch with the time-signal. In fact, as soon as the crown is put back, the second hand starts again and is perfectly synchronous with the reference watch used for time adjustment. In the photographs below (center and right) it is possible to appreciate the complex lever play controlling the zero-reset device: when the gray lever is displaced after the crown is extracted, a de-

flection spring (blue, left side) locks the balance, the hammer lever (brown) acts upon the heart-shaped eccentric (green) to zero the hand, while the stop-lever (fuchsia) holds it in place. The broken lines show the respective positions taken by the different elements, as soon as the winding crown is put in place again. The photograph below on the right shows the zero-reset system as it appears on the movement from the dial side. The brass-color wheel above is the one on whose internal side the hour hand is fastened, while the minute hand is positioned on the coaxial steel pivot. In a lower position, perpendicularly, one can see the pivot coming out from the jewel on which the small second hand is mounted.

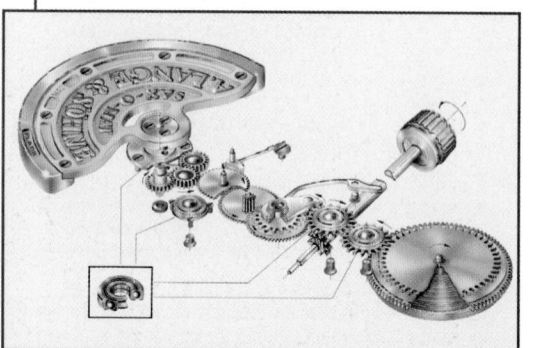

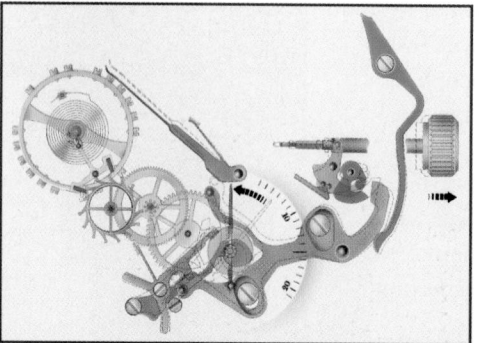

LANGEMATIK BIG DATE   REF. 308.021

Movement: mechanical, automatic winding, A. Lange & Söhne SAX-O-MAT 921.4 caliber. Hand-finished and hand-engraved.
Functions: hour, minute, small second, date.
Case: 18 kt yellow gold, three-piece case (Ø 37 mm, thickness 9.7 mm), polished and brushed finish; flat sapphire crystal; rectangular date corrector pusher at 10; gold crown; case back attached by 6 screws, displaying the movement through a sapphire crystal. Water-resistant to 3 atm.
Dial: solid silver, silvered; applied gold bâton markers; luminescent dots at quarters on a printed minute track; luminescent gold Alpha hands. **Indications:** small second at 6 (with zero-set device), gold-bordered patented big date with double window at 12.
Strap: crocodile leather, hand-stitched; gold clasp.
Also available: with bracelet; white gold, black dial, leather strap and bracelet; platinum, gray dial, leather strap and bracelet (on request); pink gold, silvered or black dial, leather strap.

LANGEMATIK BIG DATE   REF. 358.031

The Langematik version with date display adopts the original oversized date formed by combining an element for the tens with four arms (one of which without writings for the days from 1 to 9 and the other three with the numbers 1, 2 and 3 for the two-digit days), superimposed on a disc for the units (numbered from 0 to 9). The visual result is an easy-to-read oversized date display within a double window hiding the step created by the superimposition of both elements.
The photograph shows the pink-gold version with black dial. This color was obtained by a galvanization process: the silver base is dipped into a chemical bath with a zinc compound; at the passage of an electric current a color layer is deposited on the surface. This treatment offers the advantage of ensuring a longer life and an effective protection against oxidization spots.
Also available: with silvered dial; in white gold with black dial, strap or bracelet; in platinum with gray dial, strap or bracelet on request; in yellow gold with strap or bracelet.

LANGEMATIK JUBILEE   REF. 302.025

Movement: mechanical, automatic winding, A. Lange & Söhne 921.4 SAX-O-MAT caliber. Hand-finished and hand-engraved.
Functions: hour, minute, small second.
Case: platinum, three-piece case (Ø 37 mm, thickness 8.5 mm), polished and brushed finish; flat sapphire crystal; white-gold crown; numbered back, attached by 6 screws, displaying the movement through a sapphire crystal. Water-resistant to 3 atm.
Dial: solid silver, white enameled; Roman numerals, the 12 red; railway minute track; blued steel Alpha hands. **Indications:** small second at 6 (with zero-set device).
Strap: crocodile leather, hand-stitched; platinum clasp.
Yearly production limited to 500 pieces.
Also available: standard; in platinum, gray-rhodium-plated dial, leather strap and bracelet (on request); in pink gold, champagne dial, leather strap and bracelet; in white gold, black dial, strap or bracelet.

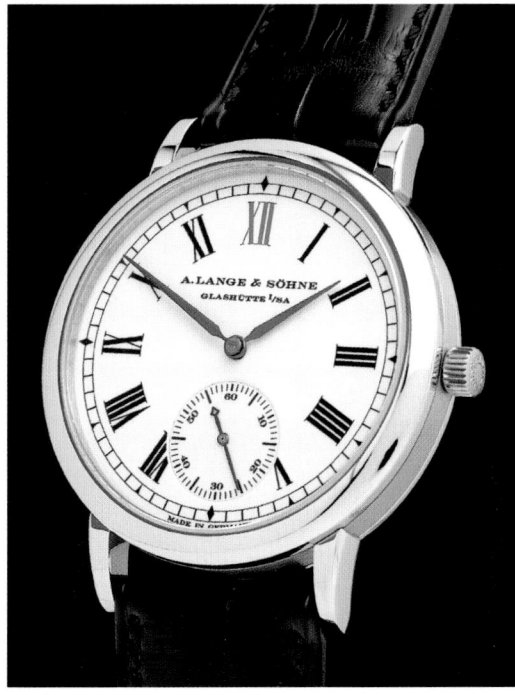

LANGEMATIK JUBILEE

Born in 1997, the automatic movement called SAX-O-MAT by A. Lange & Söhne adopts very modern and original technical solutions. It was the first automatic wristwatch in the world which was provided with the zero-reset system that zeroes and stops the second hand, when the crown is pulled out and until it is pushed in again; furthermore, it is equipped with a 3/4 rotor (i.e. its surface occupies 3/4 of the total), integrated in the movement's volume and supported by a double bearing, a traditional ball bearing and an adjustable jewel bearing. It is realized in solid gold, with a segment in platinum, and finely hand-engraved. These characteristics are added to its very high technical and constructive features that correspond to the tradition of the House: gold balance with compensation screws and hand-engraved bridge, endstones on the escape wheel (with stone-holding plate in polished steel), balance-lever regulation by micrometer screw and swan-neck regulator spring and some jewels placed within gold settings (which are not held in place by screws).

A. LANGE & SÖHNE

LANGEMATIK-PERPETUAL   REF. 310.025

Movement: mechanical, automatic winding, A. Lange & Söhne 921.4 SAX-O-MAT caliber (L1,921.4 base + perpetual calendar module). Hand-finished and hand-engraved. **Functions:** hour, minute, small second, 24 hour, perpetual calendar (date, day, month, year, moon-phase). **Case:** platinum, three-piece case (Ø 38, thickness 10.2 mm), polished and brushed finish; flat sapphire crystal; white-gold crown; rectangular pusher at 10 for the whole calendar correction; 3 additional

correctors on the middle; case back attached by 6 screws displaying the movement through a sapphire crystal. Water-resistant to 3 atm. **Dial:** solid silver, gray-rhodium-plated; zones decorated with circular beads; applied rhodium-plated gold Roman numerals; luminescent dots on a printed railway minute track; luminescent rhodium-plated gold Alpha hands. **Indications:** month at 3, 4-year cycle at 4, small second (with zero-set device) and moon-phase at 6, day and 24 hours day-night at 9, patented big date with double window bordered in rhodium-plated gold at 12. **Strap:** crocodile leather, hand-stitched; platinum clasp. **Also available:** with bracelet on request; in yellow gold, leather strap and bracelet.

LANGEMATIK-PERPETUAL   REF. 310.221

A. Lange & Söhne opens the XXIth century as well as its second life decade by a new movement made up by the SAX-O-MAT and a perpetual calendar module. The pusher on the middle, that in big-date watches is used to correct the day of the month, here offers the possibility of making all the calendar indications simultaneously advance (date, day, month, year, moon-phase), while the three classical correctors on the case allow to act individually on moon-phase, day

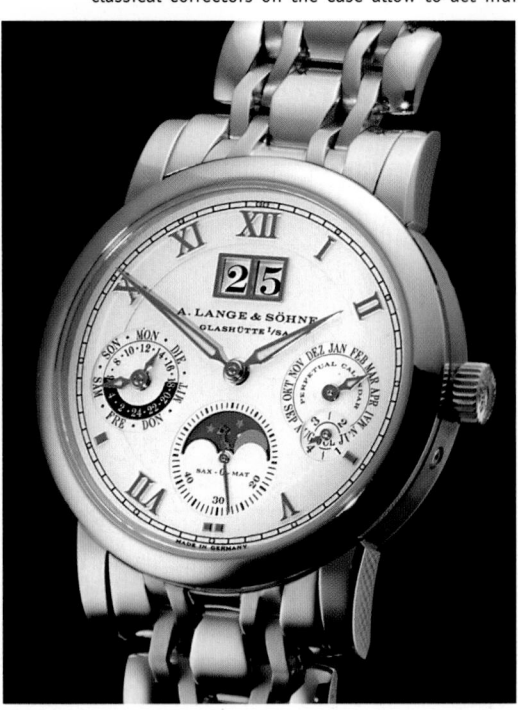

of the week, month and year.

Another peculiarity of this movement is given by the fact that it is possible to rotate the hands in both ways in any period of the day, even at the crucial day change, i.e. at midnight, without causing damages to the mechanism.

The photograph shows the 18 kt yellow gold version with silvered dial. The bracelet has a classical fold-over clasp.

Also available: with leather strap; in platinum with strap or bracelet on request.

LANGE 1 TOURBILLON   REF. 704.025

Movement: mechanical, manual winding, A. Lange & Söhne L961.1 caliber with tourbillon. Hand-finished and hand-engraved.
Functions: hour, minute, small second, date, power reserve.
Case: platinum, three-piece case (Ø 39 mm, thickness 9.75 mm), polished and brushed finish; flat sapphire crystal; rectangular date corrector pusher at 10; white-gold crown; case back attached by 6 screws, displaying the movement

through a sapphire crystal. Water-resistant to 3 atm.
Dial: solid silver, gray-rhodium-plated; aperture on the tourbillon; applied rhodium-plated gold Roman numerals and lozenge markers; printed minute track; rhodium-plated gold Alpha hands.
Indications: off-center hour and minute at 9 with hour and small second ring between 7 and 8, engine-turned (guilloché); patented big date with double window bordered in rhodium-plated gold at 1, power reserve at 3.
Strap: crocodile leather, hand-stitched; platinum clasp.
Limited edition of 150 pieces.
Also available: in pink gold, 250 pieces.

LANGE 1 TOURBILLON

Exactly 100 year from the birth of the pocket tourbillon watch signed A. Lange & Söhne and called "Tourbillon of the Century", presented at the Universal Exhibition of Paris in 1900, Lange now proposes a wristwatch model, Lange 1 Tourbillon. Maintaining the positive features of the famous Lange 1 (patented big-date watch with double barrel with an autonomy of three days, power reserve display on the dial and off-center hour at 9), this new Saxon master-

piece is the first tourbillon watch in the world to have such features.

Made up by 378 elements, the L 961.1 caliber is provided with bridges and pillar-plate realized in alpaca (a copper-nickel-zinc alloy, also known by the names of German silver or pak-tong), jewels set in gold settings locked by blued steel screws and bridges chased by hand (the 3/4 one is emphasized by the typical "Glashütte polishing" process).

The tourbillon carriage, according to the Saxon House's tradition, rotates on diamond bearings. A balance with gold compensation screws and a Breguet balance spring complete its technical description.

DATOGRAPH   REF. 403.035

Movement: mechanical, manual winding, A. Lange & Söhne 951.1 caliber. Hand-finished and hand-engraved.
Functions: hour, minute, small second, date, chronograph with fly-back feature and 2 counters.
Case: platinum, three-piece case (Ø 39 mm, thickness 10.8 mm), polished and brushed finish; flat sapphire crystal; rectangular pushers, date corrector pusher at 10; white gold crown; case back attached by 6 screws displaying the movement through a sapphire crystal. Water-resistant to 3 atm.
Dial: solid silver, black (coloring obtained by galvanization); silvered zones; applied rhodium-plated gold bâton markers and Roman numerals; luminescent rhodium-plated gold Alpha hands, counter hands in rhodium-plated and burnished steel.
Indications: minute counter at 4, small second at 8, patented big date at 12 with double window, bordered in rhodium-plated gold, center second counter, minute track with divisions for 1/5 of a second, tachometer scale.
Strap: crocodile leather, hand-stitched; platinum clasp.

DATOGRAPH

Datograph is an extremely sophisticated chronograph, provided with a big-sized date display, exactly jumping hour counter, fly-back device and several other constructive features that make it be a unique piece on the watch market. Its heart is a completely new movement, made up by 390 components and adopting traditional but complex technical solutions, such as for instance the column-wheel and the typical architecture with a three-quarter pillar-plate and hand-engraved balance bridge. Its original hour counter with exactly jumping minutes, advancing by a notch just when the chronograph hand ends the 60th second (a complex technique, realized by an endless stepped wheel).

As far as mechanics is concerned, the following features are worthwhile noting: the separate bridge of the second wheel, the chronograph control lever with a steady shaft supported on both sides, the adjustable chronograph interlocking lever, the control lever of the minute counter mounted on jewels on both sides (like a wheel) and the pivots of the escape wheel with endstones.

LANGE 1   REF. 110.029

Movement: mechanical, manual winding, A. Lange & Söhne, 901.0 caliber. Hand-finished and hand-engraved.
Functions: hour, minute, small second, date, power reserve.
Case: 18 kt white gold, three-piece case (Ø 38.5 mm, thickness 10 mm), polished and brushed finish; flat sapphire crystal; rectangular date corrector pusher at 10; white gold crown; case back attached by 6 screws, displaying the movement through a sapphire crystal. Water-resistant to 3 atm. **Dial:** solid silver, clad with mother-of-pearl. **Indications:** off-center hour and minute at 9; applied rhodium-plated gold lozenge markers and Roman numerals; printed minute track; rhodium-plated gold Alpha hands; patented big date bordered in rhodium-plated gold with double window at 1, power reserve at 3, small second between 4 and 5.
Strap: crocodile leather, hand-stitched; white gold clasp.
Also available: with bracelet; in yellow gold, silver or champagne dial, leather strap, bracelet; pink gold, black or silvered dial, bracelet platinum, gray or black dial, leather strap, bracelet on request.

LANGE 1

In 1994, Lange 1 was the first watch of the House of Glashütte after the reunification of Germany and thus it became almost a symbol of the rebirth of a great tradition thanks to which once the Saxon watchmakers were able to compete with the Swiss, as far as quality and precision are concerned. Thanks to its great simplicity, Lange 1 offered high quality features, among which the (patented) big date display whose design recalls the famous five-minute clock of Semper's Opera house in Dresden. Another very original feature for a wristwatch (much imitated today) is the quick-acting pusher corrector positioned at 10 o'clock, that is much more practical with respect to the crown system, due to the frequent need for date advance in the months having less than 31 days or in case of stop, even though the latter event is not very probable because of the three-days autonomy (72 hours displayed on the dial), thanks to the availability of a double winding barrel.

The photograph shows the versions in white gold with case and dial enriched by brilliants.

A. LANGE & SÖHNE

1815 "UP AND DOWN"   REF. 221.025

Movement: mechanical, manual winding, A. Lange & Söhne L 942.1 caliber. Hand-finished and hand-engraved.
Functions: hour, minute, small second, power reserve.
Case: 18 kt pink gold, three-piece case (Ø 36 mm, thickness 8 mm), polished and brushed finish; flat sapphire crystal; pink gold crown; case back attached by 6 screws, displaying the movement through a sapphire crystal. Water-resistant to 3 atm.
Dial: solid silver, silvered; printed Arabic numerals; printed railway minute track; pink-gold Alpha hands.
Indications: small second at 4, power reserve at 8.
Strap: crocodile leather, hand-stitched; white gold clasp.
Also available: in yellow gold, silvered dial, leather strap; in platinum, silvered dial, leather strap or bracelet (on request).

1815   REF. 206.032

Movement: mechanical, manual winding, A. Lange & Söhne L941.1 caliber. Hand-finished and hand-engraved.
Functions: hour, minute, small second.
Case: 18 kt pink gold, three-piece case (Ø 36 mm, thickness 7.1 mm), polished and brushed finish; flat sapphire crystal; pink gold crown; case back attached by 6 screws, displaying the movement through a sapphire crystal. Water-resistant to 3 atm.
Dial: solid silver, silvered; printed Arabic numerals; printed railway minute track; pink-gold Alpha hands.
Indications: small second at 6.
Strap: crocodile leather, hand-stitched; pink gold clasp.
Also available: in yellow gold, silvered dial, leather strap, with bracelet; in platinum, silvered dial, leather strap or bracelet (on request).

SAXONIA   REF. 105.035

Movement: mechanical, manual winding, A. Lange & Söhne L941.3 caliber. Hand-finished and hand-engraved.
Functions: hour, minute, small second, date.
Case: platinum, three-piece case (Ø 34 mm, thickness 9 mm), polished and brushed finish; flat sapphire crystal; rectangular date corrector pusher on case side; white-gold crown with embossed logo; case back attached by 6 screws, displaying the movement through a sapphire crystal. Water-resistant to 3 atm.
Dial: solid silver, black (coloring obtained by galvanization); applied rhodium-plated gold lozenge markers on the minute track; rhodium-plated gold Alpha hands.
Indications: small second at 6, big date at 12 bordered in rhodium-plated gold.
Strap: crocodile leather, hand-stitched; platinum clasp.
Also available: with rhodium-plated dial; with bracelet (on request); in yellow gold, silver or champagne dial, leather strap; in white gold, blue dial, leather strap, bracelet; in white gold with brilliants (on request); with closed bottom (on request).

SAXONIA   REF. 105.022

As a patriotic homage to Saxony, this model is driven by a manual movement with hours, minutes, small seconds, derived from a caliber of "1815" with the addition of a patented big date display whose visualization field is up to 5 times wider than on traditional watches. Blued screws are in contrast with the gold of settings and gilded engravings on the "three-quarter" pillar-plate, as in all Lange models, with a finish obtained by the original "Glashütte polishing"

process (a response to the typical Genevan decoration "Côtes de Genève"), in alpaca (a metal alloy made up at least for a half by a mixture of copper, nickel and zinc with a color similar to silver, for which reason it is also called German silver).
According to the tradition, the balance lever has an accurate balance-spring regulation by micrometer screws and "swan-neck" regulator spring. The bridge supporting the balance is decorated entirely by hand. At the endstone of the escape wheel one perceives the polished steel plate acting as an end-stone support in one of the most "stressed" areas of the movement. The photograph shows a piece in yellow gold with silvered dial.

CABARET   REF. 107.027

Movement: mechanical, manual winding, A. Lange & Söhne L931.3 caliber. Hand-finished and hand-engraved.

Functions: hour, minute, small second, date.

Case: 18 kt white gold, three-piece rectangular case (size 36 x 25.5 mm, thickness 9 mm); curved sapphire crystal; date corrector on case side at 2; white gold crown; case back attached by 6 screws, displaying the movement through a sapphire crystal. Water-resistant to 3 atm.

Dial: solid silver, blue (coloring obtained by oxidizing vaporization); applied rhodium-plated gold lozenge markers and Roman numerals; rhodium-plated gold Alpha hands.

Indications: small second at 6, rhodium-plated gold bordered patented big date with double window at 12.

Strap: crocodile leather, hand-stitched; white gold clasp.

Also available: in platinum, black dial, leather strap, bracelet on request; in yellow gold, champagne or silvered dial, leather strap, bracelet; in pink gold with silvered or black dial, leather strap, bracelet; in white gold jewel version (on request).

CABARET   REF. 157.132

In A. Lange & Söhne's catalogue, the Cabaret is the first men's model having a rectangular case. It is worthwhile pointing out that the House of Glashütte was able to propose an absolutely unusual architecture for its shaped watch that stands out also because of the slight curve of its profile. According to the House's tradition, the movement adopted, the 931.3 caliber, was created expressly for this model and adapts to the rectangular shape of its case. Its technical and aesthetic characteristics are typical for the renewed tradition of A. Lange & Söhne: decorated pillar-plate at three quarters in natural alpaca, jewels set in screwed-on gold settings, hand-engraved balance bridge, balance-lever regulation system by micrometer screw and swan-neck regulator spring.

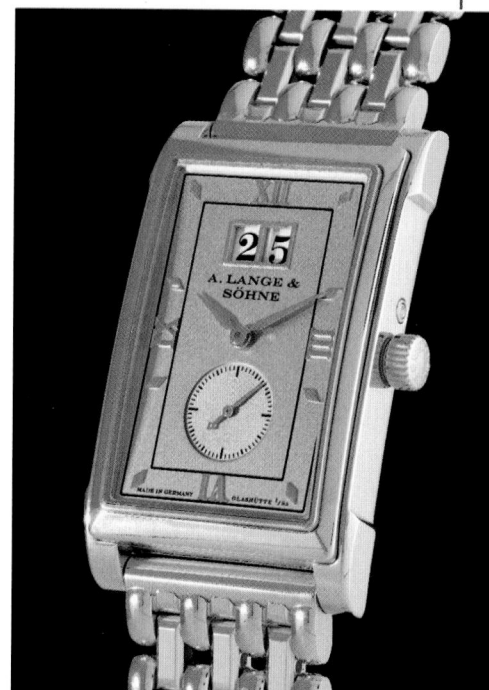

The versions in pink gold, like the one shown in the photograph with silvered dial, were realized in 1998.

Also available: with leather strap; with black dial.

ARKADE   REF. 103.035

Movement: mechanical, manual winding, A. Lange & Söhne L911.4 caliber Hand-finished and hand-engraved.

Functions: hour, minute, small second, date.

Case: platinum, two-piece rectangular case (size 29 x 22 mm, thickness 8.4 mm); flat sapphire crystal; date corrector on case side at 2; white gold crown; case back attached by 4 screws, with sapphire crystal aperture. Water-resistant to 3 atm.

Dial: solid silver, black (coloring obtained by galvanization); applied rhodium-plated gold lozenge markers and Roman numerals; rhodium-plated gold Alpha hands.

Indications: small second at 6, patented big date at 12 with double window, bordered in rhodium-plated gold.

Strap: crocodile leather, hand-stitched; platinum clasp.

Also available: with bracelet (on request); in white gold, blue dial, leather strap, bracelet; in yellow gold, champagne dial, leather strap, bracelet; as jewel-watch (on request).

ARKADE

The Arkade collection, a particularly fascinating synthesis of watchmakers' and refined goldsmiths' arts, is inspired by the arcades of the yard of the Dresden Castle and includes all of the quality characteristics of the German House, from the mysterious secret how the big date display can be adapted to a small-sized watch to the peculiarities of movements, to the skillfulness of embellishing cases and bracelets with stones.

The collection proposes bracelets worked by hand and provided with recessed clasps or leather straps, simple or jewel versions.

The photograph shows a very precious model with diamond pavé. The colors of stones (F and G of the USA scale of 22 diamond colors, going from C to Z, excluding A, B and U) is "Top Wesselton", as the Scandinavian scale is called, commonly used for the stones that we define as "extra white", corresponding to the II-Ird and IVth position of the scale of values. On the dial, the sapphire hour markers show up, as the only color spots in this highly refined realization.

AUDEMARS PIGUET

an historical perspective

More than 125 years ago, two men joined forces to create a watch company that would come to be known as one of the finest in the world. Today, the legacy of Audemars Piguet—one of tradition and excellence—thrives.

Internationally renowned as a creator of complicated timepieces and supreme sport watches, Audemars Piguet is one of just a handful of luxury watch companies that produces and assembles its own complete timepieces. This is in keeping with the ideals of its founding fathers.

It was in 1875 in the hills of the now famed Vallée de Joux that Jules Audemars, a third-generation watchmaker, set up a small workshop in his parents' farmhouse. His exacting standards of excellence and his high-quality craftsmanship made Audemars a watchmaker in demand — sought after by companies to create their complex timepieces.

However, Audemars was driven by a desire to create watches under his own name—timepieces that were of the highest quality. In pursuit of his dream, he joined forces with his good friend Edward-Auguste Piguet, also a third-generation watchmaker. Together they conceived and created complicated timepieces wherein craftsmanship and performance reigned supreme. This creed has been adhered to by Audemars Piguet generation after generation ever since.

Over the ensuing century, the Audemars and Piguet children, grandchildren and great grandchildren have been intimately involved with the family business. Thanks to their dedication to the founding philosophies, Audemars Piguet has become one of the most successful privately owned luxury watch brands in the world.

unveiling

masterpieces

Today, Audemars Piguet deftly combines high-tech materials and state-of-the-art computer aided design with superb old-world watchmaking. The result is masterpiece after masterpiece. To remain exclusive, Audemars Piguet creates only about 17,000 watches per year for worldwide distribution. These timepieces run the gamut from the futuristic Millenary Collection to high-jeweled lines to the sporty and distinctive look of the famed Royal Oak.

Additionally, Audemars Piguet continues to create especially complex watches along the lines of those introduced by its forefathers. Indeed, the newest complicated watches pay homage to both the past and the future—as they are complications of the finest nature.

Going above and beyond expectations—typical of Audemars Piguet—the brand recently unveiled five masterpieces that were the featured highlights of a traveling exhibition throughout America.

A world's first is the Jules Audemars Dynamograph—an incredibly precise watch with superb chiming powers. The Dynamograph allows the mainspring to be maintained within ideal winding limits by indicating precisely when the movement should be rewound. A winding gauge on the barrel determines the position of the Dynamograph pointer, supplying immediate information on current mainspring stress. Rewinding the movement as soon as the pointer moves beyond the zone of ideal stress shown on the indi-

cator keeps the watch at peak precision.

The Dynamograph has been further enhanced by a chiming grand strike mechanism that features three hammers, their trips and three gongs of varying pitch. A sliding mechanism allows the wearer to select the grand strike (sounding hours and quarters automatically), the lesser strike (sounding the hours only), or silence. The minute repeater is activated by a pushpiece.

This unique watch also houses two barrels: one provides a 48-hour power reserve, which powers the movement and commands the Dynamograph indicator. The second barrel powers the striking mechanism and commands its reserve indicator. In all, the 57-jeweled hand-wound movement consists of 491 components. Naturally, this masterpiece is housed in 18-karat white gold or platinum. The invention of this timepiece is a tribute to Audemars Piguet's commitment to innovation and craftsmanship.

Audemars Piguet has also unveiled a number of "world-first" timepieces that pay respect to perpetual calendars, the sun and the moon. The Jules Audemars Metropolis Perpetual Calendar watch combines a perpetual calendar with a display of local time in the world's 24 time zones. The self-winding movement of the Metropolis Perpetual Calendar houses 42 jewels and 423 parts. Featuring a 40-hour power reserve, the elegant watch has a subdial at 6:00 that provides local time in the major cities of the world. Night and day are indicated on the 24-hour ring by the colors blue and white.

Another elaborate timepiece is the Jules Audemars Equation of Time watch, which features a pair of subdials that display the time of sunrise and sun-

AUDEMARS PIGUET

set. The watch houses a perpetual calendar with astronomical moon display that will run for 122 consecutive years without needing a correction. Because sunrise and sunset times depend on latitude and longitude, each watch must be calibrated to correspond to the place determined by its owner. Currently, sunrise and sunset cams are available for 16 major cities of the world.

Tourbillons are an important part of the Jules Audemars collection, as evidenced by the Canapé Tourbillon watch with 70-hour power reserve indicator and a novel patented winding mechanism, and by the Tourbillon with Large-Size Date. This multi-function complicated timepiece consists of 443 individual parts and features the tourbillon, large-size date, perpetual calendar and minute repeater. It is housed in a platinum case to enhance the sound of the one-piece gongs that were hand-made by a single Audemars Piguet specialist.

Audemars Piguet also offers complicated timepieces in its Edward Piguet collection, including a Chiming Minute Repeater that houses an exclusive new development: the striking-work indicator of

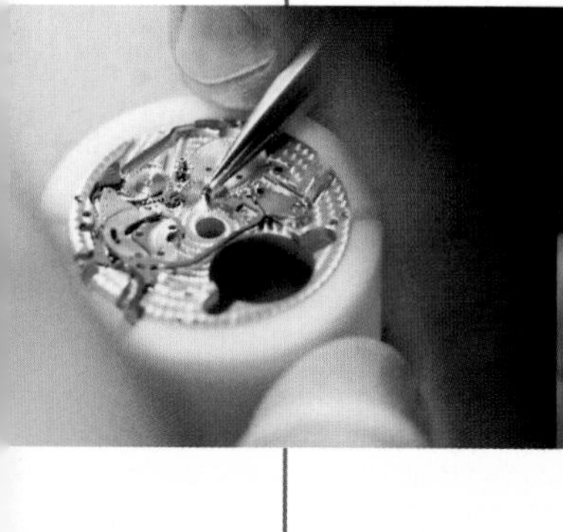

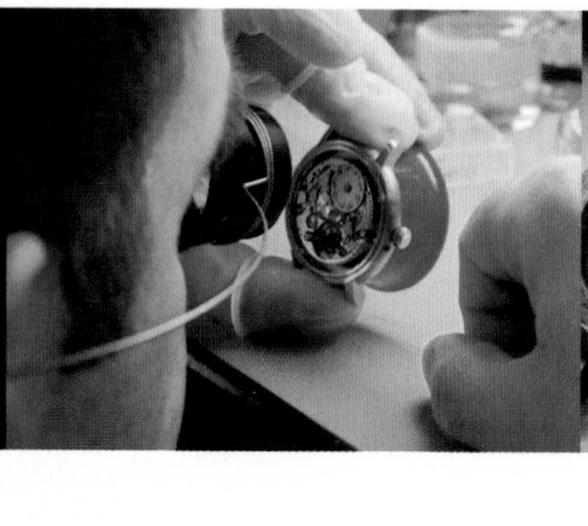

TOP

A peek at the inner workings of the new Equation of Time watch.

BOTTOM

Audemars Piguet's master watchmakers have set a tourbillon with 70 hours of power reserve into the curved rectangular Canapé case.

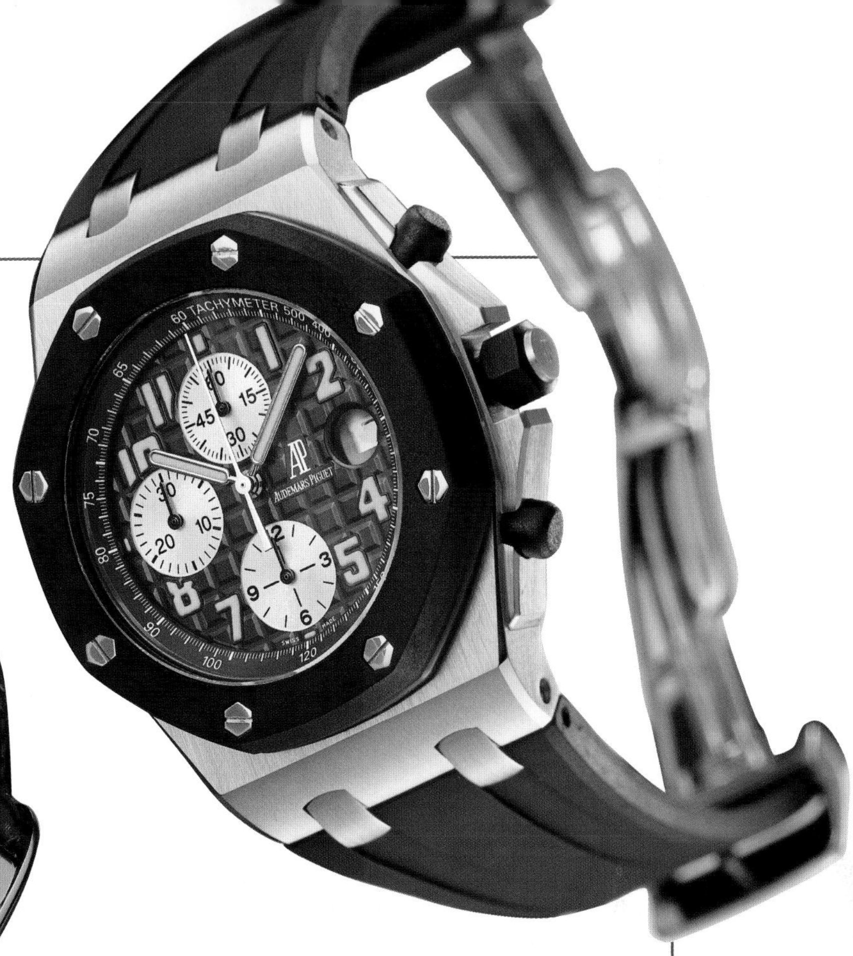

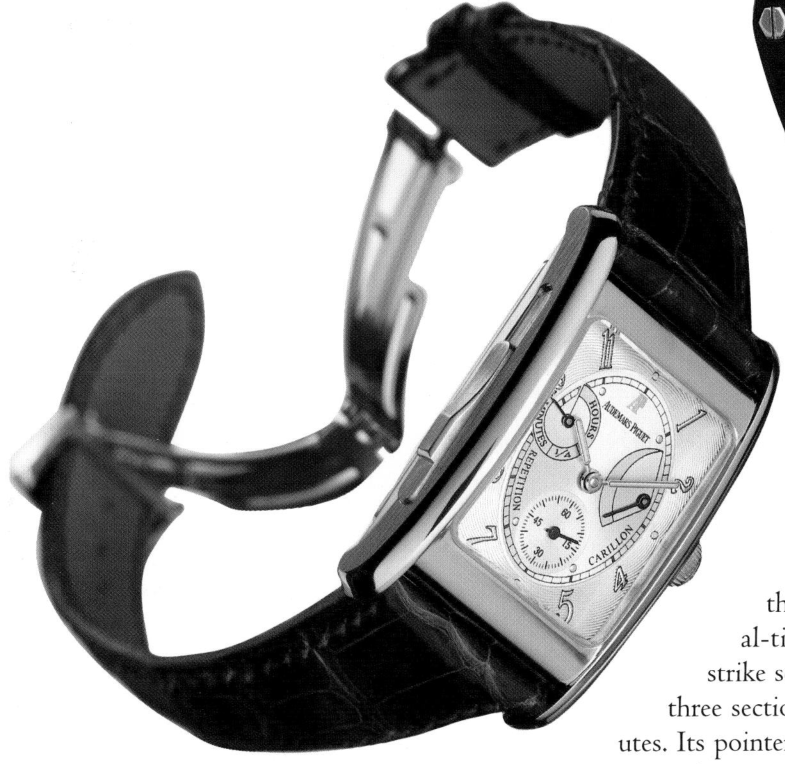

the minute repeater provides corresponding real-time information on the dial. The repeater's strike sequence is inscribed on a sub-dial divided into three sections: one each for the hours, quarters and minutes. Its pointer instantly positions itself over the appropriate segment, as determined by the uncoiling of the repeater mechanism's mainspring. The watch also includes a power reserve indicator pointer controlled by a cone-shaped sensor device created in unusually small dimensions.

And, of course, Audemars Piguet continues to unveil timepieces in its incredibly successful Royal Oak series and in its very feminine and alluring women's collections. In striking contrast, the Royal Oak sports rubber straps and bezel accents, while the Promesse series of jeweled women's watches thins down and dons a variety of gemstones. With Audemars Piguet, one is sure to always find originality that is both cutting-edge and surprisingly traditional.

TOP LEFT

Called the Edward Piguet Chiming Minute Repeater, this striking timepiece is crafted in platinum.

TOP RIGHT

The Rubber-Clad Royal Oak Offshore Chronograph is water resistant to 100 meters and features a soft-iron inner shield to protect against magnetic fields.

BOTTOM RIGHT

The New Promesse offers sleeker, sexier lines and is accompanied by a striking new jewelry collection.

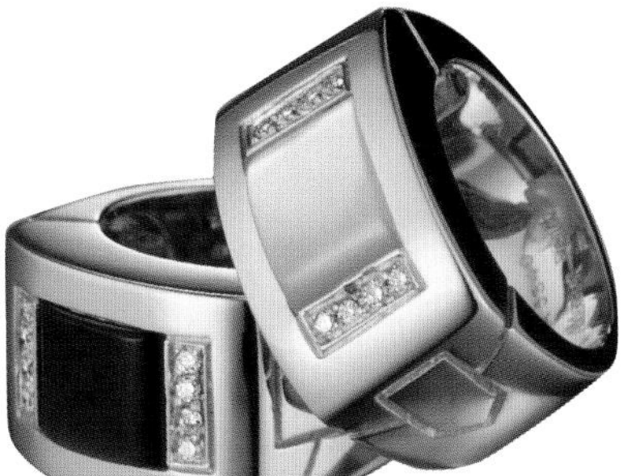

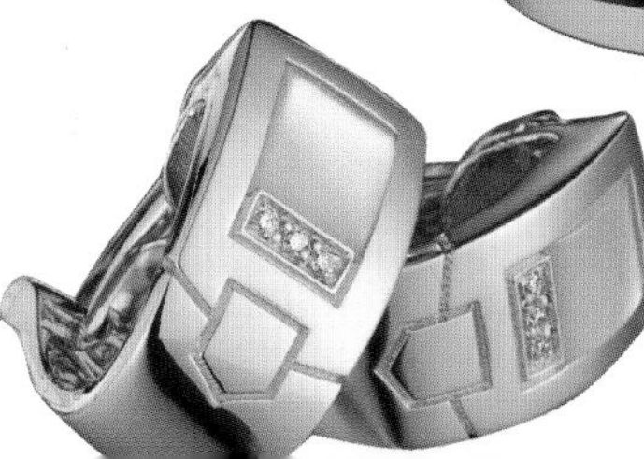

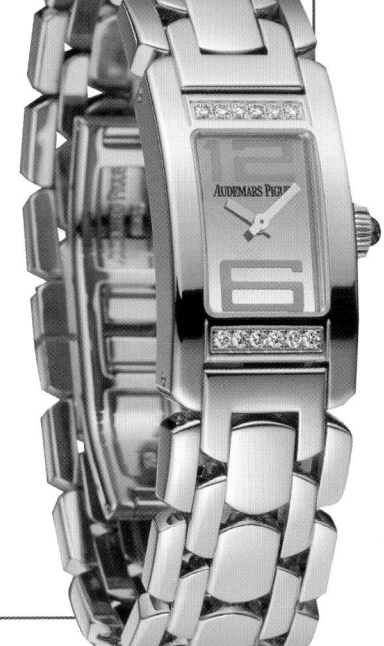

AUDEMARS PIGUET

N.B. *The photographs of Audemars Piguet watches were reduced by 8% with respect to those of other Brands.*

JULES AUDEMARS GRANDE COMPLICATION   REF. 25806OR.0002.01

Movement: automatic winding, A. Piguet 288 5 caliber, made up by more than 600 elements. Hand-made and hand-finished (Côtes de Genève pattern and beveled). **Functions:** hour, minute, small second, perpetual calendar (date, day, month, year, week, moon-phase), minute repeater, split-second chronograph with 2 counters.
Case: 18 kt pink gold, three-piece case (Ø 42 mm, thickness 13.5 mm); flat

sapphire crystal; middle with 5 correctors and slide repeater on case side; pink gold crown and pushers (with coaxial split-second pusher); snap-on back. Moisture protection.
Dial: silvered; applied pink-gold bâton and cabochon markers; burnished gold leaf style hands.
Indications: minute counter and day of the week at 3, month and four-year cycle at 6, date and small second at 9, week and moon phase at 12, center split-second counters, minute track with divisions for 1/5 of a second.
Strap: crocodile leather; pink-gold fold-over clasp. Limited edition of 5 pieces a year.
Also available: in yellow gold and platinum.

JULES AUDEMARS DYNAMOGRAPH   REF. 25945BC.0.0001CR/01

Movement: manual, A. Piguet 2891 caliber. Hand-made and hand-finished, decorated with Côtes de Genève pattern and beveled.
Functions: hour, minute, small second, petite and grande sonnerie, minute repeater, sonnerie power reserve. **Case:** 18 kt white gold, three-piece case (Ø 39 mm, thickness 10.9 mm), polished and brushed finish; curved sapphire crystal; on the middle: slide contact for the selection of the grande sonnerie (strikes

the hours and quarters automatically en passant by three timbres) or of the mute position and repeater pusher at 10; white gold crown; back fastened with 5 screws, displaying the movement through a sapphire crystal. Moisture protection.
Dial: silvered with guilloché central perimeter, second counter decorated with circular beads and bordered with white gold; applied white-gold Roman numerals and logo; white-gold leaf style hands. **Indications:** sonnerie power reserve at 1, dynamograph (barrel-spring force indicator) between 4 and 5, small second at 6.
Strap: crocodile leather; white-gold fold-over clasp. Limited edition.
Also available: in platinum.

JULES AUDEMARS GRANDE SONNERIE CARILLON   REF. 25825OR.0.0002/01

Movement: mechanical, manual winding, Audemars Piguet 2890 caliber. Produced and finished by hand (Côtes de Genève and beveled).
Functions: hour, minute, small second, grande and petite sonnerie, minute repeater.
Case: 18 kt pink gold, three-piece case (Ø 39 mm, thickness 10.26 mm), polished and brushed finish; curved sapphire crystal; slide-contact at 2 to select

the grande sonnerie (strikes the hours and the quarters en passant by three timbres), the petite sonnerie (strikes the hours) or the mute position; minute repeater pusher at 10 on the middle; pink-gold crown; case back attached by 5 screws.
Dial: silvered, engine-turned (guilloché); applied pink-gold bâton markers and Roman numerals; printed minute track with 5 minute progression; pink-gold bâton hands.
Indications: small second at 6.
Strap: crocodile leather; pink-gold clasp.
Also available: in platinum.

JULES AUDEMARS REPETITION CARILLON DAME   REF. 25818OR.0.0002|01

Movement: mechanical, manual winding, Audemars Piguet 2873 caliber, made up by 340 elements (enclosed in 2 ccm), 33 jewels, 21,600 vibrations per hour, 48 hours power reserve. Hand-finished (Côtes de Genève and beveled).
Functions: hour, minute, small second, minute repeater.
Case: 18 kt pink gold, three-piece case (Ø 28 mm, thickness 8.65 mm); curved sapphire crystal; repeater slide on the middle; pink gold crown; closed snap-on back.

Dial: silvered, engine-turned (guilloché) hour ring; brushed center disc, additional zone decorated with circular beads; applied pink-gold bâton markers and Roman numerals; printed minute track with 5 minute progression; pink-gold bâton hands, blued bâton small second hand.
Indications: small second at 6.
Strap: crocodile leather; pink-gold clasp.
Model out of stock.
Also available: in platinum.

JULES AUDEMARS METROPOLIS Q.P.   REF. 25919PT.0.0002CR/01

Movement: automatic, extra-thin, A. Piguet, 2120/2804 caliber. Rotor with 21 kt gold segment, 42 jewels, 19,800 vibrations per hour. Realized and finished by hand, decorated with Côtes de Genève and beveled. **Functions:** hour, minute, perpetual calendar (date, day, month, year), world time.
Case: platinum, three-piece case (Ø 39, thickness 10 mm), polished and brushed finish; curved sapphire glass; middle with 3 correctors; white-gold crown; pusher for the independent hour correction of world time at 4; back attached by 5 screws, displaying the movement through a sapphire glass. Water-resistant to 2 atm.

Dial: silvered, engraved meridians and parallels, zones decorated with circular beads, with gold rim; applied white-gold Arabic numerals and cabochon markers; printed minute track with 5-minute progression; white-gold leaf style hands.
Indications: date at 3, world time at 6, day at 9, month and four-year cycle at 12,.
Strap: crocodile leather; platinum fold-over clasp shaped with the firm's logo.
Also available: in pink gold.

JULES AUDEMARS TIME EQUATION   REF. 25934BA.0.0001CR/01

Movement: automatic, extra-thin, A. Piguet 2120/2808 caliber, Realized and finished by hand. **Functions:** hour, minute, perpetual calendar (date, day, month, year, moon-phase), equation of time, sunrise and sunset hours.
Case: 18 kt yellow gold, three-piece case (Ø 39, thickness 11.7 mm), polished and brushed finish; curved sapphire glass; polished bezel with engraved digits for the equation of time indication (difference between solar and civil time in minutes); middle with 3 correctors; gold crown; back attached by 5 screws, displaying the movement through a sapphire glass. Water-resistant to 2 atm.

Dial: silvered, center and zones decorated with circular beads, with gold rim; applied faceted gold bâton and triangular markers; printed minute track with 5-minute progression; skeletonized burnished gold Alpha hands. **Indications:** four-year cycle between 1 and 2, sunset hour at 3, date and day of the week at 6, sunrise hour at 9, month and moon-phase at 12, time equation center hand with sun. **Strap:** crocodile leather; gold fold-over clasp shaped with the firm's logo.
Also available: in pink gold, black dial; white gold, dark gray dial.

JULES AUDEMARS CABINET   REF. 25948PT.0022CR/01

Movement: manual, A. Piguet, cal. 2869, with tourbillon, made up by 443 elements. Hand-finished, decorated with Côtes de Genève pattern and beveled.
Functions: hour, minute, small second, perpetual calendar (date, day, month, year), minute repeater.
Case: platinum three-piece case (Ø 43 mm, thickness 13.35 mm), polished and brushed finish; curved sapphire glass; brushed middle with date corrector between 3 and 4 and repeater slide between 8 and 10; white gold crown; snap-on back displaying the movement through a sapphire crystal. Moisture protection.

Dial: silvered, engine-turned (guilloché) central perimeter, center decorated with Côtes de Genève pattern, zones decorated with circular beads, aperture on the tourbillon; applied white-gold Roman numerals and logo; burnished white-gold leaf style hands. **Indications:** big date at 2, day of the week at 3, small second at 6 integrated in the tourbillon carriage, month at 9, four-year cycle at 10.
Strap: crocodile leather; fold-over platinum clasp. 20 pieces. Second piece of the "Tradition d'Excellence" collection, realized in 2000. Out of stock.

JULES AUDEMARS TOURBILLON   REF. 25873OR.0.0002/01

Movement: mechanical, automatic winding, Audemars Piguet caliber 2875, with tourbillon (titanium carriage). Manufactured and finished by hand (decorated with Côtes de Genève pattern and beveled).
Functions: hour, minute, date, power reserve.
Case: 18 kt pink gold, three-piece case (Ø 40 mm, thickness 11.16 mm), polished and brushed finish; curved sapphire crystal; pink-gold crown on case back; back attached by 6 screws. Moisture protection.

Dial: silvered, grained finish, aperture on the tourbillon with pink-gold edge.
Indications: off-center hour and minute at 12; applied pink-gold bâton markers and Arabic numerals; pink-gold bâton hands, blued zone hands; date at 3, power reserve at 9.
Strap: crocodile leather, hand-stitched; pink gold clasp.
Also available: in platinum.

AUDEMARS PIGUET

J. AUDEMARS TOURBILLON CHRONOGRAPH   REF. 25909BA.0.0002CR/03

Movement: mechanical, manual winding, Audemars Piguet, 2879 caliber, with tourbillon, 48 hours autonomy, 30 jewels. Balance with 21,600 vibrations per hour. Manufactured and finished by hand, decorated with Côtes de Genève pattern and beveled.
Functions: hour, minute, small second, chronograph with 2 counters.
Case: 18 kt yellow gold, three-piece case (Ø 43 mm, thickness 13.2 mm), pol-

ished and brushed finish; curved sapphire glass; gold crown and pushers; snap-on back displaying the movement through a sapphire crystal. Moisture protection.
Dial: silvered, grained, gold-bordered zone and hour ring decorated with circular beads, aperture on the tourbillon; applied gold Roman numerals; skeletonized gold leaf style hands.
Indications: minute counter at 3, small second at 6 integrated in the tourbillon carriage, center second counter, minute track.
Strap: crocodile leather, hand-stitched; gold clasp with the firm's logo shape.
Also available: in pink gold; in white gold.

JULES AUDEMARS CHRONOGRAPH   REF. 25859BA.0.0001CR/01

Movement: mechanical, automatic winding, Audemars Piguet 2226/2841 caliber. Manufactured and finished by hand, decorated with Côtes de Genève pattern. and beveled.
Functions: hour, minute, small second, chronograph with 2 counters.
Case: 18 kt yellow gold, three-piece case (Ø 40 mm, thickness 11 mm), polished and brushed finish; curved sapphire crystal; gold crown and pushers; snap-on back. Water-re-

sistant to 2 atm.
Dial: black; applied gold pointed markers and Arabic numerals; gold bâton hands, white enameled chronograph hands.
Indications: small second at 3, minute counter at 9, center second counter, minute track with divisions for 1/5 of a second.
Strap: crocodile leather, hand-stitched; gold fold-over clasp in the shape of the firm's logo.
Also available: with silvered dial; in stainless steel with black or silvered dial; in white gold with blue dial.

JULES AUDEMARS POWER RESERVE   REF. 25955OR.0.00020R/01

Movement: mechanical, manual winding, Audemars Piguet 3090/3900 caliber, autonomy 48 hours, 24 jewels, Anachron balance spring. Manufactured and finished by hand, decorated with Côtes de Genève pattern and beveled, pillar-plate decorated with circular graining.
Functions: hour, minute, small second, date, power reserve.
Case: 18 kt pink gold, three-piece case (Ø 36 mm, thickness 9.2 mm), pol-

ished and brushed finish; curved sapphire crystal; pink-gold crown; back fastened by 6 screws, displaying the movement through a sapphire crystal. Water-resistant to 2 atm.
Dial: silvered; engine-turned (guilloché) on the central perimeter; center decorated with Côtes de Genève pattern, zones bordered in pink gold and decorated with circular beads; applied pink-gold Roman numerals; pink-gold leaf style hands.
Indications: power reserve between 1 and 2, small second at 6, date at 10.
Strap: crocodile leather, hand-stitched; white-gold fold-over clasp in the shape of the firm's logo.
Also available: in white gold.

JULES AUDEMARS   REF. 15056BC.0.0001CR/02

Movement: mechanical, manual winding, Audemars Piguet caliber 3090, 48 hours autonomy, 21 jewels, balance-spring in Anachron. Hand-made and hand-finished. Bridges beveled and decorated with Côtes de Genève pattern, pillar-plate decorated with circular graining.
Functions: hour, minute, small second.
Case: 18 kt white gold, three-piece case (Ø 36 mm, thickness 8.1 mm), polished and brushed finish; curved sapphire crystal; white gold crown; case back attached by 6 screws, displaying the movement through a sapphire crystal. Water-resistant to 2 atm.
Dial: silvered, center decorated with Côtes de Genève pattern and zone decorated with circular beads; applied white-gold Roman numerals; white-gold leaf style hands.
Indications: small second at 6.
Strap: crocodile leather, hand-stitched; white-gold fold-over clasp, in the shape of the firm's logo.
Also available: in pink gold; with smooth dial, Roman numerals and markers.

MILLENARY PERPETUAL CALENDAR   REF. 25777BA.0.0002/01

Movement: mechanical, automatic winding, extra-thin, Audemars Piguet 2120/2801 QP caliber. Rotor with 21 kt gold segment. Manufactured and finished by hand, decorated with Côtes de Genève pattern and beveled.
Functions: hour, minute, perpetual calendar (date, day, month, week, year, moon-phase).
Case: 18 kt yellow gold, three-piece oval case (size 34 x 39 mm), polished and brushed finish; flat sapphire crystal; middle with 4 correctors; sapphire cabochon on yellow-gold crown; case back attached by 6 screws. Water-resistant to 2 atm.

Dial: white enameled; applied gold bâton markers; printed minute track; burnished gold Cathédrale style hands.
Indications: date at 3, moon phase at 6, week day at 9, month and four-year cycle at 12, yellow-gold pointed center week hand.
Strap: crocodile leather; gold clasp.
Also available: in pink gold: in white gold. With white dial out of stock; all versions available with silvered dial.

MILLENARY CHRONOGRAPH   REF. 25822OR.0.0067CR/01

Movement: mechanical, automatic winding, Audemars Piguet 2126/2840 caliber. Rotor with 21 kt gold segment. Manufactured and finished by hand, decorated with Côtes de Genève pattern and beveled.
Functions: hour, minute, small second, date, chronograph with 3 counters.
Case: 18 kt pink gold, three-piece oval case (size 37 x 41 mm, thickness 11 mm), polished and brushed finish; flat sapphire crystal; pink-gold crown with sapphire cabochon; case back attached by 6 screws. Water-resistant to 2 atm.

Dial: silvered; printed luminescent Arabic numerals; luminescent burnished gold bâton hands.
Indications: date with magnifying glass at 3, hour counter at 6, minute counter at 9, small second at 12, center second counter, scroll tachometer scale, telemeter scale on the flange.
Strap: crocodile leather; pink-gold clasp.
Also available: with black Arabic numerals; in stainless steel, white dial, luminescent Arabic numerals.

MILLENARY DUAL TIME   REF. 25778BA.0.0002/01

Movement: mechanical, automatic winding, produced by Audemars Piguet 2129/2845 caliber. Rotor with 21 kt gold segment. Manufactured and finished by hand, decorated with Côtes de Genève pattern and beveled.
Functions: hour, minute, date, second time zone, power reserve.
Case: 18 kt yellow gold, three-piece oval case (size 35 x 39, thickness 8.3 mm), polished and brushed finish; flat sapphire crystal; yellow-gold crown with sapphire cabochon; case back attached by 6 screws. Water-resistant to 2 atm.

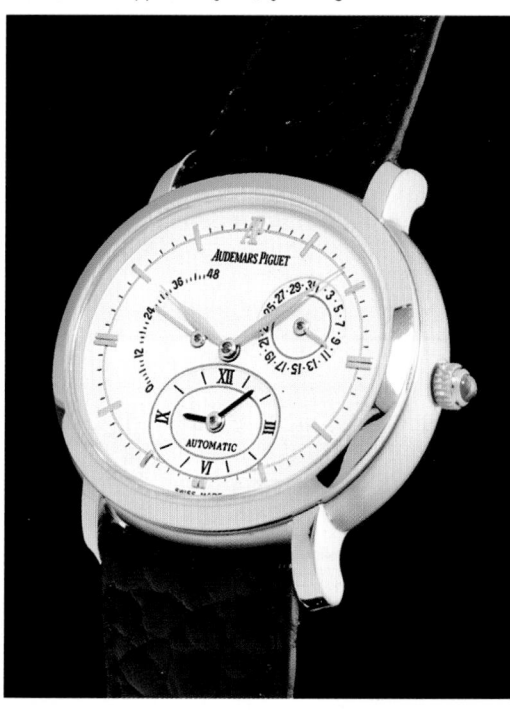

Dial: white enameled; applied gold bâton markers, printed minute track; gold leaf style hands.
Indications: date at 2, second time-zone with double hand at 6, power reserve between 8 and 11.
Strap: crocodile leather; gold clasp.
Also available: in pink gold; in white gold. With white dial out of stock; all versions available with silvered dial.

MILLENARY AUTOMATIC   REF. 14908BA.0.0001CR/01

Movement: mechanical, automatic winding, Audemars Piguet 2125 caliber. Rotor with 21 kt gold segment. Manufactured and finished by hand, decorated with Côtes de Genève pattern and beveled. **Functions:** hour, minute, second, date.
Case: 18 kt yellow gold, three-piece oval case (size 37 x 41 mm, thickness 8.2 mm), polished and brushed finish; flat sapphire crystal; yellow-gold crown with sapphire cabochon; case back attached by 6 screws. Water-resistant to 2 atm. **Dial:** silvered, grained, engraved with spider's web pattern; applied gold lozenge markers and Arabic numerals; printed minute track; gold leaf style hands. **Indications:** date at 3. **Strap:** crocodile leather, hand-stitched; gold fold-over clasp in the shape of the firm's logo.

Also available: in pink or white gold; in stainless steel with black dial luminescent Arabic numerals, white enameled dial and blue Roman numerals. Lady size: in stainless steel, black dial, lumin. Arabic numerals and white enameled dial with blue Arabic numerals; in yellow gold with silvered, guilloché or pink dial, Arabic num.; in pink gold with silvered or pink dial, Arabic num. or markers; in white gold with silvered or blue dial, Arabic num. or markers.

AUDEMARS PIGUET

EDWARD PIGUET TOURBILLON   REF. 25956OR.0.0002CR/01

Movement: mechanical, manual winding, Audemars Piguet caliber 2871 with tourbillon device. Manufactured and finished by hand, decorated with Côtes de Genève pattern and beveled.
Functions: hour, minute, small second.
Case: 18 kt pink gold, two-piece rectangular case (size 37.6 x 28.8 mm, thickness 12.5 mm), polished and brushed finish; curved sapphire crystal; pink-gold

crown; case back attached by 4 screws, displaying the movement through a sapphire crystal. Moisture protection.
Dial: silvered, engine-turned (guilloché) with "flamed" pattern and aperture on the tourbillon; applied pink-gold bâton markers and Arabic numerals; pink-gold leaf style hands. **Indications:** small second at 6 integrated in the tourbillon carriage.
Strap: crocodile leather, hand-stitched; pink gold clasp.
Also available: in white gold; with engine-turned dial (guilloché with sun pattern): in pink gold; in platinum.

EDWARD PIGUET MINUTE REPEATER CARILLON   REF. 25935PT.0.0022CR/01

Movement: mechanical, manual winding, Audemars Piguet, 2877 caliber. Manufactured and finished by hand, decorated with Côtes de Genève pattern and beveled.
Functions: hour, minute, small second, minute repeater, power reserve.
Case: platinum, two-piece, rectangular case (size 35.5 x 28 mm, thickness 10.9 mm), polished and brushed finish; curved sapphire glass; middle with re-

peater slide; white gold crown; back attached by 4 screws displaying the movement through a sapphire glass. Moisture protection.
Dial: silvered, brushed center, hour ring engine-turned (guilloché) with wave pattern, zone decorated with circular beads; printed Arabic numerals and luminescent applied white-gold round markers; printed railway minute track; luminescent white-gold bâton hands.
Indications: sonnerie power reserve between 2 and 3, small second at 6, sonnerie on/off display at 10.
Strap: crocodile leather; platinum clasp in the shape of the firm's logo. Limited edition of 20 pieces.

EDWARD PIGUET CHRONOGRAPH   REF. 25925OR.0.0001CR/01

Movement: mechanical, automatic winding, Audemars Piguet 2385 caliber (Frédéric Piguet 1185 base). Manufactured and finished by hand, decorated with Côtes de Genève pattern and beveled.
Functions: hour, minute, small second, date, chronograph with 3 counters.
Case: 18 kt pink gold, two-piece rectangular case (size 35.5 x 28.7 mm, thickness 12 mm); curved sapphire crystal; pink-gold crown; pink-gold oval push-

ers; case back attached by 4 screws. Moisture protection.
Dial: black, engine-turned (guilloché) hour ring; luminescent applied pink-gold markers and printed gilded Arabic numerals; luminescent pink-gold bâton hands. **Indications:** minute counter at 3, date between 4 and 5, small second at 6, hour counter at 9, center second counter, white railway minute track.
Strap: crocodile leather, hand-stitched; pink-gold fold-over clasp in the shape of the firm's logo.
Also available: in white gold.

EDWARD PIGUET GENTS   REF. 15121BC.0.0002CR/01

Movement: mechanical, automatic winding, Audemars Piguet caliber 2140. Manufactured and finished by hand, decorated with Côtes de Genève pattern and beveled.
Functions: hour, minute, second, date.
Case: 18 kt white gold, two-piece rectangular anatomically carved case (size 35.5 x 27 mm, thickness 9.9 mm), polished and brushed finish; curved sap-

phire crystal; white-gold crown; case back attached by 4 screws. Moisture protection.
Dial: silvered; engine-turned (guilloché with "flame" pattern); applied white gold Arabic numerals and bâton markers; white-gold leaf-style hands. **Indications:** date at 3.
Strap: crocodile leather; white-gold fold-over clasp.
Also available: with smooth black dial, printed Arabic numerals; in stainless steel; in pink gold; in white gold.

CANAPÉ TOURBILLON — REF. 258760R.0002/01

Movement: mechanical, manual winding, Audemars Piguet 2871 caliber, with tourbillon. Manufactured and finished by hand, decorated with Côtes de Genève pattern and beveled.
Functions: hour, minute, small second.
Case: 18 kt pink gold, two-piece rectangular case (size 40.5 x 23.7 mm, thickness 12.8 mm); curved sapphire crystal of considerable thickness; big mobile

curl-shaped lugs (the design of the case and lugs reminds that of a sofa called "canapé", and the idea is taken from an Audemars Piguet model of the Forties); pink gold crown; case back attached by 4 screws, displaying the movement through a sapphire crystal. Moisture protection.
Dial: silvered, curved, with an aperture on the tourbillon; applied pink-gold bâton markers and Arabic numerals; printed railway minute track; pink-gold bâton hands.
Indications: small second at 6 integrated in the tourbillon carriage.
Strap: crocodile leather, hand-stitched; pink-gold fold-over clasp in the shape of the firm's logo. Edition limited to 25 numbered pieces.

CANAPÉ TOURBILLON POWER RESERVE — REF. 25942PT.O.0022CR/01

Movement: mechanical, manual winding, Audemars Piguet 2878 caliber, with tourbillon. Manufactured and finished by hand, decorated with Côtes de Genève pattern and beveled.
Functions: hour, minute, small second, power reserve.
Case: platinum, two-piece rectangular case (size 40.5 x 23.7 mm, thickness 12.8 mm); curved sapphire glass of considerable thickness; big curl-shaped

mobile lugs (the design of case and lugs reminds that of a sofa called "canapé" and the idea is drawn from an Audemars Piguet model of the Forties); white gold crown; back attached by 4 screws with sapphire crystal window. Moisture protection.
Dial: silvered, curved, aperture on the tourbillon, power reserve; engine-turned (guilloché) with sun pattern; applied white-gold square markers and Arabic numerals; printed railway minute track; white-gold bâton hands. **Indications:** small second at 6 integrated in the tourbillon carriage, power reserve at 12.
Strap: crocodile leather, hand-stitched; fold-over platinum clasp in the shape of the firm's logo.

CANAPÉ GENTS — REF. 150691BC.0.0002CR/01

Movement: mechanical, automatic winding, Audemars Piguet caliber 2140. Manufactured and finished by hand, decorated with Côtes de Genève pattern and beveled.
Functions: hour, minute.
Case: 18 kt white gold, two-piece rectangular case (size 38.5 x 23.6 mm, thickness 11.1 mm); curved sapphire crystal of considerable thickness; big

curl-shaped mobile lugs (the design of case and lugs reminds that of a sofa called "canapé" and the idea is drawn from an Audemars Piguet model of the Forties); white-gold crown; case back attached by 8 screws; Moisture protection.
Dial: white, curved; luminescent Roman numerals and applied white-gold bâton markers with luminescent dots; luminescent white-gold bâton hands.
Strap: crocodile leather, hand-stitched; white-gold fold-over clasp in the shape of the firm's logo.

PROMESSE — REF. 67461BC.Z.0023LZ/01

Movement: quartz, Audemars Piguet 2508 caliber. Manufactured and finished by hand, decorated with Côtes de Genève pattern and beveled.
Functions: hour, minute.
Case: 18 kt white gold, two-piece rectangular case (size 31.7 x 18 mm, thickness 6.6 mm), anatomically curved; two rows of brilliants set at poles; curved sapphire crystal; white-gold crown with sapphire cabochon; case back attached by 4 screws,. Moisture protection.
Dial: sky-blue, curved; two embossed Arabic numerals (6 and 12), tone on tone; white-gold bâton hands.

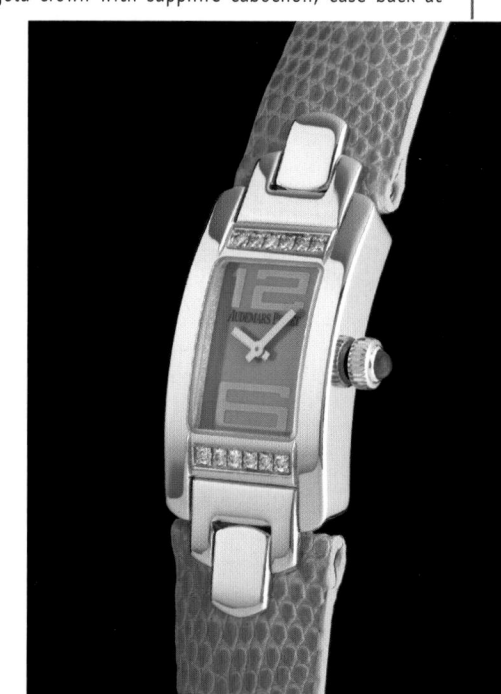

Strap: lizard skin, hand-stitched; white-gold attachment made up by a fixed link and a jointed central element; white-gold clasp.
Also available: in various color combinations of dial and strap; with bracelet; in many other jewel versions.

AUDEMARS PIGUET

ROYAL OAK PERPETUAL CALENDAR   REF. 25820ST.0.0944ST/01

Movement: mechanical, automatic winding, extra-thin, Audemars Piguet 2120/2802 caliber. White-gold skeleton rotor. Hand-finished and hand-decorated. **Functions:** hour, minute, perpetual calendar (date, day, month, year, moon phase). **Case:** stainless steel, two-piece case (Ø 38.5 mm, thickness 9.5 mm), polished and brushed finish; flat sapphire crystal; octagonal bezel with gasket and 8 recessed hexagon nuts in white gold, fastening the 8 white-gold through

screws of the case back; back displaying the movement through a sapphire crystal; 4 correctors on the middle; hexagonal screw-down crown. Water-resistant to 2 atm. **Dial:** gray; applied white-gold bâton markers; white-gold bâton hands; printed minute track. **Indications:** date at 3, moon phase at 6, day at 9, month and four-year cycle at 12. **Bracelet:** brushed stainless steel; fold-over clasp with safety pusher.
Also available: with sapphire blue dial; yellow gold gilded dial; platinum and stainless steel black Grande Tapisserie dial; platinum Tuscany blue dial. Medium size with blue Clous de Paris dial Ref. 25800: in stainless steel; in yellow gold. Squelette Ref. 25829: in steel; yellow gold; in platinum.

ROYAL OAK ANNUAL CALENDAR   REF. 25920BA.0.0789BA/01

Movement: mechanical, automatic winding, Audemars Piguet 2224/2814 caliber (Ø 26 mm, 11'''1/2, thickness 4.85 mm), made up by 228 elements, autonomy 38 hours, 35 jewels, 28,800 vibrations per hour (vph). Manufactured and finished by hand, decorated with Côtes de Genève pattern and beveled.
Functions: hour, minute, annual calendar (date, month).
Case: 18 kt yellow gold, three-piece case (Ø 37 mm, thickness 10 mm), polished and brushed finish; flat sapphire crystal; octagonal bezel with gasket and 8 recessed hexagon nuts in white gold, fastening the 8 white-gold through screws of the case back; 2 correctors on the middle; hexagonal screw-down crown. Water-resistant to 5 atm.

Dial: dark blue, decorated with Grande Tapisserie pattern; luminescent applied white enameled bâton markers and hands.
Indications: month at 5 (months with 31 days in red), red pointed center date hand.
Bracelet: yellow gold, brushed finish; gold fold-over clasp with safety pusher.
Also available: silvered dial with Grande Tapisserie pattern; in stainless steel.

ROYAL OAK DUAL TIME   REF. 25730ST.0.0789ST/06

Movement: mechanical, automatic winding, Audemars Piguet 2129/2845 caliber. Manufactured and finished by hand, decorated with Côtes de Genève pattern and beveled.
Functions: hour, minute, date, second time zone, power reserve.
Case: stainless steel, two-piece brushed case (Ø 36 mm, thickness 9.5 mm); flat sapphire crystal; octagonal bezel with gasket and 8 recessed white-gold hexagon nuts fastening the 8 white-gold through screws of the case back; hexagonal screw-down crown. Water-resistant to 5 atm.

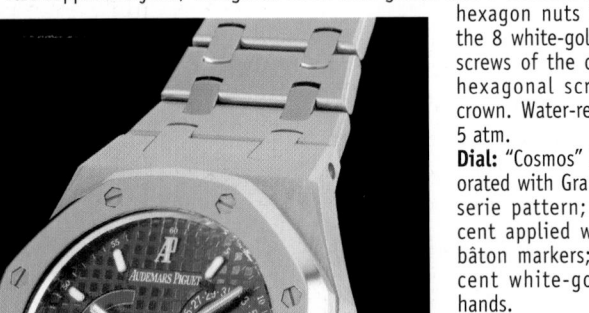

Dial: "Cosmos" blue, decorated with Grande Tapisserie pattern; luminescent applied white-gold bâton markers; luminescent white-gold bâton hands.
Indications: date at 2, second time-zone with double hand at 6, power reserve between 8 and 11.
Bracelet: stainless steel, brushed finish; fold-over clasp with safety pusher.
Also available: black or silvered Grande Tapisserie dial; in steel/yellow gold with silvered Grande Tapisserie dial; in yellow gold with silvered Grande Tapisserie dial.

ROYAL OAK DAY-DATE MOON PHASE   REF. 25594BA.0.0789BA/05

Movement: mechanical, automatic winding, Audemars Piguet 2124/2825 caliber. Manufactured and finished by hand, decorated with Côtes de Genève pattern and beveled.
Functions: hour, minute, day-date, moon phase.
Case: 18 kt yellow gold, two-piece brushed case (Ø 36 mm, thickness 8.5 mm); flat sapphire crystal; octagonal bezel with gasket and 8 recessed white-gold hexagon nuts fastening the 8 white gold through screws of the case back; hexagonal screw-down crown. Water-resistant to 10 atm.

Dial: silvered, decorated with Grande Tapisserie pattern; luminescent applied gold bâton markers; luminescent gold bâton hands.
Indications: date at 3, moon phase at 6, day at 9.
Bracelet: yellow gold, brushed finish; fold-over clasp with safety pusher.
Also available: stainless steel and yellow gold, with silvered Grande Tapisserie dial; in stainless steel with "cosmos" blue, black or silvered Grande Tapisserie dial.

ROYAL OAK CHRONOGRAPH   REF. 25960BA.O.1185BA/01

Movement: mechanical, automatic winding, Audemars Piguet 2385 caliber (Frédéric Piguet 1185 base). Manufactured and finished by hand, decorated with Côtes de Genève pattern and beveled.

Functions: hour, minute, small second, date, chronograph with 3 counters.

Case: 18 kt yellow gold, three-piece case (Ø 39 mm, thickness 11 mm), polished and brushed finish; flat sapphire crystal; octagonal bezel with gasket and 8 re-

cessed white-gold hexagon nuts fastening the 8 white-gold through screws of the case back; hexagonal gold screw-down crown; gold pushers with case protection. Water-resistant to 5 atm. **Dial:** silvered, decorated with Grande Tapisserie pattern; counters decorated with circular beads; luminescent applied square gold markers; luminescent gold bâton hands. **Indications:** minute counter at 3, date between 4 and 5, small second at 6, hour counter at 9, center second counter, minute track.

Bracelet: yellow gold, brushed finish; fold-over clasp with safety pusher.

Also available: w. blue Clous de Paris dial; white gold silvered Gr. Tapisserie dial; stainless steel Gr. Tapisserie black or "cosmos" blue or silvered dial.

ROYAL OAK CHRONOGRAPH   REF. 25860ST.0.1110ST/01

The Chronograph belonging to the Royal Oak family is driven by a movement derived from Frédéric Piguet, modified and set up by Audemars Piguet, so that it matches the latter's quality standard: its rotor is in 18 kt gold and finished with a Côtes de Genève pattern. The bridges of the balance and winding device are decorated with a Côtes de Genève, the others with a circular graining pattern. The whole is also beveled. This chronograph is one of the rare models

of the Royal Oak family that has a really removable case back (three-piece case), whereas the others are mostly characterized by a one-piece case with only one opening from the bezel (two-piece case). On the contrary, the case fastening system remains unchanged with its through screws and nuts on the back. The pushers are inserted in, and protected by, elements integrated in the middle in hexagonal shape like the winding crown.

The photograph shows the version with stainless steel case and bracelet.

ROYAL OAK FOUNDATION   REF. 15100ST.0.0789ST/01

Movement: mechanical, automatic winding, Audemars Piguet 2225 caliber. Manufactured and finished by hand, decorated with Côtes de Genève pattern and beveled. Commemorative pink-gold rotor with embossed A.P. logo and oak leaves. **Functions:** hour, minute, second, date. **Case:** stainless steel, two-piece case (Ø 37 mm, thickness 8,3 mm), polished and brushed finish; flat sapphire crystal; hexagonal screw-down crown; octagonal bezel with gasket and 8 recessed

white-gold hexagon nuts fastening the 8 white-gold through screws of the case back; back displaying the movement through a sapphire crystal; hexagonal screw-down crown. Water-resistant to 5 atm. **Dial:** "Cosmos" blue, decorated with Grande Tapisserie pattern, in the central part with an embossed royal oak; luminescent applied white-gold markers; luminescent white-gold bâton hands, printed white minute track with 5 minute progression. **Indications:** date at 3.

Bracelet: brushed steel; fold-over clasp with safety pusher.

Limited edition of 450 pieces. The proceeds of sales contribute in sustaining the Swiss "Time for the Trees" Foundation. **Also available:** in yellow gold, silvered dial, 50 pieces.

"TIME FOR THE TREES" FOUNDATION

Why should a high horology House like Audemars Piguet go to the swamps of Kuala Selangor in Malaysia, among crabs and poisonous snakes? Why should it be committed with the destiny of cork oaks in Spain, where it is exploited to an extreme extent, or in that of a forest in Southern France destroyed by fire? This is the answer: for "Time for the Trees" — a charitable foundation created under Swiss law in 1992 on the occasion of the 20th anniversary of Royal Oak — committed in the pro-

tection of environment and in particular of forests. Of course, Audemars Piguet's mission is and remains the manufacture of prestigious mechanical watches and for this reason the Foundation asked for, and obtained, the help and advice of the major experts in the world in the field of environment protection. It would take too much time to list all the projects performed or under way, to the founding of which the realization of special series - such as the one photographed on this page, dominated by the style theme of the Royal Oak, realized in 1999 in a limited series of 450 pieces in stainless steel and 50 in gold - contributes in an effective way.

AUDEMARS PIGUET

ROYAL OAK AUTOMATIC   REF. 14790ST.O.0789ST/09

Movement: mechanical, automatic winding, Audemars Piguet 2125 caliber. Manufactured and finished by hand, decorated with Côtes de Genève pattern and beveled. **Functions:** hour, minute, second, date.
Case: stainless steel, two-piece case (Ø 37 mm, thickness 8.2 mm), polished and brushed finish; flat sapphire crystal; octagonal bezel with gasket and 8 recessed hexagon nuts in white gold fastening the 8 white-gold through screws

of the case back; hexagonal screw-down crown. Water-resistant to 5 atm.
Dial: black, decorated with Grande Tapisserie pattern; luminescent applied steel bâton markers; luminescent steel bâton hands; printed minute track with 5 minute progression.
Indications: date at 3.
Bracelet: brushed steel; double fold-over clasp with safety pusher.
Also available: with Grande Tapisserie" cosmos" blue, silvered or Clous de Paris dark-gray dial; Pilot black dial, leather strap, bracelet; steel/yellow gold, Clous de Paris dark gray or silvered Grande Tapisserie dial, bracelet; yellow gold, silvered Grande Tapisserie dial; with Pilot black dial, luminescent Arabic numerals, leather strap.

ROYAL OAK AUTOMATIC   REF. 14790ST.O.0789ST/08

The history of Royal Oak started in 1651 after the battle of Worcester, when Charles II of England and Scotland, fleeing from the parliamentary forces, found refuge in such a noble tree. Later on, a whole fleet of ships of the Royal Navy took on the name of "Royal Oak" in honor of this event. In 1972, Audemars Piguet, inspired by the octagonal shape of the mouths of the canons of these war ships, realized the first stainless steel Royal Oak which in little time

became such a wanted model that the factory was led to complete the initial series by integrating it with models in new shapes and materials. In the conception of this great classic of modern horology, a particular attention was devoted to the bracelet. Each link, decreasing in section and size, requires manual assembly and accurate care by watchmakers. This attention is imposed by the will to achieve a perfect result in terms of flexibility and rigidity at the same time. Such features allows the bracelet to perfectly adapt to the wrist. The photograph shows the version with Cosmos blue dial.

ROYAL OAK AUTOMATIC   REF. 14800ST.O.0009ST/14

Movement: mechanical, automatic winding, Audemars Piguet 2125 caliber. Hand-finished and hand-decorated. **Functions:** hour, minute, second, date.
Case: stainless steel, two-piece case (Ø 37 mm, thickness 8.2 mm), polished and brushed finish; flat sapphire crystal; octagonal bezel with gasket and 8 recessed hexagon nuts in white gold fastening the 8 white-gold through screws of the case back; hexagonal screw-down crown. Water-resistant to 5 atm.

Dial: "Pilot" glossy black; luminescent Arabic numerals; printed minute track with luminescent dots; luminescent white enameled bâton hands.
Indications: date at 3.
Strap: leather; double fold-over safety clasp.
Also available: with bracelet; in yellow-gold, leather strap.

ROYAL OAK JUMBO   REF. 15202ST.O.0544ST/01

Movement: mechanical, automatic winding, extra-thin, Audemars Piguet 2121 caliber. Manufactured, finished and by hand and decorated with Côtes de Genève, beveled.
Function: hour, minute, date.
Case: stainless steel, two-piece case (Ø 39 mm, thickness 8 mm), polished and brushed finish; flat sapphire crystal; octagonal bezel with gasket and 8 recessed hexagon nuts in

white gold fastening the 8 white-gold through screws of the case back, displaying the movement through a sapphire crystal; hexagonal screw-down crown. Water-resistant to 5 atm.
Dial: silvered, Grande Tapisserie decoration; luminescent applied steel bâton markers and hands; printed minute track with five-minute progression.
Indications: date at 3.
Bracelet: brushed steel; fold-over clasp with safety pusher.
Also available: in yellow-gold.

ROYAL OAK OFFSHORE CHRONOGRAPH REF. 25721ST.0.1000ST/0

Movement: automatic, A. Piguet cal. 2226/2840. Hand-finished and hand-decorated. Protected against magnetic fields by a special ductile metal frame.
Functions: hour, minute, small second, date, chronograph with 3 counters.
Case: stainless steel, three-piece case (Ø 42 mm, thickness 15 mm), polished and brushed finish; flat sapphire crystal; octagonal bezel (joints in Therban) and 8 recessed white-gold hexagon nuts fastening the 8 steel through screws (silver joints) of the case back (joints in Therban); hexagon screw-down crown; pushers coated with a silicone layer. Water-resistant to 10 atm. **Dial:** blue, Clous de Paris decoration; luminescent applied white-gold oval markers; luminescent white-gold bâton hands. **Indications:** date with magnifying glass at 3, hour counter at 6, minute counter at 9, small second at 12, center second counter, minute track with divisions for 1/5 of a second, tachometer scale on the flange.
Bracelet: brushed stainless steel; fold-over clasp. with safety pusher.
Also available: velcro strap; yellow or blue dial, shark-skin strap; titanium dark-gray dial bracelet; yellow gold gilded or blue dial bracelet; other dial colors and leather straps.

ROYAL OAK OFFSHORE CHRONO RUBBER   REF. 25940SK.0.0002CA/01

Synthetic materials ever since played an outstanding role in Royal Oak Offshore models from a functional and aesthetic point of view. In fact, compounds such as Therban, used for gaskets (visible or hidden), and Silicone, used for the coating of crowns and pushers, characterize this family, created as a hypertechnical evolution of the classical Royal Oak collection. In the new chronograph, rubber constitutes the dominant aesthetic element. The bezel consists of a steel core, fastened on the case back by the usual through screw and nut system, and coated with a layer of black rubber. Years of studies and experiments allowed to achieve an optimal union between steel and rubber and to preserve the latter from wear. The whole is completed by a rubber strap and a dial characterized by the "Grande Tapisserie" decoration; on the anthracite background it is possible to distinguish silvered zones and highly luminescent embossed markers.

ROYAL OAK OFFSHORE DAY-DATE MONTH REF. 25807ST.0.1010ST/01

Movement: automatic, A. Piguet, 2127/2827 caliber. Rotor with 21 kt gold segment. Manufactured and finished by hand, decorated with Côtes de Genève pattern and beveled. Protected against magnetic fields by a ductile metal frame.
Functions: hour, minute, small second, full calendar (date, day, month).
Case: stainless steel, three-piece case (Ø 37 mm, thickness 14.5 mm), polished and brushed finish; flat sapphire crystal; octagonal bezel (joints in Therban) and 8 recessed hexagon nuts in white-gold fastening the 8 steel through screws (silver joints) of the case back (joints in Therban); 2 correctors on the middle; hexagonal screw-down crown coated with a silicone layer. Water-resistant to 10 atm.
Dial: blue, Clous de Paris; applied white-gold luminescent bâton markers; white-gold luminescent bâton hands. **Indications:** small second at 6, day and month below 12, white enameled pointed center date hand with reading on the flange.
Bracelet: brushed steel; fold-over clasp with safety pusher.
Also available: with leather strap; in yellow gold, leather strap or bracelet; many other color combinations of dials and leather straps.

ROYAL OAK OFFSHORE AUTOMATIC LADY   REF. 77151ST.0.0009/01

Movement: mechanical, automatic winding, Audemars Piguet 2140 caliber. Rotor with 21 kt gold segment. Manufactured and finished by hand, decorated with Côtes de Genève pattern and beveled. Protected against magnetic fields by a special ductile metal frame.
Functions: hour, minute, second, date.
Case: stainless steel, three-piece case (Ø 30 mm, thickness 10 mm), polished and brushed finish; flat sapphire crystal; octagonal bezel (joints in Therban) and 8 recessed hexagon nuts in white gold fastening the 8 steel through screws (silver joints), of the case back (joints in Therban); hexagonal screw-down crown coated with a silicone layer. Water-resistant to 10 atm.
Dial: blue, decorated with Clous de Paris pattern; luminescent applied white-gold oval markers; railway minute track on the flange; luminescent white-gold bâton hands. **Indications:** date at 3.
Strap: shark-skin, hand-stitched; steel fold-over safety clasp.
Also available: bracelet; yellow gold, leather strap or bracelet; many other color combinations of dials and leather straps.

BAUME & MERCIER

tradition with style

*T*his fine Swiss watchmaking company traces its roots back to the 1500s when the French Baume family moved to Switzerland and began crafting timepieces. Several generations of Baumes continued to engage in the trade. It wasn't until the early 1830s, however, that the firm was officially founded as The Societé Baume Frères.

At that point, four Baume brothers were working together to create elegant, technically precise watches. The Baume name came to be recognized as a symbol of fine craftsmanship and ingenuity. The brothers won numerous accolades and awards at international fairs for their timepieces, and continued to perpetuate their craft by passing their watchmaking know-how on to their children.

In 1918, William Baume and his close friend, jeweler Paul Mercier, joined forces and formed Baume et Mercier. Located in Geneva, the Baume & Mercier watchmaking house focused on creating innovative watches for men and women. Throughout the 20th century, Baume & Mercier regularly produced timepieces that were on the cutting-edge of style and fashion. Such watches included ultra-thin automatics, a turning fork watch, the distinguished octagon shaped Riviera and the Galaxy collection that made an international splash when it was unveiled in 1973.

Today, under the auspices of the Richemont Group, Baume & Mercier continues to produce high-style watches. Its key collections include the Linea, the Hampton and the CapeLand. The Linea is a sleek, elegant line of women's timepieces. Crafted in steel, the round watch features a domed sapphire

crystal and an ingenious interchangeable bracelet system. The new editions are offered with either a supple three-row link bracelet or a vast array of colorful wrap-around patent leather straps. In 2001, Baume & Mercier also introduced the Linea with varying degrees of Top Wesselton VVSI diamonds adorning the dial and bezel for scintillating appeal.

Also in 2001, Baume & Mercier unveiled a gem-set Hampton M (for mini) to round out the Hampton collection. This striking curved, rectangular watch demonstrates the brand's creative spirit. Baume & Mercier has given the vintage rectangular look of the Hampton a decidedly modern flair in this Hampton M. Precisely 22 Top Wesselton VVSI diamonds adorn the case of the watch. What's more, it houses an 11mm movement—one of the smallest movements available on the market.

On the more rugged side, Baume & Mercier has extended its very successful CapeLand collection of sports watches by adding the CapeLand S—an automatic chronograph watch that is an officially certified chronometer. Water resistant to 200 meters, the watch features a unidirectional rotating bezel, crown protection system and a security clasp—making it ideal for any sports occasion. It is offered with either a satin-polished link bracelet or a rubber strap.

BEDAT & Cᵒ

an historical perspective

"It may seem a little presumtuous to talk about history with regard to a firm that is only five years old,"

says a modest Christian Bedat. But in just five short years, this entrepreneur and designer – in partnership with his mother, long-time watch veteran Simone Bedat — has built a small legacy of luxury, authenticity and originality.

BEDAT & Cᵒ was incorporated in late 1996. However, the Bedats had spent a good deal of time prior to that researching and developing the philosophy and product niche of the brand that would bear their name. They had already identified a need for a purely Swiss-made brand of elegant, refined watches that were both timeless and modern in design. They had already delineated a strict code of ethics and quality standards by which the brand would adhere; and they had already developed a close bond between themselves and the suppliers who would carry their creative ideas to fruition.

In 1997, BEDAT & Cᵒ unveiled its first watches at the World Watch, Clock and Jewelry Show in Basel. The striking new designs, the Swiss origins and the personalities behind the brand made it an immediate success. By 1998, BEDAT & Cᵒ was ready to tackle the important, extremely competitive U.S. market. Beginning slowly in just eleven retail outlets, the brand nonetheless received incredible attention. It wasn't long before luxury retailers took note and began placing orders for the bold and beautiful BEDAT & Cᵒ watches.

In December 2000, BEDAT & Cᵒ wisely formed an alliance with the Gucci Group, wherein the Group purchased 85 percent of the brand. According to Christian Bedat, continuing Chief Executive Officer and Creative Director, "The alliance does not change the strategy or the dynamism of the brand. It simply gives us a great infrastructure in different countries around the world to grow to new heights."

Bedat & Co

unveiling
masterpieces

Remaining true to its founding philosophies, BEDAT & Co remains consistent with its product offerings and precision watchmaking. The brand's four key collections are identified by numbers rather than names as part of both a global marketing strategy and as a demonstration of the brand's unique tie to tracking time.

In 2001, the No. 7 collection was the brightest star in the lineup. It was Christian Bedat's intention to increase the men's wristwatch perception. By adding some important technical timepieces to the collection with bolder, stronger appeal, Bedat hopes to bring the balance of men's and women's watches to an even 50/50 representation.

"Just because we are part of the Gucci Group, it does not just open doors automatically. We still have to work hard to continue our product and philosophy. In fact, I think we must be even more creative than in the past, if that is possible," says Bedat.

The new No. 7 timepieces include a striking ChronoAutomatic and an Annual Calendar watch. Based on the case shape of the successful No. 7 ChronoPocket – a curved, rectangular watch of distinction – the new No. 7 models incorporate technical excellence with typical BEDAT & Co style. Each is water resistant to 50 meters.

Created in either steel, 18-karat yellow and rose gold, or platinum, the ChronoAutomatic offers 12-hour, 30-minute and 60-second counters. It also features a date indicator between 4:00 and 5:00, and 40 hours of power reserve. The No. 7 Annual Calendar has an attractive readout system, with date at 12:00 and month at 8:00. A subdial located between 4:00 and 6:00 to indicate the seconds lends the finishing touch to a harmoniously balanced design. The Annual Calendar is crafted in steel, or in 18-karat yellow and rose gold.

Bedat has indicated that in 2002, another evolution of the No. 7 Annual Calendar is to be unveiled, along with some striking new No. 7 timepieces for women.

CHRONOLOGY

1996 Mother and son team Simone and Christian Bédat establish BEDAT & Cº in Geneva on October 8th.

1997 The company launches its first collection in April. The line is distributed in Switzerland and Austria and carries three main lines: N°3, N°7 and N°8.

1998 BEDAT & Cº begins its distribution in the United States with 11 doors.

1999 The ChronoPocket is launched in April. BEDAT & Cº USA is founded

2000 The ladies' reversible N° 33 is introduced. December - BEDAT & Cº forms an alliance with the GUCCI GROUP.

2001 BEDAT & Cº's distribution reaches 100 doors in the USA.

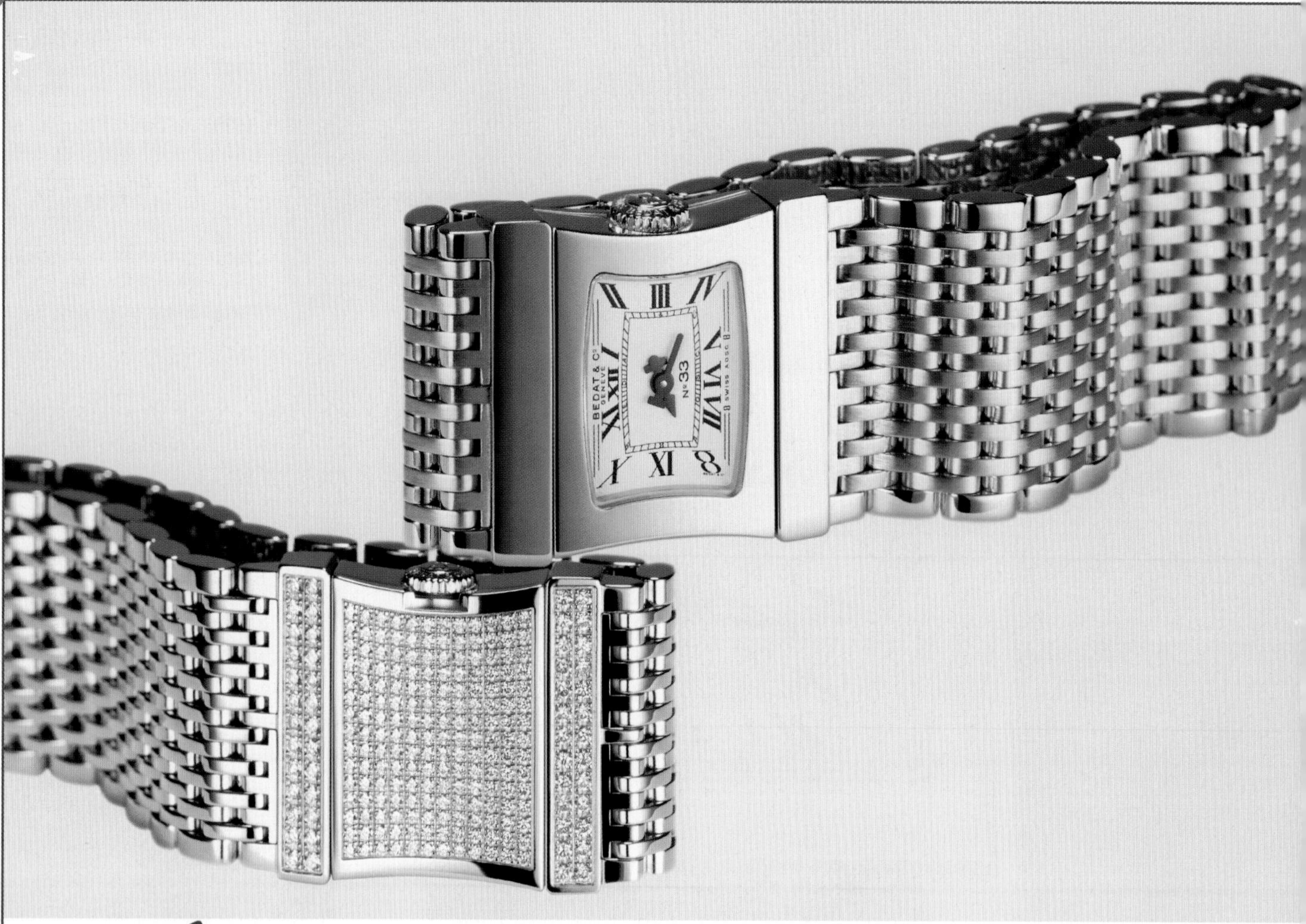

the spirit

In 2001, BEDAT & Co actively delved into the prestigious world of sailing. For the second consecutive year, the brand sponsored a Formula 40 trimaran, which has aptly been named "The Spirit of BEDAT & Co". The boat participates in the Bol d'Or competition on Lake Leman – one of the most important water races held in Europe.

According to Bedat, the links between sailing and timekeeping –speed and precision– were key in making the decision to become a part of this sport. Sponsorship of the boat gives BEDAT & Co a premiere entrée into this exciting arena – bringing the brand further consumer exposure and keeping it in sync with the luxury field.

As has always been the primary goal of Bedat, luxury and continued innovation reign supreme in its product direction. For that reason, the brand has unveiled several new pieces in its ladies' collections in both the No. 3 (barrel shaped watches) and the No. 33 (reversible watches) series.

Primarily, the additions in these lines include elaborately embellished diamond cases, more refined accents such as diamond markers or diamond edging on cases and bracelets, and more color. Particularly in the No. 3 series, color steals the spotlight with straps ranging form lavender to yellow, orange to teal and sea foam to red.

All BEDAT & C° timepieces are accompanied by the brand's A.O.S.C. certificate – the company's own quality seal that guarantees Swiss origin of the watch and all of its parts, and that certifies that the timepiece meets the brand's strict standards of manufacturing. An integral part of BEDAT & C°'s five-year guarantee, the A.O.S.C. certificate further states that each watch is crafted of gold, steel or platinum, that gemstones are precious or semi-precious, and that the leather straps are fully padded and hand stitched. Every BEDAT & C° watch is engraved with an individual serial number to track its authenticity in true luxury style.

BEDAT & C°

Movement: quartz. ETA calibre 4 7/8 E01.001, 5 jewels.
Functions: hour, minute.
Case: barrel shaped case completely integrated in the bracelet. Stainless steel, curved sapphire crystal, case back attached by screws. Crown identified with Bedat & C° logo and trademarks. Inside casing ring in metal. Water resistant to 5 atm.

Bracelet: stainless steel. Bedat & C° steel folding clasp.
Dial: Bedat & C° guilloche, black. Diamond hour markers. Bedat & C° own designed hands. Logo at 8 o'clock.
Also available: Bedat & C° guilloche, white. Diamond hour markers. Same price.
Bedat & C° guilloche, white roman.
Note: Swiss origin of each components certified with the Bedat & C° trademark Swiss A.O.S.C. and the hallmark.

Movement: quartz. ETA calibre 4 7/8 E01.001, 5 jewels.
Functions: hour, minute.
Case: barrel shaped case completely integrated in the bracelet. Stainless steel, curved sapphire crystal, case back attached by screws. Crown identified with Bedat & C° logo and trademarks. Inside casing ring in metal. Water resistant to 5 atm.

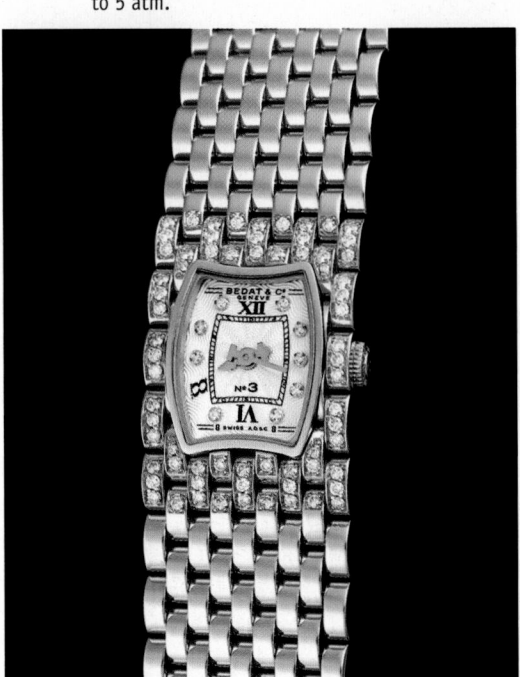

Diamonds: set with 77 Top Wesselton VVSI diamonds (0.54 cts).
Bracelet: stainless steel. Bedat & C° steel folding clasp.
Dial: Bedat & C° guilloche, white. Diamond hour markers. Bedat & C° own designed hands. Logo at 8 o'clock.
Also available: Bedat & C° guilloche, black. Diamond hour markers.
Note: Swiss origin of each components certified with the Bedat & C° trademark Swiss A.O.S.C. and the hallmark.

Movement: quartz. ETA calibre 4 7/8 E01.001, 5 jewels.
Functions: hour, minute.
Case: barrel shaped case completely integrated in the bracelet. Stainless steel, curved sapphire crystal, case back attached by screws. Crown identified with Bedat & C° logo and trademarks. Inside casing ring in metal. Water resistant to 5 atm.

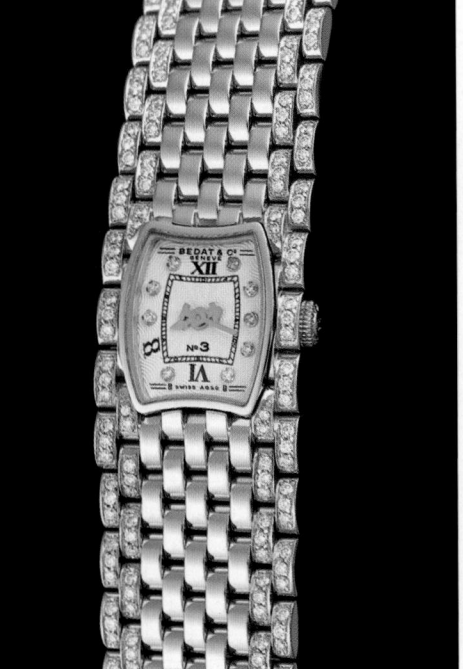

Bracelet: stainless steel. Bedat & C° steel folding clasp.
Diamonds: set with 287 Top Wesselton VVSI diamonds (2.18 cts).
Dial: Bedat & C° guilloche, white. Diamond hour markers. Bedat & C° own designed hands. Logo at 8 o'clock.
Also available: Bedat & C° guilloche, black. Diamond hour markers. Same price.
Bedat & C° guilloche, white roman numerals.
Set with 144 (only one row) Top Wesselton VVSI diamonds (1.18 cts).
White or black, diamond markers dials.
Note: Swiss origin of each components certified with the Bedat & C° trademark Swiss A.O.S.C. and the hallmark.

Movement: quartz. ETA calibre 4 7/8 E01.001, 5 jewels.
Functions: hour, minute.
Case: barrel shaped case completely integrated in the bracelet. Stainless steel, curved sapphire crystal, case back attached by screws. Crown identified with Bedat & C° logo and trademarks. Inside casing ring in metal. Water resistant to 5 atm.

Bracelet: stainless steel. Bedat & C° steel folding clasp.
Diamonds: set with 606 Top Wesselton VVSI diamonds (4.66 cts).
Dial: Bedat & C° guilloche, white. Diamond hour markers. Bedat & C° own designed hands. Logo at 8 o'clock.
Also available: Bedat & C° guilloche, black. Diamond hour markers.
Note: Swiss origin of each components certified with the Bedat & C° trademark Swiss A.O.S.C. and the hallmark.

BEDAT & C⁰ N. 3   REF. 314.011.610

Movement: mechanical, automatic winding, ETA calibre 8‴ 2000/1, 20 jewels.
Functions: hour, minute, center seconds, date at 6 o'clock with Bedat & C⁰ logo replacing the date 8.
Case: stainless steel, barrel shaped. Curved sapphire crystal. Case back attached by screws. Crown identified with Bedat & C⁰ logo and trademarks. Inside casing ring in metal. Water resistant to 5 atm.
Bracelet: stainless steel. Bedat & C⁰ steel folding clasp.
Strap: provided with the bracelet in the packaging. Black Grosgrain satin fully padded with Bedat & C⁰ lining. Regular steel buckle.
Dial: Bedat & C⁰ guilloche, silver. Luminescent Bedat & C⁰ own designed hands. Logo at 8 o'clock.
Also available: Bedat & C⁰ guilloche, white roman numerals.
Bedat & C⁰ guilloche, white, diamond hour markers.
Bedat & C⁰ guilloche, blue, diamond hour markers.
Note: Swiss origin of each components certified with the Bedat & C⁰ trademark Swiss A.O.S.C. and the hallmark.

BEDAT & C⁰ N. 3   REF. 314.051.109

Movement: mechanical, automatic winding, ETA calibre 8‴ 2000/1, 20 jewels.
Functions: hour, minute, center seconds, date at 6 o'clock with Bedat & C⁰ logo replacing the date 8.
Case: stainless steel, barrel shaped. Curved sapphire crystal. Case back attached by screws. Crown identified with Bedat & C⁰ logo and trademarks. Inside casing ring in metal. Water resistant to 5 atm.
Diamonds: set on the bezel and the sides with 181 Top Wesselton VVSI diamonds (1.99 cts).
Bracelet: stainless steel. Bedat & C⁰ steel folding clasp.
Strap: provided with the bracelet in the packaging. Black Grosgrain satin (as shown) fully padded with Bedat & C⁰ lining. Regular steel buckle.
Dial: Bedat & C⁰ guilloche, white, diamond hour markers. Luminescent Bedat & C⁰ own designed hands. Logo at 8 o'clock.
Also available: set only on the bezel with 121 Top Wesselton VVSI diamonds (0.99 cts). Bedat & C⁰ guilloche, white, diamond hour markers.
Note: Swiss origin of each components certified with the Bedat & C⁰ trademark Swiss A.O.S.C. and the hallmark.

BEDAT & C⁰ N. 3   REF. 314.303.800

Movement: mechanical, automatic winding, ETA calibre 8‴ 2000/1, 20 jewels.
Functions: hour, minute, center seconds, date at 6 o'clock with Bedat & C⁰ logo replacing the date 8.
Case: 18K solid gold, barrel shaped. Curved sapphire crystal. Steel case back attached by screws. Steel crown identified with Bedat & C⁰ logo and trademarks. Inside casing ring in metal. Water resistant to 5 atm.
Bracelet: 18K solid gold. Bedat & C⁰ steel folding clasp.
Strap: provided with the bracelet in the packaging. Black Grosgrain satin fully padded with Bedat & C⁰ lining. Regular steel buckle.
Dial: Bedat & C⁰ guilloche, antique white roman numeral. Luminescent Bedat & C⁰ own designed hands. Logo at 8 o'clock.
Also available: Bedat & C⁰ guilloche, white, diamond hour markers.
Note: Swiss origin of each components certified with the Bedat & C⁰ trademark Swiss A.O.S.C. and the hallmark.

BEDAT & C⁰ N. 3   REF. 314.515.800

Movement: mechanical, automatic winding, ETA calibre 8‴ 2000/1, 20 jewels.
Functions: hour, minute, center seconds, date at 6 o'clock with Bedat & C⁰ logo replacing the date 8.
Case: 18K solid white gold, barrel shaped. Curved sapphire crystal. Steel case back attached by screws. Steel crown identified with Bedat & C⁰ logo and trademarks. Inside casing ring in metal. Water resistant to 5 atm.
Bracelet: 18K solid white gold. Bedat & C⁰ steel folding clasp.
Strap: provided with the bracelet in the packaging. Black Grosgrain satin fully padded with Bedat & C⁰ lining. Regular steel buckle.
Dial: Bedat & C⁰ guilloche, antique white roman numeral. Luminescent Bedat & C⁰ own designed hands. Logo at 8 o'clock.
Also available: Bedat & C⁰ guilloche, white, diamond hour markers.
Note: Swiss origin of each components certified with the Bedat & C⁰ trademark Swiss A.O.S.C. and the hallmark.

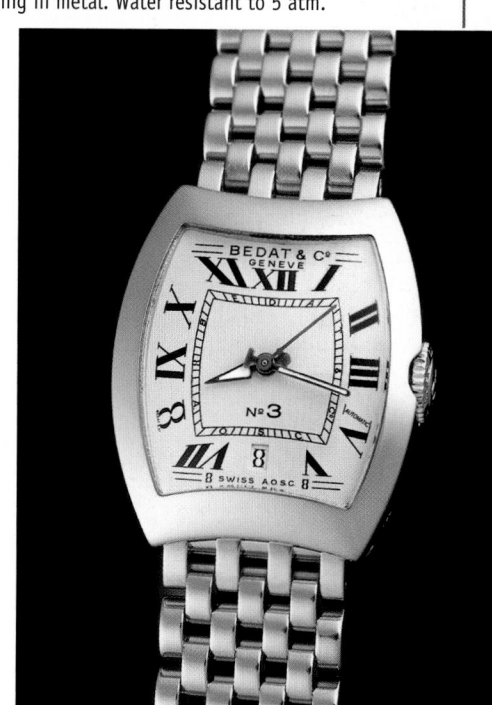

BEDAT & C°

Movement: quartz, ETA calibre 4 7/8 E01.001, 5 jewels.
Functions: hour, minute.
Case: curved, reversible case in 18K solid gold. Curved solid gold case back attached by screws. Solid gold crown identified with Bedat & C° logo and trademarks. Inside casing ring in metal. Water resistant to 5 atm.
Bracelet: reversible solid gold: one side all shiny finish, other side mat finish for center links and shiny finish for the side links. No clasp, attachment to the case with a "snap-in" mechanism.
Dial: Bedat & C° guilloche, antique white roman numeral. Bedat & C° own designed hands. Logo at 8 o'clock.
Also available: case back set with 180 Top Wesselton VVSI diamonds (1.09 cts). Bracelet set on shiny side with 52 Top Wesselton VVSI diamonds (0.59 cts). Bedat & C° guilloche, antique white diamond hour markers dial.
Note: the case and the bracelet being separately reversible, there are four ways to wear the watch. Swiss origin of each components certified with the Bedat & C° trademark Swiss A.O.S.C. and the hallmark.

Movement: quartz, ETA calibre 4 7/8 E01.001, 5 jewels.
Functions: hour, minute.
Case: curved, reversible case in 18K solid gold . Curved solid gold case back attached by screws. Solid gold crown identified with Bedat & C° logo and trademarks. Inside casing ring in metal. Water resistant to 5 atm.
Diamonds: bezel set with 121 Top Wesselton VVSI diamonds (0.74 cts).

Bracelet: reversible solid gold: one side all shiny finish, other side mat finish for center links and shiny finish for side links. No clasp, attachment to the case with a "snap-in" mechanism.
Dial: Bedat & C° guilloche, antique white, diamond markers. Bedat & C° own designed hands. Logo at 8 o'clock.
Also available: case back set with 180 Top Wesselton VVSI diamonds (1.09 cts). Bracelet set on shiny side with 52 Top Wesselton VVSI diamonds (0.59 cts).
Note: the case and the bracelet being separately reversible, there are four ways to wear the watch. Swiss origin of each components certified with the Bedat & C° trademark Swiss A.O.S.C. and the hallmark.

Movement: quartz, ETA calibre 4 7/8 E01.001, 5 jewels.
Functions: hour, minute.
Case: curved, reversible case in 18K solid white gold. Curved sapphire crystal. Curved solid white gold case back attached by screws. Solid gold crown identified with Bedat & C° logo and trademarks. Inside casing ring in metal. Water resistant to 5 atm. **Diamonds:** bezel set with 112 Top Wesselton VVSI diamonds (0.70 cts), case back set with 180 Top Wesselton VVSI diamonds (1.1 cts).
Bracelet: reversible solid white gold: one side all shiny finish, other side mat finish for center links and shiny finish for side links. No clasp, attachment to the case with a "snap-in" mechanism.
Diamonds: shiny finish side set with 52 Top Wesselton VVSI diamonds (0.59 cts).
Dial: Bedat & C° guilloche, white, pave with 126 Top Wesselton diamonds (0.56 cts). Bedat & C° own designed hands.
Also available: plain white gold, diamond dial. Other diamonds executions are available.
Note: the case and the bracelet being separately reversible, there are four ways to wear the watch.

Swiss origin of each components certified with the Bedat & C° trademark Swiss A.O.S.C. and the hallmark.
Same watch showed from reversed side.

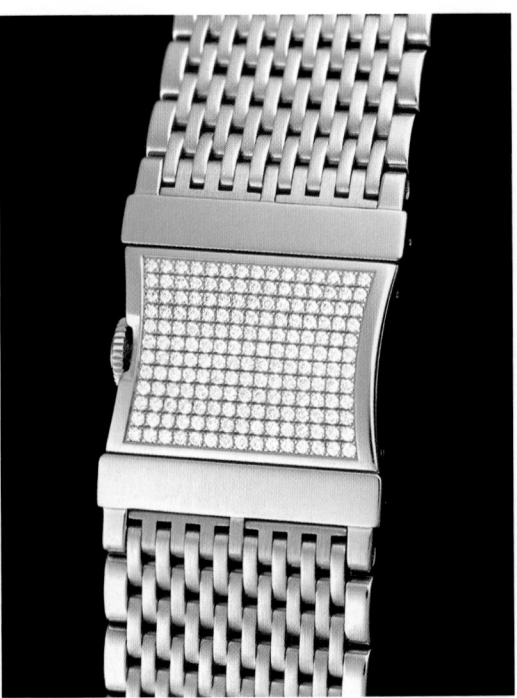

BEDAT & C° N. 7   REF. 728.510.109

Movement: mechanical, automatic winding, ETA calibre 8''' 2000/1, 20 jewels.
Functions: hour, minute, center seconds, date at 6 o'clock with Bedat & C° logo replacing the date 8.
Case: stainless steel, three pieces, square, curved case. Curved sapphire crystal. Case back attached by screws. Crown identified with Bedat & C° logo and trademarks. Inside casing ring in metal. Water resistant to 5 atm.
Diamonds: set with 14 princess cut Top Wesselton VVSI diamonds (1.51 cts).
Strap: satin, fully padded with Bedat & C° lining. Bedat & C° steel folding clasp.
Dial: Bedat & C° guilloche, white, diamond markers. Bedat & C° own designed hands. Logo at 8 o'clock.
Note: Swiss origin of each components certified with the Bedat & C° trademark Swiss A.O.S.C. and the hallmark.

BEDAT & C° N.7   REF. 728.550.109

Movement: mechanical, automatic winding, ETA calibre 8''' 2000/1, 20 jewels.
Functions: hour, minute, center seconds, date at 6 o'clock with Bedat & C° logo replacing the date 8.
Case: stainless steel, three pieces, square, curved case. Curved sapphire crystal. Case back attached by screws. Crown identified with Bedat & C° logo and trademarks. Inside casing ring in metal. Water resistant to 5 atm.
Diamonds: set with 14 princess cut Top Wesselton VVSI diamonds (1.51 cts) and 129 full cut Top Wesselton VVSI diamonds (1.91 cts).
Strap: satin, fully padded with Bedat & C° lining. Bedat & C° steel folding clasp.
Dial: Bedat & C° guilloche, white, diamond markers. Bedat & C° own designed hands. Logo at 8 o'clock.
Note: Swiss origin of each components certified with the Bedat & C° trademark Swiss A.O.S.C. and the hallmark.

BEDAT & C° N. 7   REF. 728.850.109

Movement: mechanical, automatic winding, ETA calibre 8''' 2000/1, 20 jewels.
Functions: hour, minute, center seconds, date at 6 o'clock with Bedat & C° logo replacing the date 8.
Case: stainless steel, three pieces, square, curved case. Curved sapphire crystal. Case back attached by screws. Crown identified with Bedat & C° logo and trademarks. Inside casing ring in metal. Water resistant to 5 atm.
Diamonds: set with 14 princess cut topazes (1.44 cts) and 129 full cut Top Wesselton VVSI diamonds (1.91 cts).
Strap: satin, fully padded with Bedat & C° lining. Bedat & C° steel folding clasp.
Dial: Bedat & C° guilloche, white, diamond markers. Bedat & C° own designed hands. Logo at 8 o'clock.
Note: Swiss origin of each components certified with the Bedat & C° trademark Swiss A.O.S.C. and the hallmark.

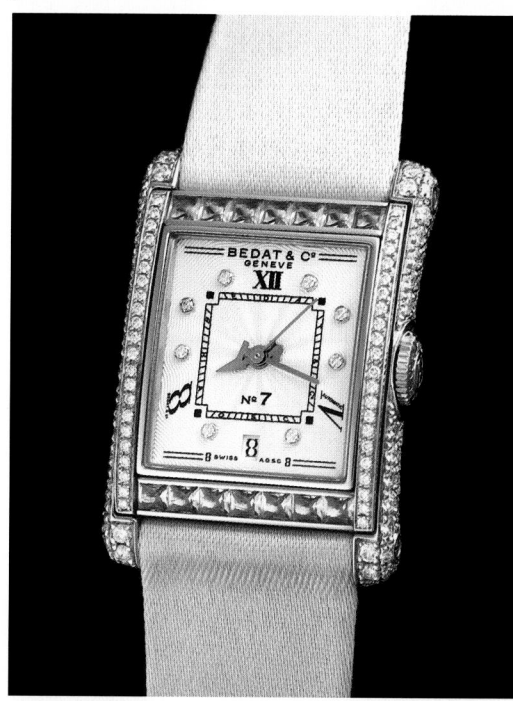

BEDAT & C° N. 7   REF. 728.087.109

Movement: mechanical, automatic winding, ETA calibre 8''' 2000/1, 20 jewels.
Functions: hour, minute, center seconds, date at 6 o'clock with Bedat & C° logo replacing the date 8.
Case: stainless steel, three pieces, square, curved case. Curved sapphire crystal. Case back attached by screws. Crown identified with Bedat & C° logo and trademarks. Inside casing ring in metal. Water resistant to 5 atm.
Diamonds: set with 14 princess cut blue sapphire (3.22 cts).
Strap: satin, fully padded with Bedat & C° lining. Bedat & C° steel folding clasp.
Dial: Bedat & C° guilloche, white, diamond markers. Bedat & C° own designed hands. Logo at 8 o'clock.
Also available: set with pink or yellow sapphire.
Note: Swiss origin of each components certified with the Bedat & C° trademark Swiss A.O.S.C. and the hallmark.

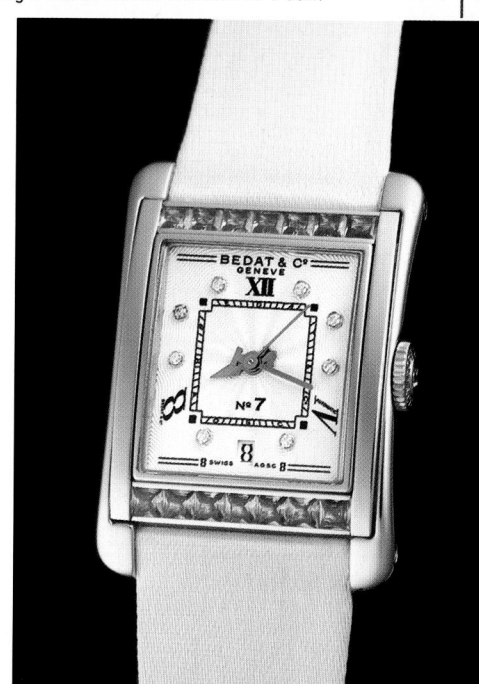

BEDAT & Co

BEDAT & Co N. 7   REF. 728.030.109

Movement: mechanical, automatic winding, ETA calibre 8''' 2000/1, 20 jewels.
Functions: hour, minute, center seconds, date at 6 o'clock with Bedat & Co logo replacing the date 8.
Case: stainless steel, three pieces, square, curved case. Satin and polish finish. Curved sapphire crystal. Case back attached by screws. Crown identified with Bedat & Co logo and trademarks. Inside casing ring in metal. Water resistant to 5 atm.

Diamonds: case sides set with 85 Top Wesselton VVSI diamonds (1.71 cts).
Strap: satin, fully padded with Bedat & Co lining. Bedat & Co steel folding clasp.
Dial: Bedat & Co guilloche, white, diamond markers. Bedat & Co own designed hands. Logo at 8 o'clock.
Also available: Bedat & Co guilloche, black, diamond hour markers.
Note: Swiss origin of each components certified with the Bedat & Co trademark Swiss A.O.S.C. and the hallmark.

BEDAT & Co N. 7   REF. 788.056.109

Movement: mechanical, automatic winding, ETA calibre 8''' 2000/1, 20 jewels.
Functions: hour, minute.
Case: stainless steel, three pieces, rectangular, curved case. Curved mineral crystal. Case back attached by screws. Crown identified with Bedat & Co logo and trademarks. Inside casing ring in metal. Water resistant to 5 atm.
Diamonds: set with 205 natural yellow diamonds (2.99 cts).

Strap: fully padded with Bedat & Co lining and hand stitched alligator. Bedat & Co steel folding clasp.
Dial: Bedat & Co guilloche, white, diamond markers. Bedat & Co own designed hands. Logo at 8 o'clock.
Note: Swiss origin of each components certified with the Bedat & Co trademark Swiss A.O.S.C. and the hallmark.

BEDAT & Co N. 7   REF. 728.050.109

Movement: mechanical, automatic winding, ETA calibre 8''' 2000/1, 20 jewels.
Functions: hour, minute, center seconds, date at 6 o'clock with Bedat & Co logo replacing the date 8.
Case: stainless steel, three pieces, square, curved case. Curved sapphire crystal. Case back attached by screws. Crown identified with Bedat & Co logo and trademarks. Inside casing ring in metal. Water resistant to 5 atm.

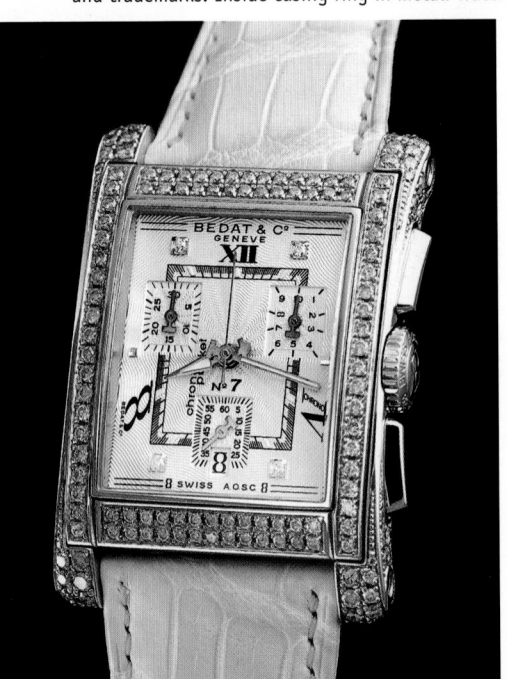

Diamonds: set with 185 Top Wesselton VVSI diamonds (2.23 cts).
Strap: satin, fully padded with Bedat & Co lining. Bedat & Co steel folding clasp.
Dial: Bedat & Co guilloche, white, diamond markers. Bedat & Co own designed hands. Logo at 8 o'clock.
Also available: Bedat & Co guilloche, black, diamond markers.
Same model set on bezel only with 108 diamonds (0.56 cts); white or black diamond markers dial.
Note: Swiss origin of each components certified with the Bedat & Co trademark Swiss A.O.S.C. and the hallmark.

BEDAT & Co N. 7   REF. 778.056.109

Movement: quartz. ETA calibre 10 Ω 251.471, 23 jewels.
Functions: hour, minute, small second, chronograph with 3 counters, date at 6 o'clock with Bedat & Co logo replacing the date 8.
Case: stainless steel, three pieces, rectangular, curved case. Curved sapphire crystal. Case back attached by screws. Crown identified with Bedat & Co logo and trademarks. Inside casing ring in metal. Water resistant to 5 atm.

Diamonds: set with 185 natural yellow diamonds (2.84 cts).
Strap: fully padded with Bedat & Co lining and hand stitched crocodile. Bedat & Co steel folding clasp.
Dial: Bedat & Co guilloche, white, diamond markers. Bedat & Co own designed hands. Logo at 8 o'clock.
Note: Swiss origin of each components certified with the Bedat & Co trademark Swiss A.O.S.C. and the hallmark.

BEDAT & C° N. 7 — REF. 728.313.809

Movement: mechanical, automatic winding, ETA calibre 8''' 2000/1, 20 jewels.
Functions: hour, minute, center seconds, date at 6 o'clock with Bedat & C° logo replacing the date 8.
Case: curved 18K yellow and rose gold, three pieces, square case. Satin and polish finish. Curved sapphire crystal. Steel case back attached by screws. Crown identified with Bedat & C° logo and trademarks. Inside casing ring in metal. Water resistant to 5 atm.
Bracelet: 18K gold. Bedat & C° steel folding clasp.
Dial: Bedat & C° guilloche, antique white, diamond markers. Bedat & C° own designed hands. Logo at 8 o'clock.
Also available: on satin strap.
Note: Swiss origin of each components certified with the Bedat & C° trademark Swiss A.O.S.C. and the hallmark.

BEDAT & C° N. 7 — REF. 728.330.809

Movement: mechanical, automatic winding, ETA calibre 8''' 2000/1, 20 jewels.
Functions: hour, minute, center seconds, date at 6 o'clock with Bedat & C° logo replacing the date 8.
Case: curved 18K yellow and rose gold, three pieces, square case. Satin and polish finish. Curved sapphire crystal. Case back attached by screws. Crown identified with Bedat & C° logo and trademarks. Inside casing ring in metal. Water resistant to 5 atm.
Diamonds: set with 85 Top Wesselton VVSI diamonds (1.71 cts).
Strap: satin, fully padded with Bedat & C° lining. Bedat & C° steel folding clasp.
Dial: Bedat & C° guilloche, white, diamond markers. Bedat & C° own designed hands. Logo at 8 o'clock.
Also available: on gold bracelet.
Note: Swiss origin of each components certified with the Bedat & C° trademark Swiss A.O.S.C. and the hallmark.

BEDAT & C° N. 7 — REF. 718.310.800

Movement: mechanical, automatic winding, ETA calibre 8''' 2000/1, 20 jewels.
Functions: hour, minute, center second, date at 6 o'clock with logo Bedat & C° logo replacing the date 8.
Case: yellow and rose gold, three pieces, rectangular shaped, curved case (satin and polished finish). Curved sapphire crystal. Case back attached by screws. Crown identified with Bedat & C° logo and trademarks. Inside casing ring in metal. Water resistant to 5 atm.
Strap: fully padded with Bedat & C° lining and hand stitched leather. Bedat & C° steel folding clasp.
Dial: Bedat & C° guilloche, antique white roman numerals. Bedat & C° own designed hands. Logo at 8 o'clock.
Also available: Bedat & C° guilloche, black indexes.
All dials available on solid gold bracelet.
Note: Swiss origin of each components certified with the Bedat & C° trademark Swiss A.O.S.C. and the hallmark.

BEDAT & C° N. 7, CHRONOPOCKET — REF. 778.310.810

Movement: quartz. ETA calibre 10 Ω 251.471, 23 jewels.
Functions: hour, minute, small second, chronograph with 3 counters, date at 6 o'clock with Bedat & C° logo replacing the date 8.
Case: solid 18K yellow and rose gold, curved, three pieces, rectangular case. Curved sapphire crystal. Steel case back attached by screws. Crown identified with Bedat & C° logo and trademarks. Inside casing ring in metal. Water resistant to 5 atm.
This ChronoPocket is sold as a complete set. The watch transforms itself into a refined pocket watch, a desk watch, a wrist chronograph with a choice of three straps in leather, alligator and water resistant material.
Strap: fully padded with Bedat & C° lining and hand stitched alligator and leather. Bedat & C° steel folding clasp.
Chain: solid silver pocket chain with yellow gold end-pieces transforming the watch into a pocket watch.
Dial: Bedat & C° guilloche, antique white, indexes. Bedat & C° own designed hands. Logo at 8 o'clock.
Note: Swiss origin of each components certified with the Bedat & C° trademark Swiss A.O.S.C. and the hallmark.

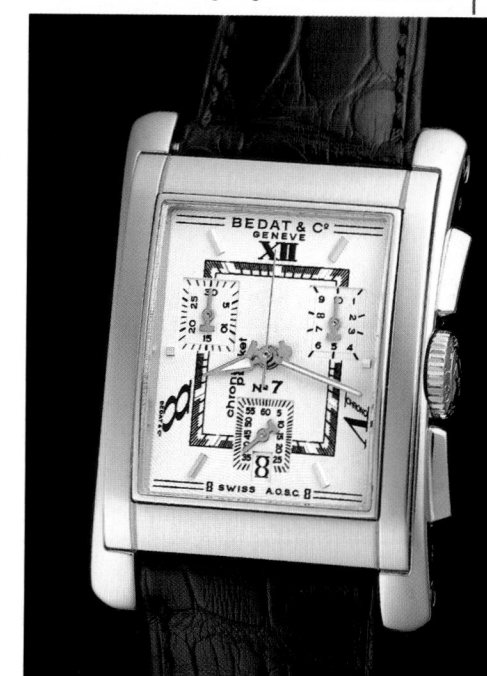

BEDAT & Co

BEDAT & Co N. 7, CHRONOPOCKET   REF. 778.010.320

Movement: quartz. ETA calibre 10 Ω 251.471, 23 jewels.
Functions: hour, minute, small second, chronograph with 3 counters, date at 6 o'clock with Bedat & Co logo replacing the date 8. **Case:** stainless steel, curved, three pieces, rectangular case. Curved sapphire crystal. Steel case back attached by screws. Crown identified with Bedat & Co logo and trademarks. Inside casing ring in metal. Water resistant to 5 atm. This ChronoPocket is sold as a complete

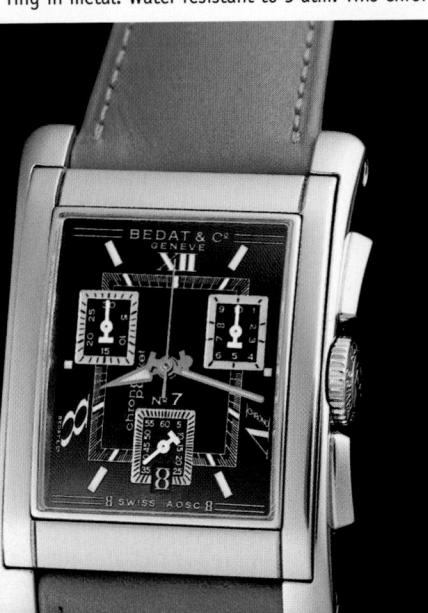

set. The watch transforms itself into a refined pocket watch, a desk watch, a wrist chronograph with a choice of three bracelets in leather, steel and water resistant material.
Bracelet: steel bracelet, steel folding clasp.
Strap: fully padded with Bedat & Co lining and hand stitched leather. Bedat & Co steel folding clasp.
Chain: solid silver pocket chain with steel end-pieces transforming the watch into a pocket watch.
Dial: Bedat & Co guilloche, black, indexes. Bedat & Co own designed hands. Logo at 8 o'clock.
Also available: Bedat & Co guilloche, white or blue indexes. **Note:** Swiss origin of each components certified with the Bedat & Co trademark Swiss A.O.S.C. and the hallmark.

BEDAT & Co N. 7, CHRONOPOCKET   REF. 778.010.610

Movement: quartz. ETA calibre 10 Ω 251.471, 23 jewels.
Functions: hour, minute, small second, chronograph with 3 counters, date at 6 o'clock with Bedat & Co logo replacing the date 8.
Case: shown as a desk watch. Stainless steel, curved, three pieces, rectangular case. Curved sapphire crystal. Steel case back attached by screws. Crown identified with Bedat & Co logo and trademarks. Inside casing ring in metal. Water re-

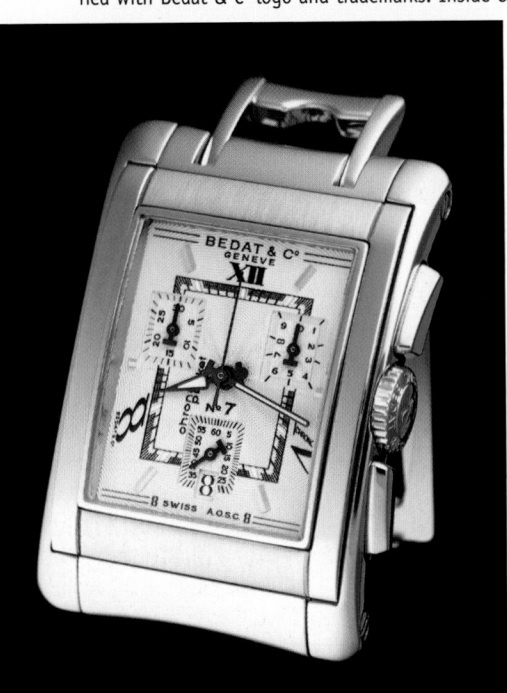

sistant to 5 atm. This ChronoPocket is sold as a complete set. The watch transforms itself into a refined pocket watch, a desk watch, a wrist chronograph with a choice of three bracelets in leather, steel and water resistant material.
Bracelet: steel bracelet, steel folding clasp. **Strap:** fully padded with Bedat & Co lining and hand stitched alligator and leather. Bedat & Co steel folding clasp. **Chain:** solid silver pocket chain with end-pieces transforming the watch into a pocket watch. **Dial:** Bedat & Co guilloche, silver, indexes. Bedat & Co own designed hands. Logo at 8 o'clock. **Note:** Swiss origin of each components certified with the Bedat & Co trademark Swiss A.O.S.C. and the hallmark.

BEDAT & Co N. 7, CHRONOPOCKET   REF. 778.510.810

Movement: quartz. ETA calibre 10 Ω 251.471, 23 jewels.
Functions: hour, minute, small second, chronograph with 3 counters, date at 6 o'clock with Bedat & Co logo replacing the date 8.
Case: solid 18K white gold, curved, three pieces, rectangular case. Curved sapphire crystal. Steel case back attached by screws. Crown identified with Bedat & Co logo and trademarks. Inside casing ring in metal. Water resistant to 5

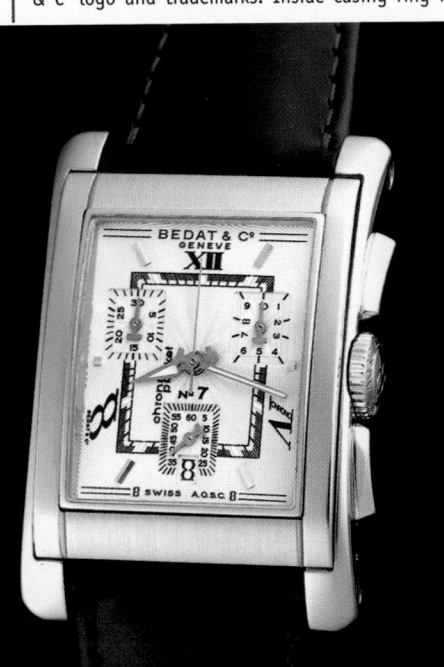

atm. This ChronoPocket is sold as a complete set. The watch transforms itself into a refined pocket watch, a desk watch, a wrist chronograph with a choice of three straps in leather, alligator and water resistant material.
Strap: fully padded with Bedat & Co lining and hand stitched alligator and leather. Bedat & Co steel folding clasp.
Chain: solid silver pocket chain with steel end-pieces transforming the watch into a pocket watch.
Dial: Bedat & Co guilloche, antique white, indexes. Bedat & Co own designed hands. Logo at 8 o'clock.
Note: Swiss origin of each components certified with the Bedat & Co trademark Swiss A.O.S.C. and the hallmark.

BEDAT & Co N. 7, CHRONOPOCKET   REF. 778.910.610

Movement: quartz. ETA calibre 10 Ω 251.471, 23 jewels.
Functions: hour, minute, small second, chronograph with 3 counters, date at 6 o'clock with Bedat & Co logo replacing the date 8.
Case: platinum, curved, three pieces, rectangular case. Curved sapphire crystal. Steel case back attached by screws. Crown identified with Bedat & Co logo and trademarks. Inside casing ring in metal. Water resistant to 5 atm.

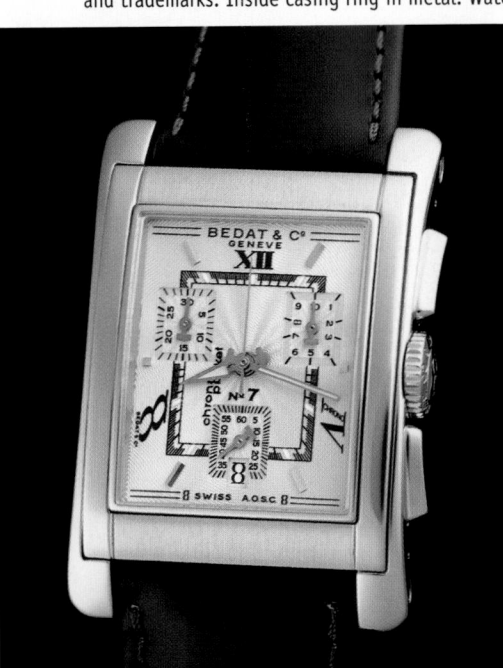

This ChronoPocket is sold as a complete set. The watch transforms itself into a refined pocket watch, a desk watch, a wrist chronograph with a choice of three straps in leather, alligator and water resistant material.
Strap: fully padded with Bedat & Co lining and hand stitched alligator and leather. Bedat & Co steel folding clasp.
Chain: solid silver pocket chain with steel end-pieces transforming the watch into a pocket watch.
Dial: Bedat & Co guilloche, silver, indexes. Bedat & Co own designed hands. Logo at 8 o'clock.
Note: Swiss origin of each components certified with the Bedat & Co trademark Swiss A.O.S.C. and the hallmark.

BEDAT & C° N. 7   REF. 708.010.100

Movement: mechanical, automatic winding, ETA calibre 8''' 2000/1, 20 jewels.
Functions: hour, minute, center second, date at 6 o'clock with logo Bedat & C° logo replacing the date 8.
Case: stainless steel, three pieces, barrel shaped, curved case (satin and polished finish). Curved sapphire crystal. Case back attached by screws. Crown identified with Bedat & C° logo and trademarks. Inside casing ring in metal. Water resistant to 5 atm.
Strap: fully padded with Bedat & C° lining and hand stitched leather. Bedat & C° steel folding clasp.
Dial: Bedat & C° guilloche, white roman numerals. Bedat & C° own designed hands. Logo at 8 o'clock.
Also available: Bedat & C° guilloche, white or black indexes.
Bedat & C° guilloche, antique white, Arabic numerals.
All dials available on steel bracelet.
Note: Swiss origin of each components certified with the Bedat & C° trademark Swiss A.O.S.C. and the hallmark.

BEDAT & C° N. 7   REF. 718.010.100

Movement: mechanical, automatic winding, ETA calibre 8''' 2000/1, 20 jewels.
Functions: hour, minute, center second, date at 6 o'clock with logo Bedat & C° logo replacing the date 8.
Case: stainless steel, three pieces, rectangular shaped, curved case (satin and polished finish). Curved sapphire crystal. Case back attached by screws. Crown identified with Bedat & C° logo and trademarks. Inside casing ring in metal. Water resistant to 5 atm.
Strap: fully padded with Bedat & C° lining and hand stitched leather. Bedat & C° steel folding clasp.
Dial: Bedat & C° guilloche, white roman numerals. Bedat & C° own designed hands. Logo at 8 o'clock.
Also available: Bedat & C° guilloche, white, blue or black indexes.
All dials available on steel bracelets.
Note: Swiss origin of each components certified with the Bedat & C° trademark Swiss A.O.S.C. and the hallmark.

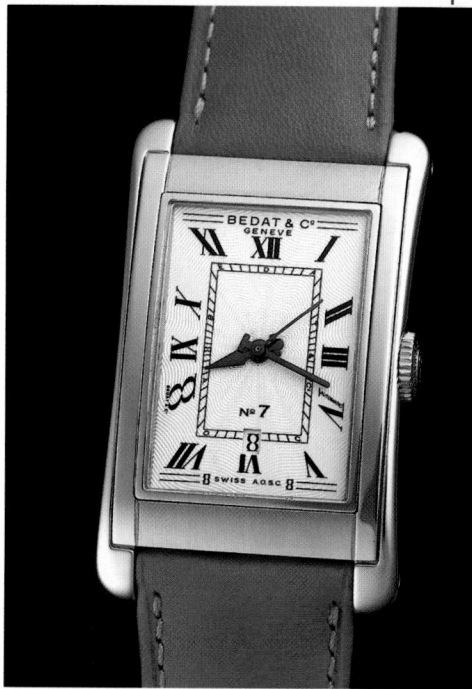

BEDAT & C° N. 7   REF. 728.010.100

Movement: mechanical, automatic winding, ETA calibre 8''' 2000/1, 20 jewels.
Functions: hour, minute, center second, date at 6 o'clock with logo Bedat & C° logo replacing the date 8.
Case: Stainless steel, three pieces, square shaped, curved case. Satin and polish finish. Curved sapphire crystal. Case back attached by screws. Crown identified with Bedat & C° logo and trademarks. Inside casing ring in metal. Water resistant to 5 atm.
Strap: fully padded with Bedat & C° lining and hand stitched leather. Bedat & C° steel folding clasp.
Dial: Bedat & C° guilloche, white roman numerals. Bedat & C° own designed hands. Logo at 8 o'clock.
Also available: Bedat & C° guilloche, white or black indexes.
Bedat & C° guilloche, black or white with diamond markers.
All dials available on steel bracelet.
Note: Swiss origin of each components certified with the Bedat & C° trademark Swiss A.O.S.C. and the hallmark.

BEDAT & C° N. 7   REF. 788.010.100

Movement: mechanical, automatic winding, ETA calibre 8''' 2000/1, 20 jewels.
Functions: hour, minute, center second, date at 6 o'clock with logo Bedat & C° logo replacing the date 8.
Case: stainless steel, three pieces, rectangular shaped, curved case (satin and polished finish). Curved mineral crystal. Case back attached by screws. Crown identified with Bedat & C° logo and trademarks. Inside casing ring in metal. Water resistant to 5 atm.
Strap: fully padded with Bedat & C° lining and hand stitched leather. Bedat & C° steel folding clasp.
Dial: Bedat & C° guilloche, white roman numerals. Bedat & C° own designed hands. Logo at 8 o'clock.
Also available: Bedat & C° guilloche, white or black indexes.
Bedat & C° guilloche, white with diamond markers.
All dials available on steel bracelet.
Note: Swiss origin of each components certified with the Bedat & C° trademark Swiss A.O.S.C. and the hallmark.

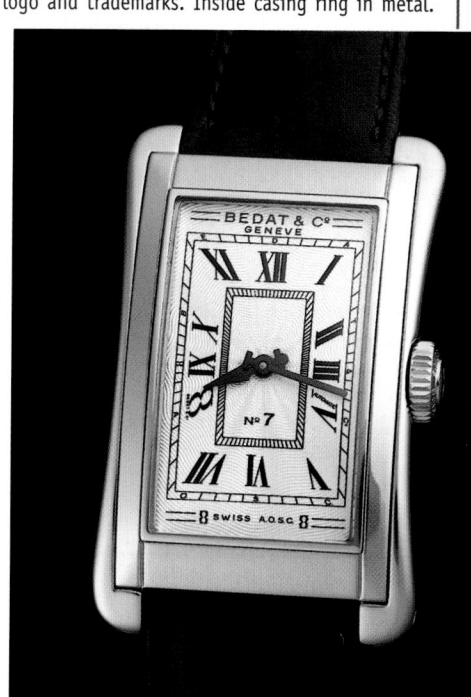

BEDAT & C°

Movement: mechanical, automatic winding. Annual Calendar calibre.
Functions: hour, minute, small second at 4 o'clock, date at 12 o'clock with Bedat & C° logo replacing the date 8, month at 8 o'clock.
Case: stainless steel, three pieces, rectangular shaped, curved case (satin and polished finish). Curved and bevelled sapphire crystal. Case back attached by screws. Crown identified with Bedat & C° logo and trademarks. Inside casing ring in metal. Water resistant to 5 atm.

Strap: fully padded with Bedat & C° lining and hand stitched leather. Bedat & C° steel folding clasp.
Dial: Bedat & C° guilloche, black, indexes. Bedat & C° own designed hands. Logo at 8 o'clock.
Also available: Bedat & C° guilloche, silver, indexes or antique white, roman numerals.
Note: Swiss origin of each components certified with the Bedat & C° trademark SWISS A.O.S.C. and the hallmark.

Movement: mechanical, automatic winding. Annual Calendar calibre.
Functions: hour, minute, small second at 4 o'clock, date at 12 o'clock with Bedat & C° logo replacing the date 8, month at 8 o'clock.
Case: stainless steel, three pieces, rectangular shaped, curved case (satin and polished finish). Curved and bevelled sapphire crystal. Case back attached by screws. Crown identified with Bedat & C° logo and trademarks. Inside casing ring in metal. Water resistant to 5 atm.

Strap: fully padded with Bedat & C° lining and hand stitched leather. Bedat & C° steel folding clasp.
Dial: Bedat & C° guilloche, silver, indexes. Bedat & C° own designed hands. Logo at 8 o'clock.
Also available: Bedat & C° guilloche, black, indexes or antique white, roman numerals.
Note: Swiss origin of each components certified with the Bedat & C° trademark SWISS A.O.S.C. and the hallmark.

Movement: mechanical, automatic winding. Annual Calendar calibre.
Functions: hour, minute, small second at 4 o'clock, date at 12 o'clock with Bedat & C° logo replacing the date 8, month at 8 o'clock.
Case: stainless steel, three pieces, rectangular shaped, curved case (satin and polished finish). Curved and bevelled sapphire crystal. Case back attached by screws. Crown identified with Bedat & C° logo and trademarks. Inside casing ring in metal. Water resistant to 5 atm.

Strap: fully padded with Bedat & C° lining and hand stitched leather. Bedat & C° steel folding clasp.
Dial: Bedat & C° guilloche, antique white, roman numerals. Bedat & C° own designed hands. Logo at 8 o'clock.
Also available: Bedat & C° guilloche, black or silver, indexes.
Note: Swiss origin of each components certified with the Bedat & C° trademark SWISS A.O.S.C. and the hallmark.

Movement: mechanical, automatic winding. Annual Calendar calibre.
Functions: hour, minute, small second at 4 o'clock, date at 12 o'clock with Bedat & C° logo replacing the date 8, month at 8 o'clock.
Case: solid 18K yellow and rose gold, three pieces, rectangular shaped, curved case (satin and polished finish). Curved and bevelled sapphire crystal. Case back attached by screws. Crown identified with Bedat & C° logo and trademarks. Inside casing ring in metal. Water resistant to 5 atm.

Strap: fully padded with Bedat & C° lining and hand stitched leather. Bedat & C° steel folding clasp.
Dial: Bedat & C° guilloche, antique white, roman numerals. Bedat & C° own designed hands. Logo at 8 o'clock.
Note: Swiss origin of each components certified with the Bedat & C° trademark SWISS A.O.S.C. and the hallmark.

BEDAT & Co N. 7   REF 768.010.316

Movement: mechanical, automatic winding, ETA calibre 12 1/2 2894.
Functions: hour, minute, center second, date at 4 o'clock with Bedat & Co logo replacing the date 8. Chronograph functions: recorder of second, minute (30) and hour (12).
Case: stainless steel, three pieces, rectangular shaped, curved case (satin and polished finish). Curved saphhire crystal. Case back attached by screws. Crown identified with Bedat & Co logo and trademarks. Inside casing ring in metal. Water resistant to 5 atm.
Strap: fully padded with Bedat & Co lining and hand stitched leather. Bedat & Co steel folding clasp.
Dial: Bedat & Co guilloche, black, indexes. Bedat & Co own designed hands. Logo at 8 o'clock.
Also available: Bedat & Co guilloche, antique white or silver, indexes.
Note: Swiss origin of each components certified with the Bedat & Co trademark SWISS A.O.S.C. and the hallmark.

BEDAT & Co N. 7   REF 768.010.610

Movement: mechanical, automatic winding, ETA calibre 12 1/2 2894.
Functions: hour, minute, center second, date at 4 o'clock with Bedat & Co logo replacing the date 8. Chronograph functions: recorder of second, minute (30) and hour (12).
Case: stainless steel, three pieces, rectangular shaped, curved case (satin and polished finish). Curved saphhire crystal. Case back attached by screws. Crown identified with Bedat & Co logo and trademarks. Inside casing ring in metal. Water resistant to 5 atm.
Strap: fully padded with Bedat & Co lining and hand stitched leather. Bedat & Co steel folding clasp.
Dial: Bedat & Co guilloche, silver, indexes. Bedat & Co own designed hands. Logo at 8 o'clock.
Also available: Bedat & Co guilloche, antique white or black, indexes.
Note: Swiss origin of each components certified with the Bedat & Co trademark SWISS A.O.S.C. and the hallmark.

BEDAT & Co N. 7   REF 768.010.810

Movement: mechanical, automatic winding, ETA calibre 12 1/2 2894.
Functions: hour, minute, center second, date at 4 o'clock with Bedat & Co logo replacing the date 8. Chronograph functions: recorder of second, minute (30) and hour (12).
Case: stainless steel, three pieces, rectangular shaped, curved case (satin and polished finish). Curved saphhire crystal. Case back attached by screws. Crown identified with Bedat & Co logo and trademarks. Inside casing ring in metal. Water resistant to 5 atm.
Strap: fully padded with Bedat & Co lining and hand stitched leather. Bedat & Co steel folding clasp.
Dial: Bedat & Co guilloche, antique white, indexes. Bedat & Co own designed hands. Logo at 8 o'clock.
Also available: Bedat & Co guilloche, black or silver, indexes.
Note: Swiss origin of each components certified with the Bedat & Co trademark SWISS A.O.S.C. and the hallmark.

BEDAT & Co N. 7   REF 768.310.800

Movement: mechanical, automatic winding, ETA calibre 12 1/2 2894.
Functions: hour, minute, center second, date at 4 o'clock with Bedat & Co logo replacing the date 8. Chronograph functions: recorder of second, minute (30) and hour (12).
Case: solid 18K yellow and rose gold, three pieces, rectangular shaped, curved case (satin and polished finish). Curved saphhire crystal. Case back attached by screws. Crown identified with Bedat & Co logo and trademarks. Inside casing ring in metal. Water resistant to 5 atm.
Strap: fully padded with Bedat & Co lining and hand stitched leather. Bedat & Co steel folding clasp.
Dial: Bedat & Co guilloche, antique white, roman numerals. Bedat & Co own designed hands. Logo at 8 o'clock.
Note: Swiss origin of each components certified with the Bedat & Co trademark SWISS A.O.S.C. and the hallmark.

BERTOLUCCI

an historical perspective

The year 2002 marks the fifteenth anniversary of Bertolucci. This premiere Swiss watch brand with immediately recognizable appeal has enjoyed tremendous international success. Today, the brand is sold in 30 countries around the globe and is well poised for even greater growth.

First unveiled in 1987 by Remo Bertolucci—a designer with a dream to create a watch with a unique and individualistic look—Bertolucci has fast become both a coveted men's and women's brand. From the start, Bertolucci insisted on designing timepieces with a true artistic quality about them. His first designs featured elegantly sculpted bracelets that emulated the water-caressed pebbles found on a lake's shore. Integrated bracelets kept the design theme intact, and the Bertolucci look soon became a trademark.

Year after year since its inception, Bertolucci has unveiled collections that respect art and craftsmanship. In fact, a specially selected team of designers, watchmakers and artisans work tirelessly together in workshops near the enchanting Lake of Neuchâtel. Every watch undergoes multiple quality checks to ensure the finest craftsmanship and precision. Additionally, all Bertolucci watches are individually finished and hand polished to achieve the utmost quality in final texture and appeal.

Last year, in an effort to further advance its development and enhance its geographic and marketing presence internationally, Bertolucci agreed to an acquisition. A luxury group of private and institutional investors with global marketing expertise purchased the Bertolucci brand. While currently only about 10,000 Bertolucci timepieces are created annually, the plan is to double production over the coming years in order to make the brand a little more accessible while still maintaining exclusivity.

While the CEO and Managing Directors are new to the Bertolucci brand, they remain true to the sense of precision and quality that built it. In fact, Bertolucci's son and family remain intimately involved in the business, further ensuring that the essence of Bertolucci boldly continues. Indeed, the collections unveiled under the new regime consistently demonstrate Bertolucci's commitment to form and function and to art and beauty.

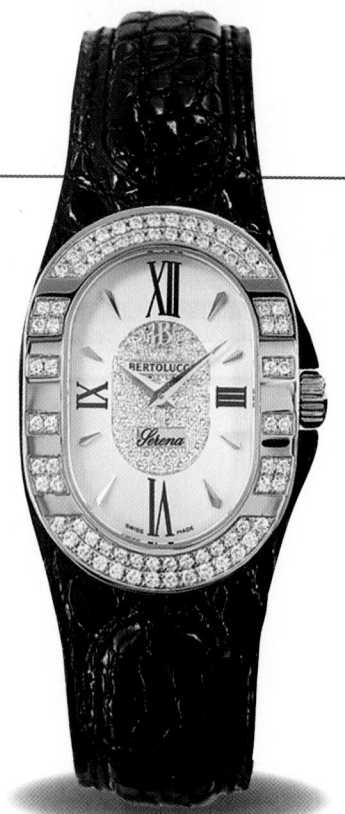

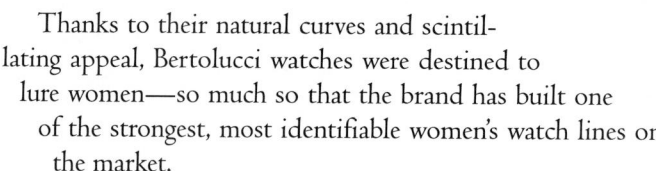

women's
wonders

Thanks to their natural curves and scintillating appeal, Bertolucci watches were destined to lure women—so much so that the brand has built one of the strongest, most identifiable women's watch lines on the market.

Among the most coveted timepieces are the Serena line, which won the impressive Public Grand Prix prize several years ago because of its innovative design style; the Poeme line of high-jeweled watches; Vir, with both classically elegant styles; and a jewelry series of Vir watches set with diamonds and gemstones.

The Serena line of incredibly feminine and yet futuristic watches is a collection that has taken the world by storm. To create this true haute couture timepiece, Bertolucci set a curved oval watch case into a striking custom-created strap and accented it with brilliant colors, diamonds and gemstones. The Serena line, which features a registered design, at once offers modernity and freshness, sensuality and individuality.

Beautifully expressive, the Serena was designed to be worn by women of the world—women who enjoy leisure activities, boardroom litigations and languid evenings. Launched just four years ago, Serena has grown by leaps and bounds in terms of colorful expression and knows no boundaries when it comes to creativity. From the initial allure of the curves of the case, straps and convex sapphire crystal, Serena garnered more and more of the spotlight each time a new model was

CHRONOLOGY

1911 A highly respected workshop for assembling mechanical watches, the Mimo Watch company is founded in the Bienne area and run by Robert Chopard.

1936 Marcel Michelotti begins his apprenticeship here and buys the company about ten years later.

1968 Michelotti's daughter, Pierrette, marries Remo Bertolucci and both join the family company—she as general manager and he as purchasing and sales manager; Remo Bertolucci begins working in the watch assembly workshop at Mimo Watch, owned by his father-in-law, this same year.

1973 Bertolucci branches into the private label sector. He is interested in watch design and, after an increasing number of contracts, starts up his own company, creating collections inspired by art and savoir-faire.

1987 Both Bertolucci SA and Bertolucci Distribution SA are founded this year and the company launches its first line of watches. The Pulchra collection is produced with all the qualities advocated by Remo Bertolucci-elegance, sobriety and a certain timeless nobility. It is the forerunner of the famous Vir.

1994 The company moves to Neuchâtel. The lakeside location is an inspiration for Bertolucci creations.

1998 Bertolucci launches the Serena collection in response to the needs and expectations of the market. Designed with the young in mind, it is a natural extension of the brand's product range and will be developed along with the other lines, particularly the Vir.

1999 Twelve years after the introduction of the Pulchra, Remo Bertolucci creates the Uomo, a watch for men only.

2001 Bertolucci agrees to sell the brand to a consortium of global marketing savvy private and institutional investors for the purpose of enriching Bertolucci's marketing presence internationally; In November, Bertolucci SA enters a joint venture with Bellport Time Group to increase distribution dramatically in the North American markets. Bellport Time Group owner Steven Butler will head the association, Bertolucci North America LLC.

unveiled. Women adored the look of the superimposed leathers and grains that offered depth and texture. When Bertolucci bedecked the Serena with diamonds, the result was spectacular success.

Now Serena has donned a wealth of different gemstones. The jewelry versions include sky blue or pale pink straps, accented with matching blue or pink sapphires and diamonds on the watchcase. Additionally, a center oval dial of 60 diamonds or gemstones reflects the beauty of the bezel and offers breathtaking appeal.

This year, too, Bertolucci adds a few new models to the Poeme and Vir collections. Poeme, a high-jeweled line that offers unusual bracelet links and cushioned square cases, now comes with varying amounts of pavé—set diamonds on the bracelet links. The case is encrusted with diamonds, and diamond markers enhance the mother-of-pearl dials.

Vir for women also comes with or without diamonds on the dial, bezel and case to bracelet attachment. There are several high-jeweled Vir models, including one whose bracelet, bezel, case and entire dial is set with pavé diamonds in 18-karat white gold for stunning appeal. In contrast, Bertolucci never forgets the practical, crafting simply elegant Vir models in steel, 18-karat gold and two-tone versions for true versatility.

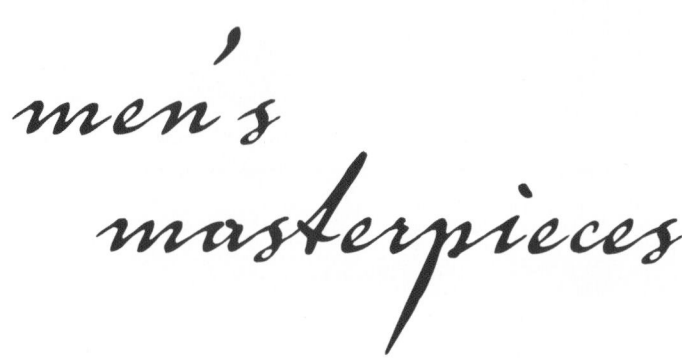

men's

masterpieces

Certainly Bertolucci also caters to men with two very important collections: Uomo and Vir. From the inception of the brand, Bertolucci was developed as a timepiece that attracted the sophisticated yet sporty man. A watch of character, Bertolucci timepieces quickly gained in popularity amongst men of taste. Today, Uomo and Vir continue to steal the limelight.

Uomo was first unveiled two years ago to celebrate the new millennium. A watch of infinite character, Uomo features a striking round case with sculptural appeal. Timepieces meant for people of action, the Uomo has a bold and rugged, yet surprisingly classic, sporty look.

The newest Uomo collection remains focused on the powerful steel pieces, but also deftly infuses two-tone models of steel and 18-karat gold. The Uomo timepieces offer sporty elegant appeal that move wonderfully from day to night, from boat to boardroom. Within the Uomo series are striking chronographs and chronometers officially certified by the COSC. Most models in the Uomo collection are water resistant to at least 100 meters and feature curved sapphires with anti-reflective treatment.

In true Bertolucci style, each part of the timepiece has been treated with the utmost attention to detail and beauty. The case and buckle of each steel Uomo is made from a single piece of metal. The bracelet is a true work of art requiring no less than 400 operations to complete.

Mother-of-pearl dials remain important, and applied markers are key.

The Vir collection — the line that has defined the brand's signature and has stood as its flagship since its inception—remains a vital part of Bertolucci's character. Both a classic and timeless piece, the Vir offers elegant style thanks to its softer line and unusual pebble-shaped bracelet links. Vir is available with a variety of dial colors, including white, midnight and copper.

In the newest versions, Bertolucci mixes satin and polished finishes for aesthetic beauty. One particularly impressive piece is an all-steel satin-finish Vir bracelet watch. The Vir models for men are available with either quartz or automatic movements. The automatic versions are officially certified chronometers accompanied by the COSC certificate.

The COSC certification is especially important in Bertolucci's Vir Plongeur line of unidirectional ratchet bezel diving watches. These striking timepieces feature luminescent hands and markers, as well as date at 3:00 and a protected crown. Again, reconfirming Bertolucci's flair for detail, each of these watches requires more than 400 different processes and operations on its way to final creation.

BLANCPAIN

masterpieces unveiled

Blancpain's roots date back 267 years to 1735, when Jehan-Jacques Blancpain embraced the tradition of watchmaking. Intent upon creating his own components and timepieces to the most exacting of standards, Blancpain began a legacy of luxury watchmaking that continues today.

Following the philosophy of its founding father, Blancpain regularly offers technical masterpieces that belie its innovative spirit and creative determination. This is a brand that embodies the benchmark of traditional watchmaking heritage—regularly unveiling handcrafted timepieces that preserve its conceptual integrity.

By 1988, Blancpain had achieved its goal of designing and producing six masterpieces in watchmaking and was the first manufacturer in the world to offer all six of them simultaneously. Those feats include the ultra-slim watch, the moonphase date calendar watch, the split-seconds chronograph, perpetual calendar watch, tourbillon, and minute repeater.

Since then, Blancpain has regularly unveiled masterpieces that have garnered international recognition, including the first women's self-winding moonphase watch and the smallest self-winding chronograph. In 1991, Blancpain unveiled its famed "1735" in tribute to its heritage. This most complex timepiece was six years in the making and houses 740 parts that offer numerous important functions. Another particularly challenging

TOP

The Blancpain Manufacture.

LEFT

Jehan-Jacques Blancpain.

BOTTOM LEFT

The Quattro houses four important watchmaking complications in its platinum case: tourbillon, perpetual calendar, Flyback chronograph, split-seconds chronograph.

BOTTOM RIGHT

The Grande Date features 100 hours of power reserve and a two-digit date readout that is double the size of most standard dates.

accomplishment is the ultra-complex Self-winding Tourbillon Split-Seconds Flyback Chronograph, which was unveiled in 1999.

In 2001, the brand topped many of its previous feats when it unveiled the Quattro, featuring four important watchmaking complications neatly fitted into a striking 42mm platinum case. The Quattro houses a tourbillon regulator, self-winding flyback chronograph, split-seconds feature and perpetual calendar. The watch's self-winding mechanism features a platinum rotor and provides 40 hours of power reserve. The 39-jeweled movement consists of 432 parts—all painstakingly finished by hand and carefully assembled.

Recognizing the need for easy readability and the classic styling that watch connoisseurs crave, Blancpain has also introduced a 100-hour self-winding Grande Date watch. The new oversized date display utilizes digits that are twice as large as those in standard systems. The self-winding mechanism is housed in a classically elegant red gold or white gold case that is 38mm in diameter and is water resistant to 50 meters.

In a sportier venue, Blancpain has also unveiled the new Monaco Y.S. Flyback chronograph to celebrate the brand's second consecutive involvement with the Monaco Yacht Show. Prince Rainier gave his approval for Blancpain's Monaco Y.S. watch to bear on its dial the principality's emblem: the flag of red and white diamonds. The watch, housed in the steel Aqua Lung case and created in a limited edition of 300 pieces, is equipped with a self-winding flyback chronograph movement, the smallest and thinnest of its kind. Its 308 components, all decorated by hand, can be viewed through a transparent caseback. The Monaco Y.S. is water resistant to 100 meters.

And, of course, Blancpain continues to appeal to women through its creations. The newest Blancpain Flyback chronograph for women has been unveiled with a diamond-studded 18-karat white gold case that is complemented by a pastel blue strap and dial for supreme elegance.

BOUCHERON

an historical perspective

For 144 years, the name Boucheron has been intimately linked to the world of haute joaillerie and fame. In 1858 Frédéric Boucheron opened his first shop in Paris where he unveiled his masterpieces—incredible works of art that were inspired by nature. Elegant flowers and butterflies, artfully crafted to impeccable standards, immediately captured the heart and soul of French and British aristocracy. Boucheron had begun his legacy.

Boucheron's intricate technique added a lightness of touch and a finesse to his pieces that were virtually unrivaled at the time. Word of his unique talent spread quickly and royalty and socialites around the world sought his creations. In 1893, Boucheron was the first jeweler to open a shop in the prestigious Place Vendôme, where it remains today.

Generation after generation, Boucheron has continued in the path of its founding father—turning out innovative masterpieces that combine daring and cunning beauty with traditional craftsmanship. Adhering to excellent standards of perfection in all that it creates, the brand has built an international empire. Each Boucheron timepiece and jewelry creation is a work of art inspired by passion and translated into reality with painstaking attention to detail.

It is no wonder that Gucci Group would take note of the global accomplishments of Boucheron and aspire to bring the brand under its umbrella. In late 2000, Gucci Group acquired Boucheron, extending its involvement in the highly profitable product categories of jewelry and watches and adding excellent luxury perfumes to its fragrance portfolio.

Timepieces have been a vital part of Boucheron's collection since its inception. Delicate works of art, the first Boucheron watches were sublimely intricate châtelaines that often were adorned with diamonds, gemstones and pearls. These were followed by pendant watches and later by wristwatches worn on ribbons and on soft fabric and leather straps.

BOUCHERON

unveiling masterpieces

1858 28-year-old Frédéric Boucheron opens his first jewelry shop in an arcade in Galerie de Valois in the Palais Royal, the Parisian center for fashionable women.

1887 Boucheron's first jewelry wristwatches for women are created alongside the classical chatelaine watches worn as brooches.

1893 Boucheron is the first modern jeweler to move to Place Vendôme, close to the new Opera quarter which is the symbol of Parisian luxury.

1900 Boucheron incarnated Belle Epoque creativeness in the art of jewelry and his pieces attracted considerable attention at the Universal Exposition.

1902 Frédéric Boucheron's son, Louis, uses his training as a civil engineer to further his father's craft. Like his father, he seeks great purity of line, exact proportion and absolute rigor of execution.

1920s Watches figure more prominently into Boucheron's creations and are usually made of platinum set with brilliants, their sparkle contrasting greatly against the deep black of onyx.

1932 Louis Boucheron's eldest son, Fred, joins the firm and specialized in gemstones. His talisman is a seven-carat sapphire.

1948 Boucheron introduces the Rectangular watch, the invention that features interchangeable straps to fit any occasion. With its brilliant design, this creation immediately sets new standards for jewelry timepieces. This concept is patented and will be furthered developed nearly 50 years later in 1996 with the B.E.S.T. (Boucheron Easy System Technology) buckle—an extra-thin buckle designed to allow the strap length to be adjusted immediately.

1991 To comply with modern tastes, the Rectangular watch of 1948 is redesigned with a godron gold case and cabochon-cut winders and named "Reflet."

1998 Boucheron celebrates its 140 years with the creation of a special 140-piece limited-edition watch.

1999 The Diamant draws inspiration from its extra-thin watch (3.3mm thick) originally created in 1947. The case has cut-off corners and is covered with "pointes de diamant" or nail head ornamentation. It is created only in gold, as gold is the only metal malleable enough to produce the finely chiseled pattern.

2000 Boucheron is acquired by Gucci Group; To celebrate the new millennium, Boucheron has created the World Heritage 2000 watch, which symbolizes its partnership with UNESCO to protect the world's natural and cultural heritage. This collection consists of 223 timepieces: 23 unique platinum watches, each with a lacquered engraving depicting one of the 23 major endangered sites in the world. The other 200 timepieces are made of yellow gold and depict five of these exceptional sites—Abu Simbel, Angkor, the Everglades, Saint Sophia and the Alhambra in Grenada, that is, 5 series of 40 numbered watches. A percentage of the sales has been donated to UNESCO to restore a Renaissance staircase in the Alhambra in Grenada and renovate the mosaics in the church of Saint Sophia in Istanbul.

2001 Boucheron develops its High Jewelry watches Collections. Round, rectangular or square, each model exists in a jewelry version: full-paved diamonds, colored diamonds, colored sapphires, to name a few. Once again, Boucheron brilliantly confirms its expertise as a jeweler and watchmaker, continuing the over one hundred and forty years of tradition renewed by infinite creativity.

TOP ACROSS

TOP LEFT

Andie MacDowell chose to wear the Eva necklace during the 2001 Cannes Film Festival.

ABOVE

Gong Li is wearing the Diamant watch made of white gold.

TOP RIGHT

Marie Gillain wore the Hiva necklace made of diamonds and cultured pearls at the 2001 Cannes Film Festival.

RIGHT

Shu Qui chose the Armide clip earrings made of diamonds and white gold during the 2001 Cannes Film Festival.

FACING PAGE

TOP LEFT

The Lyre is set with sapphires and diamonds on white gold.

CENTER

The Reflet high-jewelry watch is meticulously set with diamonds on white gold.

BOTTOM

The Diamant high-jewelry watch is set with princess-cut diamonds on white gold.

THIS PAGE

CENTER

This high-jewelry watch features diamonds on white gold.

Precious stones are extremely important components in Boucheron's most recent introductions. Always remaining true to its passions as a jeweler, the great house masterfully sets diamonds and sapphires onto its timepieces for dazzling appeal.

Boucheron bedecks its elegant square Diamant watch with baguette-shaped sapphires, offset by round diamonds, for shimmering beauty. In typical Boucheron style, each watch is a blend of elegance and contemporary styling. The dial consists of 128 diamonds, offset by 16 sapphires of pink, yellow or blue. The case is outlined with 40 baguette sapphires of matching hue, attesting to the masterful prowess of this "Jeweler of Time."

BOUCHERON

automatic talent

Indeed, decade after decade, Boucheron has been on the cutting edge of design and fashion with its timepieces. In fact, in 1948 the brand unveiled a unique rectangular timepiece. The elegant watch—with its elongated shape and distinctive godrons—featured a patented sliding-clasp system that enabled the wearer to easily and quickly change straps. This was an immediate success and women clamored for the invention that allowed them to change their looks as often as they changed their moods.

In addition to its bejeweled timepieces for women, Boucheron is a master at designing men's watches. In fact, the brand has been creating men's watches of distinction for decades. The ribbed case design indicative of Boucheron timepieces, along with the classic dials and harmonious proportions, has made them watches of elegance and individuality.

TOP LEFT
These Reflet watches are crafted of steel and diamonds, and feature interchangeable bracelets.

BOTTOM
These Diamant watches feature colored sapphires and diamonds on gold.

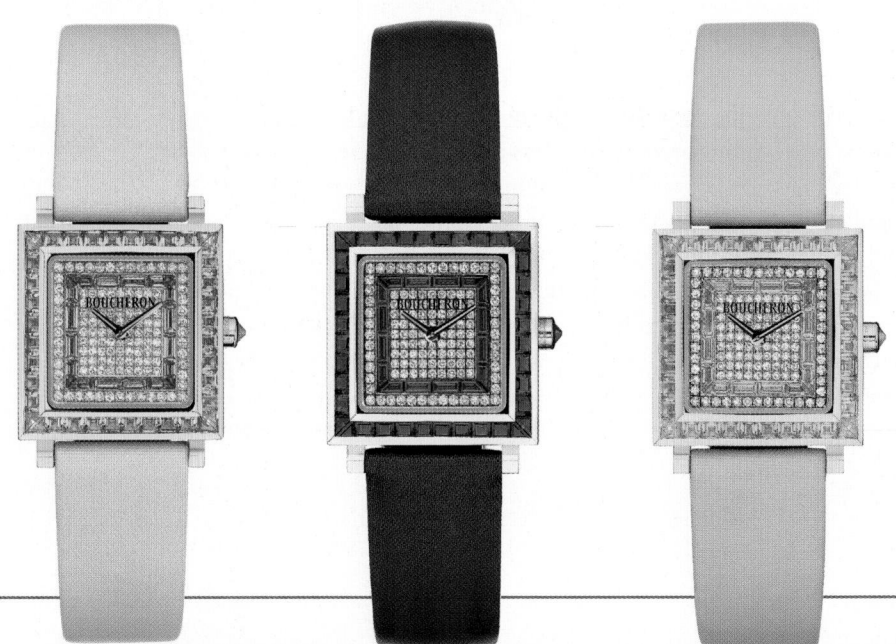

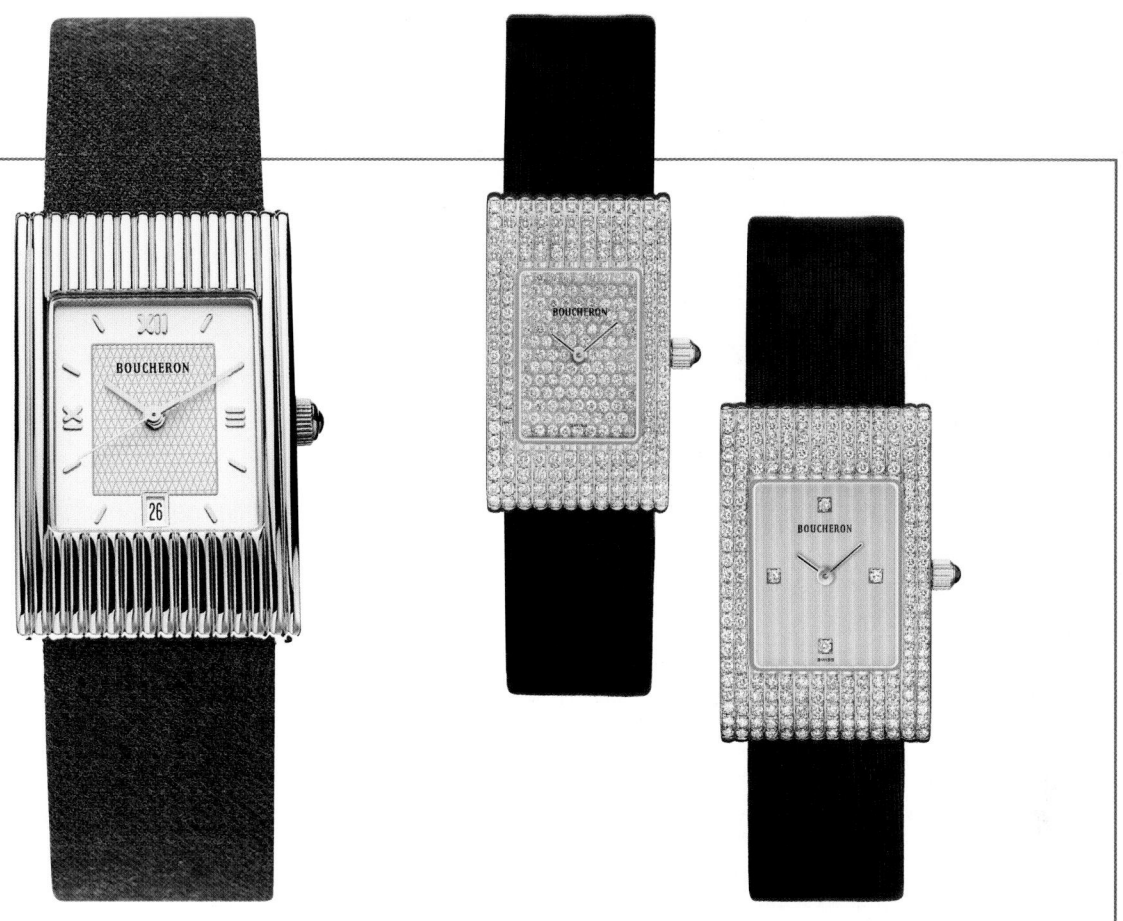

TOP LEFT

Crafted in steel, the Reflet watch is classic.

TOP RIGHT

These Reflet watches are crafted of steel and diamonds, and feature interchangeable bracelets.

BOTTOM

These 18-karat yellow-gold Diamant watches house automatic movements.

High technology also enters the Boucheron scene in the form of a new large-sized Automatic Diamant watch. Renowned for its original style, the Diamant is immediately recognizable due to its diamond-point, hand-decorated bezel. The tiny pyramid design etched on the case and bezel of this watch sometimes is carried through onto the dial and the bracelet.

The new large-sized Diamant watches feature the Piguet 951 automatic movements and are water resistant to 30 meters. Crafted in 18-karat gold, these watches offer a bold look that is characteristic of the brand. As with all Boucheron timepieces, the newest additions are entirely Swiss made and assembled in Boucheron's Swiss workshops according to the highest levels of excellence.

Indeed, in each of Boucheron's three collections, the jeweler's art combines deftly with the watchmaker's talent for creations that are not just timekeepers but ornaments of beauty and works of art. This is the Boucheron legacy—one with a future as strong as its past.

BREGUET

art and time

Since its inception in 1775, Breguet has been a brand dedicated to the essential values of tradition, art, elegance and a deep mastery of the horological field. Abraham-Louis Breguet was not only the founder of this legendary brand, but has also been dubbed the "father of watchmaking" thanks to his inventive spirit and ingenious soul.

Breguet worked tirelessly to perfect man's tracking of time. His insatiable desire to build the most complex, technically excellent timepieces led to patents and awards that garnered the brand international acclaim and legacy status. Breguet's mastery of complications yielded a host of inventions, including the famed tourbillon escapement. In fact, the year 2001 marked the 200th anniversary of the tourbillon.

Over the centuries, Breguet's owners have remained steadfast in the philosophies and guidelines of its founding father. Today, under the auspices of watch conglomerate Swatch Group, the brand continues to produce luxury timepieces of the highest caliber that embody the spirit of Breguet.

BELOW LEFT

A rendition of the Breguet Tourbillon Classique created in homage to the 200th anniversary of the tourbillon. The coverlid is engraved with the words "Breguet à Versailles."

BELOW

From the Classique Collection, this 18-karat rose-gold Anniversary Tourbillon watch features a tourbillon regulator and 50 hours of power reserve. It is crafted in a limited edition of 200 pieces.

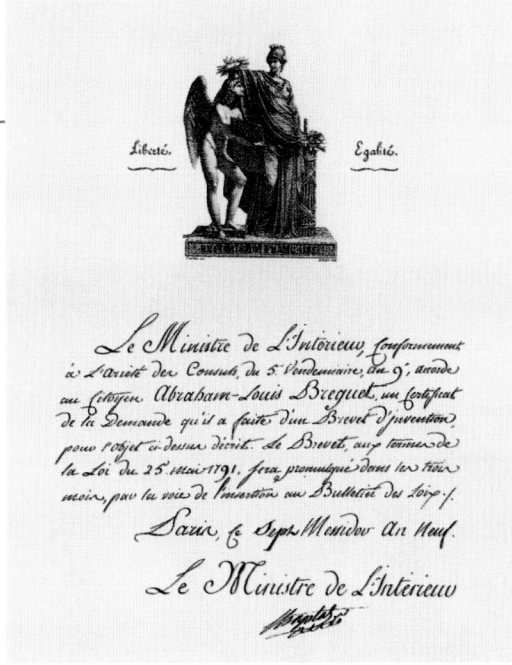

In fact, it was the intent of Nicholas G. Hayek, president and chief executive of Swatch Group, to celebrate the anniversary of the tourbillon in style—at the Palace of Versailles this past September. (In light of the tragic events of September 11, 2001, Hayek postponed the gala for a later date.) At that event, the brand was slated to unveil an horological tribute to Breguet to commemorate the 200th anniversary of the tourbillon. That tribute is the 56-piece, limited-edition Tourbillon Classique.

The Tourbillon Classique collection will be created with 28 pieces in 18-karat pink gold and 28 in 18-karat white gold. The striking timepiece features an 18-karat gold coverlid that is engine-turned by hand and inscribed with the words "Breguet à Versailles." Each watch is individually numbered and features a sapphire caseback for viewing the movement.

In addition to this timepiece, Breguet has unveiled several other new models in its Classique collection of complex timepieces. Among them is a 200-piece limited-edition Anniversary Tourbillon regulator watch in 18-karat rose gold. It houses a hand-wound movement, chased by hand, and bears the Breguet signature.

Another key timepiece is the Classique Reference 3680BA, a self-winding mechanical watch with power-reserve indicator of 38 hours. Crafted in 18-karat yellow or white gold with fluted case band, the watch exudes the grand aesthetic style of elegance for which Breguet is known. The dial is silvered gold, hand engraved and features the hour indications in a large off-centered subdial with Roman numerals. The watch also features a date calendar ring on the outer portion of the dial that displays Arabic numerals. A center-positioned serpentine pointer depicts the date. Of course the hands are blued steel Breguet hands.

In typical Breguet style, the timepieces unveiled in 2001 reflect the company's commitment to elegance and refinement with respect to the founding values. In these watches, as in the watches Abraham-Louis Breguet crafted centuries ago, technical perfection and aesthetic excellence reign supreme.

BREITLING

an historical perspective

Perhaps no other brand befits its calling card as succinctly as Breitling. Billed as "Instruments for Professionals," the timepieces created by this 118-year-old, privately owned watch company are truly technical marvels that masterfully blend form and function.

Since its inception in 1884, Breitling has focused clearly on creating watches equipped to time events perfectly. It was one of the first companies to create stopwatches and chronographs in the late 1800s and one of the first brands to be used by officials to hunt down speeding motorists in the early 1900s. Indeed, by the mid-1930s, Breitling had become synonymous with critical timing, and already was establishing its foothold in the world of aviation—having signed a contract in 1939 with the British Air Ministry to make flight chronographs for the Royal Air Force.

Firmly entrenched in the technical timing arena, Breitling quickly solidified its reputation for advanced technology and design integrity. Over the decades, the brand has unveiled numerous technological advancements in timekeeping and has garnered international acclaim for the functionality and distinct styling of its watches. Today, Breitling remains inextricably linked to the aviation world.

The brand's product-launches and activities represent a commitment to the professional aviation arena that is almost unparalleled. One of its timepieces that has won Breitling worldwide recognition is the Emergency watch. Designed for pilots and flight crews, the Emergency will broadcast a signal enabling search and rescue units to home in on its wearer's location. In the event of a crash or other emergency, the watch, with its built-in micro-transmitter broadcasting on the 121.5 MHz aircraft emergency frequency, serves as a complement to the aircraft's distress signals.

Other high-performance instruments include the Cosmonaute (which won honors in space travel with NASA's Mercury Program) and special edition watches honoring international flight teams. Such collections include watches for the USAF Thunderbirds, the US Navy Blue Angels and Top Gun, Britain's Royal Air Force, France's Patrouille de France, and Italy's Frecce Tricolori.

Privately owned and operated by the Schneider family in Grenchen, Switzerland, Breitling proudly continues in the footsteps of Léon Breitling, founding father—focusing on precision, performance and perfection in all it creates.

THIS PAGE
TOP

Bertrand Piccard (left) was the Swiss pilot in charge of the Orbiter 3 and its voyage. He was joined by British pilot, Brian Jones on their nearly 22-day circumnavigation of the globe.

BOTTOM

Representing the ultimate in luxury and refinement, this Chronomat is crafted in steel with an 18-karat gold bezel and houses an automatic movement.

FACING PAGE

The ChronoAvenger M1 watch is a World Premiere. It is water resistant and operational at a depth of 1,000 meters.

BREITLING

unveiling masterpieces

Always on the cutting edge in terms of technological advancements, it is not unusual for Breitling to unveil World Premiere timepieces. Such is the case with its recent ChronoAvenger MI watch. This is the only chronograph that is both water resistant and still operational at a depth of 1,000 meters.

Taking into account the fact that its clientele rely on their Breitling timepieces as technical instruments, the company spent long hours perfecting this unprecedented technical accomplishment. It has been achieved by the principle of magnetic pushpieces, Breitling's proprietary patented device that enables the wearer to activate the chronograph controls essentially through the metal of the case. Working on the basis of an ordinary pushpiece, Breitling's engineers integrated a magnet at the end of the stem. Pressing the pushpiece will shift the magnetic field and move the contact blades inside the watch. The electrical contact established therein is what starts and stops the chronograph. The high-performance ChronoAvenger MI is crafted from titanium and fitted with a screw-lock crown and decompression valve. What's more the ChronoAvenger MI houses the extremely precise SuperQuartz™ Caliber B73 movement.

The SuperQuartz™ technology is a breakthrough in precision and reliability. Because Breitling has recognized the importance of quartz technology, and yet wished to remain true to its creed of excellence, the brand initiated the relentless pursuit of higher accuracy. After lengthy and painstaking research and development, the SuperQuartz™ technology was born—resulting in a system that enables the quartz battery to be 10 times more accurate than other quartz timepieces.

THIS PAGE

LEFT

The SuperQuartz™ technology enables ten times more accuracy than a regular quartz battery.

BOTTOM LEFT

Providing a dual display of measured times, the Hercules offers optimal legibility and provides a 24-hour military time display.

BOTTOM RIGHT

The Hercules is an ultra-large chronograph chronometer measuring 44.8mm in diameter.

FACING PAGE

TOP LEFT

The Callisto has been redesigned. While retaining its original characteristics, it is now suitable for wrists of all sizes. It is water resistant to 200 meters.

TOP RIGHT

In the spirit of an era, Breitling has revived the Montbrillant Datora in honor of this bestseller from the 1940s. It is a high-frequency automatic chronograph chronometer.

BOTTOM LEFT

The Navitimer Olympus offers chronograph and perpetual calendar functions.

BOTTOM RIGHT

Breitling's flagship watch since 1952, this new steel Old Navitimer features the famed slide-rule bezel of the original Navitimers and houses a self-winding mechanism.

Thanks to the inclusion of a tiny thermometer in the watch, the sophisticated system also corrects the rate in accordance with temperatures. The result of these efforts is the SuperQuartz™— a thermocompensated chronometer-certified movement that has a maximum rate-variation of 15 seconds per year (as compared to around two and a half minutes per year on a standard quartz watch). All of Breitling's quartz watches (which comprise only about 20 percent of Breitling's total collections) now house the ultra-efficient SuperQuartz™ technology.

Additionally, in 2001 Breitling refocused its attention on the flagship Navitimer product line. Symbolizing the brand's mastery in the field of mechanical chronographs, the Navitimer has been a signature of Breitling since its introduction fifty years ago. (It had been an immediate international success thanks to its capability to execute the calculations that a flight plan requires.) Today's Navitimers, while updated, continue to reflect the design's unique spirit.

The recently unveiled Navitimer Olympus houses a mechanism composed of approximately 250 parts and enables measurement of short times and simultaneous display of date, day, month and moonphase. Equipped with the famed slide-rule bezel—a hallmark of the Navitimer—the Olympus is essentially a mechanical chronograph chronometer with perpetual calendar that requires adjustment only once every leap year.

These newest timepieces and technologies underscore Breitling's unflagging commitment to excellence and innovation. This is a brand that will continue to bring its heritage and roots to the forefront of tomorrow.

CARTIER

an historical perspective

*F*or nearly a century and a half, the legendary
name of Cartier has been recognized and revered
for its exquisite jewels and extraordinary creations.
Few could have known 155 years ago that the young
lad beginning a modest business in Paris was actually
establishing the foundation for future international greatness.

THIS PAGE

TOP

This exquisite necklace features
four strands of multicolored
pearls with a center diamond of
50.41 carats.

BOTTOM

Combining serious
craftsmanship with whimsical
beauty, this Tank Basculante
watch features diamonds on
the case and the Cartier name
set in diamonds on the
reverse side of the case.

FACING PAGE

The Tortue watch in
18-karat white gold is
ensconced in 4.42 carats of
diamonds. It houses the
manual-wind workshop-
crafted caliber 430MC
whose bridges are decorated
with the intertwined double
C of Cartier's logo.

In 1847, Louis-François Cartier was an eager and ambitious 28-year-old jeweler. He began his trade by creating elegant pieces of jewelry that used only the finest stones he could procure. It was Cartier's ultimate dream to be commissioned by the royal heads of France and he strove to design and produce the most regal jewelry and timepieces worthy of their attention. Within just a few short years, he had sold a cameo necklace to a countess and later gleaned the admiration of Princess Mathilde Bonaparte, Napoleon III's cousin, with one of his exquisite pieces. So captivating was Cartier's work that just six years after opening his shop, his dream came true: He was commissioned by the Empress Eugenie to create a sterling silver tea service. From that moment on, the procession of prominent customers has continued uninterrupted.

Over the centuries, Cartier has catered to kings, queens, czars, political figures, socialites and celebrities. Generation after generation, the Cartiers built their international brand upon creative genius and technical mastery. Magnificent jewels were regularly acquired, set and resold. Indeed, the great House of Cartier quickly became synonymous with jeweled masterpieces that commanded the highest prices on the market.

In 1972, shortly before the last of the fourth generation of Cartiers stepped down, a group of astute business investors gained control of the Paris-based company. The leaders of this group—today known as the prestigious Richemont Group—were steadfastly determined to remain true to Cartier's creeds of excellence and innovation. Indeed, Cartier continued its introduction of luxury product lines and, under the vigilant Richemont Group leadership, has opened Cartier boutiques around the world.

Indeed, this magnificent brand continues to amaze and beguile aficionados with its exquisite works—carrying on the creative visions of Cartier's jewelry and watches.

unveiling masterpieces

TOP LEFT

The Hexagonal Riviere Lanières watch features nearly 20 carats of diamonds.

TOP RIGHT

The Baignoire Allongée watch in 18-karat white gold features the new Cartier dial of white gold with sword-shaped hands and the Cartier C logo.

CENTER

The Tank Américaine watch with Arabic numerals features an anthracite gray moiré guilloché dial.

BOTTOM CENTER

"Pretty in Pink" aptly applies when referring to this new 32mm Pasha watch with automatic movement.

BOTTOM RIGHT

Cartier's signature is engraved at the heart of the Pasha tourbillon automatic movement. The watch features a single grid-shaped bridge. It is created in a limited edition of 20 pieces.

Cartier had been creating jeweled timepieces for decades, but it was in 1911 that the brand unveiled the Santos—a line that is still in production today. The Santos was based on a watch that had been made by Louis Cartier a few years earlier for his friend, inventor Alberto Santos-Dumont. In 1919, Louis Cartier designed another significant watch—the Tank—in tribute to the American tank commanders who assisted France during World War I. The sleek square case has since become an icon for the brand. To this day, Cartier has continued creating wristwatch masterpieces.

Among the 2001 introductions were dazzling jeweled watches, sophisticated complications and simply elegant renditions. Witness to the Cartier passion and detail, the new jewelry watch collection features eye-catching forms of exquisite workmanship. One example is the Cartier Tortue watch in 18-karat white gold. The entire case of this barrel-shaped timepiece is adorned with round diamonds totaling 4.42 carats. Similarly, the Tank Americaine and the Tank Basculante for women have both been set with varying degrees of diamonds on the case, bezel and dial.

In a special collection of Lanières watches, Cartier weaves fine geometric patterns into the dials and intricate bracelets. Some are diamond accented, others, like the Hexagonal Riviere Lanières watch in 18-karat white gold is totally diamond bedecked, with nearly 20 carats of baguette- and square-cut diamonds on its case and bracelet.

The new timepieces for men are equally exceptional. In the true spirit of Cartier, the Collection Privée Cartier Paris is the epitome of Cartier's timeless classics. Form and function come together in an expression of the creative alignment between Cartier's watchmakers and designers in these models. Among the new pieces are the Tank à vis, in platinum or in 18-karat yellow gold, and the Tortue watch in platinum. Each of these watches houses a new type of movement: the 437 MC movement. In each of these movements, the index assembly is cut out and engraved in the shape of the C in Cartier's logo. Other new pieces are complications whose movements themselves are objects of beauty. These include the Tortue perpetual calendar watch and the Pasha with Tourbillon escapement.

TOP LEFT

Crafted in 18-karat yellow gold, the Tank à vis watch with guilloché dial houses the manual-wind caliber 437 movement.

TOP RIGHT

The striking new Roadster from Cartier features an interchangeable strap and bracelet. It comes in a variety of different dial colors and finishes and is crafted in either 18-karat gold or steel.

BOTTOM

The magnificent Panthère Clock is a work of technology and art unsurpassed. It took Cartier's master watchmakers and jewelers more than 2,000 hours to create.

Additionally, this past year Cartier unveiled a majestic Mystery Clock. A stunning demonstration of art, jewelry and timekeeping, the Panthère Clock took Cartier's master artisans 2,270 hours to create. It features a satin-finished hematite base with a rock-crystal tower upon which the pale blue chalcedony clock bezel is attached. The famed Cartier panther sits atop the clock. He is bedecked with 2,400 diamonds weighing approximately 130 carats and with 65 cabochon-cut sapphires. The hour pointer of the clock is totally diamond adorned.

On the cusp of 2002, Cartier unveiled the Roadster, a watch designed for performance and style. An exclusively masculine vision of time, the Roadster is a high-tech, modern timepiece with an interchangeable bracelet and strap to offer a grand choice between sport and elegance. The bracelet version is bold, while the leather version is classically sophisticated with its triple-tiered padded design. The Roadster's dial is immediately distinctive and different. It features an outer ring, decorated with circles, on which the Roman or Arabic numerals lie. The continuous spirals enhance a luminous oval center with a touch of metal in the middle for a relief effect. This unique timepiece offers a balance between strength and beauty due to its sculpted form. It is crafted in 18-karat gold or stainless steel.

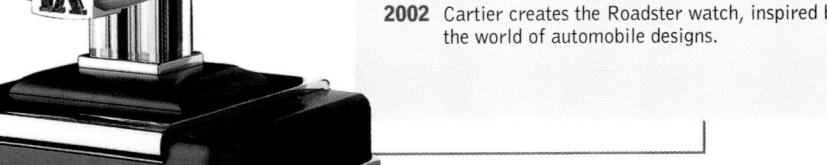

As is typical of Cartier, all of these masterpieces attest to the brand's tradition and expertise, to its commitment to perfection, and to its undying spirit of innovation.

CÉDRIC JOHNER

an historical perspective

Cédric Johner is driven by passion.
His training as both a watchmaker and jeweler,
along with his innate talent and creativity,
has sparked him to develop one of the most unusual
and masterful watch collections of today.

It was just five years ago that Johner, having worked for some of Geneva's finest watchmaking houses, came out from behind the scenes and developed his own collection of mechanical and automatic watches crafted in the great Swiss tradition. In his mind, he had long envisioned the shape of the case that would become his signature and the base of every watch he would create. It would be two years, however, before he fashioned it precisely to meet his exacting standards.

In 1996, Johner perfected his first watchcase and named it "Abyss." Its unusual shape is a mixture of spherical and geometrical design, a harmonious blending of sensual yet sober form. The sleek case is rounded on the sides, yet is fitted with a six-sided crystal that offers brilliant equilibrium to the piece. Each case is created and finished completely by hand—a tradition Johner has adhered to since its inception.

By 1997, Johner had begun creating the first four watches in his Abyss collection: a regulator, a jumping hour and two classically elegant hour, minute, second timepieces. In 1998, Johner unveiled his timepieces to the world at the Basel Watch, Clock and Jewelry Fair, and continued to create additional elaborate timepieces, adding dual time zones, perpetual calendars and similar complications. Because of their complex nature and bold design, Johner's timepieces have received much international attention.

Today, in his Vandoeuvres workshops just outside of Geneva, Johner creates his own dials, bracelets, movements, and cases to completion. He insists on every watch being handmade and hand finished, guaranteeing an incredibly exclusive line of production: only about 200 Cédric Johner watches are created annually.

THIS PAGE

TOP

Cédric Johner.

LEFT

Johner's name and the series number are engraved on the back of every timepiece.

BOTTOM

A look at the Caliber 10 movement with Geneva Seal.

FACING PAGE

The Bi-Retrograde Abyss watch houses Johner's new Automatic Caliber 10 movement.

unveiling

masterpieces

Because Johner is a watchmaker obsessed with beauty and perfection, he insists on creating only the most unusual masterpieces of high technology. Using the signature Abyss case in 2001, Johner unveiled a new movement and four striking new models— a bi-retrograde perpetual calendar, a tourbillon, a minute repeater, and a chronograph split-hand.

Focusing on excellence in technology and design, Johner and his team of master watchmakers have unveiled the Caliber 10— a movement so meticulously crafted that it has earned the right to bear the prestigious Geneva Seal. Given only to Geneva watchmakers of the highest eminence, the Seal constitutes a degree of watchmaking attesting to the highest standards in Switzerland.

Johner's Caliber 10 automatic movement features a 22-karat gold, oscillating rotor and 65 hours of power reserve. It is exquisitely hand finished and engraved, and bears the Cédric Johner name and the Poinçon de Genève Seal. Johner has chosen to utilize the Caliber 10 without the Geneva Seal in his

THIS PAGE

TOP

Crafted in 18-karat red gold, the Tourbillon Abyss watch features 110 hours of power reserve.

LEFT

Johner's new Minute Repeater movement.

BOTTOM LEFT

This Perpetual Calendar watch is crafted in red gold and houses an automatic movement. The dial is hand guillochéd with ruthénium.

BOTTOM RIGHT

This is one of the novelty Cédric Johner pieces for 2001: the Dual Time. It is crafted in steel 316 L.

FACING PAGE

TOP

Cédric Johner also creates striking bejeweled timepieces for women.

BOTTOM

Johner's Abyss cases are handcrafted in three different sizes.

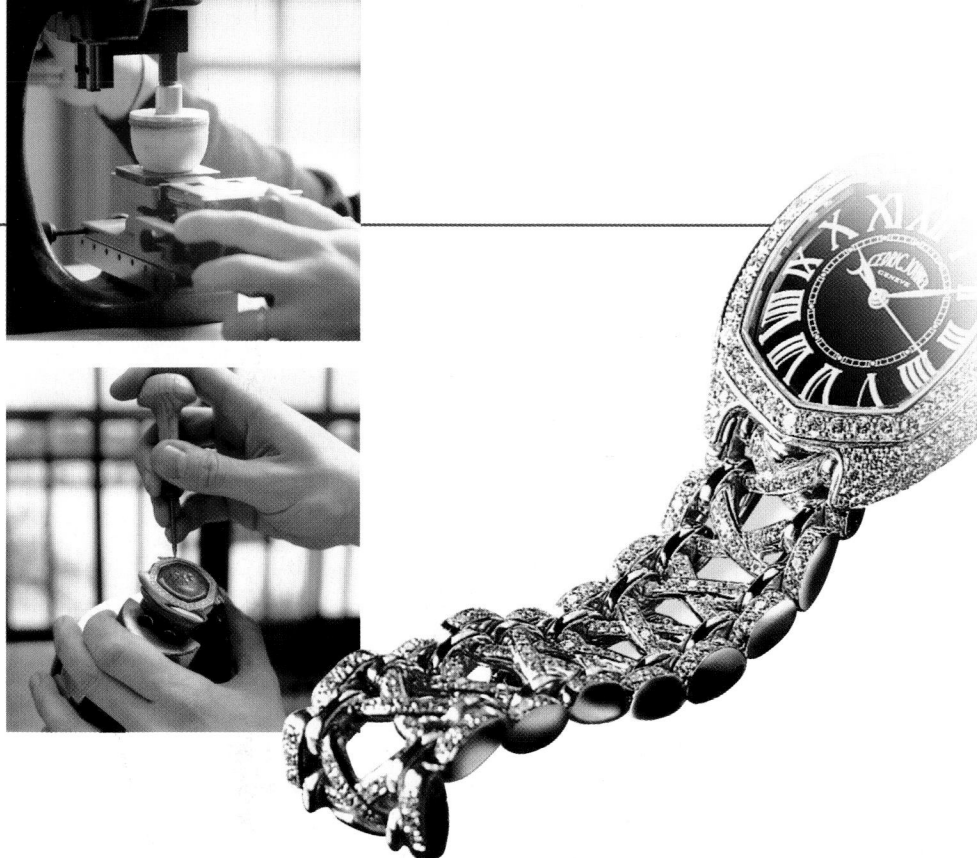

CHRONOLOGY

1992-1995
Having worked as jeweler and watchmaker for some of the great houses of Geneva, Cédric Johner begins to actively pursue his dream of launching his own watch company.

1996 A workshop is set up in the Johner family home; Johner utilizes wax as his design model and in it the first Abyss takes shape. He decides now that every step that can be done by hand will be.

1996-1997
Johner receives further training from the Horology School of Geneva.

1997 Two important institutions are established—the brand "Cédric Johner" and the company "Watch Concept Sarl"—by the Cédric Johner team of three (Cédric, his wife and one jeweler).

1998 The new brand presents for the first time at the Basel Watch, Clock and Jewelry Fair. Critiques are quite favorable but the number of sales is not; Work begins on new complication, Perpetual Calendar in platinum; A model for ladies is created with a new, hand-engraved case.

1999 This year's showing at the Basel Fair is much more profitable and encouraging. Cédric Johner is popular in the Middle East and Singapore; Dual time and 24-hour complications are implemented; The company works on a special, hand-guillochéd dial; "Cédric Johner S.A." is instated in September.

2000 The workshops are relocated to a beautiful house in front of the Mont-Blanc in Vandoeuvres, Switzerland; Two new Abyss models are introduced: a limited edition of 10 chronographs on ValJoux 72 in red gold, and also the Bi-Retrograde, a retrograde perpetual calendar; The first two watchmakers join the company and another jeweler is trained; An association is established between Cédric Johner S.A. and two Society of Watchmakers to create a new workshop of dials.

2001 Cédric Johner presents five new models at the Basel Fair: His new Caliber 10. This automatic movement with micro-rotor has 65 hours of power reserve. The Geneva Seal is obtained in April and versions are available with or without the Seal; The Tourbillon Abyss has 110 hours of power reserve and the movement is guillochéd entirely by hand (no dial/Caliber 80); The unveiling of a 5-piece limited-edition of a Chronograph "column-wheel" split-hands in white gold with Caliber 79; The Caliber 01, Cédric Johner's new movement for ladies' timepieces, is refined. A Minute Repeater, the most complicated in his new collection, is introduced.

---

new bi-retrograde perpetual calendar Abyss watch. This striking 18-karat rose-gold watch features a guillochéd, silvered dial with moonphase at 6:00.

Also in 2001, Johner unveiled his striking Tourbillon Abyss. He worked tirelessly to create this world premiere: a tourbillon movement that is entirely hand guillochéd and acts as the dial of the watch. The decoration of the bridges, barrel and carriage have been designed and executed personally by Johner. The movement is decorated in such a way that various shades of gray develop, giving it depth and beauty as a dial. The watch has 110 hours of power reserve and is housed in an 18-karat red-gold case, offering subtle elegance.

Taking on another of watchmaking's most complicated accomplishments, Johner has also unveiled his Minute Repeater. A new complication for this young genius, the minute repeater movement is hand assembled in the Vandoeuvres workshops. It has been developed and designed to exquisite perfection, and features a matte-finishing technique employed years ago that Johner sought to revive.

As with all Cédric Johner timepieces, the movements and dials of these intricate watches are hand created with the utmost attention paid to every detail. The brand's gold bracelets, available in white, yellow or red gold, have been designed and created by Johner and are exclusively manufactured in the company's workshops. Dials are offered in guilloché or engraved versions, with various colored Arabic or Roman numerals, and can be enhanced with precious stones. In fact, the choices are limitless, and it is Johner's dream that his exclusive clientele will personalize their own watches—from case colors to dials to individualized engravings on the movements.

Johner's name, the series number and movement specifications are hand engraved on each timepiece in order to track the history of the watch and to ensure exclusivity for its owner.

CEDRIC JOHNER

ABYSS PERPETUAL CALENDAR BI-RETRO   REF. 5397/4

Movement: mechanical, automatic winding, 97 caliber (GP Manufacture 3100 caliber base + Agenor calendar module).
Functions: hour, minute, perpetual calendar (date, day, month, year, moon-phase).
Case: 18 kt pink gold, two-piece case, in curved tonneau shape (size 47 x 38.5 mm, thickness 11 mm); hexagonal curved sapphire crystal; 2 correctors on the middle; pink-gold crown; back attached by 4 screws, displaying the movement through a sapphire crystal. Water-resistant to 2 atm.

Dial: silvered, engine-turned (guilloché) with sun pattern; printed Roman numerals; black enameled pink-gold leaf style hands.
Indications: date and day of the week with retrograde hands at 3 and 9, moon-phase at 6, month and four-year cycle at 12.
Strap: crocodile leather; pink-gold clasp.
Also available: with silvered engine-turned (guilloché) dial: in yellow gold (same price) or white gold; in platinum with engine-turned (guilloché) ruthenium dial. All versions are available also with dials on request.

ABYSS PERPETUAL CALENDAR LARGE SIZE   REF. 4891/4

Movement: mechanical, automatic winding, ETA 2892A2 caliber + Agenor calendar module. **Functions:** hour, minute, second, perpetual calendar (date, day, month, year, moon-phase).
Case: 18 kt white gold, two-piece case, in curved tonneau shape (size 47 x 38.5 mm, thickness 11 mm); hexagonal, curved sapphire crystal; 3 correctors on the middle; white-gold crown; back attached by 4 screws, displaying the movement through a sapphire crystal. Water-resistant to 2 atm.

Dial: gray, rhodium-plated, engine-turned (guilloché); printed Roman numerals; black enameled gold leaf style hands.
Indications: date at 3, moon phase at 6, day of the week at 9, month and four-year cycle at 12.
Strap: crocodile leather; white-gold clasp.
Also available: in yellow gold, silvered engine-turned (guilloché) dial; in pink gold, rhodium-plated engine-turned (guilloché) dial; in platinum, blue engine-turned (guilloché) dial. Medium Size: with silvered or ruthenium dial: in yellow or pink gold, or white gold; in platinum. All versions are available also with dials on request.

ABYSS CHRONOGRAPH   REF. 5372/4

Movement: mechanical, automatic winding, Valjoux 72 caliber. Entirely assembled and finished by the House. Decorated with circular graining and Côtes de Genève patterns, beveled.
Functions: hour, minute, small second, chronograph with three counters.
Case: 18 kt pink gold, two-piece case, in curved tonneau shape (size 47 x 38.5 mm, thickness 13.5 mm); hexagonal, curved sapphire crystal; drop-shaped pink-gold pushers; back attached by 4 screws, displaying the movement through a sapphire crystal. Water-resistant to 2 atm.

Dial: gray, ruthenium-plated, engine-turned (guilloché); brushed hour ring; printed Roman numerals; pink-gold leaf style hands.
Indications: minute counter at 3, hour counter at 6, small second at 9, minute track with divisions for 1/5 of a second.
Strap: crocodile leather; pink-gold fold-over clasp. Limited edition of 10 pieces.
Also available: with silvered engine-turned (guilloché) dial. Available also with dials on request.

ABYSS TWO TIME ZONE   REF. 4824/4

Movement: mechanical, automatic winding, ETA 2892A2 caliber + Agenor module.
Functions: hour, minute, second, second time-zone time, 24 hours.
Case: 18 kt white-gold, two-piece case, in curved tonneau shape (size 47 x 38.5 mm, thickness 11 mm); hexagonal, curved sapphire crystal; white-gold crown; drop-shaped white-gold pusher at 9 for second time-zone time adjustment; back attached by 4 screws, displaying the movement through a sapphire crystal. Water-resistant to 2 atm.

Dial: gray, ruthenium-plated, engine-turned (guilloché) center; white screen-prints; Arabic numerals; rhodium-plated leaf style hands.
Indications: date with magnifying glass at 6, 24 hours at 12, second time-zone time with red enameled bâton center hand.
Strap: crocodile leather; white-gold clasp.
Also available: with silvered dial: in stainless steel; yellow or pink gold; in platinum. Sport model: stainless steel, white dial, black Roman numerals. All versions can be purchased with dial on request.

ABYSS JUMPING HOUR LARGE SIZE   REF. 4827/4

Movement: mechanical, manual winding, Jacquet Baume 1727 caliber (antique A. Schild base).
Functions: jumping hour, minute, small second.
Case: 18K white gold, two-piece case, in curved tonneau shape (size 47 x 38.5 mm, thickness 11 mm); hexagonal, curved sapphire crystal; white-gold crown; back attached by 4 screws, displaying the movement through a sapphire crystal. Water-resistant to 2 atm.
Dial: black enameled polished with white screen-prints; railway track with five-minute progression in Arabic numerals on the external ring; rhodium-plated leaf style minute hands, thread style second hands.
Indications: jumping hour at 12, small second at 6, center minute.
Strap: crocodile leather; white-gold clasp.
Also available: with different dials: in stainless steel, pink gold, yellow gold, platinum.
Medium Size: in stainless steel, yellow gold, pink gold, platinum; strap or bracelet; with different dials.

ABYSS RETROGRADE SECOND   REF. 5330/4

Movement: mechanical, automatic winding, ETA 2892 caliber + Agenor module for retrograde seconds.
Functions: hour, minute, retrograde small second.
Case: 18K pink gold, two-piece case, in curved tonneau shape (size 47 x 38.5 mm, thickness 11 mm); hexagonal, curved sapphire crystal; pink-gold crown; back attached by 4 screws, displaying the movement through a sapphire crystal. Water-resistant to 2 atm.
Dial: silvered, engine-turned (guilloché) with sun pattern at the center and brushed hour ring, with black screen-prints; Arabic numerals; black enameled gold leaf style hands.
Indications: small second at 6 with blued retrograde hand.
Strap: crocodile leather; pink-gold clasp.
Also available: in white gold; stainless steel; with different dials. Ruthenium-plated dial: in yellow gold, platinum. Continuous small seconds: in stainless steel, yellow gold, pink gold, white gold, platinum; with different dials; jewels versions.

ABYSS REGULATOR MEDIUM SIZE   REF. 5250/3

Movement: mechanical, automatic winding, Jacquet Baume 876500 caliber.
Functions: hour, minute, small second.
Case: 18 kt yellow gold, two-piece case, in curved tonneau shape (size 41 x 34 mm, thickness 11 mm); hexagonal, curved sapphire crystal; yellow-gold crown; back attached by 4 screws. Water-resistant to 2 atm.
Dial: black enameled polished con white screen-prints; round markers on printed railway track; white enameled gold leaf style hands.
Indications: off-center hours at 12 with Roman numerals, small second at 6, center minute.
Strap: crocodile leather; fold-over gold clasp.
Also available: in pink gold (same price), white gold, in stainless steel, in platinum. Also in the version Grand Modèle. All versions can be purchased with dial on request.

ABYSS 24 HOURS LARGE SIZE   REF. 5293/4

Movement: mechanical, automatic winding, ETA 2892 caliber modified for hour display on a 24-hour basis.
Functions: 24 hour, minute, second.
Case: 18 kt yellow gold, two-piece case, in curved tonneau shape (size 47 x 39 mm, thickness 11 mm); hexagonal, curved sapphire crystal; yellow-gold crown; back attached by 4 screws. Water-resistant to 2 atm.
Dial: black enameled polished; Arabic numerals and railway minute track printed in brushed silver; rhodium-plated gold leaf style hands.
Strap: crocodile leather; yellow-gold fold-over clasp.
Also available: with Roman numerals on dial; in pink gold (same price), in white gold, in steel, in platinum; in white gold with silvered and mother-of-pearl dial. Medium Size: in stainless steel; in yellow or pink gold or white gold (also with brushed silvered dial; in platinum. Also with dials on request.

CHARLES OUDIN

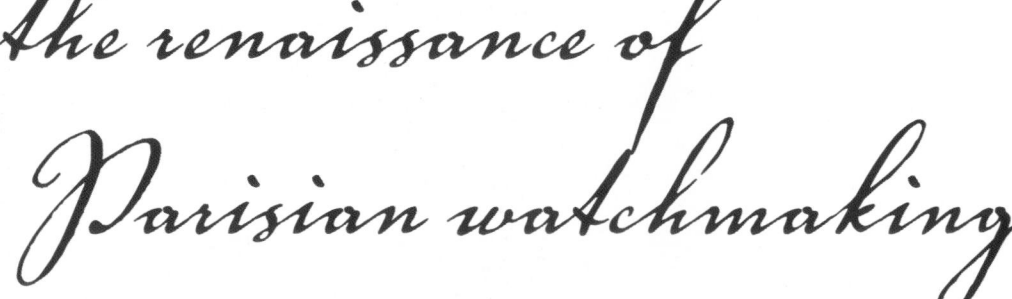

the renaissance of Parisian watchmaking

Once chronometer-maker to the French navy and watchmaker by appointment to the leading dynasties of 18th-century Europe, the Charles Oudin brand rediscovers a master watchmaker and a glorious past in a very Parisian collection of jewelry watches at its embassy located at 8 Place Vendôme.

It takes more than the revival of a name to create a brand with a collection of fine watches. The name Charles Oudin has re-emerged with consummate elegance and the courage to revive the French capital's talents in jewelry- and watchmaking. Although the recognized home of fine watch-making is now in Switzerland, there was a time when the masters of horology hailed from France and England. Abraham-Louis Breguet, for example, left Switzerland for Paris in the 18th century to become one of the greatest watchmakers in history. He established his business in the heart of the capital—the Palais Royal—and it was with Breguet that the young Charles Oudin, born in Clermont in 1772, took his first watchmaking steps. A floor mosaic at 52 Palais Royal testifies to Charles Oudin's presence and to his title as chronometer-maker to the navy. Charles Oudin's time-pieces, with their unique, custom-made styling, are the products of Paris's greatest talents, while their movements demonstrate the technical disciplines of Swiss manufacture.

Charles Oudin's apprenticeship with Breguet left him with an extraordinary aesthetic sense and a creative capacity that was constantly asserted. Many timepieces bearing his signature are featured in auction sales and even in the private museums of prestigious Swiss watch manufac-turers, serving as evidence of his association with the leading horological firms of his era.

The young watchmaker's desire for independence, however, led him to part company with his master and to set up shop at number 52 Palais Royal. Surrounded by the Paris Opera, the Carnavalet Museum, the Louvre, and the Comédie Française, the Palais Royal had a turbulent history but remained a cultural center where members of refined society could meet talented artists and craftsmen. Charles Oudin soon became the darling of Europe's royal families for whom he created original and valuable timepieces. Among his clientele: the czar and czarina of Russia, the king and queen of Spain, the king of Portugal, and the empress Josephine.

It is a stroll through history that leads to reflection and brings the name of Charles Oudin to the forefront of France's great tradition of quality watchmaking.

TOP

The entire Charles Oudin collection is inspired by the Palais Royal in Paris.

CENTER LEFT

This mother-of-pearl watch fob was made for the daughter of Czar Nicolas II around 1840-1860. It is decorated with enamel "M" that designates the imperial Russian kingdom.

CENTER RIGHT

The symbol of the czar of Russia, for whom Charles Oudin did a great deal of custom work.

BOTTOM

With its rivulets of diamonds, the Royal collection is reflection of the many fountains of Paris.

a unique style between past and present

Commemorating the life and work of a great watch-maker, today's Charles Oudin collection renews its ties with Parisian expertise. Attracting artists and craftsmen of considerable talents, Paris remains one of the last world capitals in which exceptional objects are designed and created in their entirety.

The Charles Oudin collection subtly weaves an aesthetic link between the past and the present. Their typically Parisian nature gives Charles Oudin timepieces an instantly recognizable style. Although inspired by the classic creations of the past, the bold originality of their manufacture makes them resolutely contemporary.

The name of Charles Oudin evokes in many the 18th-century golden age of horological science. Today it stands for technical innovation, the skills necessary to produce made-to-order creations and manage a business enterprise. We owe this renaissance to a French business family from the Doubs that has been involved in watchmaking for more than five generations. The Berthet family has workshops at Villers-le-Lac

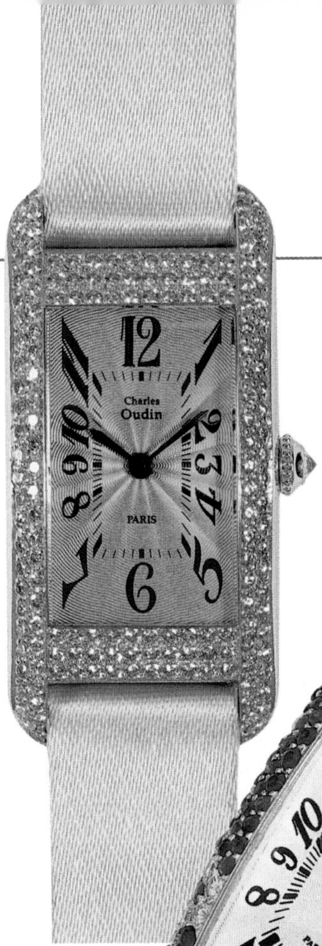

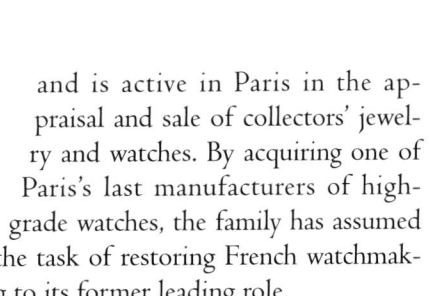

TOP

Part of the Royal collection, this Fountain watch is a cascading beauty of pink gold and diamonds.

CENTER

Sapphires with diamond, ruby and emerald accents bring this Royal to life.

BELOW LEFT

A delicate work of art and beauty, this ladies' watch features black and white diamonds on the case and black and white mother-of-pearl inlay on the dial.

BELOW RIGHT

A tribute to women in art, the Crea watch exudes a retro appeal that is striking with this mother-of-pearl inlaid dial.

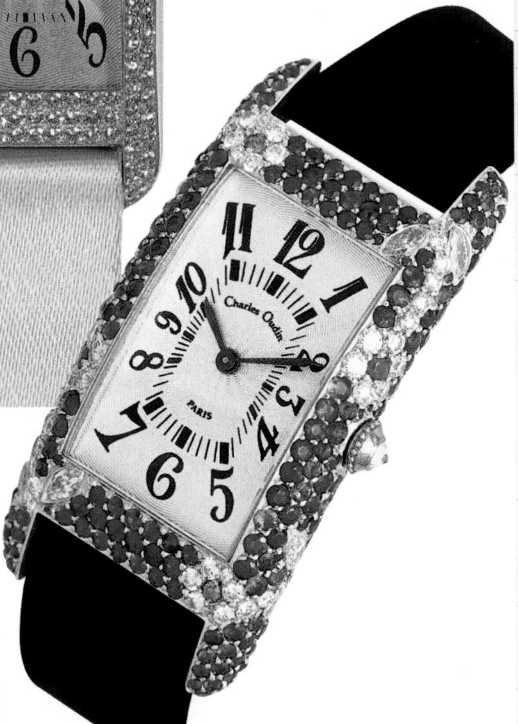

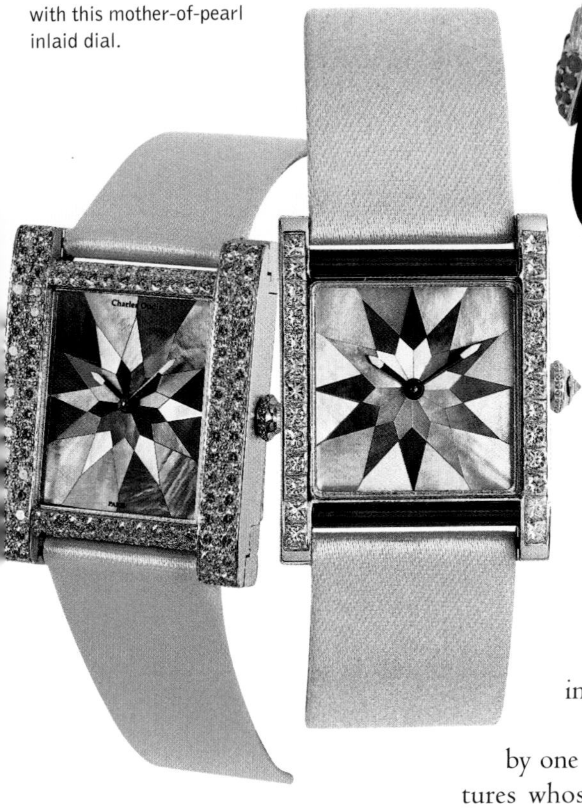

and is active in Paris in the appraisal and sale of collectors' jewelry and watches. By acquiring one of Paris's last manufacturers of high-grade watches, the family has assumed the task of restoring French watchmaking to its former leading role.

The platinum and gold cases are made by one of the few remaining Parisian manufactures whose craftsmen possess the finely honed skills and experience that attracts orders from the greatest names in luxury for the realization of precious cases for limited-series timepieces. The gemstones are set by the expert hands of craftsmen accustomed to meeting the standards of the city's prestigious jewelry houses.

CHRONOLOGY

1772	Charles Oudin is born in Clermont, France.
1790	Oudin is a pupil of Abraham-Louis Breguet.
1804	Oudin establishes his own watchmaking shop in the Palais Royal 52.
1805	He creates a repeating watch for the empress Josephine.
1806	Oudin is awarded an honorable mention at the Paris Exhibition for a self-winding watch and a watch with moonphases and synodic months; First watch wound by means of a key fitted into the pendant.
1819	Citation is awarded at the Paris Exhibition for a watch with equation of time.
1840	A miniature Six Pence watch is presented to Queen Victoria.
1859	Invention of first Crucifix watches.
1860	The company becomes watchmaker to the Pope; introduces first world-time watches; Invents first keyless miniature watch (13mm) is created for the Countess de Bastard.
1860-1914	Several high-grade, highly complicated watches are produced for distribution in the United States and South American markets.
1862	Universal Exhibition in London. The company presents a unique gold and rock-crystal timepiece with mounted quarter-repeater and set with diamonds; A new type of watch created with just 10 square pieces (as opposed to the usual 129) allows the wearer to view the time in darkness; A Crucifix watch is crafted for the Pope; Watches with tuning diapasons are created for musicians.
1863	The Mourning watch, along with a mother-of-pearl watch, is made for the empress of Russia; Ivory watches with level escapements are made for royalty of Italy and Greece.
1867	Mantel regulator is made for Napoleon III; The brand becomes horloger to Italian and Russian royalty.
1920s	First collection of wristwatches in platinum and gold appear in the Charles Oudin line for both men and women.
1998-2000	The new collection of platinum and gold wristwatches with complications, and the new collection of ladies' jeweled wristwatches are introduced.
2001-2002	Launching of the brand's first floral jewelry wristwatches: The Lily, Pansy, Tulip, and Rose; Unveiling of the first self-winding tourbillon wristwatch with 120°power-reserve.

made-to-order

horology

In an increasingly competitive industry, Charles Oudin has one asset that is virtually out of reach for even the greatest watch manufacturers driven by marketing and financial considerations: custom-made horology.

Such a luxury usually is only possible in a family-owned enterprise in which the family members exude perfect control over its own production. Charles Oudin is firmly positioned in this exclusive niche with a production that can be, and is, personalized. A model can thus be made with a variety of gem settings—as a unique piece or in a small series—without straining customers' budgets.

Inspired by the Palais Royal, the models in the Charles Oudin collection are named for the flowers growing in its magnificent gardens or in honor of cultural and architectural features of the building.

The Lily, Pansy, Tulip, and Rose models, for example, assume the shapes of these flowers while the period models recall the feminine elegance typical of Paris. They are fitted with a choice of straps of every color, in plain or moiré satin, leather or shagreen. The Precious

TOP

The fountains of France were a great inspiration to Oudin.

TOP RIGHT

This navy Chronometer was made at the beginning of the 19th century.

LEFT

From the Historique collection, this elegant Regulator is crafted in 18-karat gold.

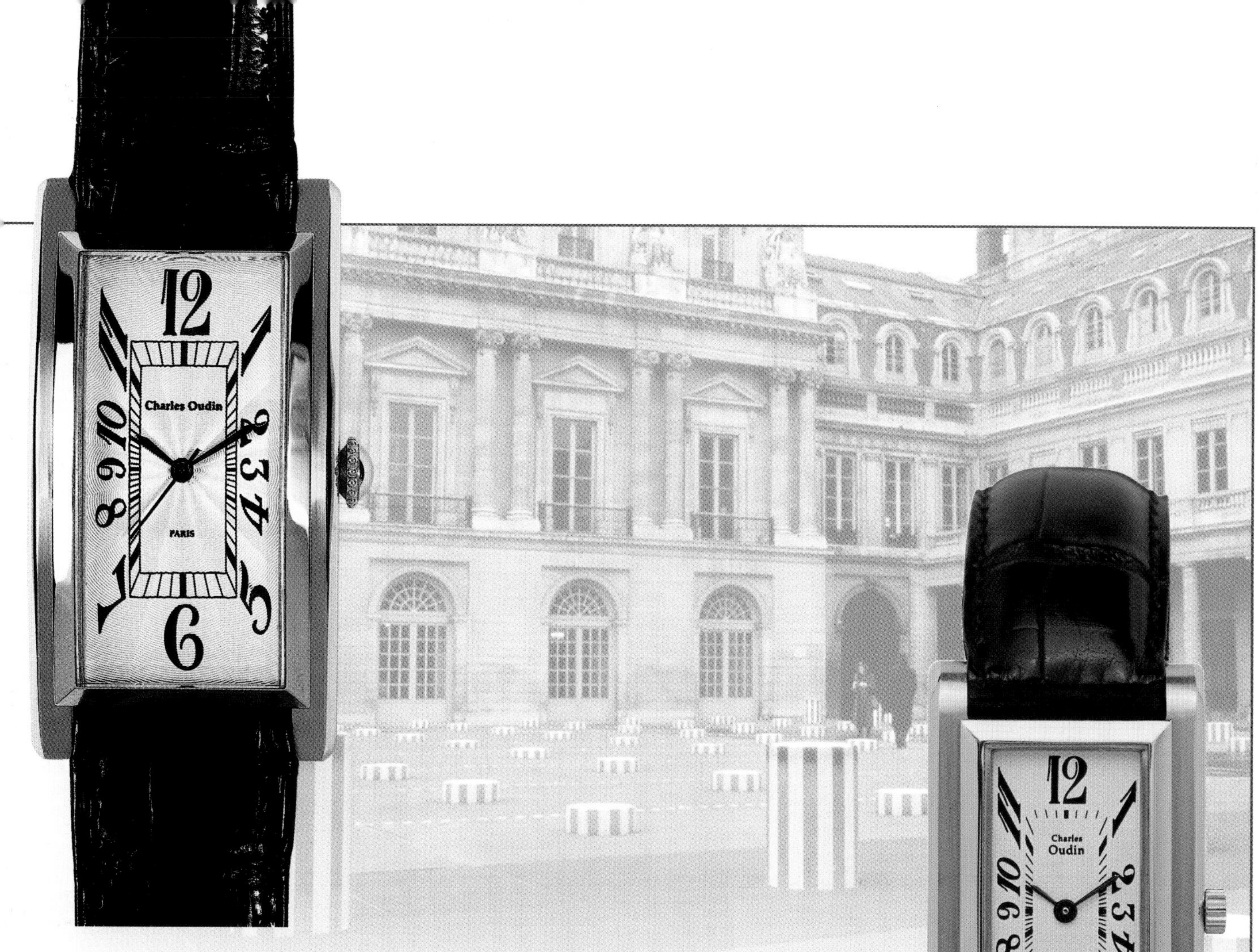

collection also is inspired by nature in its settings of the most precious gemstones—sapphires, rubies, emeralds and diamonds—that adorn time with outstanding elegance. Each is made in a limited series and exemplifies the skills of the most talented craftmasters. The Art Déco collection features mother-of-pearl dials, which are masterpieces of meticulous decoration.

For women as for men, the Fontaine or Palais models, inspired by the fountains and the imposing architecture of the Palais Royal, have regal bearings. The wide rectangular case allows every extravagance. Set with black or white diamonds, rubies and emeralds, these elegant creations express, in their most simple versions, the fashion-transcending quality that contributes to their enduring values.

The pure and structured lines of the Column modes recall the celebrated Buren pillars of the Palais Royal forecourt, while the Historique collection evokes the prestigious past of the naval horologist with the Régulateur watch which will certainly attract lovers of bygone watchmaking techniques.

Thanks to its flawless track record, this great name in French horology has returned to its natural place among the best watch-dealers of the Middle East who serve a wealthy clientele seeking exceptional items of luxury. Present also on New York's Madison Avenue, the name Charles Oudin has already been welcomed by the city's demanding customers. In Paris, it is only at 8 Place Vendôme where the lady of fashion may, by appointment, realize the dream of time made-to-measure.

ABOVE

From the Royal Collection for men, this Palais watch was inspired by the sleek lines and columns of the Palais Royal.

CENTER RIGHT

This Column watch is elegantly crafted in 18-karat gold.

BOTTOM RIGHT

This watch from the Art Déco Column collections is a perfect link between past and present.

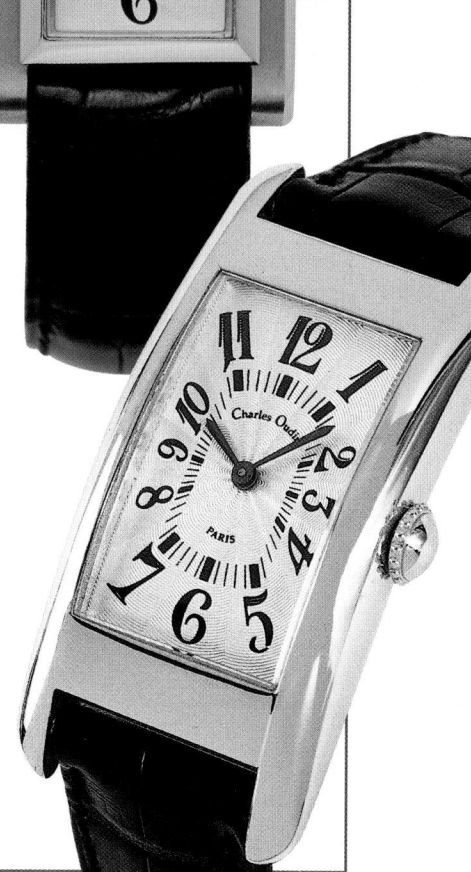

CHARLES OUDIN

CURVEX   REF. 200 W

Movement : Swiss mechanical, manual winding or quartz.
Functions : hour, minute.
Case : 18K white gold, two-piece case, size 21x45mm, thickness 7mm, sapphire glass, back attached by 8 screws.
Dial : white guilloché or plain, Arabic numerals, blued steel bâton-style hands.
Strap : crocodile leather, white gold and clasp.

Also available : yellow gold, red gold, framed by set diamonds.

COLUMN   REF. 410 Y

Movement : Swiss mechanical, manual winding or quartz.
Functions : hour, minute.
Case : 18K yellow gold, two-piece case, rectangular, size 21x39mm, thickness 6.5mm, sapphire glass, back attached by 4 screws.
Dial : white guilloché or plain, Arabic numerals, blued steel bâton-style hands.
Strap : crocodile leather.

Also available : white gold, red gold.

REGULATOR   REF. 108

Movement : Swiss mechanical, automatic winding or quartz.
Functions : hour, minute, small second.
Case : 18K white gold, two-piece case, diameter 35mm, thickness 10.8mm, sapphire glass.
Indication : off-center hour in Roman numerals at 12, center minute, small second at 6.

Dial : blued steel Breguet lozenge hands.
Strap : crocodile leather.
Also available : diameter 38mm, yellow gold.

BRANCARD   REF. 400 W/W

Movement : Swiss mechanical, automatic winding or quartz.
Functions : hour, minute.
Case : 18K white gold, two-piece case, rectangular curved, size 25x47mm, thickness 8.5mm, curved sapphire glass, back attached by 8 screws.
Dial : white guilloché or plain, Arabic numerals, blued steel bâton-style hands.
Strap : crocodile leather, white-gold strap.

Also available : yellow gold, red gold, or bicolor.

CHARLES OUDIN

RETRO   REF. 503 W/DDS

Movement : Swiss mechanical, automatic winding or quartz.
Functions : hour, minute.
Case : 18K white gold, two-piece case, size 24x33mm thickness 4.5mm, sapphire glass, framed by set brillants, back attached by 4 screws, gold crown with faceted diamond.
Dial : white guilloché or plain, Roman numerals, blued steel bâton-style hands.
Strap : crocodile leather, white-gold clasp with diamonds.
Also available : yellow gold and red gold.

BRANCARD   REF. 401 R/DDS

Movement : Swiss mechanical, automatic winding or quartz.
Functions : hour, minute.
Case : 18K red gold, two-piece case, rectangular curved, size 25x47mm, thickness 8.5mm, curved sapphire glass, framed by set brillants, back attached by 8 screws, gold crown with faceted diamond.
Dial : red guilloché or plain, Arabic numerals, blued steel bâton-style hands.
Strap : satin, red-gold clasp with diamonds.
Also available : yellow gold and white gold.

CREA   REF. 621 W/DDS

Movement : Swiss mechanical, automatic winding or quartz.
Functions : hour, minute.
Case : 18K white gold, two-piece case, rectangular, size 27x33mm, thickness 6.8mm, sapphire glass, framed by set brillants, back attached by 4 screws, gold crown with faceted diamond.
Dial : mother-of-pearl marquetry, blued steel bâton-style hands.
Strap : satin, white-gold clasp with diamonds.
Also available : princess-cut diamond and stone dials.

ROYAL   REF. 203 FLORALE

Movement : Swiss mechanical, manual winding or quartz.
Functions : hour, minute.
Case : 18K white gold, two-piece case, rectangular curved, size 23x45mm, thickness 7.5mm, curved sapphire glass, framed by set Urals Russian demantoïd garnets, brillants, rubies, sapphires, back attached by 8 screws, gold crown with faceted diamond.
Dial : white guilloché or plain, Arabic numerals, blued steel bâton-style hands.
Strap : satin, white-gold clasp with diamonds.

CHARRIOL

an historical perspective

*P*hilippe Charriol is a man of many talents. Charged with an energy and creativity that drives him to seek perfection in all he does, Charriol claims a multitude of successes in his life. An avid ice racer, automobile racer and philanthropist, Charriol has always been a man with vision. It was his dream to create an elaborate collection of watches, jewelry and accessories that would bear his name.

After spending 13 years with Cartier, where he ultimately served as president of the Les Must de Cartier divisions in Asia and North America, Charriol struck out on his own. In 1986, this self-proclaimed Renaissance man created the Philippe Charriol® brand of luxury products.

Influenced by his love of art and antiquity, Charriol unveiled a collection of 18-karat gold and steel watches that was inspired by the twisted cable designs of the ancient Celts. His first collection, which targeted a sophisticated and worldly clientele, garnered such international attention that it was an immediate success. Called the Celtic collection, this cable style has since become an icon for the brand.

It didn't take long for Charriol to unveil a multitude of new timepiece collections, a complete jewelry collection, leathergoods, accessories, and eyewear. In fact, in just 15 years, Charriol has become such a noted brand that it has established a worldwide network of 600 Charriol Corners and 42 boutiques.

"I work like an alchemist to create my special style," says Charriol. Indeed, each of his collections has a mark of difference, a signature look that is at once sporty yet elegant—with an air of modernity that bespeaks Charriol's sense of style.

While the Celtic collection continues to redefine beauty with its round and square watch versions, other series have also risen to stellar success. Perhaps top among them is the Colvmbvs collection of watches and jewelry. This collection offers striking, bold lines and a sophisticated appeal.

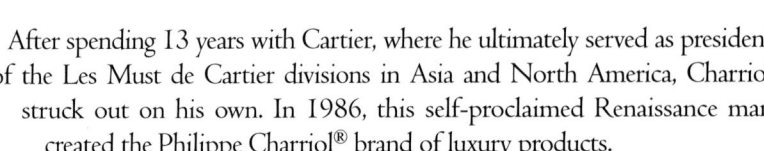

TOP

Philippe Charriol.

ABOVE

Charriol's first timepieces were inspired by the twisted cable designs of the ancient Celts. Called the Celtic collection, this cable style has since become an icon for the brand.

LEFT

The Jet Set tonneau chronograph for women is a refreshing and exciting collection of diamond and steel timepieces.

BOTTOM

The Tonneau bracelet features a unique design of curved links, screws and a sapphire cabochon to emulate the beauty of the tonneau watch.

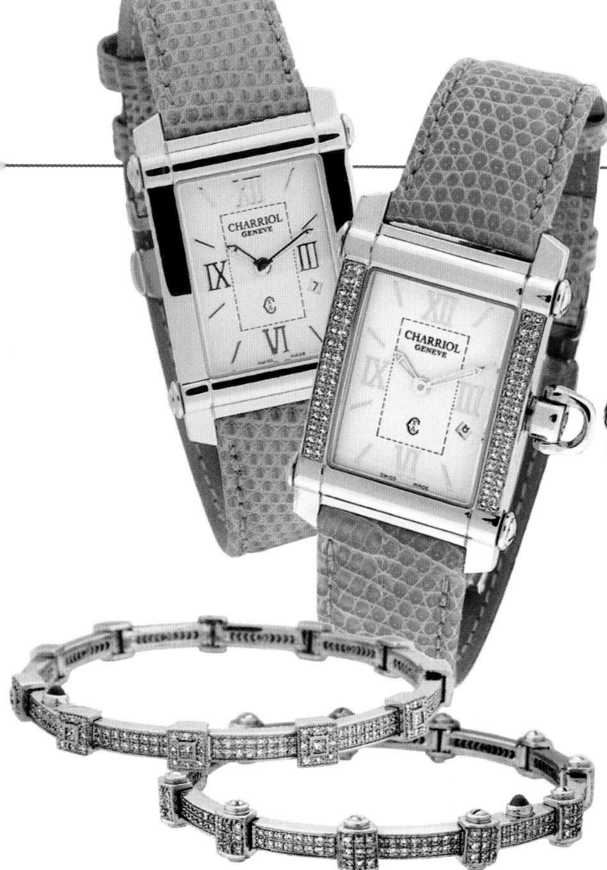

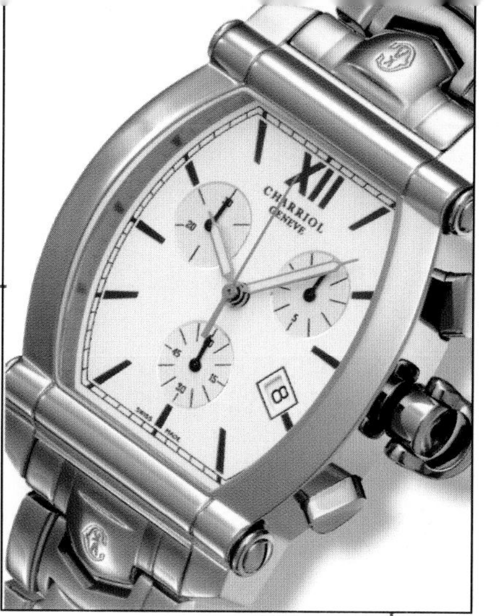

The newest Colvmbvs watches include a distinctive tonneau-shaped chronograph in a brazenly oversized case. This timepiece features an integrated bracelet of intricate links that emulates the design of the case. Charriol has also unveiled a rectangular Colvmbvs for women—crafted in 18-karat gold or steel and adorned with two rows of diamonds on either side of the case. This rectangular version is also available with a bracelet as its tonneau sibling for chic and elegantly sporty appeal. The Colvmbvs features striking pink or blue straps and comes with or without diamonds on the case sides. A collection of striking all-diamond bracelets complements the Colvmbvs collection.

Always on the edge of style and artistry, Charriol has also unveiled the Colvmbvs Jet Set for women. This striking collection of ladies' tonneau-shaped chronographs features mother-of-pearl dials in brilliant colors with contrasting subdials. The Jet Set with a pink dial and pink strap sports blue subdials, while a blue-dial version features pink subdials. There is also a white mother-of-pearl dial with blue-gray subdials and a pale gray strap. The watch is further enhanced with double rows of diamonds on each side of the gently curved case for added femininity.

Complementing the tonneau Jet Set is a Tonneau bracelet collection fashioned in a one-of-a-kind design. It features curved attachments as the links and sports screws and other details apparent in the Jet Set watch line. An innovative approach, the bracelet is adorned with diamonds and features a single blue sapphire cabochon on one of the links to emulate the watch crown.

In a bold move, Charriol has added striking blue and purple renditions to its captivating Megeve Collection. Designed to resemble the picturesque French Alpine resort for which it is named, the Megeve collection features an interplay of faceting, radiant colored dials and sapphire crystals, and scintillating stud-set diamonds. The diamonds are placed randomly across the watch dial to emulate snowflakes, and there are three rows of diamonds across the bottom of the dial to depict the fallen snow. A work of conceptual magnitude, the Megeve is a unique expression of harmony and elegance. It is created in a limited edition of just 2,000 pieces and is complemented by a jewelry collection.

As with all Philippe Charriol timepieces, the newest watches are made in Switzerland to the exacting standards of Charriol himself.

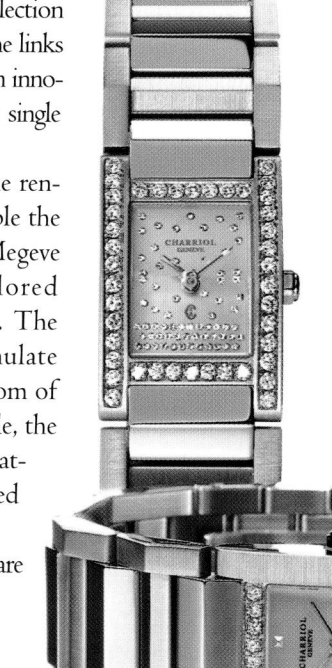

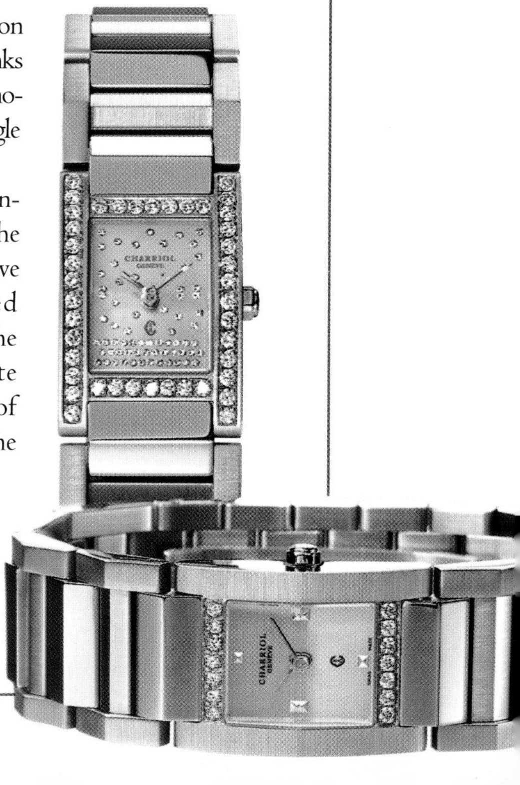

TOP LEFT

Color brightens the spirit in these Colvmbvs Twin watches, available with or without diamonds.

TOP CENTER

This Colvmbvs rectangular curved watch is decorated with two rounded bars and studded with four round-headed screws. It is armed with either a quartz or automatic movement.

ABOVE

The Colvmbvs name symbolizes the spirit of enterprise, and the innovative Colvmbvs bracelets are a charming expression of that artistic flair.

TOP RIGHT

The Colvmbvs Tonneau chronograph offers powerful lines and features a patented Integrated Hinged crown.

BOTTOM

The Megeve is a striking combination of colors, diamonds and shimmering inventiveness. The watch is designed to emulate the snow-covered French Alpine resort for which it is named.

CHAUMET

an historical perspective

Chaumet's history is one of romance, intrigue and grandeur. Originally founded in 1780 by Marie-Etienne Nitot, Chaumet's rise ran parallel to Napoleon's glory. The keen-sighted Nitot was brilliant and confident enough in his creations to offer the Emperor impressive jewels and was quickly appointed the Royal family's jeweler. The great house of Chaumet designed the imperial sword, the tiaras and all of the finery for the empresses Josephine and Marie-Louise. It was the regal beginning of what was to become Chaumet's legacy.

Decade after decade, century after century, Chaumet has continued in this fine tradition of creating the most exquisite jewels for the finest clientele. A master at flawlessly interpreting the styles of each epoch, Chaumet's archives are rich with spirited designs that reflect the Romantic period of the early 1800s and the splendor and beauty of cameos and lockets popular during the late 1800s.

In 1875, Joseph Chaumet married the daughter of the head of the firm and perpetuated the family tradition of creating masterpieces of art and elegance. He gave the house the name of Chaumet and formally registered it.

Under Joseph Chaumet's creative genius, the house entered a new era of grandeur: Art Nouveau. Lilies, waterfalls and butterfly wings propelled Chaumet to new heights. The firm quickly transitioned into the geometrics of the 1920s and 1930s, followed by the glitz of the 1940s and the diamonds of the 1950s. In 1969, Chaumet opened it boutique in the prestigious Place Vendôme.

Today, the House of Chaumet is an international trendsetter. Its five diverse jewelry and watch collections push the frontiers and echo themes of harmony and passion. For more than two centuries, Chaumet has stirred emotions and is committed to fulfilling heart-quickening dreams forever more.

THIS PAGE

"L'Echarpe" is a fringe of diamonds set in 18-karat white gold.

FACING PAGE

LEFT

Steel "Class One" watch, rotating bezel, pavé with diamonds, rubber strap.

BOTTOM

Steel "Class One" watch, pavé with pink sapphires, rubber strap.

Class One

This new creation from Chaumet is deliberately sporty in style. Each model is water resistant to 100 meters and several styles exist, including two new chronographs and a diamond-adorned jewelry version. With the variety of bezel, dial and bracelet choices, 14 different versions comprise the line.

The first dive-watch collection created by the House of Chaumet, the Class One has gained international popularity, particularly with the daring association of diamonds, steel and rubber. Most recently Chaumet unveiled two chronograph models in a larger 41mm size for men.

The new Joaillerie versions are crafted in steel and are combined with a rubber strap. Each watch features white diamonds, black diamonds or pink sapphires—the ultimate expression of Chaumet's pace-setting creativity.

Khésis
Collection

Chaumet selected the name Khésis for its first distinctly feminine watch created exclusively for women and unveiled to the world in 1995. Simply translated, Khésis means "sun" in the Navajo language, and the sun is the emblem of Place Vendôme, home of Chaumet's landmark boutique.

The Khésis collection is a romantic blend of sleek style and innovative spirit. Its case is decidedly contemporary and the curved case design offers incredible sensuality. In its various renditions, the Khésis offers women a glorious choice of moods.

Capturing the spirit of our time, Chaumet offers a striking steel version of the Khésis that is elegantly set with diamonds. The striking high-polished link bracelet with rice-grain effect offers a suppleness that feels wonderful against the skin. Chaumet further sets the pace with a choice of dials, including tone-on-tone gray, black or white with diamond hour-markers or Roman numerals.

Created in two sizes (the smaller Classic Lady and the larger Top Lady) and in 18-karat yellow or white gold in addition to the steel, the Khésis collection ranges from the sportiest chic look to the most bedazzling. In 18-karat gold, white or yellow, it is supremely elegant. When adorned further with pavé diamonds, it transforms into a stunning work of art; and when totally bedecked from end to end in princess-cut diamonds, this work of art becomes gloriously regal.

Indeed, the extensiveness of the Khésis collection allows women to express themselves according to their lifestyles.

TOP RIGHT

Steel "Khésis" watch with diamond bezels.

LEFT

Steel "Khésis" watch, bracelet and ring "Khésis" in white gold.

Style de Chaumet

The Style de Chaumet collection of watches and jewelry embodies the emotion of lines and curves, of contours and balance. A dynamic venture into the world of bold elegance and sleek proportions, Style de Chaumet watches are the epitome of self-expression.

The different variations found in this collection are created around either rectangular, square or round cases crafted in either 18-karat yellow or white gold or in steel. Designed for men and women, the Style de Chaumet watches come with either a metal link bracelet or in a variety of straps. In the spirit of Chaumet, straps range from leather to fabric, from soft-grained padded renditions to exotic crocodile to ultra-shimmering patent-leather versions.

Dials, too, run the gamut from mother-of-pearl to tone-on-tone depictions to a variety of irresistible colors. Pastels are particularly important, as Chaumet offers pale blue, pink, green or yellow dials with color-coordinated satin straps and diamond markers. Diamond accents are also offered on some of the versions, with bezels and cases paved for shimmering elegance. One particularly coveted model is the square Style de Chaumet that is entirely encrusted with diamonds—dial, case and bracelet—for stunning appeal.

The Style de Chaumet watches are offered in large and small sizes with either quartz or automatic movements. Additionally, Chaumet offers several chronograph models.

With its simplicity of volume and purity of form, the Style de Chaumet collection is the epitome of the brand's style.

TOP LEFT

Large model yellow-gold "Style de Chaumet" rectangular watch on a crocodile band. Two "Anneau" rings in 18-karat yellow gold, one set with pavé diamonds.

TOP RIGHT

Square "Style de Chaumet" watch in white gold with pavé diamonds, mother-of-pearl dial and diamond index.

The Mihewi Watch

Following in the successful footsteps of the manchette trend that the brand launched with the Khésis in 1995, Chaumet's Mihewi is a collection destined for women with bold style and a taste for the sensual. An exquisite piece of jewelry, the Mihewi is a link bracelet with a small watch square dial ensconced in it.

Mihewi watches are elegantly sculpted in 18-karat gold or in steel and feature multiple dial variations ranging from classic white to contemporary gray and even diamond pavé. The outside links of the bracelet are curved and sensuous, while the center link is harmoniously integrated to join with the watch dial. The aesthetic force of its design gives it a fashion-forward look.

One particularly arresting model features 18-karat gold outer links and all-diamond pavé center links, with a pavé diamond dial. The Mihewi collection is Chaumet's rendition of the combination of daring and generous.

TOP

Yellow-gold "Anneau" rings. Yellow-gold "Mihewi" watch.

BOTTOM

Steel "Mihewi" watch.

Night Spirit

Crafted to embody the spirit of the glamorous evening, the Night Spirit watch marks a return to elegance and glory. Destined for the refined woman of passion, the watch offers an interplay of shadow and light with its black satin strap or white gold bracelet mingled with the shimmering sparkle of a pavé diamond dial and case. The new Joaillerie watch from Chaumet, the Night Spirit is available only in 18-karat white gold with either a natural mother-of-pearl dial or a diamond pavé dial.

ABOVE

"Night Spirit" watch in white gold entirely covered with pavé diamonds on a black satin bracelet.

CHAUMET
PARIS

CHOPARD

the pulse

*O*ne of the finest luxury watch and jewelry companies in the world, Chopard is a brand with true heart and soul. For decades, this legendary firm has gracefully reached well beyond the scope of creating masterpieces. It has branched into the worlds of celebrities and automobile racing, of charities and philanthropy.

Since 1963, Chopard President Karl Scheufele and his wife Karin have run the company with a driving dedication to creativity and perfection. Today, they are joined by their son and daughter, Karl-Friedrich Scheufele and Caroline Gruosi-Scheufele. With a family valor and strength that is pervasive, Chopard has grown by great measures. The innovative spirit of each of these individuals has been the unifying factor and the propelling force behind Chopard's involvements, products and on-going success.

The astonishing success story of this dynamic brand is four-fold: in times rife with conglomerate-owned firms, Chopard has held fast as an independent family-owned business; in times when the majority of watch companies have parts made elsewhere and watches that are simply assembled on site, Chopard is one of just a handful of watch companies left in the world that creates its own timepieces from movement to fruition; at a time when the mode seems to be simply refining existing lines, Chopard continues to create new and innovative masterpieces. Finally, Chopard is a company that has regularly partnered with celebrity-studded events and with charitable foundations around the world to raise funds for various causes—often by creating special timepieces and donating the proceeds.

According to Chopard Vice-President Caroline Gruosi-Scheufele, "When one is fortunate enough to have a life filled with delights, it is essential to think of others. It is right to help those for whom life is a trial."

For this reason, Chopard actively extends its business and creativity to a broad range of areas with the ultimate goal of reviving hope and developing the future.

AGENCE DE LA FABRIQUE DE MONTRES
L.U.C.

CHOPARD

the passion

It was the passionate determination of Karl-Friedrich Scheufele that led the development of Chopard to become a complete Manufacture. Having received such high international respect for its creations, Karl-Friedrich wanted to take Chopard to the ultimate level—he wanted Chopard to produce its own movements.

Indeed, he was the driving force behind the 1996 unveiling of the first movement entirely designed and assembled in the Chopard workshops. This caliber, called the L.U.C. in honor of founder Louis-Ulysse Chopard, was so meticulously produced according to the strictest criteria that it received the highly coveted Poinçon de Genève, the hallmark of quality and excellence.

Since then, a succession of L.U.C. movements has continued to confirm the brand's natural status as a prestige watch Manufacture.

Chopard's extraordinary achievements and international acclaim have not altered the brand's vision of reality. For years, Chopard has actively supported a variety of patronage activities around the world in fields such as art, culture, sports, medicine and ecology.

In fact, for more than 12 years Chopard has annually teamed with famed tenor José Carreras in the fight against leukemia. The singer was stricken with the disease in 1987 at the peak of his career. After a long battle and several bone marrow transplants, Carreras regained his health but vowed to fight leukemia on behalf of others. He set up the first José Carreras Foundation and turned to his friend Karl Scheufele to help establish additional foundations.

Today, Karl Scheufele is also president of the Carreras Foundation in Geneva and vice president of the Carreras Foundation in Germany. Each year, Carreras holds

José Carreras Foundation

José Carreras Charity Concert in Gstaad:

TOP LEFT

José Carreras and Karl Scheufele, president of Chopard.

TOP CENTER

José Carreras, Julia Carreras and Christine Scheufele.

TOP RIGHT

José Carreras and Karin Scheufele.

LEFT AND BELOW

The 2000 José Carreras watch is available in two versions: one with a black dial surrounded by a piano keyboard and one with a slivered dial circled by symbols representing musical notes. Both versions are fitted with a caliber L.U.C. 3.96 movement and have the logo of the "Gran Teatre del Liceu" on the back sapphire crystal. The tenor's signature is engraved on the case.

Elton John AIDS Foundation

TOP LEFT

Elton John watch with mechanical chronograph and automatic winding.

FAR RIGHT

Elton John watch with quartz movement and mechanical chronograph. Case, dial and buckle are solid gold and set with diamonds.

White Tie and Tiara Ball:

TOP CENTER

Sir Elton John and Caroline Gruosi-Scheufele.

TOP RIGHT

Kevin Spacey, Sir Elton John and Sean "P. Diddy" Combs.

CENTER

Sir Elton John wearing the Elton John bejeweled watch designed by Chopard.

LEFT

Sarah Ferguson wearing a set from Chopard's Pushkin collection with diamonds and black pearls.

benefit concerts whose proceeds go to the foundation. In September 2001, Chopard organized a concert with the tenor in the prestigious setting of the Menuhin Festival Gstaad. The proceeds of this evening, Sfr. 400,000, were donated to the José Carreras Foundation for the fight against leukemia.

Chopard is also a staunch supporter of the Elton John AIDS Foundation and in 2001, in conjunction with this Foundation, unveiled a striking collection of watches—the profits of which will be devoted to the Foundation. A special celebrity- and royalty-filled White Tie & Tiara Ball was held in Sir Elton John's Windsor home last summer. To help raise millions of dollars in Elton John's fight against AIDS, Chopard gave all in attendance a preview of the limited-edition watches created in honor of the Foundation. Named "Elton John," the self-winding chronographs range from rubber-clad straps to diamond-bedecked beauties.

CHOPARD

the style

FESTIVAL
INTERNATIONAL
DU FILM
CANNES

Chopard

THIS PAGE

LEFT

2001 Palme d'Or ceated by Chopard, official sponsor of Cannes Film Festival.

TOP CENTER

Fawaz Gruosi and Caroline Gruosi-Scheufele.

RIGHT

Adriana Karembeu wearing earrings with diamonds and pearls from the Haute Joaillerie collection.

CENTER

Jerry Hall wearing a stunning necklace from the Haute Joaillerie collection.

FACING PAGE

TOP LEFT

Isabelle Huppert wearing the diamond Heart necklace with matching earrings from the Haute Joaillerie collection.

TOP RIGHT

Caroline Gruosi-Scheufule and HRH Prince Albert of Monaco.

LEFT

Caroline Gruosi-Scheufele and Sean Penn.

RIGHT

Charlotte Rampling wears earrings from the Pushkin collection.

Caroline Gruosi-Scheufele, responsible for Haute Joaillerie design and the brand's forays into accessories and perfume, succinctly sums up the firm's philosophy: "Chopard stands for creativity, excellent quality and exclusiveness."

Indeed, these are the tributes that have garnered the brand international accolades in the world of jewelry and watches. With inimitable style and grace, Chopard regularly has unveiled jeweled masterpieces that are unique and wonderful works of wearable art. From its world-renowned Happy Diamonds collection to its La Vie en Rose and Ice Cube series of watches and jewelry to its extreme haute joaillerie pieces, Chopard is a brand synonymous with exquisite expression and the spirit of inspiration.

Because Chopard truly "creates the stuff of which dreams are made," it was inevitable that the brand would partner with one of the most important international extravaganzas in the film world: The International Film Festival in Cannes. At this festival, movies are sold and marketed with zeal and panache. Top producers, actors and actresses come out en masse—many of whom are Chopard customers—to celebrate each other's successes and magical moments on screen.

For more than four years, Chopard has been an official partner of this French cultural institution, and has even created the prestigious Golden Palm award and the Mini Palms for the best film, actor and actress. Many of the celebrated stars attending the Festival wear Chopard jewelry, not just for the walk up the famous steps, but also as part of their personal wardrobes. In addition to adorning celebrities such as Patricia Arquette, Melanie Griffith, Liv Ullmann, Jean-Claude Van Damme and a myriad of others, Chopard hosts a number of important events throughout the 12-day Festival.

During the 2001 Festival, for instance, Chopard and Warner jointly organized an evening for 400 guests in honor of contending film, "The Pledge," starring Sean Penn and Robin Wright Penn. The event was held in a setting specially created by Chopard's chief interior designer on the beach of the Man Ray Hotel. At another affair, Chopard presented the first photos of a book the brand is sponsoring on behalf of UNESCO in its work for child war victims. This event was held in honor of the film, "Christmas of the Heart."

Chopard was also one of just 10 international jewelers asked by The Diamond Information Center, which sponsors AMFAR, to create an exceptional diamond piece to be auctioned in fall 2001. Caroline Gruosi-Scheufele designed The Fantasy Necklace, featuring 66 diamonds of various fancy cuts surrounded by another 3,660 diamonds. A percentage of the proceeds was donated to AMFAR.

Indeed, the list of events and involvements is extensive and, for Chopard, it is an honor to be so inextricably and actively woven into the world of the Cannes Film Festival.

1000 MIGLIA

the precision

In addition to the broad range of art, culture and medicine with which Chopard has aligned itself, the brand also is associated closely with the world of fine sports.

Since 1988, Chopard has been intimately involved with the legendary Mille Miglia vintage car race as its official sponsor. As passionate patrons and collectors, Karl and Karl-Friedrich Scheufele also take part in the race each year behind the wheel of one of the family's vintage cars.

Indeed, the symbiosis between these extraordinary cars and the superior timepieces of Chopard is all encompassing. They each offer impeccable technical excellence and superb aesthetics. Thus, it comes as no surprise that Chopard annually creates a new Mille Miglia timepiece in tribute to the event.

TOP LEFT

Karl-Friedrich Scheufele (left) and Jacky Ickx.

TOP RIGHT

Mille Miglia 2001 in titanium with a tachometric scale engraved on the bezel.

LEFT

Karl-Friedrich Scheufele.

In 2001, the Mille Miglia watch was a titanium-encased self-winding chrono-graph with tachometric scale engraved on the bezel. The certified chronometer is an exceptional timekeeper, whose rubber strap replicates the Dunlop racing tire treads from the 1960s. This past year, too, a limited number of 200 pieces were created in 18-karat yellow and white gold.

the prestige

In 2001, Chopard took part in a very important polo event hosted by HRH The Prince of Wales. In answer to a request from Prince Charles, at the polo tournament Chopard unveiled a limited-edition series of watches—the sale of which would benefit The Prince's Foundation.

In a gala evening dinner, HRH The Prince of Wales welcomed 300 guests. The following day, the guests enjoyed a formal polo tournament at the prestigious Cirencester Polo Park, followed by a luncheon. During the entire event, the Chopard Prince Charles watch was available for sale, and the total proceeds thereof were shared between three entities chosen by The Prince's Foundation: Breakthrough Breast Cancer, Breast Cancer Research and Gurkha Welfare Trust.

Taking the project to heart, Caroline Gruosi-Scheufele began sketching a strong and masculine watch designed exclusively for the event. It is a large tonneau-shaped watch housing a L.U.C. movement. Entirely crafted by Chopard

FACING PAGE

TOP

The Prince of Wales
polo team at Cirencester
Polo Park.

BOTTOM

The Prince Charles watch is
fitted with a mechanical
caliber, the L.U.C. 4.96
movement with an
off-centered microrotor.

THIS PAGE

TOP

Caroline Gruosi-Scheufele and
HRH The Prince of Wales.

RIGHT

Engraved back of the
Prince Charles watch.

CENTER

Caroline Gruosi-Scheufele and
her husband Fawaz Gruosi.

BOTTOM

Mr. and Mrs. J.B. Kent and
Mrs. Bloomingdale.

it is a feat of creativity and craftsmanship befitting of royalty. It was created in a limited edition of 200 pieces, many of which were sold at the event and the remainder of which are sold only through Chopard's 50 boutiques around the world. This watchmaking work of art has become a precious symbol of the fight against cancer.

These selfless involvements and these fights for justice by one of the world's finest watchmakers solidifies the brand further as one on an extraordinary mission. Indeed, asked what distinguishes Chopard from others, Caroline Gruosi-Scheufele aptly answers, "Our style, our family, and our commitment to more than jewelry and watches."

CHOPARD

L.U.C QUATTRO   REF. 16/91863

This new manual winding movement of the LUC family by Chopard leaves the constructive qualities and technical sophistication of the 1.96 caliber unchanged, which are essential for the quality standard recognized by the "Geneva Seal". In the present movement, the space left free by the removal of the winding micro-rotor and related elements is used to introduce a second couple of superimposed barrels, linked with the first one. Thus the working

autonomy is increased up to the prestigious target of 216 hours, i.e. 9 days. However, in order to exploit always the best part of the motive force produced by the four barrels, before its drop causes a reduction of the amplitude of the balance vibrations, it is recommended to proceed to manual winding once a week.
The photograph shows a piece with platinum case and blue dial.

L.U.C. QUATTRO   REF. 16/1863

Movement: mechanical, manual winding, L.U.C. 1.98 caliber produced by Chopard's workshops at Fleurier. Mounted, decorated and finished entirely by hand (Côtes de Genève pattern) and beveled. Officially certified chronometer (C.O.S.C.). Hallmarked with the "Geneva Seal".
Functions: hour, minute, date, small second, power reserve.
Case: 18 kt pink gold, three-piece case (Ø 38 mm, thickness 9.6 mm); curved

sapphire glass; pink-gold crown; back attached by 8 screws, displaying the movement through a sapphire glass. Water-resistant to 3 atm.
Dial: silvered, center hand-turned (guilloché) with sun pattern, brushed hour ring, zone decorated with circular beads; applied faceted pink-gold pointed markers; printed minute track; pink-gold Dauphine hands.
Indications: date and small second at 6, power reserve at 12.
Strap: crocodile leather; pink-gold clasp.
Also available: in white gold (same price); in yellow gold; in platinum. All versions are available with black, blue or silvered dial.

L.U.C TONNEAU 6.96   REF. 16/2267

Movement: automatic, tonneau-shaped, L.U.C. 6.96 caliber produced by Chopard's workshops at Fleurier. Mounted and finished entirely by hand; bridges decorated with Côtes de Genève pattern. Officially certified chronometer (C.O.S.C.). **Functions:** hour, minute, date, small second.
Case: 18 kt white gold, three-piece tonneau-shaped, anatomically curved case (size 38.5 x 40 mm, thickness 10 mm); curved sapphire glass; white-gold

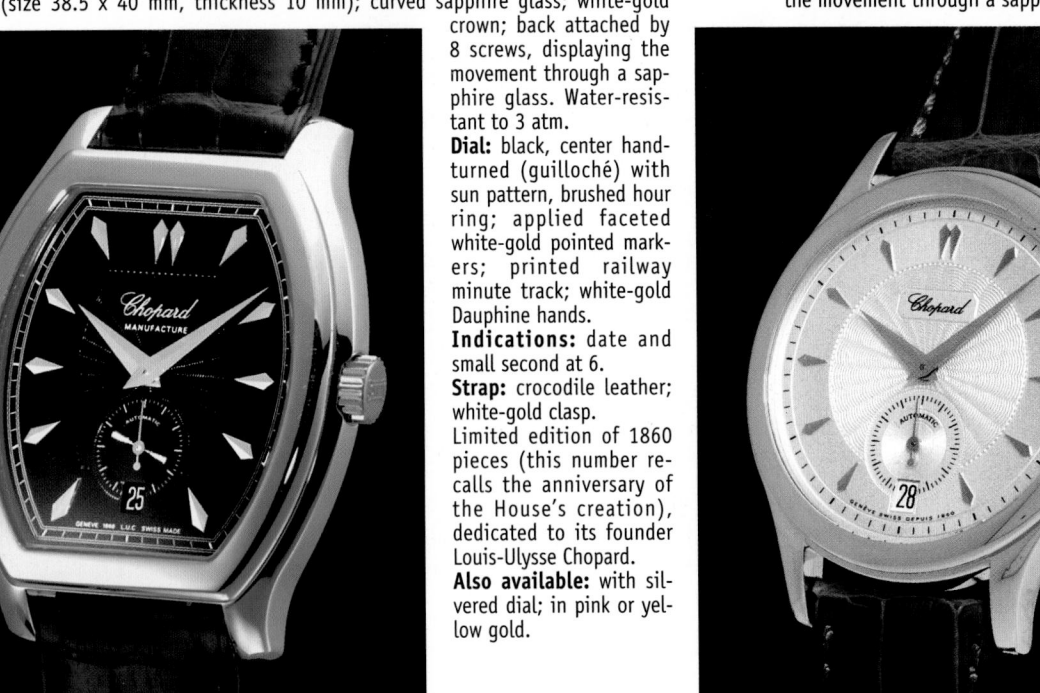

crown; back attached by 8 screws, displaying the movement through a sapphire glass. Water-resistant to 3 atm.
Dial: black, center hand-turned (guilloché) with sun pattern, brushed hour ring; applied faceted white-gold pointed markers; printed railway minute track; white-gold Dauphine hands.
Indications: date and small second at 6.
Strap: crocodile leather; white-gold clasp.
Limited edition of 1860 pieces (this number recalls the anniversary of the House's creation), dedicated to its founder Louis-Ulysse Chopard.
Also available: with silvered dial; in pink or yellow gold.

L.U.C "1.96"   REF. 16/1860/2

Movement: mechanical, automatic winding, L.U.C 1.96 caliber produced by Chopard's workshops at Fleurier. Mounted and finished entirely by hand. Hallmarked with the "Geneva Seal". **Functions:** hour, minute, small second, date.
Case: 18 kt pink gold, three-piece case (Ø 36 mm, thickness 8 mm); curved sapphire crystal; pink-gold crown; case back attached by 8 screws, displaying the movement through a sapphire crystal. Water-resistant to 3 atm.

Dial: silvered gold, center hand-turned (guilloché), brushed hour ring; applied pink-gold pointed markers; printed minute track; pink-gold Dauphine hands. **Indications:** small second and date at 6.
Strap: crocodile leather; pink-gold clasp.
Numbered edition of 1860 pieces, a homage to Louis-Ulysse Chopard who founded the firm in 1860.
Also available: with black dial; in white gold with silvered, black, gilded or coppered dial (same price); in yellow gold with black or silvered dial; in platinum with silvered, black, gilded or coppered dial. With L.U.C 3.96 movement (without "Geneva Seal"), white or coppered dial and silvered zone 1860 pieces; in white or pink gold; in yellow gold.

L.U.C SPORT   REF. 15/8200

Movement: mechanical, automatic winding, L.U.C 4.96 caliber produced by Chopard at the workshops in Fleurier. Mounted and finished entirely by hand, double barrel. Screw heads and rotor with "black nickel" finish. Officially certified "chronometer" (C.O.S.C.). **Functions:** hour, minute, second, date.
Case: stainless steel, three-piece brushed case (Ø 40 mm, thickness 10 mm); curved sapphire crystal; screw-down crown; case back attached by 8 screws, displaying the movement through a sapphire crystal. Water-resistant to 10 atm.

Dial: black, center hand-turned (guilloché) with lozenge pattern, hour ring decorated with circular beads; applied pointed rhodium-plated brass markers; printed minute track with luminescent square markers on the flange; luminescent rhodium-plated brass Dauphine hands.
Indications: date at 3.
Bracelet: brushed stainless steel, double fold-over clasp.
Limited edition of 2000 numbered pieces.
Also available: with rubber strap; in yellow gold with rubber strap; in white gold with rubber strap. All versions available with blue, black, white or pearl-gray dials.

MILLE MIGLIA 2000 CHRONOGRAPH   REF. 16/8407

Movement: mechanical, automatic winding, ETA 2892A2 caliber plus Dubois Dépraz chrono module. Officially certified "chronometer" (C.O.S.C.).
Functions: hour, minute, small second, date, chronograph with 3 counters.
Case: titanium, three-piece brushed case (Ø 40 mm, thickness 13 mm); curved sapphire crystal with antireflective treatment on both sides; case back attached by 8 screws, displaying the movement through a sapphire crystal. Water-resistant to 5 atm. **Dial:** anthracite gray with circular graining finish (the same used in the Thirties for the instrument panels of sport cars), silvered flange and counters, decorated with circular beads, luminescent Arabic numerals; luminescent rhodium-plated brass bâton hands. **Indications:** small second at 3 (with the famous red arrow as a symbol for racing), date between 4 and 5, hour counter at 6, minute counter at 9, center second counter, minute track with divisions for 1/5 of a second and triangular markers, tachometer scale on the flange. **Strap:** rubber (reproducing the tread of Dunlop Racing tires of the Sixties); titanium clasp.
Also available: in yellow gold, 250 pcs; in white gold 250 pcs.

ST. MORITZ CHRONOGRAPH   REF. 26/8390

Movement: mechanical, automatic winding, Frédéric Piguet 1185 caliber. 21 kt gold rotor.
Functions: hour, minute, second, date, chronograph with 3 counters.
Case: stainless steel, three-piece case (Ø 37.5 mm, thickness 10.7 mm); antireflective flat sapphire crystal; bezel fastened by 8 steel screws; screw-down crown; rectangular pushers; case back attached by 8 screws, displaying the movement through a sapphire crystal. Water-resistant to 10 atm.
Dial: blue, counters decorated with circular beads; applied stainless steel bâton markers (12 in Roman numerals); luminescent bâton hands.
Indications: minute counter at 3, date between 4 and 5, small second at 6, hour counter at 9, minute track with divisions for 1/5 of a second and luminescent dots on the flange.
Strap: Kevlar fiber; double fold-over steel clasp.
Also available: with single clasp with bracelet; black or white dial. Automatic (white, gray, blue or coppered dial, bracelet): in stainless steel; yellow gold; white gold; steel/yellow gold Lady's size.

HAPPY SPORT CHRONOGRAPH   REF. 28/8267-23

Movement: electromechanical, Frédéric Piguet 1270 caliber.
Functions: hour, minute, small second, date, chronograph with 3 counters.
Case: stainless steel, three-piece case (Ø 38.5 mm, thickness 10.5 mm); 7 top-Wesselton quality brilliants (totaling 0.39 carats) individually set and fluctuating between two flat sapphire crystals; sapphire cabochons on crown, pushers and lugs; case back attached by 8 screws. Water-resistant to 3 atm. **Dial:** white, silvered counters decorated with circular beads; printed Roman numerals; blued steel bâton hands.
Indications: hour counter at 3, date between 4 and 5, small second at 6, minute counter at 9, center second counter, railway minute track.
Bracelet: steel; double fold-over clasp.
Also available: iolite cab., strap, brac.; sapphire cab., strap; ruby cab., strap; ruby cab., mother-of-pearl dial, brac. Mother-of-pearl dial: yellow gold, sapphire cab., strap, brac.; yellow gold, ruby cab., strap, brac.; white gold, sapphire cab., strap, brac.; white gold, ruby cab., strap, brac. Bezel with brilliants: yellow gold, mother-of-pearl dial, sapphire cab., strap, brac.; white gold, sapphire cab., strap, brac.; in other jewel versions.

CHOPARD

CHRONOGRAPH PERPETUAL CALENDAR SEASONS — REF. 36/1224

Movement: automatic (autonomy 43 h), Jaeger-LeCoultre 889/2152 caliber base, Dubois-Dépraz perp. calendar and chrono modules. Balance with micrometer regulation of spiral and Kif shock-absorber. Beveled and decorated with Côtes de Genève pattern; rotor with 21 kt yellow-gold segment, skeletonized, personalized and engine-turned (circular graining). **Functions:** hour, minute, small second, 24-hour indication, perpetual calendar (date, day, month, week, season, year, moon-phase), chronograph with 3 counters.

Case: 18 kt yellow gold, 3-piece case (Ø 40.8, thickness 12.6 mm); antireflective curved sapphire crystal; 4 correctors on the middle; gold crown and rectangular pushers; case back attached by 8 screws, displaying the movement through a sapphire crystal. Water-resistant to 5 atm. **Dial:** gold, white enameled, silvered zones; printed Roman numerals; leaf style hands. **Indications:** moon phase and week at 3; day, hour counter and 24-hour display at 6; minute counter, month and year at 9; date, small second and season at 12; center second counter, minute track with divisions for 1/5 of a sec. **Strap:** crocodile leather; hand-engraved gold clasp. **Also available:** (50 pieces each type) guilloché dial; pink gold; in platinum.

TONNEAU PERPETUAL CALENDAR — REF. 36/92249

Movement: mechanical, automatic winding, Jaeger-LeCoultre 888 caliber base and perpetual calendar module developed by Chopard. **Functions:** hour, minute, 24-hour indication, perpetual calendar (date, day, month, year, moon phase). **Case:** platinum, three-piece tonneau-shaped case (size 36.50 x 34.40 mm, thickness 8.85 mm); flat sapphire crystal; 4 correctors on the middle; white gold crown; case back attached by 8 screws. Water-resistant to 3 atm.

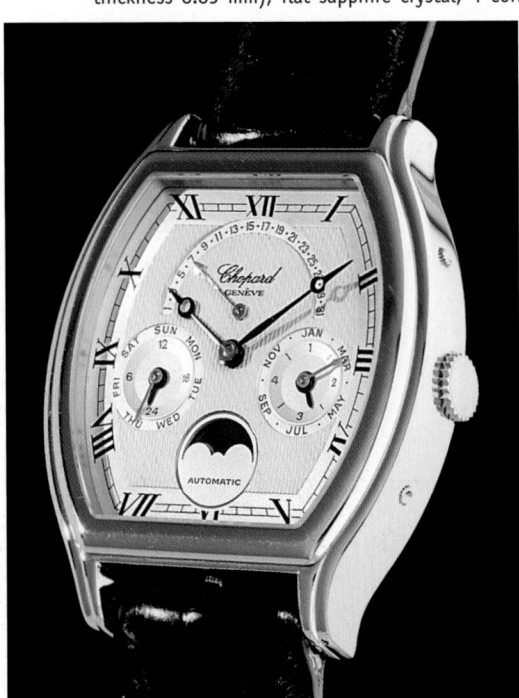

Dial: silvered, engine-turned (guilloché); printed Roman numerals and railway minute track; blued steel Breguet hands. **Indications:** month and four-year cycle at 3, moon phase at 6, day and 24-hour display at 9, date with retrograde hand at 12. **Strap:** crocodile leather, hand-stitched; platinum clasp. **Also available:** white dial: in yellow gold; pink or white gold.

CHRONOGRAPH RATTRAPANTE — REF. 34/1243

Movement: mechanical, automatic winding, Frédéric Piguet 1186. Beveled, Côtes de Genève and circular graining finish. 18 kt gold rotor. **Functions:** hour, minute, small second, date, split-second chronograph with 3 counters. **Case:** 18 kt white gold, three-piece case (Ø 38 mm, thickness 11.7 mm); antireflective curved sapphire crystal; white-gold crown and rectangular pushers (for the split-second feature at 10); case back attached by 8 screws, displaying the movement through a sapphire crystal. Water-resistant to 3 atm.

Dial: gold, silvered; zones with circular beads; printed Arabic numerals; white-gold luminescent bâton hands. **Indications:** minute counter at 3, date between 4 and 5, small second at 6, hour counter at 9, center split-second counters, minute track with divisions for 1/5 of a second. **Strap:** crocodile leather; hand-engraved white-gold clasp. **Also available:** in yellow gold. Both versions available with white or silvered dial.

IMPERIALE CHRONOGRAPH — REF. 37/3157.

Movement: mechanical with electric drive controlled by a quartz crystal, Frédéric Piguet 1270 caliber. **Functions:** hour, minute, small second, date, chronograph with 3 counters. **Case:** 18 kt pink gold, four-piece case (Ø 37 mm, thickness 9 mm); flat sapphire crystal; brand and progressive number engraved on the left middle side; pink-gold octagonal crown, pushers and lugs with ruby cabochons; case back attached by 8 screws. Water-resistant to 3 atm.

Dial: white, counters silvered; applied round faceted markers, pink-gold bâton hands. **Indications:** hour counter at 3, date between 4 and 5, small second at 6, minute counter at 9, center second chrono counter, railway minute track with divisions for 1/5 of a second. **Strap:** crocodile leather, central attachment; pink-gold clasp. **Also available:** in white gold; in yellow gold; with sapphire cabochons; in yellow gold; pink or white gold; with brilliants on bezel and central attachment, sapphire cabochons Ref. 37/3168-23: in yellow gold; white gold.

CLASSIC FOR GENT   REF.17/3450

Movement: mechanical, manual winding, produced by Frédéric Piguet, 6.10 caliber. Bridges finished with Côte de Genève and beveled, pillar-plate with circular graining.
Functions: hour, minute.
Case: 18 kt white gold, two-piece case, rectangular, curved (size 31.5 x 28 mm, thickness 7.5 mm); curved sapphire glass; bezel and lugs set with brilliants; back attached by 4 screws. Water-resistant to 3 atm.
Dial: white; printed Roman numerals; blued steel leaf style hands.
Strap: lizard skin; white-gold clasp.
Also available: yellow gold.

ICE CUBE   REF. 13/6858/42

Movement: mechanical, automatic winding, ETA 2000 caliber. **Functions:** hour, minute.
Case: 18 kt burnished white gold, two-piece anatomically curved case (size 31.5 x 31.3 mm, thickness 8.5 mm); entirely studded with square-cut pink sapphires; curved sapphire crystal; recessed burnished gold crown; curved case back attached by 4 screws. Water-resistant to 3 atm.
Dial: white gold, studded with brilliants, blued steel bâton hands.
Strap: pink satin; white-gold clasp.
Also available: with blue sapphires; entire brilliant pavé; dial with black brilliants.

LA STRADA   REF. 41/6866/8

Presented in 1997, the La Strada collection is made up by necklaces, bracelets, rings and earrings characterized by big-sized elements in half-moon shape; of course this is also the motive met in the watches of the same family. The La Strada timepieces, proposed in numerous combinations according to the subtle psychology of the feminine universe, have two case sizes, while the movement can be manual - the Omega 730 old-timer - or quartz.

The photograph shows the bigger version (size 39.5x32 mm, thickness 9.8 mm) in 18 kt white gold with three rows of diamonds on bezel sides and a mother-of-pearl dial with a small second zone driven by a quartz movement.

LA STRADA   REF. 41/6619/9

Movement: mechanical, manual winding, Omega 730 caliber (realized in 1968), rectangular shape, size 16.4 x 9 mm, thickness 3.2 mm, 17 jewels, 21,660 vibrations per hour, power reserve 48 hours.
Functions: hour, minute.
Case: 18 kt yellow gold, two-piece case (domed rectangular case, made up by 4 full-volume elements and case back), anatomically curved (size 30 x 18.5 mm, thickness 9 mm); with double brilliant pavage on strap attachments; curved sapphire crystal; brand engraved on the left middle side; gold crown; curved case back attached by 4 screws. Water-resistant to 3 atm.
Dial: white, curved; printed Arabic numerals and railway minute track; gold bâton hands.
Strap: crocodile leather, recessed and fastened by lateral screws; gold clasp.
Also available: in pink gold; in yellow gold; without brilliants: in yellow gold; in pink or white gold; in other jewel versions; with quartz movement.

CHRONOSWISS

an historical perspective

In the words of Gerd-R. Lang, master watchmaker and founder of the Chronoswiss watch brand, "Watches are the world's most precise mechanical machines. But they'll never be able to explain the phenomenon of time."

THIS PAGE

TOP LEFT

Gerd-R. Lang, watchmaker extraordinaire.

TOP RIGHT

Lang personally signs the guarantee for every watch.

BOTTOM

The Tourbillon movement.

FACING PAGE

Chronoswiss unveils its first Tourbillon timepiece with Regulator dial.

A very interesting man and an astute master watchmaker, Lang is passionate about time and tracking it. He readily admits that the ticking that emanates from within a beautiful watchcase is a "loveable thing." Indeed, Lang has poured his heart and soul into creating elegant watchcases and intricately finishing mechanical watch movements that come together in masterful works of art.

In love with the tradition of watchmaking, Lang founded Chronoswiss in 1983 in Munich, Germany. Adhering to the strictest codes of excellence and technical prowess, Lang insisted that only mechanical timepieces in special and limited editions would ever be produced.

Initially, Lang purchased limited-edition, out-of-use special movements that he could embellish and improve upon. His timepieces so deftly embodied the spirit of heritage, combined with bold elegance, that they became international- ly recognized and coveted. Regularly, Chronoswiss has won awards and accolades for its technical mastery and artistic presentation.

Since 1990, the company has manufactured its watches exclusively, creating no more than 7,000 timepieces annually. Every component of Chronoswiss watches is produced in Switzerland, demonstrating the successful melding of the German spirit of enterprise and Swiss precision. Lang in- sists on meticulous hand finishing of movements, dials and cases, and, because each Chronoswiss timepiece is an expression of Lang's philosophy, he personally signs the certificate of guarantee that accompanies each watch.

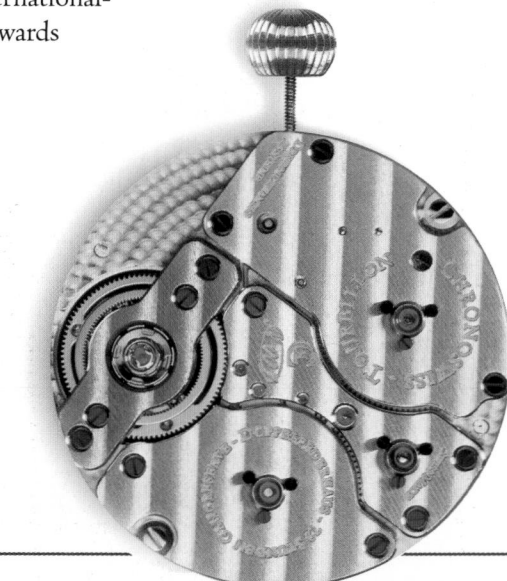

unveiling

masterpieces

Following its creed to make only fine mechanical timepieces that mark time with ultimate precision, Chronoswiss has unveiled its first tourbillon wristwatch. Housed in the very distinct fluted-bezel, 19-piece Chronoswiss case, the Tourbillon Regulator features a sterling silver guilloché dial that offers unparalleled, depth, dimension and beauty. In typical Chronoswiss style, the Regulator dial displays the hours in a subdial at 12:00, while the blued minute hand rotates around the entire face. An aperture at 6:00 allows viewing of the tourbillon, which was developed by Progress-Watch of Biel, Switzerland. The Chronoswiss logo in solid gold is artistically worked into the design of the tourbillon. This striking watch is available in platinum, 18-karat gold, gold and steel, or in steel.

Also in 2001, on the timelessly elegant side, Chronoswiss unveiled a new water-resistant Klassik Chronograph and a diamond Kairos model. The Klassik Chronograph, which made its debut in 1989 with much success, is an automatic winding chronograph of superb beauty. Until this past year, however, the nostalgic watch was not water resistant. Thanks to a special design of the pushpiece mechanism and the internal sealing system, there is no change in the look of the timepiece—a feat that took some time to accomplish. The watch is offered in 18-karat red or yellow gold, or in steel.

For years, recognizing that women appreciate mechanical timepieces, too, Chronoswiss has created smaller timepieces. The newest Kairos is available in two sizes, Kairos Lady and Kairos Medium, and glistens even more brightly with 60 brilliant VVSI Top Wesselton diamonds around the bezel for ultimate appeal.

THIS PAGE

TOP

The new Kairos watches are enhanced by 60 VVS1 Top Wesselton brilliants on the bezel.

TOP LEFT

Gerd-R. Lang at work.

LEFT CENTER

The Klassik Chronograph is now water resistant to 100 meters with no visible change in the striking appearance of the watch thanks to a specially created system.

BOTTOM CENTER

The ultra-bright Timemaster utilizes Super-LumiNova in its creation.

BOTTOM RIGHT

The Timemaster Diver watch is water resistant to 100 meters.

FACING PAGE

TOP

Lang's antique Jaguar XK 120.

LEFT CENTER

Team Chronoswiss in the Sieger Silvretta Classic race. Shown are Josefine Müller and Gerd-R. Lang.

RIGHT CENTER

The Bordmaster mounts easily and offers precise timing inside the cockpit.

BOTTOM

Years in the making, the Bordmaster for automobiles consists of a set of two separate timers.

CHRONOLOGY

1983 Gerd-Rüdiger Lang steps onto the horological scene with Chronoswiss, exceeding "expert" expectations with his mechanical watches.

1988 Chronoswiss is the first watchmaker to transfer the Regulator dial—used in large, precision timepiece clocks—to the wristwatch.

1990 The brand begins to exclusively manufacture its own models, producing between six thousand and eight thousand a year throughout the 1990s.

1992 The world premiere of the Swiss-patented, two-handed Rattrapante; Lang co-writes *Chronograph-Wristwatches*; The brand publishes its third catalog, *Chronoswiss—Faszination der Mechanik*.

1993 Chronoswiss introduces Cabrio, a European-patented reversible wristwatch; The Orea watches feature the first serially produced white enamel dials in several years.

1994 Unveiling of the internationally patented Grand Régulateur, which is awarded First Prize by the Italian magazine, *Orologi*.

1995 World premiere of Opus, the first serially produced, automatic, skeletonized chronograph.

1996 The Opus, an automatic skeleton chronograph, is chosen Watch of the Year by *Armbanduhren* magazine; Delphis is introduced and registers for a Swiss patent. Delphis is the first watch to combine a unique system of analog, digital and retrograde time displays.

1997 Chronoswiss serves as the official timekeeper for the Super Touring Car Cup; Delphis wins the third prize and Watch of the Year from *Armbanduhren* magazine.

1998 Pathos—the Swiss-patented, first skeletonized, self-winding fly-back chronograph—is introduced; The Delphis Jump Hour receives the Golden Balance Award from *Uhren* magazine; The Opus wins Watch of the Year honors from *World Photo Press* magazine in Japan; Chronoswiss's advertising campaign, Personality, earns the brand a Finalist Award at The New York Festival; The brand's first subsidiary is founded in Bellport, NY (Long Island) USA.

1999 Pathos is awarded First Prize and the Innovation Prize by *Chronos* magazine; Gerd-R. Lang and Josefine Müller win the Silvretta Classic Car Rally behind the wheel of a Jaguar XK 120 in Montafon, Austria.

2000 *Uhren* magazine honors Chronoswiss's Tora Chronograph with the Golden Balance/International Watch Award; *Signs of the Times—Tick-Talk: A Timely Book* is published in German as Chronoswiss's fourth catalog.

On the sportier side, Chronoswiss has expanded its very successful Timemaster series. First unveiled in the year 2000, the Timemaster is based on watches made for pilots and divers in the 1930s and '40s. This oversized rugged watch, with its 22-piece case, offers ultra-bright readability without a hint of radiation. Using an innovative Super-LumiNova C3 compound, the watch has up to 100 times higher intensity than traditional luminous materials. The new version offers a sweep seconds hand, two-day power reserve and bold new straps. It is water resistant to 100 meters and is designed for extreme sports.

An avid lover of vintage automobiles, and a prominent participant in key auto races, Gerd-R. Lang is obsessed with perfect timing—on the wrist and in the car. The great similarities between automobiles and timepieces in terms of high-level technology, tradition and emotions, stirred Lang to develop an in-car timing system based on the early 1900s car clock models. The result is the Bordmaster: an on-board, vintage-styled set of timers with Bordtimer and Stopmaster instruments.

The Bordtimer is a precision clock that indicates the time of day and/or the trip time. The Stopmaster is a functional fifth-of-a-second stop clock with a central 60-minute and peripheral 12-hour hand. The top-quality manual winding mechanisms feature shock absorption systems and are reserved exclusively for Chronoswiss. The timers are housed in solid aluminum cases and feature scratch-resistant, reflex-free sapphire crystals. On both models, a rotating bezel with marker enables the owner to set important targets or start times. This on-board system is the result of many years of experience, accumulated by Lang as an enthusiastic racing pilot and embodies the spirit of the traditional technology and conventional mechanics employed by Chronoswiss.

CHRONOSWISS

RÉGULATEUR À TOURBILLON   REF. CH 3121 R

Movement: mechanical, automatic winding, with flying tourbillon, Chronoswiss C361 caliber, Progress 6361.101 caliber base. Decorated with Côtes de Genève and circular graining. **Functions:** hour, minute.
Case: 18 kt pink gold, three-piece case (Ø 37 mm, thickness 10.5 mm); antireflective flat sapphire crystal; knurled bezel; brushed middle; crown with gold rim; screwed-on knurled back, displaying the movement through a sapphire crystal. Water-resistant to 3 atm.

Dial: solid silver, silvered, engine-turned (guilloché) by hand, aperture on the tourbillon; hour zone decorated with old-basket pattern; brushed hour ring; blued steel Poire hands hands.
Indications: off-center hour at 12 with printed Roman numerals, center minute with printed railway track and 5-minute progression
Strap: crocodile leather; screwed attachment; pink-gold clasp.
Also available: in yellow or while gold; in platinum, in steel and yellow gold; in steel. Bracelet only: steel, steel and yellow gold.

RÉGULATEUR   REF. CH 1223 KU

Movement: mechanical, automatic winding, Chronoswiss C122 caliber. **Functions:** hour, minute, small second.
Case: stainless steel, three-piece case (Ø 38 mm, thickness 10.3 mm); antireflective flat sapphire crystal; knurled screwed-on bezel; brushed middle; screwed-on knurled back, displaying the movement through a sapphire crystal. Water-resistant to 3 atm.

Dial: coppered; printed railway track with 5-minute progression; blued steel Stuart hands.
Indications: off-center hour at 12 with Roman numerals, center minute, small second at 6.
Strap: ostrich skin; screwed attachment; steel clasp.
Also available: with silver or black enameled dial; in steel and yellow gold, silver dial; in yellow gold, silver dial. Bracelet only: steel, steel and yellow gold; yellow gold.

CHRONOSCOPE   REF. CH 1523

Movement: mechanical, automatic winding, Chronoswiss C125 caliber, Enicar base modified by the addition of a chronograph module, 11'''3/4 (Ø 26.80 mm, thickness 6.80 mm), 30 jewels, 21,600 vibrations per hour. Pink gilded skeletonized rotor. **Functions:** hour, minute, small second, chronograph with one counter. **Case:** stainless steel, three-piece case (Ø 37 mm, thickness 12.25 mm); antireflective curved sapphire glass; knurled screwed-on bezel; brushed

middle; crown with with coaxial chronograph pusher; screwed-on knurled back displaying the movement through a sapphire glass. Water-resistant to 3 atm.
Dial: white enameled; blued steel Stuart hands.
Indications: off-center hour at 12 with printed Roman numerals, small second at 6, center minute and second counters, internal railway minute track and external 360° scale to measure fractions of a second with divisions for 1/6 of a second.
Strap: crocodile leather; screwed attachment; steel clasp.
Also available: in steel and yellow gold; white or yellow gold. Bracelt only: steel.

DELPHIS   REF. CH 1421 R

Movement: mechanical, automatic winding, Chronoswiss C 124 caliber, Enicar base modified to support digital jumping hour display and retrograde minute. Gilded rotor. **Functions:** jumping hour, minute, small second.
Case: 18 kt pink gold, three-piece case (Ø 38 mm, thickness 11 mm); flat antireflective sapphire crystal; knurled screwed-on bezel; brushed middle; crown with gold rim; screwed-on knurled back, displaying the movement through a

sapphire crystal. Water-resistant to 3 atm.
Dial: solid silver, silvered, second zone hand-turned (guilloché) with sun and old-basket patterns.
Indications: jumping hour in a window at 12, minute track and printed markers, blued stainless steel center retrograde Stuart hand, small second at 6.
Strap: crocodile leather; screwed attachment; pink-gold clasp.
Also available: in yellow gold; yellow or pink gold & stainless steel; steel; white gold; platinum; mother-of-pearl dial: steel, yellow gold & stainless steel, yellow gold.

CHRONOGRAPH RATTRAPANTE REF. CH 7321

Movement: automatic, Chronoswiss C 732 caliber, Valjoux 7750 caliber base modified to support the split-second chronograph and off-center hours and minutes functions. Rolled gold skeletonized rotor; blued screws, Côtes de Genève and circular graining finish. **Functions:** hour, minute, small second, split-second chronograph with 3 counters. **Case:** 18 kt yellow gold, three-piece case (Ø 38 mm, thickness 15.5 mm); antireflective curved sapphire crys-

tal; screwed-on knurled bezel; brudhed middle, crown and splitting pusher at 10; gold rim; screwed-on knurled back, displaying the movement through a sapphire crystal. Water-resistant to 3 atm. **Dial:** silvered, off-center hour and minute at 3 with printed Roman numerals and blued stainless steel Stuart hands. **Indications:** hour counter at 6, small second at 9, minute counter at 12, center second and split-second counters, minute track with divisions for 1/5 of a second and 5-second progression. **Strap:** crocodile leather; screwed attachment; gold clasp. **Also available:** in yellow gold & stainless steel. Bracelet only in steel, steel and yellow gold, yellow gold.

CHRONOGRAPH CHRONOMETER REF. CH 7523CD

Movement: mechanical, automatic winding, Chronoswiss C741 caliber Valjoux 7750 caliber base, modified to position the hand date at 3. Côtes de Genève and circular graining finish; blued screws; gilded and skeletonized rotor. Officially certified "chronometer" (C.O.S.C.). **Functions:** hour, minute, small second, date, chronograph with 3 counters. **Case:** stainless steel, three-piece case; (Ø 38 mm, thickness 14.7 mm); antireflective curved sapphire crystal; screwed-

on knurled bezel; brushed middle; screwed-on knurled back, displaying the movement through a sapphire crystal. Water-resistant to 3 atm. **Dial:** solid silver, silvered, engine-turned (guilloché); printed Arabic numerals, blued steel Breguet lozenge hands. **Indications:** date at 3, hour counter at 6, small second at 9, minute counter at 12, center second, minute track with divisions for 1/4 of a second. **Strap:** crocodile leather; screwed attachment; stainless steel clasp. **Also available:** in stainless steel and yellow or pink gold; in yellow or pink gold. With silver or black enameled dial. Bracelet only: in steel, stainless steel and yellow gold, yellow gold.

CHRONOGRAPH TORA REF. CH7423

Movement: automatic, Chronoswiss 742 caliber, Valjoux 7750 caliber base. Côtes de Genève and circular graining finish; skeletonized gilded rotor. **Functions:** hour, minute, small second, date, second time-zone time, 24-hour indication, chronograph with 3 counters. **Case:** stainless steel, three-piece case (Ø 38, thickness 15.5mm); antireflective curved sapphire crystal; screwed-on knurled bezel, brushed middle; pushers with non-skid finish: at 10 for fast second time-zone time correc-

tion, burnished; screwed-on knurled back, displaying the movement through a sapphire crystal. Water-resistant to 3 atm. **Dial:** solid silver, silvered, engine-turned (guilloché); printed Arabic numerals; blued steel Breguet lozenge hands. **Indications:** date at 3, hour counter at 6, small second and second time zone 24-hour (day-night) at 9, minute counter at 12, center second, minute track with divisions for 1/4 of a second. **Strap:** crocodile leather; screwed attachment; stainless steel clasp. **Also available:** black enameled dial; in stainless steel and yellow gold with silver dial; in yellow or white gold with silver dial. Bracelet only in steel, steel and yellow gold, yellow gold.

CHRONOGRAPH OPUS REF. CH 7523S

Movement: mechanical, automatic winding, Chronoswiss C741S caliber, Valjoux 7750 caliber base, modified to position the hand date indicator at 3,. Hand-skeletonized, rhodium-plated pillar-plate and bridges; blued screws; skeletonized rotor. **Functions:** hour, minute, small second, date, chronograph with 3 counters. **Case:** stainless steel, three-piece case (Ø 38, thickness 15 mm); antireflective curved sapphire crystal; screwed-on knurled bezel; brushed

middle; screwed-on knurled back, displaying the movement through a sapphire crystal. Water-resistant to 3 atm. **Dial:** solid silver, silvered, skeletonized; printed minute track; blued stainless steel Breguet hands. **Indications:** date at 3, hour counter at 6, small second at 9, minute counter at 12, center second counter, minute track with divisions for 1/5 of a second. **Strap:** crocodile leather, hand stitched; screwed attachment; stainless steel clasp. **Also available:** in yellow or pink gold & stainless steel; in yellow, pink or white gold. Bracelet only in steel; yellow gold & stainless steel; yellow gold.

CHRONOSWISS

CHRONOGRAPH LUNAR   REF. CH 7523LSW

Movement: mechanical, automatic winding, Chronoswiss C755 caliber, Valjoux 7750 caliber base. Rolled gold skeletonized rotor, blued screws.
Functions: hour, minute, small second, date, moon phase, chronograph with 3 counters. **Case:** stainless steel, three-piece case (Ø 38 mm, thickness 15 mm); antireflective curved sapphire crystal; screwed-on knurled bezel; brushed middle; screwed-on knurled back, displaying the movement through a sapphire crystal. Water-resistant to 3 atm.

Dial: solid silver, black enameled, engine-turned (guilloché); printed Arabic numerals; white enameled Breguet lozenge hands.
Indications: moon phase at 3, hour counter at 6, small second at 9, minute counter at 12, center second, minute track with divisions for 1/4 of a second, red-pointed center arrow-shaped date hand.
Strap: crocodile leather; screwed attachment; stainless steel clasp.
Also available: with silver dial; in yellow gold & stainless steel, with silver dial; in yellow, white or pink gold, silver dial; in platinum, silver dial. Bracelet only: steel; yellow gold & stainless steel; yellow gold.

LUNAR   REF. CH 9322

Movement: mechanical, automatic winding, Chronoswiss C931 caliber, ETA 2892A2 caliber base + full calendar module. Gilded skeletonized rotor.
Functions: hour, minute, center second, full calendar (date, day, month, moon phase). **Case:** stainless steel and 18 kt yellow gold, three-piece case (Ø 37 mm, thickness 10.7 mm); antireflective flat sapphire crystal; screwed-on knurled bezel; brushed middle with 4 correctors; crown with gold rim;

screwed-on knurled back, displaying the movement through a sapphire crystal. Water-resistant to 3 atm. **Dial:** solid silver, silvered, engine-turned (guilloché), zone decorated with old-basket pattern; brushed hour ring; printed Arabic numerals and minute track with 5-minute progression; rolled gold Breguet lozenge hands. **Indications:** date and moon phase at 6; day and month at 12. **Strap:** crocodile leather; screwed attachment; stainless steel & yellow gold clasp.
Also available: in stainless steel and pink gold, silver dial; in yellow or pink gold, silver dial; in while gold, silver dial; in steel, silver or black enameled dial. Bracelet only: steel, steel and yellow gold, yellow gold.

CHRONOGRAPH KLASSIK   REF. CH 7401 R SW

Movement: mechanical, automatic winding, Chronoswiss, C741 caliber, Valjoux 7750 caliber base, modified to position the hand date at 3. **Functions:** hour, minute, small second, chronograph with 3 counters.
Case: 18 kt pink gold, three-piece case (Ø 37, thickness 14.3 mm); horn-shaped lugs. antireflective curved sapphire crystal; rectangular pushers and crown with gold rim; snap-on back, displaying the movement through a sapphire crystal. Water-resistant to 3 atm.

Dial: black enameled, counters decorated with circular beads; applied pink-gold-plated square markers and Roman numerals; pink-gold-plated Railway hands. **Indications:** date at 3, hour counter at 6, small second at 9, minute counter at 12, center second, tachometer scale, minute track with divisions for 1/5 of a second.
Strap: crocodile leather; pink-gold clasp.
Also available: in pink gold & stainless steel; in steel. With silver or black enameled dial, also with pulsometer scale..

OREA AUTOMATIC   REF. CH 1263

Movement: mechanical, automatic winding, Chronoswiss caliber C 121.
Functions: hour, minute, small second.
Case: stainless steel, three-piece case (Ø 36.5 mm, thickness 8 mm); flat sapphire crystal; knurled bezel; onyx cabochon crown; screwed-on knurled case back with mineral glass bull's eye. Water-resistant to 3 atm.
Dial: white enameled; printed Arabic numerals and railway minute track; blued stainless steel Stuart hands.

Indications: small second at 6.
Strap: ostrich skin; screw connection; stainless steel clasp.
Price: 4.750.000 lire.
Also available: stainless steel and yellow gold; yellow or rose gold; with Roman numerals.

CHRONOSWISS

TIMEMASTER — REF. CH 6233 SW

Movement: mechanical, automatic winding, Chronoswiss C672 caliber.
Functions: hour, minute, second.
Case: stainless steel, three-piece case (Ø 43 mm, thickness 13 mm); antireflective curved sapphire crystal; knurled bezel turning in two ways with luminescent marker; brushed middle; oversized and jutting crown (the related tube is integrated in the case) allowing operations also with gloves; screwed-on knurled back, displaying the movement through a sapphire crystal. Water-resistant to 10 atm.
Dial: black enameled; luminescent baton and triangular markers and Arabic numerals; printed railway minute track; white enameled Railway hands.
Strap: extensible cowhide leather strap allowing to wear it on a pilot's suit; screwed attachment; steel fold-over clasp; furnished with a case containing spare accessories and an additional crocodile leather strap.
Also available: with luminescent dial, black Arabic numerals; version with crown on the right. Bracelet only: steel.

CABRIO — REF. CH 2673 SW

Movement: mechanical, automatic winding, ETA 2670 caliber, completely hand-assembled and hand-finished. Rolled gold skeletonized rotor. **Functions:** hour, minute, second.
Case: stainless steel, rectangular-shaped reversible case (size 32.3 x 23.3 mm, thickness 8.3 mm); flat sapphire crystal; case back attached by 8 screws, displaying the movement through a sapphire crystal. Water-resistant to 3 atm.
Dial: black enameled; printed bâton markers and railway minute track; applied Roman numerals; stainless steel bâton hands.
Bracelet: steel; screwed attachment; recessed double fold-over clasp.
Also available: with silver or copper dial, leather strap; in steel and yellow gold, leather strap, silver dial; in yellow gold, leather strap, silver dial.

KAIROS MEDIUM — REF. CH 2823KM

In 1995 Chronoswiss presented two new sizes of the most classical watch of their catalog: Kairos. The medium type, whose size is limited to a diameter of 34 millimeters and 8.3 mm thickness, is operated by the automatic movement ETA 2892-2 which is housed also by the larger model. This 21 jewel movement, completely hand-assembled and hand-finished by the House's watchmakers, has a diameter of 25.6 millimeters and a thickness of 3.6. The balance mounts an Incabloc shock-resistant system, in Glucydur, having a frequence of 28,800 vibrations per hour (vph) and the balance-spring is a first quality Nivarox. The rotor is skeletonized and in rolled gold. In the photograph the version with steel case and crocodile leather strap with stainless steel clasp.
Also available: with black dial; with steel bracelet; in steel and yellow gold, silvered dial, leather strap or bracelet; in yellow gold, silvered dial, leather strap. Large size (Ø 38 mm); little size (Ø 30mm).

KAIROS MEDIUM — REF. CH 2823 MDSW

Movement: mechanical, automatic winding, ETA 2892A2 caliber. Skeletonized rolled gold rotor.
Functions: hour, minute, second, date.
Case: stainless steel, three-piece case (Ø 34, thickness 8.7 mm); antireflective flat sapphire crystal; screwed-on bezel, set with diamonds; brushed middle; screwed-on knurled back, displaying the movement through a sapphire crystal. Water-resistant to 3 atm.
Dial: solid silver, black, engine-turned (guilloché); white Arabic numerals and Breguet hands.
Indications: date at 6.
Bracelet: stainless steel; screwed attachment; stainless steel fold over safety clasp.
Also available: with silvered dial; with leather strap. With knurled bezel without diamonds: in stainless steel, black or silvered dial, steel bracelet or leather strap; in steel and yellow gold, silvered dial, leather strap or bracelet; in yellow gold, silvered dial, leather strap. Large size (Ø 38 mm); little size (Ø 30mm).

CLERC

an historical perspective

Heir to a longstanding family tradition handed down from one generation to the next, Clerc has been cultivating a taste for exceptional watchmaking since 1874. For more than 125 years, the watches bearing this well-recognized signature have consistently been known for their avant-garde design and exceptional quality. The new collection designed by Gérald Clerc pursues the path laid by the original founders of the family firm in Paris—namely a will to create unique and sophisticated watches.

Clerc has always been skilled in capturing the spirit of the times. In the aftermath of World War I, the popularity of wristwatches inspired the brand to design new creations combining precious stones and time display. During successive periods, they developed jewelry watches and classic models. Gérald Clerc continues to draw inspiration for his own collections from this rich heritage, thereby perpetuating the founders' goals: the pursuit of elegance and unwavering standards of craftsmanship.

Throughout its history, Clerc has signed prestigious creations for highly recognized personalities. The Clerc name is associated with crowned heads such as Princess Grace of Monaco; heads of state such as General Charles de Gaulle, Khrushchev, Sheikh Abdullah El Zawir; artists including Salvador Dali, Paco Rabanne, Françoise Hardy, and Maurice Chevalier; and more recently, Michael Douglas, Jack Scalia and Ewan McGregor.

THIS PA[GE]

TOP LEFT

Gérald Clerc oversees every aspect of design and development.

TOP RIGHT

Clerc's original flagship location after its inception in 1874.

BOTTOM LEFT

This one-of-a-kind Clerc bangle bracelet watch, circa 1920, is elegantly crafted in platinum and bedecked in diamonds.

FACING PAGE

Princess Grace Kelly of Monaco.

distinctive styling

For sporty appeal, Clerc offers the CXX Chronograph®. Designed for extreme conditions and professional use, this diving watch features mechanical complications in several combinations. Water resistant to 300 meters and fitted with a rotating bezel, screw-locked crown and natural rubber strap, this diving watch is made to confront the elements. The CXX Chronograph was designed and developed in cooperation with a team of diving professionals well acquainted with the underwater world. Handcrafted in Switzerland, each Clerc CXX Chronograph is individually numbered and comes with a 3-year international warranty.

The CI25® bracelet design is graced with a natural, flowing feel, encircling the wrist so gently that its touch could almost go unnoticed. The CI25 rectangular cuff watch is enhanced by a fine row of diamonds on the case, and is also available as a stunning piece of jewelry with diamonds spilling over the case and bracelet.

TOP LEFT

This striking pink sapphire watch attests to the technical prowess in gemsetting mastered by Clerc.

TOP RIGHT

C125 rectangular cuff watch is available in vibrantly-colored leather straps.

BOTTOM

From the C125 collection of ladies' watches, this steel bracelet with diamonds houses a precision quartz movement.

CLERC

exceptional creations

The C-Collection® of timepieces is a powerful modern design combined with a level of excellence and quality synonymous with Clerc. A perfect blend of elegance and technology, the watches in this series are fashioned and sculpted from solid steel or 18-karat gold. Gold versions are stamped with the prestigious Clé de Genève quality hallmark. Handcrafted in Geneva, each Clerc C-Collection watch is individually numbered and comes with a 3-year international warranty.

As an extension of the C-Collection, Clerc has unveiled the C-Collection Complications series, which includes a men's steel automatic Power Reserve and Two-Timer Power Reserve.

Montres Clerc created a precedent by opening the path into the delicate art of marrying precious stones with the chilled elegance of steel. In addition to rubies, diamonds and blue sapphires, Clerc has added black diamonds and pastel colored sapphires to what is known as the Red, White & Blue® collection. Handcrafted in Switzerland, each of these watches is individually numbered and comes with a 3-year international warranty.

CONCORD

an historical perspective

Nearly 100 years ago, in 1908, Concord Watch Company was founded on the principles of achieving aesthetic and technical excellence in all it creates.

Its first timepieces were elegant and sophisticated works of art that bespoke perfection. Focusing on superb craftsmanship and insisting that technology and intricacy come together in unbridled beauty, Concord soared to international acclaim.

THIS PAGE
BOTTOM

The La Scala Stainless Steel Diamond Chronograph houses a multi-function quartz movement.

FACING PAGE

Concord's La Scala Stainless Steel Diamond Chronograph is especially appealing in an array of pastel hues with color-coordinated soleil dials and alligator straps.

Being one of the first to master the ultra-thin movement enabled the brand to offer innovative and distinctive women's watches. In the 1920s and '30s, Concord secured its reputation as a jeweler extraordinaire by producing scintillating, ultra-thin diamond and gemstone watches set in platinum that captured hearts and commanded attention around the world.

Throughout the ensuing decades, Concord continually set new standards in watchmaking sophistication and innovation. In 1979, the watchmaker impressed and delighted the world with its introduction of the Delirium—the thinnest watch ever made. This quartz timepiece measured just under 2mm. Within a year, Concord had already outdone itself, unveiling the Concord Delirium IV, which broke the 1mm barrier. This striking feat of technical prowess set a world record for watch thinness that still stands today.

Concord is a brand that prides itself on successfully combining technological achievement with sophisticated design. Among its exquisite, one-of-a-kind introductions are spectacularly jeweled creations such as the Saratoga Exor in three different breathtaking renditions—one each in ruby, emerald and sapphire—housing tourbillon, minute repeater and perpetual calendar.

Today, this master watchmaker continues to create specialty pieces that complement its innovative collection of bold and beautiful timepieces. Additionally, the brand—ever the pacesetter in the sophisticated art of watchmaking—focuses on design as the premier factor in each creation—ensuring an immediately recognizable timepiece every time.

Concord's collection of cutting-edge designs runs the gamut from the geometrically inspired and strikingly elegant La Scala to the classically bold Impresario with coin-edged detail to the avant-garde Crystale with sapphire crystal case. Each one of Concord's timepieces reflects the brand's commitment to its founding philosophies of unparalleled style and enduring appeal.

CONCORD

sleek sophistication

Most recently, Concord focused intently on its forward-thinking, smoothly sculpted La Scala family of timepieces, which was first introduced in 1997. Boldly uniting stainless steel and gemstones for a fashion emphasis that is at once both timely and timeless, Concord has carved a new niche for itself in the world of color and creativity.

Concord has unveiled unisex models, pale pastel-coordinated ladies' models, dramatic chronographs and high-tech versions of the La Scala Stainless Steel timepieces that excite the eye with black PVD cases, rubber straps and even black or champagne diamonds. Already a statement of bold individuality thanks to its unique reflection of architectural elements, the La Scala Stainless Steel collection rises to new heights with the latest renditions.

In typical Concord style, women are the center of attention in the newest collection, which offers unsurpassed versatility. The La Scala Stainless Steel Diamond Chronograph is offered either on a strap or bracelet and easily can be switched back and forth by an authorized Concord retailer. The collection includes an elegantly detailed pink, blue or silvertone soleil dial, a choice of three diamond case variations and a multitude of interchangeable alligator straps in sophisticated shades. Designed to maximize wardrobing options, this dramatic and colorful chronograph can be changed in accordance with fashion trends, season or whim.

THIS PAGE
TOP LEFT

This year, Concord's La Scala Stainless Steel timepieces are accentuated by sophisticated black diamonds.

TOP RIGHT

Concord's newest ad campaign, "be late."

BOTTOM

The La Scala Stainless Steel ladies' model with full diamond bezel and diamond case-to-bracelet attachments features an elegant mother-of-pearl dial with diamond markers.

FACING PAGE
TOP

The unisex-sized La Scala Stainless Steel Diamond Chronograph offers black and white diamonds in elegant proportions.

BOTTOM

Scintillating champagne diamonds accent these striking renditions of the La Scala Stainless Steel Diamond Chronograph with a matte tan or white alligator strap.

CHRONOLOGY

1908 Concord Watch Company SA is founded in Bienne, Switzerland as a manufacturer of high-quality watches, particularly for the American market.

1909 An American subsidiary is opened in New York City.

1918 Following World War I, Concord secures its reputation as jeweler extraordinaire, producing private-label platinum watches brilliant with diamonds, emeralds, rubies and sapphires.

1945 President Harry Truman presents Concord Ring Clock, the first portable eight-day winding travel alarm clock, to heads of state, including Winston Churchill and Joseph Stalin, at the Potsdam Conference.

1969 Concord Watch Company is purchased by Gedalio Grinberg and incorporated into North American Watch Corporation in New York City.

1979 Launch of the quartz-powered Concord Delirium, the thinnest watch in the world (1.98mm). Soon, Delirium IV will break the 1mm barrier, a world record that will remain unchallenged.

1980 Launch of Concord Mariner, a versatile sport watch that is both water resistant and elegantly thin.

1986 Introduction of the highly acclaimed Concord Saratoga, an elegant sport luxury watch of artistic symmetry and sophisticated design.

1995 Concord sets new standards in watchmaking with spectacularly jeweled, one-of-a-kind timepieces such as Saratoga Exor, one of the most expensive watches ever made.

1998 Introduction of the contemporary, yet classic Concord Impresario Collection with signature coin-edge detailing, and the extraordinarily precise Impresario Mechanique Collection.

1999 Concord makes its way to the Academy Awards as diamond Veneto and Mira models are worn on the red carpet by Whoopi Goldberg and Geena Davis, respectively.

2000 Celebrating the new millennium, Concord introduces La Scala Stainless Steel, an updated version of its signature 18-karat gold La Scala; A new lifestyle advertising campaign boldly encourages consumers to "be late."; Concord's one-of-a-kind, movie-themed Crystale watches are worn by Hollywood elite at the Academy Awards.

2001 La Scala Stainless Steel Diamond Chronograph offers unmatched versatility with a choice of colored dials and diamond cases, on bracelet and/or with a wide range of colored alligator straps. La Scala Stainless Steel timepieces are included in the Oscar gift basket for award presenters and winners.

The original ladies' La Scala Stainless Steel watches on bracelets don diamonds of varying degrees, creating shimmering style statements. Several feature diamond bezels, diamond case-to-bracelet attachments, and diamond markers on exquisite mother-of-pearl dials. Always the trendsetter, Concord has also incorporated the increasingly popular black diamond into its stainless steel La Scala.

Daring to be different, the brand has added meticulously cut black diamonds and interplayed them with their white counterparts for a dramatic look that exudes magnificence and mystery at the same time. These striking black beauties also adorn the newest unisex-sized La Scala Stainless Steel Chronograph. With its combined polished and satin-finished case, the multi-function quartz chronograph is set with 30 black diamonds with 12 white diamond case accents.

Color plays a dramatically important role in the brand's line this year, too, as the La Scala Stainless Steel Diamond Chronograph offers exuberance with fancy colored champagne diamonds. This exceptional sport luxury watch combines form, function and finesse with its crisp dial with diamond markers. The watch is offered with either a coordinating white or tan alligator strap for a sophisticated and distinct style. These gemstone models are the perfect complement to the unisex chronographs that feature pink, blue or silvertone dials and color-coordinated straps.

harmony reinterpreted

As with all great things, Concord continually seeks to accomplish more and offer more to its discerning customers. The overall effect is a fresh harmony of color, material, technology and precision.

Cleverly combining the scintillating black diamond with the dramatic impact of high technology, the watchmaker offers a PVD-coated steel case for a dark and mysterious rendition of the unisex-sized La Scala Stainless Steel Diamond Chronograph. The PVD heating process used on steel produces a high fashion, durable black coating that offers high-tech appeal. The polished black case is then fully set with black diamonds for a sleek look that is accented only by the most striking colored straps—red, white, blue or yellow.

Concord has also incorporated some cutting-edge materials into its men's line. The newest men's La Scala Stainless Steel Chronograph utilizes a black rubber strap, a blue/black or silvertone soleil dial, and a color-coordinated cabochon-sapphire crown.

While high-tech materials and stainless steel with precious stones have become an all-important statement, Concord recognizes that its sophisticated customer still craves the stunning

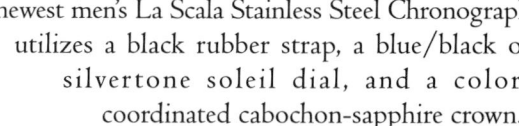

TOP LEFT

Concord cleverly combines PVD technology with stunning black diamonds for a dramatic edge in this high-performance La Scala Stainless Steel Diamond Chronograph.

TOP RIGHT

The La Scala Stainless Steel Chronograph has fresh appeal with a silvertone or blue/black soleil dial.

BOTTOM

This La Scala Stainless Steel Chronograph sports a black rubber strap for high-tech appeal.

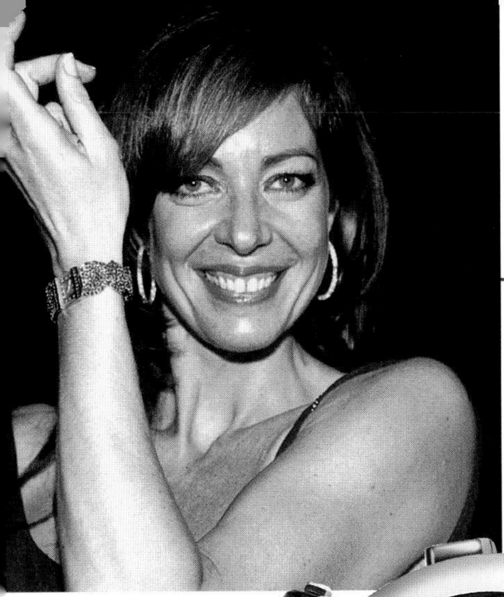

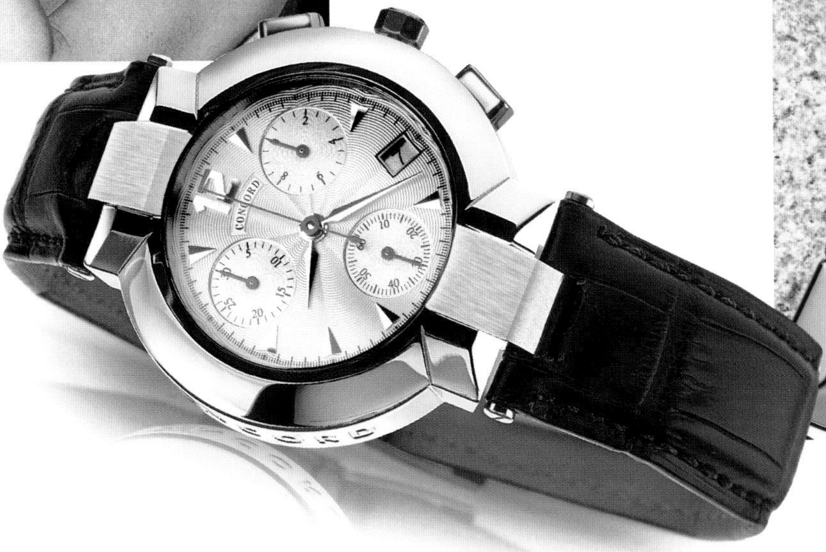

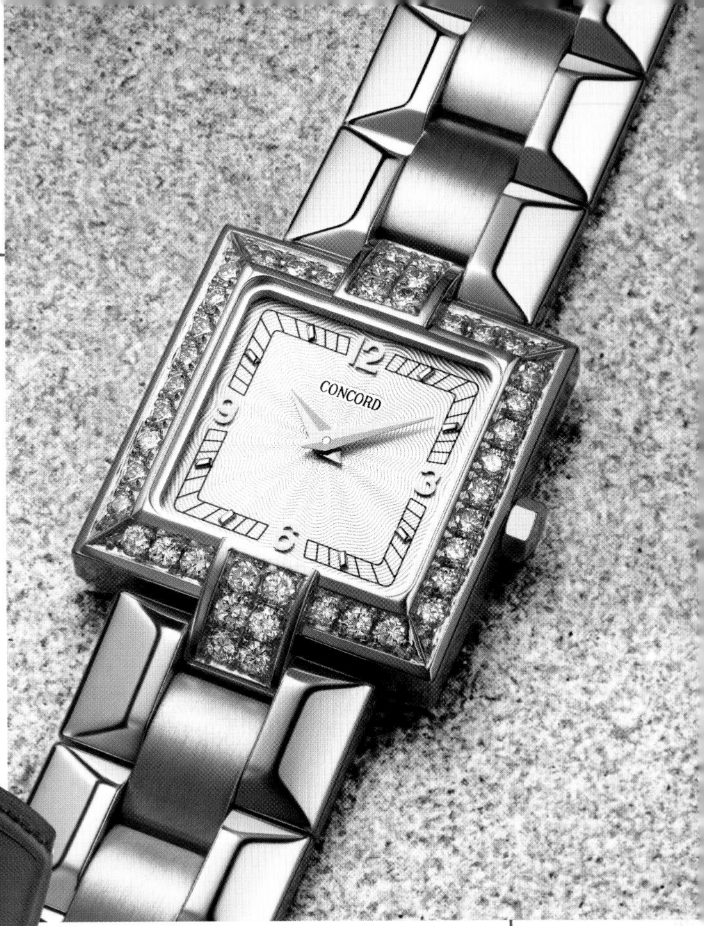

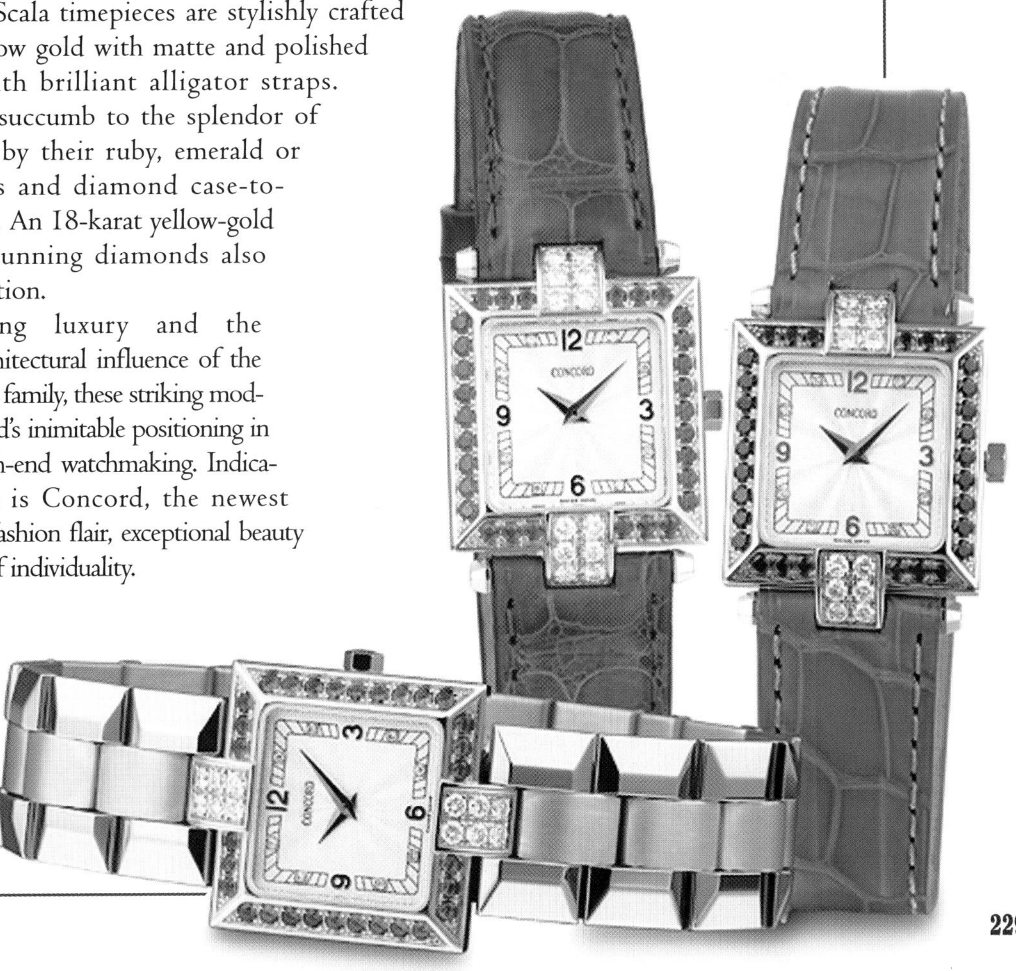

TOP LEFT

Actress Allison Janney of "American Beauty" wore a special one-of-a-kind timepiece designed by Concord and inspired by the Best Picture-winning film. The "American Beauty" watch featured a bracelet made of interlocking ruby-set "rose" petals.

TOP CENTER

A noteworthy addition to the La Scala Stainless Steel Chronograph collection is this striking men's soleil dial version.

TOP RIGHT

The square La Scala is elegantly crafted in 18-karat yellow gold and accented with a full diamond bezel for exquisite sheen.

BOTTOM

Concord never forgets its heart and soul—the brand now reinterprets the 18-karat gold square La Scala with precious gems for alluring beauty.

18-karat gold models that earned the brand international acclaim. Thus, the original square La Scala has been reinterpreted with precious gems.

Alluringly opulent, yet seductively understated, the new square La Scala timepieces are stylishly crafted in 18-karat yellow gold with matte and polished bracelets or with brilliant alligator straps. They elegantly succumb to the splendor of color provided by their ruby, emerald or sapphire bezels and diamond case-to-bracelet accents. An 18-karat yellow-gold version with stunning diamonds also graces the collection.

Epitomizing luxury and the sophisticated architectural influence of the Concord La Scala family, these striking models verify the brand's inimitable positioning in the world of high-end watchmaking. Indicative of all that is Concord, the newest timepieces offer fashion flair, exceptional beauty and a true sense of individuality.

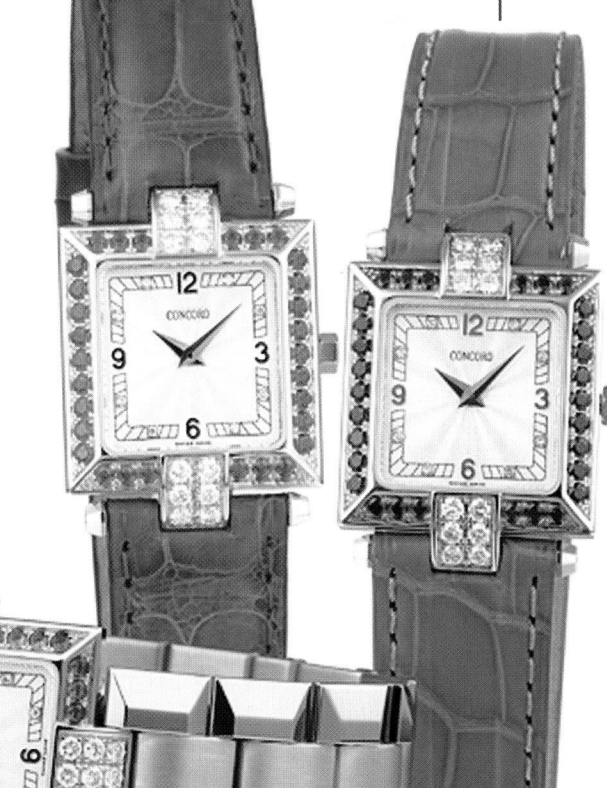

CONCORD

MINUTE REPEATER CARILLON DAME

Movement: mechanical, hand winding with 45 hours autonomy.
Functions: hours and minutes; hour, quarter and minute repeater with chime.
Shape: round.
Diameter: mm 24.25.
Thickness: mm 5.00.
Jewels: 33.
Balance: with adjusting screws in gold, with two arms.
Frequency: 18,000 vibrations per hour.
Spiral: flat, first quality.
Shockabsorber system: Kif.
Note: the pillar-plate is decorated with circular graining pattern, the bridges with Côtes de Genève and beveled. The spiral adjustment system, the repeater hammers and the screw heads are specular-polished and beveled. A third hammer (not visible in the photograph because it is concealed under the other two), which strikes a third timbre, makes this very small-sized movement be the smallest wrist "Chime" that was ever produced. On the dial side (see photograph) between 5 and 8 there are the different components (with respect to the corresponding caliber used also by other Houses) realized on an exclusive basis for Concord to activate the chime function.

A MUSICAL CASKET

To celebrate its 90th anniversary, Concord (founded in Bienne in 1908) put together, in an extraordinary casket, three couples of unique pieces, all animated by refined movements with minute repeater and "dressed" with the Impresario case, presented last year in Basel. The six men's and lady's models have cases in pink gold, platinum and platinum with brilliants. The men's model (Ø 35 mm) is animated by a movement with hand winding, developed in cooperation with a specialized atelier. The following elements are worthwhile noting: the regulator adjustment system by micrometer screw and swan-neck shaped check spring, the endstone of the escapement wheel in a steel collet held in place by a screw and the gullet teeth of the ratchet wheel to improve the rolling and silencing. The lady version possibly mounts an even more sophisticated movement that the man version. In fact, the chime is housed in a very small sized space (here we see the dial face). As a result, the sound of the minute repeater is transformed into a little wrist concert. The lady version with a Ø 27 mm platinum case with diamonds on bezel and dial (bottom), houses a two-stage slide which, on that side of the case middle, interrupts the appearing knurling typical of the Impresario case.

IMPRESARIO MINUTE REPEATER   REF. 52-G4-0215-2204-31/977

Movement: mechanical, hand winding, developed by Concord in cooperation with a specialized atelier; regulator adjustment system by micrometer screw, endstone on the escapement wheel. Decorated with Côtes de Genève pattern and beveled.
Functions: hours, minutes, minute repeater.
Case: 18 kt pink gold, two-piece (Ø 35 mm, thickness 10.5 mm); smooth sapphire crystal; spider-shaped lugs; grooved case middle; pink gold crown; snap-on back with a sapphire crystal bull's eye. Water-resistant to 3 atm.
Dial: silvered with graining pattern, with the different levels profiled with a thin engine-turned (guilloché) thread, applied pink-gold-plated Roman numerals at the quarters; screen-printed dial-train; pink-gold-plated Alpha hands.
Strap: crocodile leather; pink gold clasp.
Unique piece.
Also available: in lady's size, unique piece Ref. 52-G5-02160-2205-31/977.

IMPRESARIO MINUTE REPEATER LADY   REF. 81-G5-0260-2205-31/999S

Movement: mechanical, hand winding, developed by Concord in cooperation with a specialized atelier; chime sonnerie with three hammers, endstone on the escapement wheel. Decorated with Côtes de Genève pattern and beveled.
Functions: hours, minutes, minute repeater, chime.
Case: platinum, two-piece (Ø 27.3 mm, thickness 10 mm); smooth sapphire crystal; spider-shaped lugs; bezel with baguette cut diamonds with invisible embedding (24 stones, 1.59 kt); grooved case middle; platinum crown with an embedded rosette cut diamond; snap-on back with a sapphire crystal bull's eye. Water-resistant to 3 atm.
Dial: white gold; diamonds with flush and invisible embedding in the central disc; trapezoidal cut diamond markers, with invisible embedding; screen-printed dial-train; blued steel leaf style hands.
Strap: crocodile leather; platinum clasp set with baguette diamonds.
Unique piece.

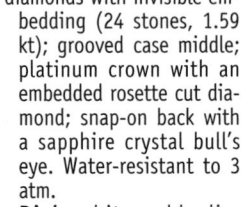

IMPRESARIO MAESTRO MASTERPIECE REF. 80-J6-0212-0000-1/0019

Movement: mechanical, manual winding, Concord caliber J6, developed by the House in cooperation with a specialized factory; with tourbillon and steel carriage. Beveled three-block mirror finish and Côtes de Genève finished.

Functions: hour, minute, perpetual calendar (day, date, month), chronograph with 2 counters, minute repeater.

Case: platinum (platinum weight 86 gr.), two-piece (Ø 38 mm, thickness 14 mm); spider-shaped lugs; 2 correctors on the grooved case side; white gold repeater slide on case side; white gold crown and pushers; flat sapphire crystal; snap-on back displaying the movement through a sapphire crystal.

Dial: silvered, engine turned (guilloché), aperture on the tourbillon; applied bâton markers; printed minute track; Alpha hands.

Indications: minute counter and day at 3, month at 9, date at 12, second central counter, minute track with divisions for $1/5$ of a second.

Strap: crocodile leather; platinum clasp.

Single piece. 10 year guarantee.

Once again Concord choose the stage of the Basel Show to present their last masterpieces of mechanic engineering. The two great complications are realized as single pieces and presented in the Impresario Maestro Masterpiece collection. The common features are the tourbillon (with hand-finished and hand-polishes steel carriage), the chronograph with 2 counters and the minute repeater. The platinum model has also the perpetual calendar feature, while the pink gold model has the power reserve. Their realization took one year and a half, due to both the intrinsic mechanic complexity (the first is made up by 525 parts and 38 jewels for a total of 9.25 mm height, and the second by 441 parts and 38 jewels for 7.65 mm), and the high general level of finish of all the components of the movement and case, even of the hidden ones. The Impresario Maestro Masterpieces are presented in a valuable case with an authenticity certificate and a 10 year guarantee.

IMPRESARIO MAESTRO MASTERPIECE REF. 80-J6-0212-0000-1/0019

IMPRESARIO MAESTRO MASTERPIECE REF. 52-J7-0212-0000-1/0020

Movement: mechanical, manual winding, Concord caliber J7, developed by the House in cooperation with a specialized factory; with tourbillon and steel carriage. Beveled three-block mirror finish and Côtes de Genève finished.

Functions: hour, minute, small second, chronograph with 2 counters, power reserve, minute repeater.

Case: 18 kt pink gold (gold weight 55 gr.), two-piece (Ø 38 mm, thickness 12 mm); spider-shaped lugs; grooved case side; pink gold crown and pushers; flat sapphire crystal; pink gold repeater slide on case side; snap-on back, displaying the movement through a sapphire crystal.

Dial: silvered engine turned (guilloché), aperture on the tourbillon; applied bâton markers; printed minute track; Alpha hands.

Indications: minute counter at 3, small second at 9, power reserve at 12, center second counter, minute track with divisions for $1/5$ of a second.

Strap: crocodile leather; pink gold clasp.

Unique piece. 10 year guarantee.

IMPRESARIO MAESTRO MASTERPIECE

The "minor" model (though it is a relatively minor watch, because its price exceeds 250,000$) of the new complicated ones recently presented by Concord, belongs to the Maestro Masterpiece collection. Made of 18 kt pink gold, it combines a minute repeater and a two-counter chronograph with the indication of the power reserve. For its realization - and the same is true for the model provided with a perpetual calendar - technicians and watchmakers have been working for over one year and a half, due to its intrinsic mechanical complexity (its movement, a caliber J7 Concord, is made up by 441 parts) as well as to the general high level of its finish which involves all the components of movement and case, obviously including those which cannot be seen. The Impresario Maestro Masterpiece models are supplied in a prestigious case and are accompanied by a certificate of authenticity and 10-years guarantee.

CONCORD

IMPRESARIO CHRONOGRAPH   REF. 14-G9-0211-2202-1/231BA

Movement: mechanical, automatic winding, Zenith El Primero caliber 41.1. Côtes Circulaires finished rotor, circular graining finished bridges. Officially certified "chronometer" (C.O.S.C.).
Functions: hour, minute, small second, chronograph with 3 counters, full calendar (date, day, month).
Case: stainless steel, two-piece case (Ø 38 mm, thickness 12.2 mm); spider-

shaped lugs; flat sapphire crystal; grooved case side; 1 corrector on case side; elliptic pushers; snap-on back displaying the movement through a sapphire crystal. Water-resistant to 3 atm.
Dial: silvered, engine turned (guilloché); applied pointed markers (Arabic numeral 12); printed minute track; Alpha hands.
Indications: small second at 9, minute counter at 3, hour counter at 6, month at 2, date between 4 and 5, day at 10, center second counter, minute track with divisions for $^1/5$ of a second.
Strap: crocodile leather; stainless steel clasp.
Also available: with bracelet; black dial; pink gold silvered dial, leather strap, with bracelet; brown or blue crocodile leather strap.

IMPRESARIO CHRONOGRAPH

In this model, as in many others of the Impresario collection, Concord adopted the Zenith movements, subsequently refined and decorated according to their high-level specifications. In this case we are in front of a Zenith El Primero caliber, in the version with complete calendar. It is worthwhile noting the personalization of decorations (Côtes Circulaires on the rotor and circular graining on bridges) and the eccentric screw system for the precise regulation

of the regulator; the screw is flame-blued and its head is hand-polished. Zenith El Primero, up to now the only chronograph with a balance working frequency of 36,000 vibrations per hour (vph), underwent also the C.O.S.C. tests and obtained the chronometer certification.

IMPRESARIO GMT   REF. 14-G6-0220-2204-1/251

Movement: mechanical, automatic winding, Zenith Élite caliber 682. Côtes Circulaires finished rotor, circular graining finished bridges. Officially certified "chronometer" (C.O.S.C.).
Functions: hour, minute, small second, date, second time zone, 24-hour indication.
Case: stainless steel, two-piece case (Ø 35 mm, thickness 8 mm); spider-

shaped lugs; flat sapphire crystal; grooved case side; 1 corrector on case side; crown for the adjustment of the second time zone; snap-on back displaying the movement through a sapphire crystal. Water-resistant to 3 atm.
Dial: silvered, engine turned (guilloché); applied pointed markers (Arabic numerals 6 and 12); printed minute track; Dauphine hands.
Indications: date at 3, red painted second-time-zone central hand, small second at 9.
Strap: crocodile leather; stainless steel clasp.
Also available: black dial; pink gold, silvered dial; brown, blue or bordeaux crocodile leather strap.

IMPRESARIO POWER RESERVE   REF. 14-G8-0220-2204-4/261BA

Movement: mechanical, manual winding, Zenith Élite "HW". Officially certified "chronometer" (C.O.S.C.).
Functions: hour, minute, small second, date, power reserve.
Case: stainless steel, two-piece case (Ø 35 mm, thickness 8 mm); spider-shaped lugs; flat sapphire crystal; grooved case side; snap-on back displaying the movement through a sapphire crystal. Water-resistant to 3 atm.

Dial: black, engine turned (guilloché); applied pointed markers (Arabic numerals 6 and 12); printed minute track; Dauphine hands.
Indications: date between 4 and 5, power reserve at 2, small second at 9.
Strap: crocodile leather; stainless steel clasp.
Also available: silvered dial; pink gold, silvered dial; brown or blue crocodile leather strap.

IMPRESARIO SMALL SECOND   REF. 52-G7-0220-2203-1/242RE

Movement: mechanical, automatic winding, Zenith Élite caliber 680. Côtes Circulaires finished rotor, circular graining finished bridges. Officially certified "chronometer" (C.O.S.C.).
Functions: hour, minute, small second, date.
Case: 18 kt pink gold, two-piece case (Ø 35 mm, thickness 7 mm); spider-shaped lugs; flat sapphire crystal; grooved case side; snap-on back displaying the movement through a sapphire crystal. Water-resistant to 3 atm.
Dial: silvered engine turned (guilloché); applied pointed markers (Arabic numerals 6 and 12); printed minute track; Alpha hands.
Indications: date between 4 and 5; small second at 9.
Strap: crocodile leather; pink gold clasp.
Also available: black crocodile leather strap.

SARATOGA PERPETUAL CALENDAR "BOUTIQUE"

Concord, since the beginnings, made itself familiar with jeweller's craft. In fact, one must not forget that in 1915 they produced, for the account of clients such as Tiffany and Cartier, mostly very sophisticated watches, in platinum and studded with diamonds, emeralds, rubies and sapphires. It is the beauty of these stones that inspired the creation of four Perpetual Calendars of the Saratoga collection called "Boutique". The photograph shows the version with brilliants and emeralds set on the bezel, but there are also three models with rubies, sapphires or only diamonds, always set on the bezel riders and alternating with brilliants. These "colored" versions have also cabochons on the crown and leather straps of the same color tone as the stones chosen. All the dials of these jewel-watches are in mother-of-pearl (sky-blue for the version with sapphires) with silvered center zone decorated with refined engine turned (guilloché) pattern.
Also available: with rubies, sapphires or only diamonds.

RECTANGULAR   REF. 14-36-0622-2113-4/131BA

Movement: quartz, next with mechanical movement and automatic winding.
Functions: hour, minute, center second, date.
Case: steel, two-piece rectangular-curved case, polished and brushed (at lugs and without crown 37.8 mm, width 26.3 mm, thickness 7.2 mm); curved sapphire crystal; crown with case protection; case back attached by 4 screws. Water-resistant to 3 atmospheres.
Dial: black, guilloché at center and brushed hour ring; applied pointed markers (Arabic numerals 6 and 12); luminescent dots on the printed railway minute track; luminescent sword style hands.
Indications: date at 3.
Strap: leather, stainless steel fold-over clasp.
Also available: strap in brown, bordeaux, green or blue leather; with bracelet; with dial bordeaux, silvered, green, blue or salmon. In the same versions, in lady's size.

CRYSTALE

Movement: mechanical, manual winding, extra-thin, Frédéric Piguet 8,10 caliber, entirely skeletonized and hand-chased.
Functions: hour, minute.
Case: platinum, two-piece case (size 30.5 x 25.5 mm); flat sapphire glass of considerable thickness; white-gold crown; back attached by 4 screws, displaying the movement through a sapphire crystal. Water-resistant to 3 atm.
Dial: consisting of an adapter element for the movement, decorated with circular graining pattern and the skeletonized movement; blued steel Alpha hands.
Strap: crocodile leather; platinum clasp.
Also available: in white gold or white gold and diamonds.

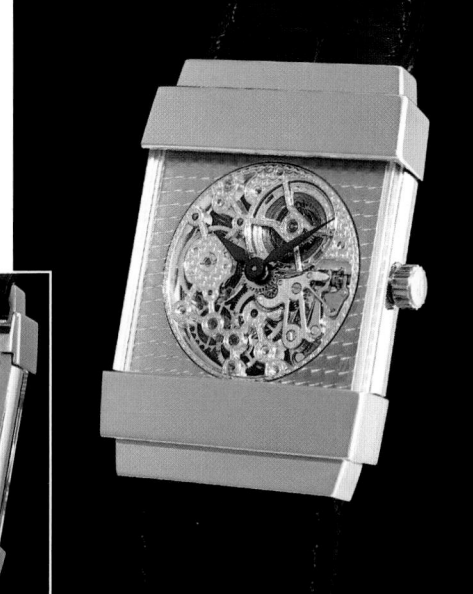

CONCORD

LA SCALA

Movement: quartz, ETA.
Functions: hour, minute.
Case: 18 kt white gold, two-piece case with two set brilliants; flat sapphire glass; octagonal white-gold crown; brand engraved on the middle; back attached by screws. Water-resistant to 3 atm.
Dial: white gold, high-polished; 1 row of brilliant around the central disc, 1 row of mother-of-pearl pieces and embossed logo below 12; 2 rows of brilliants on the external ring with embossed white-gold Roman numerals at quarters; white-gold Dauphine hands.
Bracelet: white gold and brilliant set in central links; fold-over clasp.

LA SCALA

Movement: quartz, ETA.
Functions: hour, minute.
Case: stainless steel, two-piece case; bezel with 22 set brilliants; flat sapphire glass; hexagonal crown; brand engraved on the middle; back attached by screws. Water-resistant to 3 atm.
Dial: mother-of-pearl; 10 brilliant markers, 12 and 6 applied rhodium-plated Arabic numerals; rhodium-plated Dauphine hands.
Bracelet: stainless steel; fold-over clasp.

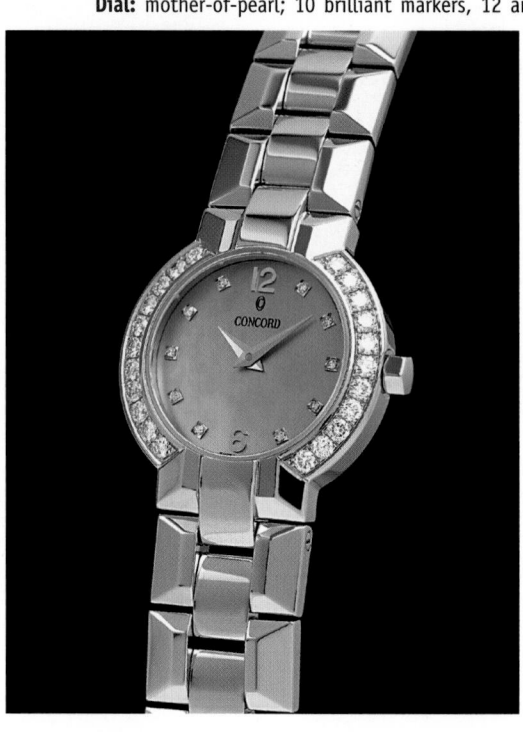

LA SCALA

The polished case with its rounded shape, characterizing the La Scala family, many years after its launching, becomes again the protagonist in a series of both extra-luxury proposals in gold and less sophisticated and modern versions in stainless steel or combined with rubber straps. For the latter, that are in no way inferior to the others in terms of elegance, Concord chose dials in silvered tones for men (also with diamonds), while white and blue mother-of-pearl, also luckily combined with set brilliants as hour markers, was reserved for ladies. "Luxury" versions are meant for more sophisticated and selected customers who prefer (yellow or white) gold as a symbol for elegance and brilliants set on cases, dials and bracelets, within artistic geometries. Precious details also distinguish dials in white, blued or pink mother-of-pearl decorated with sun pattern to make it particularly luminous, while bracelets have jointed links of the same material as the case. They come in numerous variants, among which the precious example shown in the photograph in yellow gold with brilliant and white mother-of-pearl.

LA SCALA

Movement: quartz, ETA.
Functions: hour, minute.
Case: 18 kt white gold, two-piece case with two set brilliants; flat sapphire glass; octagonal white-gold crown; brand engraved on the middle; back attached by screws. Water-resistant to 3 atm.
Dial: white gold, high-polished; 1 row of brilliant around the central disc, 1 row of mother-of-pearl pieces and embossed logo below 12; 2 rows of brilliants on the external ring with embossed white-gold Roman numerals at quarters; white-gold Dauphine hands.
Bracelet: white gold and brilliant set in central links; fold-over clasp.

LA SCALA CHRONOGRAPH

Movement: quartz, ETA.
Functions: hour, minute, small second, date, chronograph with 3 counters.
Case: stainless steel, two-piece case; flat sapphire glass; rectangular pushers; octagonal crown; brand engraved on the middle; back attached by screws. Water-resistant to 3 atm.
Dial: black with blue zones, engine-turned (guilloché) with sun pattern; bâton markers, 12 applied rhodium-plated Arabic numeral; rhodium-plated Alpha hands.
Indications: tenths of a second at 2, date at 4, small second at 6, minute counter at 10, center second counter, minute track with divisions for 1/5 of a second.
Bracelet: polished and brushed stainless steel; fold-over clasp.

LA SCALA CHRONOGRAPH

The new La Scala chronograph versions use stainless steel as the advanced material par excellence. Concord, after having presented the model in yellow gold in 1997, is looking out for a vaster public, still using the same quartz movement and the same design elements in a modern and unconstrained interpretation. For gentlemen, dials have silver or black-blue tones with sun-pattern engravings and bracelets or rubber straps; for ladies, the chronograph becomes also an accessory both elegant and useful. Pastel colors coat dials and straps as well, but more precious variants have brilliants on bezels and markers. On the other hand, the series with stainless steel cases and bezels bordered by black and white diamonds is particularly sophisticated and conspicuous. In fact, the union of these two stones, accurately cut by Concord's craftsmen, generates mysterious and fascinating versions in both men's and ladies' size. The photograph shows the sober version for gentlemen with a silvered dial.

LA SCALA CHRONOGRAPH

Movement: quartz, ETA. **Functions:** hour, minute, small second, date, chronograph with 3 counters.
Case: stainless steel, two-piece case; 30 black brilliants set on the strap attachments; flat sapphire glass; rectangular pushers; octagonal crown; brand engraved on the middle; back attached by screws. Water-resistant to 3 atm.
Dial: silvered, engine-turned (guilloché) with sun pattern; 7 brilliant markers, 12 applied rhodium-plated Arabic numeral; rhodium-plated Alpha hands.
Indications: tenths of a second at 2, date at 4, small second at 6, minute counter at 10, center second counter, minute track with divisions for 1/5 of a second.
Strap: crocodile leather; central attachment; steel fold-over clasp.

LA SCALA CHRONOGRAPH

Movement: quartz, ETA. **Functions:** hour, minute, small second, date, chronograph with 3 counters.
Case: 18 kt yellow gold, two-piece case; bezel with 22 set brilliants; flat sapphire glass; yellow-gold rectangular pushers; yellow-gold octagonal crown with sapphire cabochon; brand engraved on the middle; back attached by screws. Water-resistant to 3 atm.
Dial: yellow gold; center disc in mother-of-pearl; gold ring with brilliant pavé; hour ring in mother-of-pearl with 12 brilliant markers on the printed minute track; gold Dauphine hands.
Indications: tenths of a second at 2, date at 4, small second at 6, minute counter at 10, center second counter.
Bracelet: yellow gold with brilliants set on the central links; fold-over clasp.

DANIEL JEANRICHARD

an historical perspective

Daniel JeanRichard is a brand whose historical roots date back centuries but whose true success lies in a philosophy and strategy built in just the past decade.

It was in the early 1990s that visionary and watch strategist Dr. Luigi Macaluso pursued his dream to reinstate the brand to its rightful place in Swiss watchmaking heritage. After all, Daniel JeanRichard had been a legend in Neuchâtel watchmaking for nearly 300 years thanks to his creative talent and foresight. In fact, even today a majestic statue of JeanRichard stands tall in the square outside a key watchmaker's School in LeLocle, Switzerland.

In the late 17th century, Daniel JeanRichard—a goldsmith apprentice—became preoccupied with the meticulous art of watchmaking and eventually changed careers. Driven by the desire to produce his own timepieces, JeanRichard was among the first to create machinery that made watch parts and to introduce watch production to his region. He was committed to creating timepieces of superior standards in terms of both artistic beauty and craftsmanship. This dedicated craftsman began training others in the valley as watchmakers, engravers, dial- and casemakers. In fact, he is credited with bringing the profitable watchmaking venue to the Neuchâtel valley. Even after his death in 1741, JeanRichard's watchmaking legacy lived on.

The name survived its founder and underwent manifold changes over the ensuing centuries: changing hands, changing locations, and bowing to the power of the quartz era. In the 1980s, Dr. Macaluso became enthralled with the stories of Daniel JeanRichard. He shared the man's commitment to, and passion for, watchmaking. Macaluso purchased the brand and, with careful determination and a strict code of excellence, set up the production of Daniel JeanRichard in the world's prestigious watchmaking town of La Chaux-de-Fonds, Switzerland—where sister company Girard-Perregaux (both brands being owned by the Sowind Group) is headquartered.

Focusing on product development and brand strategy, Macaluso relaunched Daniel JeanRichard as a brand committed to innovation, originality and top-quality craftsmanship. Retro designs, combined with striking modernity and premiere craftsmanship piloted Daniel JeanRichard watches to the forefront of many international markets.

Today, less than 10 years since Macaluso began his rebuilding, the brand is known globally for its distinctive look and meticulous craftsmanship. Always daring to be different, and never forsaking the details, Daniel JeanRichard has stolen the hearts of watch lovers with truly creative spirits.

unveiling masterpieces

The Daniel JeanRichard brand is intended for seekers of originality and individuality. Every timepiece is created in the great watchmaking tradition in terms of techniques and craftsmanship, but sports an artistic edge that pushes the limit.

The entire collection is based around four principal, highly innovative lines, including the TV Screen, Chronoscope, Diverscope and Bressel (the nickname by which watchmaker Daniel Jean-Richard had been called).

With its modern view of timekeeping, Daniel JeanRichard turned heads when it first unveiled its signature line: the TV Screen. In fewer than five years, this striking series has become the center of attention due to its boldly updated retro styling. Based on the look and shape of original television screens from the 1940s, the TV Screen is known for its distinctive cushion-cornered square case.

THIS PAGE
TOP

The TV Screen Lady watch houses a quartz movement in a polished steel or 18-karat gold case. Dial color choices abound. There are also mother-of-pearl dial versions with diamond markers and diamond bezels.

BOTTOM

The TV Screen Chronograph Rattrapante Automatic is offered in the large-sized case in polished steel.

FACING PAGE
BOTTOM

Now available in large or medium sizes, the TV Screen Chronograph Automatic offers new dials, strong readability and rubber strap options.

The TV Screen watch comes in several sizes, including large, medium and a newly introduced women's size. Indeed, the TV Screen Lady watch features a steel case more discreet in size. Available in 18-karat gold or stainless steel, with or without diamonds, the TV Screen Lady offers an array of mother-of-pearl dial colors and strap colors for fashionable flair.

Another important new TV Screen model is a Chronograph Rattrapante Automatic in large size for men. This mechanical split-second chronograph movement with automatic winding is set in a polished stainless steel case. The pushers for the chronograph are square and the dial is incredibly clean and elegant, with 60-second and 30-minute counters. The watch exudes an elegant yet sporty appeal thanks to the crocodile strap with stitching in contrasting colors.

For those less concerned with split-second timing, Daniel JeanRichard unveils the TV Screen Chronograph Automatic in large and medium sizes. The watch houses a mechanical chronograph movement with automatic wind. It has new dials with large numbers for optimum readability, features 60-seconds, 30-minutes and 12-hour counters, and comes with either a rubber or crocodile strap.

239

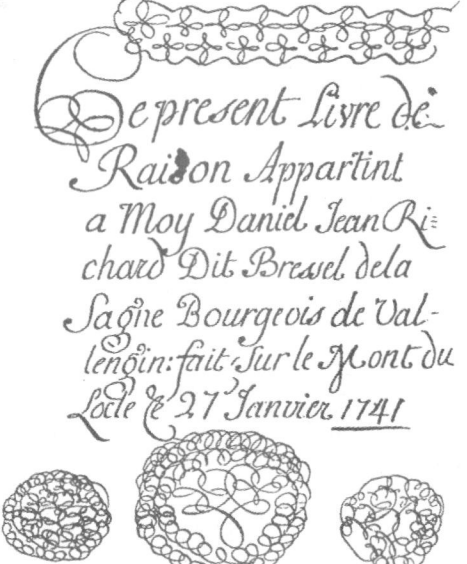

rounding out

Daniel JeanRichard also recently unveiled a TV Screen version of the Chronoscope—a series that has also enjoyed success internationally. The newest model, the TV Screen Chronoscope Automatic, comes in a large-sized case that closely emulates the TV Screen. In fact, the TV Screen lines define the outer case, which is then complemented by a round, brushed steel bezel to bring the design of both lines together. Water resistant to 50 meters, the watch houses a mechanical chronograph movement with automatic winding and a calendar window.

Recognizing the needs of today's consumers to remain high-tech, Daniel JeanRichard has unveiled the Chronoscope Automatic watch set in a round titanium case and accented with a black rubber strap. The mechanical chronograph movement with automatic wind is water resistant to 100 meters.

Similarly, the new Diverscope Automatic watch with mechanical movement has also been unveiled in titanium, but this timepiece is water resistant to 300 meters. In style typical of the brand, the watch features an easy-to-read dial and interior swivel bezel.

TOP

Water resistant to 300 meters, the Diverscope Automatic features titanium case and rubber strap with calendar window on dial.

TOP

This pocket watch is signed "Daniel JeanRichard, Le Locle, beginning 17th C."

BOTTOM LEFT

This version of the Bressel Chronograph Automatic comes in a polished steel 43mm case with tachometric scale.

BOTTOM RIGHT

Sizing down a bit, this Bressel Chronograph Automatic is housed in a 37mm case. It is available with either a brilliant silver dial with telemetric scale or a black dial with tachometric scale.

Several new models have also come into play in the elegant, classically round Bressel line. Each is an Automatic Chronograph—one is in the signature oversized 43mm case and the other is in a smaller 37mm case. Both are water resistant to 50 meters and feature tachometric scales and crocodile straps. The larger model has a polished steel case, while the smaller model has a satin-finished case. What's more, the 37mm watch offers a choice of either silver dial with telemetric scale or black dial with tachometric scale.

Indeed, the key for Daniel JeanRichard is to offer choice and selection but to always pay attention to the details and strive to offer a watch that combines distinctive styling and function.

According to Ron Jackson, head of the brand in the U.S. market, "Daniel Jean-Richard fits a special niche where we meet the demands of consumers who want to be different and insist on stylized mechanical watches."

DANIEL JEANRICHARD

TV SCREEN MAXI CHRONO FLY-BACK BIG-SIZED DATE   REF. 51016

Movement: mechanical, automatic winding, DJR 51 caliber 13'''1/4 (Valjoux 7750 caliber base modified by Jacques Baume), with fly-back feature, 28 jewels, 28,800 vibrations per hour.
Functions: hour, minute, small second, date, fly-back chronograph with three counters.
Case: 18 kt pink gold, three-piece case, in curved square shape (size 41 x 38.5

mm, thickness 14.2 mm); curved sapphire crystal; pink-gold rectangular pushers and crown; back attached by 4 screws. Water-resistant to 5 atm.
Dial: white, counters decorated with circular beads; applied gold-plated brass Arabic numerals; gold-plated brass Dauphine hands.
Indications: minute counter at 3, hour counter at 6, small second at 9, big date in a double window at 12, center fly-back second counter, railway minute track, tachometer scale.
Strap: crocodile leather; pink-gold clasp.
Also available: in stainless steel, black dial and luminescent Arabic numerals, strap with fold-over clasp, bracelet

TV SCREEN MAXI CHRONO TWO COUNTERS   REF. 30016

Movement: mechanical, automatic winding, DJR 30 caliber, 13'''1/4 (ETA 2824/2 caliber base + Dubois Dépraz 2020 caliber chrono module), 51 jewels, 28,800 vibrations per hour.
Functions: hour, minute, small second, chronograph with 2 counters.
Case: stainless steel, three-piece case, in curved square shape (size 41 x 38.5 mm, thickness 14.2 mm); curved sapphire crystal; rectangular pushers; snap-on back. Water-resistant to 5 atm.

Dial: opaline, counters decorated with circular beads; blue printed bâton markers and applied gold-plated brass Arabic numerals at 6 and 12; blued steel leaf style hands.
Indications: small second at 3, minute counter at 9, center second counter, railway minute track with divisions for 1/5 of a second, tachometer scale.
Strap: crocodile leather; steel fold-over clasp.
Also available: with bracelet.

TV SCREEN   REF. 24006

Movement: mechanical, automatic winding, DJR 24 caliber, 11'''1/2 (ETA 2824-2 caliber base), 25 jewels (11'''1/2), 28,800 vibrations per hour.
Functions: hour, minute, second, date.
Case: stainless steel, three-piece case, curved square shape (size 37 x 35 mm, thickness 12.7 mm); curved mineral crystal; back attached by 4 screws. Water-resistant to 3 atm.

Dial: white enameled; printed Roman numerals and railway minute track; blued steel leaf style hands.
Indications: date at 3.
Strap: crocodile leather; steel fold-over clasp.
Also available: with bracelet; Arabic numerals: black, pink, blue, silvered dial; in shot-blasted steel: with black dial and luminescent Arabic numerals, rubber strap with buckle or ivory dial with printed Arabic numerals, crocodile leather strap with fold-over clasp. Maxi Size Ref. 24016 (size 41x38.5, thickness 13.2 mm), shot-blasted steel, black dial and luminescent Arabic numerals, rubber strap with buckle or ivory dial with printed Arabic numerals, crocodile leather strap with fold-over clasp.

RECTANGULAR CAMBRÉ   REF. 26008

Movement: mechanical, automatic winding, DJR 26 caliber, 7'''3/4 (ETA 2671 caliber base), with 25 jewels, 28,800 vibrations per hour.
Functions: hour, minute, second.
Case: stainless steel, two-piece case, rectangular, cambered (size 34 x 26 mm, thickness 10.35 mm); curved mineral crystal; back attached by 4 screws. Water-resistant to 3 atm.

Dial: mat black enameled; luminescent Arabic numerals; printed railway minute track; luminescent white enameled bâton hands.
Strap: leather; steel fold-over clasp.
Unique version.

BRESSEL CHRONO GMT   REF. 54012

Movement: mechanical, automatic winding, DJR 54 caliber 13'''1/4 (Valjoux 7750 caliber base + modified Jacques Baume 8104 caliber for the second time-zone time display), 28 jewels, 28.800 vibrations per hour.
Functions: hour, minute, small second, date, second time-zone time, 24 hours, chronograph with three counters.
Case: stainless steel, three-piece case (Ø 43 mm, thickness 14.5 mm); curved mineral crystal; pump-type pushers; screwed-on back. Water-resistant to 5 atm.

Dial: opaline, counters decorated with circular beads and brushed external ring with printed 24-hours day-night display; printed bâton markers; blued steel leaf style hands.
Indications: minute counter at 3, date between 4 and 5, hour counter at 6, small second at 9, center second counter, second time-zone time 24-hours day-night display with red arrow-pointed center hand, minute track with divisions for 1/5 of a second.
Strap: crocodile leather; steel fold-over clasp.
Unique version.

BRESSEL CHRONO 37 MM   REF. 25042

Movement: mechanical, automatic winding, DJR 25 caliber 11'''1/2 (ETA 2824-2 caliber base + Dubois Dépraz 2020 caliber chrono module), 51 jewels, 28,800 vibrations per hour.
Functions: hour, minute, small second, chronograph with three counters.
Case: stainless steel, three-piece case (Ø 37 mm, thickness 14.3 mm); curved sapphire crystal; pump-type pushers; back fastened by 6 screws. Water-resistant to 5 atm.

Dial: blue, counters decorated with circular beads; printed bâton markers (12 in applied Arabic numerals); rhodium-plated brass leaf style hands.
Indications: small second at 3, hour counter at 6, minute counter at 9, center second counter, minute track with divisions for 1/5 of a second, tachometer scale.
Strap: crocodile leather; steel fold-over clasp.
Also available: with silvered dial.

CHRONOSCOPE   REF. 25020M

Movement: mechanical, automatic winding, DJR 25 caliber 13'''1/4 (ETA 2824-2 caliber base + Dubois Dépraz 2020 chrono module), 51 jewels (13'''1/4), 28,800 vph. **Functions:** hour, minute, small second, chronograph with 3 counters. **Case:** shot-blasted steel, 3-piece case (Ø 43, thick. 14.5 mm); curved mineral crystal; pushers with case protection; screw-down winding crown at 3, with case protection, screw-down crown at 9 for the adjustment of the two-way turning flange, with case protection; screwed-on back. Water-res. to 10 atm. **Dial:** mat black; flange with minute track for diving times, with luminescent markers; luminescent square markers; luminescent white enameled bâton hands. **Indications:** small second at 3, hour counter at 6, minute counter at 9, center second counter, minute track with divisions for 1/2 of a second. **Bracelet:** shot-blasted steel; recessed double fold-over clasp.
Also available: leather or rubber strap; polished steel silvered or black dial, white counters or blue dial silvered counters, leather strap or bracelet (same price); titanium black dial, luminescent markers, leather or rubber strap. Steel version: silvered dial and 12-hours indication on flange.

CHRONOSCOPE DIVER   REF. 24020P

Movement: mechanical, automatic winding, DJR caliber 24, 11'''1/2 (ETA caliber 2824-2 base), 25 jewels, 28.800 vibrations per hour.
Functions: hour, minute, second, date.
Case: steel with mat black PVD (Physical Vapor Deposit) treatment, three-piece case (Ø 43 mm, thickness 13.65 mm); curved mineral crystal; screw-down crowns at 3 (for hour and date corrections) and at 9 (for the adjustment of the two-way turning flange) with case protection; screwed-on back. Water-resistant to 33 atm.
Dial: mat black enameled; polished flange with minute track, for the calculation of diving times; luminescent square markers; printed minute track with five-minute progression with luminescent dots; luminescent white enameled bâton hands.
Indications: date at 3.
Strap: rubber; buckle in steel with black PVD treatment.
Also available: with bracelet; in titanium, black enameled dial, luminescent markers, rubber or leather strap. Date between 4 and 5, in polished steel, black enameled dial and luminescent Arabic numerals, rubber strap or bracelet.

DANIEL MINK

an historical perspective

In the world of watchmaking, Daniel Mink is relatively young. Founded just under 30 years ago, this brand has nonetheless made its mark in the timekeeping arena. One of the finest watchmaking brands on the market today, Daniel Mink is committed to traditional Swiss watchmaking techniques, technical advancement and contemporary design.

Over the years, the brand has introduced striking timepieces that—as the company's creed succinctly summarizes—"Redefine the Measure of Time." Owned for more than five years by The Montreux Group, LC, Daniel Mink offers a powerful blend of past, present and future in its timepieces. Because its owners are insistent that the brand focus more strongly on the technical art of mechanical watchmaking, the product mix has been rejuvenated in such a way as to deftly combine cutting-edge style and technical prowess.

Under the direction of The Montreux Group, the Daniel Mink product offering has grown to seven substantial collections—each produced with the strictest attention to detail. The mechanical portion of the Daniel Mink line has experienced the most growth over the past few years. In fact, approximately 75 percent of the brand's total timepiece production is mechanical. Among the key mechanical watch collections are the Skeleton, Tonneau (a line of complex mechanical watches), Intrinsic (a line of COSC-certified chronometers) and Titus (a moonphase, calendar and chronograph series).

Of course, quartz also plays a role in the Daniel Mink line in collections such as the Vevé and the Diamanche. For these timepieces, the brand uses only ETA movements and focuses on every detail of design. Bracelets are meticulously assembled, diamonds adorn cases and bezels, and mother of pearl enhances dials. In typical Daniel Mink style, every watch is crafted only in 18-karat gold or fine surgical-grade steel. All of these factors ensure that Daniel Mink timepieces are creations of aesthetic beauty, powerful styling and quality technology.

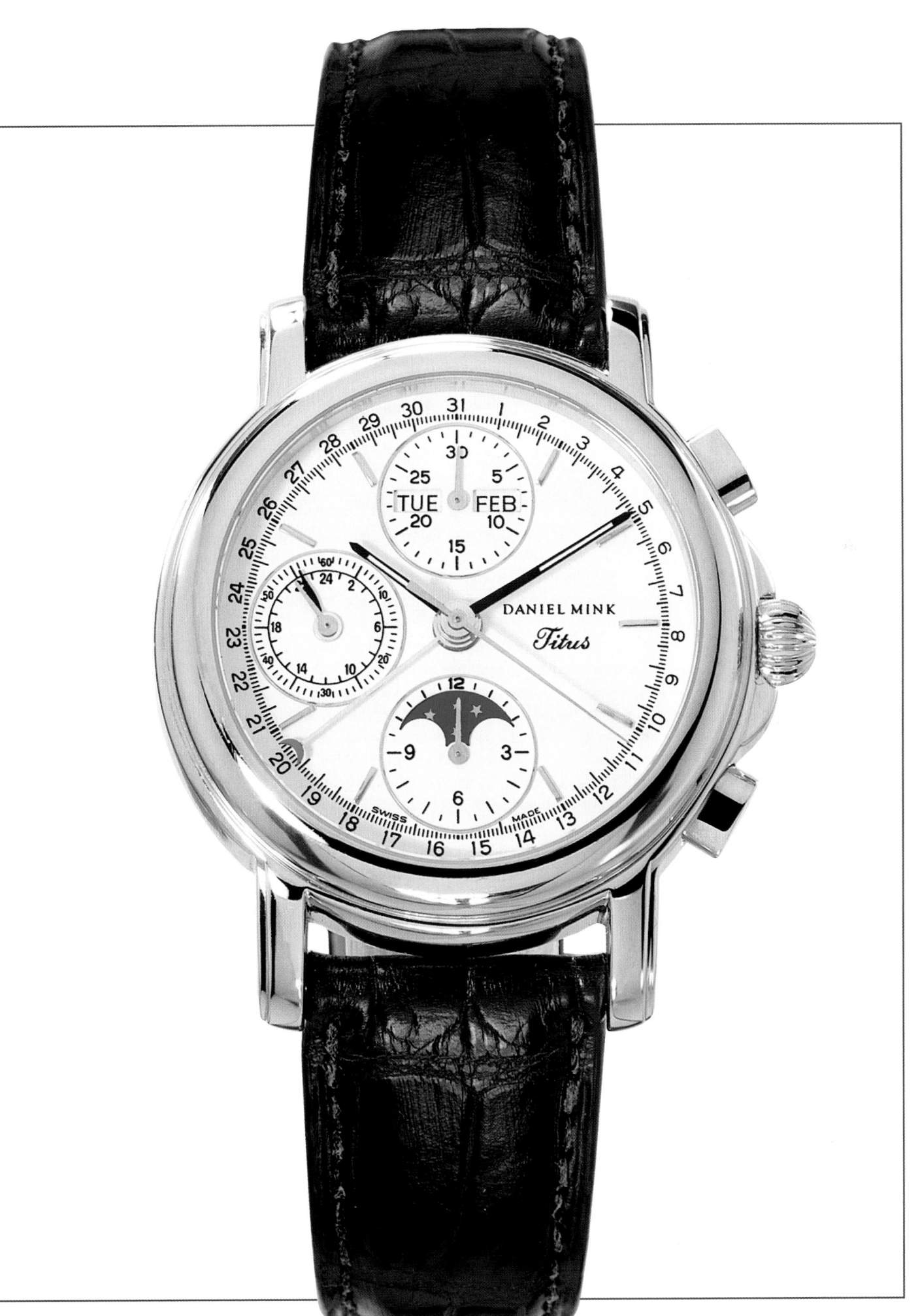

DANIEL MINK

unveiling masterpieces

The newest Daniel Mink creations unveiled this past year revolve around the Vevé, the 1900, and the Skeleton series, but there were also new introductions in the Titus and Tonneau collections. In fact, 2001 was predominantly a year of expansion and evolution for Daniel Mink as the brand rounded out almost all of its key collections.

In the Titus series of square and round mechanical watches introduced just about two years ago, Daniel Mink unveiled a mechanical Chronograph Moonphase watch with automatic winding. Crafted in steel, the watch offers moonphase at 6:00, small second, and 24-hour indication. It is offered with black or white dial, Arabic numerals and black alligator strap. There is also a version with a vanilla-scented rubber strap that features luminescent digits. The dial of this version is black with red accents for easy readability and striking design. Each of these watches features an exhibition back for viewing the movement.

Perhaps the most striking change in the Daniel Mink line this past year is the Vevé collection. A series of elegant, fashion-forward timepieces, the Vevé received a completely new look. By paying close attention to detail, Daniel Mink brought this collection from an avant-garde square-cased series to a stunning, slender rectangular series that is at once both traditional and classic. The sleek new versions are crafted in stainless steel, house quartz movements and feature domed crystals. The Vevé is offered with a choice of dial colors, including pale blue,

THIS PAGE

TOP LEFT

The new Vevé offers a sleek, elegant appeal.

TOP RIGHT

This Vevé is crafted in steel and features a vivid blue dial.

BOTTOM LEFT

The 1900 Chronograph model is crafted in steel and features an exhibition caseback.

BOTTOM CENTER

From the 1900 series, this new model features 55 full-cut black diamonds on the bezel. The dial is silver sunbrushed with black Roman numerals.

BOTTOM RIGHT

The bezel of this 1900 watch is set with 55 diamonds and is accented with a white mother-of-pearl dial and diamond markers.

FACING PAGE

RIGHT CENTER

The 1900 is available in steel with embossed rubber strap.

BOTTOM

This Titus Moonphase watch houses an automatic movement.

CHRONOLOGY

1980 One of the early collections to carry the Daniel Mink name, The Monte Carlo, is among the first dress timepieces to sport a rubber bracelet.

1982 The Arx collection is launched. Designed by Remo Bertolucci, it is the first watch produced in 18-karat gold for Daniel Mink and features a grid over the dial.

1988 Introduction of the Radica/Locman collection, which features bezels made of briarwood from the Mediterranean coast.

1993 After much research, The 1900 collection is launched at the Basel Fair, answering a demand for the unique. Although a difficult watch to manufacture with its Clous De Paris design, every detail is studied and executed. This marks the first watch to feature the Clous De Paris design on the bracelet and it is considered the signature collection of Daniel Mink.

1997 After many years under family management, Daniel Mink ownership is passed to The Montreux Group.

2000 This is a very important and intense product launch year for the Daniel Mink brand. Daniel Mink Switzerland is re-emerging internationally, due largely to its new collections: Titus, Diamanche, Skeleton, Vevé and Tonneau. Many of these new collections represent a step toward more technical creations from Daniel Mink.

2001 Daniel Mink enriches and expands six of its seven collections; The brand launches an international communication and advertising campaign with the tag line "Redefine The Measure Of Time," its largest effort to date; Daniel Mink watches are seen regularly on the wrists of celebrities such as Claudia Schiffer, Cher, Patrick Ewing, Bill Clinton, and Jennifer Capriati to name a few.

mother of pearl, silver, and black. It is also available without diamonds, or with 32 or 64 diamonds on the case.

Daniel Mink also unveiled diamonds in its 1900 collection, with new models donning either colorless diamonds or black diamonds on the bezels. The 1900 collection has been one of Daniel Mink's best sellers since its introduction in 1993. A signature line for Daniel Mink, the watch is immediately recognizable thanks to its highly distinctive textured round case or bracelet. The new models, crafted in steel, offer various dial colors, including mother-of-pearl selections, and come with either bracelets or straps. The diamonds are meticulously set in single or double rows on the bezel.

In its Skeleton line, Daniel Mink has unveiled a steel semi-skeleton called Open Heart. Demonstrating its love for fine watchmaking and technical expertise, Daniel Mink has created the Open Heart with a fully engraved automatic movement that is totally visible in the back and partially visible through an aperture in the front. Also underway is a limited-edition Skeleton chronograph. This skeleton watch will be created in 18-karat white or pink gold and only 25 pieces are being made of each for worldwide distribution. Each is individually numbered on the front of the dial.

As with all Daniel Mink timepieces, the newest watches are crafted with the utmost respect for Swiss watchmaking tradition, detailing and design.

247

DANIEL MINK

TONNEAU DAY/DATE MOONPHASE   REF. 3258 SVR

Movement: mechanical, automatic winding, ETA 2892-2 engine-turned rotor and bridges, personalized DANIEL MINK.
Functions: hour, minute, center second, day, date, month and moonphase.
Case: stainless steel, two-piece (height 32mm-width 32mm-thickness-9mm) sapphire crystal, caseback attached with 4 screws displaying movement, water resistant to 3atm.

Dial: silvered, lumines-cent Arabic numerals, gunmetal-blue sword-style hands.
Indications: moonphase at 6, printed date track, day and month in aper-tures at 12.
Strap: alligator leather, stainless steel clasp.
Also available: black dial with applied Arabic numerals and baton markers.
Price: available upon request.

TONNEAU   REF. 3229 CR

Movement: mechanical, automatic winding, ETA 2892-2 engine-turned rotor and bridges, personalized DANIEL MINK.
Functions: hour, minute, center second, date.
Case: stainless steel, two-piece (height 32mm-width 32mm-thickness 7mm) mineral crystal, caseback attached with 4 screws displaying movement, water resistant to 3 atm.

Dial: cream with brown Arabic numerals, printed minute track, chocolate-brown sword-style hands.
Indications: date at 6:00.
Strap: alligator leather, stainless steel clasp.
Also available: matte black or silvered versions.
Price: available upon request.

TONNEAU FLY-BACK CHRONOGRAPH   REF. 3292MBK

Movement: mechanical, 29 jewels, automatic winding, valjoux 7750 with fly-back feature allowing the chronograph's second hand to start again imme-diately after a zero setting, using only the pusher at 4.
Functions: hour, minute, small second, chronograph with fly-back feature and 2 counters.
Case: stainless steel, two-piece (height 37mm width 35mm thickness 13mm)

curved sapphire crystal, rectangle pushers with case protectors, caseback attached with 4 screws, water resistant to 3 atm.
Dial: black enameled, white Arabic numerals, printed minute track, luminescent baton-style hands, red accents.
Indications: minute counter at 3, small sec-onds at 9, center second counter, minute track.
Bracelet: stainless steel with safety locking clasp
Also available: white enameled dial, alligator strap.
Price: available upon request.

TONNEAU   REF. 3229 SVR

Movement: mechanical, automatic winding, ETA 2892-2 engine-turned rotor and bridges, personalized DANIEL MINK.
Functions: hour, minute, center second, date.
Case: stainless steel, two-piece (height 32mm-width 32mm-thickness 7mm) mineral crystal, caseback attached with 4 screws displaying movement, water resistant to 3 atm.

Dial: silvered with lumi-nescent Arabic numerals, printed minute track, luminescent baton-style hands, red accents.
Indications: date at 6:00.
Strap: alligator leather, stainless steel clasp.
Also available: black with white Arabic numer-als or creme versions.
Price: available upon request.

TONNEAU CHRONOGRAPH   REF. 3232 SVR

Movement: mechanical, automatic winding, ETA 2894-2, 37 jewels, engine-turned rotor and bridges, personalized DANIEL MINK.
Functions: hour, minute, small second, chronograph with 3 counters.
Case: stainless steel, two-piece (height 32mm, width 32mm, thickness 9mm), sapphire crystal, caseback attached with 4 screws displaying movement, water resistant to 3 atm.
Dial: silvered, applied Roman numerals and baton markers, mother-of-pearl subdials, printed minute track, blued leaf-style hands.
Indications: small second at 3, hour counter at 6, minute counter at 9, center second counter.
Strap: alligator leather, steel clasp.
Also available: matte black, exploding luminescent Arabic numerals.

TITUS DAY/DATE MOONPHASE SQUARE   REF. 1222SVR

Movement: mechanical, automatic winding ETA 2892-2 engine-turned rotor and bridges, personalized DANIEL MINK.
Functions: hour, minute, center second, day, date, month and moonphase.
Case: stainless steel, two-piece (33mm, thickness 10mm) curved crystal, 4 pushers on case sides, skeletonized snap-on back displaying movement.
Dial: silvered guilloché with sun pattern, applied Arabic numerals and baton markers, printed date track, blued sword-style hands.
Indications: moonphase at 6, day and month in apertures at 12, date with red-tipped center hand.
Strap: alligator leather, stainless steel clasp.
Also available: blue guilloché with sun pattern, applied Roman numerals.

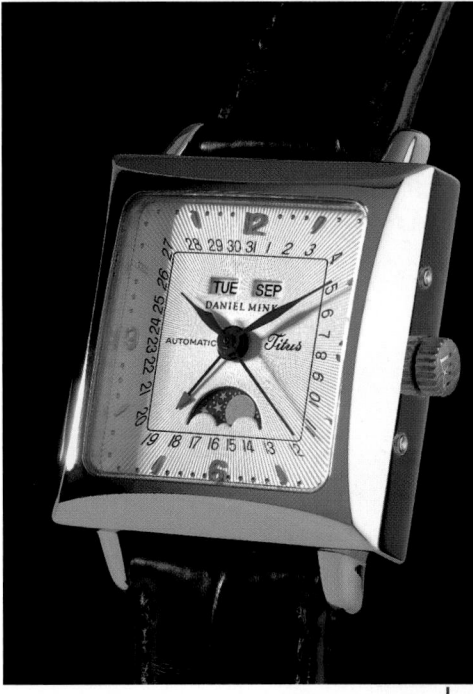

TITUS MOON PHASE CHRONOGRAPH   REF. 7041 WH

Movement: mechanical, automatic winding, Valjoux 7751 personalized DANIEL MINK.
Functions: hour, minute, small second, 24-hour indication, chronograph with 3 counters, day date month and moonphase.
Case: stainless steel, three-piece (Ø 38mm, thickness 13mm) sapphire crystal, drop-shaped pushers, one pusher on case side, screw-on case-back displaying movement.
Dial: white, applied baton markers, luminescent baton-shaped hands, printed date and minute track.
Indications: hour counter and moonphase at 6, small second and 24-hour indication at 9, minute counter, day and month in apertures at 12, center second counter and date indicator with red-tipped half-moon center hand.
Strap: alligator leather fastened by 4 screws, steel clasp.
Also available: matte black with luminescent Arabic numerals.

TITUS DAY/DATE MOONPHASE ROUND   REF. 1221BL

Movement: mechanical, automatic winding, ETA 2892-2 engine-turned rotor and bridges, personalized DANIEL MINK.
Functions: hour, minute, center second, day, date, month and moonphase.
Case: stainless steel, three-piece (Ø 38mm, thickness 10mm) curved crystal, 4 pushers on case sides, skeletonized back attached by 4 screws displaying movement.
Dial: blue guilloché with sun pattern, applied Roman numerals and baton markers, printed date track, luminescent baton-style hands.
Indications: moonphase at 6, day and month in apertures at 12, date with red-tipped center hand.
Strap: alligator leather, stainless steel clasp.
Also available: silvered guilloché with sun pattern, applied Arabic numerals.

DANIEL MINK

TITUS SPORT CHRONOGRAPH   REF. 3270BLK

Movement: mechanical, automatic winding, valjoux 7750 personalized DANIEL MINK.
Functions: hour, minute, second, day and date, chronograph with 3 counters.
Case: stainless steel, three-piece (Ø 40mm thickness 14mm) sapphire crystal, screw-down crown, screw-on caseback, see-through back displaying movement, water resistant to 5 atm.

Dial: matte black with yellow accents, white Arabic numerals, printed minute track and tachymeter, black and white baton-style hands.
Indications: day at 3, hour counter at 6, small second at 9, minute counter at 12, center second counter and tachymeter scale.
Strap: matte black alligator.
Also available: rubber (vanilla scented), stainless steel deployment buckle.
Price: available upon request.

TITUS SPORT CHRONOGRAPH   REF. 3270RBK

Movement: mechanical, automatic winding, valjoux 7750 personalized DANIEL MINK.
Functions: hour, minute, second, day and date, chronograph with 3 counters.
Case: stainless steel, three-piece (Ø 40mm thickness 14mm) sapphire crystal, screw-down crown, screw-on caseback, see-through back displaying movement, water resistant to 5 atm.

Dial: matte black, luminescent Arabic numerals, printed minute track, luminescent burnished-steel Sport hands with red accents.
Indications: day at 3, hour counter at 6, small second at 9, minute counter at 12, center second counter and tachymeter scale.
Strap: rubber (vanilla scented); stainless steel deployment buckle
Also available: Black alligator strap
Price: available upon request.

OPEN HEART SKELETON STEEL   REF. 3252RW

Movement: mechanical, automatic winding, ETA 2824 25 jewels, modified with skeleton under the balance, rotor personalized DANIEL MINK.
Functions: hour, minute and center second.
Case: stainless steel, three-piece (Ø 36mm thickness 9mm) sapphire crystal, skeleton caseback, water resistant to 3 atm.
Dial: white with Roman numerals, with aperture to balance, sword-style hands.

Strap: black genuine alligator, steel clasp.
Also available: white dial with black Arabic numerals and brown alligator strap.
Price: available upon request.

SKELETON STEEL   REF. 6050 GRY

Movement: mechanical, automatic winding, ETA 2892/2, hand skeletonized.
Functions: hour, minute and center second.
Case: stainless steel, three-piece (Ø 36mm, thickness 8mm), sapphire crystal with Daniel Mink imprint, skeleton caseback attached with 4 screws, water resistant to 5 atm.
Dial: black Roman numerals on gray beveled ring, black baton hands.

Strap: alligator leather fastened by 4 screws, steel clasp.
Also available: black dial with white Roman numerals.

DANIEL MINK

SKELETON GOLD   REF. 4945 CHBR

Movement: mechanical, automatic winding, ETA 2892/2 hand-skeletonized.
Functions: hour, minute and center second.
Case: 18K yellow-gold, three-piece (Ø 34mm, thickness 8mm), sapphire crystal with Daniel Mink imprint, fluted bezel, skeleton snap-on caseback.
Dial: black Roman numerals on beveled ring, black baton hands.
Strap: alligator leather, golden clasp.
Also available: black alligator strap.

INTRINSIC RESERVE DE MARCHE STEEL   REF. 2940 STMBL

Movement: mechanical, automatic winding ETA 2892/A2 guilloché rotor and bridges, personalized DANIEL MINK.
Functions: hour, minute, center second, date, power reserve and 24-hour indication.
Case: stainless steel, three-piece (Ø 35mm, thickness 11mm) sapphire crystal, screw-on caseback displaying movement, water resistant to 10 atm.
Dial: blue enameled, printed Roman numerals, Breguet style hands.
Indications: date at 3, power-reserve meter at 6, 24-hour indicator at 12.
Bracelet: stainless steel duo-fold clasp.
Also available: assorted dials and alligator straps.

COLLECTION 1900 STEEL CHRONOGRAPH   REF. 1950DA527200

Movement: mechanical, automatic winding, Valjoux 7750 personalized DANIEL MINK.
Functions: hour, minute, second, day and date, chronograph with 3 counters.
Case: stainless steel, three-piece (Ø 40mm, thickness 3mm) sapphire crystal Clous de Paris design on bezel, crown (screw-down) and pushers, screw-on caseback with engraved sapphire crystal displaying movement, water resistant to 10 atm.
Dial: matte black with red accents, white Roman numerals, tachymeter and steel baton hands.
Indications: day and date at 3, hour counter at 6, small second at 9, minute counter at 12, center second counter and tachymeter scale.
Bracelet: stainless steel, Clous de Paris design, duo-fold clasp with safety pushers.
Also available: white guilloché or silver guilloché with blue subdials.

COLLECTION 1900 STEEL & GOLD CHRONOGRAPH   REF. 1950DA627300

Movement: mechanical, automatic winding, Valjoux 7750 personalized DANIEL MINK.
Functions: hour, minute, second, day and date, chronograph with 3 counters.
Case: stainless steel with 18K yellow gold bezel, three-piece (Ø 40mm, thickness 3mm) sapphire crystal Clous de Paris design on bezel, crown (screw-down) and pushers, screw-on caseback with engraved sapphire crystal displaying movement, water resistant to 10 atm.
Dial: white guilloché, black Roman numerals, tachymeter and black sword-style hands.
Indications: day and date at 3, hour counter at 6, small second at 9, minute counter at 12, center second counter and tachymeter scale.
Bracelet: stainless steel, Clous de Paris design, duo-fold clasp with safety pushers.

DAVID YURMAN

an historical perspective

In terms of watchmaking history, 23 years may seem like a drop in the bucket. But in that amount of time David Yurman and his wife Sybil have built an internationally acclaimed jewelry and watch brand. In fact, since they began their company in 1979, Yurman has become virtually a household name for those who love beauty and luxury.

Recognized today as the man responsible for developing the concept of brand-name jewelry in the United States, Yurman has masterfully combined the aesthetics and crafts-manship of fine jewelry and watches with fashion. He deftly brings together the dynamics of fluidity and movement, of balance and harmony in his creations.

An American icon, Yurman was not trained in the art of jewelry making. In fact, he came to it circuitously—as a sculptor who had apprenticed with some of the finest, including Jacques Lipchitz and Theodore Rozark. Sybil was an accomplished painter, whose works now grace the walls of Yurman's studio and boutiques. Together, the two joined forces, not only in marriage, but in work, as well.

Within five years of founding their company, Yurman's designs had taken off. He had launched with a highly stylish, yet very timeless Cable collection that has since become the brand's signature look. In fact, Yurman's incredible copyrighted Cable collection may well be one of the most imitated designs in the world. After all, people only copy the best and most successful styles. Yurman, however, protects his trademarked designs with a fierceness that is necessary in this business. In what could be considered a landmark case, Yurman was awarded a trade dress for his signature Cable collection in a federal court—thus enabling him to claim market-ownership of his overall cable look.

During the 1980s and 1990s, the company's growth was phenome-nal. Yurman's jewelry collections grew; sterling silver was accompanied by gold; gemstones entered the scene with panache; timepieces came onto the scene in full-force.

Today, the Yurman collection is extensive. Nonetheless, each product line remains true to the Yurman philosophy of timeless design and fashion flair.

THIS PAGE

TOP

David and Sybil Yurman with Sir Elton John, who received the David Yurman Humanitarian Award at the 2000 GQ Men of the Year ceremony.

TOP LEFT

Created by Yurman, this bronze angel sculpture was presented to Sir Elton John.

BOTTOM

David Yurman's Madison Avenue Flagship store in New York City.

FACING PAGE

The Thoroughbred DualTime™ houses an automatic movement that displays two time zones. It is crafted in a steel and sterling silver case with either an all-metal bracelet or a rubber-sculpted and steel bracelet.

DAVID YURMAN

unveiling masterpieces

In the early 1990s, the Yurmans recognized a void in their line and they set about developing a watch collection. In 1995 Yurman unveiled his first watches, a complement to his Cable jewelry collection that garnered immediate international acclaim. A product of love, passion and perfection, the Cable Watch Collection® naturally embodied the spirit of the jewelry that had come before it.

Flawlessly marrying Yurman's signature style with the finest Swiss watchmaking, the collection of bracelet watches grew quickly. Precious metal joined the sterling silver bracelets and cases, with two-tone renditions and solid 18-karat gold models making their debut. In 1998, a contemporary strap-version of the Cable collection was unveiled, and Yurman has been creating watches for men and women that have captured hearts and souls alike ever since.

In 1999, after two years of tireless design and development, Yurman unveiled a new timepiece series to the world. The Thoroughbred Luxury Watch Collection™ offered a fresh look that nonetheless successfully reinterpreted the classic and unique Yurman style. It had taken David and Sybil hundreds of hours of research and countless trips to Switzerland to find a premier Swiss watch house that could successfully interpret and fulfill Yurman's designs. (To celebrate the launch of the Thoroughbred™ series, Yurman created the David Yurman Humanitarian Award, which was given to Steven Spielberg at the 1999 GQ Men of the Year Awards ceremony. This has since become an annual tradition and the second David Yurman Humanitarian Award (for the year 2000) was given to Elton John for his work with Aids.)

Taking his Thoroughbred collection even further in 2000, Yurman unveiled the Women's Thoroughbred™ Luxury Timepiece Collection. Once again bringing together Swiss craftsmanship, precision engineering and unique styling, Yurman launched a winner. These newest watches featured an exclusive cable bracelet consisting of sterling silver cable tubes, each of which rolls independently creating a sleek, fluid bracelet.

The year 2001 was another milestone in Yurman's quest for perfecting his timepieces. In October 2001, Yurman created a separate division of the brand. By establishing Yurman Timepieces, Yurman is making a commitment and dedication to the field of luxury watchmaking. This division serves as a fusion between art and science. Yurman's watches are 100 percent American designed and 100 percent Swiss made.

All Yurman watches feature only the finest Swiss automatic and quartz movements and parts. Dials are available in porcelain, lacquer, or mother of pearl. Cases are gold, silver or steel. Crystals are sapphire, and every watch is water resistant to at least 30 meters.

The newest timepieces unveiled under the watchful eye of the Yurman Timepiece division attest to the brand's pursuit of technical excellence in addition to superlative design. The Thoroughbred Limited Edition Chronograph, for instance, is a striking combination of form and function.

Two different models have been created of this COSC-certified, 37-jeweled automatic chronograph watch. One Thoroughbred Chronograph model is crafted in 18-karat gold and another model is crafted in steel with a platinum bezel and a platinum dial. Only 50 pieces of each will ever be produced. The Thoroughbred Chronograph has an exhibition sapphire caseback for viewing of the movement. Each watch is numbered on the caseback and is hand-signed by Yurman. So special are these timepieces that they are sold in custom-made, automatic winding boxes.

Yurman's Thoroughbred Dual Time™ watch also is a striking instrument of rugged elegance. The watch allows the wearer to view the time in two zones via an automatic GMT movement. The watch is available in a stainless steel case with sterling silver insets and comes with either a black or white enamel dial. While an alligator strap or a stainless steel bracelet is available, this watch also comes with a unique, rubber-infused steel cable bracelet that is indicative of Yurman's signature style and creative renditions.

Indeed, Yurman has crossed the borders of time with the innovative flair evident in his watchmaking efforts. This American icon now offers a new view of timekeeping—one firmly planted in both American design and Swiss heritage.

DAVID YURMAN

LARGE THOROUGHBRED   REF. T3030AL-ST-BRAC

Movement: mechanical, automatic winding, ETA 2892/A2, 21 jewels, 28,800 vibrations per hour.
Functions: hour, minute, sweep second, date.
Case: oxidized and high-polished sterling silver and high-polished steel 6-piece case (Ø 35mm, thickness 11mm); domed, anti-reflective sapphire crystal; caseback displays the movement through a sapphire crystal; caseback attached by 4 screws; water resistant to 3 atm.
Dial: blue enamel dial applied in 12 layers; feuille hands; applied baton markers and David Yurman logo.
Indications: date at 3.
Bracelet: combination of high-polished and brushed stainless steel, recessed deployant clasp.
Also available: gold case; gold bracelet; alligator strap.
Price: upon request.

MIDSIZE THOROUGHBRED   REF. T3138QM-ST-RDGA

Movement: quartz movement, ETA 955.432, stop device and interrupter, long life, 7 jewels.
Functions: hour, minute.
Case: oxidized and high-polished sterling silver and high-polished steel 6-piece case (Ø 32mm, thickness 9mm); domed, anti-reflective sapphire crystal; bezel set with diamonds (64 stones); caseback attached by 4 screws; water resistant to 3 atm.
Dial: natural black mother-of-pearl dial; applied markers set with diamonds; applied David Yurman logo; feuille hands.
Strap: alligator strap with deployant clasp.
Also available: gold case; steel or gold bracelet.
Price: upon request.

LADIES THOROUGHBRED   REF. T3144QS-88-BRACD

Movement: quartz movement, ETA 956.032, long life, 7 jewels.
Functions: hour, minute.
Case: high-polished 18K yellow-gold 6-piece case (Ø 25mm, thickness 7mm); domed, anti-reflective sapphire crystal; bezel set with diamonds (43 stones); caseback attached by 4 screws; water resistant to 3 atm.
Dial: natural white mother-of-pearl dial; applied markers set with diamonds; applied Arabic numerals and David Yurman logo; feuille hands.
Bracelet: high-polished 18K yellow-gold bracelet with pavé set diamonds (56 stones); recessed deployant clasp.
Also available: calf, alligator, or gros-grain strap; gold bracelet.
Price: upon request.

CABLE CAPRI   REF. T9514M-88-ADIBKGR

Movement: quartz movement, ETA 280.002, 7 jewels.
Functions: hour, minute.
Case: high-polished 18K yellow-gold 6-piece case (Ø 21mm, thickness 9mm); sapphire crystal; bezel and lugs set with diamonds (80 stones); water resistant to 3 atm.
Dial: natural white mother-of-pearl dial; applied markers set with diamonds; applied markers; feuille hands.
Strap: black gros-grain and leather strap with gold buckle.
Also available: alligator or moiré strap.
Price: upon request.

CLASSIC CABLE — REF. T1010M-SS-GG

Movement: quartz movement, ETA 280.002, 5 jewels.
Functions: hour, minute.
Case: high-polished 18K yellow-gold 2-piece case (Ø 21mm, thickness 9mm); sapphire crystal; water resistant to 3 atm.
Dial: natural white mother-of-pearl dial; applied Roman numerals and markers, feuille hands.
Bracelet: oxidized and high-polished sterling silver and high-polished 18K yellow-gold cable bracelet.
Also available: gold cable bracelet; gold cable bracelet accented with precious and semi-precious stones.
Price: upon request.

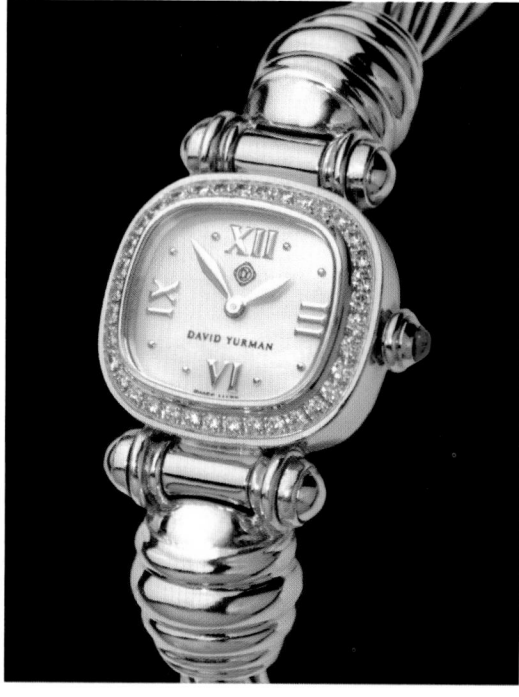

LIM. EDIT. THOROUGHBRED CHRON. — REF. T3065AC-SP-BRACR

Movement: mechanical, automatic winding, ETA 2894, 37 jewels, 28,800 vibrations per hour.
Functions: hour, minute, second, date, chronograph with 3 counters.
Case: high-polished steel with brushed platinum bezel 8-piece case (Ø 41mm, thickness 13mm); domed, anti-reflective sapphire crystal; caseback displays the movement through a sapphire crystal; caseback attached by 4 screws; water resistant to 3 atm; limited edition of 50, signed and numbered on caseback.
Dial: brushed platinum dial; feuille hands; applied Arabic numerals and David Yurman logo.
Indications: center flyback second counter; small second at 3; date between 4 and 5; hour counter (12h) at 6; minute counter (30') at 9.
Bracelet: brushed and high-polished steel with black rubber bracelet; recessed deployant clasp.
Also available: black alligator strap.
Price: upon request.

LIM. EDIT. THOROUGHBRED CHRON. — REF. T3066AC-88-BKMA

Movement: mechanical, automatic winding, ETA 2894-2, 37 jewels, 28,800 vibrations per hour.
Functions: hour, minute, second, date, chronograph with 3 counters.
Case: high-polished 18K yellow-gold 8-piece case (Ø 41mm, thickness 13mm); domed, anti-reflective sapphire crystal; caseback displays the movement through a sapphire crystal; caseback attached by 4 screws; water resistant to 3 atm; limited edition of 50, signed and numbered on caseback.
Dial: black enamel dial applied in 12 layers; feuille hands; applied Arabic numerals and David Yurman logo.
Indications: center flyback second counter; small second at 3; date between 4 and 5; hour counter (12h) at 6; minute counter (30') at 9.
Strap: black alligator strap with deployant clasp.
Price: upon request.

THOROUGHBRED DUALTIME® — REF. T3062AD-ST-BRAC

Movement: mechanical, automatic winding, ETA 2893-2, 21 jewels, 28,800 vibrations per hour.
Functions: hour, minute, sweep second.
Case: oxidized and high-polished sterling silver and high-polished steel 6-piece case (Ø 41mm, thickness 13mm); domed, anti-reflective sapphire crystal; caseback displays the movement through a sapphire crystal; caseback attached by 4 screws; water resistant to 3 atm.
Dial: white enamel dial applied in 12 layers with gray guilloché subdial; feuille hands; applied baton markers and David Yurman logo.
Indications: date at 3; red painted center second-time-zone 24-hour hand.
Bracelet: high-polished and brushed steel bracelet; recessed deployant clasp.
Also available: alligator strap; black dial on alligator strap or steel and rubber bracelet.
Price: upon request.

de GRISOGONO

an historical perspective

Fawaz Gruosi is an artist of many talents, and internationally known jeweler passionate about his work. His creativity, his discriminating eye for the exceptional and his drive for perfection and originality have set him apart from others.

THIS PAGE
TOP

Fawaz Gruosi.

BOTTOM

Romance is back in black. This one-of-a-kind heart necklace is elegantly set with 81.7 carats of black diamonds and 49.4 carats of heart-shaped emeralds.

FACING PAGE

Instrumento Nº Uno is depicted here in platinum with a white-gold dial elegantly set with 365 diamonds. The case is set with 572 diamonds.

For more than 20 years, Gruosi worked behind the scenes for some of the world's finest jewelry houses—regularly turning out masterpieces of wearable art and beauty. But it had always been his dream to establish his own boutiques and to create jewelry under his own name.

In 1996, Gruosi followed that dream and struck out on his own, opening his first de Grisogono boutique in Geneva. That was also the year he discovered the gemstone that would become his signature, and mark his innovative debut onto the stage of haute couture jewelry.

Glancing through a book, Gruosi came upon a photo of the famed 190-carat Black Orlov diamond. Intrigued, he traveled the world visiting diamond mines and collecting enough of these jet-black beauties to create one of the most unique jewelry collections in the world. A man who views things differently than most, Gruosi built his entire premiere collection around this little-known stone. The risk paid off— the jewels of de Grisogono were an immediate success.

Today there are de Grisogono boutiques in Geneva, Gstaad, London and Rome. A true haute couture jeweler, Gruosi continues to invent breathtaking one-of-a-kind and limited-edition necklaces, earrings, bracelets and rings that bespeak the mysteries of the black diamond. Daring and defiant in his approach, Gruosi has adorned a mobile telephone with 240 diamonds and has even unveiled a creative new watch collection that also bears his black diamond hallmark.

de GRISOGONO

mystére

Seduced by the dark luster and mysterious allure of black diamonds, Gruosi followed his heart and used these gems as the focal point of his work. In his creations, he often associates black diamonds with pearls, white diamonds, and other gemstones for striking contrast.

Recognized today as the jeweler who launched the love affair between the black diamond and women around the world, Gruosi has mastered the stone. It is arguably the most difficult diamond to cut and polish due to its inclusions and inner color flecks. This did not deter Gruosi, however. Instead, he endeavored to find the cuts and settings that best displayed the quintessence of the stone. According to him, black diamonds have long been underrated. Now, thanks to his vigilance and creativity, they are enjoying the attention they have long deserved.

In each of the past five years, his collections have become ever more daring, bold and original. Sometimes his intriguing designs include a hint of humor; sometimes a sensually feminine mystique emerges. Indeed, each new piece of de Grisogono jewelry is a unique expression.

Among some of his black masterpieces are striking dome rings that combine black and white diamonds to varying degrees; eternity and wedding bands that feature black on white and white on black diamond combinations; and an extensive collection of earrings that dangle with wonderful mixtures of black and white stones. The de Grisogono necklaces and bracelets are also incredibly stunning and captivating, with themes of nature, flowers, animals and hearts pervading.

TOP LEFT

de Grisogono's Geneva boutique.

TOP CENTER

Set in 18-karat white gold, this stunning necklace is bejeweled with approximately 100 carats of black diamonds.

LEFT CENTER

This striking black and white depiction of the Instrumento Nº Uno is housed in a blackened steel case with black diamond accents.

BOTTOM

These two rings can be worn separately or stacked. Each is set with just over 2 carats of diamonds and topped with a stunning South Sea pearl.

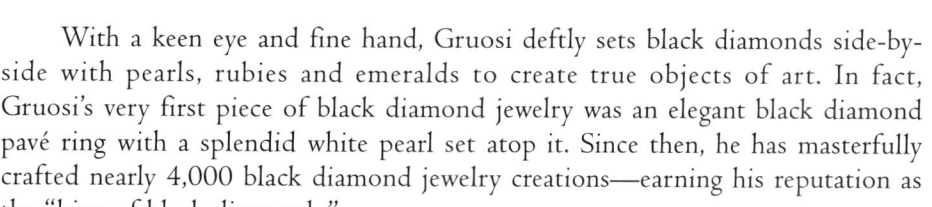

With a keen eye and fine hand, Gruosi deftly sets black diamonds side-by-side with pearls, rubies and emeralds to create true objects of art. In fact, Gruosi's very first piece of black diamond jewelry was an elegant black diamond pavé ring with a splendid white pearl set atop it. Since then, he has masterfully crafted nearly 4,000 black diamond jewelry creations—earning his reputation as the "king of black diamonds."

The majestic and mystical allure of black diamonds has led celebrities and royalty all over the world to these stunning stones. Baroness Nadine de Rothschild, for instance, owned a black diamond brooch that had been a gift from her husband; actress Salma Hayek was seen wearing a specially made black diamond suite from de Grisogono; and Natasha Andress wore striking black and white diamond and South Sea pearl earrings from de Grisogono to a celebrity event last year.

Becoming increasingly creative with black diamonds, Gruosi eventually turned his sights to timepieces. In the late 1990s he unveiled to the world a man's watch entirely set with square-cut black diamonds. Not only was it an immediate success, but even to this day, there is a waiting list for this design. This was Gruosi's entrée into the world of watchmaking—a field he has since pursued with vigor.

colour

THIS PAGE
TOP LEFT

Creativity and a true sense of color reign supreme in this white- and yellow-gold bracelet. It is set with 118 carats of rubies and 44 carats of black diamonds.

TOP CENTER

An 8.95-carat amethyst is the center stone of this ring. It is flanked by nearly 5 carats of rubies.

TOP RIGHT

Symmetry is elegant in these ruby and emerald earrings.

BOTTOM LEFT

Gruosi deftly mixes 5 carats of emeralds with turquoise drops for a daring new take on color.

BOTTOM RIGHT

These 18-karat yellow-gold earrings are set with 4.8 carats of white diamonds and finished with two lovely coral drops.

FACING PAGE
TOP LEFT

Color is all-important in de Grisogono's watch collection as well. This piece features a bezel set with diamonds and a crown set with a natural black diamond.

TOP RIGHT

Part of the new Icy Diamonds collection, this ring is set with approximately 12 carats of gray Icy Diamonds mixed with sapphires and white diamonds.

LEFT CENTER

From the new Icy Diamonds collection, this ring is set with white diamonds and approximately 7 carats of yellow Icy Diamonds.

BOTTOM RIGHT

Platinum and blue make a wonderful combination in these Instrumento Nº Uno watches with automatic movements.

While black is definitely the chic hallmark of de Grisogono, color is also a favorite. In fact, Gruosi has masterfully woven color into his collections every year—often offering unusual mixtures of precious and semiprecious stones, or of oddly contrasting colors.

This past year, for instance, he unveiled cascading earrings of shimmering white diamonds set in 18-karat gold ending with tear-shaped coral drops, and deep green emerald earrings set in blackened white gold ending with tear-shaped turquoise drops. In another rendition of the same earring design, he offered one ruby earring ending in an emerald ball and one emerald earring ending in a ruby ball. In an eye-catching ring, Gruosi combined a nearly 9-carat amethyst center stone with nearly 5 carats of rubies on the ring shank for a red/purple look that is definitively haute couture.

In 2001, de Grisogono also moved into another daring category: lunar diamonds. Calling them "Icy Diamonds," Gruosi was attracted to the milky, almost opalescent appearance of these diamonds. This foray into the world of milky diamonds is similar to the awakening of sleeping beauties with the grace of a simple touch. By using these forgotten stones in his creations, de Grisogono breathes new life into them.

CHRONOLOGY

1996 Opening of de Grisogono on rue du Rhône in Geneva; Launching of the world's first black diamond jewelry collection.

1997 de Grisogono confirms its international presence by opening a boutique in London at 3, Burlington Gardens.

1998 Following the rich and famous to their winter vacation resorts, de Grisogono opens a boutique at the Palace Hotel in Gstaad.

1999 Further attesting to the great success and popularity of de Grisogono with the Italian ladies, Fawaz Gruosi inaugurates a boutique at the Hotel de Russie in Rome.

2000 Gruosi unveils the first de Grisogono watch collection, Instrumento Nº Uno.

2001 Grand opening of the new Geneva boutique at rue du Rhône 27; Launching of de Grisogono's latest mystery—the Icy Diamonds collection.

2002 Presentation of the new de Grisogono watch collection, Instrumento Doppio.

Essentially, the opaque effect of these stones is due to their physical and chemical characteristics. Depending on the nature of the internal particles, waves of different colors can be seen in a single diamond. It is this imbalance that appeals to Gruosi, and it is his determination to "balance that imbalance" in his creations. He hand-selects these stones, carefully mixing and matching the right colors to unite them later with pearls, sapphires or black diamonds in their finished forms.

Instrumento
Nº Uno

Driven by a passion, Gruosi is hardly the type to rest on his laurels. With a highly successful jewelry collection under his reigns, it was time to tackle the watchmaking arena.

It was just a few years after launching his jewelry line that he unveiled his first black diamond men's watch. From there, he set to work creating the black diamond Ice Cube for Chopard. Requiring 76 perfect black diamonds, the black Ice Cube was an important feat. It took Gruosi two years to collect enough uniformly colored black diamonds to create the watch.

In the year 2000, Gruosi unveiled his own timepiece collection to the world at the International Watch, Clock and Jewelry Fair in Basel. Called Instrumento Nº Uno, the collection was based on one significantly bold, cushioned-square shape. It garnered immediate attention thanks to the design and the stylistic elements. For the collection, de Grisogono used black diamonds mixed with colored stones or white diamonds. The straps were textured stingray that offered even more depth and dimension to the watches. Men and women alike were enchanted by the collection and it has become as successful as everything else de Grisogono fashions.

TOP

The bezel of this watch is set with 148 white diamonds and the hinges are set with an additional 36 diamonds to enhance the pink-gold case and dial. The watch houses a mechanical movement with automatic wind.

LEFT

This Instrumento Nº Uno watch is crafted in 18-karat pink gold with pink mother-of-pearl dial and red stingray strap.

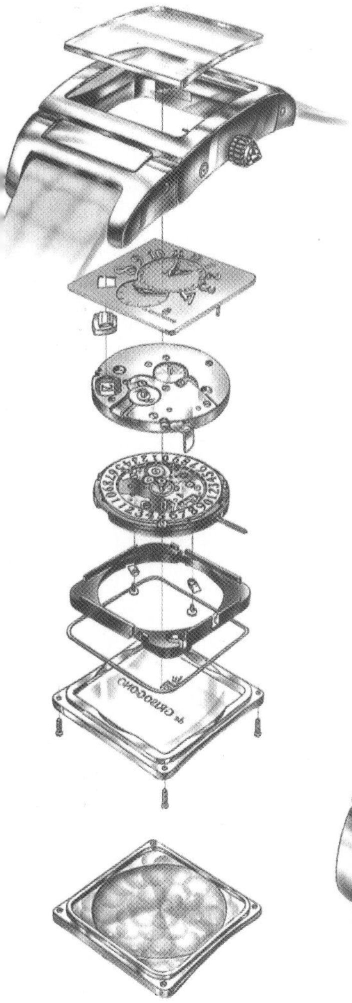

The newest timepieces unveiled in 2001 further build upon the initial Instrumento Nº Uno concept. Using platinum, gold and steel cases, de Grisogono unveiled colored straps with coordinated colored stones, colored mother-of-pearl dials and colored gold, with a particular emphasis on pink gold and blackened gold. Every watch houses an automatic movement and features a large date at 7:30. There is a subdial on each watch that offers a dual time zone function.

The amazing difference between each of the Instrumento Nº Uno timepieces stems from the various decorations of the dials and cases. Dials are often guilloché in contrasting patterns from one dial to the second time-zone dial. Varying degrees of diamonds and gemstones are used, ranging from no stones to totally adorned watches. Sometimes, black diamonds are offset by white diamonds, rubies or emeralds. Indeed, considering that this vast line of timepieces is based on one model, it is difficult to find redundancy—only further attesting to the creative genius of Gruosi.

TOP LEFT

Every Instrumento Nº Uno watch features two dials, one that marks the local time and a smaller one that marks the second time zone.

TOP RIGHT

The square case of every Instrumento Nº Uno is 33mm by 33mm. This one is crafted in steel with a copper-colored dial. It is water resistant to 30 meters.

BOTTOM

The bracelet versions of the Instrumento Nº Uno feature an articulated design that replicates the shape of the case.

DeLaneau

an historical perspective

Since its establishment in 1880, DeLaneau has been dedicated to combining the finest Swiss craftsmanship with haute joaillerie techniques and innovative style. Provocative, exciting and different, DeLaneau watches are designed to upstage everything one wears, but not to upstage the wearer.

While DeLaneau has always created gemstone watches, it is only in the past 30 years that it has gained international recognition for its high-jeweled masterpieces. DeLaneau's superb gemsetting and original designs may well be unparalleled in today's market. In fact, in the past three years, the brand has been actively designing and introducing one of the most scintillating collections of haute joaillerie watches.

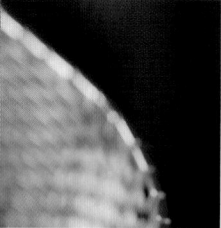

DeLaneau's meticulous craftsmanship is so time-consuming and excessively precise that only about 1,500 watches are produced in a year. Some of the most special pieces and elaborate custom orders can take more than a year to create.

The driving design force behind this private brand is Cristina Thévenaz. Young, chic and consumed by the belief that women should be capricious and daring, Thévenaz strives to create the most romantic and exquisitely feminine timepieces one can imagine. Indeed, exotic, sensual and intriguing best describe DeLaneau's timepieces. Even its watches for men are elegantly sculpted or architecturally inspired for an air of bold and sexy sophistication.

Technically referred to as a watch brand, DeLaneau is more about a state of mind, a style, and lifestyle, than it is about telling time.

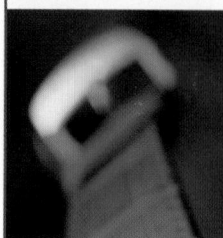

RIGHT

First Lady limited series watch in white gold set with round diamonds (6.00cts) and 28 square-cut pink sapphires (3.91cts). Pink mother-of-pearl dial with fancy numerals and a diamond-paved centre.

unbridled feminity

The newest collection from DeLaneau is the Les Capricieuses series of bejeweled beauties. Designed to set free one's natural impulses, the Les Capricieuses series symbolizes individuality and freedom.

The collection consists of three sensational high-jeweled watches, each of which celebrates one of three women whose charisma entranced the world and whose every move struck a chord of sensual nonconformity. Marlène Dietrich epitomized mystique and allure; Joséphine Baker's exotic dancing scandalized a city; and Ginger Rogers' high-heeled twirling left men and women alike breathless. These are the legends upon which the Les Capricieuses collection is built.

Marlène Dietrich was a woman who seemed hard to impress. She responded almost indifferently to the extraordinary or the outrageous. Therefore, DeLaneau chose to name one of its most exquisite watch-making phenomena after her. The Marlène bracelet watch breaks all conventions of watch and jewelry making. It is a latticework of golden mesh, formed into a sleekly supple bracelet set off by a tassel of pearls. In the middle of this golden shimmer is a golden ribbed dome that lifts to reveal a baguette watch in a semi-cylindrical case beneath. This "secret" watch is made in 18-karat white or yellow gold and features onyx cabochons.

THIS PAGE
TOP&BOTTOM

Marlène bracelet watch in yellow gold set in diamonds on the case and on the mounting of the ruby tassel, gold batons and onyx cabochons (1.83cts).

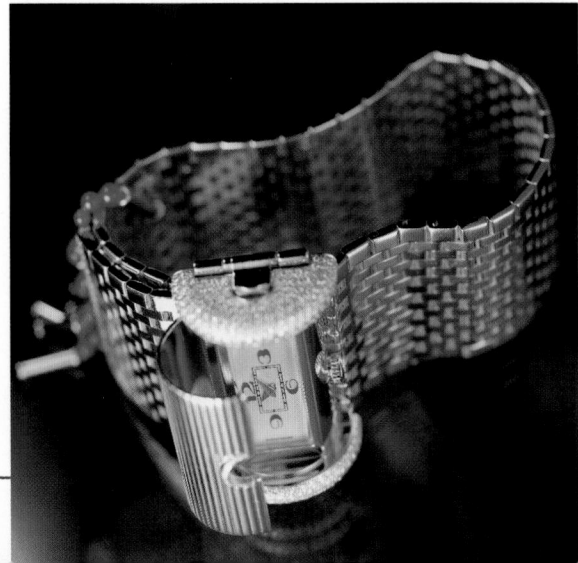

The Joséphine is designed to celebrate the free spirit of its namesake. The long-chained watch embodies the skills of Geneva's finest jewelers and watchmakers and features a patented shutter design that opens to reveal the dial. Created in either 18-karat yellow or white gold, the watch glimmers with accents of diamonds, onyx and a ruby cabochon. It features a stunning 12-row tassel of Akoya, onyx, ruby and many other precious pearls. Several versions exist of the Joséphine, each one more enticing than the next.

The Ginger Butterfly watch recalls the desirable Ginger Rogers and her extravagant dance routines with Fred Astaire. This amazing woman captured the hearts of men and women alike. As such, it is only befitting that DeLaneau select bedazzling sapphires for this exquisite series. Every watch features a selection of perfectly matched sapphires that capture the subtleties of light and color. Each piece is individually made and therefore unique.

Perhaps more so than any other DeLaneau timepieces, these luxury watches are designed to break the mold, to evoke the sensual, seductive side of anyone.

magical masterpieces

A variety of striking new models also grace the key DeLaneau ladies' collections and the three key men's collections.

For women, the most important DeLaneau watch collections include the Butterfly and the First Lady. The Butterfly is an exquisite, artfully interpreted rendition of its namesake. The case is curved in a butterfly pattern that is enhanced by diamonds or gemstones for luxurious color that emulates nature. Crafted in 18-karat white or yellow gold, the timeless interpretations of the Butterfly watches are created with anywhere from 2 carats to more than 7 carats of diamonds and sapphires. Some versions simply have a gemstone case and bezel, other versions include a diamond pavé dial, and yet others are fully encrusted with diamonds from end to end. The newest versions feature pastel straps and elegant color-coordinated gemstones.

The First Lady collection is a dramatically elegant reinterpretation of Art Deco designs. Representative of the brand's distinctive styling, the First Lady watches combine gold, diamonds and gemstones with mother-of-pearl dials in striking tonneau-cases and inverted-tonneau dial shapes. The unique mix of geometric patterns is available in a several combinations.

Perhaps the most striking of the First Lady timepieces is the First Lady Jewelry collection. These exquisitely feminine watches are among the most sought after of DeLaneau's creations. The brand's jewelers handset each and every watch individually, combining fancy-cut gemstones and diamonds in imaginative ways. Available in two sizes, the First Lady watches feature pearl, diamond or gold Milanese bracelets. Soft leather straps in a vast array of striking pastel and bright colors are also available.

The men's collections are also striking in their presentation. Sculpted edges, polished gold and bold difference mark each one of the key collections.

One of them is the Three Time Zones collection, a chronograph design patented 15 years ago. This bold, round watch houses an automatic movement. The round case features a main dial with small, round dials, one above the 12 and one below the 6, serving as case-to-bracelet attachments. Each of the smaller dials depicts a different time zone. Every rendition of this watch is a provocative statement of individuality and worldliness.

All DeLaneau timepieces are created in Switzerland under the watchful eye of Thévenaz who insists that all of the brand's watches answer to the call of the free-spirited soul.

DUBEY & SCHALDENBRAND

Cinette Robert: the soul of Dubey Schaldenbrand timekeepers

an historical perspective

In a luxury industry dominated by financial groups that lean toward mass production of timepieces, Dubey & Schaldenbrand's outstanding feature is that this trademark belongs to the high-quality segment where movements are the sinews of war. It was only thanks to Cinette Robert's atypical path and original personality that the house could take a pride in carrying on its glorious history.

This enthusiastic woman who collected movements, was able to cause the heart of each model in the Dubey & Schaldenbrand collection to beat with the exclusive movements of her precious collection. Thus, she offered collectors and lovers of beautiful watches limited series of high-quality pieces and kept alive the exclusive spirit of the brand.

Francinette Robert (affectionately called "Cinette") was born in Les Ponts-de-Martel, a small village of two thousand souls located in the Sagne valley in the Neuchâtel Canton, where watchmakers' creativity never lacked. While most families of this region are devoted to the watchmaking industry, this is not the case of the Roberts. Although her mother devised technical plans for the prestigious Martel watch company from home, only Cinette's great-grandfather had been an actual watchmaker. According to Cinette, this could be the only origin of her unlimited passion for watch handicrafts. As a young girl, Cinette acted as a messenger between her home and the enterprise for which her mother worked and became accustomed to the peculiar atmosphere of watchmakers' workshops. The Martel company (which employed about one hundred workers) cooperated with the most important houses to produce exclusive calibers such as the Universal chronograph or Zenith's famous El Primero model. In this enterprise, Cinette was initially hired as an administration employee in 1960 and worked there until 1963. Very quickly she developed a real cult for watchmaker sciences, but her professional ambition led her first into the banking world of Zürich, Switzerland's first financial center. Here she learned the severity of figures, but the position lacked the emotions she searched for and Cinette decided to return to her first love: beautiful watch movements.

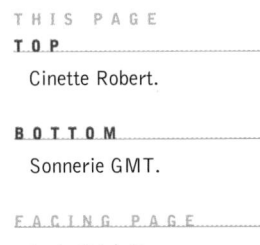

273

DUBEY & SCHALDENBRAND

She made her debut as a manager at Mathey-Tissot, a movement factory cooperating with important houses (such as Vacheron Constantin, Girard-Perregaux, Breguet, and Gübelin) essentially for the realization of exceptional pieces. She held this position for 15 years; it offered her a unique and irreplaceable experience. Soon she discovered that very creative watchmakers often work in small independent workshops, and not within big structures. For this reason, Mathey-Tissot also assigned to them overhauling and repairs of complicated pieces. Particular ties were therefore secured between this rigorous and passionate woman and fine craftsmen. At that time, she met Georges Dubey, who had an intense relationship with the Mathey-Tissot company.

But when the quartz era began, Cinette did not accept the explanation that the mechanical watch crafts were bound to disappear; she preferred to leave such an industry which no longer corresponded to her expectations. Following her belief that mechanical timepieces were here to stay, she established a business of her own devoted to the production and marketing of old watches and movements. Therefore, when presented with the opportunity, she did not hesitate to go to England to glean even further knowledge from the most prestigious auction sale houses.

an interesting search

Thanks to her direct contacts with the watchmakers of her region, little by little Cinette bought many stocks of components, which allowed her to recover old calibers. To this end she built extensive archives and this activity broadened her technical knowledge to a great extent. Furthermore, apart from owning an extraordinary collection of pocket watches and movements, she possesses valuable books on watchmaking, which contain the secrets of the most important mechanical realizations ever invented. Soon collectors, museums and passionate individuals were among her list of privileged customers.

With great emotion she admits that, when travelling abroad, she finds it difficult to resist the temptation to buy a new piece if she learns that the watchmaker is a fellow-countryman of hers. She can imagine the craftsman's work and personality as well as the trajectory of the timekeeper who must have experienced the most secret of adventures. But the status of an independent venture is not always very easy to hold. Therefore, to allow herself to get on with her passion for watches, she divided her activity into the trades of pocket watches and wristwatches—two different classifications for two different classes of customers.

1995 was an important year in Cinette Robert's life, as well as the House's. Just 24 hours after receiving the offer to buy Dubey & Schaldenbrand, she accepted and launched into her new adventure. Why choose this brand and not another? Her answer: She was personally acquainted with Georges Dubey; greatly respected and admired him as the owner of a very interesting patent of a split-second chronograph; and Dubey was a creator of consistently high-quality and even exceptional movements—some of which were included in Cinette's own collection. These were sufficient reasons to stimulate the interest of a mechanical watch expert such as Cinette.

THIS PAGE

LEFT

Aerodyn Celebrity.

LEFT CENTER

Aerodyn Celebrity movement.

BOTTOM

Cinette Robert at work.

FACING PAGE
BOTTOM

Lady acier, with automatic movement.

Dubey & Schaldenbrand —yesterday and today

CHRONOLOGY

Just after World War II in 1946, watchmaker Dubey, who was then working as a teacher at the Technicum of La Chaux-de-Fonds, created his first caliber: a split-second chronograph with a mobile pointer, a mechanism developed from one of the principles of French watchmaker Josepf Winnerl (1870). Dubey's high-performance split-second chronograph was much cheaper than those of Breitling, Butex or Patek Philippe and it was used very frequently in important sporting events and for military purposes.

The system of this movement, called Index Mobile, is as simple as it is brilliant—it does not require a column-wheel nor pincer-like levers—but at the same time is quite clever. A central wheel (placed at the center of the chronograph) allows the positioning of a central axis on the dial and its connections directly to a pusher. A kind of brake allows the split-second hand to be stopped by depressing a pusher on the crown until the time reading is taken. The hand that is still in use recoils a balance-spring lying on the dial that is hooked over the short ends of both second hands. After releasing the pusher, a return spring ensures that the stopped second hand catches up with its traveling companion. This invention of the Index Mobile was patented all over the world and led to a huge business success for Dubey.

René Schaldenbrand, another highly intelligent and experienced watchmaker, joined Dubey and together they created the Dubey & Schaldenbrand Watch Company that undoubtedly possesses a unique know-how in the field of watch complications. Soon the company attracted a large following of collectors interested in the realization and restoration of complex pieces, although its production did not yet exceed 2,000 pieces per year.

Today the brand is addressing a customer segment of connoisseurs and collectors with a yearly output of around 5,000 pieces marketed all over the world in equal proportions: Europe, Asia and the United States of America. Visionary Cinette Robert was able to keep up the spirit of this exceptional company within the purest of watchmaking tradition, thus maintaining the spirit of the founding fathers. Here, the classical art of fine watchmaking is combined with the advanced technology of modern mechanical movements. The watches produced in limited series adopt exclusive movements and the standard collection consists of exclusive Dubey & Schaldenbrand developments on the basis of either Eta or Valjoux calibers.

Movements receive special attention from highly skilled engravers, creating individual works of art because the patterns are always slightly different. Naturally, this contributes greatly to the exclusive quality of each piece. Only after a watch's individual elements have been polished and plated are they assembled and ready to undergo the elaborate testing procedures to ensure precise, accurate performance. And only upon passing are they eventually enclosed in their cases.

Among these precision timepieces from Dubey & Schaldenbrand are the: Vintage Carré Cambré, Aerodyn Vintage, Jumping Hour, Regulator, Gran'Chrono Astro, Carré Cambré Martel, Sonnerie GMT, and the Lady Celebrity. The flowing lines of the Aerodyn models look particularly flattering on anyone's wrist despite the unusual size of the watch. The decorative work covering the dials with refined guilloché patterns has made these timepieces appreciated collectors' items at acceptable prices.

CHRONOLOGY

1946 Georges Dubey, professor at the Ecole d'Horlogerie in La Chaux-de-Fonds, during his holidays develops a new split-second chronograph system that he calls "Index Mobile"; He joins master watchmaker René Schaldenbrand and creates the trademark Dubey & Schaldenbrand.

1947 Dubey's patent application for the split-second chronograph is filed in Switzerland, France and the USA.

1948 More complementary patent applications are filed.

1950 The production of gentlemen's automatic watches reaches its peak; The Dubey & Schaldenbrand collection is enriched by the addition of an alarm.

1960 A new 6 3/4" automatic ladies' watch is produced as well as an 11 1/2" caliber with power reserve.

1970 Chronographs are the fashion and production follows its rhythm.

1980 The popularity of quartz movements does not upset Dubey & Schaldenbrand. They will never make them. On the contrary, Georges Dubey devotes his talent to the restoration of antique watches, minute repeaters, perpetual calendars, Jack-o'-the-clocks, grand sonneries, etc.

1990 As of this year Georges Dubey has reassembled 17 tourbillon pocket watches—an impressive record.

1995 Cinette Robert acquires Dubey & Schaldenbrand with the vision of selling high quality watches all over the world.

2001 5,000 watches are exported to 30 different countries.

DUBEY & SCHALDENBRAND

GRAN'CHRONO ASTRO

Movement: mechanical, automatic winding, modified Valjoux 7751 caliber. Gilded and engraved; skeletonized rotor.
Functions: hour, minute, full calendar (date, day, month), moon phases, chronograph with 2 counters.
Case: stainless steel, two-piece case, in curved tonneau shape (size 49 x 37.5 mm, thickness 15.3 mm); curved sapphire crystal; drop-shaped pushers; back

attached by 6 screws, displaying the movement through a sapphire crystal. Water-resistant to 3 atm.
Dial: silvered, engine-turned (guilloché); printed markers on a railway minute track; luminescent blued steel Alpha hands.
Indications: moon phase and hour counter at 6; day, month and minute counter at 12; center second and date.
Strap: crocodile leather; stainless steel fold-over clasp.
Also available: with simple clasp; with stainless steel bracelet; in pink gold with leather strap. All versions are available with silvered, black or blue dial.

GRAN'CHRONO

Movement: mechanical, automatic winding, modified Valjoux 7750 caliber, with 25 jewels. Hand-decorated, with gold-plated pillar-plates and bridges; skeletonized rotor.
Functions: hour, minute, date, chronograph with 2 counters.
Case: stainless steel, two-piece case, in curved tonneau shape (size 49 x 37.5 mm, thickness 15.5 mm); curved sapphire crystal; drop-shaped pushers; back

attached by 6 screws, displaying the movement through a sapphire crystal. Water-resistant to 3 atm.
Dial: blue, engine-turned (guilloché) with sun pattern; gilded printed pointed markers; luminescent steel lozenge hands.
Indications: date and hour counter at 6, minute counter at 12, center second counter, railway minute track.
Strap: crocodile leather; stainless steel fold-over clasp.
Also available: in pink gold; with black or silvered dial.

AERODYN JUMP HOUR

Movement: mechanical manual winding, old make, Vintage 1960 caliber.
Functions: jumping hour, minute, small second. **Case:** stainless steel, two-piece case, in curved tonneau shape (size 43 x 32.5 mm, thickness 11.4 mm); curved sapphire crystal, antireflective on both sides; back attached by 7 screws displaying the movement through a sapphire crystal. Water-resistant to 3 atm.
Dial: blue, guilloché with sun pattern; small second zone decorated with cir-

cular neads; white printed minute track, steel hands, Dauphine minute hand. **Indications:** jumping hour at 12, center minute, small second at 6.
Strap: crocodile leather, steel clasp. Limited edition of 300 pieces.
Also available: with black or silvered dial; with steel bracelet; in pink gold with black dial and crocodile leather strap, limited edition of 100 pieces.

AERODYN DUO

Movement: mechanical, automatic winding, modified ETA 2892-2A caliber (exclusive model D&S), with 23 jewels. Balance with 28,800 vibrations per hour.
Functions: hour, minute, second, date, second time-zone time, 24 hours.
Case: stainless steel, two-piece case, in curved tonneau shape (size 43 x 32.5 mm, thickness 11.5 mm); curved sapphire glass; crown for the regulation of all functions (normal position clockwise for winding, first click clockwise for the adjustment of the second time zone, counterclockwise for date correction, second click clockwise for main time correction); back attached by 7 screws. Water-resistant to 3 atm.
Dial: bright blue; printed white Arabic numerals and luminescent dots on the printed railway minute track; luminescent steel Sports hands.
Indications: date at 6, 24 hour at 9, second time zone with double hand at 12.
Bracelet: steel; fold-over clasp.
Also available: with leather strap (with simple or fold-over clasp); in pink gold, leather strap. All versions are available with silvered dial and pink numerals or black and pink numerals or black and white numerals.

AERODYN RÉGULATEUR

REF. D794212B11

Movement: mechanical, manual winding, old make, Peseux 7040 caliber. Entirely hand-engraved; totally redesigned bridges.
Functions: hour, minute, small second.
Case: 18 kt pink gold, two-piece case, in curved tonneau shape (size 43 x 32.5 mm, thickness 11.7 mm); curved sapphire crystal, antireflective on both sides; back attached by 7 screws, displaying the movement through a sapphire crystal. Water-resistant to 3 atm.

Dial: silvered, engine turned (guilloché) with old-basket pattern, zones decorated with circular beads; printed Roman numerals and railway minute track; pink-gold-plated Breguet hands.
Strap: crocodile leather; pink gold clasp.
Available: limited edition of 30 pieces with silvered dial and 20 with black dial.

AERODYN DATE

Movement: mechanical, automatic winding, modified ETA 2892 caliber.
Functions: hour, minute, small second, big sized date.
Case: stainless steel, two-piece case, in curved tonneau shape (size 43 x 32.5 mm, thickness 11.7 mm); curved sapphire crystal, antireflective on both sides; back attached by 7 screws. Water-resistant to 3 atm.
Dial: silvered, engine turned (guilloché), zones decorated with circular beads; printed Roman numerals and railway minute track; blued steel leaf style hands.
Indications: small second at 6; big-sized date at 12.
Bracelet: in stainless steel; fold-over clasp.
Also available: in pink gold.

CARRE CAMBRE DIPLOMATIC

Movement: mechanical, automatic winding, modified ETA 2892A2 caliber (exclusive model D&S), with 23 jewels. Balance with 28,800 vibrations per hour.
Functions: hour, minute, second, date, second time-zone time, 24 hours.
Case: stainless steel, two-piece, in curved cambered shape (size 34 x 34 mm, thickness 9.5 mm); antireflective curved sapphire glass; crown for the regulation of all functions (normal position, clockwise for winding, first click clockwise for the adjustment of the second time zone, counterclockwise for date correction, second click clockwise for main time correction); back attached by 4 screws. Water-resistant to 3 atm.

Dial: white; printed black Arabic numerals and railway minute track; blued steel leaf style hands.
Indications: date at 6, 24 hour at 9, second time zone with double hand at 12.
Strap: crocodile leather; steel clasp.
Also available: with fold-over clasp; in pink gold. Both versions are available with white dial and black numerals, black and silvered numerals or blue and silvered numerals.

CARRE CAMBRE CALENDAR

Movement: mechanical, automatic winding, modified ETA 2892A2 caliber.
Functions: hour, minute, small second, big sized date.
Case: stainless steel, two-piece, in curved cambered shape (size 34 x 34 mm, thickness 9.9 mm); antireflective curved sapphire glass; back attached by 4 screws. Water-resistant to 3 atm.
Dial: silvered, engine-turned (guilloché); applied blued steel cabochon markers and Arabic numerals 3 and 9; blued steel Alpha hands; printed minute track.
Indications: small second at 6; big-sized date at 12.
Strap: crocodile leather; steel clasp.
Also available: in pink gold.

EBEL

an historical perspective

The year 2001 marked the momentous occasion of the 90th anniversary of this prestigious brand. It was in 1911, in La Chaux-de-Fonds—the heart of Swiss watchmaking—that Eugène Blum and his wife Alice Lévy founded Ebel. A combination of their initials (Eugène Blum Et Lévy), Ebel was founded on a philosophy of design and harmony.

When the brand unveiled its first wristwatch in 1912, it garnered immediate acclaim with its timeless character and boldly modern flair. Ebel quickly built its reputation by creating luxury platinum and gold, diamond- and gemstone-set watches that adhered to a guiding principle of pursuit of style.

Throughout the ensuing decades, Ebel's development was marked by numerous distinctions. The brand won preeminent awards, developed a variety of new systems and patents in watchmaking, and became a vital source of movements for other prestigious brands. During World War II, Ebel was a key supplier of watches to the British Army, and afterward, continued its expansion. By 1956 Blum had inaugurated a new factory. During the rough years of quartz innovation, which left many Swiss watch companies paralyzed, Ebel continued to grow.

Innovative new spirit blew through the company in the 1970s when third-generation Ebel launched the Sport Classic into the world in 1977—a line that would set the tone for all future Ebel collections. Based on the concept of soft lines and the elimination of sharp angles, the Sport Classic features a simple case structure and integrated wave-like bracelet. It became an emblem of the brand and its forward-thinking, cutting-edge design.

Since then, Ebel has unveiled striking new products that have earned spots in the international limelight. Among the key introductions were the Beluga in 1985 and the 1911 in 1986.

In 1999 the brand was taken over by the internationally famed LVMH luxury group. The acquisition of Ebel by LVMH has offered great opportunities to the brand for marketing and product development. In fact, Ebel has since launched evolutions of the brand's greatest successes—bringing it to new levels of accomplishment. Indeed, the dynamism and long-term vision that is indicative of LVMH now backs Ebel—whose renewed aim is to regain a dominant position in the world market for haute horlogerie.

THIS PAGE

TOP

Eugène Blum and his wife Alice Lévy.

BOTTOM

Ebel automatic movement Caliber 137.

FACING PAGE

The concept of the Classic Wave is based on a sphere.

279

unveiling

masterpieces

vis inclinées
(centre sphère)

SPHERES

According to Managing Director Guillaume Brochard, Ebel will focus on "a narrower range of its most powerful products. To achieve this," he says, "we are grounding our efforts on the strong historical values of designs and watchmaking know-how that represent Ebel's distinctive heritage."

Ebel watches not only offer sensual shapes, originality and subtle elegance in their designs, but also focus on technical quality. Since 1999, Ebel has organized the complete Manufacture of its watches within its new production facility in La Chaux-de-Fonds. Here the cases, bracelets and movements are created, assembled and fitted together with the utmost attention to detail and precision—guaranteeing both craftsmanship and daring, innovative style.

Indeed, the newest collections reflect this commitment. Among the pillars of the brand are the Sport Classic, Beluga and 1911—and these are the key lines that have most recently been boldly updated and brazenly unveiled.

In fact, the new Classic Wave takes its inspiration from the Sport Classic watch and pays

THIS PAGE
TOP LEFT

The Classic Wave Senior is distinctly weighty and rugged, projecting an unmistakably powerful personality.

CENTER

A sketch of Classic Wave.

BOTTOM LEFT

This Classic Lady has a case and bracelet crafted in gold and steel and a white dial with Roman numerals.

FACING PAGE
BOTTOM

Classic Wave lady bicolor with diamonds on the bezel.

tribute to its emblematic wave design. A watershed for Ebel, the expressive wave bracelet offers flowing lines, balanced proportions and incredible comfort. Subtly, the Sport Classic has been refined to enhance its appeal and has become the Classic Wave.

To achieve the artful blend of contemporary appeal and timeless value that is the Ebel signature, the brand turned to a creative team of two brothers, Renato and Marco Scarinzi. Drawing upon the ingenuity of the original integrated one-piece case and bracelet design, the Scarinzi brothers elevated it to new style heights.

The fundamental goals were to lend more volume and substance to the watch while preserving its essence. This was achieved by creating a gold-and-steel version that juxtaposed the colors and finishes for emphasized appeal, and by elongating the case to give it a more powerful visual effect.

Several versions of the Classic Wave now exist—each available in three sizes: mini, ladies' or gents'. Additionally, a wide range of refined dial choices is offered. In the mini and ladies' versions, the Classic Wave offers a host of feminine touches including diamond markers, mother-of-pearl dials and gem-set bezels. The gents' models offer bold style and sleek lines so that the entire collection exudes emotional, sensual and chic undertones.

1911 Ebel brand is founded by Eugène Blum and his wife, Alice Lévy. "Ebel" is derived from a combination of their initials: Eugène Blum Et Lévy.

1912 Launch of the first Ebel wristwatch.

1914 The brand wins gold medal at the Swiss National Exhibition in Bern; First sales to the Austro-Hungarian markets.

1925 Ebel is awarded the Grand Prix in the Decorative Arts Exhibition in Paris.

1929 Ebel launches the "baguette" movements for jewelry watches; Wins Diploma of Honour at the Barcelona Exhibition; Son Charles-Eugène Blum joins the company.

1930 Launch of Ebello, a self-winding travel watch.

1932 Company launches the travel Mignonette model.

1935 The brand receives Diploma at the Universal Exhibition in Brussels; Ebel is the first Swiss watch company to use the Western Electrique system for precision testing.

1939-1945 Ebel is a key supplier of watches to the British army.

1955 Launch of the 96 Piguet caliber, the world's thinnest movement (1.7mm). It enjoys worldwide success, particularly in America.

1956 The company builds a new factory and expands production.

1957 Charles Blum co-founds the Communauté d'Horlogerie de Précision.

1968 Alice Lévy Blum steps down from the Chairmanship of the Board of Directors at the age of 88.

1970 Pierre-Alain Blum, the founders' grandson, joins Ebel.

1977 Ebel introduces the Sport Classic model.

1983 The Perpetual Calendar Chronograph debuts.

1985 Ebel unveils the Beluga line.

1986 Launch of 1911 model; Ebel acquires the Villa Turque, the mansion built by Le Corbusier in 1916-1917 in La Chaux-de-Fonds.

1994 Majority of interest in the Ebel Group is acquired by Investcorp.

1995 Launch of Le Modulor Chrono 1911 chronograph.

1997 Introduction of the Beluga Steel model.

1998 Launch of the Beluga Manchette model.

1999 Ebel is acquired by the LVMH Group in October; Launch of the E-Type model.

2000 The company launches the Type E Chronograph 137 Ebel movement, certified chronometer.

2001 Classic Wave, the new 1911 model and the new Beluga Manchette are introduced.

reaching

new heights

This past year also ushered in a seductive introduction of the Beluga Manchette. Since its creation, the Beluga watch has enticed women around the world with its multiple facets of femininity. Originally unveiled in a round case-shape, the Manchette model was added about three years ago. Today, a daringly innovative, refined version joins the ranks.

The new Beluga Manchette offers a striking array of spectacular straps of all colors and textures. Patent leather offers evening glamour, while textured fabric makes an intriguing round-the-clock appearance. Pastel hues and vibrant colors intermingle beautifully with diamond markers and diamond bezels to create luminous virtuosi. These newest selections of Beluga Manchette watches, created in stainless steel, offer black or mother-of-pearl dials, pastel, gray or black straps, and scintillating diamond accents.

Crafted in gold for the Round Beluga, or in steel with diamonds set on the case and dial, they are a glowing tribute to femininity thanks to their curves, purity, sensuality and radiance.

Created in 1985, the original model with its discreet and refined elegance is still one of the brand's bestsellers; a timeless yet still contemporary watch, graceful, attractive and even seductive...perhaps like the women who wear it. Feminine to the core, Beluga quite obviously delights in showing that it has plenty of surprises in reserve, even for longstanding admirers. Pared down to sparkling essentials, the new dials feature four diamonds at 12, 3, 6 and 9:00.

THIS PAGE
TOP
Beluga Manchette dons a black calf leather strap and diamonds on the case.

BOTTOM LEFT
The Beluga Manchette with a steel case, a rose fabric strap, mother-of-pearl dial, and case set with 14 baguette-cut pink sapphires.

FACING PAGE
BOTTOM LEFT
Simple elegance and harmony of balance, as seen in this 1911 watch, are hallmarks of Ebel's designs.

RIGHT
Beluga with a fuchsia dial.

The softly striated or sunray effect adds to the sense of refined purity and is typical of Ebel's concern for the details that make the difference. For an added touch of trendy glamour, a blushing fuchsia dial tells the world that this timelessly elegant watch also likes to capture the spotlight on certain occasions.

Powerfully symbolizing Ebel's commitment to watchmaking tradition, the 1911 series carries distinctive characteristics of the brand—such as the soft hexagonal case and five functional bezel screws. The newest pieces, however, are more expressive and assertive, offering a wealth of new dials and a stronger sense of balance and beauty.

The reinterpretations of the 1911—for both women and men—are infused with energy gathered from new mixtures of materials and colors. Bracelet versions are in steel or steel-and-gold mixtures; straps include pastels for women and the rugged, yet classically elegant stitched brown or black alligator for men.

Remaining true to its creed of quality, Ebel's new men's 1911 watches are automatic calibers. There is also a resolutely masculine, COSC-certified chronometer chronograph. The crisp design of this elegant watch with black dial and 12-hour, 30-minute and 60-second counters disguises the top-quality automatic Caliber 137 (with 200 parts) that lies within.

Indeed, quality, perfection and timeless elegance have been the core of the Ebel philosophy since its inception—and will remain the guiding principles for its creations of the future.

EBEL

CLASSIC WAVE SENIOR	REF. 9187F41/0225

Movement: quartz, Ebel 187 caliber.
Functions: hour, minute, second.
Case: stainless steel, single-piece brushed case; domed sapphire glass with antireflective treatment; polished bezel fastened with 5 screws; steel crown. Water-resistant to 5 atm.
Dial: silvered, engine-turned (guilloché); applied curved steel Roman numer-

als; round domed hands.
Bracelet: stainless steel; triple-blade folding clasp.
Also available: blue galvanized, mat black, white mat dial; in steel with diamond bezel, mat white dial; in steel and yellow gold with steel bracelet and PVD treatment or with strap; rhodium-galvanized, white or mat ivory dial, silvered guilloché: in steel and yellow gold with diamond bezel, mat white dial; in yellow gold with gold bracelet or strap: black enameled, silvered dial; in yellow gold with diamond bezel and silvered dial.

CLASSIC WAVE SENIOR	REF. 8187F41/6235137

Movement: quartz, Ebel 187 caliber.
Functions: hour, minute, second, date.
Case: 18 kt yellow gold, single-piece brushed case; domed sapphire glass with antireflective treatment; polished bezel fastened with 5 screws; gold crown. Water-resistant to 5 atm.

Dial: silvered; applied curved gold Roman numerals; gold baton hands. **Indications:** date at 3.
Strap: crocodile leather; gold triple-blade folding clasp.
Also available: black enameled dial; in yellow gold with diamond bezel, silvered dial; in steel and yellow gold with steel bracelet and PVD treatment or with strap; rhodium-galvanized, white or mat ivory dial, silvered guilloché: in steel and yellow gold with diamond bezel, mat white dial; in steel with blue galvanized, mat black, mat white, silvered, guilloché dial; in steel with diamond bezel and mat white dial.

CLASSIC WAVE LADY	REF. 1090F21/9725

Movement: quartz, Ebel 687 caliber. **Functions:** hour, minute. **Case:** stainless steel and 18 kt yellow gold, single-piece brushed case; domed sapphire glass with antireflective treatment; polished bezel fastened with 5 screws; gold crown. Water-resistant to 5 atm. **Dial:** mother-of-pearl; applied curved gold Roman numerals and 10 set diamonds; round domed hands. **Bracelet:** stainless steel with PVD treatment; triple-blade folding clasp. **Also available:** with slate-

gray, black enameled, mat ivory, mat white dial; in steel and yellow gold diamond bezel, mother-of-pearl dial applied Roman numerals, mat white or mother-of-pearl dial diamond markers; in steel with mat white, rhodium-galvanized, blue guilloché dial or mother-of-pearl applied Roman numerals, mat white, blue guilloché or mother-of-pearl dial and diamond markers; in steel with diamond bezel mother-of-pearl dial applied Roman numerals, mat white or mother-of-pearl dial diamond markers; in yellow gold (bracelet also with diamonds); mother-of-pearl dial Roman numeral or diamond markers; in yellow gold diamond bezel Roman numeral or diamond markers.

CLASSIC WAVE MINI	REF. 8157F14/9725

Movement: quartz, Ebel 157 caliber. **Functions:** hour, minute. **Case:** 18 kt yellow gold, single-piece brushed case; domed sapphire glass with antireflective treatment; bezel with set diamonds, fastened with 5 screws; gold crown. Water-resistant to 5 atm. **Dial:** mother-of-pearl; applied curved gold Roman numerals and 10 set diamonds; round domed hands. **Bracelet:** gold; triple-blade folding clasp. **Also available:** bezel with diamonds or simple bezel; mother-of-pearl dial applied

Roman numerals; in steel and yellow gold (stainless steel bracelet with PVD treatment) mat white, mat ivory or mother-of-pearl dial applied Roman numerals, mat white, black enameled or mother-of-pearl dial diamond markers; in steel and yellow gold diamond bezel, mother-of-pearl dial applied Roman numerals, mat white or mother-of-pearl dial applied Roman numerals, mat white or mother-of-pearl dial: in steel with mat black, silvered, blue galvanized, blue guilloché or mother-of-pearl dial applied Roman numerals, mat white or mother-of-pearl dial diamond markers, mat white or mother-of-pearl dial applied Roman numerals, mother-of-pearl dial diamond markers.

CHRONO 1911   REF. 9137240/14735138

Movement: mechanical, automatic winding, Ebel 137 caliber. Officially certified "chronometer" (C.O.S.C.).
Functions: hour, minute, small second, date.
Case: stainless steel, three-piece brushed case; flat sapphire glass with antireflective treatment; polished bezel fastened with 5 screws; steel crown. Water-resistant to 3 atm.

Dial: blue with sun pattern; zones decorated with circular beads; cabochon markers and applied curved steel Roman numerals, luminescent dots on the flange; luminescent steel baton hands. **Indications:** minute counter at 3, date between 4 and 5, hour counter at 6, small second at 9, center second counter, minute track with divisions for 1/5 of a second.
Strap: crocodile leather; screwed attachment; steel fold-over clasp.
Also available: with bracelet; with black dial; in steel and gold with strap or bracelet, silvered or black dial; in yellow gold with strap or bracelet and silvered dial.

1911 CHRONOGRAPH

In 1995, after an over five years lasting work, Ebel presented the "1911" automatic movement, whose design had been totally reviewed by Ebel's specialists, mainly as far as the reduction of thickness is concerned (31 mm diameter and 6.4 mm thickness, compared with the original 8 mm). Each "1911" movement undergoes individually all the "chronometer" tests of the Swiss Bureau, whose certificate proves excellent working accuracy.

Through the aperture on the case back, protected by a sapphire crystal glass, one can see in the foreground the harmony of the beautiful rotor, hand-decorated with Côtes de Genève.

NEW 1911 SENIOR   REF. 9330240/15635134

Movement: mechanical, automatic winding, Ebel 330 caliber (GP 3300 caliber base).
Functions: hour, minute, second, date.
Case: stainless steel, three-piece brushed case; flat sapphire glass with antireflective treatment; polished bezel fastened with 5 screws; screwed-on crown; back fastened with 8 screws. Water-resistant to 10 atm.

Dial: black; applied curved steel Roman numerals and luminescent dots; minute track printed on the flange; luminescent steel baton hands. **Indications:** date at 3.
Strap: crocodile leather; screwed attachment; steel fold-over clasp.
Also available: with bracelet; with vanilla, silvered or blue (sun pattern) dial; in steel and yellow gold with strap on request or bracelet, slate-gray or silvered dial; in yellow gold with strap or bracelet and black or silvered dial, Lady's size with quartz movement.

NEW 1911 MINI   REF. 9090211/16835130

Movement: quartz, Ebel 690 caliber.
Functions: hour, minute.
Case: stainless steel, three-piece brushed case; flat sapphire glass with antireflective treatment; bezel with set diamonds; screwed-on crown; back fastened with 8 screws. Water-resistant to 10 atm.
Dial: mother-of-pearl; applied curved steel Roman numerals and set diamonds; minute track printed on the flange; luminescent steel baton hands.
Strap: crocodile leather; screwed attachment; steel fold-over clasp.
Also available: with bracelet; simple bezel with silvered, mother-of-pearl or black dial and diamond markers; in steel and gold with strap or bracelet, mother-of-pearl or black dial, diamond markers; diamond bezel, mother-of-pearl dial and diamond markers; in yellow gold with strap or bracelet, simple or diamond bezel with mother-of-pearl dial and diamond markers.

EBEL

ROUND BELUGA LADY
REF. 9157428/982050

Movement: quartz, Ebel 157 caliber.
Functions: hour, minute.
Case: stainless steel, two-piece case; curved sapphire glass; bezel with set diamonds; back fastened with 4 screws. Water-resistant to 3 atm.
Dial: mother-of-pearl; applied curved steel Roman numerals and set diamonds; steel baton hands.

Bracelet: steel; triple-blade folding clasp.
Also available: simple bezel with blue, silvered, white or black dial or black with 8 diamonds, anthracite or fuchsia with 4 diamonds; blue or silvered dial without diamonds; in yellow gold with simple or diamond bezel with mother-of-pearl dial and diamond markers.

ROUND BELUGA LADY
REF. 8157421/19950

Movement: quartz, Ebel 157 caliber.
Functions: hour, minute.
Case: 18 kt yellow gold, two-piece case; curved sapphire glass; gold crown; back fastened with 4 screws. Water-resistant to 3 atm.
Dial: mother-of-pearl; markers with set diamonds; gold baton hands.
Bracelet: gold; triple-blade folding clasp.

Also available: diamond bezel with mother-of-pearl dial and diamond markers; in steel with simple or diamond bezel with blue, silvered, white, black or mother-of-pearl dial and 8 diamonds, anthracite or fuchsia with 4 diamonds, blue or silvered without diamonds.

BELUGA MANCHETTE
REF. 9057A21/19950

Movement: quartz, Ebel 057 caliber.
Functions: hour, minute.
Case: stainless steel, two-piece case; curved sapphire glass; back fastened with 4 screws. Water-resistant to 3 atm.
Dial: mother-of-pearl; markers with set diamonds; steel baton hands.
Bracelet: stainless steel; triple-blade folding clasp.

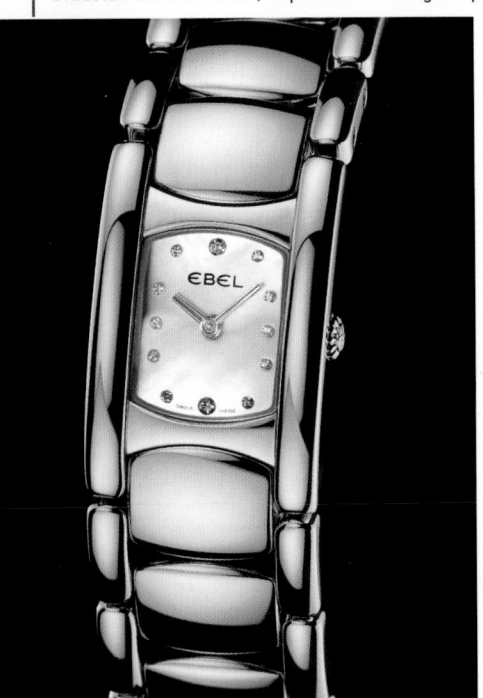

Also available: with fabric or calfskin strap; diamond bezel: with white, black or anthracite gray dial with 4 diamonds, mother-of-pearl dial and 4 diamonds and applied markers; in yellow gold with strap or bracelet: simple or diamond bezel.

BELUGA MANCHETTE
REF. 9057A21/19950

Movement: quartz, Ebel 057 caliber.
Functions: hour, minute.
Case: stainless steel, two-piece case; bezel with set diamonds; curved sapphire glass; back fastened with 4 screws. Water-resistant to 3 atm.
Dial: black; markers with set diamonds at quarters; steel baton hands.
Strap: calfskin; triple-blade folding clasp.

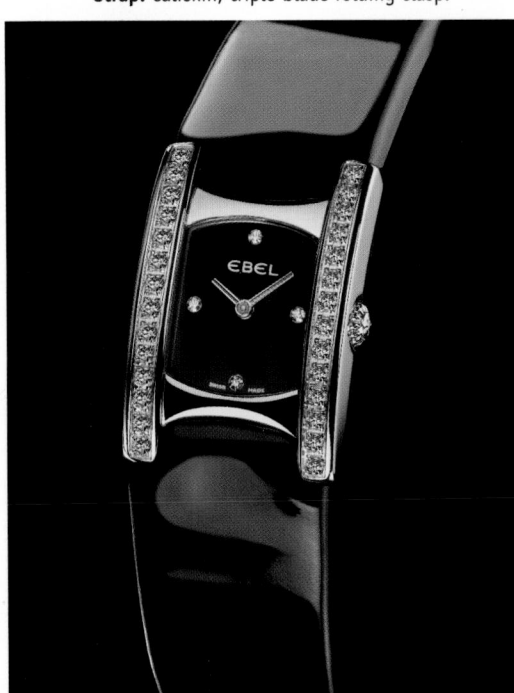

Also available: with fabric strap; bezel without diamonds: white or anthracite gray dial with 4 diamonds, mother-of-pearl dial with 4 diamonds and applied markers; mother-of-pearl dial and 12 diamonds; in yellow gold with strap or bracelet: simple or diamond bezel.

SATYA MINI   REF. 8057B18/991050

Movement: quartz, Ebel 057 caliber.
Functions: hour, minute.
Case: 18 kt yellow gold, two-piece case; curved sapphire glass; bezel and horizontal bands with diamonds; gold crown; back fastened with 4 screws. Water-resistant to 3 atm.
Dial: mother-of-pearl; markers with set diamonds; gold Alpha hands.
Bracelet: gold; triple-blade folding clasp.
Also available: bezel and horizontal bands without diamonds; in white gold.

SATYA MINI   REF. 3057B11/9985

Movement: quartz, Ebel 057 caliber.
Functions: hour, minute.
Case: 18 kt white gold, two-piece case; curved sapphire glass; white-gold crown; back fastened with 4 screws. Water-resistant to 3 atm.
Dial: mother-of-pearl; markers with set diamonds; white-gold Alpha hands.
Bracelet: white gold; triple-blade folding clasp.
Also available: bezel and horizontal bands with diamonds; in yellow gold.

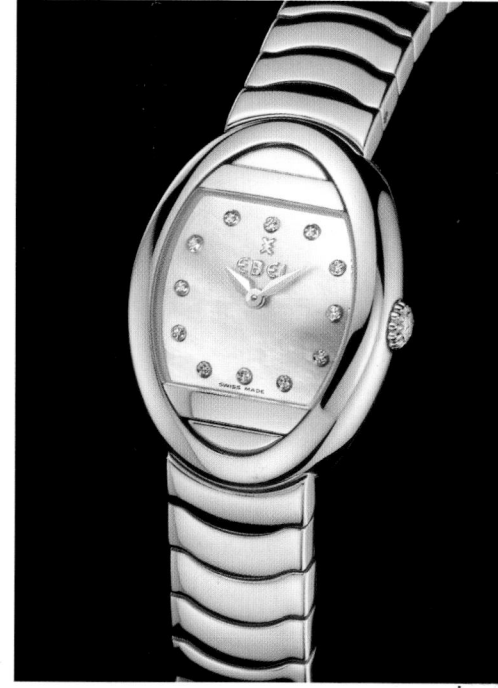

TYPE E CHRONOGRAPH   REF. 9137C51/5316

Movement: mechanical, automatic winding, Ebel 137 caliber. Hand-engraved rotor. Officially certified "chronometer" (C.O.S.C.).
Functions: hour, minute, small second, date, chronograph with 3 counters.
Case: stainless steel, three-piece brushed case; slightly curved sapphire glass with antireflective treatment; bezel with engraved and polished hour markers; polished steel drop-shaped pushers; back fastened with 8 screws, displaying the movement through a sapphire crystal. Water-resistant to 10 atm.
Dial: black; applied steel curved baton markers, 12 Arabic numeral and luminescent; skeletonized chuck hands with luminescent tips. **Indications:** minute counter at 3, date between 4 and 5, hour counter at 6, small second at 9, center second counter, minute track with divisions for 1/5 of a second, tachometer scale on the flange.
Bracelet: brushed steel with E-shaped links; triple-blade folding clasp with engraved logo.
Also available: with slate-gray or silvered dial; white or black dial with rubber strap.

CHRONOGRAPH, PERPETUAL CALENDAR   REF. 3136901/35

Movement: mechanical, automatic winding, Ebel 136 caliber (40.0 caliber + perpetual calendar module realized by Ebel).
Functions: hour, minute, small second, perpetual calendar (date, day, month, year, moon phase), chronograph with 3 counters.
Case: 18 kt yellow gold, three-piece brushed case (Ø 40 mm, thickness 12 mm); flat sapphire glass with antireflective treatment; polished bezel fastened with 5 white-gold screws; 4 correctors on the middle; hexagonal white-gold crown with case protection. Water-resistant to 3 atm.
Dial: ivory; applied yellow-gold Roman numerals, yellow-gold baton hands.
Indications: minute counter and date at 3, moon-phase and hour counter at 6, small second and week day at 9, four-year cycle and month at 12; center second counter, minute track with divisions for 1/5 of a second, tachometer scale on the flange.
Strap: crocodile leather; yellow-gold, triple-blade folding clasp.
Also available: with bracelet.

FRANCK MULLER

unveiling masterpieces

O*ne of the youngest Swiss watch brands to make a true impact on the world of watchmaking, Franck Muller celebrates its 10th anniversary this year. Named for the master watchmaker whose dream was to create complications of a new breed, Franck Muller has woven his own web of watchmaking art and technology this past decade.*

It was in 1992 that Muller first launched his own collection. Having created timepieces for some of the world's finest brands, he was ready to strike out on his own. His complex watches, his meticulous craftsmanship and attention to detail, as well as his exclusivity and savvy marketing, quickly propelled him to the forefront. Today, Franck Muller timepieces enjoy a coveted spot at the top of the connoisseur list.

Working in a beautifully refurbished castle and new surrounding facilities in the hills of Genthod outside of Geneva, Muller's watchmakers tirelessly craft movements and timepieces to exacting standards. Known as Watchland, the Franck Muller complex is home to a team of expert watchmakers, engravers, designers and other craftsmen—who this past year turned out a myriad of Muller's designs in limited and exclusive editions.

In typical Muller style and tradition, he has unveiled an extraordinary complication that he calls the Caliber 2001—A Whirlwind of Light. The striking watch houses the Imperial Tourbillon with a raised cage that elevates it up to the light above the dial. The aesthetic procedure required more than a year of technical study and a patent was filed for the technique. Additionally, the Caliber 2001 houses a retrograde hour and minutes indicator made possible by the addition of a double fly-back module. The two mechanisms are partially interlocked. This extraordinary arrangement of crossing over and superimposing the parts is also a patented technique. The watch is created in solid platinum only.

Some of Muller's other important introductions in 2001 were built within the famed tonneau-shaped Cintrée Curvex case. For the first time, Muller has combined the supreme Grande and Petite Sonnerie with the Perpetual Calendar function in a Cintrée Curvex case. These exquisite complications will chime the hours and quarters and track time and moonphases for years to come. The movement consists of 500 pieces and 50 rubies. The watch is also available with the Minute Repeater function.

Additionally, in 2001, Muller combined the Cintrée Curvex Chronograph with his renowned Imperial Tourbillon. The column-wheel chronograph has a 72-hour power reserve and offers a 30-minute counter. This exquisite watch is created in Muller's signature four colors of gold (yellow, white, pink and green) and in platinum.

In a more modern vein, Muller has also unveiled six new Transamerica models. Available only in steel, but in limited editions, the Transamerica has been an important edition in Muller's sporty collections. Among the models unveiled in 2001 is a self-winding Classic Transamerica Diver's Watch with rotating bezel, the Grand Réveil GMT Big Ben self-winding alarm watch with second GMT time zone and 24-hour indicator, the World Wide Transamerica with second time zone and the Bi-Retro Seconds watch. There is also an all-new chronograph model and a Transamerica Lady—smartly clad with a self-winding movement and available in 18-karat yellow, red or white gold, or in steel. It comes in a variety of pastel colors with coordinated dials and straps.

The retro-inspired Long Island collection of rectangular timepieces has been so successful that women have clamored for their own version. Now Muller complies, introducing the Long Island Lady. The newest art deco pieces come in two sizes and are available in a variety of colors including pink, blue, green, black or white straps with color-coordinated sun-designed guilloché dials. The Long Island Lady watches are available with either a mechanical or quartz movement.

Coming full circle, Muller has also unveiled a jewelry collection to round out his haute horologerie and couture.

FRANCK MULLER

RONDE CALIBER 2001

Movement: mechanical, automatic winding, with tourbillon device, Franck Muller 2001 caliber, tourbillon carriage jutting from the dial (patented system), module for retrograde hours and minutes (patent pending).
Functions: hour, minute, small second.
Case: platinum, three-piece brushed case (Ø 43 mm, thickness 14.2 mm); curved sapphire crystal; white-gold crown; snap-on back with engravings.

Dial: solid silver, black enameled; printed Arabic numerals on silver platelets fastened with blued steel screws, white painted Stuart hands.
Indications: retrograde hours between 8 and 12, retrograde minutes between 12 and 4, small seconds at 6 with white painted serpentine hand integrated in the tourbillon carriage.
Strap: crocodile leather, hand-stitched; screwed attachment; white-gold clasp.
Unique piece.

RONDE DIAMOND CHRONOGRAPH AUTOMATIC   REF. 7000 CC D

Movement: automatic, Franck Muller 7000 caliber (Valjoux base), 42 hours autonomy, 25 jewels (Ø 30 mm, th. 7.90 mm), special patented escapement, 28,800 vph, first quality balance-spring with micrometer screw regulation, Incabloc shock-absorber system. Platinum rotor. Beveled and decorated with Côtes de Genève and circular graining patterns, blued screws. **Functions:** hour, minute, small second, chronograph with three counters. **Case:** stainless steel, three-piece case (Ø 39 mm, thickness 13.4 mm) with brilliant pavé; curved sapphire crystal; snap-on back. Water-resistant to 3 atm.

Dial: silvered, decorated with circular beads, black enamel zones, applied star-shaped markers, 12 in Arabic numerals in nickel-plated steel, leaf-style nickel-plated steel hands.
Indications: hour counter at 3, minute counter at 6, small seconds at 9, center second, minute track with divisions for 1/5 second.
Strap: crocodile leather, hand-stitched; screwed attachment; steel clasp.
Also available: with bracelet; in white, pink, red or yellow gold with strap or bracelet; in platinum with strap or bracelet; in other jewel versions; Ø 36 mm. Dial: black, silvered, green, blue or bordeaux.

TRANSAMERICA GRAND RÉVEIL GMT   REF. 2000 BIG BEN O

Movement: mechanical, automatic winding, Franck Muller 7850 caliber, 45 hours autonomy, 36 jewels, 28,800 vph, flat balance-spring, Incabloc shock-absorber system. Platinum rotor. Beveled and decorated with Côtes de Genève pattern, blued screws. **Functions:** hour, minute, second, date, second time-zone time, 24 h display, sonnerie.
Case: stainless steel, three-piece tonneau-shaped,

anatomically curved case (size 43.5 x 39.7 mm, thickness 13.8 mm); curved sapphire crystal; round bezel; crowns at 2 for sonnerie setting and at 4 for hour, second time-zone and date settings; back fastened by 4 screws. Water-resistant to 3 atm.
Dial: black enameled, guilloché with sun pattern, luminescent Arabic numerals, blued steel lozenge hands.
Indications: date (referred to main time) and second time-zone time on 24 hours at 6, sonnerie with red serpentine center hand.
Bracelet: stainless steel; recessed double fold-over clasp.
Also available: with silvered dial and leather strap.

TRANSAMERICA DOUBLE RETROGRADE SECONDS   REF. 2000 DSR O

Movement: mechanical, automatic winding, Franck Muller 2800 GR caliber, 42 hours autonomy, 21 jewels (Ø 26,20 mm). Balance with 28,800 vph, flat balance-spring, Incabloc shock-absorber system. Platinum rotor; blued screws, Côtes de Genève finish, beveled.
Functions: hour, minute, small second.
Case: stainless steel, three-piece tonneau-shaped, anatomically curved case (size 43.5 x 39.7 mm, thickness 14 mm); round bezel; curved sapphire crystal; back, fastened by 4 screws. Water-resistant to 3 atm.

Dial: silvered, guilloché with sun pattern with translucent enamel; luminescent Arabic numerals and blued stainless steel lozenge hands.
Indications: small second wit two retrograde hands at 6 and 12, each indicating 30 seconds alternately.
Bracelet: stainless steel; recessed double fold-over clasp.
Also available: with black dial and leather strap.

CINTRÉE CURVEX GRANDE ET PETITE SONNERIE, QP   REF. 7850 GS QP

Movement: mechanical, automatic winding, Franck Muller RFM7850 caliber, 50 jewels, two barrels for movement and sonnerie to be wound by alternating the crown's rotation way.

Functions: hour, minute, perpetual calendar (date, day, month, year, moon phase), minute repeater, grande and petite sonnerie.

Case: white gold, two-piece tonneau-shaped, anatomically curved case (size 41.5 x 35.2 mm, thickness 13.8 mm); curved sapphire crystal; repeater slide, grande and petite sonnerie selector and 4 correctors on the middle; white-gold crown; back fastened by 4 screws.

Dial: silvered, guilloché, curved, printed Arabic numerals, blued steel Stuart hands.

Indications: date at 3, moon phase at 6, day at 9, month and 4-year cycle at 12.

Strap: crocodile leather, hand-stitched; white-gold clasp.

Also available: in yellow, pink or red gold; in platinum.

CINTRÉE CURVEX TOURBILLON IMPÉRIALE CHRONO   REF. 7850 T CHR

Movement: mechanical, automatic winding, with tourbillon device, Franck Muller TFC 01 caliber, 21,6000 vph, 72 hours autonomy.

Functions: hour, minute, small second, chronograph with 2 counters.

Case: 18 kt white gold, two-piece case tonneau-shaped, anatomically curved case (size 41.5 x 35.2 mm, thickness 14.2 mm); curved sapphire crystal; white-gold crown and oval pushers; back fastened by 4 screws, displaying the movement through a sapphire crystal.

Dial: black enameled, zones white enameled, curved, with an aperture on the tourbillon; luminescent Arabic numerals, luminescent blued steel lozenge hands.

Indications: minute counter at 3, small seconds at 6 integrated in the tourbillon carriage, center second, minute track.

Strap: crocodile leather, hand-stitched; white-gold clasp.

C. CURVEX CHRONO PERPETUAL CALENDAR BIRETRO   REF. 6850 CC QP B

Movement: mechanical, automatic winding, Franck Muller 5888 BR caliber, 45 hours autonomy, 45 jewels (Ø 26.20 mm), 21,600 vph, flat balance-spring, Incabloc shock-absorber system. Platinum rotor. Hand-finished. **Functions:** hour, minute, perpetual calendar (date, day, month, year, moon phase), chronograph with three counters. **Case:** 18 kt white gold, two-piece tonneau-shaped, anatomically curved case (size 40 x 34 mm, thickness 14 mm); curved sapphire crystal; 4 correctors on the middle; white-gold crown and 2 oval pushers with case protection; back fastened by 4 screws. Water-resistant to 3 atm. **Dial:** flinqué, black, silvered zones with circular beads and ring; curved; luminescent Arabic numerals, luminescent blued steel lozenge hands. **Indications:** date at 3 and day at 9 with retrograde hand, minute counter at 3, moon phase at 6, hour counter at 9, month and 4-year cycle at 12, center second, railway minute track. **Strap:** crocodile leather, hand-stitched; white-gold clasp. **Also available:** blue or silvered dial, fold-over clasp; bracelet; in yellow, pink or red gold, strap or bracelet; in platinum, strap or bracelet. Ref. 7850: in yellow, pink, white or red gold, strap or bracelet; in platinum, strap or bracelet.

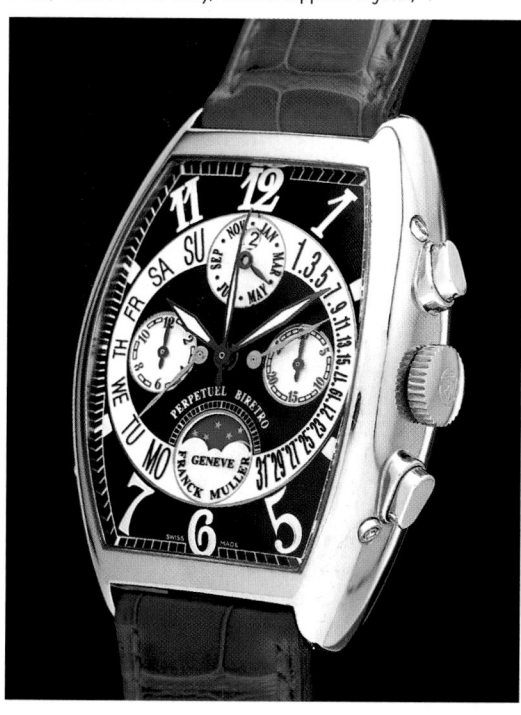

CINTRÉE CURVEX CHRONOGRAPH MASTER BANKER   REF. 7850 CC MB

Movement: automatic, Franck Muller 7000 caliber, 42 hours autonomy, 25 jewels (Ø 30, th. 7.90 mm), special patented escapement, 28,800 vph, first-quality balance-spring with micrometer screw regulation, Incabloc shock-absorber system. Platinum rotor. Beveled and finished with Côtes de Genève and circular graining patterns. **Functions:** hour, minute, small second, date, 3 time-zones time, chronograph with two counters. **Case:** 18 kt pink gold, two-piece tonneau-shaped, anatomically curved case (size 41.5 x 35, thickness 13.8 mm); curved sapphire crystal; corrector on the middle; screw-down pink-gold crown and oval pushers with case protection; back fastened by 4 screws. Water-resistant to 3 atm. **Dial:** flinqué, black, silvered zones with circular beads and ring; curved; luminescent Arabic numerals, luminescent blued steel lozenge hands. **Indications:** date at 3, second time-zone time at 6, small second at 9; minute counter and third time-zone time at 12, center second, railway minute track with divisions for 1/5 second. **Strap:** crocodile leather, hand-stitched; pink-gold clasp. **Also available:** blue or silvered dial, fold-over clasp; bracelet; yellow or red gold, platinum, steel.

F.P. JOURNE-INVENIT ET FECIT-

an historical perspective

François-Paul Journe is an independent master watchmaker whose timepieces embody the spirit of the 18th and 19th centuries. Each of the 700 watches he creates annually, is designed and developed by him personally and handmade according to the strictest watchmaking standards.

When François-Paul Journe set up his workshops in Geneva in 1999 to produce his own watches under the Invenit et Fecit label, he had just two watchmakers working with him. Three years later, there are 15 producing the three models in his collection: the Resonance wrist-chronometer; the Tourbillon Souverain with "remontoir;" and the remarkable Octa five-day automatic caliber for the Octa Automatic, Octa Chronograph, and Octa Perpetual Calendar.

F.P. Journe defines himself as an inventor and maker of watches. He is not, he emphasizes, a manufacture, the title claimed by companies that make their own watch components.

"If I had the plant, machinery and specialists to manufacture every part, my annual production of watches (currently around 700 timepieces) would keep (my watchmakers) busy for only a few days a year," says Journe. He goes on to explain that the term "manufacture" is largely a myth. According to Journe, "The reality is that (most watchmakers) depend on outside suppliers for key parts, especially balance-springs and escapements. But most of the brands buy finished movements ready for casing up; they only have to manage a couple of suppliers. We manage 40."

Journe's business is to invent the watches of the future and to implement these inventions into functioning prototypes. Research and Development consumes 40% of the time and resources of his teams in the construction studio, mechanical and watchmaking workshops. Before a prototype goes into production, its manufacturing feasibility is tested in a small pre-series, which could include unique variations of the model.

The workshops are divided into three sections, each dedicated to a particular model . Under the direction of Journe's "chef d'atelier" Georges Alessio, each watchmaker—including Journe himself—builds an entire watch from A to Z, poising the balance, assembling the movement, adjusting and testing it. For the tourbillon, for instance, the process can take up to eight weeks.

F.P. Journe-Invenit et Fecit-

Limited series

Each watch has its own file, which includes details of its adjustment and performance. When the watch is returned to the workshops for a repair or servicing, it is attended to by the watchmaker who made it.

F.P. Journe employs Swiss and French watchmakers with broad experience in a variety of movements. But regardless of how experienced they are, each one comes to F.P. Journe as an apprentice. "The watch schools teach the conventional standard calibers," explains Journe. "Our watchmakers have to adapt to a new horological environment, which can take three to four months.

They must also be competent in all the major disciplines: assembly; timing; casing up; even mechanical work and tooling."

F.P. Journe's watchmaking operation is divided into two independent companies. Montres Journe SA handles the administration, marketing and sales, while TIM is the manufacturing arm. They both occupy an Art Deco building on Geneva's left bank, not far from the city's banking district.

F.P. Journe plans to increase his production over the next few years to reach an optimum output of 1,500 watches per year. The watches are sold exclusively to 32 retailers in North America, Europe, the Middle East and Asia.

1977 François-Paul Journe graduates from the Paris School of Watchmaking. His graduation piece is the most difficult of horological feats: a tourbillon escapement in a fob watch, commissioned by a collector.

1978 Journe begins working in the workshop of his uncle (a noted restorer of antique timepieces at St. Germain des Prés, Paris) and here Journe builds his first Tourbillon pocket watch.

1983 Journe first applies the phenomenon of resonance to watchmaking in a resonance-system pocket watch.

1984 Creation of the first self-winding pocket chronometer with remontoir.

1985 Journe sets up his first workshop at rue de Verneuil in Paris and manufactures the self-winding pocket chronometer with remontoir and retrograde perpetual calendar.

1986 Journe creates a tourbillon pocket watch with remontoir, displaying a planetarium, solar time, moonphase and power reserve.

1987 Creation of the Pendule Sympathique, commissioned by Asprey's; F.P. Journe receives an award from the Fondation de la Vocation, Bleustein Blanchet.

1989 Journe receives the Balancier d'Or award at the Watchmakers Convention in Madrid; A new workshop is established in Switzerland with a small group of inventors who specialize in developing innovative watch movements for brands.

1994 Journe receives the Prix Gaïa award for Best Watchmaker from Switzerland's international Musée de l'Homme et du Temps, at La Chaux-de-Fonds.

1996 F.P. Journe establishes TIM SA, Geneva, designing exclusive calibers for major brands.

1999 Launching of the F.P. Journe "Invenit et Fecit" brand (distributed by Montres Journe SA, Geneva) with the Souverain collection. With it came two technical breakthroughs: the resonance-system chronometer, the world's first wristwatch to use resonance to achieve precision; and the Tourbillon Souverain, the world's only mechanical wristwatch that maintains its rate throughout the development of its mainspring.

2000 Introduction of the Octa collection which houses automatic movements with integrated complications; New workshops and showroom are established in the rue de l'Arquebuse, in the heart of Geneva.

2000 The unique Sonnerie Souverain makes its debut; The Octa caliber is introduced, the first to combine automatic winding with a long power reserve and precision adjustment; François-Paul Journe and the House of Harry Winston form a creative association to create 18 exclusive chronometers together.

FACING PAGE

CENTER

The Tourbillon Souverain is a world premiere work of art and technical mastery.

THIS PAGE

TOP

An inside look at the Chronometer A Resonance movement.

BOTTOM

The Chronometer A Resonance in platinum houses a manual-wind mechanical movement. The first wristwatch working with resonance physical phenomenon.

the Octa—
one size fits all

It took François-Paul Journe more than 20 years to perfect his first wristwatch, but the revolutionary resonance-system chronometer that came out in 1999 established him as the new standard-bearer of pure horology, restoring the watch to its rightful status as an exercise in precision and function.

In an age when watches have become branded commodities, F.P. Journe revives the spirit of the 18th and 19th centuries, when a timepiece was a strategic instrument, invented and fashioned by the scientific celebrities of their eras.

F.P. Journe's latest invention, the automatic Octa watch, is a new, multipurpose construction of extreme complexity, integrating different mechanical complications in the same structure without changing the size of the movement. The movement's future evolution is thus designed into the caliber, without the need for add-on modules.

Each Octa complication is an original design because it must conform to a common baseplate with holes and recesses cut for other complications. It also has to fit into a 1mm-high space.

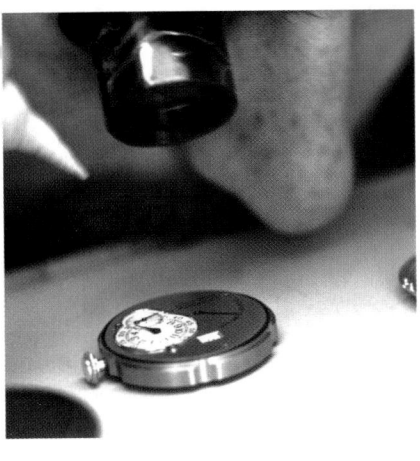

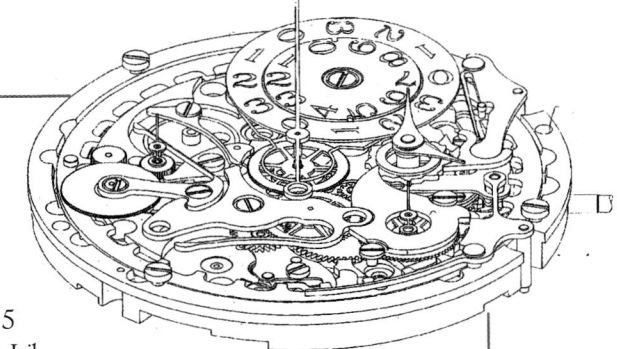

The Octa is the first caliber to combine automatic winding with a long (at least 5 days') power reserve and precision adjustment. Like all of F.P. Journe's watches, the Octa has a free-sprung chronometer balance of Journe's own design, with four opposing weights for close dynamic adjustment. The mainspring maintains the amplitude of the balance, and thus a constant rate, for 120 hours of the total power reserve.

Many watches with long power reserves require small balance-wheels, which are susceptible to shocks and disturbances. The Octa's compact construction allows a large (10.1mm) balance to be fitted, giving greater inertia and stability.

The first Octa model, introduced in 2000, incorporated a 120-hour power-reserve indicator and Journe's patented large date with separate numerals. Later that year, F.P. Journe produced the Octa chronograph, which features zero-restart as well as zero-stop functions and a 60-minutes register. The watch displays the large date and the hours, minutes and small seconds on Journe's trademark dial.

F.P. Journe designed an ultra-thin version of the classic column-wheel chronograph to fit into the 1mm-high space under the dial. This space is shared by the twin concentric discs of the large date display. The column-wheel has been flattened into a cam-wheel and its profiled rim, instead of columns, acts on the chronograph levers. A single, sliding lever zeroes both the chronograph seconds and minutes, disengaging their brakes as it strikes specially profiled heart-pieces to zero the hands. These two innovations allow the entire chronograph's work to be reduced to three mechanical levels.

The third Octa complication integrates an annual calendar with a retrograde (fly-back) date into the automatic, five-day movement with the same dimensions (30mm x 5.7mm) as the first two Octas. The calendar displays the days and months through separate windows, advances instantaneously and is self-adjusting for months with 29, 30 and 31 days. This means that in non-leap years, when February has 28 days, the date must be advanced manually by one day on March 1st.

The annual calendar is a particularly elegant mechanism, driven by an internally toothed great wheel that surrounds the movement. The retrograde date-hand, which rides up its scale on the curve of a snail cam, is held on the precise, correct date by twin sprung-racks acting on a pinion. The design controls the fly-back, reduces the forces required, and distributes them evenly throughout the mechanism.

The first Octa annual calendars are expected to be ready in 2002. Further developments of this revolutionary caliber have yet to be announced, but there is a clue: the slightly decentralized winding rotor allows access from the movement to future indications at the back of the watch.

Indeed, F.P. Journe remains focused on perfecting movements and taking the level of mechanical watchmaking to new heights with his highly individualized style.

F. P. JOURNE INVENIT ET FECIT

TOURBILLON SOUVERAIN

Movement: mechanical, manual winding, with tourbillon and constant force remontoir. Original concept and production by F.P. Journe, 1498 caliber (patented system). **Functions:** hour, minute, power reserve 42 h.
Case: platinum, two-piece numbered case (Ø 38.3 mm, thickness 9.1 mm); curved sapphire crystal; white-gold knurled crown; back attached by 6 screws displaying the movement through a sapphire crystal. Water-resistant to 3 atm.

Dial: 18K gold, aperture on the tourbillon; solid silver engine-turned (guilloché) zones; blued steel hands in an exclusive shape.
Indications: off-center hour and minute at 3 with printed Arabic numerals and railway minute track with five-minute progression, power reserve at 12.
Strap: crocodile leather; platinum clasp.
Also available: case in pink gold; with bracelet in platinum or gold; dial in white, yellow and pink gold.
Journe's Tourbillon Souverain is equipped with a constant force device (partly visible through the aperture at 6) that compensates the force of the escapement, thus allowing a more accurate balance isochronism.

LIMITED SERIE IN RUTHENIUM

The movements of Tourbillon and Resonance Chronometer, two worldwide premières which adopt rather unusual solutions and have recently been proposed in a new 40 millimeter diameter size with ruthenium-clad dials and movements, are a hit among the public that loves technique. Both manual-winding wristwatches are produced in a limited series of 99 pieces each and have a power reserve of respectively 42 and 40 hours.

FROM LEFT: The device is loaded each second and allows a constant energy transmission. The design of this model is very particular: the off-center engine-turned (guilloché) hour and minute dial in solid silver, is kept in place on the 18K solid gold base by a polished steel ring fastened with three screws. Through the wide sapphire crystal on the case back one may notice, on the big rear bridge, the long slot inside which the bending spring of said constant force device is visible.

SONNERIE SOUVERAINE UNIQUE PIECE

Movement: mechanical, manual winding. Original concept and production by F.P. Journe, 1996 caliber.
Functions: hour, retrograde minute, power reserve, minute repeater, grande and petite sonnerie.
Case: platinum, numbered two-piece case (Ø 38 mm, thickness 11 mm); curved sapphire crystal; knurled white-gold crown and pushers (for the repeater at 2, for the selection of the grande or petite sonnerie and mute at 4); snap-on back displaying the movement through a sapphire crystal. Water-resistant to 3 atm.

Dial: 18K gold; solid silver engine-turned (guilloché) shaped center zone and applied brushed solid silver minute ring; printed Arabic numerals; blued steel hands in an exclusive shape.
Indications: power reserve at 2, mute, petite or grande sonnerie at 4, retrograde center minute with 5-minute progression.
Strap: crocodile leather; platinum clasp.
Unique piece.

SONNERIE SOUVERAINE

This is an extraordinary single piece presented by F. P. Journe: a platinum watch with minute repeater (actuated by means of a pusher at 2) and grande and petite sonnerie (pusher at 4). The design of the gold dial is very peculiar with the center hour display on a shaped solid silver engine-turned (guilloché) zone, the retrograde minute display in a circle sector and an aperture on the hammers of the grande (top) and petite (bottom) sonnerie at 10.

CHRONOMETRE A RESONANCE

Movement: mechanical, manual winding. Original concept and production by F.P. Journe. Working with resonance phenomenon.

Functions: hours and minutes of two different time zones, small second, power reserve 40 h.

Case: platinum, numbered two-piece case (Ø 38,3 mm, thickness 9,20 mm); curved sapphire crystal; knurled white-gold crowns (at 12 for winding and time adjustment on both dials, at 4 for the automatic synchronization of the seconds hands); back attached by 6 screws displaying the movement through a sapphire crystal. Water-resistant to 3 atm.

Dial: 18K gold; symmetric solid silver engine-turned (guilloché) zones; printed Arabic numerals and railway minute track with five-minute progression; blued steel hands in an exclusive shape.

Indications: symmetric off-center double time display (hour, minute, small second), power reserve at 11.

Strap: crocodile leather; platinum clasp.

Also available: case in pink gold; with bracelet in platinum or gold; dial in white, yellow and pink gold.

CHRONOMETRE A RESONANCE

F. P. Journe is a skillful watch-maker, capable of designing and entirely realizing all of the components of a watch, distinguishing himself because of the highly original technical and creative solutions chosen. That is also the case of this world premiere GMT, where local time and the time of a second time zone are indicated in two silver engine-turned (guilloché) zones kept in place on the 18K solid gold base by the usual polished steel rings. Time adjustment on both dials is actuated by means of the single crown at 12: pulled out by one click and turned counterclockwise, it sets the time of the left dial and clockwise the time of the right dial. A world premiere in a wristwatch (the crown at 4 can be pull to reset the seconds).

Through the sapphire crystal of the case back it is possible to admire the unusual "motor" characterized by the combination of two symmetric but independent movements on a single pillar-plate. The vibrations of both balances are synchronized by the natural principle of resonance offering more accuracy.

OCTA RESERVE DE MARCHE

Movement: mechanical, automatic winding. Entirely designed and produced by F. P. Journe. 22K gold rotor, personalized and engine-turned (guilloché).

Functions: hour, minute, small second, date, power reserve 120h.

Case: platinum, numbered two-piece case (Ø 38.3 mm, thickness 10 mm); curved sapphire crystal; knurled white-gold crown; back attached by 6 screws displaying the movement through a sapphire crystal. Water-resistant to 3 atm.

Dial: 18K gold; solid silver engine-turned (guilloché) zones; blued steel hands in an exclusive shape.

Indications: off-center hour and minute at 3 with printed Arabic numerals and railway minute track with five-minute progression, small second between 4 and 5, power reserve at 9, patented big-sized date with double disc below 11.

Strap: crocodile leather; platinum clasp.

Also available: in pink gold; with bracelet in platinum or gold; dial in white, yellow and pink gold.

OCTA CHRONOGRAPHE

Movement: mechanical, automatic winding. Original concept and production by F.P. Journe. 22K gold rotor; power reserve 120h; personalized and engine-turned (guilloché). Three level chronograph mechanism, flattened to just 1 mm, combines zero-stop and zero-restart features. **Functions:** hour, minute, small second, large date, chronograph with two counters.

Case: platinum, numbered two-piece case (Ø 38 mm, thickness 10,30 mm); curved sapphire crystal; knurled white-gold crown and pushers; back attached by 6 screws, displaying the movement through a sapphire crystal. Water-resistant to 3 atm.

Dial: 18K gold; solid silver engine-turned (guilloché) zones; blued steel hands in an exclusive shape.

Indications: off-center hour and minute at 3 with printed Arabic numerals and railway minute track with five-minute progression, small second between 4 and 5, minute counter at 9, large date at 11, center second counter.

Strap: crocodile leather; platinum clasp.

Also available: case in pink gold; with bracelet in platinum or gold; dial in white, yellow and pink gold.

FRÉDÉRIQUE CONSTANT

an historical perspective

Just fourteen years ago, the Frédérique Constant watchmaking brand was born. What the brand may lack in long years of heritage, however, it makes up for in technical artistry. This is a brand that deftly mixes microtechnology and state-of-the-art computer-aided design with Swiss watchmaking knowledge. The result is cutting-edge, elegant timepieces that function with precision.

Family owned and operated, Frédérique Constant is the brainchild of Peter C. Stas. Interestingly, Stas is not a watchmaker, but rather an astute Dutch businessman with a passion for watches and a keen entrepreneurial sense. In the mid 1980s, while employed by a Dutch firm, Stas traveled to Switzerland where he visited watch factories and garnered a genuine interest in the field. He began developing his own ideas for creating affordable mechanical wristwatches. Later, when he was transferred to Hong Kong, he solidified relationships with several watch experts and even hand-assembled a dozen of his own watches.

In 1988 Stas met Aletta Bax, who took a strong interest in his watchmaking plans. Together, the two created a name from their respective family histories: Frédérique, after Aletta's great-grandmother, and Constant in honor of Peter's great-grandfather, who had been involved in making clock dials, and the brand was officially born.

In 1991, the married couple opened a small office for the fledgling watchmaking enterprise and attended a single exhibition where the company received orders for 370 watches. In late 1991, Frédérique Constant set up a workshop in Geneva and assembly commenced under the direction of Stas's closest friend and watchmaking colleague, Philippe Bouchet.

The brand's first automatic mechanical wristwatches arrived on the scene in 1992—and that year the company garnered orders for 3,000 watches. Thanks to a creative strategy, identifiable look and defined pricepoint, Frédérique Constant was well on its way to success.

FRÉDÉRIQUE CONSTANT

evolution of time

In the past decade, Frédérique Constant has enjoyed much international attention. Following a creed to produce affordable mechanical watches with a distinctive look, the brand's watchmakers have spent long hours in the research and development stages that guide the creation of its timepieces.

Just two years after the appearance of its first automatic wristwatches, Frédérique Constant introduced the Heart Beat collection of mechanical timepieces. The introduction of the Heart Beat drew immediate attention and garnered such acclaim that even today, eight years later, Frédérique Constant creates a Heart Beat model in each of its key collections. The Heart Beat automatic watch has a three-spoke balance wheel with a hairspring that beats 28,800 times per hour. The balance wheel rotates clockwise and counter-clockwise, and its constant rotation (hence, the name "Heart Beat") is visible through the dial aperture. It offers both an alluring and mystifying appeal.

In 1995, Frédérique Constant exhibited it timepieces at the Basel Watch, Clock and Jewelry Show for the first time. Orders poured in from countries around the world for the creative styles and unusual technical developments from Frédérique Constant. Within two years, Stas

THIS PAGE

TOP CENTER

The Highlife™ Heart Beat Day/Date is an interesting watch wherein the wearer can view the constant rotation of the balance wheel through an aperture.

TOP RIGHT

Aletta and Peter Stas in the new atelier.

BOTTOM LEFT

The Slim Automatic is an ultra-slim automatic watch in the Highlife™ collection.

FACING PAGE

TOP LEFT

From top: New atelier; Solving a technical issue; First quality control.

TOP RIGHT

The Highlife™ Ladies Round watches feature black or white dials with contrasting numerals for added appeal.

BOTTOM

The Highlife™ Ladies Round is now available in an array of brightly colored straps.

expanded the enterprise and, in 1997, established an office just outside of Geneva. That year, the brand produced 24,000 watches.

In response to a request from the Dutch Olympic Sailing Team, which needed a stringent timer created for the then-recently adjusted signals, Frédérique Constant unveiled the patented Yacht Timer in 1998 after two years of research. The brand has been developing innovative variations on the design ever since.

Today, the Frédérique Constant line of timepieces is quite varied and caters to both men and women. It encompasses complicated timepieces, sport chic watches, the Heart Beat series, the Highlife™ series of classically elegant watches and an 18-karat gold and gemstone collection. In fact, the 18-karat gold collection includes limited-edition pieces such as the Grandgala (which elegantly includes diamonds in unusual settings on the cases and dials), the Dansant (tonneau- and rectangular-shaped watches featuring diamond-set grids over the sapphire crystals), and the Allure (created in round, oval or square shapes with 18-karat white-gold bracelets or lizard straps). Only 99 pieces of each of these series will ever be produced.

All Frédérique Constant timepieces are created in Switzerland and are sold in 36 countries around the world. In a quest to expand, the brand recently opened a new atelier in Chêne-Bourg, a small suburb of Geneva, for watch and movement assembly. This past year, 50,000 watches were produced there.

303

FRÉDÉRIQUE CONSTANT

passion

unveiled

Underscoring Frédérique Constant's zeal for life and newness, the brand's new ad campaign elegantly focuses on passion. With the philosophy "Live Your Passion," the brand encourages men and women to pursue their passions—whether it is art, chess or watchmaking—and to succeed. With this concept as its core, Frédérique Constant unveils its newest collections—watches that venture further into the realm of complications and functions.

One very important Frédérique Constant collection is the Highlife™ range of men's and women's watches. New to the series are several key timepieces for both. The Tourbillon Highlife™, crafted in platinum or in 18-karat rose gold, features an elegant round case with unusual Arabic numerals on the enameled dial that flow elegantly around the face of the watch. The tourbillon is visible via an aperture at 6:00 and the solid gold brand emblem is situated on the dial at 3:00. The Highlife™ Tourbillon watch features a hand-wound movement with 23 rubies and bridges decorated with the Côtes de Genève seal. Only 99 pieces of each of the three models (platinum, 18-karat with black or silver dial) will ever be created.

Joining the Tourbillon is the new Highlife™ Triple Time watch. Created specifically for international travelers, the automatic watch presents the time in three dimensions: the traditional 12-hour clock dial, the 24-hour clock indicator and the 24 time zones in an outer ring on the dial. Crafted in steel, the watch houses an automatic movement with 42 hours of power reserve. It is water resistant to 100 meters and features a galvanized silver dial with bold Arabic numerals and luminescent hands.

Additionally, Frédérique Constant has unveiled some striking new Highlife™ models for women. There are several round versions,

available either with leather strap or with steel bracelet. Dial choices are black or silver, with contrasting Arabic numerals. These particular watches feature quartz movements and display the hours, minutes and date. A very modern square version has also been unveiled—the Highlife™ Carree. This stunning timepiece comes in an array of bright and pastel colored straps with coordinated mother-of-pearl dials. The dials feature varying degrees of diamonds for updated styling that remains timeless.

In addition to the Highlife™ collection, Frédérique Constant has unveiled the Yacht Timer Mark II. The exclusive countdown functions include the traditional countdown of 10 and 5 minutes, as well as the official 6- and 3-minute countdown introduced for the Atlanta Games. It features a black dial to enhance the visibility of its functions, which are indicated in bold nautical colors.

Finally, an important new men's collection has joined the ranks. Aptly called Persuasion, these large, bold watches come in several versions, each of which is characterized by Roman numerals as opposed to Arabic numerals. The Persuasion Business Timer is a square quartz model with day, date, month and moonphase readout. There is also an automatic version and eight different Persuasion Heart Beat models.

The creative and innovative spirit of the Frédérique Constant timepieces was enhanced this past year when the brand appeared at La Palmerai de l'Hotel Martinez in Cannes during the 54th International Film Festival. At this meeting and interview place for international stars, Frédérique Constant presented its timepieces in the center of the Hotel to allow a select few to discover the Highlife™. Several stars chose their favorites, and Frédérique Constant watches now grace their wrists.

FESTIVAL DE CANNES
9-20 mai 2001

54e
FESTIVAL
INTERNATIONAL
DU FILM

GEORGES V

an historical perspective

*A*dventures of men, works by artists revealing themselves in original creations, final realizations of concepts devised ages ago—Georges V opens new horizons within a universe that everyone deemed already established: very high horology.

When two men meet—men who both possess wills to revolutionize the world of luxury by proposing their artistic interpretations—a break in conventional values is unavoidable. The self-financed Georges V company, originating from the idea that luxury products very often lack any kind of soul, is eager to realize the dream of its founders: to manufacture a limited quantity of pieces corresponding to differentiated standards.

The young Georges V company intends to attract collectors of a philosophy of life based on symbols and refined tastes by offering to them a rich and unique collection.

To breathe life into watches, cigars, and other complete collections of luxury items is a difficult project. Fortunately, the brand's founders were able to invest the skills they'd acquired through years of answering to public demand for something more than price, more than subjective rarity. The public wanted style, it wanted precision, and it wanted them in one watch. Creating objects of art entails not just the simple manufacturing of a product design, but rather the much harder task of giving that design a soul. Round shapes, characteristic choices, tastes, or even evocations refer to artistic decisions that are sometimes difficult to translate.

Pasquale Gangi is a man fond of beauty and originality. What he tries to create is, above all, a complete universe of values to which everyone is free to cling. The luxury of life is already a miracle in itself, and to make people want to take part in his sensations encourages him to advance even further in his creations. The five senses have great credit in his enterprise. As an artist, he is devoted to everyday life without pretenses. Therefore, the materials chosen for his watches must mesh together naturally. If they are forced, the pieces lose their greatness. His vision—his sense of aesthetics; his resolution—to make his perception accessible to everyone.

René Schmidlin, a great industrial entrepreneur of the Jura, is a professional committed to high-quality watch production. He registered the name "Georges V" as a visionary about twenty years ago, intending to use it only when he founded a company worthy of the title. When he met Gangi, a man committed to watchmaking like no one Schmidlin had ever known—and ready to invest heavily in this far-reaching project with respect to both financial and intellectual resources—Schmidlin had found the appropriate time and partner with whom to launch his adventure, Georges V.

an inspiration in design

As far as creativity is concerned, Georges V admittedly draws its inspiration from the past, Gangi and Schmidlin are Epicureans who draw upon the round tastes of a certain wine or cigar inside the opulence of a club armchair. They leave a little part of their souls in each object they create. There is no doubt about it: these aesthetes have very developed and exquisite tastes, earning them the utmost of trust among faithful followers of their company. Gangi and Schmidlin have appointed the artists who bring to fruition what they intend to offer to all those who wish to enjoy their own principles of life.

From the outset, Georges V did not only intend to create watches, but aimed at a global target. Of course, their watch collection represents an important part of the activity of this young house. Time is the main luxury. One must play with it to use it as a leitmotif.

These watches, designed like functional and original jewels, possess the unique distinc-

TOP

The V 6000 Tourbillon, shown here in yellow gold on a leather strap with slate-gray dial, is also available in platinum, white or pink gold; with diamonds, rubies, emeralds and sapphires; on a metal bracelet; with a white dial.

TOP RIGHT

The V 5000 Chrono-flyback Quantième Perpetual features moonphase at 3:00. Crafted in yellow gold with 38 rubies and a slate-gray dial on a metal bracelet, the V 5000 houses a bidirectional, automatic movement. The watch is also available in platinum, white or pink gold; with diamonds, rubies, emeralds and sapphires, on a leather strap; with a white dial.

BOTTOM

Crafted in yellow gold, this V 4000 Quantième Perpetual displays 21 rubies, a slate-gray dial, and a metal bracelet. The movement is bidirectional, automatic, and the moonphase function is visible at 6:00. The V 4000 is also crafted in platinum, white or pink gold; with diamonds, rubies, emeralds and sapphires; on a leather strap; with a white dial.

tion of being created, by passionate men. The object creates harmony; the model defines the taste. The designers of Georges V watches rightly make it their ambition to create an environment corresponding to the idea of luxury as proposed by Gangi and Schmidlin.

These very new horology tools are evidently an ode to a passion for beauty, a dream of the exceptional, and the production of a strong symbol of a true identity by artists' hands. These watches are, rather than mere accessories, rousing examples of what the brand's strong identity asserts with a certain pride: a unique character.

The general aspect of a product is only one of the elements that determines a customer's choice. Gangi and Schmidlin, along with the persons who assist them, search for something more substantial than easy recognition due to a pleasing image of design. In this search for an absolute timepiece, nothing is simple and easy.

"I want to produce like I would like to consume," asserts Gangi, the great arranger of the collections. And this idea is the foundation of the enterprise's entire philosophy. That's why Georges V watches, animated by original movements realized and mounted independently by René Schmidlin's companies, announce a new era in horology at the dawn of the third millennium.

Rectangular or square-round with sensual contours and suggestively full-shaped curves, the timepieces in each of Georges V's lines, affirm the mastered technical challenge and a skin-deep sensitivity that demands only to be shared.

Modern in design with their bold shapes and relentless readability, the "T," "Q" and "V" models—named for alphabetic characters that imply strength in other areas of imagination—play with all the analogies possible to imagine.

GEVRIL

an historical perspective

There was a talented watchmaker from the Le Locle Valley in the mid-1700s who left his mark on the progression of tracking time. Jacques Gevril lived during a time when clockmakers and watchmakers, including his good friend Daniel JeanRichard, were laying the foundation for the future of their craft.

Gevril was a known restorer of timepieces in La Chaux-de-Fonds, where he left his name on numerous watch and clock movements as he rose to success. In 1758, he answered a call from the King of Spain to accept the appointment as Watchmaker to the Crown. He moved to Madrid where he set up a modest workshop and serviced the royal family with his clocks and timepieces for years.

Gevril had apprenticed under the creed that one must have an authentic command of the art of watchmaking, so as a true master of his craft, he continued to insist on only the finest workmanship. His creations became the pinnacle of style, gracing the salons of the royal palace and rewarding Gevril with a position of prestige in the history of time.

It is in this spirit of quality and invention that Gevril lives today. Purchased in 2001 by First SBF Holding, Inc., the brand now operates under the watchful eye of president Samuel Friedmann, who has been involved in the watch industry for years. Friedmann is determined to adhere to strict standards in both the design and creation of Gevril watches.

Every timepiece is completed in Gevril's workshops in Switzerland using only the finest Swiss-made cases, bracelets, movements and parts. It is Friedmann's goal to unveil innovative Gevril designs crafted in old-world tradition.

THIS PAGE

TOP LEFT

Lugano, Switzerland in 1891.

BOTTOM

The Soho Deluxe in stainless steel with bracelet.

FACING PAGE

The Soho Deluxe is a Complete Calendar watch with day, date, month and moonphase indications. It is displayed here upon its wood mechanical winding box.

classic elegance

The hallmarks of Gevril watches are the exquisite details, elegant dials and mechanical movements. These are hallmarks that not only remain intact but also are being further built upon by Friedmann in his plan for the brand.

Swiss-born Friedmann, who comes from a long line of family members involved in the creation and sale of timepieces, has planned an exciting launch of the Gevril brand under his post. Focusing on refining the strongest existing product lines, unveiling innovative new designs with fresh style, and launching an all new marketing and image campaign, Friedmann is well equipped to infuse fresh attitude into the Gevril brand.

Important collections include the entire New York series, named for city neighborhoods: Soho, Chelsea, Greenwich, Madison and Gramercy watches. The Soho Deluxe is a Complete Calendar watch with day, date, month and moonphase indicator. The watch houses a 25-jeweled automatic movement and is water resistant to 50 meters. It features a silvered guilloché dial and transparent caseback. Created in a limited edition of 100 pieces in gold and 500 pieces in steel, this elegant watch is sold in an inlaid cherry wood mechanical winding box.

Similarly, the Chelsea is also a calendar watch. Its 25-jeweled automatic movement offers date and moonphase at 6:00 and day and month readout at 12:00. It has a depth and strength of character thanks to its silvered guilloché dial. The Greenwich watch is a 100-meter water-resistant chronograph that houses a 51-jeweled automatic movement. The dial of this timepiece is unusually clean and elegant in either black or white guillochéd patterns.

The Gevril Madison with Roman numeral dial is another popular timepiece because of its classic appeal. It features a date readout at 3:00 and a subseconds hand at 6:00. The Gramercy, a 50-meter water-resistant watch, houses a 31-jeweled automatic regulator movement. The watch is further enhanced by a bracelet design that is intricately assembled without revealing screws. With its elegant regulator dial, the Gramercy attests to Gevril's respect for tradition.

1722 Jacques Gevril is born in Le Locle, Switzerland.

1743 Gevril creates his first chronometer with different dials in stainless steel.

1744 Gevril designs his first repetition dial.

1749 Son of Jacques, Moyse Gevril is born in Le Locle, Switzerland.

1758 Jacques Gevril becomes the first exporter of Swiss watches when he and the famed horloger Pierre Jaquet-Droz embark on an historic journey to Madrid to present his masterpiece to the King of Spain.

1784 Moyse Gevril achieves the status of master clockmaker and makes imitations of self-winding watches.

1800 The Gevril family extends its craft to include enameling as well as creating faces for watches and clocks.

1810 A watch from this era and signed "Gevril à Genève" will be displayed in the Musée d'Horlogerie in Geneva nearly 200 years later.

1827 A school for watchmaking is founded in Le Locle.

1867 The famous exhibition in Paris displays a timepiece associated with Gevril within its collection of the world's most exclusive chronometers.

1910 Aiding mechanical watch production, the "machine a' pointer de Dixi S.A." is invented in Gevril's hometown and is a popular tool among Le Locle watchmakers.

1918-1930
In Le Locle, a series of new mechanical branches open two important factories, Dixi I and Dixi II specifically designed for precise, mechanical executions. These factories use diverse, fully equipped automatic machines that are capable of handling all aspects of precision watchmaking.

1959 Author Alfred Chapues pens *Grands Artisans De La Chronometrie* and includes Jacques Gevril as an important contributor to the history of fine Swiss watchmaking in La Locle.

1990s The Gevril watch company continues in the spirit and tradition of the legendary Jacques Gevril, headed by the Swiss company UTC (international distributors of Audemars Piguet, Breguet, Breitling, Bertolucci and Girard-Perregaux); Gevril designs an exclusive line to honor its namesake.

1994 Gevril patents the unlocked crown indicator; A journalist with a Ph.D in philology, Dr. Phillipe Roland Carrera of Peseux, Switzerland records the history of Gevril in his book, aptly titled *Gevril*.

1995 Gevril launches 15 Degree which features an exchangeable bezel, the UCI mechanism and 24 hours on 360 degrees with a caliber of B0110.

1999 Gevril introduces the TriBeCa, an automatic chronograph limited to 500 pieces.

2001 Gevril is acquired by First SBF Holding, Inc. and spearheaded by Samuel Friedmann; The brand is faithful to tradition—in the Gevril workshop, production revels in the astute craftsmanship and spirit of 250 years ago.

2002 Gevril introduces two brand new collections: The high-tech, sporty Sea Clouds and the Lafayette. The Lafayette is the first line just for ladies and is crafted with mother-of-pearl dials and set with diamonds possessing the colors of the rainbow.

GEVRIL

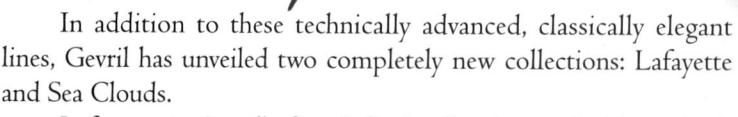

unveiling masterpieces

In addition to these technically advanced, classically elegant lines, Gevril has unveiled two completely new collections: Lafayette and Sea Clouds.

Lafayette is Gevril's first ladies' collection and offers a high fashion, haute couture look. The watches in the Lafayette collection make their debut in a palette of colors ranging from pale green, to pink, pale blue and even white. They have color-coordinated mother-of-pearl dials, or, in some cases, white mother-of-pearl dials. A total of 16 models exist that run the gamut from watches with no diamonds to watches with diamond dials, diamond bezels and diamond cases. Each Lafayette model is produced in a limited edition of just 500 pieces and the diamond-adorned watches feature only Top Wesselton diamonds.

Recognizing a woman's love for versatility and change, Friedmann has developed the Lafayette collection with interchangeable straps and may even offer interchangeable bezels. The line made its debut first in America in early 2002, and is being introduced to Switzerland and Austria later this year.

In addition to this strikingly modern watch for women, Gevril has also introduced a high-tech sports line called the Sea Clouds. Inspired by a well-known 200-meter yacht, the Sea Clouds watches are all water resistant to 200 meters and demonstrate a rugged elegance. The collection consists of six models: three in steel and three in steel-and-gold. Focusing on technical advancement and precision, Gevril offers a Sea Clouds Chronograph, a GMT and a Sea Clouds Automatic.

As with all of Gevril's timepieces, the newest watches are crafted of the finest materials. They house movements procured from private Swiss sources and then specially hand finished by Gevril's artisans. Watch cases are hand engraved and hand polished. Straps are made of only the finest sections of Louisiana crocodile that lend large-grain patterns for ultimate elegance.

The end result of all of this careful planning and attention to detail ensures that each and every Gevril watch is beautifully crafted— inside and out.

GEVRIL

TRIBECA SKU# R005/2 REF. 2101

Movement: D&D 2020/2824, automatic, 51 jewels.
Functions: chronograph.
Case: stainless steel, 37mm diameter, water resistant to 10 atm, hesalite crystal, tachymetric bezel in black enamel, stainless steel caseback.
Dial: black with white zones, numerals appliques/luminous.
Indications: small seconds at 3, hour counter at 6, minute counter at 9.

Bracelet: stainless steel bracelet.
Also available: leather strap.
Note: 500-piece limited edition.
Price: $3995

TRIBECA SKU# R004 REF. 2103

Movement: D&D 2020/2824, automatic, 51 jewels.
Functions: chronograph.
Case: stainless steel, 37mm diameter, water resistant to 10 atm, hesalite crystal, tachymetric bezel in polished steel, stainless steel caseback.
Dial: white with black zones, numerals appliques/luminous.
Indications: small seconds at 3, hour counter at 6, minute counter at 9.

Bracelet: stainless steel bracelet.
Also available: leather strap.
Note: 500-piece limited edition.
Price: $3995

TRIBECA SKU# R006/1 REF. 2104L

Movement: D&D 2020/2824, automatic, 51 jewels.
Functions: chronograph.
Case: 18K yellow gold, 37mm diameter, water resistant to 5 atm, hesalite crystal, black enamel bezel, 18K yellow-gold caseback.
Dial: champagne with black zones, numerals appliques/luminous.
Indications: small seconds at 3, hour counter at 6, minute counter at 9.

Strap: crocodile with 18K gold buckle.
Also available: 18K solid gold bracelet.
Note: 100-piece limited edition.
Price: $7495

TRIBECA SKU# R006/2 REF. 2105L

Movement: 2020/2824, automatic, 51 jewels.
Functions: chronograph.
Case: 18K yellow gold, 37mm diameter, water resistant to 5 atm, hesalite crystal, black enamel bezel, 18K yellow-gold caseback.
Dial: black with champagne zones, numerals appliques/luminous.
Indications: small seconds at 3, hour counter at 6, minute counter at 9.

Strap: crocodile with 18K gold buckle.
Also available: 18K solid gold bracelet.
Note: 100-piece limited edition.
Price: $7495

SEA CLOUD — REF. 3104

Movement: ETA 2824, 25 jewels.
Functions: date-automatic.
Case: stainless steel 316L, 40mm diameter, water resistant to 20 atm, sapphire crystal with anti-glare treatment on both sides, unidirectional bezel in 18K gold with raised minute indicators to control diver timing, screw-on stainless steel 316L caseback.
Dial: black, luminescent hands, numerals appliques/luminous.
Indications: date at 6.
Bracelet: stainless steel with logo in 18K gold.
Note: 500-piece limited edition.
Price: $3995

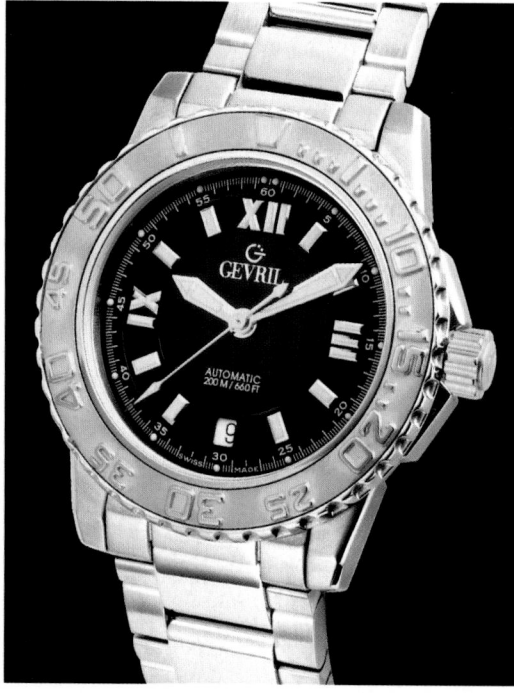

SEA CLOUD — REF. 3107

Movement: D&D 2020/2824, automatic, 51 jewels.
Functions: chronograph, 40-hour power reserve.
Case: stainless steel 316L, 40mm diameter, water resistant to 20 atm, sapphire crystal with anti-glare treatment on both sides, unidirectional bezel in 18K gold with raised minute indicators to control diver timing, screw-on stainless steel 316L caseback.
Dial: black, luminescent hands, numerals appliques/luminous.
Indications: small seconds at 3, hour counter at 6, minute counter at 9.
Bracelet: stainless steel with logo in 18K gold.
Note: 500-piece limited edition.
Price: $5995

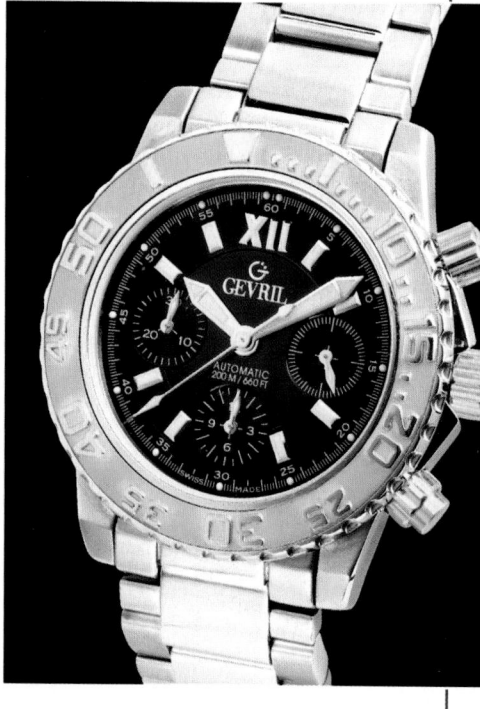

SEA CLOUD — REF. 3102

Movement: ETA 2893-2, automatic, 21 jewels.
Functions: GMT, date, 40-hour power reserve.
Case: stainless steel 316L, 40mm diameter, water resistant to 20 atm, sapphire crystal, unidirectional bezel in stainless steel 316L with third time zone, screw-on stainless steel 316L caseback.
Dial: black, luminescent hands, numerals appliques/luminous.
Indications: date at 6, second time-zone hand-painted red.
Bracelet: stainless steel.
Also available: steel and gold.
Note: 500-piece limited edition.
Price: $3995

SEA CLOUD — REF. 3103

Movement: D&D 2020/2824, automatic, 51 jewels.
Functions: chronograph, 40-hour power reserve.
Case: stainless steel 316L, 40mm diameter, water resistant to 20 atm, sapphire crystal with anti-glare treatment on both sides, unidirectional bezel in stainless steel 316L with raised minute indicators to control diver timing, screw-on stainless steel 316L caseback.
Dial: black, luminescent hands, numerals appliques/luminous.
Indications: small seconds at 3, hour counter at 6, minute counter at 9.
Bracelet: stainless steel.
Note: 500-piece limited edition.
Price: $4995

GEVRIL

LAFAYETTE — REF. 2902

Movement: D&D 2020/2824, automatic, 21 jewels.
Functions: chronograph.
Case: stainless steel, 37mm diameter, case is water resistant to 10 atm, hesalite crystal, polished-steel bezel, stainless steel caseback.
Dial: blue natural mother of pearl, raised metallic Arabic numerals.
Indications: small seconds at 3, hour counter at 6, minute counter at 9.

Strap: Louisiana crocodile.
Also available: diamond dial and/or diamond bezel.
Note: 500-piece limited edition.
Price: $4495

LAFAYETTE — REF. 2911

Movement: D&D 2020/2824, automatic, 51 jewels.
Functions: chronograph
Case: stainless steel, 37mm diameter, water resistant to 10 atm, hesalite crystal, bezel with 56 Top Wesselton diamonds (1 carat), stainless steel caseback.
Dial: pink natural mother of pearl, raised metallic Arabic numerals.
Indications: small seconds at 3, hour counter at 6, minute counter at 9.

Strap: Louisiana crocodile.
Also available: diamond dial.
Note: 500-piece limited edition.
Price: $7495

LAFAYETTE — REF. 2914

Movement: D&D 2020/2824, automatic, 51 jewels.
Functions: chronograph.
Case: stainless steel, 37mm diameter, case is water resistant to 10 atm, hesalite crystal, bezel with 56 Top Wesselton diamonds (1 carat), stainless steel caseback.
Dial: white natural mother of pearl, raised metallic Arabic numerals.

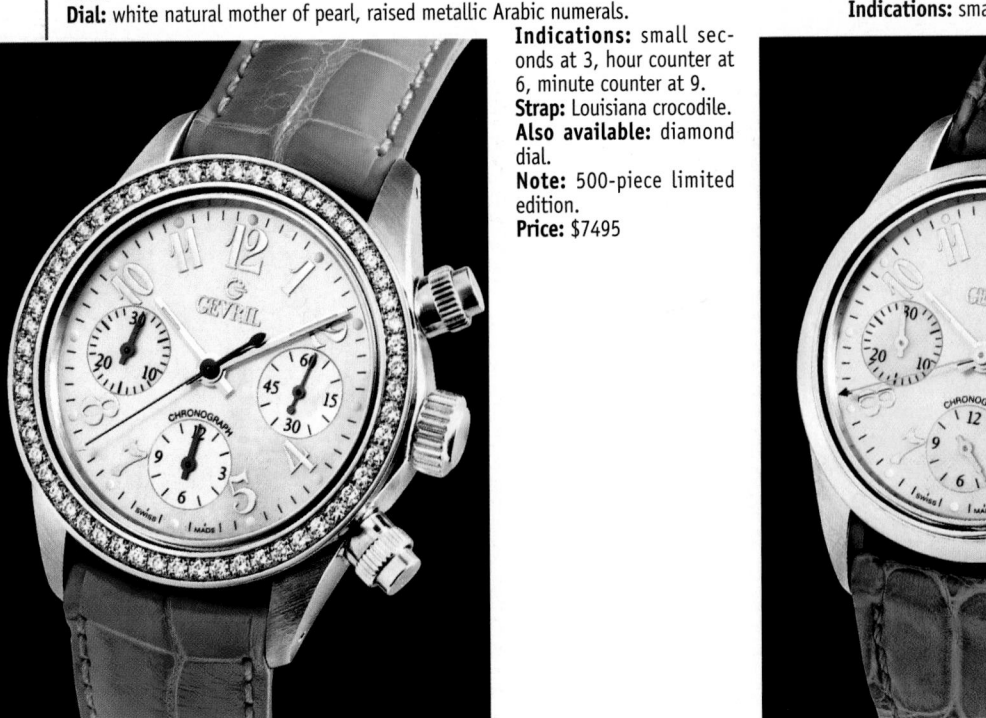

Indications: small seconds at 3, hour counter at 6, minute counter at 9.
Strap: Louisiana crocodile.
Also available: diamond dial.
Note: 500-piece limited edition.
Price: $7495

LAFAYETTE — REF. 2903

Movement: D&D 2020/2824, automatic, 51 jewels.
Functions: chronograph.
Case: stainless steel, 37mm diameter, case is water resistant to 10 atm, hesalite crystal, polished-steel bezel, stainless steel caseback.
Dial: green natural mother of pearl, raised metallic Arabic numerals.
Indications: small seconds at 3, hour counter at 6, minute counter at 9.

Strap: Louisiana crocodile.
Also available: diamond dial and/or diamond bezel.
Note: 500-piece limited edition.
Price: $4495

SOHO DELUXE   SKU# R012   REF. 2605L

Movement: D&D 9200/2824, automatic, 25 jewels.
Functions: complete calendar, day/date/month and moonphase.
Case: 18K gold, 39mm diameter, water resistant to 5 atm, sapphire crystal, 18K yellow-gold bezel.
Dial: silvered, guillochéd, Roman numerals.
Indications: day at 4 and 5, month at 7 and 8, moonphase at 12, date indicator painted red.
Strap: crocodile
Also available: 18K solid gold bracelet.
Note: 100-piece limited edition, accompanied by exclusive wooden winding box.
Price: $9995

CHELSEA   SKU# R011   REF. 2305L

Movement: D&D 9310/2824, automatic, 25 jewels.
Functions: complete calendar, day/date/month and moonphase.
Case: 18K yellow gold, 39mm diameter, water resistant to 5 atm, sapphire crystal, 18K yellow-gold bezel.
Dial: silvered, guillochéd, Roman numerals.
Indications: day and month at 12, date and moonphase at 6.
Strap: crocodile.
Also available: 18K solid gold bracelet.
Note: 100-piece limited edition.
Price: $8495

MADISON   SKU# R013   REF. 2505L

Movement: ETA 2895, automatic, 30 jewels.
Functions: subdial second date.
Case: 18K yellow gold, 39mm diameter, water resistant to 5 atm, sapphire crystal, 18K yellow-gold bezel.
Dial: silvered, guillochéd, Roman numerals.
Indications: date at 3, small seconds at 6.
Strap: crocodile.
Also available: 18K solid gold bracelet.
Note: 100-piece limited edition.
Price: $6995

GRAMERCY   SKU# R014   REF. 2405L

Movement: JB 876/2824, automatic, 31 jewels.
Functions: regulator.
Case: 18K yellow gold, 39mm diameter, water resistant to 5 atm, sapphire crystal, 18K yellow-gold bezel.
Dial: silvered, guillochéd, Roman numerals.
Indications: hour counter at 12, minute counter at center, small seconds at 6.
Strap: crocodile.
Also available: 18K solid gold bracelet.
Note: 100-piece limited edition.
Price: $7995

GEVRIL

GREENWICH SKU# K0111/1   REF. 2201

Movement: ETA 2924, automatic, 51 jewels.
Functions: chronograph.
Case: stainless steel, 39mm diameter, water resistant to 10 atm, sapphire crystal, stainless steel bezel and caseback.
Dial: silver, Roman numerals.
Indications: small seconds at 3, hour counter at 6, minute counter at 9.

     Bracelet: stainless steel.
     Price: $2495

GREENWICH SKU# K01111/2   REF. 2202

Movement: ETA 2924, automatic, 51 jewels.
Functions: chronograph.
Case: stainless steel, 39mm diameter, water resistant to 10 atm, sapphire crystal, stainless steel bezel and caseback.
Dial: silver, Roman numerals.
Indications: small seconds at 3, hour counter at 6, minute counter at 9.

     Bracelet: stainless steel.
     Note: 500-piece limited edition.
     Price: $2495

SOHO DELUXE   REF. 2602L

Movement: D&D 9200/2824, automatic, 25 jewels.
Functions: complete calendar, day/date/month and moonphase.
Case: stainless steel, 39mm diameter, water resistant to 5 atm, sapphire crystal, stainless steel bezel.
Dial: silvered, guillochéd, Roman numerals.
Indications: day at 4 and 5, month at 7 and 8, moonphase at 12, date indicator painted red.
     Strap: crocodile.
     Note: 500-piece limited edition.
     Price: $4495

MADISON   REF. 2502L

Movement: ETA 2895, automatic, 30 jewels.
Functions: subdial second date.
Case: stainless steel, 39mm diameter, water resistant to 5 atm, sapphire crystal, stainless steel bezel.
Dial: silvered, guillochéd, Roman numerals.
Indications: date at 3, small seconds at 6.

     Strap: crocodile.
     Note: 500-piece limited edition.
     Price: $2495

SOHO DELUXE SKU# R008   REF. 2601

Movement: D&D 9200/2824, automatic, 25 jewels.
Functions: complete calendar, day/date/month and moonphase.
Case: stainless steel, 39mm diameter, water resistant to 5 atm, sapphire crystal, stainless steel bezel.
Dial: silvered, guillochéd, Roman numerals.
Indications: day a 4 and 5, month at 7 and 8, moonphase at 12, date indicator painted red.
Bracelet: stainless steel.
Note: 500-piece limited edition.
Price: $4995

MADISON SKU# R009   REF. 2501

Movement: ETA 2895, automatic, 30 jewels.
Functions: subdial second date.
Case: stainless steel, 39mm diameter, water resistant to 5 atm, sapphire crystal, stainless steel bezel.
Dial: silvered, guillochéd, Roman numerals.
Indications: date at 3, small seconds at 6.
Bracelet: stainless steel.
Note: 500-piece limited edition.
Price: $2995

GRAMERCY   REF. 2402L

Movement: JB 876/2824, automatic, 31 jewels.
Functions: regulator.
Case: stainless steel, 39mm diameter, water resistant to 5 atm, sapphire crystal, stainless steel bezel.
Dial: silvered, guillochéd, Roman numerals.
Indications: hour counter at 12, minute counter at center, small seconds at 6.
Strap: crocodile.
Also available: stainless steel bracelet.
Note: 500-piece limited edition.
Price: $3495

CHELSEA SKU# R009   REF. 2302L

Movement: D&D 9310/2824, automatic, 25 jewels.
Functions: complete calendar, day/date/moonphase.
Case: stainless steel, 39mm diameter, water resistant to 5 atm, sapphire crystal, stainless steel bezel.
Dial: silvered, guillochéd, Roman numerals.
Indications: day and month at 12, date and moonphase at 6.
Strap: crocodile.
Also available: stainless steel bracelet.
Note: 500-piece limited edition.
Price: $3995

GIRARD-PERREGAUX

an historical perspective

*F*ew companies can boast 211 years of consistently superb watchmaking. Girard-Perregaux can—but chooses not to. Girard-Perregaux does not tout its laurels or brag about its myriad of incredible watchmaking achievements. Instead, this quietly proud premier watch Manufacture with an illustrious past subtly reigns supreme.

THIS PAGE
TOP

This cross-shaped jeweled watch was created by Girard-Perregaux around 1870.

BOTTOM

The Vintage 1945 Tourbillon features a tourbillon movement with patented automatic-winding system.

FACING PAGE

The Vintage 1945 with power-reserve readout, date and sub-seconds hand is created in 18-karat yellow, white or pink gold.

With its foundation established in Geneva in 1791 by Jean François Bautte, the Girard-Perregaux Manufactory has been firmly established in the heart of Switzerland's watchmaking center—La Chaux-de-Fonds—since 1854. In that veritable eye of excellence, generation after generation of watchmakers has passed on expertise and ancestral secrets. These insights have propelled Girard-Perregaux's levels of craftsmanship and technical prowess to unprecedented heights resulting in several "world firsts."

This legendary house has an exemplary history—one filled with highly coveted inventions and awards. Famed for its Tourbillon with three Gold Bridges (first built in the 1860s by Constant Girard and still created in wonderful variations today), renowned for its Opera One, its Vintage series and for its technical masteries, this watchmaker extraordinaire has long produced luxury timepieces in the grandest tradition, combining technical excellence with innovative thinking and unusual design.

Today in the hallowed halls of the brand's workshops, nearly 20,000 watches are made annually—each handcrafted to the most exacting details. Under the vigilant eye of leader Dr. Luigi Macaluso, who has owned and spearheaded the company for the past 10 years, Girard-Perregaux thrives. A purist with a driving passion for perfection, Macaluso insists on superior quality in all that is developed by the brand. He consistently pushes the limits and soars.

A member of the Sowind Holding Company, Girard-Perregaux manufactures its own movements, cases, bracelets and watch parts. It is one of but a handful of elite Manufactures to have such status and capabilities. It is this completely integrated positioning, along with a strategy of independence, that keeps Girard-Perregaux firmly on the cutting edge decade after decade, century after century.

vintage

fine

Among the courageous choices made throughout its history, the Girard-Perregaux Manufactory has consciously opted for independence. By steering clear of acquisitions and mergers with larger conglomerates, the brand relishes the status that its singular ownership offers. Girard-Perregaux is free to make its own choices in terms of products, development and strategies.

Deliberately consistent and requiring incredible discipline, these choices primarily focus on long-term prospects that ensure uniformity and perfection. It is Macaluso's goal to further develop the Girard-Perregaux manufacturing concept to its fullest—completing its range of watch mechanisms and techniques, and creating an immediately identifiable style.

This is a mastery Girard-Perregaux has deftly achieved with its many intricate and complicated timepieces. Additionally, when the brand launched a timepiece collection six years ago that was based on a 1945 model, it garnered immediate international acclaim. The Vintage 1945 series is now Girard-Perregaux's largest area of growth in terms of both sales and new product developments.

Within the clean and inviting rectangular, retro-styled Vintage case, the Manufacture has expertly placed the greatest number of its movement capabilities.

There is a magnificent automatic Tourbillon with one Gold Bridge, an automatic column-wheel chronograph, Grande date and power-reserve versions and a variety of ladies' styles.

In fact, among its most recent introductions, Girard-Perregaux unveiled the Vintage 1945 Tourbillon in platinum with a new black satin dial that features large appliqué numerals to match the case, and a classic Vintage 1945 with automatic winding that features a second-hand subdial, power reserve and elegant calendar window offset between 1:00 and 2:00. Another incredibly striking model in the sleek, ergonomically curved case is the Vintage 1945 with large date window at 12:00 and second-hand subdial and moonphase indicator at 6:00. The overall look achieved by this elegant design is a harmonious balance of legibility and beauty. Each of these distinctive timepieces is created in 18-karat yellow, white or rose gold.

With the introduction of the Vintage series, and with its own movement and casemaking capabilities, Girard-Perregaux was better positioned to move strongly into the creation of ladies' watches. The Vintage 1945 is especially sought after by women drawn to its sleek yet definitive style. The newest models for women feature mechanical movements with automatic winding. There is also a column-wheel chronograph model. Each is created in the three colors of gold and in powerful new pastel versions that coordinate dial and strap for striking appeal.

Girard-Perregaux also introduced an all-new series of Vintage 1945 Lady Joaillerie watches set with diamonds and color-coordinated dials and straps.

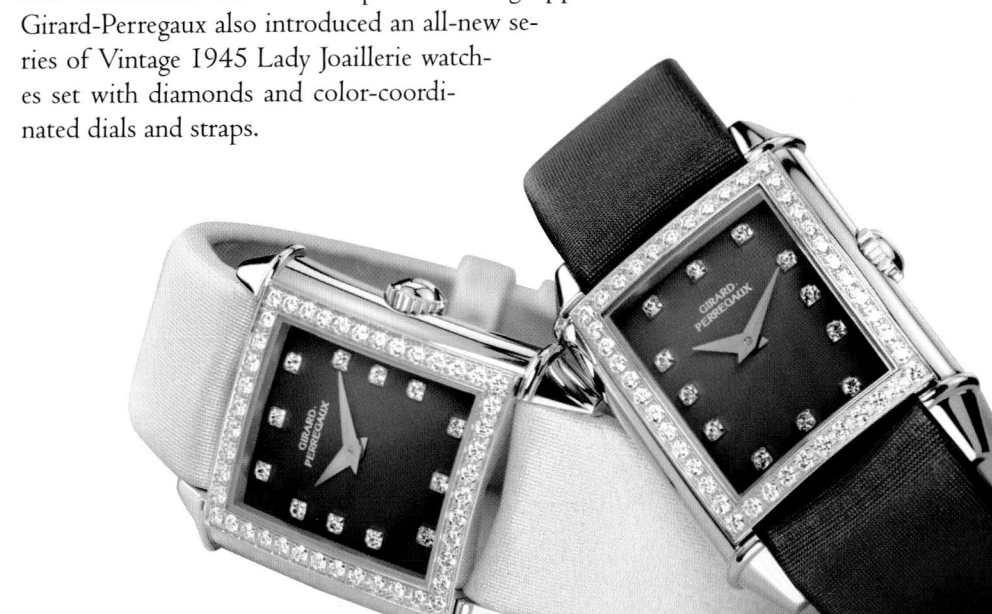

classic elegance

With the incredible success of the Vintage 1945 for women firmly rooted, Girard-Perregaux embarked on a mission to create distinctive women's watches that were unlike anything else in the company's line. Classic refinement and technological advancement were the driving philosophies behind these creations.

In no time at all, Girard-Perregaux had garnered the attention of elite women around the world with the Ladies Chronograph watches it unveiled. The brand has since elaborated the line, adding new models regularly.

Most recently, Girard-Perregaux unveiled the Petite Chronograph Lady Joaillerie—an incredible diamond-adorned chronograph watch with softly hued mother-of-pearl dials and matching straps in pastel tones. Housing the manufactured mechanical column-wheel movement with automatic winding, the watch offers distinct styling and a wonderful fit due to elongated lugs that curve and hug the wrist. The Chronograph Grand Classique, already existing and thriving in the collection, also donned color-coordinated brilliance in 2001, with pastel models capturing the most attention.

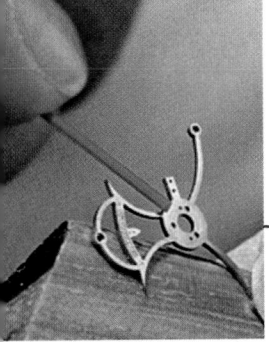

FACING PAGE

TOP

The Chronograph Grand Classique houses a mechanical movement with automatic wind.

CENTER

These splendid Grand Classique models feature date and sub-seconds hand.

BOTTOM

Featuring a mechanical chronograph movement with automatic wind and flyback function, this Grand Classique is created in a 40mm gold or steel case.

THIS PAGE

TOP

The Traveller II is a dual time zone watch with alarm function.

BOTTOM

Dubbed the "ww.tc," this striking watch tells time around the world and features a day/night ring.

In typical Girard-Perregaux style, another important Grand Classique watch joining the collection this year is a flyback chronograph with automatic-winding mechanism. Elegantly chic in steel or 18-karat yellow, white or rose gold, the flyback chronograph features a sapphire crystal and caseback to allow viewing of the movement. Honoring the spirit of classic elegance, Girard-Perregaux also unveiled a simple mechanical version of the Grand Classique with small seconds subdial at 9:00 and date window at 3:00.

Joining Classic Elegance (as Girard-Perregaux refers to this striking collection of beauties) is the Traveller II and the ww.tc. Reflecting the needs of its demanding clientele, Girard-Perregaux offers the chic and elegant Traveller II dual time zone watch with alarm function. Housed in steel or in any of the three colors of gold, the Traveller II features a mechanical movement with automatic wind. The ww.tc—Hours of the World Chronograph Automatic watch—was unveiled first in 2000 and, in 2001, was crafted in a host of new colors and renditions. The world time chronograph features a complex system with day/night ring and calendar window.

All of these classically superb timepieces attest to Girard-Perregaux's ongoing commitment to design and perfection.

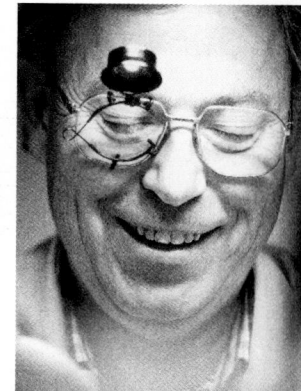

technical

excellence

By adeptly forging ahead in microtechnology and microelectronics, and combining its technical knowledge with stylistic advances, Girard-Perregaux remains on the forefront with its watches—well poised for the third millennium. Function and precision—ever important to the brand's timepiece development—remains key. As a result, Girard-Perregaux continues to produce instruments of elegance and action.

The new Opera Two is representative of the brand's technical excellence. Building on the Opera One, which was introduced in 1999 as a Tourbillon with Gold Bridges and the Westminster Chimes, the Opera Two demonstrates the new levels of Girard-Perregaux's watchmaking savoir-faire. The sophisticated mechanisms of this complicated timepiece include Tourbillon with three Gold Bridges, Minute Repeater and Perpetual Calendar. Housed in either 18-karat yellow, white or pink gold, or in platinum, the watch features an aperture through which three of the four strike hammers are visible—the fourth hammer is visible only when striking. The hand-wound movement with 75-hours of power reserve houses the Westminster chimes for the repeater.

Forging ahead, too, with its commitment to performance and excellence in the pour Ferrari line, Girard-Perregaux has achieved even greater exclusivity in this series.

"With great emotion and appreciation for the Ferrari family of product, Girard-Perregaux will now focus specifically on creating limited edition pieces that

THIS PAGE
LEFT

Opera Two features the complex three Gold Bridges, Minute Repeater and Perpetual Calendar.

FACING PAGE
TOP LEFT

Dr. Luigi Macaluso (left) and Luca Cordero Di Montezemolo, President of Ferrari.

TOP RIGHT

The limited edition F1 2000 is crafted in steel with carbon fiber or silver dial.

BOTTOM

A rubber-strapped version of the F1 2000 offers sporty appeal.

commemorate an occasion or a car," said Ron Jackson, head of Girard-Perregaux in the all-important American market.

This past year, the brand unveiled a new 42-hour power-reserve, 63-jeweled chronograph: the pour Ferrari FI 2000. This striking automatic chronograph pays tribute to Ferrari's double victory in the Formula I 2000 World Championships. The watches are available in steel or in 18-karat yellow, white or red gold with carbon fiber dials, and feature either steel bracelets or hand-sewn leather or rubber straps. The back of the case is engraved elegantly with the profile of the victorious car.

This timepiece, as with the entire pour Ferrari line, symbolizes a collaboration of the two great companies whose philosophies are based on quality and performance. Both brands share the same taste for refined details and cultural traditions and their successful co-branding relationship is unique in the industry.

GIRARD-PERREGAUX

OPERA ONE   REF. 99760

Movement: mechanical, manual winding, GP 9899 caliber, with tourbillon device mounted on three 18 kt pink-gold bridges, Westminster Carillon with four hammers and four gongs tuned on the notes E-C-D-G. Realized, finished, chased and decorated totally by hand by the firm's watchmakers.
Functions: hour, minute, small second, minute repeater, carillon.
Case: 18 kt pink gold, three-piece case (Ø 40 mm, thickness 13 mm); antire-

flective curved sapphire crystal; repeater slide on the middle; pink-gold crown; back attached by 6 screws, displaying the movement through a sapphire crystal. Water-resistant to 3 atm.
Dial: gold, black enameled; aperture on the tourbillon and on three carillon hammers (G, C, D; E is hidden); applied pink-gold bâton markers and Arabic numerals; pink-gold Dauphine hands.
Indications: small second at 6, integrated in the tourbillon carriage.
Strap: crocodile leather, hand-stitched; gold clasp. Produced in a few pieces per year.
Also available: in yellow or white gold; in platinum. Black or ivory dial.

OPERA TWO   REF. 99740

Movement: mechanical, manual winding, GP 9897 caliber, with tourbillon device mounted on three 18 kt pink-gold bridges, 37 jewels, 21,000 vibrations/hour. Westminster Carillon with four hammers and four gongs tuned on the notes E-C-D-G. Realized, finished, chased and decorated totally by hand by the firm's watchmakers.
Functions: hour, minute, small second, minute repeater, carillon, perpetual calendar (date, day, month, year).

Case: 18 kt pink gold, three-piece case (Ø 40 mm, thickness 15 mm); antireflective curved sapphire crystal; repeater slide on the middle; pink-gold crown; back attached by 6 screws, displaying the movement through a sapphire crystal.
Dial: ivory; aperture on the tourbillon and on three carillon hammers (G, C, D; E is hidden); applied pink-gold counter crowns; pink-gold-plated Dauphine hands.
Indications: date at 3, day at 9, month and year at 12.
Strap: crocodile leather, hand-stitched; pink-gold clasp.
Produced by 10 pieces per year. **Also available:** in yellow or white gold; in platinum.

TOURBILLON WITH THREE GOLD BRIDGES PRESIDENT   REF. 99800

Movement: mechanical, manual winding, GP 9800 caliber, with tourbillon device mounted on three 18 kt pink-gold bridges, 75 hours autonomy, 20 jewels, 21,600 vibrations per hour. Movement mounted upside down, hand-fitting at the pillar-plate. Silvered and chased pillar-plate. Realized, finished and decorated totally by hand by the firm's watch-makers. **Functions:** hour, minute, small second.
Case: 18 kt yellow gold, three-piece case (Ø 38 mm, thickness 12.7 mm), pol-

ished and brushed finish; antireflective curved sapphire crystal; gold crown; back attached by 6 screws, displaying the movement through a sapphire crystal. Water-resistant to 3 atm.
Dial: silvered; printed Roman numerals and railway minute track; blued steel leaf style hands. **Indications:** small second at 6, integrated in the tourbillon carriage.
Strap: crocodile leather, hand-stitched; gold clasp.
Also available: in pink or white gold. Black dial and applied Arabic numerals or silvered dial and printed Roman numerals.

TOURBILLON WITH THREE GOLD BRIDGES AUTOMATIC   REF. 99250

Movement: mechanical, automatic winding, GP 9600 caliber, with tourbillon device mounted on three 18 kt pink-gold bridges, over 40 hours autonomy, 21,600 vibrations per hour. Rotor positioned under the power barrel (patented system). Rhodium-plated and chased pillar-plate and barrel cover. Realized, finished and decorated entirely by hand by the firm's watchmakers.
Functions: hour, minute, small second.

Case: 18 kt pink gold, three-piece case (Ø 38 mm, thickness 10 mm), polished and brushed finish; antireflective flat sapphire crystal; pink-gold crown; back attached by 6 screws. Water-resistant to 3 atm.
Dial: 3 solid gold tourbillon bridges, arabesqued pillar-plate, barrel and tourbillon are all visible; pink-gold Dauphine hands.
Indications: small second at 6, integrated in the tourbillon carriage.
Strap: crocodile leather, hand-stitched; pink-gold clasp.
Also available: in yellow or white gold or platinum.

GIRARD-PERREGAUX

CHRONO RATTRAPANTE TOURBILLON MIN. REPEATER   REF. 99700

Movement: mechanical, manual winding, GP 9898 caliber, with tourbillon device, 32 hours autonomy, 44 jewels, 18,000 vibrations per hour. Realized, finished and decorated by hand by the firm's watchmakers.
Functions: hour, minute, small second, split-second chronograph with 2 counters, minute repeater.
Case: platinum, three-piece case (Ø 40, thickness 15 mm), polished and brushed finish; curved sapphire crystal; brushed bezel; white-gold crown and pushers (splitting pusher on the crown); back attached by 4 screws, displaying the movement through a sapphire crystal. Water-resistant to 3 atm.
Dial: black; printed white Arabic numerals and minute track; white-gold Dauphine hands.
Indications: minute counter at 3, small second at 9, center second and split-second counters, minute track with divisions for 1/5 of a second.
Strap: crocodile leather, hand-stitched; white-gold clasp.
The model shown is out of stock. It is available only with ivory dial.
Also available: in yellow or pink gold, in white gold.

CHRONO WW.TC   REF. 49800

Movement: automatic, GP 3387 cal., 13''' (GP 3100 base + modules), 45 hours power reserve, 18 kt gold rotor, 63 jewels. Decorated with Côtes de Genève pattern and beveled. Realized and finished by hand by the firm's watchmakers.
Functions: hour, minute, small sec., date, world time, 24 hours, chronograph with 3 counters. **Case:** 18 kt yellow gold, 3-piece case (Ø 43, thick. 13.6 mm), polished and brushed finish; antireflective curved sapphire crystal; screw-down crowns (at 9 for town disc control) and rectangular gold pushers; back attached by 6 screws, displaying the movement through a sapphire crystal. Water-resistant to 3 atm.
Dial: ivory; lumin. applied gold-plated cabochon markers (Arabic 12); lumin. gold-plated leaf style hands. **Indications:** date at 01:30, small sec. at 3, hour counter at 6, minute counter at 9, center sec. counter, minute track; external turning flange with reference town names for 24 time zones, internal ring with 24-hours day/night turning together with the main hour.
Strap: crocodile leather, hand-stitched; gold foldover clasp. Photograph reduced by 10%.
Also available: bracelet: pink gold; white gold, strap and bracelet; platinum, strap or bracelet.

CHRONO SPORT 40 MM   REF. 49560

Movement: mechanical, automatic winding, GP 3370 cal., 45 hours power reserve, 28,800 vph, 63 jewels, 13'''. Decorated with Côtes de Genève pattern and beveled. Manufactured, mounted, finished and decorated by hand by the firm's watchmakers. **Functions:** hour, minute, small sec., date, chronograph with 3 counters. **Case:** 18 kt pink gold, three-piece case (Ø 40, thickness 12.65 mm), polished and brushed finish; antireflective curved sapphire crystal; pink-gold crown and pushers; back attached by 7 screws. Water-resistant to 3 atm.
Dial: ivory; zones decorated with circular beads; applied gold-plated brass bâton markers (Arabic 12); gold-plated brass leaf style hands.
Indications: small second at 3, date between 4 and 5, hour counter at 6, minute counter at 9, center sec. counter, minute track with divisions for 1/5 of a second, tachometer scale.
Strap: crocodile leather, hand-stitched; pink-gold clasp.
Also available: bracelet: yellow or white gold, strap and bracelet; in steel with black or blue dial, silvered zones, applied markers or white dial and applied Arabic numerals.

PETIT CHRONO 32 MM   REF. 80450

Movement: automatic, GP 3080 cal., 10'''1/2, 36 hours power reserve, 18 kt gold rotor, 38 jewels, 28,800 vph. Decorated with Côtes de Genève pattern and beveled. Modified, mounted, adjusted, finished and hand-decorated by the firm's watchmakers. **Functions:** hour, minute, small second, chronograph with 2 counters. **Case:** 18 kt yellow gold, 3-piece case (Ø 31.5, thickness 11.7); antireflective curved sapphire crystal; gold crown and pushers; back attached by 5 screws, displaying the movement through a sapphire crystal. Water-resistant to 3 atm. **Dial:** silvered, counters in mother-of-pearl; luminescent Roman numerals and applied markers in gold-plated rolled brass with set brilliants; luminescent burnished steel leaf style hands. **Indications:** minute counter at 3, small sec. at 9, center sec. counter, minute track with divisions for 1/5 of a second. **Strap:** crocodile leather; gold clasp. **Also available:** pink gold; white gold; jewel versions. Black dial, lumin. Arabic numerals or silvered dial, mother-of-pearl counters, 8 brilliant markers; or all mother-of-pearl, 8 brilliant markers; skeletonized dial, applied Arabic numerals: yellow or pink gold, silvered zones; white gold, rosé zones.

GIRARD-PERREGAUX

GP POUR FERRARI "F310B"   REF. 90260

Movement: mechanical, automatic winding, GP 3170 cal., 44 jewels, 28,800 vph. **Functions:** hour, minute, small second, 24-hour indication, perpetual calendar (date, day, month, year, moon phase), chronograph with 3 counters.
Case: titanium, 3-piece case (Ø 40, thickness 13 mm), brushed; antireflective curved sapphire crystal; 2 correctors on the middle; screw-down crown; back attached by 8 screws, with the "F310B" silhouette and the Grand Prix races won.

Water-resistant to 3 atm.
Dial: carbon fiber; luminescent Arabic numerals; luminescent rhodium-plated brass bâton hands.
Indications: moon-phase and 24-hour display at 3, week day and hour counter at 6, month over a four-year cycle and minute counter at 9, date and small second at 12, center second counter, tachometer scale.
Strap: crocodile leather, hand-stitched; titanium fold-over clasp. Wooden red China lacquer case with rotating winding device.
Also available: yellow or pink gold, white gold. Black dial with luminescent Arabic numerals or ivory dial with applied Arabic numerals. "F50", realized in 1996 for the 205th G.P. and 50th Ferrari anniversaries (same versions).

CHRONOGRAPH RATTRAPANTE S.F. FOUDROYANTE   REF. 90200

Movement: automatic, GP 8020 caliber, 13''', 45 hours power reserve, 40 jewels, 28,800 vph. Decorated with Côtes de Genève pattern and beveled. Modified, hand-finished and decorated by the firm's watchmakers.
Functions: hour, minute, split-second chronograph with two counters and "foudroyante" feature. **Case:** 18 kt yellow gold, three-piece case (Ø 40, thickness 14.6 mm), polished and brushed finish; antireflective curved sapphire crys-

tal; gold crown and pushers (splitting pusher coaxial with the crown); back attached by 7 screws with engraved "1929-1999". Water-resistant to 3 atm.
Dial: ivory; applied gold-plated brass triangular markers and Arabic numerals; gold-plated brass leaf style hands. **Indications:** minute counter at 3, eighths-of-a-second counter with "lightning" hand at 9, center split-second counters, minute track with divisions for 1/5 of a sec., tachometer scale.
Strap: crocodile leather, hand-stitched; gold fold-over clasp. Limited ed. of 750 numbered pcs; delivered in a special case.
Also available: pink or white gold; platinum, leather strap; black dial, applied markers or lumin. Arab. numerals; titanium, carbon fiber dial.

GP POUR FERRARI "F1-2000 WORLD CHAMPION"   REF. 49560

Movement: automatic, GP 2280 caliber, 13''', auton. 45h, 57 jewels, 28,800 vph. Decorated with Côtes de Genève pattern and beveled. Realized and finished by hand. **Functions:** hour, minute, small second, date, chronograph with 3 counters.
Case: 18 kt white gold, 3-piece case (Ø 40, thick. 13 mm), polished and brushed finish; antireflective curved sapphire crystal; white gold screw-down crown and pushers; back fastened by 7 steel screws with the car that won the 2000 Formula 1

World Championship. Water-resistant to 3 atm. **Dial:** anthracite; silvered zones with circular beads; applied rhodium-plated brass bâton markers (12 Arabic) and luminescent rhodium-plated brass bâton hands. **Indications:** small second at 3, date at 04:30, hour counter at 6, minute counter at 9, center second counter, minute track with divisions for 1/5 of a second and tachometer scale. **Strap:** crocodile leather; white gold buckle. 2001 pieces. Wooden case with "Ferrari red" lacquer.
Also av.: ivory dial; bracelet; yellow gold ivory or anthracite dial silvered zones; pink gold coconut fiber strap, cream dial, bracelet; stainless steel, carbon fiber or silvered dial red, black, yellow zones, rubber strap, coconut fiber strap, bracelet.

GP POUR FERRARI "275 LE MANS"   REF. 80900

Movement: automatic, GP 2280 caliber, 13''', autonomy 45 hours, 57 jewels, 28,800 vibrations per hour. Decorated with Côtes de Genève pattern and beveled. Realized and finished by hand by the firm's watchmakers.
Functions: hour, minute, small second, 24-hour indication, chronograph with 3 counters.
Case: stainless steel, three-piece case (Ø 39.5 mm, thickness 13.9 mm), pol-

ished and brushed finish; antireflective curved sapphire crystal; screw-down crown; back attached by 8 screws, with the engraved profile of the Ferrari 275 of Le Mans. Water-resistant to 5 atm.
Dial: black, grained pattern; silvered zones decorated with circular beads; printed white bâton markers (12 Arabic); luminescent white enameled brass bâton hands.
Indications: small second at 3, hour counter at 6, 24-hour display at 9, center second and minute counters, minute track with divisions for 1/5 of a second; tachometer scale.
Strap: crocodile leather; stainless steel clasp.
Also available: with silvered dial, black zones, rubber strap; with bracelet.

GRAND CLASSIQUE CHRONOGRAPH RETOUR EN VOL   REF. 49580

Movement: mechanical, automatic winding, GP 337A caliber, 13''', autonomy 45 hours, 63 jewels, 28,800 vibrations per hour. Decorated with Côtes de Genève pattern and beveled. Realized, mounted, regulated, finished and decorated by hand by the firm's watchmakers.

Functions: hour, minute, small second, fly-back chronograph with 3 counters.

Case: 18 kt yellow gold, three-piece case (Ø 40 mm, thickness 13 mm); antire-

flective curved sapphire crystal; gold crown and pushers; back attached by 7 screws. Water-resistant to 3 atm.

Dial: ivory; applied gold-plated brass bâton markers (Arabic 12); luminescent gold-plated brass leaf style hands.

Indications: small second at 3, date between 4 and 5, hour counter at 6, minute counter at 9, center fly-back second counter, minute track, tachometer scale.

Strap: crocodile leather, hand-stitched; gold clasp.

Also available: bracelet: pink or white gold, strap and bracelet; in steel with strap and bracelet. Black or ivory dial.

GRAND CLASSIQUE SMALL SECOND   REF. 49520

Movement: mechanical, automatic winding, GP 3300 caliber, 11'''1/2, autonomy 50 hours, 27 jewels, 28,800 vibrations per hour. Decorated with Côtes de Genève pattern and beveled. Realized, mounted, regulated, finished and decorated by hand by the firm's watchmakers.

Functions: hour, minute, small second, date.

Case: 18 kt pink gold, three-piece case (Ø 38 mm, thickness 9 mm), polished

and brushed finish; antireflective curved sapphire crystal; pink-gold crown; back attached by 6 screws, displaying the movement through a sapphire crystal. Water-resistant to 3 atm.

Dial: gray with sun pattern; zone decorated with circular beads; applied pink-gold-plated brass bâton markers and Arabic numerals; printed minute track; luminescent pink-gold-plated brass leaf style hands.

Indications: date at 3, small second at 9.

Strap: crocodile leather, hand-stitched; pink-gold clasp.

Also available: in yellow or white gold. With silvered dial and printed Roman numerals or blue, gray or ivory dial and applied markers.

NEW CHRONO 7000   REF. 70300

Movement: mechanical, automatic winding, GP 2280 caliber, autonomy 46 hours, 57 jewels, 13''', 28,800 vibrations per hour. Beveled and decorated with Côtes de Genève pattern. Modified, mounted, adjusted, finished and hand-decorated by the firm's watchmakers.

Functions: hour, minute, small second, date, chronograph with 3 counters.

Case: stainless steel, two-piece case (Ø 38, thickness 11.8 mm); antireflective

flat sapphire crystal; bezel with engraved tachometer scale; ogival pushers; back attached by 6 screws. Water-resistant to 5 atm.

Dial: mat black, counters decorated with circular beads; luminescent bâton markers, 12 in Arabic numerals; luminescent white enameled hands.

Indications: small second at 3, date between 4 and 5, hour counter at 6, minute counter at 9, center second counter, railway minute track.

Bracelet: stainless steel; recessed double fold-over clasp.

Also available: with leather strap; pink gold & stainless steel, leather strap, bracelet. White or black dial, luminescent markers; silvered dial, applied Arabic numerals.

TRAVELLER II 40 MM   REF. 49350

Movement: automatic, GP 2291 caliber, 31 jewels; 28,800 vibrations per hour. Realized and finished by hand by the firm's watchmakers. **Functions:** hour, minute, second, date, second time-zone time, 24-hour indication, alarm.

Case: 18 kt yellow gold, three-piece case (Ø 40 mm, thickness 13.8 mm), polished and brushed finish; antireflective curved sapphire crystal; gold crown at 2 for hour, second time-zone and date setting, at 4 for alarm setting; back at-

tached by 6 screws. Water-resistant to 3 atm.

Dial: ivory; applied gold-plated brass Arabic numerals; luminescent dots on the printed railway minute track; luminescent gold-plated brass Dauphine hands. **Indications:** date at 6 (referred to central time), second time-zone time and 24-hour display below 12, sonnerie with red arrow-pointed luminescent center hand, dedicated minute track with divisions for 10 minutes.

Strap: coconut fiber, hand-stitched; gold clasp.

Also available: anthracite or blue dial applied Arabic numerals or black luminescent or applied Arabic numerals; stainless steel, strap, bracelet; pink gold, leather strap; white gold, strap. Ø 38 mm Ref. 49400.

GIRARD-PERREGAUX

VINTAGE 1945 TOURBILLON SOUS UN PONT D'OR   REF. 99850

Movement: mechanical, automatic winding, GP 9600 caliber, with a tourbillon mounted on a 18 kt pink-gold bridge, autonomy 48 hours, 32 jewels (size 28.6 x 28.6 mm), 28,800 vibrations per hour. Engine-turned (guilloché) and beveled. Realized, mounted, adjusted, finished and decorated by hand by the firm's watchmakers.
Functions: hour, minute, small second.

Case: 18 kt pink gold, two-piece case, in square anatomically carved shape (size 32 x 31 mm, thickness 12.5 mm); antireflective curved sapphire crystal; pink-gold crown; snap-on back. Water-resistant to 3 atm.
Dial: ivory, aperture on the tourbillon, curved; applied pink-gold Arabic numerals; printed minute track; pink-gold Dauphine hands.
Indications: small second at 6 integrated in the tourbillon carriage.
Strap: crocodile leather, hand-stitched; pink-gold clasp.
Also available: in yellow or white gold; in platinum. Ivory or anthracite dial with applied Arabic numerals.

VINTAGE 1945 BIG DATE MOON-PHASE   REF. 25800

Movement: mechanical, automatic winding, GP 3330 caliber, 50 hours autonomy, 32 jewels, 28,800 vibrations per hour. Decorated with Côtes de Genève pattern and beveled. Realized, mounted, regulated, finished and decorated by hand by the firm's watchmakers.
Functions: hour, minute, small second, date, moon-phase.
Case: 18 kt pink gold, two-piece square, anatomically curved case (size 32 x 32 mm, thickness 11 mm); antireflective curved sapphire crystal; pink-gold crown; a corrector on the middle; snap-on back displaying the movement through a sapphire crystal. Water-resistant to 3 atm.

Dial: ivory, curved; applied gold-plated brass Arabic numerals and triangular markers; printed minute track; gold-plated brass Dauphine hands.
Indications: small second and moon-phase at 6, double-disc big date at 12.
Strap: crocodile leather, hand-stitched; pink-gold fold-over clasp.
Also available: in yellow or white gold, leather strap or bracelet. With black or ivory dial and applied markers.

VINTAGE 1945 CHRONOGRAPH   REF. 25990

Movement: automatic, GP 3080 caliber (Ø23.3 mm, thickness 6.28 mm), 36 hours autonomy, 38 jewels, 28,800 vibrations per hour. Finished and decorated by hand by the firm's watch-makers.
Functions: hour, minute, small second, chronograph with 2 counters.
Case: 18 kt pink gold, two-piece rectangular, anatomically curved case (size 31 x 30 mm, thickness 13 mm); antireflective curved sapphire crystal; pink gold crown and rectangular pushers; snap-on back. Water-resistant to 3 atm.
Dial: silvered, engine-turned (guilloché) center, curved; applied faceted gold-plated brass Arabic numerals and triangular markers; gold-plated brass Dauphine hands.
Indications: minute counter at 3, small second at 9, center second counter; minute track.
Strap: crocodile leather, hand-stitched; pink-gold fold-over clasp.
Also available: with bracelet in yellow gold; in white gold, leather strap or bracelet. With anthracite or silvered dial and applied markers, or black dial with applied Arabic numerals (yellow, pink or white gold); with pink, yellow, green, blue dial and applied Arabic numerals (white gold).

VINTAGE 1945 SMALL SECOND POWER RESERVE   REF. 25850

Movement: mechanical, automatic winding, GP 33R0 caliber, 50 hours autonomy, 27 jewels, 11'''1/2, 28,800 vibrations per hour. Decorated with Côtes de Genève pattern and beveled. Realized, mounted, regulated, finished and decorated by hand by the firm's watchmakers.
Functions: hour, minute, small second, date, power reserve.
Case: 18 kt pink gold, two-piece square, anatomically curved case (size 32 x 32 mm, thickness 11.5 mm); antireflective curved sapphire crystal; pink gold crown; snap-on back displaying the movement through a sapphire crystal. Water-resistant to 3 atm.

Dial: glossy black, curved; applied gold-plated brass Arabic numerals; printed white railway minute track; gold-plated brass Dauphine hands.
Indications: date between 1 and 2 with magnifying lens, power reserve between 4 and 5, small second and moon-phase at 9.
Strap: crocodile leather, hand-stitched; pink-gold fold-over clasp.
Also available: in yellow or white gold. With silvered or black dial and applied Arabic numerals.

GIRARD-PERREGAUX

VINTAGE 1945 DATE SMALL SECOND   REF. 25960

Movement: automatic, GP 3200 caliber, 42 hours autonomy, 27 jewels, 10'''1/2, 28,800 vibrations per hour. Beveled and decorated with Côtes de Genève pattern. Finished and decorated entirely by hand by the firm's watchmakers.

Functions: hour, minute, small second, date.

Case: 18 kt yellow gold, two-piece square-curved case (size 28 x 28 mm, thickness 8.9 mm); antireflective curved sapphire crystal; gold crown; snap-on back displaying the movement through a sapphire crystal. Water-resistant to 3 atm.

Dial: silvered, engine-turned (guilloché) center, curved; applied gold-plated brass Arabic numerals and triangular markers, printed minute track; gold-plated brass Dauphine hands.

Indications: date at 6, small second at 9.

Strap: crocodile leather, hand-stitched; gold clasp.

Also available: with bracelet; with black dial and luminescent or applied Arabic numerals; with anthracite dial and applied markers; in pink gold; in white gold with pink, yellow, green, blue dial and applied Arabic numerals, leather strap or bracelet.

RICHEVILLE TONNEAU CHRONOGRAPH   REF. 27500

Movement: mechanical, automatic winding, GP 2280 caliber. Finished and decorated entirely by hand by the firm's watchmakers.

Functions: hour, minute, small second, chronograph with 2 counters.

Case: stainless steel, three-piece tonneau-shaped case (size 37 x 35 mm, thickness 11.5 mm); antireflective flat sapphire crystal; drop-shaped pushers, with case protection; back attached by 7 screws. Water-resistant to 3 atm.

Dial: blue enameled, engine-turned (guilloché) counters; printed oversized Arabic numerals and railway minute track; luminescent rhodium-plated brass lozenge hands.

Indications: small second at 3, minute counter at 9, center second counter.

Strap: crocodile leather; stainless steel clasp.

Also available: with bracelet with silvered dial and applied Arabic numerals or with ivory, black or blue enameled dial with luminescent Arabic numerals.

1970 CHRONOGRAPH RATTRAPANTE   REF. 90120

Movement: mechanical, automatic winding, GP 8298 caliber, 31 jewels, 28,800 vibrations per hour. Modified, mounted, adjusted, finished and hand-decorated by the firm's watchmakers.

Functions: hour, minute, small second, split-second chronograph with 2 counters.

Case: 18 kt yellow gold, two-piece brushed square carved case (size 38 x 38 mm, thickness 14.8 mm); antireflective curved sapphire crystal; rectangular pushers, splitting pusher on the gold crown; back attached by 5 screws. Water-resistant to 3 atm.

Dial: ivory; applied gold-plated brass Arabic numerals; gold-plated brass Dauphine hands.

Indications: minute counter at 3, small second at 9, center second and split-second counters, minute track with divisions for 1/5 of a second.

Strap: crocodile leather, hand-stitched; gold clasp; precious wood case and authenticity certificate.

Also available: in pink gold; in steel. With black dial and luminescent Arabic numerals or ivory dial and applied Arabic numerals.

1970 CHRONOGRAPH   REF. 25980

Movement: mechanical, automatic winding, GP 2280 caliber, 28,800 vibrations per hour. Modified, mounted, adjusted, hand-finished and hand-decorated by the firm's watchmakers.

Functions: hour, minute, small second, 24-hour indication, chronograph with 2 counters.

Case: stainless steel, three-piece brushed case (size 38 x 38 mm, thickness 14.8 mm); antireflective curved sapphire crystal; screw-down crown; rectangular pushers; back attached by 7 screws. Water-resistant to 3 atm.

Dial: ivory; applied rhodium-plated brass Arabic numerals; printed minute track; rhodium-plated brass leaf style hands.

Indications: small second at 3, 24-hour display at 9, center minute counter (with arrow-shaped point) and second counter, minute track with divisions for 1/5 of a second.

Strap: crocodile leather, hand-stitched; stainless steel clasp.

Also available: in yellow or pink gold; in white gold. With ivory dial and applied Arabic numerals or black dial and luminescent Arabic numerals.

GLASHÜTTE

the return of a German watchmaking tradition

In the mid-1800s in the Saxony region of Germany, watchmaking as a trade took root. Astute watchmakers of this area perfected their trades, and one by one, new companies were formed—yielding a variety of brands. It was in this environ that the roots of what is today called Glashütte took shape. Founded in 1845, Glashütte was dedicated to excellence and quickly attained quality status.

The German brand produced fine watches even in the face of the turmoil and upheavals of World War I. Unfortunately, the watchmaking trade here was thwarted by World War II bombings and political unrest. At the end of the war, the city of Glashütte came under the control of the East German government, which merged the various watch brands of the region into one company in 1951. The elegant timepieces that had heretofore made a name for themselves became mostly forgotten outside of East Germany.

Following the German reunification in 1990, the dream of the return of German watchmaking became a

TOP

The Alfred Helwig Tourbillon 2 houses the Glashütte Original manufactured movement, caliber 41-02, with manual winding and a one-minute flying tourbillon.

ABOVE

The Glashütte Original movement, caliber 60, is a manual-wind, classic column-wheel chronograph with flyback mechanism.

BOTTOM

The Senator Karree "Up and Down" watch is created in either 18-karat rose gold or steel and is strikingly elegant.

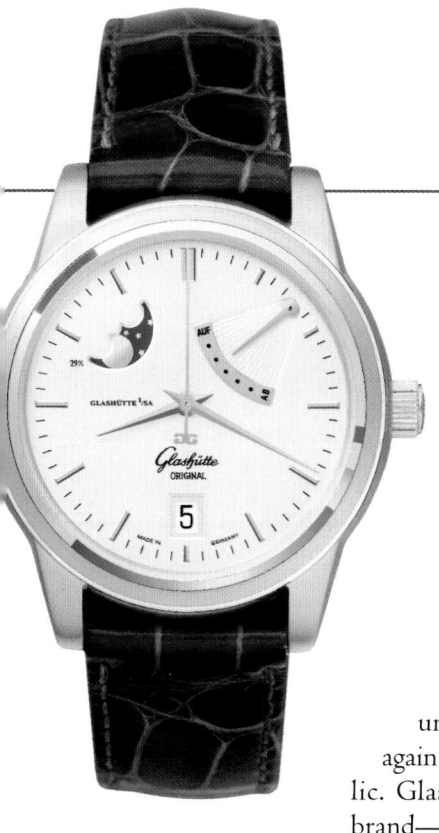

possibility again. Several of the companies whose watchmaking had been stifled throughout the past 40 years, immediately set about reestablishing their brands. Such was the case with Glashütte. In 1994, the Glashütte Original brand was established. Based on its fine roots and with a loyalty to traditional values, Glashütte embarked on a quest to create some of Germany's finest complex mechanical timepieces.

When the first watches of the brand were unveiled to the world in 1996, Glashütte once again found itself in the discriminating eye of the public. Glashütte was not intimidated; the elements of the brand—excellent craftsmanship, elegant design, interesting history, and dedication to survival—came together in a winning formula for success. Within a few short years, Glashütte had garnered the attention of connoisseurs and collectors with its exclusive movements and timepieces. In late 2000, the brand was purchased by The Swatch Group, which was determined to maintain Glashütte's purity of tradition.

Building on its past, the company is once again producing watches that are mechanical masterpieces. Designing, developing and producing its own movements gives Glashütte an edge. All watches are created in limited editions with the utmost attention paid to every detail. The timepieces unveiled in 2001 pay homage to the brand's past and reveal its lust for the future.

The Alfred Helwig Tourbillon 2 watch, which is a second edition of the Alfred Helwig Tourbillon watch unveiled in 1996, is based on a watch created by master watchmaker Alfred Helwig in Glashütte around 1920. It houses a Glashütte Original manufactured movement, caliber 41-02, with manual winding and a frontally placed one-minute flying tourbillon. The watch also offers 48 hours of power reserve, a subdial to indicate the hour and minute displays, and a retrograde date display—making it an elegant complication. Created in 18-karat rose gold, the Alfred Helwig Tourbillon 2 is being produced in a limited edition of 25 pieces for worldwide distribution.

As an addition to its Senator collection, Glashütte unveiled two new Senator "Up and Down" watches. The Senator Classic "Up and Down" offers moonphase display, date display and power-reserve readout. Housing a Glashütte Original automatic movement, the watch is crafted in 18-karat rose gold. The Senator Karree "Up and Down" offers the same features and functions as the Classic model, but is created in a square case with octagonal accents. This version is crafted in either 18-karat rose gold or in steel. It is a striking rendition of form and function—much like the rest of the stunning Glashütte collection.

TOP LEFT

Housing an automatic movement and offering power-reserve indication, the Senator Classic "Up and Down" watch is created only in 18-karat rose gold with a Louisiana crocodile strap.

TOP RIGHT

Called the PanoRetroGraph, this flyback chronograph is able to count backwards. It is crafted in platinum and features a burnished 18-karat white-gold dial.

BOTTOM

Crafted in a limited edition of 25 pieces, the Karree Tourbillon features a manual-wind movement with flying tourbillon and 48 hours of power reserve.

GUCCI

an historical perspective

This famed Italian house of design is a global phenomenon. Founded in Florence in 1921 by Guccio Gucci, the brand began as a small luggage and saddler company. Intent on providing his customers with the finest leathergoods, Gucci started his company on the principles of perfection and quality. Certainly he could not have imagined that he was laying the foundation of a great legacy, nor could he have envisioned the international stir that his brand would create.

In everything he produced, Gucci remained true to a proud tradition of excellence and style. He developed relationships with the best Florentine craftsmen, employing them and their families to handcraft his designs. Word of Gucci's quality and innovative flair quickly spread throughout Europe and the rest of the world. The company flourished and, within just a few decades, had become a definitive leader in the world of high quality luxury goods.

Gradually Gucci began expanding its product offerings beyond the leathergoods arena. Branching out from luggage and handbags, the brand unveiled silk scarves, accessories, fragrances and a wide range of other products. In the late 1960s, Gucci took an interest in developing watches and licensed this part of the business to a savvy entrepreneur and designer, Severin Wunderman. Wunderman opened Severin Montres to create and distribute Gucci time-pieces and the firm grew to be one of the largest and most profitable manufacturers of watches.

In 1997, Gucci acquired the Severin Montres business in order to gain direct control over the design, production and distribution of its watches. It was the goal of the company to redefine and reposition the watch collection to more closely reflect the overall image and quality standards of the brand. A complete revamping was in order and Gucci Group's Creative Director, Tom Ford, would see to it that the design and development of the timepieces added to his creative flow and luxury standards.

unveiling

masterpieces

Not one single Gucci product emerges without being developed and nurtured personally under the watchful and innovative eye of Tom Ford. The brand's watches are no exception. Ford works closely with a creative team, technical experts and watchmakers to develop new timepieces. He is continuously shaping a collection that reflects the modern design aesthetic found in all Gucci products.

Indeed, the Gucci watch line, like its brand counterparts, has garnered recognition as an international luxury brand. The Italian design and modern styling of the timepieces are aesthetically advanced and are matched by superior standards of Swiss watchmaking. Gucci uses top-quality surgical steel or 18-karat gold for its cases and bracelets, and utilizes only Swiss watch components.

In the past five years, since the brand has taken the creation of its timepieces fully in-house, a very distinct design style indicative of the fashion house has emerged. Gucci watches are

THIS PAGE

TOP

Sophisticated strength and modern styling come together in the architecturally inspired 7700. Available in two sizes for men and women, the watch features a curved sapphire crystal with anti-reflective coating.

LEFT

The asymmetrically designed 7100 has a recessed crown and a pyramid texture. The hard metal case is crafted of tungsten, cobalt, carbon and titanium.

FACING PAGE

TOP LEFT

The ultra-thin elongated 3905 features a diamond-set case and open-linked bracelet.

TOP RIGHT

The 4605 Diamond watch is set with 22 full-cut diamonds on its case.

BOTTOM

The 7905 Gold Mesh watch is crafted entirely entirely of solid 18-karat gold.

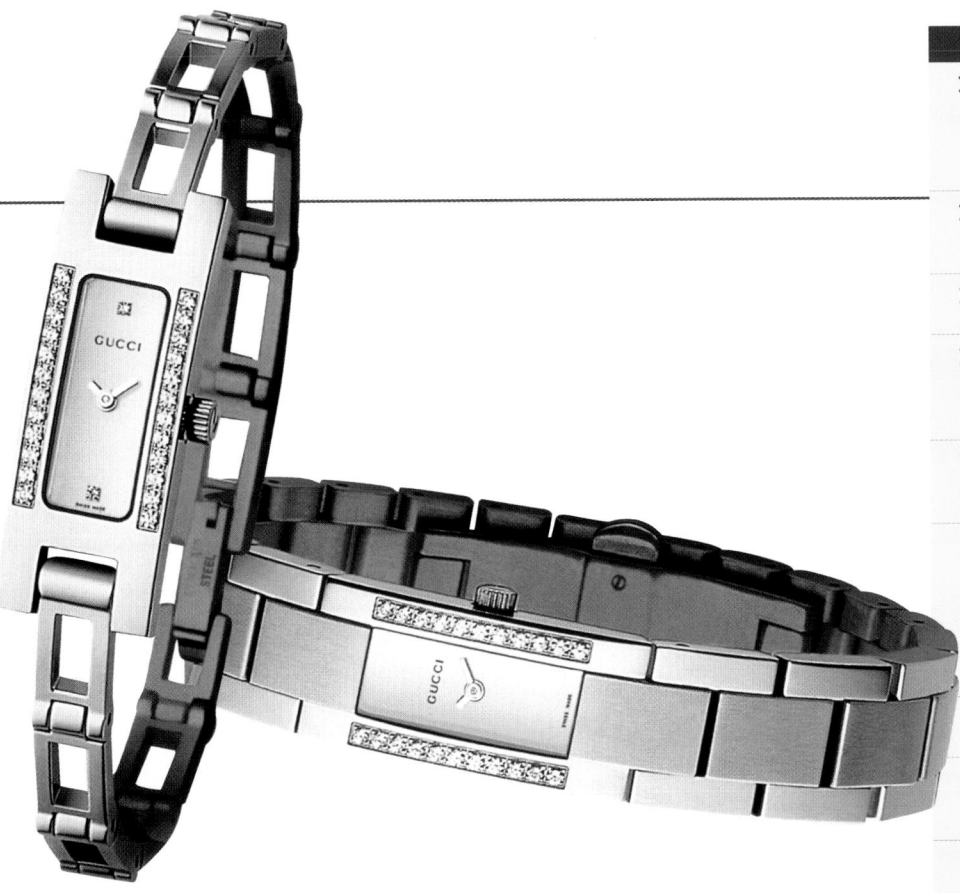

beautiful objects of classic elegance that incorporate flairs of artistic fashion. The new era of watches applies more luxurious elements—gold, crocodile or ostrich leather, fine gros-grain fabric straps, and diamond accents.

Gucci has been working with diamonds for years and has deftly mastered the technique of setting these scintillating stones in steel. In fact, this past year Gucci unveiled two models that were diamond-adorned evolutions of best sellers. The 3905 and 4605 Diamond watches are sleek, elongated rectangular watches that offer a light, airy and sensual appeal. Each of these watches is set with Top Wesselton diamonds and each comes with a choice of mother-of-pearl, black or silver dial.

Gold is also important to the Gucci brand, as evidenced by the unveiling of the 7905 Gold Mesh watch. This 18-karat solid gold square watch features a textured mesh bracelet and a jewelry clasp. The champagne dial offers a striking guilloche pattern. This watch is so universally elegant that it is offered in petite, ladies' and men's sizes.

fashion and technology

CENTER LEFT

The 6105 embodies Gucci's Italian styling with its chain-link bracelet.

CENTER RIGHT

The elegant 3905 features the brand's exclusive gros-grain fabric strap.

BELOW

Streamlined for contemporary appeal, the 5200 features Roman numerals, circular minute indicator and hand-stitched leather strap.

CENTER LEFT

The 6105 embodies Gucci's Italian styling with its chain-link bracelet.

CENTER RIGHT

The elegant 3905 features the brand's exclusive gros-grain fabric strap.

BELOW

Streamlined for contemporary appeal, the 5200 features Roman numerals, circular minute indicator and hand-stitched leather strap.

Because Gucci is first and foremost a fashion brand, the company puts a great deal of emphasis on research and development of design and materials. Its fashion-forward timepieces often incorporate a hint of Italian styling.

The 6105 for instance, is a striking statement of individuality. The oval case, which mimics the hardware of an iconic Gucci handbag, is crafted in steel and features a chain-link bracelet with jewelry clasp. Housing a quartz movement, the watch is water resistant to 30 meters. The 8505 is another interesting piece. Drawing its design influence from timepieces of the 1960s and 1970s, this steel or gold-plated watch features a bold, cushion-edged square case. Its bracelet is integrated in form and features tapered links. It comes with a variety of dial colors and offers date readout on the dial at 6:00. The distinctive retro look of the case, along with the ingenuity of the bracelet, makes this quite an eye-catching timepiece.

Technical excellence is also important to Gucci, as the brand has spent 81 years producing only top-quality products. Therefore it was important to Ford that the brand offer advanced models. The first such offering is the all-new 5600 mechanical watch. The elegantly styled watch features a 17-jeweled hand-wound movement with a seconds subdial for easy readability. This mechanical hand-wound movement represents a prestigious milestone in the road to establishing Gucci as a maker of technically

TOP

Mechanical timepieces such as the 5600 have now entered Gucci's scene as the brand forges ahead in establishing itself as a full-fledged luxury timepiece brand.

BOTTOM

The 7705 Chronograph is crafted in stainless steel and features squared subdials to complement the bold square case.

advanced timepieces. The watch, with 44 hours of power reserve, is created in a solid 18-karat gold version and in a steel version.

Complementing this new mechanical series is the 7705 Chronograph. Sporting an architectual and masculine case, the chronograph offers 1/10th of a second, seconds and 30-minute time indications on its striking square subdials. To ensure durability and function, the watch is created in stainless steel and features a curved sapphire crystal with double-sided anti-reflective coating. This timepiece is backed by a two-year international warranty. In fact, all of Gucci's watches are guaranteed for a minimum of two years.

While design and continuity of image reigns supreme at Gucci, the brand also is incredibly vigilant when it comes to timepiece performance. Its well-rounded collection, with finely finished details inside and out, attests to the fact that Gucci adheres to strict standards of production in both form and function.

HERMÈS

an historical perspective

Hermès is a company of many talents and a master of them all. This is a brand rich with history and ripe with accomplishments. It is a brand whose timepieces deftly match style with precision and elegance with international fashion flair.

Founded in Paris in 1837 by Thierry Hermès, the brand began as a maker of fine saddles, harnesses and other equestrian-related goods. With excellence as his creed and targeting the Parisian aristocracy for his clientele, Hermès quickly gained recognition for his unsurpassed artistry and craftsmanship. The Hermès brand name gained international popularity and the house won coveted awards of distinction for its workmanship and inventiveness. By the early 1900s, Hermès enjoyed a prestigious cosmopolitan clientele.

Times were changing, however, and as the automobile industry began replacing the horse-and-carriage trade, the astute Hermès family also evolved with the times. Thierry's grandson, Emile-Maurice Hermès introduced trunks, automobile accessories, luggage, gloves, and saddlebags—all of which bore the Hermès stamp of excellence.

It was also in the 1920s that Hermès turned its attention to watches. Employing its expertise in leatherwork to produce finely sewn leather straps for watches and fobs, Hermès quickly carved a niche for itself in the world of harmoniously elegant straps. It partnered with prestigious watch manufacturers to produce wristwatches, pocket watches and belt watches under its name and guidance.

In the 1930s, Hermès launched a line of incredibly recognizable handbags—including what would later come to be known as the famed Kelly bag. Additionally, it unveiled riding coats, jockey attire, and jewelry—the forerunners of today's creations. The silk Hermès used for jockeys' blouses garnered great attention and, in 1937, Hermès introduced its famed silk scarves. Designed by Robert Dumas-Hermès, the scarves demonstrated unparalleled creativity. By the mid-1950s, the House was looked upon as the reference point for demonstrating the true dynamism inherent in high-quality French products.

In 1978, when Jean-Louis Dumas-Hermès (Robert's son) took over the helm, he decided it was time for Hermès to create its own timepieces and so established La Montre Hermès S.A. in Bienne, Switzerland. The brand has since grown and the collection has significantly evolved while still remaining true to the Hermès heritage and reputation for individual style.

HERMÈS

24, FAUBOURG SAINT-HONORÉ

BIARRITZ   PARIS   CANNES

alluring time

With a vision of taste and creative design that underlies Hermès, Jean-Louis Dumas-Hermès has introduced new products and increased international distribution in the past 24 years.

"Ever since the days when its expert saddlers stitched the leather straps that enabled a fob watch to be worn on the wrist, Hermès has taken deep satisfaction in its work as a watchmaker," says Jean-Louis Dumas-Hermès. That satisfaction comes from "the joy of marrying beauty and utility, of meeting a need and ravishing the eye."

Indeed, this is a most befitting description of Hermès timepieces. Worldly, sophisticated, magical and mysterious—these are the words that define the Hermès style of timekeeping. Designed to link tradition with innovation, Hermès timepieces are authentic, timeless objects of art.

The grand Parisian design influence has given rise to a great many exciting looks, and this creativity has ensured the brand's success. Hermès collections include the internationally renowned Arceau, Clipper and Sellier series, with fine touches such as saddle stitching on leather straps, and equestrian accents inspired by horseshoes, bridals and stirrups.

The signature Kelly and Belt timepiece lines draw their influences from the key-lock of the Kelly bag and the tab straps and buckles of Hermès luggage and belts. The H-Our (with the Hermès H logo serving as the case shape and bracelet link) and Espace (with its high-tech, multi-function brilliance) lines deftly portray the fashion-forward, invigorating side of the brand.

The Kepler and Sesame models, first introduced in 1999, exemplify the brand's commitment to horology. These striking automatic mechanical timepieces push Hermès's frontiers of technical performance. The Kepler comes in a chronograph and a chronometer version, and the Sesame is a beautifully finished skeleton watch.

Hermès watches are available in solid 18-karat gold, solid sterling silver, steel, and a combination of gold and steel. They feature striking matching bracelets or elegantly stitched straps in line with the tradition of the great House. The back of each Hermès watch is engraved with the brand's distinctive signature.

HERMÈS

new masteries

Each of the timepiece collections offers definitive hints of Hermès' heritage, deftly blended with Swiss watchmaking prowess and perfection.

The Nomade collection, for instance, was unveiled in 2001 as the first Hermès watch with an autoquartz movement. It combines the precious quartz with rotor technology as an energy accumulator to achieve 45- to 100-hours of power reserve (depending on the model). The movement is housed in a bold and sophisticated case that features two H-shaped links on either side for contemporary appeal that is classically Hermès. Available in three versions (men's, women's and chronographs), the Nomade is crafted in stainless steel. The men's version can also add a compass—blending avant-garde technology with age-old timekeeping—another perfect example of Hermès at its finest.

In addition to launching the Nomade, Hermès expanded some of its key collections in 2001. It has added a very feminine mini version of the Belt ladies' watch with interchangeable leather straps, and has set the case (18-karat gold or steel) with 102 brilliant-cut diamonds for ultra shimmering appeal. Every Belt watch is sold in a set with a choice of two straps to adapt to any mood, or need. The newest diamond-adorned piece comes with a choice of elegant black or brown crocodile.

TOP RIGHT

The workshops of Hermès in Bienne, Switzerland.

LEFT

This mini-sized Belt watch joined the collection in 2001.

BOTTOM

Available this summer, the Nomade for men can be equipped with a compass.

Diamonds also join the coveted Cape Cod collection as two precious versions are added to the ranks—a mini and ladies' Cape Cod, in 18-karat yellow or white gold. Available with either a matching bracelet or leather strap, these Cape Cod watches feature alluring mother-of-pearl dials.

Recognizing that a good portion of its refined clientele is female, Hermès also unveils a men's version of the highly successful Cape Cod Double Tour watch. This striking leather-strapped timepiece, wherein the strap doubles around the wrist, is available with either a quartz or automatic movement for men.

Espace, first unveiled in 1999 as the brand's analog/digital watch, now makes a grand appearance in a strictly analog version. This modern timepiece offers bold, cutting-edge design that appeals to the most forward-thinking individuals. The new steel Espace watches come in men's and women's sizes and epitomize the words "avant garde."

Indeed, Hermès has been so firmly entrenched in watchmaking that it boasts a wonderful array of styles—each with its own exclusive message, its own alluring manner.

HUBLOT

an historical perspective

The creations of Italian designer Carlo Crocco, Hublot watches have been a major international sensation since they were first unveiled to the world 22 years ago.

Crocco, a man with a dream, invested five years into the research and development of what he considered the perfect watch. Having established his company, MDM Geneve, Crocco set about achieving his goal in 1997. He determined that the watch he was going to create would be consistent in its presentation—one that was both elegant and sporty at the same time and that would rise above changing fashion. Simplicity was key, followed by the necessary flexibility to move effortlessly from the beach to the boardroom to the ballroom.

Born out of this desire to transcend time and to shake the pangs of similarity, Hublot made its debut in 1980 with an 18-karat gold watch on a vanilla-scented rubber strap. The case was a porthole shape and featured 12 screws on the bezel to serve as hour indicators. Its clean black dial against the gold offered a sleek elegance, while the rubber strap offered a sporty chic appeal. It was a watch 20 years ahead of its time and one that captured hearts around the world.

Within months, members of European royal families were donning Hublot timepieces. The King of Spain and the King of Sweden were among the first, followed by prestigious clients from the art and entertainment industries, as well as business tycoons and political figures. All were smitten with the watch. In fact, the design was so desirable that for seven years, Crocco worked with only that one model.

In the past 10 years, Crocco has added extensions to the brand, though always remaining true to its original format. While the Classic line continues, the legendary look has also been translated into an Elegant line, a Jewelry line, a Super Professional sports line, a Power Reserve series and a Limited Edition collection. Each rendition transcends time, yet remains a classic.

TOP

Hublot and:
top row: Giorgio Armani; Antonio Banderas; and Sir Elton John.
middle row: Christopher Lambert; Luciano Pavarotti; and Sylvester Stallone.
bottom row: King Carl Gustaf of Sweden.

TOP LEFT

The Chronograph Elegant Noir features an 18-karat black-gold dial and houses an automatic movement.

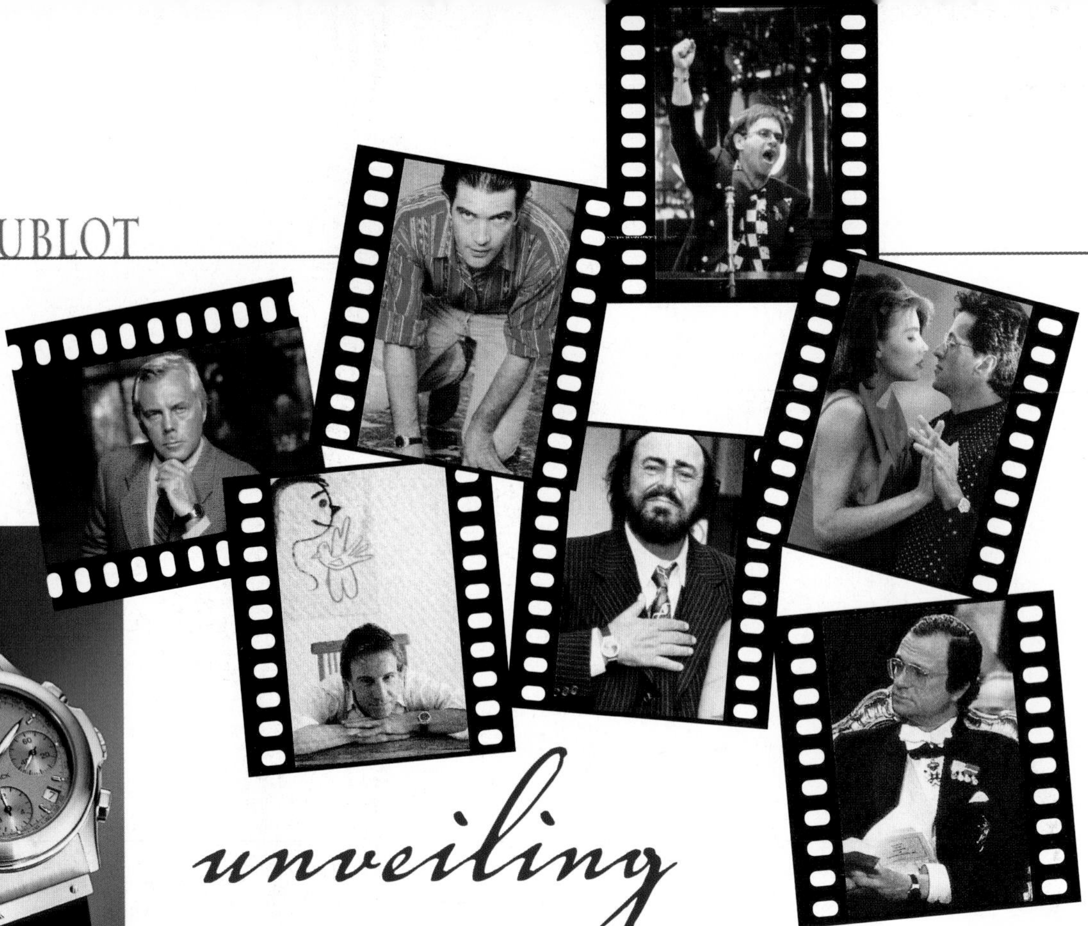

unveiling masterpieces

CENTER

The Super Professional, a 1,500-foot water-resistant dive watch, is both bold and beautiful with a fuchsia dial.

BOTTOM CENTER

This Elegant Haute Joaillerie watch is crafted in steel and set with 264 Top Wesselton diamonds and 44 pink sapphires.

BOTTOM RIGHT

Featuring an elegant hinged Cover case, this watch is set with 705 diamonds weighing 5.75 carats and 46 pink sapphires. It houses an automatic movement and is water resistant to 50 meters.

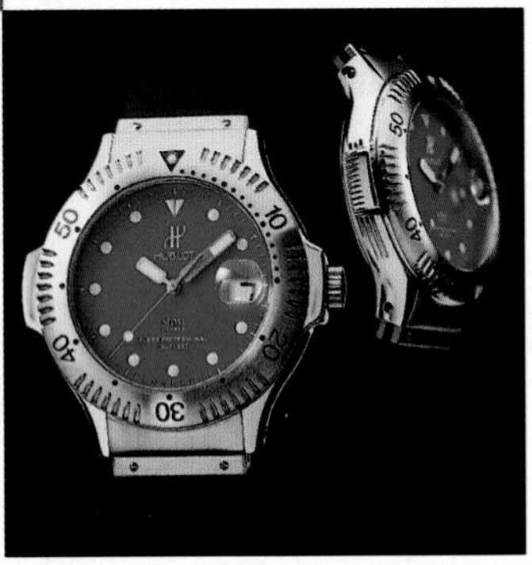

The Classic Hublot watch is based on the very first design. It is available in five sizes in 18-karat gold, steel and gold, and in steel—with and without diamonds. New additions unveiled this past year include a striking mother-of-pearl-dialed design for women. Hublot artfully has incorporated three pastel dials—blue, pink and lustrous natural white—into the Classic series. One version features a clean dial without markers; another version features color-coordinated pink or blue sapphires as the hour markers; and on the white dial, black diamonds serve to mark the hours.

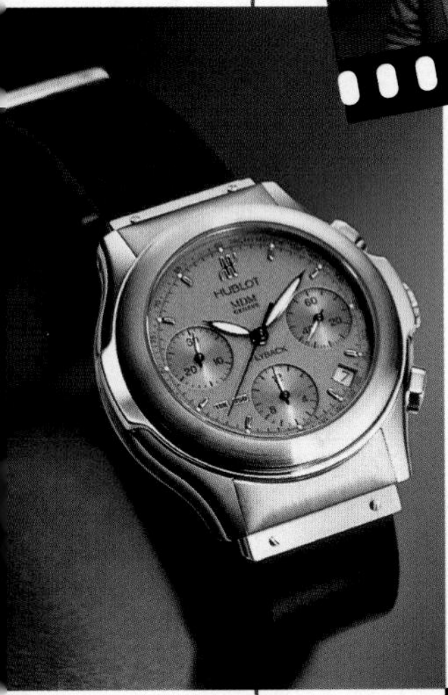

The Elegant Line, first unveiled in 1992, features a slightly larger case than the traditional model and has subtly rounded lines to offer it a softer, gentler face. In the year 2000, Hublot unveiled a Chronograph Elegant in white gold with a black-gold dial. It was an immediate hit. This past year, the brand followed suit and introduced the Chronograph Elegant in rose gold with rose-gold dial. It houses an automatic movement, is water resistant to 100 meters and is created in a limited edition of 199 pieces.

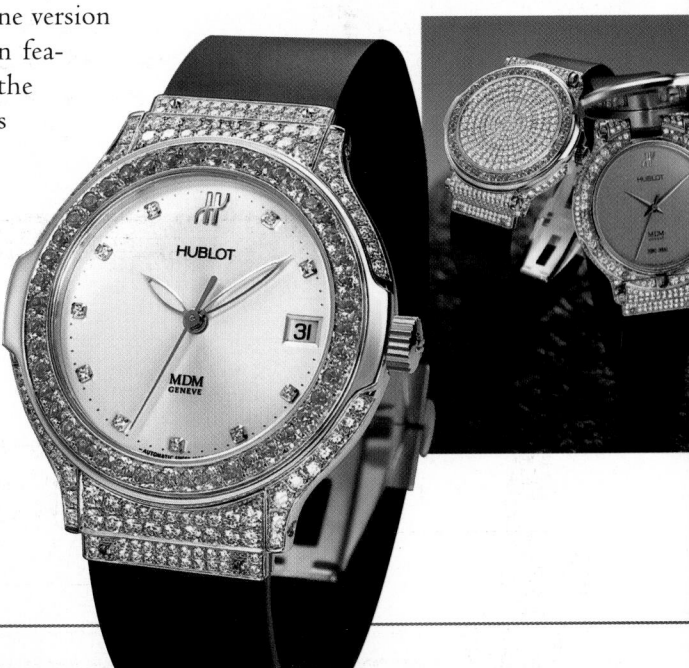

RIGHT

The year 2001 saw the introduction of a sun-brushed, burgundy lacquer dial on the Chronograph Elegant and Grand Quantième automatic models.

BELOW

The Teddy watch is crafted in steel with a pink or blue lacquer dial.

1980 Hublot watches appear at the Basel Fair and MDM president Carlo Crocco is immediately criticized for Hublot's unconventional combination of gold and rubber.

1985 The "Plongeur Professional" is presented at Montecarlo, water resistant to 300 meters, with a traditional unidirectional rotating bezel and new screw crown.

1987 Crocco creates the first automatic Hublot with a Frédéric Piguet caliber movement. The look is modern, the case bigger with smoother, rounder lines and the bezel screws disappear. This new model is the predecessor of the Elegant line.

1988 The Hublot chronograph is created. It houses an electro-mechanical Piguet movement, technologically advanced and very practical and precise.

1990 The GMT, useful to avid travelers and the second complication made by the House, is introduced. It has a new water-resistant system with a double gasket on the back and is held in place by 6 screws.

1991 Introduction of the automatic chronograph on the caliber 1185 Piguet in 350 pieces: 100 in platinum, 250 in gold.

1993 The Hublot Service is inaugurated and courtesy watches are offered to clients in substitution for their own during maintenance; The first chronograph in the Elegant line is launched in 250 platinum pieces.

1994 Improvement for the Hublot Professional with an automatic movement classic ETA 2892. It is water resistant to 30 atm with unidirectional rotating bezel and a choice of green or blue in salute to the sea's dominant colors.

1995 The Hublot Classic is presented with an automatic movement.

1996 The Colonial Bracelet is presented and wins the Best Metallic Bracelet of the Year. Production begins for a limited number of Cloisonné and Champlevé enameled models.

1997 With its rounded lines and created in gold and steel, the Elegant Chronograph is an instant success for Hublot. Its black dial is available with Arabic numerals—and called "Navy"— or with indexes.

1998 The Elegant line is enhanced with an automatic version with power reserve; The first Hublot in steel is set with diamonds.

1999 Launching of the Super Professional, a high-technology professional watch for divers that is water resistant up to 45 atm; the brand launches the ladies' automatic.

2000 20th Anniversary of Hublot; The Grand Quantième is introduced in black gold along with the Personal Engraving Cover Watch, which bears the finest of engravings on the cover and the innovative black-gold dial; Carlo Crocco's children, Federico and Guendalina, join the company to insure a family-owned Manufacture that retains absolute freedom of creation and management.

2001 A limited edition of Grand Quantième is launched in 200 pink-gold pieces; Two new versions of the Elegant Chronograph, one in black gold and one in pink gold, are introduced—both with the addition of the Flyback.

In addition to these collections, Hublot has delved into the world of jewelry watches. The family-owned business is intent on offering additions that are expertly designed and embellished in the classic and elegant tradition of the brand. Joining the already exquisite Haute Joaillerie series are several new creations. Two particular models are set beautifully with Top Wesselton diamonds and pink sapphires for luxurious style.

One model features a diamond case, pink sapphire bezel and diamond markers; the other model is an all-jeweled, hinged Cover version pavé set with 705 Top Wesselton diamonds and 46 pink sapphires. It takes several weeks of highly skilled, meticulous craftsmanship by the master setters at MDM workshops in Geneva to complete just one watch.

Of course, Hublot continues to unveil new models in its Super Professional line. This series features a steel-cased watch fitted with a screw-down crown that ensures water resistance to 1,500 feet. Its unidirectional bezel offers an exclusive locking device. The newest Super Professionals include models with striking dial colors, including a bold fuchsia version that has captivated men and women alike. Additionally, Hublot offers its specialty timepieces and limited-edition series. These unique pieces are often made-to-order pieces, although brilliant renditions of teddy bears, dogs, fish and other animals are always available in the exclusive line.

As with all Hublot watches, each of these series is individually numbered and finished with the utmost attention to detail.

HUBLOT

CHRONOGRAPH ELEGANT FLY-BACK "PINK GOLD" REF. 1810.910P.8

Movement: mechanical, automatic winding, ETA 2892A2 base + Dubois Dépraz chronograph module 2021 caliber, personalized for Hublot.
Functions: hour, minute, small second, date, fly-back chronograph with 3 counters.
Case: 18 kt pink gold, three-piece case (Ø 40 mm, thickness 12.7 mm), polished and brushed finish; flat sapphire crystal; screw-down crown; olive-shaped pushers; back attached by 6 screws. Water-resistant to 10 atm.

Dial: pink gold, grained finish; counters decorated with circular beads; applied blued steel bâton markers, applied Hublot logo at 12; luminescent blued steel leaf style hands.
Indications: small second at 3, date between 4 and 5, hour counter at 6, minute counter at 9, center second counter, minute track with divisions for 1/5 of a second with luminescent dots and tachometer scale.
Strap: rubber, reinforced with integrated steel blades and inserted in a patented attachment; pink-gold double fold-over steel clasp.
Also available: in gray gold.

ELEGANT POWER RESERVE REF. 1830.130.1

Movement: mechanical, automatic winding, ETA 2892A2 base + power reserve module.
Functions: hour, minute, second, date, power reserve.
Case: stainless steel, three-piece case (Ø 40 mm, thickness 12 mm); flat sapphire crystal; brushed bezel; screw-down crown; back attached by 6 screws. Water-resistant to 10 atm.

Dial: black; luminescent printed Arabic numerals, applied Hublot logo at 12; printed minute track; luminescent steel bâton hands.
Indications: date at 3, power reserve at 6.
Strap: rubber, reinforced with integrated steel blades and inserted in a patented attachment; double fold-over steel clasp.
Also available: with applied bâton markers.

ELEGANT AUTOMATIC REF. 1710.410B.1

Movement: mechanical, automatic winding, ETA 2892/A2 caliber, Hublot personalized. **Functions:** hour, minute, second, date.
Case: stainless steel, three-piece case (Ø 37 mm, thickness 8 mm); flat sapphire crystal; brushed bezel; screw-down crown; back attached by 6 screws. Water-resistant to 5 atm. **Dial:** silvered with sun pattern; applied blued steel bâton markers and Hublot logo at 12; printed minute track; luminescent blued steel leaf style hands.

Indications: date at 3.
Strap: rubber, reinforced with integrated steel blades and inserted in a patented attachment; double fold-over steel clasp.
Also available: stainless steel/yellow gold; blue or black dial applied bâton markers or luminescent Arabic numerals or white dial applied bâton markers; steel black or silvered dial brilliant markers; steel brilliants on bezel: black dial applied markers, black or silvered dial brilliant markers. Lady (Ø 33, th. 8.5), ETA 2000 cal., white or silvered dial applied markers, blue or black dial applied markers or luminescent Arabic numerals: steel/yellow gold; steel black or silvered dial brilliant markers; other jewel versions.

GRAND QUANTIEME REF. 1840.900.4

Movement: mechanical, automatic winding, Dubois Dépraz 14370 caliber, ETA 2892A2 base + big date and day module.
Functions: hour, minute, second, day, date.
Case: 18 kt palladium-refined white gold, three-piece case (Ø 38 mm, thickness 10.5 mm); flat sapphire crystal; brushed bezel with 12 screws at hour markers; white gold screw-down crown; back attached by 6 screws, with engraved "H 2002". Water-resistant to 5 atm.

Dial: black gold; applied white-gold firm's logo at 12; black gold Régate hands.
Indications: day of the week at 6, big date in double window at 12.
Strap: rubber, reinforced with integrated blades and inserted in a patented attachment; double white-gold fold-over clasp.
Limited edition of 100 numbered pieces.
Also available: in steel with black dial. Unlimited series.

CLASSIC AUTOMATIC   REF. 1880.100.3

Movement: mechanical, automatic winding, ETA 2892A2 caliber, personalized for Hublot.
Functions: hour, minute, second, date.
Case: 18 kt yellow gold, three-piece case (Ø 36 mm, thickness 8.6 mm); flat sapphire crystal; brushed bezel with 12 screws at hour markers; screw-down crown; case back attached by 6 screws. Water-resistant to 5 atm.
Dial: black; applied Hublot logo at 12; luminescent bâton hands.
Indications: date at 3.
Strap: rubber reinforced by integrated steel blades and inserted in the patented central attachment; double fold-over gold clasp.

Also available: with black, white or blue dial: Colonial bracelet; steel/yellow gold with strap, bracelet; steel with strap and bracelet; in white gold with black dial, strap, with "honeycomb" engine-turned blue or green dial: in steel with strap; in the same versions with quartz movement. Classic Large, Ref. 1880.100.1 (Ø 38.5 mm) with white, black or blue dial; in stainless steel; quartz versions: in steel, in steel/yellow gold, in yellow gold.

CHRONOGRAPH   REF. 1620.140.8

Movement: electric drive controlled by a quartz crystal and mechanical chronograph module, Frédéric Piguet 1270 caliber.
Functions: hour, minute, small second, date, chronograph with 3 counters.
Case: 18 kt pink gold, three-piece case (Ø 37 mm, thickness 9 mm); flat sapphire crystal; brushed bezel with engraved tachometer scale; gold-plated (80 micron) hexagonal crown; back attached by 6 gold screws. Water-resistant to 5 atm.
Dial: black; luminescent cabochon markers; luminescent bâton hands.
Indications: hour counter at 3, date and small second at 6, minute counter at 9, center second counter, minute track with divisions for 1/5 of a second.
Strap: rubber, reinforced with integrated steel blades and inserted in a patented attachment; double fold-over gold clasp.

Also available: in yellow gold with leather strap or bracelet; in yellow or pink gold & stainless steel, strap; in yellow gold & stainless steel, bracelet; in steel, strap or bracelet. All with black, blue, white or green dial (for jewel version only black dial).

SUPER PROFESSIONAL 450 MT   REF. 1850.140.1

Movement: mechanical, automatic winding, ETA 2892A2 caliber, personalized for Hublot.
Functions: hour, minute, second, date.
Case: special surgical steel alloy, three-piece case (Ø 41 mm, thickness 12.5 mm); flat sapphire crystal; one-way turning bezel with additional locking device to maintain the selected position (causing a counter clockwise rotational force of the element placed between frame and ring acting upon the lateral juts, this shall snap in by approx. 5 mm in the "safety" position, thus preventing any accidental rotation); engraved minute track, for the calculation of diving times; screw-down crown with case protection; back attached by 8 screws. Water-resistant to 45 atm.
Dial: black; luminescent round markers; printed minute track; luminescent Index hands.
Indications: date at 3.
Strap: rubber, reinforced with integrated steel blades and inserted in a patented attachment; double fold-over clasp.
Also available: with blue dial.

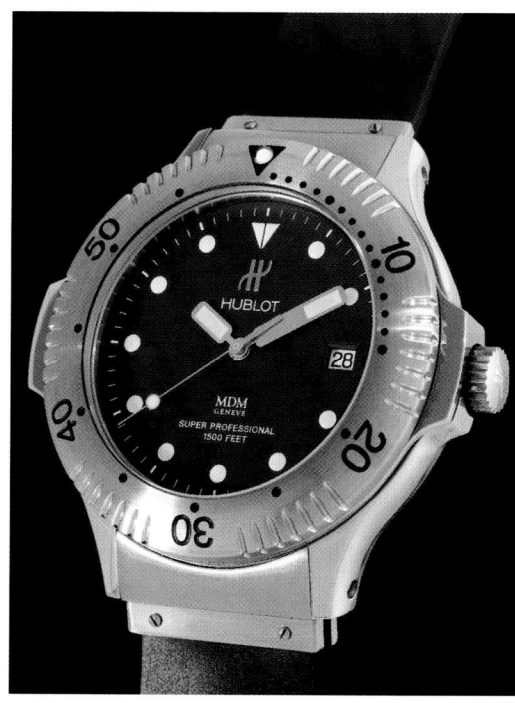

PROFESSIONAL 300 MT   REF. 1552.740.3

Movement: mechanical, automatic winding, ETA 2892A2 caliber, personalized for Hublot.
Functions: hour, minute, second, date.
Case: 18 kt yellow gold, three-piece case (Ø 36 mm, thickness 9 mm); flat sapphire crystal; counter clockwise turning bezel with engraved minute track, useful for the calculation of diving times; gold screw-down crown with case protection; back attached by 6 titanium screws. Water-resistant to 30 atm.
Dial: blue; luminescent applied cabochon markers; luminescent Index hands.
Indications: date at 3.
Strap: rubber, reinforced with integrated blades and inserted in a patented attachment; double fold-over gold clasp.
Also available: with Colonial bracelet; in yellow gold & stainless steel, strap bracelet; in steel, strap, bracelet. All versions available with green, black or blue dial.

IKEPOD

an historical perspective

Considered still in its infancy in terms of age, IKEPOD is a brand that nonetheless has built an enormous international following. First launched eight years ago at the World Watch, Clock and Jewelry Fair in Basel, this unusual line had connoisseurs buzzing as soon as it was unveiled. Indeed, the oversized, unique look of IKEPOD's timepieces typically piques curiosity and is one of the main clinching factors when it comes to purchasing the watch.

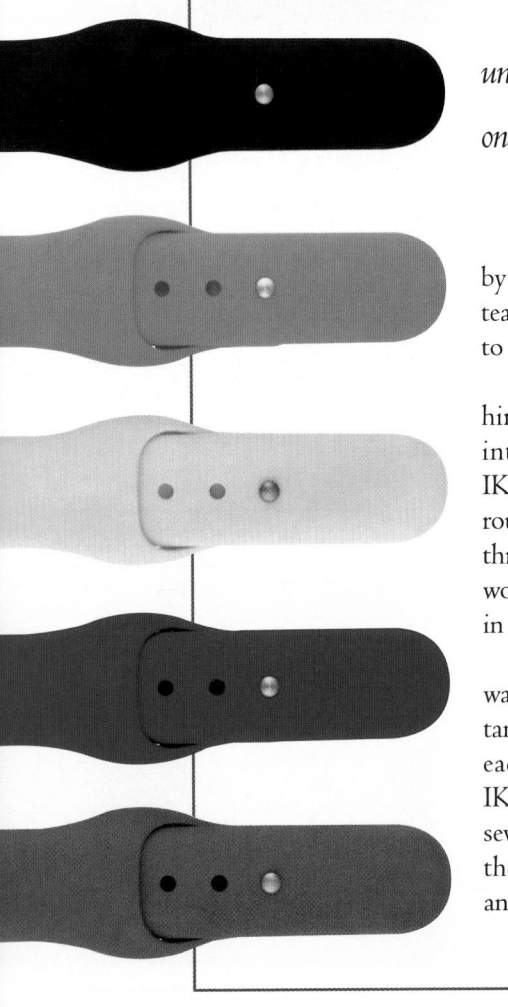

The brainchild of Swiss entrepreneur Oliver Ike, the line is designed by famed international architectural designer Marc Newson. The two teamed up nearly 10 years ago when Oliver Ike began following his dream to create a watch brand like none other that existed on the market.

Ike was drawn to the futuristic designs of Newson and approached him with the concept of developing a watch collection. Newson was intrigued by the prospect and the two men formed a partnership. IKEPOD was formed (using a combination of Ike's name and Newson's, round, pod-like design shape) and from the very start, the men agreed on three founding principles: all watches would be mechanical; all watches would be COSC-certified chronometers; and all watches would be created in limited editions only.

IKEPOD's first collection was the Seaslug, a line of automatic diving watches. Featuring a second time zone, the Seaslug watches are water resistant to 150 meters and are limited to a production of 9,999 models of each dial version worldwide. Since then, the IKEPOD line has branched out to include several important collections, including the Hemipode, Megapode, Manatee, and Tourbillon.

unveiling masterpieces

At the IKEPOD workshops in the Jura Mountain town of Bassecourt, all movements are hand finished and detailed according to strict standards of perfection. Cases also are produced and hand finished, and every timepiece the brand creates is assembled and tested before leaving the factory. All of this attention to detail, along with IKEPOD's unusual and bold styling, has made the brand a coveted force in 40 countries around the world.

Building on its international success, IKEPOD has not deviated from its formula of innovation in design and technical mastery. Among the newest timepieces unveiled to the world this past year are: diamond-adorned models, platinum versions, and an advanced, complex series including a tourbillon and world timer.

In the Hemipode collection, one of the brand's most celebrated and successful lines, IKEPOD unveiled several new timepieces in the year 2001, including a diamond chronograph. Crafted in stain-

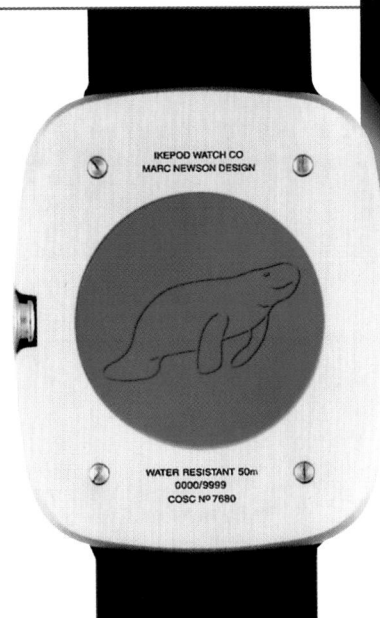

CHRONOLOGY

Early 1990s
Swiss businessman Oliver Ike and designer Marc Newson combine "Ike" and Newson's unique "pod" design to form the IKEPOD watch company.

1994 IKEPOD unveils its first line, the Seaslug, at the World Watch, Clock and Jewelry Fair in Basel.

Late 1990s
The Hemipode (so named in tribute to the endangered bird of Australia), Isopode and Megapode join the Seaslug in this futuristic brand's collection.

2000 The Manatee, honoring the endangered underwater mammal and featuring all 24 time zones, is introduced.

2001 The Hemipode collection is enhanced by the addition of a diamond chronograph (the Hemipode HO3), and the Hemipode Grand Date.

TOP

Named for the endangered sea animal, the Manatee is a world time zone watch.

BOTTOM LEFT

The Hemipode is available in a variety of models, including this Grand Date.

BOTTOM CENTER

Crafted in steel, the Seaslug GMT diving watch is water resistant to 150 meters.

BOTTOM RIGHT

IKEPOD based the functional development of the Megapode Pilot Chronograph on in-depth consultations with pilots. The watch is crafted in titanium.

less steel, the Hemipode HO3 features a dual lane of diamonds on the bezel. The watch houses a certified chronometer movement with GMT function at 6:00.

Additionally, IKEPOD has unveiled its Tourbillon in the Hemipode case. The tourbillon, first introduced in 2000, came full-circle in 2001—with final versions including platinum, gold and steel models. The watch coordinates the technical know-how of IKEPOD with the advanced design and "aura" of the brand. Housing the Caliber Ikepod IK23 automatic flying tourbillon movement, the watch offers 70 hours of power reserve and is being created in a limited edition of 23 pieces in platinum, 99 pieces in 18-karat yellow gold and 999 pieces in steel.

IKEPOD also has further perfected another collection that it originally unveiled in the year 2000: the Manatee. Offering several versions in a variety of different dial colors, IKEPOD offers this rectangular watch in a polished or matte steel case. Designed for world travelers, the watch is fitted with an ETA base movement finished by IKEPOD with a turning dial that enables the wearer to read 24 time zones simultaneously. The cities representing the 24 time zones are listed on an inner dial that turns with the movement, while an outer dial indicates the time in those zones. The caseback features an inlay with an engraving of the Manatee, the endangered sea animal for which the watch is named.

As with all IKEPOD timepieces, the newest additions are fitted with the brand's natural rubber strap. Each is accompanied by a COSC chronometer certificate and comes with an international warranty.

IKEPOD

HEMIPODE TOURBILLON VOLANT — REF. T001

Movement: mechanical, automatic winding, produced by Progress exclusively for Ikepod, 6361.101 caliber, with tourbillon device, 72 hours power reserve, 28,000 vibrations per hour. Officially certified "chronometer" (C.O.S.C.).
Functions: hour, minute.
Case: brushed steel, one-piece case with a little sapphire crystal bull's eye on the tourbillon on the back (Ø 44 mm, thickness 16.3 mm); antireflective

curved sapphire crystal. Water-resistant to 5 atm.
Dial: black, curved, golf ball surface pattern, aperture on the tourbillon; luminescent steel hands in an exclusive shape.
Strap: rubber, steel press-stud buckle and loop.
Limited edition of 999 numbered pieces.
Also available: with silvered dial; in yellow gold with gilded dial; in pink gold with pink dial; in white gold with silvered dial, 99 pieces each version (on request); in platinum with blue dial, 23 pieces (on request); with bracelet (on request).

HEMIPODE SPLIT-SECOND CHRONOGRAPH — REF. HR01

Movement: automatic, Valjoux 7750 caliber, modified for the split-second chronograph feature and offset hour display. Officially certified "chronometer" (C.O.S.C.). **Functions:** hour, minute, small second, split-second chronograph with three counters.
Case: brushed steel, one-piece case with a little sapphire crystal bull's eye on the balance on the back (Ø 44 mm, thickness 17 mm); antireflective curved sap-

phire crystal; pushers with orange head (splitting pusher at 10). Water-resistant to 5 atm.
Dial: black, silvered counters decorated with circular beads.
Indications: off-center hour and minute at 3 with printed Arabic numerals and steel hands in an exclusive shape, hour counter at 6, small second at 9, minute counter at 12, center split-second counters (orange and green enameled hands), minute track with divisions for 1/5 of a second.
Strap: rubber; steel press-stud clasp and loop.
Limited edition of 99 numbered pieces.
Also available: with silvered dial and black counters; with bracelet; in platinum, blue dial and silvered counters, strap, 23 pieces.

HEMIPODE CHRONOGRAPH CHRONOMETER GMT — REF. HB03L

Movement: automatic, Valjoux 7750 caliber modified to obtain the second time-zone. Officially certified "chronometer". **Functions:** hour, minute, small second, date, second time-zone, 24 hours, chronograph with 2 counters. **Case:** polished black steel with PVD treatment, one-piece case with a bull's eye on the balance on the back (Ø 44, thickness 17.2 mm); antireflective curved sapphire crystal on both sides; pushers (for second time-zone at 8) with orange heads. Water-resistant to 5

atm. **Dial:** mat black; luminescent steel hands in an exclusive shape. **Indications:** date at 3, 24-hour second time-zone time at 6, small second at 9, minute counter at 12, center second counter, minute track with divisions for 1/5 of a second. **Bracelet:** black polished steel with PVD treatment; recessed double fold-over clasp. Limited edition of 9.999 numbered pcs. **Also available:** silvered dial; black dial and silvered zones; silvered dial and black zones; with strap; polished steel 9,999 pcs; brushed steel or brushed steel with PVD 9,999 pcs each, leather strap or bracelet; titanium, strap or bracelet; brushed steel, brilliant bezel, white or black dial or white dial and black counters or black dial and white counters, strap, 9,999 pcs.

HEMIPODE CHRONOGRAPH CHRONOMETER GMT GOLD — REF. HG03

All the round watches signed by Ikepod have one-piece cases, i.e. middle and case back made of a single piece of metal. Therefore, to pull out the movement, the only possible access is that obtained by removing the bezel by means of a special tool. To extract the movement from the case, it is always necessary to pull out the stern (connecting the movement with the crown). Since this operation is typically performed on the back side, in this case a

"trick" has to be used, that consists in adopting a stern built in two pieces united by a dap joint, allowing to separate them at request - one half remains inside the movement and the other in the crown.
Limited edition of 999 numbered pieces.
Also available: in yellow gold with gilded dial, 999 pieces; in white gold with silvered dial, 999 pieces; in platinum with blue dial and silvered zones, 23 pcs. Cunningam model Ref. HC01 in titanium, white-blue dial with vertical stripes, strap, bracelet, 888 pieces.

HEMIPODE CHRONOGRAPH WITH OVERSIZED DATE   REF. HDG01

Movement: automatic, ETA 2892A2 caliber + modified chronograph module. Officially certified "chronometer" (C.O.S.C.).
Functions: hour, minute, small second, date, chronograph with three counters.
Case: 18 kt yellow gold, one-piece brushed case with a little sapphire crystal bull's eye on the balance on the back (Ø 44 mm, thickness 16.5 mm); antire-

flective curved sapphire crystal; semi-recessed crown; gold pushers with orange heads. Water-resistant to 5 atm.
Dial: gilded, grained, counters decorated with circular beads; luminescent gilded hands in an exclusive shape.
Indications: small second at 3, hour counter at 6, minute counter at 9, big-sized date in a double window below 12, center second counter, minute track with divisions for 1/5 of a second.
Strap: rubber; gold press-stud clasp and loop.
Limited edition of 999 numbered pieces.

HEMIPODE CHRONOGRAPH WITH OVERSIZED DATE   REF. HD02

Movement: automatic, ETA 2892A2 caliber + chronograph module modified for the big date feature. Officially certified "chronometer" (C.O.S.C.). **Functions:** hour, minute, small second, date, chronograph with 3 counters. **Case:** brushed steel, one-piece case with a little bull's eye on the balance on the back (Ø 44, thickness 16.5 mm); antireflective curved sapphire crystal; semi-recessed crown; pushers with orange heads. Water-resistant to 5 atm. **Dial:** silvered, black counters deco-

rated with circular beads; luminescent steel hands in an exclusive shape. **Indications:** small second at 3, hour counter at 6, minute counter at 9, big-sized date in a double window below 12, center second counter, minute track with divisions for 1/5 of a second. **Strap:** rubber; steel press-stud clasp and rubber loop. Limited edition of 9,999 numbered pieces.
Also available: black dial and silvered counters or all black or silvered dial; orange or green rubber strap or bracelet; brushed PVD steel, 9,999 pcs, black dial and silvered zones or silvered dial and black zones; polished PVD steel, 9,999 pcs, black dial and silvered zones or silvered dial and black zones, strap, bracelet; yellow or pink gold, strap, 999 pcs each; white gold, strap, 999 pcs.

MEGAPODE PILOT CHRONOGRAPH FLY-BACK CHRONOMETER REF. MGF02

Movement: automatic, Valjoux 7750 modified by Minerva to obtain a second time-zone time display and the fly-back feature. Officially certified "chronometer" (C.O.S.C.). **Functions:** hour, minute, small second, date, second time-zone time, 24 hours, fly-back chronograph with three counters. **Case:** brushed titanium, one-piece case with a little sapphire crystal bull's eye on the balance on the back (Ø 46, thickness 17.5 mm); antireflective sapphire crystal on both sides; crown at 3

for normal slide-rule adjustment; crown at 9 for winding, date, second time-zone time and hour. Water-resistant to 5 atm.
Dial: blue and black, counters decorated with circular beads; luminescent white enameled hands in an exclusive shape (yellow enameled counters and seconds hands). **Indications:** small second at 3, date and minute counter at 6, second time-zone time over 24 hours at 9, hour counter at 12, center fly-back second counter, minute track with divisions for 1/5 of a second, turning flange for slide-rule use and fixed black ring.
Strap: rubber; steel press-stud clasp and rubber loop.
Limited edition of 9,999 numbered pieces.
Also available: with gray and black dial; in platinum, 23 pieces.

MEGAPODE PILOT CHRONOGRAPH CHRONOMETER   REF. MG01

Movement: automatic, Valjoux 7750 modified by Minerva to obtain a second time-zone time display. Officially certified "chronometer" (C.O.S.C.).
Functions: hour, minute, small second, date, second time-zone time, 24 hours, chronograph with three counters. **Case:** brushed titanium, one-piece case with z little sapphire crystal bull's eye on the balance on the back (Ø 46 mm, thickness 17.5 mm); antireflective sapphire crystal on both sides; crown at 3 for normal slide-rule adjustment;

crown at 9 for winding, date, second time-zone time and hour. Water-resistant to 5 atm.
Dial: gray and black, counters decorated with circular beads; luminescent white enameled hands in an exclusive shape. **Indications:** small second at 3, date and minute counter at 6, second time-zone time over 24 hours at 9, hour counter at 12, center second counter, minute track with divisions for 1/5 of a second, turning flange for slide-rule use and fixed black ring.
Strap: rubber; steel press-stud clasp and rubber loop.
Limited edition of 9,999 numbered pieces.
Also available: with blue dial; in platinum, 23 pieces.

IKEPOD

ISOPODE CHRONOGRAPH CHRONOMETER   REF. ISB01

Movement: mechanical, automatic winding, ETA 2894-2 caliber. Officially certified "chronometer" (C.O.S.C.). **Functions:** hour, minute, small second, date, chronograph with three counters. **Case:** mat black steel with PVD (Physical Vapor Deposit) treatment, one-piece case with a small sapphire crystal bull's eye (Ø 39 mm, thickness 15 mm); antireflective curved sapphire crystal on both sides; pushers with orange heads. Water-resistant to 5 atm. **Dial:** black mat,

decorated with circular beads; luminescent steel hands in an exclusive shape. **Indications:** small second at 3, date between 4 and 5, hour counter at 6, minute counter at 9, center second counter, minute track with divisions for 1/5 of a second. **Bracelet:** mat black steel with PVD treatment; recessed double fold-over clasp. Limited edition of 9,999 numbered pieces.
Also available: with silvered dial, rubber strap; with polished finish 9,999 pcs, strap, bracelet; in brushed steel 9,999 pcs, with strap, bracelet; in platinum 23 pcs, strap; in yellow or pink gold with strap, 999 pcs each version; in white gold, strap, 999 pcs; in steel with brilliant bezel and white or black dial, strap, 9,999 pcs.

ISOPODE CHRONOGRAPH CHRONOMETER   REF. ISS01

Movement: automatic, modified ETA 2894-2 caliber. Officially certified "chronometer" (C.O.S.C.).
Functions: hour, minute, small second, date, chronograph with three counters.
Case: stainless steel, one-piece case with a small sapphire crystal bull's eye (Ø 39 mm, thickness 15 mm); bezel with set diamonds; antireflective curved sap-

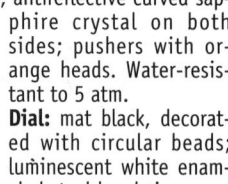

phire crystal on both sides; pushers with orange heads. Water-resistant to 5 atm.
Dial: mat black, decorated with circular beads; luminescent white enameled steel hands in an exclusive shape.
Indications: small second at 3, date between 4 and 5, hour counter at 6, minute counter at 9, center second counter, minute track with divisions for 1/5 of a second.
Strap: rubber; steel press-stud clasp and loop. Limited edition of 9,999 numbered pieces.

ISOPODE DUAL TIME   REF. ISD02

Movement: mechanical, automatic winding, ETA 2894-2 caliber modified by Arola to obtain the second time zone. Officially certified "chronometer" (C.O.S.C.).
Functions: hour, minute, second, date, second time-zone time.
Case: stainless steel, one-piece case with a small sapphire crystal bull's eye on the back (Ø 39 mm, thickness 15 mm); antireflective curved sapphire crystal

on both sides. Water-resistant to 5 atm.
Dial: white; printed bâton markers and minute track; black enameled hands in an exclusive shape.
Indications: date at 6, second time-zone with double hand at 12.
Strap: rubber; steel press-stud clasp and loop. Limited edition of 9,999 numbered pieces.
Also available: with black dial.

MANATEE GMT   REF. MN01L

Movement: mechanical, automatic winding, ETA 2893-3 caliber modified to obtain the turning disc of the time-zone reference towns. Officially certified "chronometer" (C.O.S.C.).
Functions: hour, minute, second, date, world time, 24 hours.
Case: stainless steel, two-piece brushed case (size 40 x 33 mm, thickness 9.4 mm); antireflective sapphire crystal on both sides; recessed crown; back fas-

tened by 4 screws. Water-resistant to 5 atm.
Dial: mat blue, black enameled 24-hour ring and mat black turning center disc; luminescent white and black enameled bâton hands.
Indications: world time (24-hour fixed disc, turning center with the names of the 24 time-zone reference towns).
Strap: rubber, in a single piece whose profile allows it to pass around the case; steel fold-over clasp.
Limited edition of 9,999 numbered pieces.
Also available: polished finish; in yellow, pink or white gold, 999 pcs, each version (upon request); in platinum, 23 pieces (upon request). All with blue, yellow, white or bordeaux dial.

SEASLUG ALARM GMT   REF. SA02

Movement: automatic, AS 5008 caliber. Officially certified "chronometer".
Functions: hour, minute, second, day-date, world time, alarm. **Case:** stainless steel, 3-piece brushed case (Ø 45, thickness 15.8 mm); fixed bezel with engraved names of reference towns for the 24 time zones; antireflective curved sapphire crystal on both sides; center crown for turning flange adjustment; crown at 3 for the 24-hour ring adjustment, at 2 for winding and day, date and hour adjust-

ments; crown at 4 for alarm use (setting, loading and actuation); screwed-on back with a sapphire crystal. Water-resistant to 3 atm. **Dial:** white; printed Arabic numerals; luminescent steel hands in an exclusive shape. **Indications:** date and day at 6, world time (day-night) on the counter clockwise turning flange, synchronized with the main time, corresponding to the town names on the ring, alarm with luminescent arrow-pointed center hand and dedicated scale with divisions for a quarter of an hour. **Bracelet:** brushed steel; extensible safety fold-over clasp. Limited edition of 9,999 numbered pcs. **Also available:** black dial, rubber strap; platinum, strap, 23 pcs; yellow or pink gold, strap, 999 pcs each; white gold, 999 pcs.

SEASLUG ALARM GMT   REF. SAG03

Movement: mechanical, automatic winding, AS 5008 caliber. Officially certified "chronometer" (C.O.S.C.).
Functions: hour, minute, second, date, day, world time, sonnerie.
Case: 18 kt pink gold, three-piece brushed case (Ø 45 mm, thickness 15.8 mm); antireflective curved sapphire crystal on both sides; center crown for turning flange adjustment; crown at 3 for adjusting the turning flange, crown at 2 for

winding, for day, date and hour adjustments; crown at 4 for sonnerie use (setting, loading and actuation); screwed-on back displaying the movement through a sapphire crystal. Water-resistant to 3 atm. **Dial:** white; printed Arabic numerals; luminescent steel hands in an exclusive shape.
Indications: date and week day at 6, world time (day-night) on the turning flange, corresponding to the town names on the ring, sonnerie with luminescent center arrow-pointed hand and scale with divisions for a quarter of an hour.
Strap: rubber; brushed pink gold buckle.
Limited edition of 999 numbered pieces.

SEASLUG CHRONOMETER GMT   REF. S03D

Movement: mechanical, automatic winding, ETA 2893-2 caliber. Officially certified "chronometer" (C.O.S.C.).
Functions: hour, minute, second, date, second time-zone time, 24 hours.
Case: stainless steel, three-piece brushed case (Ø 38 mm, thickness 11.5 mm); antireflective curved sapphire crystal on both sides; counter clockwise turning ring with luminescent marker and engraved minute track, for the calculation of diving

times; crown at 2, at the first click, for the second time-zone time (clockwise) and date (counter clockwise) adjustment, at the second click for winding; screwed-on back displaying the movement through a sapphire crystal. Water-resistant to 10 atm.
Dial: anthracite; white printed drop-shaped markers with luminescent dots; luminescent steel hands in an exclusive shape.
Indications: date at 3, second time-zone time over 24 hours with luminescent center arrow-pointed hand.
Strap: rubber; brushed steel clasp.
Limited edition of 9,999 numbered pieces.
Also available: with black or silvered dial; with bracelet; in punk gold with pink dial, strap, 999 pieces.

SEASLUG CHRONOMETER GMT

The automatic winding movement of this watch with double time-zone display, with or without date, is the ETA 2893-2 caliber that obtained the official C.O.S.C. chronometer certificate. The display of the second time-zone time over 24 hours is indicated by means of an independent center hand.
The case of the Seaslug model, by which the House started its collection in 1995, appears rigorous on its front side and is smoothly tapered towards the case back. Hands, markers, recesses on the case back and strap or bracelet sections follow the "orgone" design, a shape common to all works performed by designer Macro Newton. Orgone is a vital energy held to pervade nature and to be accumulated by the human body by sitting in a specially designed box. Should, in the designer's view, the shape of this watch, which probably reminds the organ box, be a good portent for him who wears the object?
This model is realized in 9,999 pieces for each dial color (silvered, anthracite, black), has a steel case, a rubber strap or steel bracelet and is water-resistant to 10 atm.

IWC

an historical perspective

IWC, International Watch Company, is a brand rich with history and ripe with accolades for its technological prowess. This is a brand that, since its inception in 1868, has clearly focused on precision timekeeping and innovative design. IWC has been propelled to the international forefront time and again thanks to its ingenuity and craftsmanship.

IWC was founded by an American intent on creating precision timepieces. Florentine Ariosto Jones began International Watch Company in Schaffhausen, Switzerland—the German-speaking region where industrialization was fueled by harnessing the power of the nearby Rhine River. Since its earliest days, IWC was known for its technically advanced movements. In the late 1800s, it unveiled its first digital watches and developed several important calibers.

By the early 1930s, IWC had produced advanced pilot watches and, throughout the ensuing decades, focused on creating functional instruments particularly useful to pilots and divers. IWC was one of the first watchmaking houses to create an anti-magnetic pilot watch, to develop and patent an automatic-winding system with date display, and to join forces in the creation of the Swiss quartz movement.

A fully integrated Manufacture, IWC is one of a handful of luxury watch firms creating and assembling its own movements, parts and watches totally in house. Its state-of-the-art workshops in Schaffhausen utilize cutting-edge technology, side-by-side with the old-world art of watchmaking.

Indeed, throughout its illustrious history, IWC has firmly established itself as one of the finest luxury brands in the world. IWC's complicated timepieces and technically advanced professional sports lines attracted the attention of luxury giant Richemont Group, which purchased the brand in 2001. Offering strong financial and marketing support, Richemont intends to back the already successful IWC brand while allowing it to remain true to its heritage of technical prowess and staunchly precise craftsmanship.

365

unveiling

masterpieces

THIS PAGE

TOP

A number of complex steps go into the manufacture of a titanium case for the GST line.

LEFT

The GST Perpetual Calendar houses a complex chronograph movement and is crafted in titanium or stainless steel. It features the IWC patented bracelet.

RIGHT TOP

The patented bracelet is articulated via spring-loaded locking pins.

RIGHT BOTTOM

IWC's unique bracelet system features an integrated pushbutton-clasp.

LEFT CENTER

The GST Chrono-Rattrapante in titanium features an automatic self-winding split-second movement.

FACING PAGE

TOP

Housing the Caliber 5000, the Portuguese 2000 automatic watch offers a power reserve of 204 hours. To ensure maximum accuracy, though, the watch is stopped mechanically after 168 hours if not worn.

CENTER

The DaVinci Split-Seconds Chronograph is created in 18-karat rose gold and houses the company's patented perpetual calendar movement.

Refusing to rest on its laurels, IWC always goes the extra steps to take its timepiece development to new heights. For example, throughout the past few years, the brand has focused its efforts on further developing its four main collections: the GST (professional sports), DaVinci (classic elegance), Portuguese (elegantly oversized), and its pilot watches.

The GST, first introduced just three years ago, is a complete line of sports watches founded on the principles of sensible design and precise timekeeping. Reliability and durability were key factors in the creation of this series. Among the GST watches: the Aquatimer diver's watch, the Automatic Alarm, the Deep One diver's watch with mechanical depth gauge and the GST Chronographs.

This past year, IWC rounded out the series with a GST Perpetual Calendar Chronograph and a Split-Seconds Chronograph. The mechanical calendar is mechanically programmed to the year 2499, requiring no adjustment of the calendar. This unique mechanism essentially recognizes and displays the correct weekday, date (including leap years), year and moonphase. IWC holds a patent on this 500-year perpetual calendar system. The GST

CHRONOLOGY

1868 American watchmaker Florentine Ariosto Jones and watchmaker-businessman Johann Heinrich Moser establish IWC, International Watch Company, in Schaffhausen; IWC produces pocket watches with the caliber Jones—a high-precision movement that is among the first that can be wound from the crown.

1880 The Company is acquired by local industrialist Johannes Rauschenbach-Vogel.

1890 The first Grand Complication in a pocket watch is introduced. It incorporates more than 1,300 mechanical parts.

1900 The first wristwatches are made for the British Royal Navy and the Imperial German Navy; An anti-magnetic watch is created as a solution for workers operating electric-powered vehicles for the Berlin public transportation system and who often encounter magnetic fields that interfere with their watches' accuracy.

1904 The Caliber 72 is created—only 300 pieces will be produced before 1918.

1929 Ernst Jakob Homberger, fourth-generation Rauschenbach, becomes the sole owner of IWC.

1940 IWC initiates a new era with the Portugieseruhr and the first Fliegeruhr, an anti-magnetic watch for aviators—the largest wristwatch by IWC—mounted on a Caliber 83.

1954 The automatic-rewinding mechanism is refined and implemented in the Ingenieur and this year's best seller, the Yacht Club; Collaborating with Swiss Houses, the mechanism "Beta 21" is perfected. It will play an important role in the 1970s when IWC unveils its first quartz model.

1978 IWC links with Ferdinand A. Porsche. The bond will last for twenty years and lead to the birth of Porsche Design by IWC; Homberger's son sells IWC to the German VDO Group and Adolf Schindling AG.

1983 Günter Blümlein assumes the management of IWC.

1985 IWC teams develop the module of a perpetual calendar. The DaVinci is the first model to hold this revolutionary mechanism that retains accuracy for at least 500 years.

1990 The Grande Complication includes the perpetual calendar and, with its 9 hands and 659 mechanical parts, is the most complicated wristwatch of the era.

1993 The company adds a manual-winding mechanism, a split-seconds function and a tourbillon with titanium cage to the perpetual calendar.

1997 The new GST collection is named for the metals it utilizes (gold, steel, titanium). These are thoroughbred chronographs: an automatic caliber 7922 with day and date, and a quartz-mechanical caliber 631, the most compact ever built.

1998 IWC perfects the readout of a second time zone on the UTC, an aviator's watch with a class of instruments familiar to IWC since the 1930s; The GST line launches the 40mm Aquatimer which is water resistant to 2,000 meters but produced only in steel and titanium (gold cannot withstand such high pressure).

2000 IWC introduces the Caliber 5000.

2001 The brand launches the Portuguese model incorporating the Caliber 5000 and automatic movement which holds up to seven days of power reserve, a continuation of IWC's patented Pellaton system; IWC mourns the death of Günter Blümlein.

Chronograph Rattrapante (split-seconds) comes with a third button designed for recording a second, or intermediate time, and is a specialty of IWC. The new GST models are available in titanium cases and bracelets, or in surgical-grade stainless steel.

While 2001 was a heavy-hitter for IWC in the sports arena, the brand also developed a new Portuguese model with the Automatic Seven-day Caliber 5000 movement. The Caliber 5000 was first unveiled in the year 2000. The automatic movement with a power reserve of seven days is a further development of IWC's patented Pellaton winding system. The carefully decorated movement consists of 286 parts in 25 sub-assemblies. The escapement generates 18,000 beats per hour, the same speed as the classical pocket watch. Because of the impressive size of the movement, the case is boldly oversized yet with a crisp and clean design.

Of course, it would not be a complete year if IWC did not focus on the ever-popular DaVinci collection. Most important is the rose-gold split-seconds chronograph. The split-seconds mechanism of this watch enables the wearer to record intermediate times. IWC has held a patent on its system since 1992. Despite the fact that the function adds another hand to the DaVinci (now displaying 10 hands) the dial remains strikingly elegant—a prerequisite for all DaVinci watches.

INTERNATIONAL WATCH CO.

IWC SPLIT SECONDS CHRONOGRAPH   REF. 3713

Movement: automatic, IWC caliber 79230, 28,800 vibrations/h, 44-hour power reserve, 29 jewels.
Functions: chronograph movement with fly-back hand, day-date indication, small second with stop device.
Case: stainless steel, sapphire glass resistant against pressure drop, soft iron inner case for protection against magnetic fields, screwed crown, water resistant to 60 m, diameter 42mm, height 16.2mm.
Dial: black Mark XI.
Bracelet: brushed steel; fold-over clasp with safety pusher.
Also available: with crocodile mat black, strap width 21/18mm.
Price: available upon request.

IWC MECHANICAL PILOT'S CHRONOGRAPH   REF. 3706

Movement: automatic, IWC caliber 7922, 28,800 vibrations/h, 44-hour power reserve, 25 jewels.
Functions: mechanical chronograph, day-date indication, small second with stop device.
Case: stainless steel, sapphire glass resistant against pressure drop, soft iron inner case for protection against magnetic fields, screwed crown, water resistant to 60 m, diameter 39mm, height 14.6mm.
Dial: black, Mark XI.
Bracelet: crocodile mat black, strap width 20/18mm.
Also available: with stainless steel bracelet.
Price: available upon request.

IWC PILOT'S CHRONOGRAPH   REF. 3741

Movement: quartz, IWC caliber 631, battery 397, life 18 mon, 25 jewels.
Functions: mechanical chronograph with quartz-controlled step motors, date indicator, small second with stop device, battery indicator (end of life).
Case: stainless steel, sapphire glass resistant against pressure drop, soft iron inner case for protection against magnetic fields, scewed crown, water resistant to 60 m, diameter 36 mm, height 10.2 mm.
Dial: black Mark XI.
Bracelet: brushed steel; double fold-over clasp.
Also available: with crocodile mat black, strap width 18/16 mm.

IWC MARK XV   REF. 3253

Movement: automatic, IWC caliber 37524, 28,800 vibrations/h, 42hour power reserve, 21 jewels.
Functions: date indicator, center second with stop device.
Case: stainless steel, sapphire glass resistant against pressure drop, soft iron inner case for protection against magnetic fields, screwed crown, water resistant to 60 m, diameter 38mm, height 9mm.
Dial: black, Mark XI.
Bracelet: stainless steel, strap width 19/16mm.
Also available: with buffalo black strap.
Price: available upon request.

IWC UTC PILOT'S WATCH   REF. 3251

Movement: automatic, IWC caliber 37526, 28,800 vibrations/h, 42 hour power reserve, 21 jewels. **Functions:** date indicator, 24-hour display, adjustment of the watch in one-hour steps, center secon with stop device.
Case: stainless steel, sapphire glass resistant against pressure drop, soft iron inner case for protection against magnetic fields, scewed crown, water resistant to 60 m, diameter 39 mm, height 13.5 mm.
Dial: black with arabical numerals.
Bracelet: brushed steel; fold-over clasp with safety pusher.
Also available: with buffalo brown strap; in platinum with crocodile glossy blue strap and blue dial.

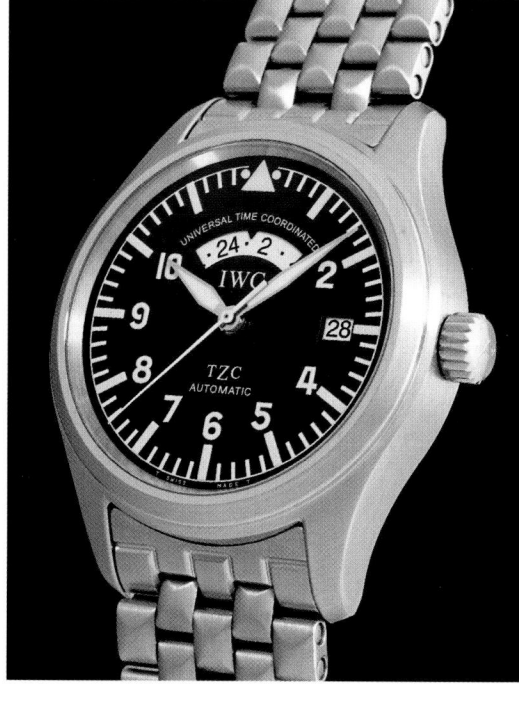

IWC LITTLE DA VINCI   REF. 3736

Movement: IWC caliber 630, 25 jewels, battery 397, life 18 months.
Functions: mechanical chronograph with quartz-controlled step motors, date indicator, perpetual indication of moon phases, small second with stop device, battery indicator (End of life).
Case: 18 kt yellow gold , sapphire glass, screwed crown, water resistant to 30 m, diameter 29mm, height 8.3mm.
Dial: white with index rhodium.
Bracelet: crocodile glossy green, strap width 15/14 mm.
Also available: in 18 kt yellow gold with crocodile nature brown strap, or 18 kt yellow gold bracelet, crocodile glossy light blue, crocodile glossy red; in stainless steel with crocodile glossy black, strap width 15/14 mm or stainless steel bracelet; in stainless steel with black dial.
Price: available upon request.

IWC DA VINCI   REF. 3750

Movement: automatic, IWC caliber 79261, 28,800 vibrations/h, 44-hour power reserve, 39 jewels.
Functions: perpetual calendar, perpetual moonphase indication, 4-digit year indication, chronograph, small second with stop device, mechanical chronograph movement.
Case: in polished stainless steel , Plexiglass, water resistant to 30 m, diameter 39mm, height 14.3mm.
Dial: black with rhodium index.
Bracelet: crocodile black mat, strap width 19/16 mm.
Also available: with stainless steel bracelet; in 18 kt yellow gold, white dial with gilt index, crocodile nature brown bracelet, strap width 19/16mm; in 18 kt yellow gold with 148 brilliants, TW, IF, 1.22 ct. and 18 kt yellow gold bracelet.
Price: available upon request.

IWC DA VINCI SPLIT-SECONDS CHRONOGRAPH   REF. 3754

Movement: automatic, IWC caliber 79251, 28,800 vibrations/h, 44-hour power reserve, 43 jewels.
Functions: mechanical chronograph movement, perpetual calendar, 4-digit year indication, perpetual moonphase indication, split-seconds hand for intermediate times, small second with stop device.
Case: 18 kt rose gold, convex Plexiglass, water resistant to 30 m, diameter 41.5mm, height 16mm.
Dial: silvered with Arabic gilt numerals.
Bracelet: crocodile matte black, strap width 20/18mm.
Also available: in platinum with crocodile mat blue strap and limited edition of 500 pieces per year.
Price: available upon request.

INTERNATIONAL WATCH CO.

IWC SL CHRONOGRAPH   REF. 3728

Movement: quartz, IWC caliber 631, battery 397, life 18 mon, 25 jewels.
Functions: mechanical chronograph with quartz-controlled step motors, date indicator, small second with stop device, battery indicator (end of life).
Case: stainless steel, three-piece brushed case (Ø 37 mm, thickness 10 mm); jointed lugs with central attachment; flat sapphire crystal; screw-down crown; polished rectangular pushers; case back attached by 5 screws. Water-resistant to 10 atm.

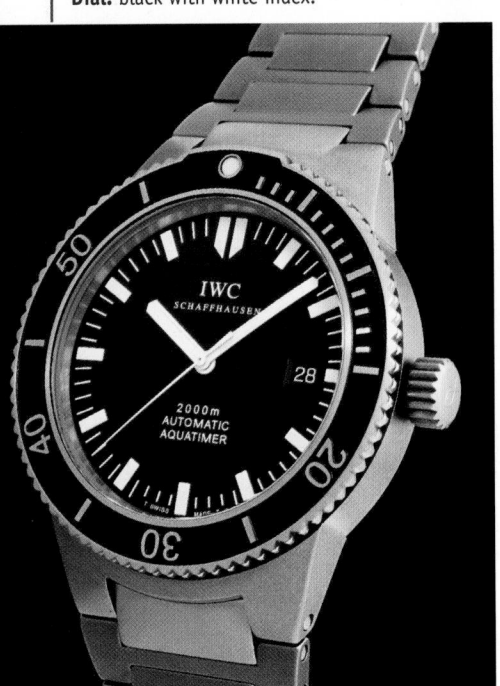

Dial: black, zones with circular beads pattern; applied rhodium-plated square markers with luminescent cabochon; luminescent white-gold bâton hands.
Indications: hour counter at 3, date between 4 and 5, small second at 6, minute counter at 9, center second counter, minute track.
Bracelet: stainless steel, brushed finish; fold-over clasp.
Also available: leather strap; in polished steel, white dial; in yellow gold, leather strap and white dial.

IWC SL AUTOMATIC   REF. 3528

Movement: automatic, IWC caliber 37524 28,800 vibrations/h, 42-hour power reserve, 21 jewels.
Functions: date indicator, central second with stop device.
Case: 18 kt yellow gold, sapphire glass, screwed crown, water resistant to 120 m, diameter 37 mm, height 10 mm).
Dial: white with gilt index.

Bracelet: crocodile mat black.
Also available: with 18 kt yellow gold bracelet. Or in polished stainless steel with nappa black, desmopan, crocodile mat black strap or stainless steel bracelet. In satin-finished stainless steel with nappa black, desmopan, crocodile mat black strap or stainless steel bracelet and black dial.

IWC GST AQUATIMER   REF. 3536

Movement: automatic, IWC caliber 37524, 28,800 vibrations/h, 42-hour power reserve, 21 jewels.
Functions: date indicator, center second with stop device.
Case: titanium, sapphire glass, screwed crown, water resistant to 2000 m, diameter 42mm, height 14.5mm.
Dial: black with white index.

Bracelet: titanium.
Also available: with Velcro band or in stainless steel with stainless steel bracelet.
Price: available upon request.

IWC GST DEEP ONE   REF. 3527

Movement: automatic, IWC caliber 8914, 28,800 vibrations/h, 38-hour power reserve.
Functions: mechanical movement, dial ring for setting diving time, diving depth display with fly-back hand to show maximum depth, IWC bracelet system with push-button release safety clasp, velcro strap and test pump.
Case: titanium, sapphire glass, screwed-crown, water resistant to 100 m, diameter 42 mm, height 14,4 mm.
Dial: black with white index.
Bracelet: titanium.

IWC GST CHRONO-AUTOMATIC   REF. 3707

Movement: automatic, IWC caliber 7922, 28,800 vibrations/h, 44-hour power reserve, 25 jewels.
Functions: mechanical chronograph movement, day/date indication, small second with stop device.
Case: stainless steel, sapphire glass, screwed crown, water resistant to 120 m, diameter 39.7mm, height 13.95mm.
Dial: silvered with gilt index.
Bracelet: stainless steel.
Also available: with black dial and rhodium index, or in titanium with titanium bracelet and black dial with white index.
Price: available upon request.

IWC GST CHRONOGRAPH   REF. 3727

Movement: quartz, IWC caliber 631, battery 397, life 18 mon, 25 jewels.
Functions: mechanical chronograph and quartz-controlled step motors, date indicator, small second with stop device.
Case: titanium, sapphire glass, screwed-crown, water resistant to 120 m, diameter 37 mm, height 11 mm.
Dial: black with white index.
Bracelet: titanium.
Also available: in stainless steel with stainless steel bracelet and black or white dial.

IWC GST PERPETUAL CALENDAR   REF. 3756

Movement: automatic, IWC caliber 79261, 28,800 vibrations/h, 44-hour power reserve, 39 jewels.
Functions: perpetual calendar, perpetual moonphase display, 4-digit year display, mechanical chronograph movement, push-button release safety clasp, IWC metal bracelet system.
Case: stainless steel, sapphire glass, screwed crown, water resistant to 120 m, diameter 43mm, height 16mm.
Dial: saumon with rhodium index.
Bracelet: stainless steel.
Also available: with rhodium dial and rhodium index, or in titanium with titanium bracelet and black dial with white index.
Price: available upon request.

IWC GST CHRONO-RATTRAPANTE   REF. 3715

Movement: automatic, IWC caliber 79230, 28,800 vibrations/h, 44-hour power reserve, 29 jewels.
Functions: mechanical chronograph movement, split-second hand for intermediate times, day and date display, push-button release safety clasp, IWC metal bracelet system.
Case: stainless steel, sapphire glass, screwed crown, water resistant to 120 m, diameter 43mm, height 16.5mm.
Dial: rhodium with rhodium index.
Bracelet: stainless steel.
Also available: with saumon dial and rhodium index, or in titanium with titanium bracelet and black dial with white index.
Price: available upon request.

INTERNATIONAL WATCH CO.

IWC PORTUGUESE SPLIT-SECONDS CHRONOGRAPH   REF. 3712

Movement: hand-wound, IWC caliber 76240, 28,800 vibrations/h, 48-hour power reserve, 31 jewels.
Functions: mechanical chronograph movement with fly-back hand, small second with stop device.
Case: stainless steel, sapphire glass, water resistant to 30 m, diameter 40.90 mm, height 12.3 mm.

Dial: silvered with Arabic gilt numerals.
Bracelet: crocodile glossy black, strap width 22/18mm.
Also available: in stainless steel with crocodile glossy brown or crocodile glossy green strap, 18 kt rose gold with crocodile glossy brown or crocodile glossy black strap.
Price: available upon request.

IWC PORTUGUESE AUTOMATIC CHRONOGRAPH   REF. 3714

Movement: automatic, IWC caliber 79240, 28,800 vibrations/h, 44-hour power reserve, 31 jewels.
Functions: mechanical chronograph movement, small second with stop device.
Case: 18 kt white gold, sapphire glass, water resistant to 30 m, diameter 40.90 mm, height 12.45 mm.
Dial: black dial with Arabic rhodium numerals.

Bracelet: crocodile glossy black, strap width 20/18mm.
Also available: in stainless steel with crocodile glossy black strap, in stainless steel with crocodile glossy black strap and silvered dial with Arabic gilt numerals, 18K rose gold with crocodile glossy brown strap.
Price: available upon request.

IWC PORTUGUESE AUTOMATIC 2000   REF. 5000

Movement: automatic (IWC patent), IWC caliber 5000, 18,000 vibrations/h, 168-hour (7 days) power reserve, 44 jewels.
Functions: mechanical movement, self-winding (IWC patent), powere reserve display, small second with stop function, precision adjustement, Breguet balance spring, rotor with 18 kt gold weight.

Case: 18 kt rose gold, plexiglass, sapphire glass back, diameter 42 mm, height 13.5 mm limited edition 750 pieces in rose gold and 1,000 pieces in stainless steel.
Dial: silvered with Arabic gilt numerals.
Bracelet: crocodile glossy brown, strap width 22/18 mm.
Also available: in stainless steel with crocodile glossy black strap and black dial with Arabic rhodium numerals.
Price: available upon request.

IWC CALIBER 5000

For the 5000 caliber, IWC was inspired by a realization of the Fifties, when the then technical manager of the Albert Pellaton manufacture conceived the automatic winding mechanism proposed here (for its technical description please refer to the movement sheets). The sizes correspond to the classical dimensions of "Lépine" pocket watches, i.e. 38.20 mm diameter and 7.20 mm thickness; 46 jewels; balance with compensation screws and fine regulation system

by screws with eccentric mass positioned at the ends of both arms; 18,000 vibrations per hour; Breguet balance spring with a further fine regulation device; 8.5 days power reserve. The first watch provided with these mechanisms is the new Portuguese Automatic 2000 model, a big-sized timekeeper, characterized by two opposed counters for small seconds (at 9) and power reserve (at 3). The movement appears on the case back side and displays a gold segment inserted in the rotor, on which the motto of the IWC House "Probus Scafusia" stands out proudly.

IWC PORTUGUESE MINUTE REPEATER   REF. 5240

Movement: hand-wound, IWC caliber 95290, 18,000 vibrations/h, 43-hour power reserve, 54 jewels.
Functions: minutes repetitions, small second with stop device.
Case: 18 kt rose gold, sapphire glass back, diameter 42 mm, height 12.3 mm, limited edition of 250 pieces in rose gold.
Dial: silvered with Arabic gilt numerals.
Bracelet: crocodile glossy brown, strap width 22/18mm.
Also available: with crocodile glossy black strap.
Price: available upon request.

IWC GRANDE COMPLICATION   REF. 3770

Movement: automatic, IWC caliber 79091, 28,800 vibrations/h, 44-hour power reserve, 21 kt gold rotor, 75 jewels.
Functions: chronograph, perpetual calendar, perpetual moonphase indication, 4-digit year indication, minute repetition, small second with stop device.
Case: platinum, sapphire glass, screwed crown, water resistant to 10 m, diameter 42.2 mm, height 16.3 mm, limited edition of 50 pieces per year.
Dial: white with gilt index.
Bracelet: crocodile glossy black strap, strap width 22/18 mm.
Also available: with platinum bracelet instead of the crocodile strap or in 18 kt yellow gold with crocodile glossy black strap and white dial with gilt index.
Price: available upon request.

IWC PORTOFINO AUTOMATIC   REF. 3513

Movement: automatic, IWC caliber 37521, 28,800 vibrations/h, 42-hour power reserve, 21 jewels.
Functions: date indicator, center second with stop device.
Case: stainless steel, sapphire glass, water resistant to 30 m, diameter 34 mm, height 8.1 mm.
Dial: white with arabical numerals.
Bracelet: collet carabou brown, strap width 18/16 mm.
Also available: 18 kt yellow gold with crocodile glossy black or crocodile nature brown strap, in stainless steel with crocodile glossy black, collet carabou black strap or stainless steel bracelet.

IWC PORTOFINO   REF. 2010

Movement: hand-wound, IWC caliber 849, 21,600 vibrations/h, 36-hour power reserve, 19 jewels.
Case: 18 kt yellow gold, sapphire glass, diameter 32 mm, height 4.8 mm (extra-flat).
Dial: white with gilt index.
Bracelet: crocodile glossy black, strap width 18/16 mm.
Also available: in 18 kt white gold with rhodium index.

JAEGER-LECOULTRE

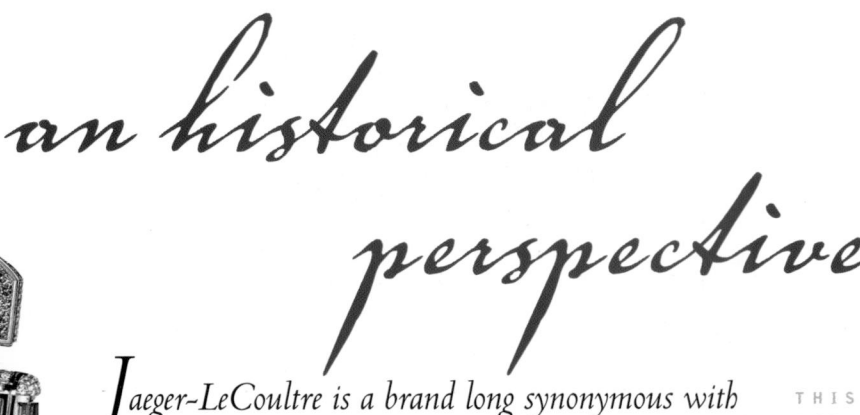

an historical perspective

Jaeger-LeCoultre is a brand long synonymous with innovation and technical prowess. For more than a century and a half, the timepieces created by this inimitable watchmaker have not only garnered international recognition, but have also generated hundreds of patents thanks to their technical excellence.

Jaeger-LeCoultre was born on the principles of perfection and detail. Founding father Antoine LeCoultre, who started his company in 1833, was enthralled with watchmaking and was obsessed with creating new and different movements. His love of watchmaking carried on through his family and in 1903 the LeCoultres joined forces with Edmond Jaeger, master of chronometers. Throughout the first half of the twentieth century, Jaeger-LeCoultre unveiled a number of world firsts, including the Caliber 101 (the smallest mechanical watch movement ever produced), the Reverso (the famed reversible watch), and the Memovox (the first automatic alarm wristwatch).

With such an esteemed and honored place in history, it is no wonder that Jaeger-LeCoultre was an object of desire for one the top luxury conglomerates in the world: Richemont Group. Indeed, Jaeger-LeCoultre's heritage and continuing respect for craftsmanship and technological advances were so akin to the philosophies and priorities of Richemont that the group purchased the brand in 2000.

According to the powers that be at Richemont, Jaeger-LeCoultre will retain its place of honor in a category where only a handful of the most elite watchmaking houses co-exist. This prestigious entity vows to continue Jaeger-LeCoultre's pursuit of excellence and innovation in all it creates—producing limited timepieces that pay homage to its roots and to the legacy of Swiss watchmaking.

unveiling masterpieces

Rich with tradition yet always on the cutting-edge of design and invention, Jaeger-LeCoultre has a varied, striking collection of time-pieces—heralded by the famed Reverso—that runs the gamut from men's to women's, complex to jeweled, sports to elegance.

First created in 1931, the Reverso—with its reversible swivel case—is a world-renowned icon. Recognized for its artistic flair, innovative industrial design and unique versatility, the Reverso has been one of the most talked about watches in history. Over the decades, Jaeger-LeCoultre has continually produced Reverso masterpieces that are breathtaking beauties in design and technical prowess. So coveted is this watch, that celebrities and royalty alike have placed special orders to the prestigious brand for custom-made Reversos.

Additionally, because collectors clamored for the Reverso, Jaeger-LeCoultre began a special 500-piece-per-year limited-edition series of very special Reversos. They ranged from the Reverso 60ème with an all-pink-gold movement, to the Tourbillon, the Répétition Minutes, Chronographe Rétrograde, Géographique, and Quantième Perpétuel.

Now, in celebration of the 70th anniversary of the Reverso, Jaeger-LeCoultre has unveiled what is perhaps the most heralded Reverso: the Reverso Platinum Number One. The second dynasty of limited pieces created to celebrate the Reverso's 70th anniversary, the newest timepiece is the first platinum Reverso with skeletonized movement. Developed according to the inventive passions of Jaeger-LeCoultre master-watchmaker Sylvain Golay, the Reverso Platinum Number One features an ultra-thin, openworked, manually wound movement that took countless painstaking hours of engraving and carving to create.

Only 500 of the swivel-cased Reverso Platinum Number One timepieces will ever be created. Each is housed in the Grande Taille case, made of more than 50 parts. There is no dial, as a transparent sapphire crystal appears on both sides of the watch with blued steel hands to indicate the time. The grandeur of this masterpiece is further enhanced by blued steel screws and 19 jewels.

Further celebrating the anniversary of this famed timepiece, Jaeger-LeCoultre has unveiled exciting Gran'Sport models. A chic addition to the world of sports watches, the Gran'Sport brings together the technical expertise of Jaeger-LeCoultre with cutting-edge innovation. New models include a sophisticated Automatique, fitted with a screw-locked crown and water resistant to 50 meters. It houses a mechanical movement with 44-hour power reserve and is polished and decorated by hand in true Jaeger-LeCoultre style.

Also, this past year, a manually wound retrograde chronograph joined the line-up. Featuring a double-gasket crown, it displays the hour, minute, center seconds, date and stop/start shutter on the front dial. The back dial features the 60-second and retrograde 30-minute counters. This Reverso Chronographe Rétrograde Gran'Sport is also offered with a new black rubber strap and coordinating slate-gray dial for ultimate appeal. The strap features an exclusive design with five godrons, integrated design and a complex clasp that is designed for rapid length adjustment to guarantee a perfect fit summer or winter, morning or night.

women's
wonders

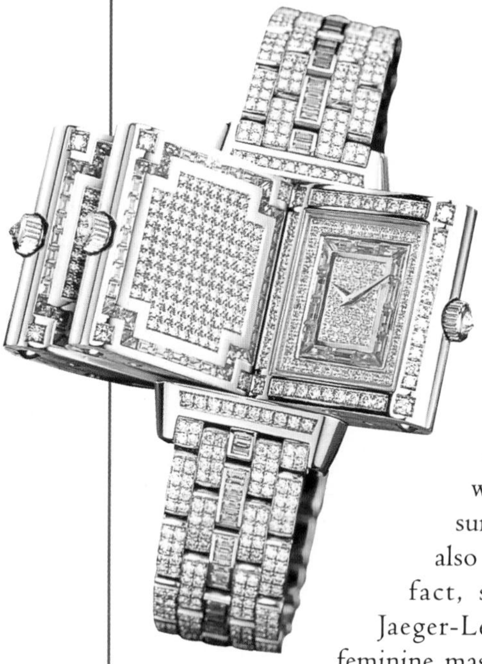

Because the great House of Jaeger-LeCoultre is dedicated to creating the finest, most wonderful timepieces in the world, it comes as no surprise that the brand is also oriented to women. In fact, since its early years, Jaeger-LeCoultre has unveiled feminine masterpieces—tiny in size but big in design—that have won awards and graced the wrists of royalty around the world.

Today, Jaeger-LeCoultre continues its tradition of excellence and beauty by adding to its Reverso timepieces for women. The Florale series, first introduced several years ago, has become quite a sensation in the world of women's watches, thanks to the truly feminine appeal. Over the past few years, Jaeger-LeCoultre's craftsmen have elegantly bedecked the Florale with various gemset motifs that have turned heads and stolen hearts.

The newest piece pays homage to the exotic Tahitian Tiaré flower. Drawn to the natural fragrance and beauty of this sovereign of the Polynesian "Garden of Eden," Jaeger-LeCoultre's gemologist Sam Wühl created an haute couture motif to depict the flower. Each watch features 168 carefully selected diamonds to illuminate the petals in electrifying beauty. Indeed, the Top Wesselton VVSI full cut diamonds total well over a carat in weight. This timepiece is sold with either an 18-karat yellow gold bracelet or a deep burgundy crocodile strap.

LEFT

A shimmering sea of pink sapphires and diamonds make this Reverso Joaillerie Baguette watch stand out at any distance.

TOP RIGHT

The Reverso Florale Tiaré with diamonds pays homage to the exotic Tahitian Tiaré flower.

RIGHT CENTER

In its Florale Feuilles Pastel, Jaeger-LeCoultre deftly blends pastel blue sapphires with diamonds for exquisite radiance.

TOP

Turning to color and coordinating cabochons, Jaeger-LeCoultre unveils the Reverso Cabochon collection.

BOTTOM LEFT

The Reverso Duetto is a graceful watch that offers a daytime classic dial and a reversible, more glamorous dial for evening.

BOTTOM RIGHT

A specialty from the great watchmaking house, the Reverso pocket watch.

Another striking model is the Florale Feuilles Pastel, wherein pale blue sapphires accented by diamonds create the flowers and design of the Reverso. In one stunning rendition, Jaeger-LeCoultre has adorned the 18-karat white-gold Reverso with 194 blue sapphires and 24 brilliant diamonds for scintillating appeal. In true Haute Joaillerie style, the brand unveils a Reverso incomparable in its radiance thanks to the fact that the 18-karat white-gold case is set with 195 diamonds and 48 baguette-cut pink sapphires. In its Montre de Poche Feuilles pocket watch, Jaeger-LeCoultre brings together 68 baguette-cut diamonds, 837 diamonds and 159 yellow sapphires on a case housing a mechanical, manually wound Caliber 823 movement with power reserve and thermometer.

Of course, not all of Jaeger-LeCoultre's timepieces for women are this elaborate. Recognizing the desire of women for understated elegance and technical beauty, the brand offers Reversos simply accented with diamonds (as on the Reverso Cabochon, where a simple pink or yellow cabochon adorns the top and bottom of the case with diamond accents), or with no diamonds at all. Thanks to the genius of the brand's watchmakers and designers—each timepiece is just as desirable as the next.

JAEGER-LeCOULTRE

MASTER GRANDE MEMOVOX   REF. 146.240.952B

Movement: automatic winding, Jaeger-LeCoultre 909 caliber, 45 hours power reserve, 36 jewels, 28,800 vph, 349 elements. Tested over 1000 hours. Constructed and decorated by hand with Côtes de Genève and circular graining patterns.
Functions: hour, minute, second, 24 hours, perpetual calendar (date, day, month, year, moon-phase), alarm. **Case:** platinum, 3-piece (Ø 41.5, thickness 15.7 mm); curved sapphire crystal; white-gold winding crown at 4, for sonnerie at 2; calendar corrector at 8; back attached by 6 screws, numbered, with "1000 hours" seal. Water-resistant to 5 atm. **Dial:** deep blue, zones with circular beads; applied white-gold pointed markers; printed minute track with luminescent dots at quarters; luminescent white-gold Dauphine hands. **Indications:** week day at 3, moon-phase and 24 hours (red-color display of the hours at which calendar corrections are not allowed) at 6, date at 9, month and two-digit year at 12, sonnerie with center arrow-pointed hand and scale with divisions for a quarter of an hour.
Strap: crocodile leather; white-gold fold-over clasp. Limited edition of 500 numbered pieces.
Also available: in pink gold with silvered dial.

MASTER PERPETUAL   REF. 140.340.804B

Movement: automatic, Jaeger-LeCoultre 889/440/2 caliber. "Master Control 1000 Hours" engraved on rotor, 22 kt pink-gold segment. Decorated with Vagues de Genève and circular graining. Tested over 1000 hours. **Functions:** hour, minute, perpetual calendar (date, day, month, year, moon phase). **Case:** 18 kt white gold, 3-piece case (Ø 37, thick. 10.6 mm); bezel fastened from behind by 4 through screws; curved sapphire crystal; whole calendar corrector at 8; white-gold crown; back fastened by 4 screws with sapphire bull's eye, hinged cover and numbered medallion. Water-resistant to 5 atm. **Dial:** rhodium-gray with sun pattern, curved; zones with circular beads decoration; applied faceted white-gold pointed markers (Arabic numeral 6); luminescent dots on the printed minute track; faceted white-gold Dauphine hands, skeletonized on the "off hours". **Indications:** week day at 3, moon phase at 6, date at 9, month and two-digit year at 12, central sector for the red-color display of the period in which calendar corrections are not allowed.
Strap: crocodile leather; white-gold fold-over clasp.
Also available: "Black" dial, sapphire back: in steel; pink gold; pink gold, silvered dial, closed case back.

MASTER GEOGRAPHIC   REF. 142.340.924.B

Movement: automatic, Jaeger-LeCoultre 929/3 caliber. Rotor with 22 kt pink-gold segment. Vagues de Genève and circular graining decoration. Tested over 1000h.
Functions: hour, minute, second, date, world time, 2nd time-zone time, power reserve. **Case:** 18 kt white gold, 3-piece case (Ø 38, thickn. 11.8 mm); bezel fastened from behind with 4 through screws; curved sapphire crystal; winding crown at 3 for the synchronization of secondary zones with the main time-zone time; world time white-gold crown at 10; date corrector at 2; back with sapphire crystal fastened by 4 screws. Water-resistant to 5 atm. **Dial:** rhodium-gray, grained, curved; zones with circular beads; applied white gold markers and printed minute track on the flange; luminescent rhodium-plated Dauphine hands. **Indications:** date at 2, 2nd time zone (night & day, two hands) and window with two-way disc for reference town names of the 24 time zones at 6, power reserve at 10. **Strap:** crocodile leather; fold-over steel clasp. **Also available:** steel, strap, silvered dial, closed case back or "Black" dial, sapphire case back; pink gold, leather strap, "Black" dial, sapphire case back or silvered dial, closed case back; in white gold, leather strap, gray dial, hinged cover.

MASTER MOON   REF. 140.640.984B

Movement: automatic, Jaeger-LeCoultre 891/448 caliber. Rotor with 22 kt pink gold segment and gilded engraving "Mater Control 1000 Hours". Vagues de Genève and circular graining decoration. Tested over 1000 hours.
Functions: hour, minute, small second, full calendar (date, day, month, moon-phase). **Case:** 18 kt white gold, three-piece case (Ø 37 mm, thickness 11.5 mm); bezel fastened by 4 screws from behind; curved sapphire crystal; 3 correctors on the middle; white gold crown; sapphire crystal back, fastened by 4 screws and protected by a hinged numbered cover. Water-resistant to 5 atm. **Dial:** rhodium-gray, grained, curved; applied white-gold pointed markers and Arabic numerals; 4 luminescent dots; luminescent white-gold Dauphine hands. **Indications:** small second and moon phase at 6, center day and month, date with half-moon center hand.
Strap: crocodile leather; white-gold fold-over clasp.
Also available: "Black" or silvered dial, sapphire case back without cover: steel, leather strap and fold-over clasp; pink-gold, leather strap and fold-over clasp. Limited series of 250 pcs., platinum with "deep blue" dial, leather strap.

MASTER GRANDE TAILLE   REF. 140.240.892B

Movement: mechanical, automatic winding, Jaeger-LeCoultre 889/1 caliber. Vagues de Genève and circular graining decoration. Tested over 1000 hours.
Functions: hour, minute, second, date.
Case: 18 kt pink gold, three-piece case, with additional ductile iron non-magnetic back (Ø 37 mm, thickness 9.8 mm); bezel fastened from behind with 4 screws; curved sapphire crystal; pink gold crown; back attached by 4 screws, numbered, with gold "1000 hours" seal. Water-resistant to 8 atm.
Dial: silvered, curved; applied pink gold Arabic numerals and pointed markers; luminescent dots on the printed minute track; luminescent pink gold Dauphine hands.
Indications: date at 3.
Strap: crocodile leather; pink-gold fold-over clasp.
Also available: in steel, leather strap with fold-over clasp or stainless steel bracelet.

MASTER MEMOVOX BLACK   REF. 144.240.947SB

Movement: mechanical, manual winding, produced by Jaeger-LeCoultre 914 caliber. Vagues de Genève and circular graining decoration. Tested over 1000 hours.
Functions: hour, minute, second, alarm.
Case: 18 kt pink gold, three-piece case (Ø 36 mm, thickness 12 mm); curved sapphire crystal; pink-gold winding crown at 4, for the sonnerie at 2 (20 seconds ringing); back with sapphire crystal. Water-resistant to 5 atm.
Dial: black, curved; turning center disc; applied faceted pink-gold Arabic numerals and pointed markers; luminescent dots on the printed minute track; luminescent faceted pink-gold Dauphine hands.
Indications: turning center disc with luminescent sonnerie pointer.
Strap: crocodile leather; pink-gold fold-over clasp.
Also available: in stainless steel.

MASTER POWER RESERVE PLATINUM   REF. 140.640.936.B

Movement: automatic winding, Jaeger-LeCoultre 928 caliber. Rotor with gilded engraving "Master Control 1000 Hours" and platinum segment. Vagues de Genève and circular graining decoration. Tested over 1000 hours. **Functions:** hour, minute, small second, date, power reserve. **Case:** platinum, three-piece case (Ø 37 mm, thickness 11.5 mm); curved sapphire crystal; date corrector on the middle; white-gold crown; back attached by 4 screws, displaying the movement through a sapphire crystal protected by a hinged cover, numbered and with the engraving "Série limitée à 250 pièces Platinum". Water-resistant to 5 atm.
Dial: deep blue, curved; applied white-gold Arabic numerals and pointed markers; luminescent dots on the printed minute track; luminescent white-gold Dauphine hands.
Indications: date at 2, small second at 6, power reserve at 10. **Strap:** crocodile leather; platinum fold-over clasp. Limited edition of 250 numbered pieces.
Also available: non limited series, coverless, "Black" dial, sapphire case back or with silvered dial, closed case back: steel, leather strap with fold-over clasp or stainless steel bracelet; in pink gold, bracelet and fold-over clasp.

MASTER ULTRA-THIN   REF. 145.340.794SB

Movement: mechanical, manual winding, Jaeger-LeCoultre 849 caliber, ultra-thin. Winding barrel with the engraving "Master Control 1000 H". Vagues de Genève and circular graining decoration. Tested over 1000 hours.
Functions: hour, minute.
Case: 18 kt white gold, three-piece case (Ø 34 mm, thickness 6 mm); bezel fastened from behind with 4 screws; curved sapphire crystal; white-gold crown; back fastened by 4 screws, displaying the movement through a sapphire crystal. Water-resistant to 5 atm.
Dial: rhodium-gray, with sun pattern, curved; applied faceted rhodium-plated Arabic numerals and pointed markers; faceted rhodium-plated Régate hands.
Strap: crocodile leather; white-gold fold-over clasp.
Also available: in steel with black dial and sapphire case back or silvered dial and closed case back with hinged cover; in pink gold, black dial and sapphire crystal case back or with silvered dial, closed case back with hinged cover; in platinum with deep blue dial and sapphire crystal case back, 250 pcs.

JAEGER-LeCOULTRE

REVERSO GRAN'SPORT CHRONOGRAPH   REF. 295.110.593

Movement: manual, Jaeger-LeCoultre 859 caliber (derived from 829 caliber), 38 jewels, 28,800 vph, made up by 317 elements. Beveled and Côtes de Genève hand-decorated. **Functions:** hour, minute, second, date, chronograph with 2 counters, chronograph working indicator. **Case:** 18 kt yellow gold, tonneau-shaped, reversible double-face case (with carrier size 43 x 28, thickness 11.5 mm; only case size 32 x 28, thickness 10 mm), engraved with sand-blasted

transverse grooves; curved sapphire crystal on both sides; gold crown and beveled rectangular pushers; back attached by 4 screws, carrier with brushed finish and circular graining decoration. Water-resistant to 5 atm. **Dial:** silvered, engine-turned (guilloché) with center panels; printed Arabic numerals; luminescent black enameled gold lozenge hands. **Indications:** chronograph on/off indicator at 5, date at 6; back face: silvered, black counter rings, engine-turned (guilloché) panels; minute counter with retrograde hand at 6, slightly off-center second counter. **Strap:** rubber; yellow gold double fold-over clasp and safety pushers (length adjustable by pushers).

REVERSO GRAN'SPORT CHRONOGRAPH   REF. 295.110.592

The original patented bracelet with five integrated links of the Reverso Gran'Sport model, shared with both the chronograph and automatic models, is not only smooth and agreeable to bear, but also anti-allergic (a characteristic that, of course, does not refer to the gold version, as this material is always well tolerated by the skin, but rather to the stainless steel version which has no nickel). The complex clasp, made up by 52 elements (the most complicated

one in the world) has an original opening system with double safety device without screws with fast lengthening feature (± 8 mm).

A further distinguishing element of the Reverso Gran'Sport is its dial, which is available silvered or anthracite with a chessboard central rectangle and "chemin-de-fer" minute track. The chronograph version displays hours, minutes, seconds and date at 6 on its front side and is provided with a chronograph mode indicator, while on the rear side a second dial shows the chronograph second and (retrograde) minute counters.

REVERSO GRAN'SPORT LADY   REF. 296.882.743

Movement: manual, Jaeger-LeCoultre 864 caliber, 19 jewels, 21,600 vph, made up by 164 elements. Beveled and Côtes de Genève hand-decorated. **Functions:** hour, minute, small second, date, day-night indicator, second time-zone time, day-night. **Case:** stainless steel, tonneau-shaped, reversible double-face case (only case size 27.5 x 24.5, thickness 9.5 mm), engraved with sand-blasted transverse grooves; 32 diamonds set on the second face; curved sapphire crystal on both

sides; corrector for the adjustment of the second time-zone time on the middle; carrier with brushed finish and circular graining decoration. Water-resistant to 5 atm. **Dial:** silvered, guilloché; "Linton" Arabic numerals; printed minute track with 3 luminescent dots; burnished steel lozenge hands. **Indications:** small second at 6, night-day at 12. **Back face:** silvered, engine-turned (guilloché) panels; applied rhodium-plated drop-shaped markers and printed blue "flower" Arabic numerals; luminescent steel bâton hands. **Indications:** second time-zone time, night-day at 6. **Strap:** polished/brushed steel; double fold-over clasp and safety pushers. **Also available:** in yellow gold with bracelet.

REVERSO GRAN'SPORT AUTOMATIC   REF. 290.880.602

Movement: mechanical, automatic winding, Jaeger-LeCoultre 960R caliber, 31 jewels, 28,800 vibrations per hour. Made up by 226 elements. Rotor with 21 kt yellow-gold segment. Beveled and hand-decorated (Côtes de Genève pattern). **Functions:** hour, minute, second, date. **Case:** stainless steel, tonneau-shaped, reversible case (with carrier size 43 x 26.5 mm, thickness 10 mm; only case size 30.5 x 26.5 mm, thickness 4 mm);

engraved sand-blasted transverse grooves; curved sapphire crystal; screw-down crown; brushed carrier decorated with circular graining pattern. Water-resistant to 5 atm. **Dial:** silvered, engine-turned (guilloché) with center panels; luminescent applied pointed markers and Arabic numerals; printed minute track; luminescent blued steel lozenge hands. **Indications:** date at 6. **Bracelet:** stainless steel, polished and brushed; double fold-over clasp with safety pushers. **Also available:** with anthracite dial; yellow gold, bracelet, silvered dial; rubber strap: yellow gold, silvered dial; stainless steel, anthracite dial.

REVERSO PERPETUAL CALENDAR   REF. 270.240.552B

Movement: manual, Jaeger-LeCoultre 855 caliber, constructed and worked entirely by hand, 50 hours power reserve, 39 jewels, 21,600 vph. Made up by 276 elements. Decorated with Côtes de Genève pattern and circular graining.
Functions: hour, minute, small second, perpetual calendar (date, day, month, year, moon phase). **Case:** 18 kt pink gold, rectangular, reversible, double-face case (with carrier size 42x26, thickness 9.8 mm; only case size 30.5x26, thickness 8.6 mm); engraved transverse grooves; curved sapphire crystal on both sides; pink-gold crown; four correctors on the middle; back fastened with 4 screws. Waterproof.
Dial: solid silver with engine-turned (guilloché) center, zones decorated with circular beads; printed Arabic numerals and minute track; blued steel bâton hands. **Indications:** day-night at 1, small second and four-year cycle at 6; rear side: day at 4, month at 8, date with retrograde hand and moon-phase at 12.
Strap: crocodile leather; pink-gold fold-over clasp. Limited edition of 500 pieces.
Also available: with bracelet.

REVERSO DUOFACE   REF. 270.240.544B

Movement: mechanical, manual winding, Jaeger-LeCoultre 854 caliber, patented. **Functions:** home-time hour, minute and small second; second time-zone hour, minute and 24-hour.
Case: 18 kt pink gold, rectangular, reversible, double-face case (with carrier size 42 x 26, thickness 9.8 mm; case size 30.5 x 26, thickness 8.5 mm); engraved sand-blasted transverse grooves; curved sapphire crystal on both sides; second time-zone corrector on the middle; pink-gold crown. Waterproof.
Dial: front dial in solid silver, Art Déco design, with engine-turned (guilloché) center, printed Arabic numerals and minute track, blued steel bâton hands; small second at 6; rear dial black, engine-turned (guilloché), with luminescent applied pink-gold pointed markers and Arabic numerals, luminescent gold lozenge hands and 24-hour display at 6.
Strap: crocodile leather; pink-gold fold-over clasp.
Also available: both dials silvered; with bracelet; in yellow gold; in steel, ostrich skin strap and fold-over clasp or bracelet; in white gold with black-rosé dials, leather strap and fold-over clasp or bracelet.

REVERSO GEOGRAPHIQUE   REF. 270.240.582B

Movement: mechanical, manual winding, Jaeger-LeCoultre 858 caliber, patented. **Functions:** hour, minute, small second, night & day indicator; second time-zone time, night & day indicator with reference towns. **Case:** 18 kt pink gold, rectangular, reversible double-face case (with carrier size 42 x 26, thickness 9.8 mm; case size 30.5 x 26, thickness 8.5 mm) with engraved transverse grooves; curved sapphire crystal on both sides; pink-gold second time-zone corrector; reference town rectangular corrector pusher on the middle; pink-gold crown. Waterproof.
Dial: front dial: solid silver, engine-turned (guilloché) center; printed Arabic numerals and minute track, blued steel bâton hands, small second at 6, night & day display at 12; black rear dial, engine-turned (guilloché), white Chinese-style Arabic numerals, luminescent pink-gold lozenge hands, reference towns at 5 and 7, GMT ± between 7 and 8, night & day display between 4 and 5.
Strap: crocodile leather; pink-gold fold-over clasp. Limited edition of 500 pieces.
Also available: with bracelet.

REVERSO DATE   REF. 270.840.357.B

Movement: mechanical, manual winding, Jaeger-LeCoultre 835 caliber (cal. 836 base + day-night display module).
Functions: hour, minute, small second, day-date.
Case: 18 kt white gold, rectangular, reversible case (carrier size 42 x 26 mm, thickness 9.8 mm; only case size 30.5 x 26 mm, thickness 8.5 mm) with engraved transverse grooves; curved sapphire crystal; date corrector on the middle; white gold crown. Waterproof.
Dial: black enameled; white enameled Chinese-style Arabic numerals; white gold lozenge hands.
Indications: small second and day-night at 6, day at 11, red arrow-pointed center date hand.
Strap: crocodile leather; white gold fold-over clasp.
Also available: without day-night display: in stainless steel, with crocodile strap and fold-over clasp, bracelet; in pink gold, crocodile leather strap and fold-over clasp or bracelet; in white gold, black dial, crocodile leather strap and fold-over clasp, bracelet.

JAEGER-LeCOULTRE

REVERSO MEMORY   REF. 255.840.822B

Movement: manual winding, Jaeger-LeCoultre 862 caliber. Modified with an original fly-back counter mechanism equipped with an "artificial release" device that allows knowing by touch whether the pusher performed its function.
Functions: hour, minute, small second, 60-minute fly-back "memento" counter.
Case: 18 kt yellow gold, rectangular, reversible double-face case (with carrier size 38.5x23, thickn. 10 mm; case only 27x23), made up by 50 elements, engraved transverse grooves; curved sapphire crystal; rectangular counter pusher at 4; case back attached by 8 screws, with gasket. Waterproof. **Front dial:** silvered, engine-turned (guilloché) center and zone; printed Arabic numerals and minute track; luminescent blued steel bâton hands, small second at 6. **Rear dial:** black, engine-turned (guilloché) center, luminescent bâton hand, for the continuous center 60-minute counter with simultaneous zeroing and restart by the pusher. **Strap:** crocodile leather; fold-over gold clasp. **Also available:** with bracelet; in steel, leather strap, fold-over clasp or bracelet; in steel and yellow gold, leather strap, fold-over clasp or bracelet.

REVERSO SUN MOON   REF. 270.340.637SB

Movement: mechanical, manual winding, Jaeger-LeCoultre 823 caliber. **Functions:** hour, minute, small second, night & day indicator, moon phase, power reserve.
Case: 18 kt white gold, rectangular, reversible (with carrier size 42 x 26 mm, thickness 9.8 mm; only case size 30.5 x 26 mm, thickness 8.5 mm) with engraved transverse grooves; curved sapphire crystal; white-gold crown; back with a rectangular aperture displaying the movement through a sapphire crystal. Waterproof.
Dial: black enameled; white painted Chinese-style Arabic numerals and railway minute track; luminescent white-gold leaf style hands.
Indications: night & day display at 2, small second and moon phase at 6, power reserve between 10 and 11.
Strap: crocodile leather; white-gold fold-over clasp.
Also available: with bracelet; in pink gold with silvered dial, leather strap and fold-over clasp or bracelet; only pink gold bracelet; only white gold bracelet.

REVERSO PLATINUM NUMBER ONE   REF. 270.640.490SB

Movement: mechanical, manual winding, Jaeger-LeCoultre 849R-SQ caliber, 19 jewels, 21,600 vph. Made up by 128 elements. Skeletonized, chased and polished by hand. **Functions:** hour, minute.
Case: platinum, rectangular, reversible (with carrier size 42 x 26.2 mm, thickness 8.8 mm; only case size 30.5 x 26 mm, thickness 7.5 mm) with engraved sand-blasted transverse grooves; curved sapphire crystal; white-gold crown with set sapphire cabochon; back with a rectangular aperture displaying the movement through a sapphire crystal.
Dial: blued steel leaf style hands.
Strap: crocodile leather; platinum fold-over clasp. Limited edition of 500 pieces.

REVERSO ART DÉCO   REF. 270.340.625B

Movement: mechanical, manual winding, tonneau-shaped, 14 kt pink gold, Jaeger-LeCoultre 822/AD caliber, made up by 134 elements. Skeletonized, hand-engraved in Art Nouveau style with "grain d'orge" pattern.
Functions: hour, minute, small second.
Case: 18 kt white gold, rectangular, reversible case (with carrier size 42 x 26 mm, thickness 9.8 mm; only case size 30.5 x.26 mm, thickness 8.5 mm) with engraved transverse grooves; curved sapphire crystal; white-gold crown; numbered back with a rectangular aperture displaying the movement through a sapphire crystal. Waterproof.
Dial: solid silver, rosé, engine-turned (guilloché) and hand-finished; applied pointed markers and white-gold cabochon; white-gold Dauphine hands.
Indications: small second at 6.
Strap: crocodile leather; white-gold fold-over clasp.
Also available: with bracelet; in pink gold with solid silver engine-turned (guilloché) dial, leather strap and fold-over clasp or bracelet.

REVERSO CLASSIC   REF. 250.140.862B

Movement: mechanical, manual winding, Jaeger-LeCoultre 846/1 caliber.
Functions: hour, minute, small second.
Case: 18 kt yellow gold, rectangular, reversible case (with carrier size 38.5 x 23 mm, thickness 7.3 mm; case only size 27 x 23 mm, thickness 6.3) with engraved transverse grooves; curved sapphire crystal; gold crown; case back attached by 8 screws, with gasket. Waterproof.

Dial: silvered; printed Arabic numerals and railway minute track, blued steel bâton hands.
Strap: ostrich skin; yellow-gold fold-over clasp.
Also available: with bracelet; in steel and yellow gold, leather strap and fold-over clasp or bracelet; in stainless steel, leather strap and fold-over clasp or bracelet; with quartz movement.
Reverso Lady: in stainless steel, leather strap and fold-over clasp or bracelet; in steel and yellow gold, leather strap and fold-over clasp or bracelet; in yellow gold, leather strap and fold-over clasp or bracelet; with quartz movement.

REVERSO DUETTO CLASSIC TAILLE   REF. 256.882.752

Movement: mechanical, manual winding, Jaeger-LeCoultre 845 caliber, autonomy 50 hours, 19 jewels, 21,600 vph. Manufactured and decorated by hand.
Functions: double hour and minute display, small second.
Case: stainless steel, rectangular, reversible, double face case (with carrier size 38 x 23 mm, thickness 10 mm; case only size 27 x 23 mm) with engraved transverse grooves; 32 brilliant-cut diamonds set on the back; curved sapphire crystal on both sides. Waterproof.

Dial: solid silver, center and zones engine-turned (guilloché); printed "Chinese"-style Arabic numerals and minute track, blued steel bâton hands. Rear side: silvered, center engine-turned (guilloché) with rim; applied yellow-gold Arabic numerals and bâton markers; yellow-gold bâton hands.
Indications: small second at 6.
Bracelet: steel; double fold-over clasp.
Also available: with strap; in yellow gold, with leather strap and fold-over clasp or bracelet; in white gold, wit leather strap and fold-over clasp or bracelet.

REVERSO DUETTO   REF. 256.142.752B

Movement: mechanical, manual winding, Jaeger-LeCoultre 865 caliber. Constructed and decorated by hand; 50 hours power reserve, 19 jewels; 21,600 vibrations per hour.
Functions: double hour and minute indication, small second.
Case: 18 kt yellow gold, rectangular, reversible, double-face (with carrier size 38.5 x 23 mm, thickness 10 mm; only case size 27 x 23 mm) with engraved transverse grooves; 32 brilliant-cut diamonds set on the second face; curved sapphire crystal on both sides; yellow-gold crown with a recessed brilliant. Waterproof.

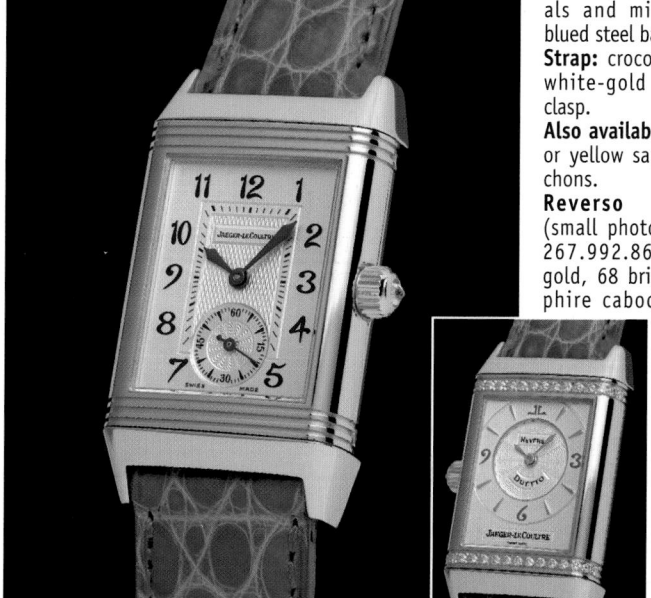

Dial: front dial: solid silver, engine-turned (guilloché) center and zone; printed Eastern style Arabic numerals and minute track; blued steel bâton hands; rear dial: silvered, with engine-turned (guilloché) center with rim, applied yellow-gold pointed markers and Arabic numerals; yellow-gold bâton hands.
Indications: small second at 6.
Strap: crocodile leather; yellow-gold fold-over clasp.
Also available: with bracelet; in white gold, with leather strap and fold-over clasp or bracelet.

REVERSO JOAILLERIE CABOCHONS "PASTEL"   REF. 267.343.001B

Movement: mechanical, manual winding, Jaeger-LeCoultre 846/1 caliber. Finished, assembled and decorated by hand. **Functions:** hour, minute.
Case: 18 kt white gold, rectangular, 116 brilliants (front and rear) and two pink sapphire cabochons, reversible case (with carrier size 33 x 21 mm, thickness 8.5 mm; only case size 22.5 x 21 mm, thickness 7.5 mm); curved sapphire crystal; white-gold crown with pink sapphire cabochon. Waterproof. **Dial:** silvered hour ring, mother-of-pearl in the middle; printed Chinese-style Arabic numerals and minute track; blued steel bâton hands.

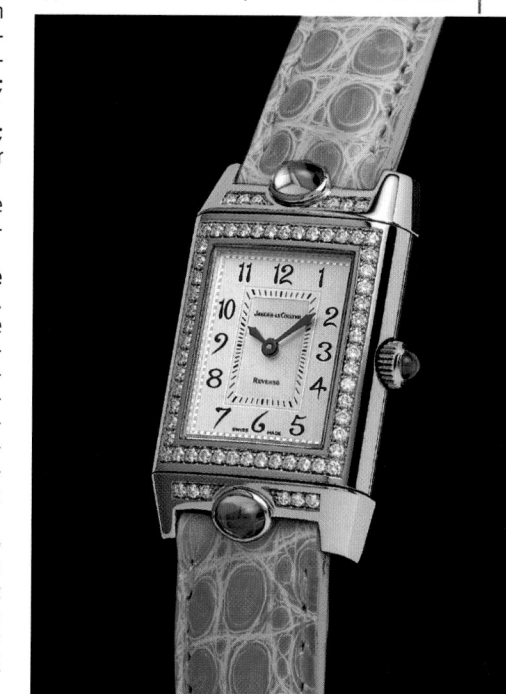

Strap: crocodile leather; white-gold fold-over clasp.
Also available: with blue or yellow sapphire cabochons.
Reverso Joaillerie (small photograph, Ref. 267.992.862V) white gold, 68 brilliants, sapphire cabochons, brilliant markers and applied Arabic numerals, Britain bracelet.
Also available: with quartz movement; in many other jewel versions.

JEAN-MAIRET & GILLMAN

an historical perspective

*W*hile Jean-Mairet & Gillman is just three years old, it draws its references for timepieces and its traditional craftsmanship from a very long line of watchmakers. It was the dream of watchmaker César A. Jean-Mairet, who founded the brand in 1999, to combine his passion for watches with a family tradition of watchmaking, mechanics and science. The result is an exclusive collection of timepieces that pays homage to heritage and classicism.

The Jean-Mairet family established itself in the regions of Neuchâtel at the beginning of the 16th century. Historical references within the watch industry can be traced as far back as 1766, when Jean-Henry Mairet invented a seven-shots pistol and a machine tool for the industry. In the 1800s, Sylvain Jean-Mairet, master horologist, became a maker of lever escapements, precision watches and chronometers. He invented a double stem-wind and perfected several lever devices. In fact, in the Musée d'Horlogerie in Le Locle, there is a carriage watch movement made by Sylvain Jean-Mairet in 1884, which he donated to the museum.

The family heritage continued into the 1900s when watchmaker André Jean-Mairet was appointed chief of workshops at the Ecole d'Horlogerie du Locle. His father had been a teacher of precision timing at the school and this was André's main area of interest. Throughout his career, André won 119 first prizes from the Observatoire de Neuchâtel for his watchmaking and secured two records for his chronometers.

On the other side of César Jean-Mairet's ancestral tree are the Gillmans, who trace their roots back to a family of scientists who traveled the world during the Victorian period. In fact, César's great-great grandparents were Robert Gillman and Caroline Bovet of the famous Bovet of Fleurier.

With such an interesting and involved family heritage, it is no wonder that César would follow in the watchmaking footsteps of his forefathers. His goal was to create an elite brand of watches that would be founded on a philosophy of sobriety and quality. In fact, these are the attributes that mark the spirit of the brand.

387

JEAN-MAIRET & GILLMAN

unveiling

masterpieces

All Jean-Mairet & Gillman timepieces are created in limited editions to ensure exclusivity. They are crafted in the finest Swiss watchmaking tradition, but offer an air of modernity geared toward today's lifestyles. Headquartered in Geneva, all Jean-Mairet & Gillman watches are handmade under the vigilant eye of César.

The first collection unveiled by Jean-Mairet & Gillman is the Grand Voyageur. The watch pays tribute to Clement Gillman, pioneer geographer who spent his life in Africa. He helped lay the foundation for understanding the roots of modern Tanzania. In his honor, the Grand Voyageur timepiece features a second time zone and a mechanical alarm.

Crafted in 18-karat yellow, white or pink gold, or in stainless steel, the Grand Voyageur houses a mechanical automatic-winding Jean-Mairet Gillman caliber 1999 with 31 jewels. The movement was mounted and adjusted by the firm's watchmakers on premises. The second time zone is indicated via a 24-hour display below 12:00. The watch features applied Breguet numerals for elegant appeal. A variety of dial colors is available, includ-

CHRONOLOGY

1999 Persuaded by friends, collectors and watchmakers, César A. Jean-Mairet initiates the development of his own collection of exclusive watches.

2000 The name "Jean-Mairet Gillman" is registered; production is completed on the Grand Voyageur, the brand's first prototype model.

2001 The company continues to develop its collection as both the Grand Voyageur and Seven Days models are perfected and prepared to enter the retail market.

2002 Two new watch models and a new version of the Grand Voyageur are introduced in Basel.

TOP

Pink was recently added to the Grand Voyageur repertoire, creating an appealing watch for women.

RIGHT

The Seven Days watch shown here with a white lacquered dial is also available with a champagne dial and blued applied numerals. It is crafted in stainless steel, 18-karat yellow, white or pink gold and houses a manual-winding movement with seven days' power reserve.

ing white, black and ivory. The company also recently unveiled a chic pink dial for women.

Another collection, the Seven Days watch series, pays homage to the Jean-Mairet ancestors. Its name refers to the seven-shots pistol created by Jean-Mairet; it is on display today in the Landesmuseum in Zurich. A sober, elegant watch, the Seven Days offers easy readability and seven days of power reserve. The watch features an anti-reflective, curved sapphire crystal and is water resistant to 3 atm. As with all Jean-Mairet & Gillman timepieces, it is crafted in each of the three colors of gold and in steel.

Most recently in the works from Jean-Mairet & Gillman are a split-seconds chronograph, and a watch the company refers to as Hora Mundi. Each will be created in limited editions, signed and numbered.

JMG
GENÈVE

LEONARD

an historical perspective

Long revered as one of the finest cutting-edge Parisian fashion houses, Leonard is a brand lavish with panache and savoir-faire. Year after year, its ready-to-wear collections, its haute couture outerwear and accessories garner international acclaim. Now this prestigious house enters the exciting world of watchmaking with scintillating style.

In 1958 Jacques Léonard and Daniel Tribouillard first established the fashion company. The brand was positioned as one of the most exclusive collections and rivaled by only the finest French fashion brands. With its bold prints, specially designed fabrics and its enticing perfumes, the brand quickly gained respect on the international market.

Throughout the ensuing decades, Leonard built boutiques worldwide: in New York, Japan and key European cities, so that today the brand stands firm with 122 boutiques around the world. Accessories of all types have joined the Leonard ranks, including tabletop designs, silk scarves and exotic men's ties.

In 2000, Leonard decided it was time to launch into watchmaking by offering a full licensing agreement to a company that bears its name and whose ambitions match its reputation. The brand turned to financial investors and Ricardo Guadalupe, a long-time watch executive with more than 15 years of experience in the luxury watch field, to establish Leonard S.A. in Geneva.

In 2001, the Leonard watch collection made its debut at the World Watch Clock and Jewelry Fair in Basel. The timepieces unveiled are firmly entrenched in the principles of personality, luxury and perfection—hallmarks of Leonard.

THIS PAGE
TOP LEFT

The Leonard Boutique in Paris.

TOP CENTER

Ricardo Guadalupe, who spent more than a dozen years at firms such as Bvlgari and Blancpain, is now partner and CEO of Leonard S.A.

BOTTOM

The Screen for women in stunning hot pink.

FACING PAGE

These Screens from Leonard are fashioned here in stainless steel and set with diamond brilliants on the case.

LEONARD

unveiling

masterpieces

In the true haute couture nature inherent in all that Leonard creates, the new horological venture, Leonard S.A., is an ambitious program of product, image and strategy that reflects the fashion house's main philosophies.

Leonard S.A. is a newly established Geneva-based company that has been granted the watch license for the creation, development, production and distribution of Leonard watches and accessories. Under the vigilant eye of Ricardo Guadalupe, CEO of Leonard S.A., the new collection focuses strongly on two product lines with very distinct, immediately identifiable looks. Tailored to the sophisticated worldly consumer, Leonard watches exude a contemporary vitality.

Each of the two Leonard collections has its roots in basic geometry. The Screen collection is a series of horizontally rectangular cases, while the Sphere collection is a series of round watches with an elongated look thanks to the curved case-to-bracelet attachment. All Leonard watches are entirely Swiss made and house either self-winding mechanical or quartz movements.

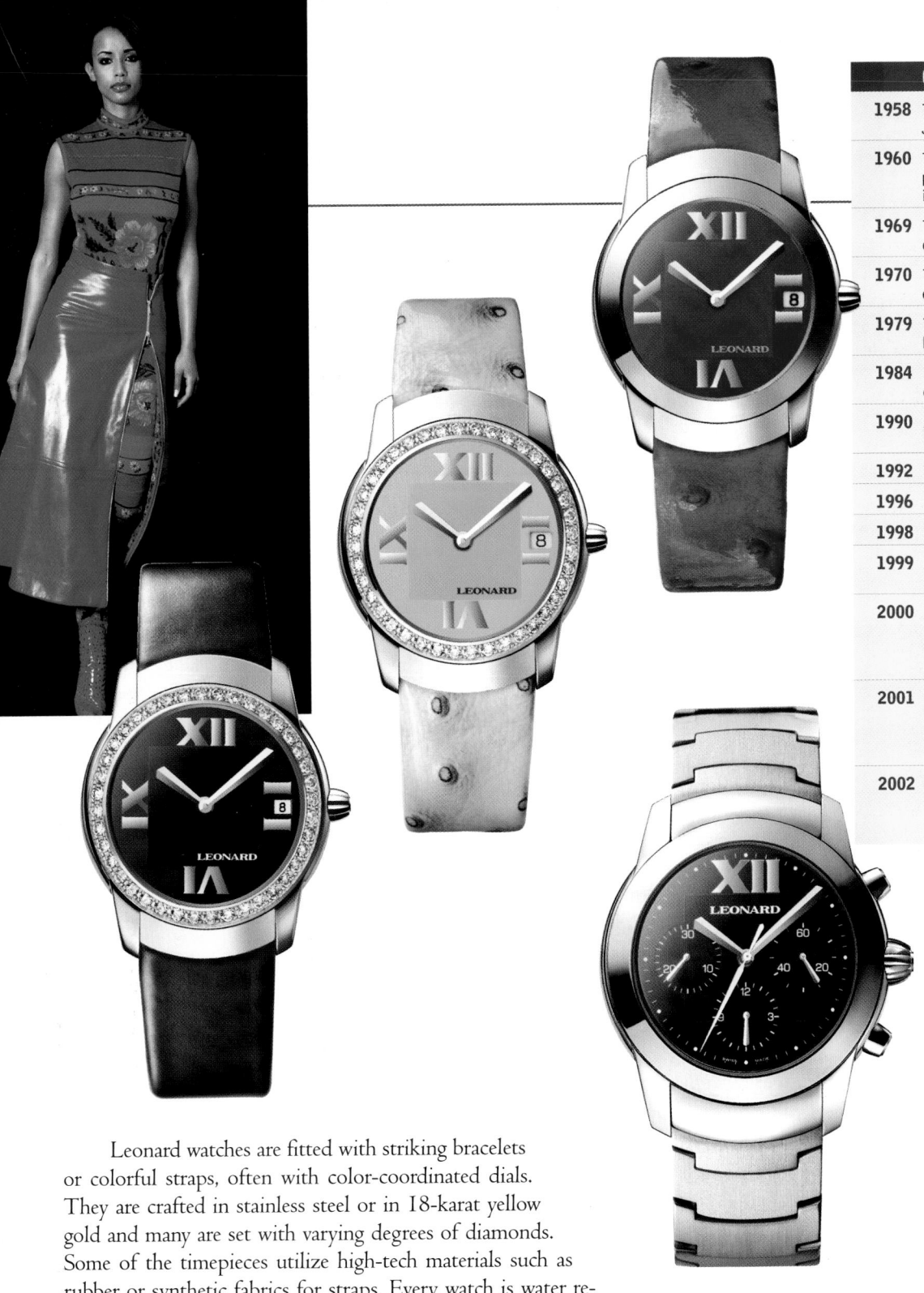

Leonard watches are fitted with striking bracelets or colorful straps, often with color-coordinated dials. They are crafted in stainless steel or in 18-karat yellow gold and many are set with varying degrees of diamonds. Some of the timepieces utilize high-tech materials such as rubber or synthetic fabrics for straps. Every watch is water resistant to 50 meters and comes with a two-year warranty.

Paying strict attention to detail, Leonard S.A. positions its watches at the top tier of the fashion market. Thanks to a past steeped in luxury watchmaking, Ricardo Guadalupe is insistent that every Leonard watch is meticulously executed and impeccably finished.

In keeping with the Leonard character and personality, Leonard S.A. will maintain a very selective distribution policy. In 2001, the brand launched its watches in three markets—Asia, America and Europe—and opened no more than 70 doors internationally. This exclusivity policy will be consistent, as the main objective is to eventually have a total of no more than 500 outlets in these major markets.

LOCMAN

MARINA DI CAMPO

an historical perspective

The Locman brand is synonymous with innovation and cutting-edge style. Locman-adorned wrists of celebrity trendsetters in America and Europe attest to the brand's growing following—and to the company's position as a leader in setting international watch trends.

Whether sparkling with diamonds, glowing with the burnished veneer of exotic woods, or gleaming with powerful aluminum and bold colors, Locman watches, in scarcely more than a decade, have captured the loyalty and shopping passions of a generation of collectors, fashion-conscious aficionados, society icons, and A-List celebrities. Stars such as Catherine Zeta-Jones, Madonna, Oprah Winfrey, Sir Elton John, Sean Combs, Sharon Stone, Michael Jordan, Elizabeth Taylor, Barbara Walters, and Carolina Herrera are among the many who choose to adorn themselves with Locman timepieces.

Founded in 1986 on picture-postcard-charming Elba, off the coast of Italy, Locman made its debut with the incomparable Radica Collection. Thirty-six unusual models featuring bezels fashioned from exotic, 300-year-old wood now comprise the Isola D'Elba and Giannutri Collections. True collectors' watches, the diverse models sport steel or gold embellishments, and feature Swiss ETA movements.

It is arguably the Diamond Aluminum Collection that has entranced consumers and connoisseurs. Introduced in the summer of 2000, the full-sized Diamond Aluminum is the first watch ever to use a featherweight aluminum case set with high-quality diamonds. A watershed of construction innovation, each watch in this unprecedented collection is emblazoned with anywhere from one to four carats of handset, full-cut diamonds of superb quality and clarity. A year-and-a-half later, Locman is still the only diamond on aluminum watch in the world.

THIS PAGE

TOP

The Isle of Elba on the coast of Italy is the seat of creative inspiration where Locman was founded.

BOTTOM

The chronograph, with four carats of diamonds, is worn by men and women. Sharon Stone chose red, while Elizabeth Taylor preferred the watch in all yellow. Sir Elton John wears classic black, Sean Combs has every color and prefers the chronos.

FACING PAGE

The Locman story is one of sporty diamonds for day and play with bold punches of color. The look is oversized, frankly fun and meant to be noticed. The mix and match opportunities of changing the straps alter the look of each watch dramatically.

unveiling creativity

With the unveiling of this totally unique diamond and aluminum watch, Locman captured the attention of the watch world. The Half Pavé features one carat of diamonds on the top of the case. The result is a blaze of sparkle intended to be sporty and fun—a playful watch that quickly has become an international status symbol and the standard for contemporary, cutting-edge watch fashion.

THIS PAGE
CENTER LEFT
Oprah Winfrey wears the red on red Mother of Pearl. Changing the red strap to white or royal blue alligator gives her three different Locman looks.

CENTER
The classic and first model, Half Pavé in black with 1 carat of diamonds.

CENTER RIGHT
A romantic mood for Locman. Powder pinks on mother-of-pearl.

FACING PAGE
TOP
Primary face colors were first used by Locman and are still bestsellers. Half Pavé featured a leather strap with saddle stitching; the Full Pavé all features alligator straps with diamond buckles.

BOTTOM RIGHT
The powerful chronograph features four carats of diamonds. A leather strap with sporty stitching makes this the ultimate diamond sport watch.

So successful was the Half Pavé Diamond Aluminum, that it has spawned several models, each with resounding success. The successor, a Full Pavé model, features a case completely encrusted with diamonds on the top and sides, as well as on the crown. The color-coordinated alligator straps are accented with a diamond buckle. This small, elegant touch is symbolic of the kind of attention that Locman pays to the tiniest of details, a hallmark of this style-conscious company.

Locman rapidly followed the Diamond Aluminum's success with a model featuring an iridescent, mother-of-pearl dial, complemented by lacquered numerals in either primary tones or romantic pastels. Each is a true jewel, with its full-pavé application and alligator strap. This model quickly became the newest must-have for music moguls, celebrities, and fashion trendsetters.

LOCMAN

A testament to Locman's powerhouse of creative talent, for Fall/Winter 2001, the company introduced the White on White collection, escalating the term "winter white" to a new level. A blizzard of pure, snowy perfection, this collection of watches features mother-of-pearl dials and white alligator straps, bedecked with diamond buckles. The flash of colored, lacquered numerals in scarlet, orange, Kelly, turquoise, pink, plum, as well as in classic black, provides the perfect counterpoint to the creamy iridescence of the face. Two carats of pavé diamonds embrace the watch while the chronograph (with black numbers only) features four carats of diamonds.

For the woman who wants the status, presence, and style of a Diamond Aluminum, but prefers a scaled-down version, the company recently introduced its diminutive, Half Size watch. This latest addition to the Locman family of watches is both subtle and bold. It is every bit the showstopper that the full-size model is, but its delicate look is perfect on a smaller wrist. This style, set with two carats of diamonds, is available with either a mother of pearl or lacquered, primary-color face.

T O P

The White on White collection is perfect for day or evening—in snowy or tropical climates it makes a fashion statement. The bright or pastel numbers dazzle against the mother-of-pearl dials all enhanced with white alligator straps.

L E F T

The Total Pavé is the newest Diamond Aluminum. It is all diamonds with no interference from numbers or embellishments to detract from the intense diamond look. It is available in two sizes, including the new Half or petite size.

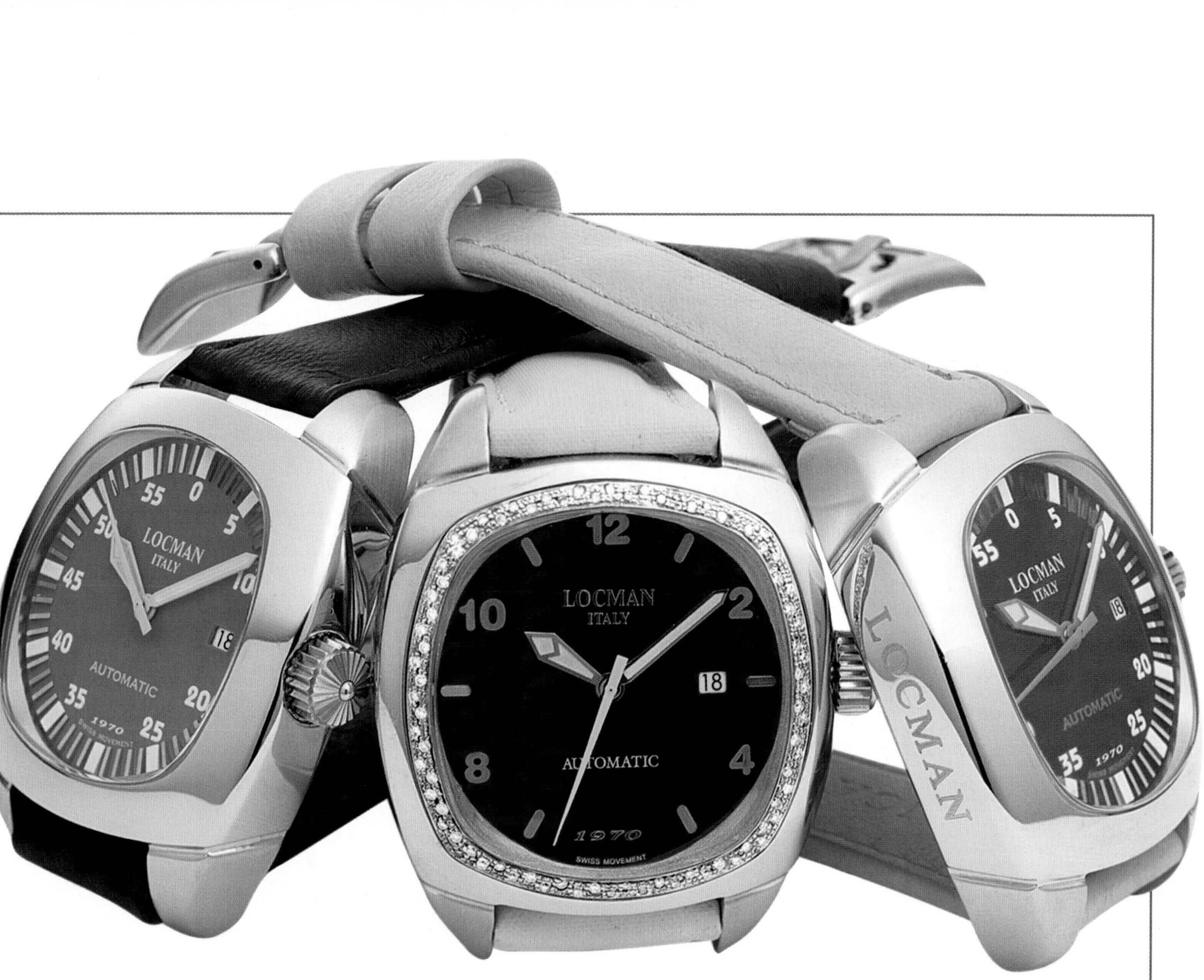

TOP

A selection of classic or primary colors enhance powerful contemporary face designs of the new "1970" with or without a thin diamond bezel. It features automatic movements with skeleton backs.

BELOW

Each bezel of a Radica watch is unique due to the graining of the wood. Enriched in color by wear, the collection now has 36 models which capture the interest of collectors'.

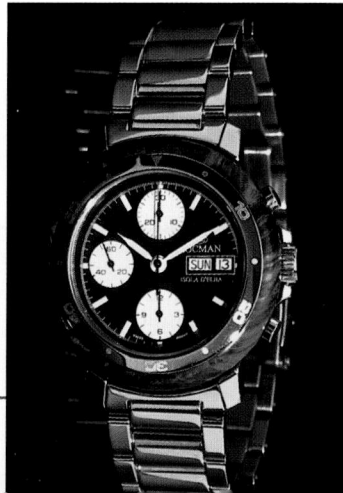

Additionally, this appealing model is available in the Total Pavé for incredible radiance. Introduced for the 2001 holiday season, this model is, without question, the ultimate in black-tie watches: Not only are there diamonds on the top, sides, and crown, but the entire face is also bejeweled—totaling an artful and audacious four carats. Locman has determined how to etch its logo inside the crystal so that the glamour of the pavé face remains uninterrupted by text.

Always at the forefront of fashion, Locman also debuted for Holiday 2001 another impressive and innovative watch. The boldly stylized "1970" is an oversized, cushion-shaped steel timepiece, which gets its power and Italian styling from its impressive, bold size and innovative color combinations. Measuring 57mm x 46mm, it is available as a quartz chronograph or an automatic with a transparent caseback. The color combinations are formidable, in attention-grabbing combinations of royal blue with orange detailing on the face; black with yellow; gray with red; and in more monochromatic combinations. Of special interest is the "1970" model featuring the skillful detailing of a rope of diamonds surrounding the bezel. The contrast between this large watch and the delicate diamond rope is magnificent.

The Locman Company always has a magic touch to change the mundane into the majestic, the prosaic into the praiseworthy. The "1970" is no different and will surely become as highly prized a collectible to the watch connoisseur as Locman's other innovative timepieces in the Diamond Aluminum and Radica Collections.

LOCMAN

MONTECRISTO CHRONOGRAPH   REF. 54GWH

Movement: mechanical, automatic winding, modified Valjoux 7750 caliber, 25 jewels, 28,800 vibrations per hour.
Functions: hour, minute, small second, chronograph with three counters.
Case: 18K yellow gold, two-piece case (Ø 37.5 mm, thickness 14.5 mm); flat sapphire crystal, antireflective on both sides; briarwood bezel; yellow-gold glass-holder bezel; waterproof 20 micron gold-plated steel crown and pushers;

back fastened by 4 screws, and nylon gasket, displaying the movement through a sapphire crystal. Waterproof.
Dial: silvered, engine-turned (guilloché), brushed zones with gold-plated steel rim and hour ring; applied faceted gold-plated steel pointed markers; blued steel Pomme hands.
Indications: minute counter at 3, hour counter at 6, small second at 9, center second, minute track and tachometer scale.
Strap: crocodile leather; gold-plated steel clasp. Limited edition of 1000 numbered pieces.
Also available: with silvered dial and blue counters.

MONTECRISTO AUTOMATIC   REF. 46GWHC

Movement: mechanical, automatic winding.
Functions: hour, minute, second, date.
Case: 18K yellow gold, two-piece case (Ø 37.5 mm, thickness 14.5 mm); flat sapphire crystal, antireflective on both sides, with magnifying glass on the date; briarwood bezel; gold glass-holder bezel; 20 micron gold-plated steel crown with case protection; back fastened by 4 screws, displaying the move-

ment through a sapphire crystal and nylon gasket. Waterproof.
Dial: silvered, engine-turned (guilloché), brushed hour ring with printed Roman numerals and applied gold-plated steel bâton markers; printed minute track; luminescent gold-plated steel bâton hands.
Indications: date at 6. Limited edition of 1000 numbered pieces.
Strap: crocodile leather; gold-plated steel clasp.

ISOLA D'ELBA CHRONOGRAPH   REF. 154GWHYC

Movement: mechanical, automatic winding, Valjoux 7750 caliber, 25 jewels, 28,800 vibrations per hour. **Functions:** hour, minute, small second, day and date, chronograph with three counters.
Case: stainless steel two-piece case (Ø 39.5 mm, thickness 14.4 mm); flat sapphire crystal; briarwood bezel with yellow-gold ring and engraved 5-minute progression; crown with case protection, waterproof; back fastened by 4

screws, with nylon gasket. Water-resistant to 3 atm.
Dial: white, gilded counters decorated with circular beads; applied gold-plated bâton markers; luminescent gold-plated bâton hands.
Indications: date and day at 3, hour counter at 6, small second at 9, minute counter at 12, center second, minute track with divisions for 1/5 of a second, tachometer scale.
Strap: crocodile leather; steel clasp.
Also available: with steel ring; with wholly briarwood bezel: gold-plated or steel case. All versions with white, blue, black or green dial, zones with matching or contrasting colors, crocodile or leather strap or metal bracelet.

ISOLA D'ELBA CHRONOGRAPH   REF. 154BKBB

Movement: mechanical, automatic winding, Valjoux 7750 caliber, 25 jewels, 28,800 vibrations per hour.
Functions: hour, minute, small second, day and date, chronograph with three counters.
Case: stainless steel two-piece brushed case (Ø 39.5 mm, thickness 14.4 mm); flat sapphire crystal; briarwood bezel with steel ring and engraved 5-minute

progression; crown with case protection, waterproof; back fastened by 4 screws, with nylon gasket. Water-resistant to 3 atm.
Dial: black; luminescent bâton markers; luminescent white-enameled steel hands.
Indications: date and day at 3, hour counter at 6, small second at 9, minute counter at 12, center second, minute track with divisions for 1/5 of a second.
Bracelet: polished steel; steel fold-over clasp.
Also available: with gold ring; with wholly briarwood bezel: gold-plated or steel case. All versions with white, blue, black or green dial, counters with matching or contrasting colors, crocodile or leather strap or metal bracelet.

ISOLA D'ELBA AUTOMATIC   REF. 44PGRL

Movement: mechanical, automatic winding, ETA 2824/2 caliber, 11'''1/2, 25 jewels, 28,800 vibrations per hour.
Functions: hour, minute, second, date.
Case: stainless steel two-piece case (Ø 39 mm, thickness 11 mm); antireflective flat mineral crystal, with magnifying glass on the date; briarwood bezel; steel glass-holder bezel; screw-down steel crown with case protection, with double gasket; back fastened by 4 screws, with nylon gasket. Water-resistant to 3 atm.
Dial: dark green; applied steel Roman numerals and cabochon markers; luminescent steel bâton hands; printed minute track and 5-minute progression.
Indications: date at 6.
Strap: leather; steel clasp.
Also available: with blue or ivory dial.

ISOLA D'ELBA AUTOMATIC MEDIUM   REF. 46YWHL

Movement: mechanical, automatic winding, ETA 2824-2 caliber, 11 '''1/2, 25 jewels, 28,800 vibrations per hour.
Functions: hour, minute, second, date.
Case: 10 micron yellow-gold-plated steel, two-piece case (Ø 35.5 mm, thickness 9.5 mm); antireflective flat mineral crystal, with magnifying glass on the date; briarwood bezel; gold-plated steel glass-holder bezel; 20 micron gold-plated steel screw-down crown with case protection, with double gasket; back fastened by 4 screws, with nylon gasket. Water-resistant to 3 atm.
Dial: ivory; applied gold-plated steel Roman numerals and cabochon markers; printed minute track and 5-minute progression; luminescent gold-plated steel bâton hands.
Indications: date at 6.
Strap: leather; 10 micron gold-plated steel clasp.
Also available: with blue or green dial.

GIANNUTRI AUTOMATIC GENTS   REF. 64SLWHC

Movement: mechanical, automatic winding, ETA 2671, 7'''3/4, 25 jewels, 28,800 vibrations per hour.
Functions: hour, minute, date.
Case: stainless steel two-piece rectangular case (size 35.5 x 26.5 mm; thickness 11 mm); lapislasuli inlays fastened with two screws on the case side; curved mineral crystal; steel crown; back fastened by 4 screws, with nylon gasket.
Dial: silvered, engine-turned (guilloché), brushed hour ring; printed round markers and Roman numerals; faceted steel Dauphine hands.
Indications: date at 6.
Strap: crocodile leather; steel clasp.
Also available: with blue engine-turned (guilloché) dial; with briarwood, black onyx or white mother-of-pearl inlays.

GIANNUTRI AUTOMATIC LADY   REF. 66GWHC

Movement: mechanical, automatic winding, ETA 2671, 7'''3/4, 25 jewels, 28,800 vibrations per hour.
Functions: hour, minute, date.
Case: 18K yellow gold, two-piece rectangular case (size 33.5 x 22 mm; thickness 11 mm); curved mineral crystal; briarwood inlays fastened with two screws on the case side; gold-plated steel crown; back fastened by 4 screws, with nylon gasket.
Dial: silvered, engine-turned (guilloché), brushed hour ring; printed round markers and Roman numerals; faceted gold-plated steel Dauphine hands. **Indications:** date at 6.
Strap: crocodile leather; yellow-gold clasp.
Also available: with blue engine-turned (guilloché) dial.

LONGINES

the spirit of time

Longines is a company rich with history and ingenuity. Since its founding in 1832, Longines has played a pioneering role in numerous technological breakthroughs and has been on the cutting edge of creativity. With a past that is mixture of invention and practicality, of modernity and tradition, Longines has enjoyed world-renowned success.

Throughout the 19th and 20th centuries, Longines regularly accrued prizes and awards at international exhibitions. In fact, the brand holds 10 first prize placements and 28 gold medals. Longines was a leader in the creation of extra-flat movements and in the concept of mechanical wristwatches.

As early as 1900, Longines had developed chronographs for timing competitive events, and led the way to improving its automatic timing systems. The reliability of the brand made it a most-coveted watch by athletes and explorers. Longines watches accompanied Amundsen, Admiral Byrd and others on their expeditions. In 1927 when Charles Lindbergh crossed the Atlantic Ocean in his solo non-stop flight from New York to Paris, Longines officially timed the trip. Later, the brand created Lindbergh's rendition of a flight watch for pilots, called the Hour Angle watch.

Decades later, Longines was recognized for its record-breaking precision with chronometer wristwatches. The brand was among the first to enter into the electronic age with miniaturized movements, and pioneered into the world of quartz-powered watches as early as 1969. The brand consistently remained on the forefront of technology in events timing and, to this day, remains intimately involved in tracking time for competitive sports.

Longines also remains committed to creating top-of-the-line timepieces. The year 2001, in fact, witnessed Longines's creation of its 30-millionth watch and the unveiling of a commemorative collection

TOP LEFT
The DolceVita Diamond series is created in the three different colors of gold and demonstrates Longines's prowess in jeweled watches.

TOP RIGHT
Varying degrees of Top Wesselton VVS diamonds bedeck the DolceVita diamond collection.

BOTTOM
Longines DolceVita Chronograph.

to mark the occasion. Called the 30 Millionth Longines Watch, the timepiece is created in a limited series of 990 pieces: 390 in yellow gold; 300 in pink gold; and 300 in white gold.

Classically elegant in its design appeal, the watch houses the self-winding Longines 990 caliber—the last movement that the firm designed and built (in 1977). For a decade, Longines produced this efficient, stable movement. In the late 1980s, the L990 caliber was purchased by Nouvelle Lémania—movement specialists who upgraded the design and continue to produce it today. The L990 is a 25-jeweled movement and offers 38 hours of power reserve.

This past year Longines also added a significant number of new models to its highly successful DolceVita Collection. This series, unveiled several years ago, was inspired by a watch originally produced by the company in 1912. Its rounded rectangular case is at once striking and thoroughly modern. The 2001 introductions are all diamond adorned.

Aptly named the DolceVita Diamond Collection, the series offers a broad choice of gold colors, strap colors, case shapes and sizes. Some models feature diamond cases, bezels and case-to-bracelet attachments, while other models feature diamonds all the way through the bracelet. In all, there are five degrees of settings and each uses only Top Wesselton VVS diamonds. There are two case shapes—square and rectangular— and each is offered in four sizes: mini ladies', ladies', medium and gents'. The watches are produced in all three colors of gold and are available with either supple, precious-metal link bracelets or in a full range of leather strap colors.

The introduction of this series is a complement to the brand's technical timepieces and demonstrates Longines's talent for creating luxurious jeweled watches.

OFFICINE PANERAI

precision at its finest

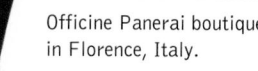

This Italian brand, famous for its oversized and extremely precise sports watches, was founded in Florence in 1860. Founder Guido Panerai specialized in creating high-precision instruments, and in a short time the brand had been granted several patents in the timekeeping and optics fields.

In the early years of the 20th century, Panerai set up a watchmaking school in its workshops in Florence for the repair and modification of timepieces. In an vital move, Panerai went on to cultivate a relationship with the Royal Italian Navy by supplying precision pocket stopwatches specifically designed for military use. During the First World War, Panerai created not just timepieces for the military, but also aiming-sights for launching torpedoes and various timers used in anti-ship mines.

In 1936, the brand unveiled its first prototype dive watch. Called the Radiomir Panerai, it was one of the first watches to use a protective devise on the crown to assure water resistance. In the Second World War, Panerai supplied Radiomir watches to the Royal Italian Navy, along with compasses and instruments for aiming, lighting and signaling.

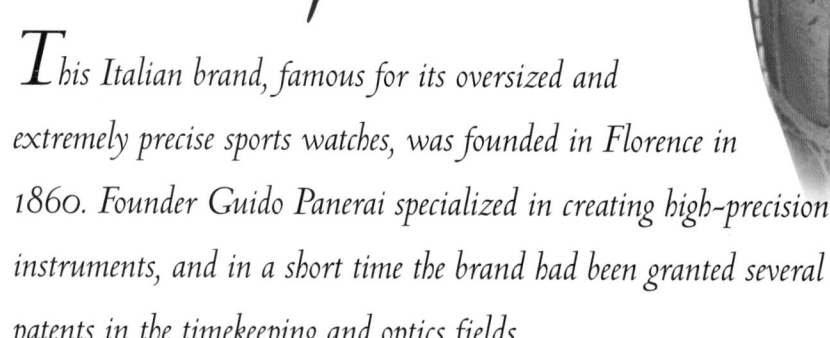

TOP LEFT

Officine Panerai boutique in Florence, Italy.

TOP RIGHT

The Panerai Luminor Amagnetic watch is crafted in titanium and features an inner iron case to protect it from magnetic fields.

BOTTOM LEFT

The Luminor Marina Automatic is crafted in steel. The 44mm case houses a COSC-certified automatic mechanical movement.

BOTTOM CENTER

This Luminor Submersible watch was developed in accordance with the NIHS (Normes de L'Industrie Horlogere Suisse, Standards of the Swiss Watchmaking Industry) standards relating to divers' watches.

BOTTOM RIGHT

Housed in Panerai's famed oversized 44mm case, the Luminor Power Reserve watch is crafted in brushed titanium and offers a power reserve of 42 hours.

Panerai's reputation for creating professional, high-precision timepieces that could endure extreme situations made the brand the reference standard for the Navy's divers and frogmen.

For more than 50 years, Panerai's watch production was reserved exclusively for the commandos of the Royal Italian Navy. The brand's watches first became available to the civilian market in 1993 when limited editions of the Luminor were created. In 1997, Officine Panerai was purchased by the Richemont Group, which was committed to continuing the brand's legacy by producing timekeeping instruments geared for professional use.

Today, Panerai's successful lines combine technical innovation with bold, oversized styling designed for use underwater. Its collection revolves around two distinct lines: the Luminor and the Radiomir. In 2001, Officine Panerai added numerous models to both of these series. As an extraordinary special edition of the Luminor, Panerai launched the Luminor Amagnetic 44mm watch. Produced in titanium, the watch is fitted with a special inner casing that protects the movement from the effects of external magnetic fields. This technological development allows the watch to be used in the presence of extreme gravitational influence. The watch is water resistant to 300 meters and features a unidirectional rotating bezel with compass indications.

The Luminor Marina Automatic 44mm watch houses an exclusive automatic mechanical movement. A certified chronometer, the new timepiece is offered in a brushed stainless steel version or in an exclusive titanium and steel version with bracelet. Only 3,000 pieces of the steel watch are being produced annually, and 1,000 of the titanium and steel version will be created annually. Panerai also unveiled two new Luminor Submersibles: a 300-meter water-resistant titanium and steel bracelet model created in a numbered edition of 500 pieces; and a 1,000-meter water-resistant steel Luminor Submersible with helium escape valve and automatic movement. Officine Panerai also unveiled a Luminor GMT and Power Reserve watch. Each model is crafted in steel and titanium with an alligator strap.

In its Radiomir collection, Panerai presented a GMT/Alarm (in a 42mm steel case and housing an automatic movement) watch and a Chrono Foudroyante (a split-seconds chronograph watch housed in a 42mm steel case). Additionally, the Radiomir Independent made its debut. This 18-karat white-gold watch is being produced in a unique limited edition of 160 numbered pieces. A jumping-seconds watch, the Independent is water resistant to 100 meters and features a transparent sapphire crystal caseback.

OMEGA

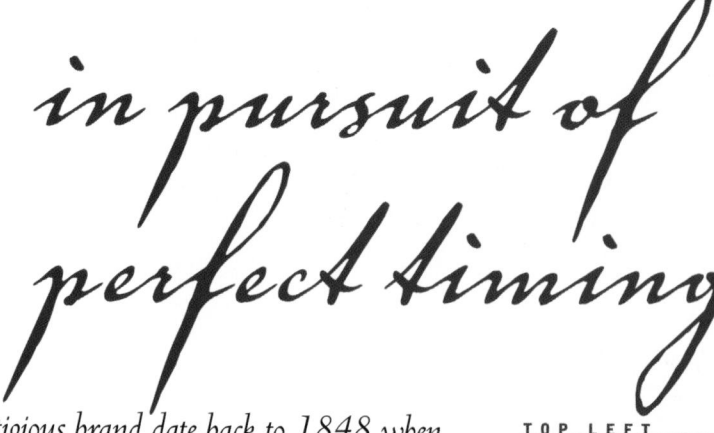

in pursuit of perfect timing

*T*he roots of this prestigious brand date back to 1848 when 23-year-old Louis Brandt founded the firm in La Chaux-de-Fonds. It was his dream to create precision timepieces whose technical prowess surpassed most other brands. Swiftly, the company rose to the challenge its founding father had set: Omega was among the first to create chronographs and chronometers.

By 1900, Omega had garnered international accolades for the technical excellence of its timepieces, as well as for design and craftsmanship. One of the first to perfect time measurement, Omega timed Olympic Games early in the century and journeyed to the surface of the moon on the wrist of Buzz Aldrin in the 1960s. Indeed, Omega has been, and continues to be, intimately involved in the U.S. space program, regularly outfitting astronauts with cutting-edge technology on the wrist.

Additionally, Omega has delved into other sports arenas, from auto racing to yacht racing, including timing the America's Cup. In 2001, Omega was the official sponsor of the "blakexpeditions" venture to the Antarctic Peninsula. Omega's Seamaster Diver 300m automatic watch accompanied divers on missions to study the water during this Antarctic expedition.

Also in 2001, Omega unveiled a wealth of new product—further defining each of its distinct watch collections for men and women. Acknowledging its history and traditional values, Omega selected 2001 to launch the Omega Museum Collection. Each year, the brand will unveil a limited-edition watch based on a design from its archives. The 2001 Museum Collection watch is a new edition of a 1938 pilot's watch. Housing a self-winding chronometer, the watch features an extra-wide leather strap that pays tribute to the early pilot habits of wearing the watch over the flight suit.

TOP LEFT
The blakexpeditions, enroute to the Antarctica.

LEFT CENTER
The Seamaster Diver 300m automatic watch was used on the blakexpeditions to the Antarctic.

BOTTOM LEFT
The 2001 Omega Museum watch is fashioned after a 1938 pilot's watch.

BOTTOM RIGHT
The Omega Museum Collection 2002 watch is crafted in 18-karat pink gold and is based on a 1951 design.

The 2002 Museum Collection watch is the first-ever Omega multiple calendar complications watch. This watch, originally called the Cosmic, was first launched in 1947 in a round rendition and was later released in a square case. The square version is now replicated in 18-karat pink gold. The square watch displays the time, date, and day of week, month and moonphase. Production is limited to 1,951 units—for the year that the square Cosmic made its debut.

In its Speedmaster collection, Omega unveiled the Broad Arrow collection, which draws its inspiration from the very first Speedmaster model. It features an exclusive Omega chronograph movement, the caliber 3303. This movement was developed by Omega and produced exclusively for the brand by Frédéric Piguet. It is a self-winding COSC-certified chronometer movement with column-wheel chronograph mechanism. The Broad Arrow is named not for the movement, but for the shape of the hands that grace the dial. The arrowhead hour hand was used on the first Speedmaster, and has since been used on the Moonphase models.

For an elegant twist, Omega also unveiled a Speedmaster Automatic with diamond bezel in the year 2001 in order to fulfill the wishes of its female clientele. Additionally, Omega unveiled the Constellation Quadra collection. Created in gold with either pastel straps or bracelets, this seductive square watch features varying degrees of diamonds on the case and dial. This successful design was followed by the launch of the Omega Constellation Bangle watch in machette shape. This chic timepiece, bedecked in diamonds, offers a dynamic, arched design that ensures a perfect fit.

In the My Choice collection, which pays tribute to Omega's ambassador, Cindy Crawford, a Ladies Mini watch appeared on the scene. Created in a limited edition of just 999 pieces, the 18-karat gold and steel watch features a diamond bezel and diamond markers for elegant beauty.

Indeed, the list of new introductions continues as Omega marches on in its pursuit of technical perfection and aesthetic bliss.

PARMIGIANI FLEURIER

an historical perspective

Parmigiani Fleurier is a brand short in history but long in tradition. For more than 25 years, master watchmaker Michel Parmigiani has garnered international recognition for his art of creating and restoring timepieces. Parmigiani is a man dedicated to perfection and to creating timepieces that herald Swiss watchmaking heritage.

THIS PAGE
TOP

Master Watchmaker, Michel Parmigiani.

BOTTOM

Parmigiani restored this Breguet Carriage Clock, originally crafted in 1821.

FACING PAGE

The all-new Forma watch houses the Parmigiani automatic Caliber 331 with 32 jewels and consisting of 186 individual parts.

In fact, Parmigiani's passion for horology has made him a man of multiple talents. He deftly and artfully restores antique watches and clocks for museums and private collectors. For decades, he masterfully engineered some of the finest timepieces for distinguished watch houses. And, for the past seven years, he has created his own Parmigiani Fleurier masterpieces.

His collections are concise and answer to the call of classic elegance. Parmigiani offers mechanical timepieces for men and women that run the gamut from timeless beauty to sport chic, from high-jeweled to meticulously complicated. Indeed, Parmigiani's roots are linked with the great traditions of watchmaking—thereby making complications his forte.

In the famed Swiss watchmaking town of Fleurier—at the Manufacture of Parmigiani Mesure et Art du Temps (The Measurement of Art and Time)—the finest artisans, engravers, jewelers and craftsmen band together to produce Parmigiani's works of art. Only about 1,000 Parmigiani timepieces are made per year, each to incredibly exacting standards of perfection. Under Parmigiani's vigilant eye, every watch is entirely hand made and finished. In fact, it takes a minimum of 400 hours of labor for a master watchmaker to assemble a Parmigiani watch. The more complicated pieces, of course, take longer to complete.

Indeed, by seeking the heritage of the land and combining it with cutting-edge technology and innovative design, Parmigiani continually produces timepieces that set the benchmark.

PARMIGIANI FLEURIER

unveiling

masterpieces

Parmigiani's deep respect for the past inspires creativity and feeds the drive to uphold the exceptional standards of craftsmanship to which the brand adheres. Had Parmigiani not spent so many countless hours restoring and studying the most precious timepieces of the world, perhaps he would not have come to develop the necessary appreciation to produce the meticulous collection that today bears his name.

In his restoration work, Parmigiani developed an understanding of how the great watchmakers of the past overcame the technological restrictions of the time period with ingenious solutions. Impressed and inspired, Parmigiani resolved to create a line devoted to the same degree of innovation. His determination is what has brought the brand international recognition. Every Parmigiani Fleurier watch is immediately recognizable as a masterpiece of unparalleled distinction.

Most recently, Parmigiani unveiled an important new movement: the automatic winding mechanical Caliber 331. This is the second Parmigiani signature movement (the first was a hand-wound mechanical 8-day movement, created two years ago) to be produced. The Caliber 331 Automatic has a power reserve of 55 hours that is stored by two spring barrels arranged in series. While the watch is worn for one hour, the mechanism accumulates power reserve of two hours.

The Caliber 331 houses 32 jewels and consists of 186 individual parts. It offers hours, minutes, seconds and date function. The bridges are hand chamfered and decorated with the Côtes de Genève seal. It is Parmigiani's intention to create the new caliber in nickel silver alloy rather than in brass, and to produce it in limited quantities.

To launch the new movement, an all-new case was designed. The timepiece is called Forma. In creating Forma for men and women, Parmigiani remained faithful to his observation of nature. The watch is composed completely of curves so as to be harmonious to the eye. Designed as a modern application of the principles of proportion known to the ancient Greeks, the Forma is reminiscent of a curved tortoise shell. Its case attachments are derived from a spiral and its crystal is shaped into a spherical sapphire dome. The curved sides of the case are derived from a curve generated by the mathematical function of the parabola.

Created in 18-karat pink, yellow or white gold, the watch features an 18-karat gold black dial with only the numeral 12. A circular chapter ring is used to indicate the time with hour and minute markers. There is also a version available with a silvered gold dial. The men's model is the first to be fitted with the Caliber 331.

The ladies' Forma is fitted with the Frédéric Piguet FP 6.15 automatic movement with platinum oscillating weight. It features a flat sapphire crystal back and is water resistant to 30 meters. It is fitted with a striking 18-karat gold bracelet that offers integrated beauty and distinction.

handcrafting time

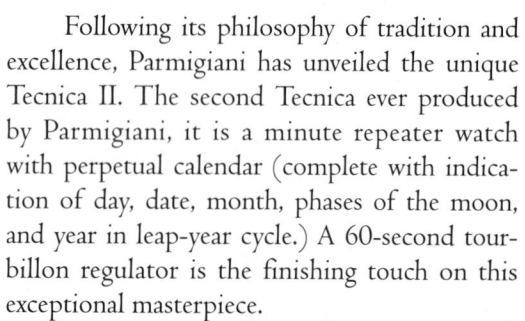

Following its philosophy of tradition and excellence, Parmigiani has unveiled the unique Tecnica II. The second Tecnica ever produced by Parmigiani, it is a minute repeater watch with perpetual calendar (complete with indication of day, date, month, phases of the moon, and year in leap-year cycle.) A 60-second tourbillon regulator is the finishing touch on this exceptional masterpiece.

The movement is intricately engraved in the form of an egg surrounded by the Greek frieze. The dial is solid 18-karat gold with an opening to view the tourbillon at 6:00. On the small month dial at 9:00, a window indicates the status reached in the leap-year cycle. The Tecnica II is housed in a platinum case and fitted with a hinged double back, on which the Greek decoration is engraved and covered with periwinkle-blue translucent enamel.

Parmigiani recognizes the needs of today's time connoisseur and so has also unveiled

FACING PAGE
BOTTOM

Striking in its clean lines and elegant form, the Toric GMT offers indication of hours, minutes sand second time zone.

THIS PAGE
TOP LEFT

Crafted in 18-karat white gold, the Toric Chronograph Rattrapante 2001 is being produced in a limited edition of 10 pieces.

RIGHT

The Basica Joaillerie is a stunning work of art with 229 rose or blue sapphires decorating the case.

the Toric GMT. A men's watch in 18-karat gold, the GMT is an automatic-wind watch that indicates hours and minutes as well as second time zone. It is at once classic and elegant. Also in the Toric collection is the Chronograph Rattrapante 2001. Created in 18-karat white gold only, the split-seconds chronograph is being made in a limited edition of 10 pieces. The manual-wind movement offers indication of hours, minutes and seconds, as well as chronograph counters for seconds, 30-minute counter and 12-hour counter. This watch features a pink salmon 18-karat gold dial and Parmigiani signature javelin-style hands in blued steel.

Women play an important role for Parmigiani, and this year the watchmaker paid homage to them with the striking Basica Joaillerie watch. Crafted in 18-karat white gold and accented in either pink or blue, the watch is set with 229 sapphires on the case. The mother-of-pearl dial features color-coordinated sapphire markers. A striking pastel-hued strap accents the piece. And, as with all of Parmigiani's masterpieces, the bridges are polished and decorated with the Côtes de Genève seal.

PARMIGIANI FLEURIER

TORIC CHRONOGRAPH RATTRAPANTE EDITION 2001

Movement: mechanical, manual winding, 27101 caliber (Venus 175 caliber base, 14'''), 21 jewels, balance with timing screws, spring with Phillips curves, 18,000 vph. Hand-chamfered bridges and mechanism, rhodium plated and Côtes de Genève finished. **Functions:** hour, minute, small second, split-second chronograph with 3 counters.
Case: 18 kt white gold, three-piece case (Ø 40 mm, thickness 14.80 mm);

bezel with double hand-engraved knurling; curved sapphire crystal; white gold crown with coaxial splitting pusher and ogival pushers; snap-on case back with engraved limited series number, displaying the movement through a sapphire crystal. Water-resistant to 3 atm.
Dial: solid gold, pink salmon; applied gold-plated points and Arabic numeral 12; blued steel Javeline hands. **Indications:** minute counter at 3, hour counter at 6, small second at 9, center second and split-second counters, minute track with divisions for 1/5 of a second, tachometer scale.
Strap: alligator leather; white gold tongue clasp. Series limited to 10 numbered pieces.

TORIC CHRONOGRAPH — REF. PF 000088/C00902

Movement: mechanical, automatic winding, caliber 19001, derived from Zenith El Primero 400 (13'''), 31 jewels, 36.000 vibrations per hour (vph); regulator with off-center screw adjustment; 22K pink gold rotor engraved and personalized by hand. Mounted by hand, beveled, decorated by hand with Côtes de Genève pattern. **Functions:** hour, minute, small second, date, chronograph with 3 counters.
Case: platinum, three-piece case (Ø 40 mm, thickness 12.5 mm); bezel with dou-

ble hand-engraved knurling; curved sapphire crystal; natural sapphire cabochon white gold crown; oval pushers; snap-on case back, knurled, displaying the movement through a sapphire crystal. Water-resistant to 3 atm. **Dial:** solid gold, eggshell, engine turned (guilloché) with barleycorn pattern; printed Roman numerals and minute track; applied white gold logo; white gold Javeline hands. **Indications:** white gold bordered date at 1:30, minute counter at 3, hour counter at 6, small second at 9, center second counter, minute track with divisions for 1/5 of a second.
Strap: crocodile leather; platinum tongue clasp.
Also available: yellow, pink or white gold. All available with slate-grey, anthracite or eggshell dial.

TORIC CHRONOGRAPH — REF. PF 000091/C00922

All the Parmigiani Fleurier watches - in men's or lady's versions, time only or complicated - have certain common technical and aesthetic features: bezel with simple or double knurling, the brand name inserted in an oval tag, elliptic lugs, Javelin type hands, a natural sapphire cabochon on the crown, pushers always of the same material as the case and the whole showing a quality without compromises. Parmigiani chose their movements very accurately - regardless if they

are rare antique calibers or modern and sophisticated mechanisms - as is the case of the El Primero high frequency device used for the automatic chronograph.
The photograph shows the version with yellow gold case and black dial, with screen-printed Roman numerals.

TORIC CHRONOGRAPH — REF. PF 000090/C00921

Movement: mechanical, automatic winding, caliber 19001, derived from Zenith El Primero 400 (13'''), 31 jewels, 36.000 vibrations per hour (vph); regulator with off-center screw adjustment; 22K pink gold rotor engraved and personalized by hand. Mounted by hand, beveled, decorated by hand with Côtes de Genève pattern. **Functions:** hour, minute, small second, date, chronograph with 3 counters. **Case:** 18 kt yellow gold, three-piece case (Ø 40 mm, thickness 12.5 mm); bezel with double

hand-engraved knurling; curved sapphire crystal; natural sapphire cabochon yellow gold crown; oval pushers; snap-on case back, knurled, displaying the movement through a sapphire crystal. Water-resistant to 3 atm. **Dial:** solid gold, eggshell, engine turned (guilloché) with barleycorn pattern; printed Roman numerals and minute track; applied yellow gold logo; yellow gold Javeline hands. **Indications:** yellow gold bordered date at 1:30, minute counter at 3, hour counter at 6, small second at 9, center second counter, minute track with divisions for 1/5 of a second. **Strap:** crocodile leather; yellow gold tongue clasp. **Also available:** platinum, yellow, pink or white gold. All available with slate-grey, anthracite or eggshell dial.

TORIC WESTMINSTER   REF. PF004184

Movement: mechanical, manual winding, with tourbillon device, 25501 caliber (G.P. Manufacture base), 42 jewels, balance wheel with timing screws, 21,600 vph, 85 hours power reserve. Hand-chamfered bridges and mechanism, rhodium plated and Côtes de Genève finished. **Functions:** hour, minute, second time-zone time, 24 hours, minute repeater, carillon. **Case:** 18 kt pink gold, three-piece case (Ø 42 mm, thickness 15 mm); bezel with hand-engraved double

knurling; curved sapphire crystal; pink gold crown with a natural sapphire cabochon; pusher for the independent adjustment of the second time-zone time at 2, repeater slide on the middle (Westminster Melody, chimes hours, quarters and minutes on four gongs by means of four strike-hammers); case back fastened by 6 pink gold screws, displaying the movement through a sapphire crystal. Wr. to 3 atm. **Dial:** made up by the pillar-plate of the movement, pink gold flange with printed minute track; blued steel Javeline hands. **Indications:** second time-zone time with independent adjustment at 2. **Strap:** crocodile leather; pink gold tongue clasp. **Also available:** in white gold.

TORIC GMT   REF. PF004578

Movement: automatic, 13301 caliber (Lemania 8815 caliber base), 11'''1/2, 38 hours autonomy, 25 jewels, 28,800 vph; balance-spring regulator system with micrometer adjustment; 22 kt pink gold rotor, engine turned (guilloché), engraved and personalized by hand. Mounted and finished by hand, rhodium plated, beveled, hand-decorated with Côtes de Genève pattern. **Functions:** hour, minute, second time-zone time.

Case: 18 kt pink gold (46 grams), three-piece case (Ø 36.20 mm, thickness 8 mm); bezel with double hand-engraved knurling; curved sapphire crystal; pink gold crown with natural sapphire cabochon; snap-on case back, knurled, displaying the movement through a sapphire crystal. Water-resistant to 3 atm.

Dial: solid gold, azure silvered, matte finish, decorated with circular beads; silvered hour ring with applied white-gold cabochon markers; printed minute track; blued steel skeleton Delta Parmigiani hands. **Indications:** second time-zone 24-hour jumping time. **Strap:** alligator leather; pink gold tongue clasp. **Also available:** in yellow gold; in white gold.

TORIC GMT   REF. PF004577

Movement: automatic, 13301 caliber (Lemania 8815 caliber base), 11'''1/2, 38 hours autonomy, 25 jewels, 28,800 vph; balance-spring regulator system with micrometer adjustment; 22 kt pink gold rotor, engine turned (guilloché), engraved and personalized by hand. Mounted and finished by hand, rhodium plated, beveled, hand-decorated with Côtes de Genève pattern. **Functions:** hour, minute, second time-zone time.

Case: 18 kt yellow gold (46 grams), three-piece case (Ø 36.20 mm, thickness 8 mm); bezel with double hand-engraved knurling; curved sapphire crystal; yellow gold crown with natural sapphire cabochon; snap-on case back, knurled, displaying the movement through a sapphire crystal. Water-resistant to 3 atm.

Dial: solid gold, azure silvered, matte finish, decorated with circular beads; silvered hour ring with applied white-gold cabochon markers; printed minute track; blued steel skeleton Delta Parmigiani hands. **Indications:** second time-zone 24-hour jumping time. **Strap:** alligator leather; yellow gold tongue clasp. **Also available:** in pink gold; in white gold.

TORIC GMT   REF. PF004579

Movement: automatic, 13301 caliber (Lemania 8815 caliber base), 11'''1/2, 38 hours autonomy, 25 jewels, 28,800 vph; balance-spring regulator system with micrometer adjustment; 22 kt pink gold rotor, engine turned (guilloché), engraved and personalized by hand. Mounted and finished by hand, rhodium plated, beveled, hand-decorated with Côtes de Genève pattern. **Functions:** hour, minute, second time-zone time.

Case: 18 kt white gold (46 grams), three-piece case (Ø 36.20 mm, thickness 8 mm); bezel with double hand-engraved knurling; curved sapphire crystal; white gold crown with natural sapphire cabochon; snap-on case back, knurled, displaying the movement through a sapphire crystal. Water-resistant to 3 atm.

Dial: solid gold, azure silvered, matte finish, decorated with circular beads; silvered hour ring with applied white-gold cabochon markers; printed minute track; blued steel skeleton Delta Parmigiani hands. **Indications:** second time-zone 24-hour jumping time. **Strap:** alligator leather; white gold tongue clasp. **Also available:** in pink gold; in yellow gold.

PARMIGIANI FLEURIER

CLASSIC QUANTIEME — REF. PF004570

Movement: mechanical, automatic winding, 13301 caliber (Lemania 8815 caliber base), 11'''1/2, 38 hours autonomy, 25 jewels, 28,800 vph; balance-spring regulator system with micrometer adjustment; 22 kt pink gold rotor, engraved and personalized by hand. Mounted and finished by hand, rhodium plated, beveled, beveled, hand-decorated with Côtes de Genève pattern. **Functions:** hour, minute, center second, date. **Case:** 18 kt pink gold (45 grams), three-piece case (Ø 36

mm, thickness 8.3 mm); knurled bezel, hand-engraved; curved sapphire crystal; pink gold crown with a natural sapphire cabochon; snap-on case back, knurled, displaying the movement through a sapphire crystal. Water-resistant to 3 atm. **Dial:** solid gold, white; blue printed Arabic numerals and minute track; blued steel Javeline hands. **Indications:** white-gold bordered date at 3. **Strap:** crocodile leather; pink-gold clasp. **Also available:** in yellow gold; in white gold. Slate-gray or eggshell dial, engine-turned (guilloché) with barleycorn pattern or porcelainized white, two applied white or pink gold cabochon markers and logo; in yellow or pink gold; in white gold; optional bezel with 60 brilliants.

CLASSIC QUANTIEME — REF. PF004565

Movement: mechanical, automatic winding, 13301 caliber (Lemania 8815 caliber base), 11'''1/2, 38 hours autonomy, 25 jewels, 28,800 vph; balance-spring regulator system with micrometer adjustment; 22 kt pink gold rotor, engraved and personalized by hand. Mounted and finished by hand, rhodium plated, beveled, hand-decorated with Côtes de Genève pattern. **Functions:** hour, minute, center second, date. **Case:** 18 kt yellow gold (45 grams), three-piece case (Ø 36.20 mm,

thickness 8.30 mm); knurled bezel, hand-engraved; curved sapphire crystal; yellow gold crown with a natural sapphire cabochon; snap-on case back, knurled, displaying the movement through a sapphire crystal. Water-resistant to 3 atm. **Dial:** solid gold, white; blue printed Arabic numerals and minute track; blued steel Javeline hands. **Indications:** white-gold bordered date at 3. **Strap:** alligator leather; yellow-gold clasp. **Also available:** in rose gold; in white gold. Slate-gray or eggshell dial, engine-turned (guilloché) with barleycorn pattern or porcelainized white, two applied white or pink gold cabochon markers and logo; in yellow or pink gold; in white gold; optional bezel with 60 brilliants.

CLASSIC QUANTIEME — REF. PF004571

Movement: mechanical, automatic winding, 13301 caliber (Lemania 8815 caliber base), 11'''1/2, 38 hours autonomy, 25 jewels, 28,800 vph; balance-spring regulator system with micrometer adjustment; 22 kt pink gold rotor, engraved and personalized by hand. Mounted and finished by hand, rhodium plated, beveled, hand-decorated with Côtes de Genève pattern. **Functions:** hour, minute, center second, date. **Case:** 18 kt white gold (45 grams), three-piece case (Ø 36.20 mm,

thickness 8.30 mm); knurled bezel, hand-engraved; curved sapphire crystal; white gold crown with a natural sapphire cabochon; snap-on case back, knurled, displaying the movement through a sapphire crystal. Water-resistant to 3 atm. **Dial:** solid gold, white; blue printed Arabic numerals and minute track; blued steel Javeline hands. **Indications:** white-gold bordered date at 3. **Strap:** alligator leather; yellow-gold clasp. **Also available:** in rose or yellow gold. Slate-grey or eggshell dial, engine-turned (guilloché) with barleycorn pattern or porcelainized white, two applied white or pink gold cabochon markers and logo; in yellow or pink gold; in white gold; optional bezel with 60 brilliants.

TORIC — REF. PF000060/C00700

Movement: mechanical, automatic winding, 13301 caliber (Lemania 8815 caliber base), 11'''1/2, 25 jewels, 28,800 vph; balance-spring regulator system with micrometer adjustment; 22 kt pink gold rotor, engraved and personalized by hand. Mounted by hand, rhodium plated, beveled, hand-decorated with Côtes de Genève pattern. **Functions:** hour, minute, second, date. **Case:** platinum 950, three-piece case (Ø 40 mm, thickness 8.8 mm); bezel with

double hand-engraved knurling; curved sapphire crystal; white gold crown with natural sapphire cabochon; snap-on case back, knurled, displaying the movement through a sapphire crystal. Water-resistant to 3 atm. **Dial:** solid gold, engine turned (guilloché) with barleycorn pattern, matt slate-grey; applied white gold hour ring with printed Roman numerals; applied white gold logo; printed minute track; white gold Javeline hands (second hand in blued steel). **Indications:** date at 3. **Strap:** crocodile leather; white gold buckle. **Also available:** in yellow gold; in white gold; in platinum. All with slate-grey or eggshell dial.

IONICA "8 DAYS" REF. PF 000340/C02041

Movement: mechanical, manual winding, manufacture caliber 110 (13'''x10'''), tonneau-curved, with power reserve of 8 days, 28 jewels; balance-spring regulator system with micrometer adjustment and regulator spring. Mounted by hand, beveled, hand-decorated with Côtes de Genève pattern.
Functions: hour, minute, small second, date, power reserve.
Case: 18K pink gold, two-piece tonneau case (height 45 mm, width 36 mm, thickness 11 mm); bezel with double hand-engraved knurling; curved mineral crystal; natural sapphire cabochon pink gold crown; case back attached by 8 gold screws, knurled and displaying the movement through a sapphire crystal. Water-resistant to 3 atm.
Dial: solid gold, eggshell, engine turned (guilloché) with barleycorn pattern; printed Arabic numerals and applied gold logo; pink gold Javeline hands.
Indications: date at 3; small second at 6; power reserve at 12 (applied gold sector).
Strap: crocodile leather; pink gold clasp.
Also available: yellow or white gold; platinum. All available with eggshell, anthracite or slate-grey dial.

IONICA "8 DAYS" REF. PF 000332/C02000

Contrasting the iron law of the market and following the certainly more expensive and complex way of the best watchmaking tradition for his Ionica tonneau, Michael Parmigiani choose to create "his" tonneau-curved movement (while today commercial logics impose also for shaped models the use of round standard movements). As a result, we have now manufacture caliber 110 of Parmigiani's Mesure et Art du Temps (this is the name of the division specialized in micromechanics inside Parmigiani Fleurier). The construction by separate bridges, which must take into account the tension exerted by the main spring dimensioned for a power reserve of 8 days, is really beautiful. In line with the best tradition are also the balance-spring regulator system with micrometer adjustment and regulator spring (swan-neck shaped). The photograph shows the version with platinum case, anthracite dial, white gold hands and logo.

BASICA JOAILLERIE REF. PF004265

Movement: mechanical, automatic winding, 34001 caliber (Frédéric Piguet 1150 caliber base), 11'''1/2, 72 hours autonomy, 29 jewels, 28,800 vibrations per hour; balance-spring regulator system with micrometer adjustment. Mounted and finished by hand, rhodium plated, decorated with Côtes de Genève pattern and beveled.
Functions: hour, minute.
Case: 18 kt white gold (26 gr), three-piece case (Ø 32.50, thickness 7,65 mm); curved sapphire crystal; lugs, bezel and middle set with 261 blue sapphires (2,35 ct); white gold crown with natural sapphire cabochon; snap-on case back, knurled, displaying the movement through a sapphire crystal. Water-resistant to 3 atm.
Dial: mother-of-pearl on solid gold base; 12 round rhodium-plated steel markers with blue sapphires set on the printed minute track and three Arabic numerals in powdered gold; blued steel Javeline hands.
Strap: alligator leather; white gold clasp set with 20 blue sapphires.
Also available: in pink gold; in yellow gold.

BASICA JOAILLERIE REF. PF004266

Movement: mechanical, automatic winding, 34001 caliber (Frédéric Piguet 1150 caliber base), 11'''1/2, 72 hours autonomy, 29 jewels, 28,800 vibrations per hour; balance-spring regulator system with micrometer adjustment. Mounted and finished by hand, rhodium plated, decorated with Côtes de Genève pattern and beveled.
Functions: hour, minute.
Case: 18 kt white gold (26 gr), three-piece case (Ø 32.50, thickness 7,65 mm); curved sapphire crystal; lugs, bezel and middle set with 261 pink sapphires (2,35 ct); white gold crown with natural sapphire cabochon; snap-on case back, knurled, displaying the movement through a sapphire crystal. Water-resistant to 3 atm.
Dial: mother-of-pearl on solid gold base; 12 round rhodium-plated steel markers with pink sapphires set on the printed minute track and three Arabic numerals in powdered gold; blued steel Javeline hands.
Strap: alligator leather; white gold clasp set with 20 pink sapphires.
Also available: in pink gold; in yellow gold.

PATEK PHILIPPE

an historical perspective

*P*atek Philippe stands out in the world of watchmaking as the epitome of perfection. It is the benchmark by which all other brands and standards are measured. Since 1839, this legendary brand has been perpetuating the tradition of Geneva fine watchmaking with a vigilance and savoir-faire that is most likely unparalleled.

Since its inception, the brand has been devoted to a philosophy of luxury and creativity. Founding father Antoine Norbert de Patek and his partner, Adrien Philippe, contributed regularly to the advancement of timekeeping. In fact, Philippe is credited with the astute invention of the winding crown—which replaced the previous key method of winding. The timepieces created by Patek Philippe were much-coveted items.

In fact, the company boasts an illustrious entourage. In 1851 the firm received an order for a watch from Queen Victoria, monarch of the United Kingdom. Victoria owned one of the first Patek Philippe keyless watches that incorporated Adrien Philippe's integrated winding and setting system. Other prominent citizens were also Patek Philippe loyal followers. The extensive list includes international writers, scientists, composers, explorers, magnates and royalty.

In 1932, dial suppliers Charles and Jean Stern took over the ownership of this prestigious brand. Dedicated to carrying on the brand's tradition of excellence, the brothers vowed to uphold Patek Philippe's philosophy and positioning. Throughout the ensuing decades, the family-owned Patek Philippe Manufacture focused on creating complex timepieces. In terms of research and development Patek Philippe has remained on the cutting edge and the brand has been awarded more than 60 patents for its inventions.

Indeed, this truly independent watchmaker has unveiled innovation after innovation throughout its 163 years. The brand's pedigree lineage, and exclusivity and dedication to technical prowess have propelled it to its well-deserved, esteemed pedestal position within the watch industry.

unveiling
masterpieces

To this day, Patek Philippe is respected and admired for the craftsmanship and creativity it consistently embodies. In its workshops in the canton of Geneva, one can witness the extraordinary contrast and combination of time-honored tradition and state-of-the-art modernity.

Within primarily glass walls, 600 technicians and master watchmakers craft an amazing blend of emotion and passion. In these ultra-modern workshops, the company produces all of its own movements, the majority of the main watch parts and, ultimately, every Patek Philippe timepiece. Because of the extensive hand craftsmanship and the painstakingly minute work involved in creating its mechanical marvels, Patek Philippe produces just about 20,000 watches annually for worldwide consumption.

Philippe Stern, master at the helm today, continues to follow in the footsteps of the brand's founders. He does not waiver when it comes to perfection or performance. This is evident in the fact that each and every one of Patek Philippe's mechanical timepieces is awarded with the coveted Geneva Seal—the ultimate hallmark of distinction.

While Patek Philippe's watch collection may seem extensive, it is, indeed, limited. The current collections for men and women include the classic, round Calatrava, the water-resistant Nautilus, the distinctive Golden Ellipse and the rectangular or tonneau-shaped Gondola. Additionally, the brand regularly unveils complications illustrating the highest watchmaking skills. Such complications include the calendar and astronomical functions, multiple time zones, extensive power reserves, skeletons, repeaters and high-jeweled watches.

In typical Patek Philippe style, the timepieces unveiled in 2001 were masterpieces of art, sophistication and technology. The Sky Moon Tourbillon, for instance, is a symphony that unites some of the rarest

THIS PAGE
TOP LEFT

The bejeweled Twenty-4® is meticulously set with 671 flawless Top Wesselton diamonds.

TOP CENTER

Patek workshops

TOP RIGHT

A watchmaker's bench

BOTTOM

The Calatrava Travel Time watch houses a manually wound movement and offers a transparent caseback.

FACING PAGE
BOTTOM

The Calatrava Travel Time in 18-karat rose or white gold features an 18-karat gold hour hand to indicate home time.

complications into one spectacular wristwatch. Deemed by Patek Philippe as the most complicated wristwatch the brand has ever built, the double-faced timepiece features a complex presentation of the night sky on its reverse side. The deep blue nocturnal face displays the movements of the stars, orbit of the moon, phases of the moon, and hours and minutes in sidereal time. The watch—a feat of fascinating factors—also houses a perpetual calendar with retrograde date display, a minute repeater and tourbillon escapement. The repeater has an especially beautiful resonance due to a refined alloy that produces a rich, full-bodied hour strike similar to the bells in a cathedral.

The Sky Moon Tourbillon is crafted in either platinum or 18-karat gold and houses a total of 686 individual parts, each meticulously finished by hand. Because of the intense engraving and craftsmanship, it takes months to complete one movement. The result is a marvel of precision engineering worthy of the Geneva Seal, which is embossed on its bridge.

Another incredible work of art is the diamond bedecked Twenty-4® haute joaillerie watch that Patek Philippe unveiled in response to the success of the first Twenty-4® watches. The early models were adorned in varying degrees of diamonds. The newest model is a stunning version in 18-karat white or rose gold that is set with a total of 671 Top Wesselton diamonds. Each watch takes several months to set with the baguette and round stones that weigh well over 30 carats.

In response to its time-conscious world traveler, Patek Philippe also unveiled an all-new Calatrava Travel Time watch in 18-karat yellow, white or rose gold. The watch indicates dual time zones with a gold hand to display home time and a black hand to indicate the second zone. A 24-hour subsidiary dial at 12:00 indicates day/night. When the dual time zone function is not needed, the gold hand tucks secretly away beneath the black hand for clean elegance. The watch features a sapphire caseback to reveal the manually wound movement. Attesting to the brand's technical prowess, this Patek Philippe mechanical movement also bears the coveted Geneva Seal.

1839 Patek, Czapek & Co. is founded in Geneva by Antoine Norbert de Patek and François Czapek. The small company produces about 200 pocket watches annually.

1842 Frenchman Jean Adrien Philippe develops the first keyless watch.

1844 The company participates in an exhibition in Paris. It is here that Patek first learns of the talented Jean Adrien Philippe. They form Patek & Co. a year later.

1851 Patek & Co. becomes Patek Philippe & Co.; The company wins a gold medal at London's Crystal Palace Exhibition (the first World's Fair); Queen Victoria purchases two Patek Philippe watches.

1856 Patek Philippe develops its first chronograph in response to the Americans' desire to time the speed of their horses to a quarter of a second.

1863 Patek Philippe invents the free mainspring, leading to the development of the automatic watch; Adrien Philippe's book on keyless pocket watches is published, earning him the title of "expert writer" by the daily *Journal de Genève*.

1868 At the request of Countess Kocewicz, Patek Philippe creates the first known Swiss wristwatch.

1877 Distinguished for his services to the Catholic Church by Pope Pius IX, the now-Count Antoine Norbert de Patek dies.

1890 Jean Adrien Philippe is awarded France's Cross of the Legion of Honor for his services.

1894 Three years after his retirement, Jean Adrien Philippe passes away.

1901 The Patek and Philippe heirs transfer the family firm into a stock corporation: Ancienne Manufacture d'Horlogerie Patek Philippe & Co. S.A.

1916-1929 Many highly complicated chronometers and astronomical watches are created for American car tycoon James Ward Packard.

1927 Patek Philippe introduces the first wrist chronograph which sells for Sfr 2,135 ($410).

1932 Even Patek Philippe is not immune from the effects of the Great Depression. The company is sold to the Stern family, a long-time provider of watch dials to Patek Philippe; The company's best-selling watch, the Calatrava, is created.

1933 Brothers Charles and Jean Stern enlist Jean Pfister to make movements in-house; The most complicated watch of its time, the Graves watch, is sold to American magnate Henry Graves, Jr. for Sfr 60,000 ($11,570). It will re-sell for $11 million at an auction 66 years later.

1942 Charles's son Henri establishes The Henri Stern Watch Agency in New York, responsible for the sales and distribution of Patek Philippe watches throughout the United States.

1948 Creation of the Electronics Division and the development of quartz technology.

1956 Patek Philippe produces the first clock powered by a battery without any moving parts.

1977 Henri Stern turns over the reins of Patek Philippe to his son, Philippe Stern.

1989 Commemorating its 150th Anniversary, Patek Philippe creates the Caliber 89, the world's most complicated mechanical timepiece. Nine years in the making, it performs 35 horological functions—33 of which are considered complications. The Caliber 89 is purchased at an auction for $3.2 million.

1996 The company obtains a patent for the annual calendar wristwatch.

1996-1997 Patek Philippe comes together under one roof with new state-of-the-art workshops in Plan-les-Ouates, Geneva.

2001 Patek Philippe's new museum displays some of the over 2,000 innovative masteries in Patek Philippe's watchmaking history.

PATEK PHILIPPE

SKY MOON TOURBILLON   REF. 5002J

Movement: manual, Patek Philippe 109 (RTO 27 PS QR SID LU CL) caliber, with tourbillon. Beveled and decorated with Côtes de Genève and circular graining pattern. Hallmarked with the "Geneva Seal". Chronometer certified by the Swiss Official Chronometer Testing Institute (C.O.S.C).
Functions: hour, minute, perpetual calendar (date, day, month, year, moon phase), minute repeater, sidereal time, heaven map, lunation period.

Case: 18 kt yellow gold, three-piece case (Ø 43 mm, thickness 16.2 mm); double curved sapphire crystal; gold crowns: at 2 for heaven map and sidereal hour, at 4 for the movement; 4 correctors and repeater slide on the middle, decorated with engraved Calatrava crosses.
Dial: gold, silvered; applied gold Roman numerals; printed minute track; gold Poire hands. **Indications:** month at 3, moon phase at 6, week day at 9, four-year cycle at 12, date with retrograde center hand. Rear side dial in blue sapphire crystal; skeletonized white enameled Poire hands.
Indications: sidereal hour, lunation period, visible heaven part.
Strap: crocodile leather; gold clasp.

TOURBILLON PERPETUAL CALENDAR MINUTE REPEATER   REF. 5016J

Movement: mechanical, manual winding, Patek Philippe RTO 27 PS QR caliber, with tourbillon. Hallmarked with the "Geneva Seal".
Functions: hour, minute, small second, perpetual calendar (date, day, month, year, moon-phase), minute repeater.
Case: 18 kt yellow gold, three-piece case (Ø 36 mm, thickness 14 mm); curved sapphire crystal; 4 correctors and repeater slide on the middle; gold crown; furnished with two snap-on case backs, one closed and the other with a sapphire crystal.

Dial: gold, silvered; applied gold Arabic numerals; gold cabochon minute track; gold Pomme and blued gold leaf style hands.
Indications: month at 3, moon phase and small second at 6, week day at 9, four-year cycle at 12, date with retrograde center hand.
Strap: crocodile leather; gold clasp.
Also available: in pink gold; in platinum with closed case back.

TOURBILLON MINUTE REPEATER   REF. 3939HJ

Movement: mechanical, manual winding, Patek Philippe RTO 27 PS caliber, with tourbillon. Hallmarked with the "Geneva Seal".
Functions: hour, minute, small second, minute repeater.
Case: 18 kt yellow gold, three-piece case (Ø 33 mm); curved sapphire crystal; repeater slide on the middle; gold crown; furnished with two snap-on case backs, one closed and the other with a sapphire crystal.

Dial: gold, white enameled; applied gold Arabic numerals; printed minute track; gold Pomme style hands.
Indications: small second at 6.
Strap: crocodile leather; gold clasp.
Also available: in pink or white gold; in platinum with closed case back.

PERPETUAL CALENDAR   REF. 5050P

Movement: mechanical, automatic winding Patek Philippe 315SQR caliber. Beveled and decorated with Côtes de Genève pattern. Hallmarked with the "Geneva Seal". **Functions:** hour, minute, center second, perpetual calendar (date, day, month, year, moon-phase).
Case: platinum, three-piece case (Ø 35 mm, thickness 10.5 mm); curved sapphire crystal; hollowed bezel; 4 correctors on the middle; platinum crown; furnished with two screwed-on case backs, one closed and the other with a sapphire crystal. Water-resistant to 2.5 atm.

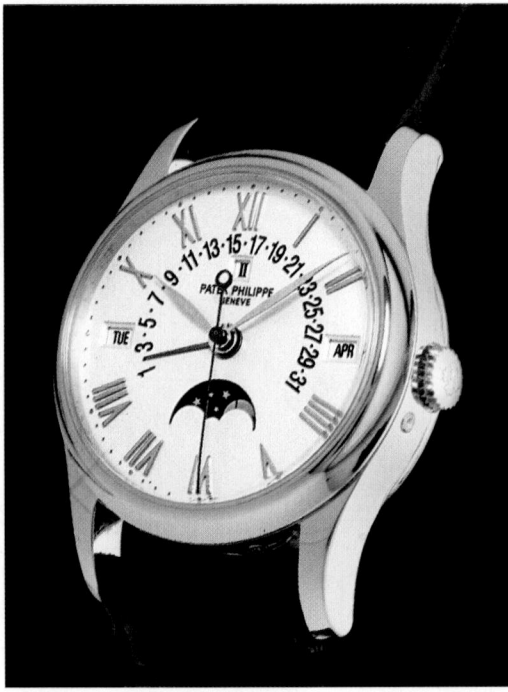

Dial: gold, silvered; applied white-gold Roman numerals; white-gold cabochon minute track; white-gold leaf style hands.
Indications: month at 3, moon phase at 6, week day at 9, four-year cycle at 12, date with retrograde center hand in black oxidized gold.
Strap: crocodile leather; platinum clasp.
Also available: with applied bâton markers; in yellow, pink or white gold. The gold versions are furnished with two screwed-on case backs, one closed and the other with a sapphire crystal bull's eye.

PERPETUAL CALENDAR — REF. 3940R

Movement: mechanical, automatic winding, Patek Philippe 240 Q caliber. 22 kt gold rotor. Beveled and decorated with Côtes de Genève pattern. Hallmarked with the "Geneva Seal".

Functions: hour, minute, 24-hour indication, perpetual calendar (date, day, month, year, moon-phase).

Case: 18 kt pink gold, three-piece case (ø 36 mm, thickness 8.5 mm); curved sapphire crystal; 4 correctors the middle; pink-gold crown; furnished with two snap-on case backs, one closed and the other with a sapphire crystal.

Dial: gold, silvered; applied pink-gold bâton and square markers; applied pink-gold cabochon minute track; pink-gold Dauphine hands.

Indications: month and four-year cycle at 3, date and moon phase at 6, week day and 24-hour indication at 9.

Strap: crocodile leather; pink-gold clasp.

Also available: in white or yellow gold; in platinum, closed case back. With silvered dial with applied markers or white dial with printed Roman numerals (black dial and Roman numerals only for platinum version).

CHRONOGRAPH — REF. 5070G

Movement: mechanical, manual winding, Patek Philippe CH 27-70 caliber. Beveled and decorated with Côtes de Genève pattern. Hallmarked with the "Geneva Seal".

Functions: hour, minute, small second, chronograph with 2 counters.

Case: 18 kt yellow gold, two-piece case (Ø 42 mm, thickness 11.7 mm); curved sapphire crystal; stepped bezel; white gold crown; white gold rectangular pushers; screwed-on back displaying the movement through a sapphire crystal. Water-resistant to 2.5 atm.

Dial: silvered; applied burnished gold Arabic numerals; burnished gold leaf style hands.

Indications: minute counter at 3, small second at 9, center second counter, minute track with divisions for 1/5 of a second, tachometer scale.

Strap: crocodile leather; fold-over clasp with logo, in yellow gold.
Yearly production limited to 250 pieces.

Also available: in yellow gold with black dial.

CHRONOGRAPH RATTRAPANTE PERPETUAL CALENDAR — REF. 5004J

Movement: mechanical, manual winding, Patek Philippe CHR 27-70 Q caliber. Beveled and decorated with Côtes de Genève pattern. Hallmarked with the "Geneva Seal". **Functions:** hour, minute, small second, 24-hour indication, split-second chronograph with 2 counters, perpetual calendar (date, day, month, year, moon phase).

Case: 18 kt yellow gold, three-piece case (Ø 37 mm); curved sapphire crystal; 4 correctors on the middle; splitting pusher on gold crown; furnished with two screwed-on case backs, one closed and the other with a sapphire crystal. Water-resistant to 2.5 atm.

Dial: gold, opaline silvered; applied gold Arabic numerals and cabochon markers; gold leaf style hands. **Indications:** minute counter and four-year cycle at 3, moon phase and date at 6, small second and 24-hour indication at 9, week day and month at 12, center second and split-second counters, minute track with divisions for 1/5 of a second.

Strap: crocodile leather; gold clasp.

Also available: in pink or white gold with silvered or black dial; in platinum with silvered or black dial.

CHRONOGRAPH PERPETUAL CALENDAR — REF. 3970 BG

Movement: mechanical, manual winding Patek Philippe CH 27-70 Q caliber. Beveled and decorated with Côtes de Genève pattern. Hallmarked with the "Geneva Seal". **Functions:** hour, minute, small second, 24-hour indication, chronograph with 2 counters, perpetual calendar (date, day, month, year, moon phase). **Case:** 18 kt white gold, three-piece case (Ø 36, thickness 12 mm); curved sapphire crystal; hollowed bezel; 4 correctors on the middle; white-gold crown; furnished with two screwed-on case backs, one closed and the other with a sapphire crystal. Water-resistant to 2.5 atm. **Dial:** gold, silvered; counters decorated with circular beads; applied white-gold bâton and square markers; white-gold bâton hands. **Indications:** minute counter and four-year cycle at 3, moon phase and date at 6, small second and 24-hour indication at 9, week day and month at 12, center second counter, minute track with divisions for 1/5 of a second.

Strap: crocodile leather; white-gold clasp.

Also available: with black dial; in pink or yellow gold with silvered dial; in platinum, black or silvered dial; with black dial and brilliants at markers.

PATEK PHILIPPE

ANNUAL CALENDAR   REF. 5036/1R

Movement: mechanical, automatic winding, Patek Philippe 315 QA IRM LU caliber, autonomy 48 hours, 21 kt gold rotor and 37 jewels (Ø 30 mm). Gyromax balance, 21,600 vph, flat balance-spring. Made up by 356 elements. Hallmarked with the "Geneva Seal". **Functions:** hour, minute, second, power reserve, annual calendar (date, day, month - keeps automatically the count of the days of months over a whole year). **Case:** 18 kt pink gold, three-piece case (Ø 36.5 mm, thickness 11 mm); curved sapphire crystal; hollowed bezel; 4 correctors on the middle; pink-gold crown; screwed-on back displaying the movement through a sapphire crystal. Water-resistant to 2.5 atm.

Dial: silvered; luminescent applied pink-gold Roman numerals, printed railway minute track; luminescent pink-gold leaf style hands.

Indications: month with hand at 3, moon-phase and date at 6, day of the week with hand at 9, power reserve at 12.

Bracelet: pink gold, double fold-over clasp.

Also available: in white gold with silvered or black dial; in yellow gold with silvered dial. Ref. 5056 platinum, slate-gray dial, strap, 250 pcs.

WORLD TIME   REF. 5110P

Movement: mechanical, automatic winding, Patek Philippe 240/188 caliber, 48 hours autonomy, 22 kt gold micro-rotor and 33 jewels. Gyromax, balance with 21,600 vibrations per hour, flat balance spring. Made up by 235 elements. Hallmarked with the "Geneva Seal". **Functions:** hour, minute, world time, 24 hours. **Case:** platinum, three-piece case (Ø 37 mm, thickness 9.65 mm), with Top Wesselton brilliant set between the lugs; curved sapphire crystal; platinum crown

with case protection; rectangular white-gold pusher at 10, for basic setting and time zone adjustments (for hours hand advancing by one-hour clicks - clockwise - and the adjustment of the 24-hours discs and reference town names for the 24 time zones - counter-clockwise); screwed-on back displaying the movement through a sapphire crystal. Water-resistant to 2,5 atm. **Dial:** blue, with engine-turned (guilloché) center; applied white-gold bâton markers; white-gold lozenge hands. **Indications:** world time, 24 hours day-night.

Strap: crocodile leather, hand-stitched; platinum fold-over clasp.

Also available: in pink or white gold with opaline dial; in yellow gold with opaline dial.

TRAVEL TIME   REF. 5134J

Movement: mechanical, manual winding Patek Philippe 215 PS FUS 24H caliber, autonomy 44 hours, 18 jewels (Ø 21.90 mm, thickness 3.35 mm). Gyromax balance, 28,800 vibrations per hour, flat balance-spring. Made up by 178 elements. Hallmarked with the "Geneva Seal".

Functions: hour, minute, small second, second time zone, 24-hour indication. **Case:** 18 kt yellow gold, three-piece case (Ø 37 mm, thickness 9.8 mm);

curved sapphire crystal; gold crown with case protection; 2 pushers on the middle (at 8 to move the GMT hand forward, at 10 to move it backward); screwed-on back, displaying the movement through a sapphire crystal. Water-resistant to 2.5 atm.

Dial: mat white; applied gold Arabic numerals; printed railway minute track; burnished gold leaf style hands (gold GMT hand).

Indications: small second at 6, 24-hour display at 12.

Strap: crocodile leather; gold buckle.

Also available: in yellow or white gold.

10 DAYS   REF. 5100R

Movement: mechanical, manual winding, Patek Philippe 28-20/220 caliber. Officially certified "chronometer" (C.O.S.C.). Hallmarked with the "Geneva Seal".

Functions: hour, minute, small second, power reserve. **Case:** 18 kt pink gold, two-piece, rectangular case (size 34.5 x 34 mm, thickness 11.8 mm), curved sapphire crystal; pink-gold crown with case protection;

back attached by 4 screws with sapphire crystal aperture and engraved "Year 2000". Water-resistant to 2,5 atm.

Dial: gray; applied pink-gold faceted pointed markers and Arabic numerals; printed minute track; faceted pink-gold Dauphine hands.

Indications: small second at 6, power reserve at 12.

Strap: crocodile leather, hand-stitched; pink-gold clasp. Realized for the 2000 celebration. Limited edition of 3000 numbered pieces (1500 in yellow gold, 750 in pink gold, 450 in white gold, 300 in platinum).

Also available: in white gold with blue dial; in yellow gold with silvered dial; in platinum with black dial.

CALATRAVA — REF. 5107J

Movement: mechanical, automatic winding, Patek Philippe caliber 315 SC. Hallmarked with the "Geneva Seal".
Functions: hour, minute, second, date.
Case: 18 kt yellow gold, three-piece case (Ø 37 mm, thickness 8.8 mm); curved sapphire crystal; screw-down gold crown, with case protection; screwed-on back displaying the movement through a sapphire crystal. Water-resistant to 2,5 atm.
Dial: opaline; applied gold faceted bâton markers; applied gold cabochon minute track; gold faceted Dauphine hands.
Indications: date at 3, with gold rim.
Strap: crocodile leather; gold clasp.
Also available: in pink or yellow gold.

CALATRAVA — REF. 5115J

Movement: mechanical, manual winding, Patek Philippe 215 PS caliber. Hallmarked with the "Geneva Seal".
Functions: hour, minute, small second.
Case: 18 kt yellow gold, three-piece case (Ø 35 mm, thickness 8.35 mm); curved sapphire crystal; bezel decorated with Clous de Paris pattern; gold crown with case protection; screwed-on back. Water-resistant to 2,5 atm.
Dial: white enameled; printed Roman numerals and minute track; black oxidized gold leaf style hands.
Indications: small second at 6.
Strap: crocodile leather, hand-stitched; gold clasp.
Also available: in white gold.

GONDOLO "CABRIOLET" — REF. 5099RG

Movement: mechanical, manual winding, Patek Philippe 215 PS caliber. Hallmarked with the "Geneva Seal".
Functions: hour, minute, small second.
Case: in 18 kt pink and white gold, three-piece square case (size 28.5 x 28.5 mm, thickness 7.7 mm), with hinged cover (opening by simultaneously pressing both octagonal pushers positioned on the lower case sides); flat sapphire crystal; pink-gold crown; back attached by 4 screws. Water-resistant to 2.5 atm.
Dial: in solid pink gold; printed Arabic numerals and railway minute track; black oxidized gold leaf style hands.
Indications: small second at 6.
Strap: leather, hand-stitched; pink and white gold clasp.
Inspired by a rare model of Art Déco design of 1928. Yearly production limited to few pieces.

SMALL SECONDS MOON-PHASE (LADY) — REF. 4857G

Movement: mechanical, manual winding, Patek Philippe 16-250PS/LU caliber. Hallmarked with the "Geneva Seal".
Functions: hour, minute, small second, moon-phase.
Case: in 18 kt white gold, three-piece case (ø 29 mm, thickness 7.8 mm), curved sapphire crystal; a corrector on the middle; white-gold crown with sapphire cabochon; snap-on back. Water-resistant to 2,5 atm.
Dial: gray with sun pattern; applied white-gold markers with set brilliants and Roman numerals (6 and 12); printed minute track; white-gold leaf style hands.
Indications: moon-phase at 4, mall second at 8.
Strap: crocodile leather; white gold clasp.
Also available: in yellow gold with white dial and blue zones.

PAUL PICOT

an historical perspective

*T*he year 2001 marked the glorious 25th
anniversary of the atelier of Paul Picot.
Established in 1976 on a philosophy of preserving
rich Swiss watchmaking tradition and promoting
technical prowess, Paul Picot is a brand dedicated to the heritage
of its country and master watchmakers.

FACING PAGE

The Technicum is a
self-winding mechanical
split-second chronograph
with calendar and power
reserve. It is a COSC-
certified chronometer.

At a time when the quartz revolution was taking the world by storm, and slapping
the Swiss watch industry in the face, one man recognized a need to reinforce the spirit of
watchmaking. Founder Mario Boiocchi, current Chairman of Paul Picot, chose the name
as a tribute to an 18th century watchmaker who built his timepieces entirely by hand, engraving and decorating the multitude of tiny pieces before assembling them and engraving
his signature.

"I had the impression that unless I reacted, I might be accused of failing to assist
a world in danger, because everything that had delight-
ed my early years was on the point of disappearing,"
said Boiocchi.

At that point, Boiocchi dedicated himself to creating a brand of innovative timepieces that could rival the
greatest masters. By elaborating on movements and creating mechanical watches housing a variety of watchmaking
complications, Boiocchi brought the brand to international acclaim.

Today, 26 years after its inception,
Paul Picot remains dedicated to creating
technically sophisticated timepieces that
will surprise and delight watch lovers
around the world.

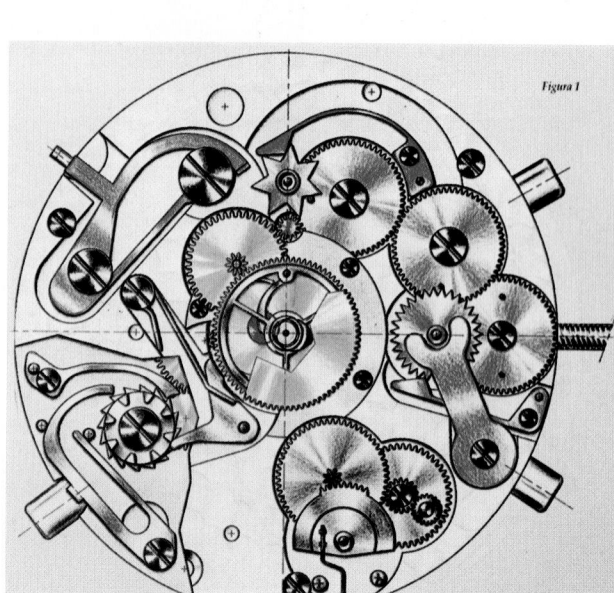

Figura 1

427

unveiling

masterpieces

Each of the enchanting and enthralling Paul Picot timepieces is a mark of technical excellence. This is a brand that pays close attention to detail and perfection. In fact, its overall design philosophy is "Nobility in Detail."

Dedicated to authenticity and enlightenment in the world of watchmaking, Paul Picot unveiled masterpiece after masterpiece. Its Technicum, considered the signature timepiece and found in the Atelier collection, is a remarkable COSC-certified chronometer watch that combines a power-reserve indicator and split-second chronograph. Although the first Technicum was unveiled more than 10 years ago in 1991, it has won international awards and become so coveted that the brand continues to introduce new versions.

The Technicum is created in stainless steel, yellow, pink and white gold, and features a solid silver dial. The automatic chronograph chronometer with central split-second function, power reserve and full calendar spent several years in the development stages. It features a self-winding caliber PP 8888, based on a Valjoux

THIS PAGE

TOP LEFT

The Firshire 1937 features a mechanical tonneau-shaped hand-wound movement. It offers a power reserve and a sub-seconds dial. This version is crafted in a limited edition.

TOP CENTER

The Firshire Power Reserve COSC-certified chronometer is a statement of elegance with calendar and power reserve.

TOP RIGHT

This 40mm oversized Atelier 1100 timepiece evokes a sense of early watchmaking. It houses 21 jewels and a solid gold rotor.

CENTER

The self-winding movement of the Firshire is tonneau shaped and elegantly engraved and finished.

BOTTOM LEFT

This 18-karat pink gold version of the Firshire 1937 is available in men's and ladies' sizes.

FACING PAGE
TOP

The Manufacture of Paul Picot.

BOTTOM RIGHT

Part of the Atelier collection, the Rattrapante 310 is crafted in 18-karat yellow gold and is a hand-winding split-seconds chronograph with full calendar and moonphase.

In the last 10 years, Paul Picot has refocused its marketing strategies to include distribution to 15 countries, propelling the brand to international success.

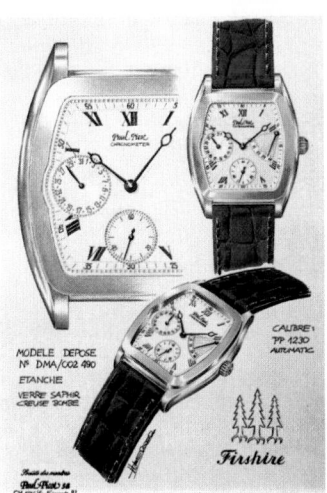

7750 movement. It features 27 jewels and a solid 21-karat gold rotor.

Also recently unveiled in the Atelier collection is the Atelier 1100. In keeping with the spirit of oversized, classic timepieces made in the 17th century, Paul Picot created the 1100 Regulator with power reserve and date function. Housed in an impressive fluted case, the watch is water resistant to 50 meters and features a sapphire caseback to allow viewing of the self-winding movement.

In its impressive Firshire collection—named for the age-old, stately fir trees that proudly mark the Jura Mountains, birthplace of Swiss watchmaking heritage—Paul Picot unveils watches that pay homage to its history and its future. Created in elegant tonneau-shaped cases, the newest Firshires combine technical refinement with harmonious detailing and classically elegant design.

The nostalgic Firshire 1937 offers a tonneau-shaped hand-wound mechanical movement replicating one first produced in 1937. The 17-jeweled caliber PP88 is visible from a sapphire caseback. Additionally, the Firshire Power Reserve flaunts a silvered guilloché dial of unparalleled simplicity and beauty. It depicts power reserve of 44 hours, sub-seconds dial at 6:00 and date subdial. The certified Chronometer houses a self-winding, 21-jeweled movement. These watches are engraved on the back with three fir trees to symbolize their heritage and watchmaking ingenuity.

Indeed, while Paul Picot is relatively young in years, the brand is rich with tradition and remains dedicated to carrying the spirit of true watchmaking well into the new millennium.

PAUL PICOT

FIRSHIRE RONDE CHRONODATE FLY-BACK   REF. 194

Movement: mechanical, automatic winding, Paul Picot 8890 caliber (Valjoux 7750 cal. base) with fly-back feature, 28 jewels, 28,800 vibrations per hour; 50 hours autonomy.
Functions: hour, minute, small second, date, fly-back chronograph with 3 counters.
Case: 18 kt pink gold, three-piece case (ø 39.6 mm, thickness 14.7 mm); curved sapphire crystal; pink-gold rectangular crown and pushers; back fastened by 4 screws. Water-resistant to 5 atm.
Dial: mat black; printed Arabic numerals; luminescent gold-plated bâton hands.
Indications: minute counter at 3, hour counter at 6, small second at 9, big date with double window at 12, center fly-back second counter, minute track.
Strap: crocodile leather; pink gold clasp.
Also available: in steel with silvered or black dial, strap, bracelet.

FIRSHIRE RONDE AUTODATE   REF. 4091/D32

Movement: mechanical, automatic winding, Paul Picot PP1120 caliber (ETA 2892A2 base + big date module), 40 hours autonomy, 26 jewels. Glucydur balance, 28,800 vibrations per hour, Nivarox 1 balance spring. Vagues de Genève finished and beveled.
Functions: hour, minute, small second, date.
Case: stainless steel, three-piece case (ø 37.5 mm, th. 9.8 mm); curved sapphire crystal; knurled snap-on back. Water-resistant to 5 atm.
Dial: black; zone decorated with circular beads; applied rhodium-plated bâton markers; printed minute track; rhodium-plated bâton hands.
Indications: small second at 6, big date with double window bordered with rhodium-plated brass at 12.
Strap: crocodile leather; stainless steel clasp.
Also available: with silvered dial. Without brilliants: strap, bracelet; in pink gold.

FIRSHIRE RONDE 2-BARRELS AUTOMATIC   REF. 181

Movement: mechanical, automatic winding, Paul Picot 8810 caliber (Lemania 8815 caliber base), with double winding barrel. Vagues de Genève decoration.
Functions: hour, minute, second, date.
Case: 18 kt pink gold, three-piece case (Ø 37 mm, thickness 7.8 mm); curved sapphire crystal; knurled snap-on case back hand-engraved with three firs as the collection's symbol. Water-resistant to 5 atm.
Dial: silvered, engine turned (guilloché) with basket pattern; applied pink gold Roman numerals; printed minute track; pink-gold-plated Régate hands.
Indications: bordered pink-gold-plated date at 3.
Strap: crocodile leather; pink gold fold-over clasp.
Also available: in steel with strap, bracelet; with brilliant bezel and markers, strap, bracelet.

FIRSHIRE TONNEAU 2000 LADY   REF. 4099/DK

New and delicate colors animate the Tonneau Firshire collection combining agreeable colors with precious brilliants. For these versions, dedicated to the feminine public, provided with quartz movements without seconds and with date display, the House adopts also mother-of-pearl dials (s. small photograph) in tones harmonizing with the straps used. Ladies can therefore afford not only shaped watches with the most classical combinations - black or white dial with Arabic or Roman numerals - but also choose among the numerous versions with diamonds set on bezels and hour markers or only on markers.
Also available: see left.

FIRSHIRE HAND WINDING PLATINUM GENTS   REF. 6003

Movement: mechanical, manual winding, Paul Picot 88 caliber (base: ETA 735 cal. of 1937 + power reserve module), autonomy 42 hours, 17 jewels; Glucydur balance, 18,000 vph, Nivarox 1 balance-spring, Incabloc shock-resistant system. Beveled, Vagues de Genève and circular graining finished. **Functions:** hour, minute, small second, power reserve. **Case:** platinum, 2-piece tonneau-shaped case (size 36x33, thickn. 10.5 mm); curved sapphire crystal; white gold screw-down crown with set brilliant; case back attached by 4 screws, displaying the movement through a sapphire crystal. Water-resistant to 5 atm. **Dial:** solid silver, guilloché; applied bâton markers (Arabic numeral 12); printed minute track; bâton hands. **Indications:** power reserve at 1, small second at 6. **Strap:** crocodile leather; white gold clasp. Limited edition. Sold in a case combined with lady's version (bottom), also in pink gold.

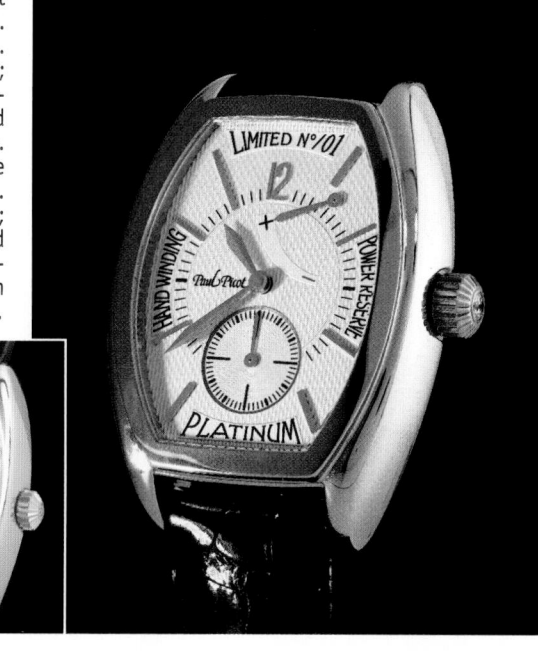

FIRSHIRE TONNEAU 2000 AUTODATA   REF. 4093

Movement: mechanical, automatic winding, Paul Picot 180 caliber (ETA 2892A2 caliber base + big date module), autonomy 40 hours, 26 jewels; Glucydur balance, 28,800 vibrations per hour, Nivarox 1 balance-spring. Vagues de Genève and circular graining finish, beveled. **Functions:** hour, minute, small second, date. **Case:** stainless steel, three-piece tonneau-shaped case (size 36 x 33.5 mm, thickness 10.7 mm); curved sapphire crystal; case back attached by 4 screws, engraved with a three fir-trees pattern as a symbol for the Firshire County. Water-resistant to 5 atm. **Dial:** silvered, engine turned (guilloché); applied rhodium-plated bâton markers; printed minute track; rhodium-plated bâton hands. **Indications:** small second at 6, big date with steel-bordered double window at 12. **Strap:** crocodile leather; steel clasp. **Also available:** with black dial; with bracelet.

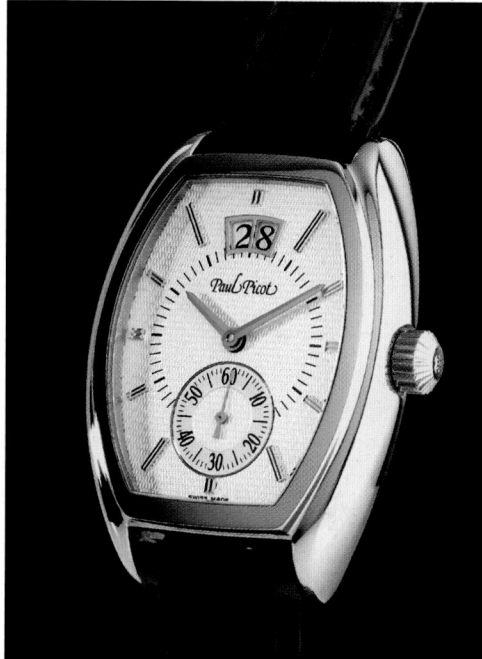

ATELIER AUTOMATIC   REF. 4025/N

The automatic watches of Paul Picot's Atelier collection are manufactured in four case sizes: the diameter goes from 27 (smallest model) to 37 mm (biggest model) and includes the intermediate sizes of 31 and 33 mm. Since the last spring, mother-of-pearl dials in pastel colors with brilliant markers have been added to an already vast series. Paul Picot, by this collection has been occupying the first ranks in worldwide watch production, as far as quality, technical content, style and accuracy of finishing are concerned. The model shown in the photograph (Ø 33 mm, thickness 9 mm) is in stainless steel. **Also available:** with bracelet; with white, green or blue mother-of-pearl dial; with brilliant bezel and markers, strap or bracelet; without brilliants, with strap or bracelet. Size Ø 31, th. 7 mm: brilliant markers, strap, bracelet; brilliant bezel and markers, strap, bracelet; without brilliants, strap, bracelet.

AMERICAN BRIDGE   REF. 4076/D58NK

Movement: quartz. **Functions:** hour, minute, date. **Case:** stainless steel, two-piece rectangular anatomically curved case (size 35 x 27 mm, thickness 9 mm); bezel with set brilliants; curved sapphire crystal; case back attached by 4 screws, engraved with the symbol of the collection. Water-resistant to 5 atm. **Dial:** blue mother-of-pearl, curved; applied Roman numerals and square markers with set brilliants; steel Régate hands. **Indications:** date at 6. **Strap:** crocodile leather; steel fold-over clasp. **Also available:** with black dial; with bracelet.

PIAGET

an historical perspective

Piaget. The name alone conjures up visions of jeweled beauties and iconic timepieces that are at once statements of elegance and mastery. Piaget's roots date back to 1874 when, at the very young age of 19, Georges Édouard Piaget founded the watchmaking establishment that still bears his name—and that continues to revel in his tradition of excellence.

A dreamer and innovator, Piaget worked diligently with lever escapement watches—perfecting them to an unprecedented degree of thinness that led him to develop such slim movements that his watches were absolute marvels of the time. These slim timepieces were quite elegant and quickly became coveted items in the Swiss watchmaking circle. Within just a few decades, Piaget's business had become such a thriving success that he was compelled to open new and larger workshops in the Swiss Jura town of La Côte-aux-Fées. Georges Édouard also chose that time to turn the family business over to his youngest child, Timothée—who continued to build the brand based on technological advancements.

Timothée, however, aspired to incorporate the finest jewels into the brand's watches and by the early 1920s had transformed the workshops into one of the most celebrated jewelry timepiece manufactures known to the world. In 1945, when he handed the business over to the third generation of Piagets, the brand had already chosen "Luxury and Precision" as its motto. The entrepreneurial spirit of this generation led to the brand's registration and, by extension, gave it an international dimension.

In 1957, Piaget unveiled the first mechanical ultra-thin movement (caliber 9P) and several years later unveiled the world's thinnest automatic movement (the famed caliber 12P), which appeared in the Guinness Book of Records. From then on, the brand has enjoyed global success as a luxury watchmaker of ultra-thin movements, ultra-thin timepieces and intricate works of art for the wrist.

From the 1960s to date, Piaget has enjoyed some of the most incredible successes in watchmaking. In the 1960s, when fourth generation Piagets took over the firm—including Yves Piaget, a creative genius still with the brand today—Piaget made several bold moves in its creations that would forever seal its reputation as an innovator and luxury watchmaker.

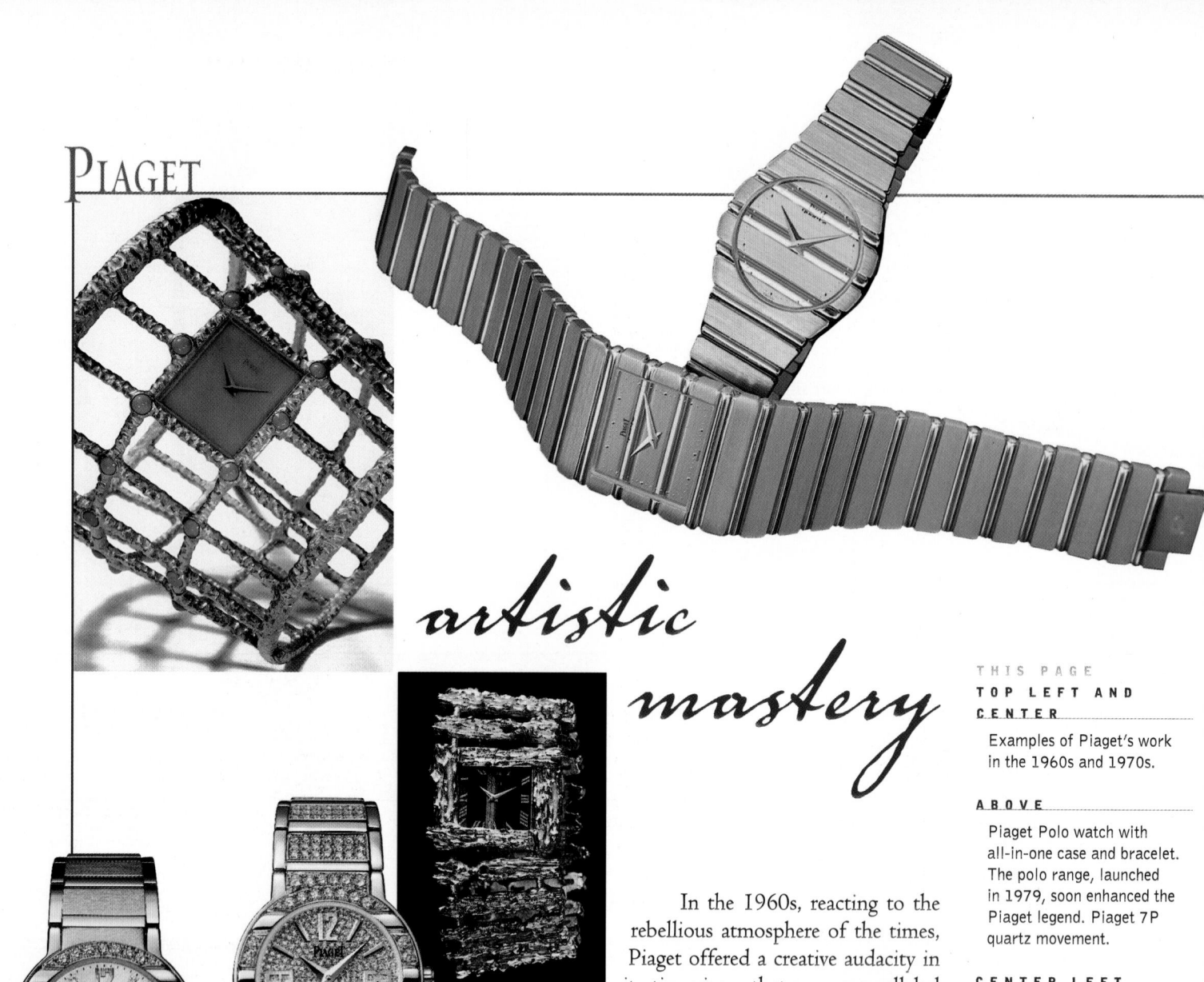

artistic mastery

THIS PAGE

TOP LEFT AND CENTER

Examples of Piaget's work in the 1960s and 1970s.

ABOVE

Piaget Polo watch with all-in-one case and bracelet. The polo range, launched in 1979, soon enhanced the Piaget legend. Piaget 7P quartz movement.

CENTER LEFT

The new ladies' Piaget Polo in 18-karat yellow gold is simply elegant.

CENTER RIGHT

Diamond accents transform this 18-karat white-gold Piaget Polo into a work of art. It is meticulously set with approximately 5.4 carats of diamonds.

FACING PAGE

TOP

This striking 18-karat yellow-gold Upstream houses a 26-jeweled, 40-hour power-reserve movement and features the unique bezel opening.

BOTTOM

The Upstream is Piaget's first foray into stainless steel. The self-winding watch is a unique blend of innovation and elegance.

In the 1960s, reacting to the rebellious atmosphere of the times, Piaget offered a creative audacity in its timepieces that was unparalleled and heralded. The brand introduced some of the most whimsical interpretive timepieces of the era: bold cuffs of brazen woven and meshed gold were born; semiprecious gemstones such as turquoise, onyx and lapis lazuli made their colorful debut as watch dials unlike any seen before. In the 1970s, diamonds and gemstones came to life in scintillating renditions that had hardly been matched, and Piaget's image as a prestigious high-jeweled watchmaker was emblazoned on the minds of women and men around the world.

The 1980s saw the entrée of what would become a legend for the brand: the Piaget Polo watch. Along with other distinctive designs such as the Dancer and the Protocole ultrathin watches, the Polo was designed as a collection for those living a luxurious lifestyle, for those with taste and refined elegance. Each of these designs became international successes and icons of the elite. With such an incredible demonstration of artistic prowess and technical excellence, Piaget became a highly desirable entity. In 1988, the Richemont Group acquired the brand, committed to continuing its fine Swiss watchmaking tradition. Indeed, in the 1990s a number of highly complicated watches, entered the scene—often bedecked in diamonds and gemstones.

Today, Piaget is renowned for its innovative sense of style, its mastery of the watchmaking profession and for its exclusivity. One of the few fully integrated manufacturers still in existence, Piaget designs and produces all of its own watches. A highly skilled team of designers, master watchmakers and gem-setters work side by side in the company's brand new, ultra-modern workshops to produce the most advanced expressions of form and function.

In fact, the year 2001 saw the unveiling of the updated Piaget Polo. Paying homage to the 1980s, the new Piaget Polo recaptures the chic irreverence of the original line and combines it with a distinctly sleek and modern elegance. The new Piaget Polo is bold, powerful and strong in its shape and profile, featuring the same seamless integrated bracelet that first made the watch so revolutionary. It now comes in 14 different versions of automatic and quartz models.

While classic elegance with updated style is important to Piaget, so, too is modernity and innovation—traits evident in the all-new Upstream. This creative watch is Piaget's first foray into the world of steel. Previously, all Piaget timepieces were crafted only of precious metals; the Upstream is offered in gold or in steel and comes in seven different models, including a chronograph version. The Upstream is a decisively masculine watch with sculptural inspiration and a Piaget movement. The distinctive design of the watch revolves around a bezel that unfolds at 12:00 for the wearer to don the watch. The bracelet features no clasp and offers a full look and feel.

PIAGET

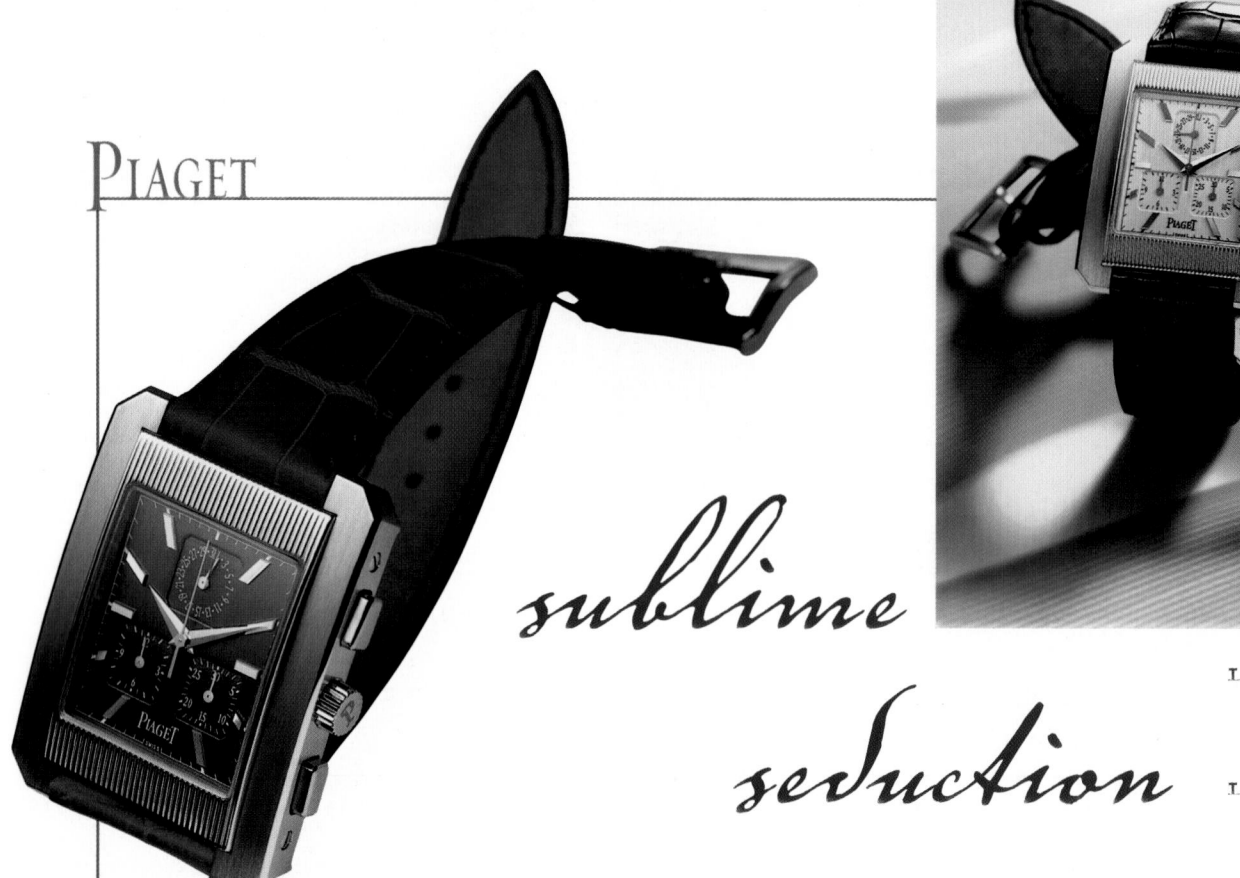

sublime seduction

Technical prowess and boldness are not the only defining marks of Piaget. This renowned jewelry watchmaker excels when it comes to creations of elegance. As a result, many of the newest timepieces are design delights for women: Among them are exciting versions of the Miss Protocole, the Miss Protocole Allongée and the haute joaillerie collections.

The first Protocole was unveiled in the 1960s and was an immediate hit. Its rectangular case shape with rounded corners made it a watch ahead of its time. In the late 1990s, Piaget began recreating the Protocole collection. In 1998, the brand unveiled its Miss Protocole collection of fashion-forward watches with interchangeable straps. The collection has since progressed with a vim and vigor characteristic of Piaget. The newest Miss Protocole models are offered with diamond accents and an array of brilliantly colored straps.

Building on the line's success, Piaget has stretched its imagination and introduced an elongated Miss Protocole Allongée rectangular watch. The vertical guilloché pattern of the case remains intact, but the new version is leaner and sleeker with squared edges on the rectangular case. Diamond accents abound, with models offering entirely diamond pavé dials and bracelets, and others offering diamond pavé cases with colorful mother-of-pearl dials.

In its high jewelry collection, Piaget has reinterpreted classical shapes—giving new perspective to the tonneau for women. Different versions have been created of the barrel-shaped watch for women, including an iridescent pastel blue mother-of-pearl

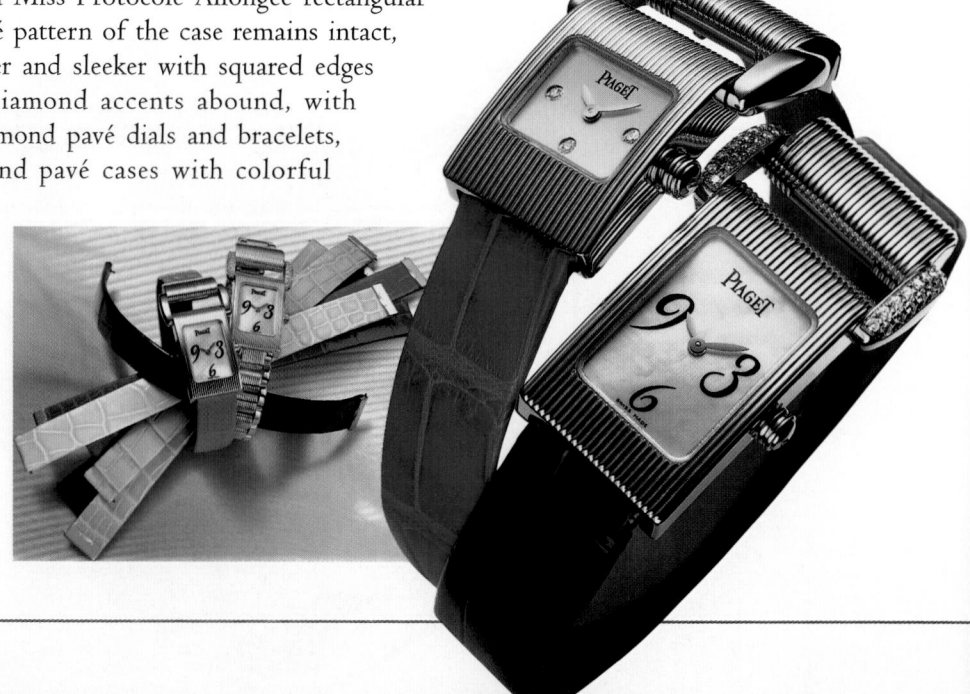

TOP RIGHT

This one-of-a-kind lady's haute joaillerie creation glows in 18-karat white gold with 2 trapeze-shaped diamonds, 162 baguette-cut diamonds, and 24 square-cut diamonds with a combined weight of 41.83 carats. This radiant beauty houses a quartz movement Piaget 201P.

CENTER LEFT

Set with 117 diamonds and accented with a pink mother-of-pearl dial and pink strap, this rectangular timepiece houses a quartz Piaget movement.

CENTER RIGHT

A statement in blue, this barrel-shaped watch is set with 1.33 carats of diamonds.

BELOW

Taking the navette form, this striking haute joaillerie watch is set with triangular- and emerald-cut diamonds weighing 41.8 carats.

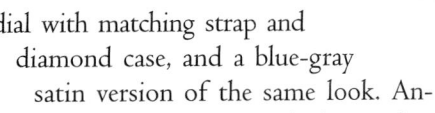

dial with matching strap and diamond case, and a blue-gray satin version of the same look. Another model exists with diamond pavé dial and case, and a third, incredibly shimmering version exists that is entirely bedecked in diamonds from end to end.

In its dazzling high jewelry geometry series, another masterpiece was unveiled that unites trapeze-cut diamonds and square diamonds. After nine months of painstaking, meticulous work by the grand masters of the jewelry profession, a unique high jewelry watch was born. The bezel is set with 9.58 carats of diamonds, the bracelet with 32.25 carats of diamonds and the dial with 2.3 carats of diamonds for a splendid radiance. The list of bejeweled watches goes on and on. In fact, the Piaget high jewelry unveilings in 2001 were among the most spectacular and extensive ever, with nearly a dozen new timepieces making their debut.

Indeed, Piaget sparkles as brightly as ever with its innate sense of tradition, modernity, elegance, glamour and refinement.

PIAGET

PIAGET POLO GOA26020	PIAGET POLO GOA26021	PIAGET POLO GOA26034	PIAGET POLO GOA26032
Men's watch in 18 kt white gold. Slate-gray dial, Dauphine hands. Self-winding movement Manufacture Piaget 504P, 11 lines, 26 jewels, 40-hour power-reserve, 21,600 vibrations/hour. Date display at 6 o'clock.	Men's watch in 18 kt yellow gold. Silvered dial, Dauphine hands. Self-winding movement Manufacture Piaget 504P, 11 lines, 26 jewels, 40-hour power-reserve, 21,600 vibrations/hour. Date display at 6 o'clock.	Ladies watch in 18 kt white gold. Dial set with diamonds, Dauphine hands. Bezel partially set with diamonds. Bracelet set with diamonds. Total carats: approx. 5.383 cts. Quartz movement Manufacture Piaget 690P.	Ladies watch in 18 kt yellow gold. Silvered dial, hour-markers set with diamonds, Dauphine hands. Bezel partially set with diamonds. Total carats: approx. 0.604 cts. Quartz movement Manufacture Piaget 690P.

UPSTREAM   REF. GOA26006

Movement: mechanical, automatic winding, Piaget 504P caliber (500P base), 11''', autonomy 40 hours. Decorated with Côtes de Genève and circular graining patterns.
Functions: hour, minute, second, date.
Case: stainless steel, four-piece tonneau-shaped case (size 34 x 33 mm, thickness 9.8 mm), brushed finish; curved sapphire crystal; hexagonal crown protected by shoulders; back attached by 8 screws. Water-resistant to 5 atm.
Dial: silvered, brushed; printed Arabic numerals and minute track; steel Dauphine hands.
Indications: date at 6.
Bracelet: steel.
Opening system: a folding bezel opening at 12 o'clock (replaces the folding clasp).
Also available: anthracite dial; in yellow gold with silvered dial, strap; in white gold with anthracite dial and strap.

PROTOCOLE XL AUTOMATIC   REF. GOA25031

Movement: mechanical, automatic winding, 500P caliber, with 40 hours autonomy, 26 jewels, 21,600 vibrations per hour. **Functions:** hour, minute, second, date.
Case: 18 kt white gold, three-piece, rectangular case with smoothed angles (size 34 x 31 mm, thickness 8 mm), polished and brushed finish; curved sapphire crystal; glass-bearing bezel decorated with ligné pattern; carriers fastened to the case by 4 screws; white gold crown; back fastened by 8 screws. Water-resistant to 3 atm.
Dial: solid gold, black, decorated with ligné pattern; printed black Roman numerals; white-gold Dauphine hands. **Indications:** date at 6.
Strap: square-scale alligators leather, hand-stitched; white gold clasp.
Also available: with silvered dial; bracelet and recessed double fold-over clasp, silvered dial, black dial; in yellow gold with silvered dial, leather strap. Jewel versions. With quartz movement, brushed silvered or black dial, applied Roman numerals.

EMPERADOR   REF. G0A25037

Movement: mechanical, automatic winding, Piaget 551P caliber (500P base), with 27 jewels. Balance with 21,600 vibrations per hour.
Functions: hour, minute, small second, power reserve.
Case: 18 kt pink gold, three-piece case, rectangular (size 33 x 32 mm, thickness 9.4 mm), polished and brushed finish; curved sapphire crystal; pink-gold crown; back attached by 4 screws; water-resitant to 3 atm.
Dial: solid gold, silvered, decorated with "Clous de Paris" pattern, brushed hour ring; printed Arabic numerals; faceted pink-gold Dauphine hands.
Indications: power reserve at 6, small second at 10.
Strap: crocodile leather, hand-stitched; pink-gold clasp.

Also available: in white gold; brilliant bezel and lugs, silvered dial with a row of brilliants and printed markers: pink gold; white gold; in other jewel versions.

ALTIPLANO   REF. G0A23093

Movement: mechanical, manual winding, ultra-thin, produced by Piaget, 430P caliber (derived from the famous Piaget 9P caliber, realized in 1956).
Functions: hour, minute.
Case: 18 kt white gold, three-piece square case (size 28x28 mm, thickness 4,3mm); flat sapphire crystal; sapphire cabochon on white-gold crown; back attached by 8 screws. Water-resistant to 3 atm.
Dial: solid gold, black, Arabic numerals; white-gold leaf style hands.
Strap: crocodile leather, hand stitched; white-gold clasp.

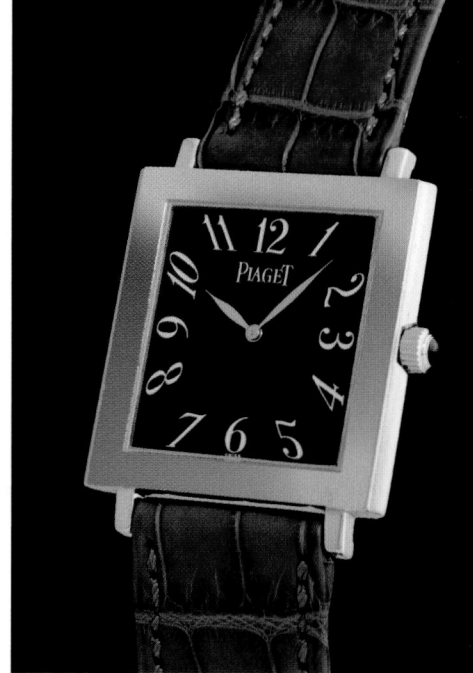

TONNEAU   REF. G0A26055

Movement: quartz, 59P caliber.
Functions: hour, minute,
Case: 18 kt white gold and brilliants (1.6 carat), two-piece, tonneau-shaped case (size 25x16 mm, thickness 5 mm); curved sapphire crystal; white gold crown with a faceted set diamond; back fastened by 4 screws. Water-resistant to 3 atm.
Dial: solid gold, pavé of square-cut diamonds (0.3 carat); 18 kt white gold applied Arabic numerals 6 and 12; white-gold Dauphine hands.
Strap: blue moiré; white-gold clasp.
Also available: with blue dial and blue navy or blue sky satin strap; with blue mother-of-pearl dial and blue lezard strap; with paved bracelet.

MISS PROTOCOLE ALLONGÉE   REF. G0A26001

Movement: quartz, 57P caliber.
Functions: hour, minute.
Case: 18 kt yellow gold, rectangular case anatomically curved (size 30x17 mm, thickness 5 mm) with upper decoration with fluted pattern; curved sapphire crystal; yellow gold crown; back fastened by 4 screws. Water-resistant to 3 atm.
Dial: white mother-of-pearl; three Arabic numerals; yellow-gold leaf style hands.
Strap: calfskin strap, attachment made of a rectangular element and upside jointed and downside recessed lugs; yellow gold clasp.
Also available: in yellow gold with brushed dial and 3 set diamonds; in yellow gold with mother-of-pearl dial, attachments set with diamonds; in white gold with mother-of-pearl dial; in yellow gold with mother-of-pearl dial, attachments set with diamonds, yellow gold bracelet. Wide collection of colourful straps on different materials (calfskin, taffetas, square-scale alligators, textile, lizard, snake skin). Yearly new straps animation on new materials (moiré, tag, ...).

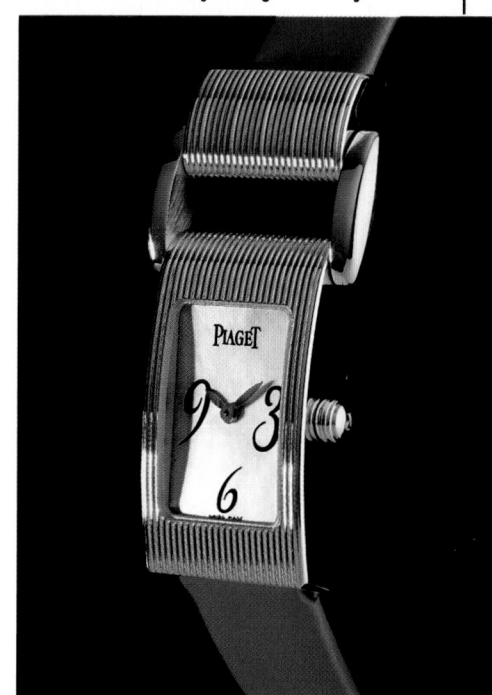

POIRAY

an historical perspective

Located on the prestigious Rue de la Paix in Paris, the Poiray boutique was purchased fourteen years ago by Nathalie Hocq-Choay. It was her dream to create a new philosophy and style of jewelry and watches. Driven by passion and perfection, Nathalie Hocq-Choay spent years developing one of the most striking and individualistic looks on the market.

Thanks to her innovative design sense, Nathalie Hocq-Choay has succeeded in attracting a jewelry following of today's finest international clientele and, in doing so, building a small empire. In only 14 years, this authentic fine jewelry house has flourished from a single boutique into 87 different outlets in France and Japan.

By focusing clearly on classic, contemporary style and refined elegance, Nathalie Hocq-Choay, chairman and sole designer of Poiray, has accelerated the brand into a leading position. The originality and craftsmanship inherent in each Poiray creation underscores the brand's endless use of fresh design techniques and its overall quest for excellence.

According to Nathalie Hocq-Choay, "An innovative approach, respecting tradition and refinement of craftsmanship — while striving for perfection and creative techniques—is the key."

Indeed this is the philosophy upon which the brand was built. Initially, Nathalie Hocq-Choay focused her attentions on developing the jewelry line. Core creations include scintillating pieces meant to fulfill a woman's every desire and mood. They are modern, easy-to-wear jewels that make bold statements of individuality. Interchangeable, stackable rings, big bold gemstone rings and brilliant pearl rings immediately catch the eye. Pendants that move and flow with the body, necklaces that drape like fabric against the skin—these are the elements that comprise the Poiray jewelry collection.

With her innovative jewelry collection firmly rooted in success, Nathalie Hocq-Choay turned her attention to timepieces in the early 1990s. Her first creations garnered high acclaim and, for the past decade, Poiray has been producing striking, versatile watches that capture the mind's imagination and the body's spirit.

sophisticated style

Like the brand's jewelry, its timepieces are crafted with emphasis on detail and creativity. The first timepieces unveiled by Poiray as the Ma Première collection offered such elegant style and sophistication that they were immediate successes. Today, this series is one of the most important to the brand. It features a striking square case with rounded corners and a notched linear design. Interchangeable straps are the hallmark of the collection and come in such a brilliant array of colors and styles that women can create new images at will. The newest straps feature tassels of beads, insets of pearls, or embossed designs. In all, there are more than 400 bracelets and straps in the collection—and even more are designed daily.

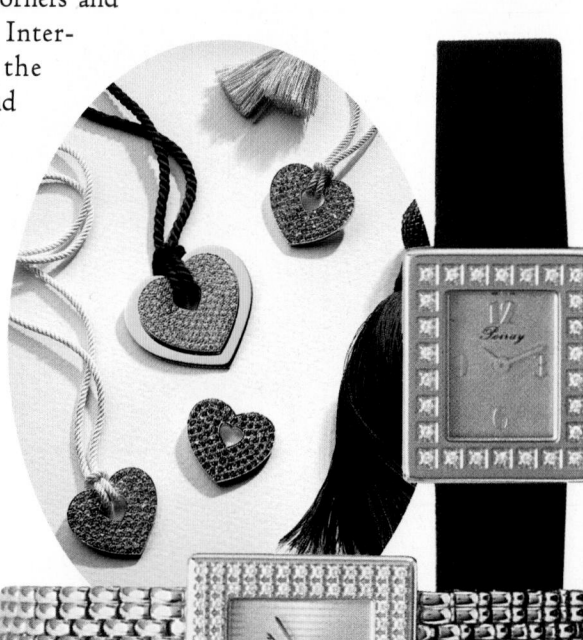

The Times 3 watch, first unveiled in 1999, has also made an indelible mark on the wrists of women who want versatility and elegance. This unusual timepiece is an interchangeable watch wherein the strap, bezel or dial can easily be changed by the woman herself to offer her a different look for every hour, every day, every occasion.

The interchangeable bracelets, bezels and dial choices consist of 54 different renditions, including an open-link bracelet, high-polished or notched bezels and a myriad of dial and strap colors, including some brilliant shades. Additionally, there is a scintillating Times 3 High Jewelry collection that offers varying amounts of diamonds on the dials and bezels. This haute joaillerie Times 3 series comes with either a bracelet, or in a strap collection of pastel hues called Sorbet.

New renditions of the Times 3 are in the form of a Times 3 Manchette for women and a Times 3 Urban for men. The Manchette features a square dial set into a large, oversized strap that shows Poiray's fashion flair. The straps are created in lizard or calf and in fabric, ranging from bright orange to purple, red, blue, black, white and gold. The dial choices include color-coordinated tones, as well as classic white or black.

The Times 3 Urban for men is designed for gentlemen who like both disciplined and daring, who like sobriety yet fun. Offered in either a quartz or automatic version, it features the signature rounded-edge square case of Poiray, but in a larger size. It is characterized by sleek, seductive lines that give it the bold yet sophisticated look that appeals to Nathalie Hocq-Choay's clients. Like the ladies' Times 3, the Urban has easy-change straps to adapt perfectly from business to evening, from jeans to tuxedo.

Indeed, with its hint of fun, flair for fashion and sleek sophistication, Poiray offers unbridled choices.

QUINTING

an historical perspective

Quinting timepieces are definitively different. Six years in the making, these exceptional watches are the world's first completely transparent chronographs. These clear masterpieces have overcome challenges of mechanics and defied technological barriers to offer an all-new look at time.

Years ago, an automotive engineer, had dreamed of creating a totally transparent watch. His designs regularly met with technological problems and watch manufacturer after manufacturer told him that a transparent wristwatch simply could not be achieved. Engineers and researchers of the Quinting manufacture didn't listen. Recognizing that conventional watchmaking processes were of no use, the Quinting manufacture enlisted the help of two highly qualified Swiss watchmaking engineers specializing in structural design and technical development of the watch. Together, those watchmakers managed the miniaturization of technology that heretofore had only been found in Cartier's Mystery Clocks.

In order to achieve the transparency they were searching for, Quinting developed a process that uses 12 specially coated sapphires. The mechanical movement is powered by four electronic motors created especially for the new technology required to operate the watch. The movement and its electronic motors were configured in a precise manner so they would fit within the watch rim and bezel. The completely new manufacturing technology was a challenge both for Quinting, which now produces its own movements, and for the subcontracting companies needed to build certain parts. Of the 230 parts and 26 subassemblies comprising the Quinting watch, all but seven parts are made exclusively for this chronograph.

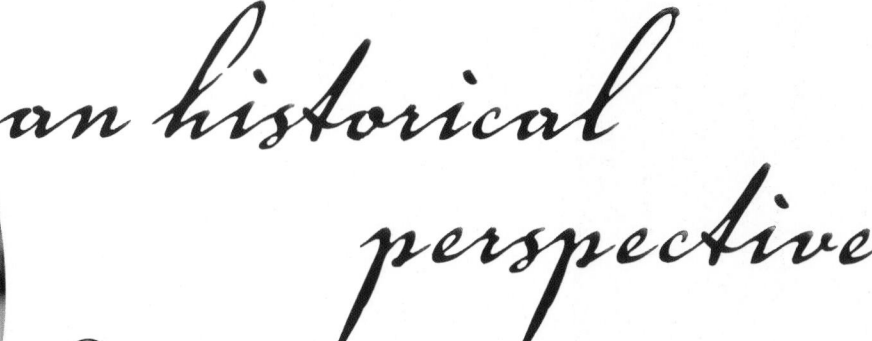

After six full years of research and development, the first Mystery Transparent Quinting watch was unveiled to the world in 1999. It received several honors and was met with overwhelming interest by collectors and connoisseurs. In 2000, a new investor as well as engineer, Pascal Berclaz bought the company with an eagerness to bring it to even higher heights. President Berclaz, the managing director of this fast-growing enterprise, is committed to developing a full range of high-tech Mystery watches whose transparency and purity can become a symbol for all who wear it.

QUINTING
MANUFACTURE D'HORLOGERIE

unveiling

masterpieces

TOP

This steel watch features a black ring and black subdials.

CENTER LEFT

The steel bracelet of this Mystery watch is incredibly flexible for comfort and elegance.

BOYTOM

In 2001, Quinting unveiled ladies' versions of the transparent chronograph.

Quinting watches are precision instruments made of the highest quality materials and manufactured entirely by hand in the company's workshops in St. Blaise, Switzerland. This totally transparent chronograph is an electrical-mechanical watch. The heart of the watch consists of 11 sapphire crystals that have been specially treated to render them virtually transparent. Six of the crystals are actually toothed wheels—each of which imparts motion to one of the watch's six hands. The mechanism of this complex watch consists of four drives or motors hidden within the watch case rim.

The technical and aesthetic value of this exceptional watch keeps orders pouring in. Nonetheless, the manufacture is limited due to the sheer nature of the craftsmanship involved. Every Quinting watch is individually numbered on the caseback and on the movement. Currently, Quinting watches are created in 18-karat yellow or white gold or in steel. Each is complemented by either a crocodile strap or a sleek metal bracelet in

CHRONOLOGY

1993 Establishment of Quinting.

1999 After six years of tireless pursuit, Quinting unveils the first Mystery Transparent watch to the world, for which its original styling receives several honors.

2001 New president Pascal Berclaz acquires the company.

2002 Quinting has its first showing at Basel; Launching of the brand's first models for ladies.

CENTER LEFT

The newest diamond-adorned versions of the Mystery chronograph feature either 1.5 or 2.8 carats of diamonds.

BOTTOM

Dubbed "Noel" and released for the 2001 holidays, this striking transparent chronograph is a mixture of harmony and beauty.

BOTTOM RIGHT

The bezels of these steel watches are each set with 1.5 carats of VVS1 Top Wesselton diamonds.

matte and polish finish. Some models feature diamonds, while others sport high-polished bezels.

Until December of 2001, Quinting watches were created only for men. However, just in time for the holidays, the brand unveiled a striking rendition for women. The bezel of the newest watch is set with Top Wesselton VVSI quality diamonds totaling 1.5 carats in weight. There is also a version with diamonds weighing 2.8 carats. These sparkling masterpieces are offset with colorful red or blue straps.

Backing its commitment to challenge, Quinting has also become involved in the world of sports' sponsorships.

REPOSSI

an historical perspective

"*My jewellery has a rich past made of adventures, sorrows, joys...just like life is.*"

Alberto Repossi

Indeed, Alberto Repossi draws inspiration for all he creates from life around him. Everywhere he goes, he spends time studying, gazing, experiencing—and then he reinterprets these moments into timeless treasures. Jeweler extraordinaire, Alberto Repossi now heads up the legendary House that has carried his family name since 1920. A third-generation jeweler, Repossi has a passion for noble metals and precious stones—a passion he translates from emotion to reality with such depth and feeling that it leaves one in awe.

Certainly since its inception, Repossi has been a brand synonymous with regal splendor and exquisite beauty. Alberto, however, has spent the last 25 years bringing the brand to new heights. Aside from his magnificent jewelry creations and his timely foray into the world of timepieces, Repossi has opened three strategically located international boutiques and has spent the past eight years acting as the official purveyor to H.R.H. Prince Rainier III of Monaco.

Repossi has created jewelry for some of the world's most renowned celebrities and royalty and has won awards for his adept and detailed work. Fantasy and fun, reality and richness all come together in Repossi masterpieces. Indeed, Repossi spends long hours meshing the technical aspects of creating jewelry with the artistic beauty of dreams.

While over the decades Repossi has created elegant and beautiful jeweled timepieces, it was Alberto's dream to branch into the world of watches with a complete line. For him, combining the technical with the splendid had already been achieved and delving into the creation of a watch line was only natural.

Today, Repossi offers jeweled and classic timepieces that deftly complement the brand's exquisite jewelry and make a mark on time all their own.

THIS PAGE
BOTTOM

Called the "Toi et Moi," this geometrical ring is composed of nearly 9 carats of diamonds.

FACING PAGE

Repossi's new ultra-slim watch comes in several versions. This model is crafted in polished stainless steel with Onyx dial set with 108 diamonds weighing .52 carats. It houses a quartz movement.

449

eye of the beholder

TOP RIGHT

HRH Princess Caroline of Hanover and Mr. Alberto Repossi.

CENTER

This ultra-flat watch is in polished stainless steel and the onyx dial is set with diamonds.

BOTTOM LEFT

The Astrum watch collection features the constellation of each Zodiac sign set in diamonds on the dials. These timepieces are housed in brushed stainless steel with brightly colored straps.

BOTTOM RIGHT

This Lady's watch is crafted in PVD-treated stainless steel to combine the magic of black with the scintillating appeal of diamonds. The dial is set with four diamonds.

FACING PAGE

TOP

Mr. and Mrs. Alberto Repossi with Tasha de Vasconselos wearing the Repossi Czarina necklace.

BOTTOM

From the Astrum collection of jewelry, this black-gold model features the zodiac sign represented by diamonds set in gold.

A perfectionist with a passion for the finest, Alberto Repossi travels the world to look for diamonds and gemstones he uses in his creations. Most of what he selects is the result of a keen sense of mood and emotion, mixed, of course, with perfection of the stone.

Known to the elite world for his cutting-edge style and depth, Repossi deftly blends colors and shapes. His ideas stem from his travels and his sketches are creative watercolor renditions that are incredibly inspiring in and of themselves. With each new rendition, Repossi brings his imagination— influenced by changing times and changing needs and desires.

In his Haute Joaillerie, femininity reigns supreme— with dazzling collar necklaces, bracelets of bows and ribbons, and floral brooches of radiant distinction. Even the high-jewelry watches Repossi has specially created for select clientele reflect a classic sense of style and beauty—donning the perfect amount of diamonds and gemstones in custom selections.

It was two years ago that Repossi finally unveiled a watch collection that he felt could reflect his style and image appropriately. Years in the thought and design process, the first Repossi collection was

called the R Monaco. The collection offered unusual case shapes, vibrant colors, and diamond accents that are indicative of Repossi.

The watchcases of the R Monaco are meticulously crafted octagons that offer bold refinement. Matched with striking, geometrical linked bracelets or brightly colored straps, the R Monaco makes a statement of strength and beauty. The case shape, along with the distinctive Repossi logo and dial design, reflects a "Place Vendôme" look and feel.

From the outset, three different sizes and attitudes (sporty, dressy and casual) of the R Monaco were offered without changing the overall character of the watch. Among the models unveiled were a diamond-adorned dress watch, several bracelet and strap pieces that were classically elegant, and some brightly colored straps with matching mother-of-pearl dial renditions that easily and quickly captured the eye and the heart.

Created in steel, or in 18-karat yellow or white gold (some diamond adorned, some not), the collection became an instantaneous hit amongst his clientele, and Repossi went on to evolve this series and to produce new and exciting additions that complement the R Monaco.

elegant

masterpieces

This past year, Alberto Repossi elected to round out his collection of elegant timepieces by adding versions that answered the needs of his prestigious and demanding customers.

Among the newest timepieces are a series of ultra-flat watches, an unusual Zodiac-inspired piece and a collection of high-powered chronographs. Each of the watches keeps the strong Repossi identity established with the octagon case, Repossi logo, Place Vendôme form and distinct styling.

Dubbed the R5 Monaco, Repossi's Ultra-flat watch is designed for evening-wear. Measuring a scant 5.09mm thick on its curved case, the R5 Monaco gives the ultimate impression of thinness. Created only in 18-karat yellow, white or pink gold, or in stainless steel set with diamonds, the sober design evokes a true sense of elegance.

Going a step further toward coordinating chosen watch and jewelry lines, Repossi also unveiled the ladies' Astrum watch collection. Complementing the Astrum jewels

collection, the watches are crafted in stainless steel—on which the constellation of each of the Zodiac signs is emulated. Proportionately sized diamonds represent big and small stars. An engraved line links the diamonds and thereby outlines the design of each sign on the watch dial for a truly unusual, yet highly personal statement.

In the creation of the Chronograph, Repossi relied on his strength in design to establish the alliance between technical features and aesthetics. The chronograph features an automatic movement that is water resistant to 50 meters. Each watch is set in either a brushed or polished stainless steel case (with or without diamonds), or in 18-karat pink gold for striking appeal.

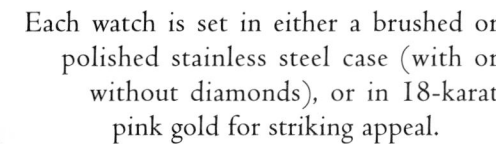

As with all Repossi timepieces, the newest watches are Swiss made, feature sapphire curved crystals and screw-on casebacks. Every watch features an engraved caseback that bears Repossi's signature, the product seal, its origin, and individual number of order. Only 2,000 Repossi watches are made annually to preserve the brand's philosophy of exclusivity.

RICHARD MILLE

The culture and love of mechanics in general, of the automobile and aviation in particular, and the passion for technical sophistication, have come together to manufacture of this modern, sophisticated, efficient, practical, powerful and reliable piece–the Richard Mille Watch.

The drive for innovation and the technical choices required thousands of hours spent on engineering design (120,000 operations), validation, tests and adjustments. Painstaking attention has been paid to every detail and every material has been tested with vigor. Each movement of this watch required more than 20,000 mechanical operations, and each consists of 267 components. ARCAP (an alloy with great mechanical properties that ensure stability over time and resistance to deformation), as well as titanium and ceramics, have been used.

The design and execution of this watch testify to an integral approach taken with the movement/case/dial-everything has been designed from a clean slate according to extremely precise and rigorous specifications. The goal was to completely integrate all elements, like a Formula I car in which the chassis and the engine are both developed according to a single specification. For example, no casing ring is necessary. Combined, this explains the exceptional quality of fabrication in the Richard Mille Watch.

With characteristic lateral ribs of improved rigidity, a large-size, and easy-to-grip hand-setting crown, easy readability, power reserve, and torque indicator display, everything in this watch has been designed to make life easier for its wearer. Moreover, the sapphire glass has been given an anti-glare treatment.

The component reliability has been studied and tested intensely. Based on research, these were implemented: a special, rapidly rotating spring barrel which balances the supply of driving power; a strengthened mainspring; optimized wheel-work with the spring barrel's teeth and the center pinion with a profile of gears—reducing friction and improving the clockwork movement. A new-generation, modular hand-setting block facilitates after-sale service due to its easy access, in which complete dismantling of the hands and dials in no longer necessary; a stiffened plate structure was added (as in car engines), thus avoiding the twisting that often affects the workability of mechanical watches. Finally, a ruby wheel located in the hour-setting module allows the hand-setting stem to be operated with gentle precision.

The titanium screws characteristic of this watch allow phenomenal screwing/unscrewing torque, thus avoiding any damage to the screw that frequently occurs with a conventional screwdriver. The particular shape of the screw head means only specialized approved retailers, who have the proper tools, can dismantle the watch. A copper washer under each screw allows optimum tightening without marking the bridges or plates. At the critical points, such as the crown wheel, wear-resistant washers, hardened and precision-ground, have been placed to protect the functional components. Thus, when taken for servicing, these washers can be replaced as soon as any major wear and tear is noted.

The radical style of this watch reflects a temperament dedicated to powerful performance. Glamour is absent-there is no embellishment, no extravagance but rather the confirmed determination to define a new vision of extreme luxury, of top-of-the-range watches. It is a Formula I, with all the qualities of use and reliability inherent in a great G.T.

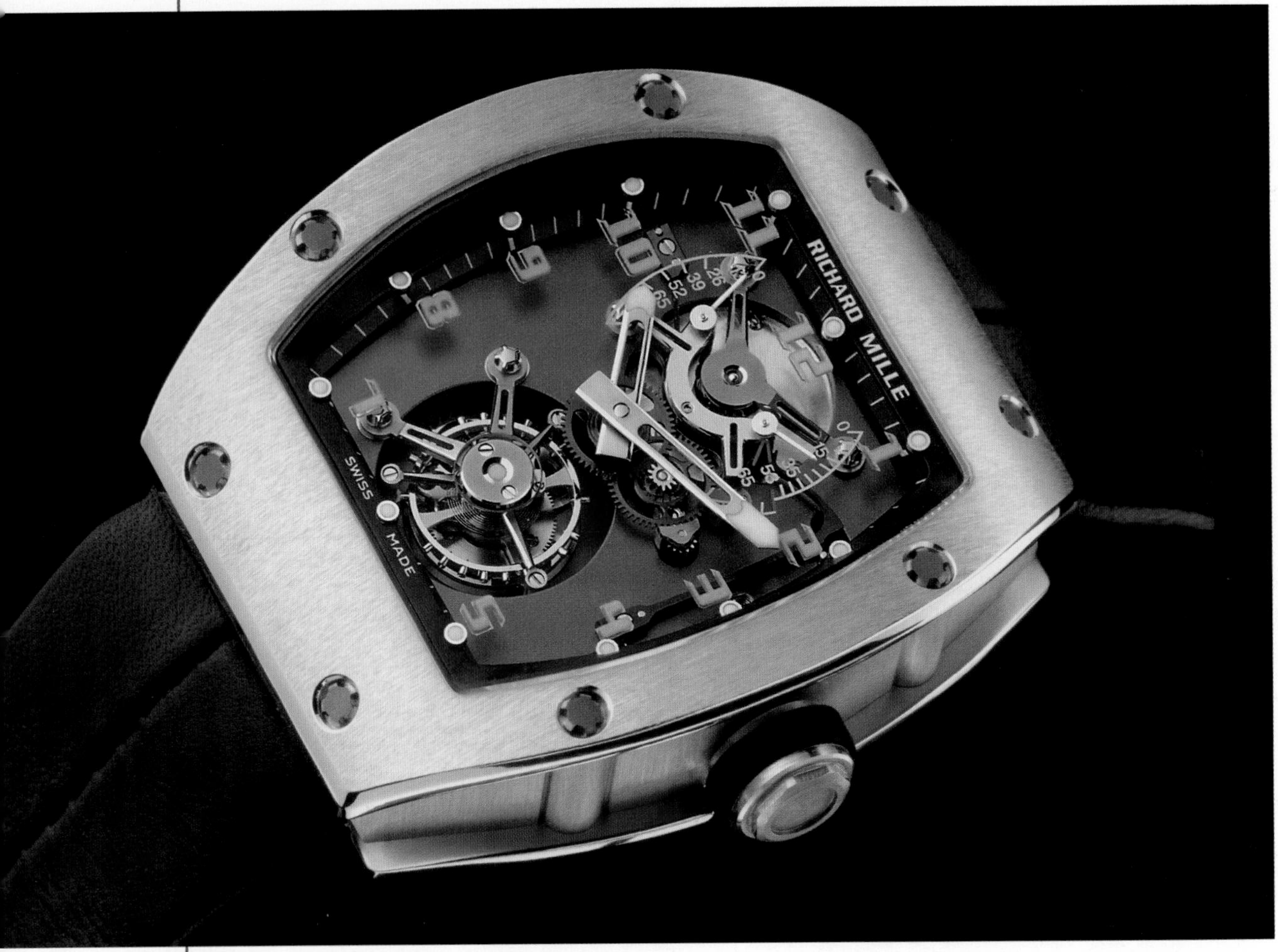

RM 001-1

This Richard Mille Tourbillon features a hand-wound movement, second time zone (RM 003), hours and minutes, 70 hours of power reserve, and torque indicator.

The torque indicator displays the main spring tension and enables optimization of the movement's timing. If the torque is below 53 dNmm, the spring is too slack; at the other extreme, if it registers above 65 dNmm, the excessive tension has an adverse affect on the running of the movement and may cause damage. These indications are visible on the numerical zone to the right of the barrel.

The Richard Mille tooth-system devised to ensure excellent torque transmission and distinct improvement in performance consists of a barrel and third-wheel pinion with central involute profile. The wheel has a central developing profile, and a pressure angle of 20 degrees promotes an effective rolling movement that compensates for differences between the centers.

The RM-001-I possesses a variable inertia balance, which provides better reliability in the event of shocks, movement assem-

TOP

Each RM 001 features 23 jewels, PVD coating and measures 30.20mm x 28.60mm.

BOTTOM

This RM 001 is crafted in pink gold and, as are all RM 001 models, is polished and beveled by hand.

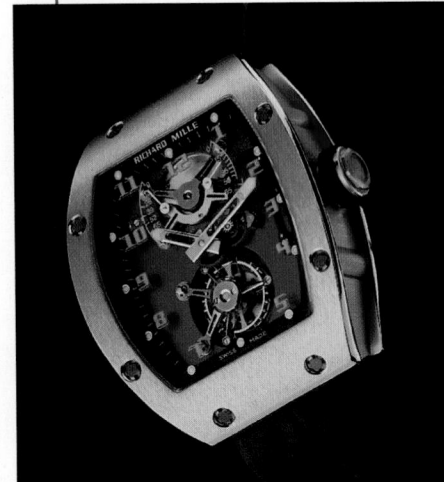

bly and disassembly. It also guarantees better chronometric results over an extended period of time. The index has been eliminated, thus providing more accurate and repetitive timing.

The movement has been fitted with a barrel that rotates at a faster speed than usual. At 6 hours per revolution (instead of 7.5 hours), the barrel has several advantages, two of which are: a greatly diminished occurrence of sticking mainsprings; an excellent mainspring curve delta for which the ideal power reserve, performance and regularity ratio has been chosen. The barrel pawl with progressive recoil adds about 20% winding gain (especially at the start of a procedure) to the device and eliminates mainspring tension. Facilitating the logical approach to maintenance and ease of use, the barrel cover is enclosed with eccentric screws.

Because the time-setting mechanism is fitted with a module against the tourbillon's caseback, mounting dismantling of the module without disturbing the hands and dial is possible. It is also easy to mount this component on the outside of the movement, so in the event of a defect, this time-setting assembly can be changed without affecting the integrity of the bottom plate.

Visible through the back of the watch, the time-setting lever is in the form of a small wheel. This improves the time-setting functions by eliminating engaging friction, now replaced by rolling friction. The more rigid stem body reduces slack during winding.

Possessing 23 jewels, the RM-00I-I is 30.20mm x 28.60mm with a thickness of 6.35mm. The tourbillon's diameter measures I2.30mm, and the balance wheel is I0mm. The balance is in GLICYDUR, the balance spring in ELINVAR and the alloy is by NIVAROX. Antichoc: KIF ELASTOR I60 B28. The endstone for the tourbillon cage is crafted in ceramic, and the stone setting is in white gold. The barrel shaft is created in nickel-free chronifer (DIN x 46 Cr I3 + S) with the following characteristics: stainless, anti-magnetic properties, suited for tempering.

The RM-00I-I features hand-polished chamfers, PVD coating, sapphire blasted milled sections and surfaces, lapped and polished ends, burnished pivots, a hand-polished locking section, and is beveled and polished by hand. The gear wheels feature concave chamfering with a diamond tool, circular-smoothed faces, and gilding (before cutting teeth).

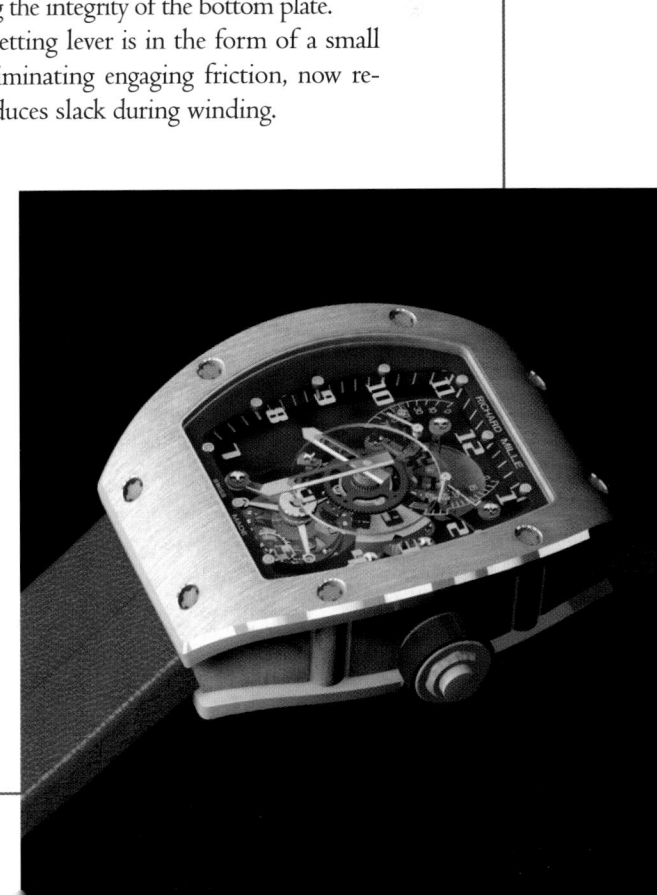

RM 004

Following the introduction of the RM 001/2 and the RM 003 tourbillons, Richard Mille launched a new-generation chronograph with several technical innovations, the RM 004.

This complication watch features: chronograph with column-wheel; split-second wheel with improved function; optimized minute counter; torque sensor; power reserve; winding-stem with neutral position; rapidly rotating spring barrel; wheel-toothing; a new escapement; ergonomic positioning of buttons.

In fact, above and beyond the indisputable precision in chronometry, intense research has resulted in a large number of improved parameters from which the Richard Mille tourbillon models have already benefited. These improvements are evident in: a new-generation spring barrel with rapid rotation; new collection of gear teeth which absorb any geometric variation affecting the center distance; new escapement design which reduces friction; special curve of the spiral which reduces the shifting of the center of gravity during performance; and a rewinding system featuring a small ruby wheel designed to eliminate scratching and friction.

With the invention of a neutral position for the winding stem, which is modeled on a gearbox, the aim is to eliminate the permanent overload of the flange. Thus, the mechanism is disconnected from the seal and the ratchet key (whose recoil relieves tension in the flange) and the piece functions safely while the crown remains tight.

The design quality of the RM 004 prevents virtually all jumping of the seconds hand, a common problem in mechanical chronographs. Vital mathematical research has enabled Richard Mille technicians to understand the causes of this phenomenon and thus determine the perfect solutions for inaccurate time display. These solutions were implemented through the manufacture of titanium gear wheels and bars, which reduced inertia. The development of innovative split-seconds pieces has made it possible to simultaneously reduce energy consumption by approximately 50% by lowering friction on the spindle, and to eliminate the jumps on stopping by working on the clips in particular.

In addition, the modern architecture evident in the RM 004 has allowed for the consistent arrangement of parts, which has greatly improved the functioning of the systems and thereby avoiding unnecessary super impositions and allowing the optimum application of technical solutions along the lines of Formula I. Moreover, access to the settings has been simplified, allowing for easier manipulation during after-sales servicing.

Finally, the main button has been positioned to accommodate the thumb rather than the index finger. This change is in response to clientele demands for a product that, while mechanically complicated and sophisticated, is easy to use.

The RM 004 has a total height of 8.90mm and the height on hands is 11.20mm. It features 21,600 A/h with 72 hours of power reserve. Physically, the hour hand is positioned in the center along with the minutes and chronograph. It displays a split-seconds wheel, minute counter, power-reserve indicator, torque sensor, and winding-stem position indicator.

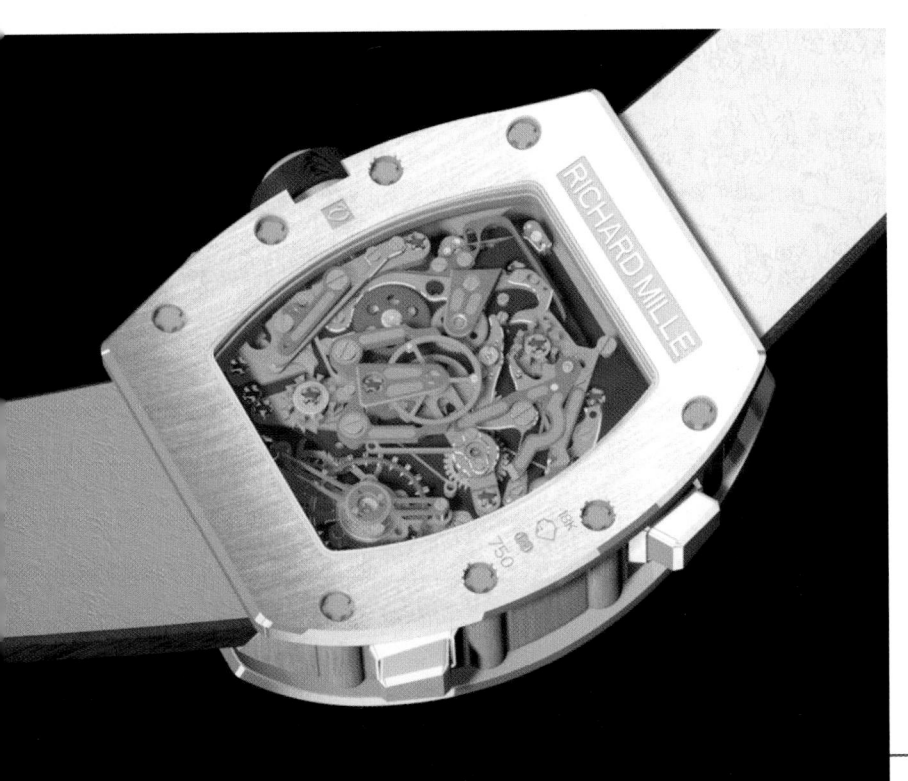

ROGER DUBUIS

art and tradition

*J*ust seven years old, the Roger Dubuis watch brand already is enjoying much international acclaim. Formed in 1995 as a partnership between entrepreneur Carlos Dias and watchmaker extraordinaire Roger Dubuis, the brand quickly stole the attention of watch lovers around the world.

Built on a philosophy of art and a respect for tradition, Roger Dubuis timepieces exude an air of marked originality. For Dubuis, who had spent 40 years as a master watchmaker for some of the world's finest brands, art is the expression of harmony, purity and authenticity. Respect, he explains, is to be paid to the glory of Swiss watchmaking heritage in general, and Geneva's tradition in particular.

For this reason, he holds steadfast to the legacy of Swiss watchmaking techniques—handcraftsmanship, mechanical precision and technical prowess—with a passion. However, Dubuis is quick to realize the roles of today and tomorrow in timekeeping, and is incredibly innovative in his case and dial designs.

Each Roger Dubuis collection is exceptional in its appearance and in the craftsmanship that goes into its making. Ranging from a unique cushioned-square case shape to incredibly oversized, vertical and horizontal rectangles, Roger Dubuis watches are immediately recognizable and distinctive. All Roger Dubuis watches are marked with the prestigious Geneva Quality Hallmark attesting to their high-watchmaking and mechanical prowess.

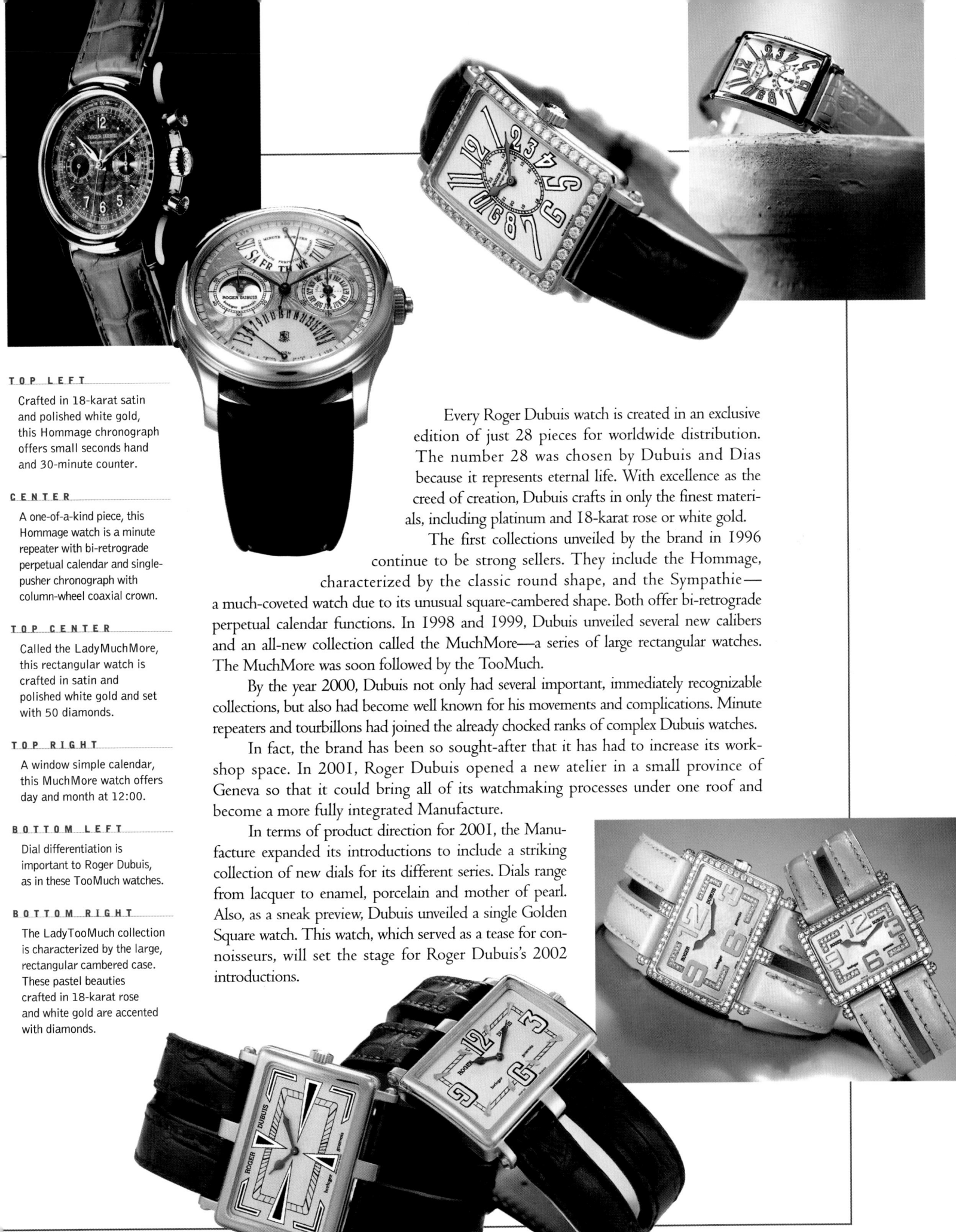

TOP LEFT

Crafted in 18-karat satin and polished white gold, this Hommage chronograph offers small seconds hand and 30-minute counter.

CENTER

A one-of-a-kind piece, this Hommage watch is a minute repeater with bi-retrograde perpetual calendar and single-pusher chronograph with column-wheel coaxial crown.

TOP CENTER

Called the LadyMuchMore, this rectangular watch is crafted in satin and polished white gold and set with 50 diamonds.

TOP RIGHT

A window simple calendar, this MuchMore watch offers day and month at 12:00.

BOTTOM LEFT

Dial differentiation is important to Roger Dubuis, as in these TooMuch watches.

BOTTOM RIGHT

The LadyTooMuch collection is characterized by the large, rectangular cambered case. These pastel beauties crafted in 18-karat rose and white gold are accented with diamonds.

Every Roger Dubuis watch is created in an exclusive edition of just 28 pieces for worldwide distribution. The number 28 was chosen by Dubuis and Dias because it represents eternal life. With excellence as the creed of creation, Dubuis crafts in only the finest materials, including platinum and 18-karat rose or white gold.

The first collections unveiled by the brand in 1996 continue to be strong sellers. They include the Hommage, characterized by the classic round shape, and the Sympathie—a much-coveted watch due to its unusual square-cambered shape. Both offer bi-retrograde perpetual calendar functions. In 1998 and 1999, Dubuis unveiled several new calibers and an all-new collection called the MuchMore—a series of large rectangular watches. The MuchMore was soon followed by the TooMuch.

By the year 2000, Dubuis not only had several important, immediately recognizable collections, but also had become well known for his movements and complications. Minute repeaters and tourbillons had joined the already chocked ranks of complex Dubuis watches.

In fact, the brand has been so sought-after that it has had to increase its workshop space. In 2001, Roger Dubuis opened a new atelier in a small province of Geneva so that it could bring all of its watchmaking processes under one roof and become a more fully integrated Manufacture.

In terms of product direction for 2001, the Manufacture expanded its introductions to include a striking collection of new dials for its different series. Dials range from lacquer to enamel, porcelain and mother of pearl. Also, as a sneak preview, Dubuis unveiled a single Golden Square watch. This watch, which served as a tease for connoisseurs, will set the stage for Roger Dubuis's 2002 introductions.

ROLEX

moments in time

Rolex. The word is practically a household name—in fact, it is one of the most recognized names in the world.

Creating fine timepieces for nearly 100 years, Rolex is a brand that has built an international image and following based on its high-powered, high-performance chronometers and chronographs.

Founded by Hans Wilsdorf, Rolex was borne on the commitment to technical ingenuity and advancement. It was one of the first brands to insist on having its timepieces rigorously tested to achieve certified-chronometer status.

This is a brand that, since its inception, has been intent on participating in the world's adventures. Rolex has made headlines while on the wrists of such adventurers as Chuck Yeager when he flew faster than the speed of sound in 1947, and Sir Edmund Hillary when he climbed Mt. Everest in 1953. Today, Rolex remains intimately involved in the rigors of sports and continues to produce watches that exceed the limits.

Among the newest timepieces unveiled this year is a collection of Oyster watches for women. First created in 1926, the Oyster laid claim to fame as the first water-resistant watch when it crossed the English Channel on the wrist of swimmer Mercedes Gleitze in 1927. The patented Oyster was deemed truly water resistant—thanks to Rolex's case design and technical expertise.

LEFT

This rounded Lady-Datejust is crafted in 18-karat pink gold with Oyster bracelet and black mother-of-pearl dial set with 10 diamonds.

BELOW LEFT

Crafted in platinum, the Lady-Datejust, with its pale blue or pink mother-of-pearl dial, combines the elegance of robust personality and simple beauty.

BELOW

This trio of 18-karat yellow-gold Lady-Datejust Oyster watches offers varying degrees of diamonds and date aperture at 3:00.

Throughout the ensuing decades, the Oyster has remained an icon for the brand. It has evolved gracefully over time without compromising its power or its identity. Now the designers and watchmakers at Rolex have joined forces to unveil the Oyster Lady-Datejust. The 2001 models are available in 18-karat yellow, pink or white gold and feature the Oyster bracelet or strap. The bezel remains fluted, but the crystal is slightly domed and the dials are striking mother-of-pearl renditions. All models are equipped with the latest generation of self-winding mechanisms because Rolex, ever in tune with market demands, recognizes the universal appeal of its self-winding timepieces.

In addition to the Oyster Lady-Datejust, Rolex has rounded out its more formal Cellini line with several new models for women. Both elegant and sensual, the Cellini watches offer a more provocative look. Among the new models is the striking, strictly female Orchid. This precious timepiece features an all-diamond case, diamond markers and a diamond-adorned bracelet. The Cellissima is a white-gold collection that includes an elegant round- or tonneau-shaped case design with diamond bezels and diamond case-to-bracelet attachments. Finally, the Cestello is a new watch with vibrantly colored strap, round Oyster case and mother-of-pearl dial. The strap is a dual-colored green-on-blue, or blue-on-green ostrich.

These recent introductions embody the spirit, technical excellence and aesthetic emphasis that characterize all Rolex timepieces.

ROLEX

OYSTER PERPETUAL COSMOGRAPH DAYTONA   REF. 116519

Movement: mechanical, automatic winding, Rolex 4130 caliber of own manufacture; 72 hours autonomy, Glucydur balance with "Microstar" micrometer regulation, 44 jewels, 28,800 vibrations per hour, Breguet balance spring. Officially certified "chronometer" (C.O.S.C.).
Functions: hour, minute, small second, chronograph with three counters.
Case: 18 kt white gold, three-piece case (Ø 40 mm, thickness 12.5 mm), pol-

ished and brushed finish; sapphire crystal; fixed bezel with engraved tachometer scale; white-gold screw-down crown with threefold gasket and case protection; screw-down pushers; screwed-on back. Water-resistant to 10 atm.
Dial: pink mother-of-pearl, counter crowns with white-gold rims; applied white-gold Roman numerals; white-gold bâton hands. **Indications:** minute counter at 3, small second at 6, hour counter at 9, center second, minute track with divisions for 1/5 of a second.
Strap: lizard skin; white-gold fold-over clasp.
Also available: with turquoise, green chrysoprase, yellow mother-of-pearl dial and lizard skin strap in matching colors.

OYSTER PERPETUAL DATE YACHT-MASTER ROLESIUM   REF. 168622

The waterproof Yacht Master is realized with three case sizes: large - diameter 40 millimeters, medium - diameter 34 millimeters, small - diameter 29 millimeters. Medium size models come with traditional dials showing steel, blue, white or champagne-color backgrounds or the white reflexes of mother-of-pearl, also combined with markers made of precious stones.
The name of the Rolesium model, shown in the photograph, is added to the

traditional versions in yellow gold or stainless steel with gold and indicates the steel alloy with the same name, used by the Genevan House for some models of the past. Today, the name Rolesium defines a new interpretation of the most recent Rolex model, characterized by the combination of stainless steel for case and bracelet with platinum for bezel and dial.
Also available: Ø 40 mm Ref. 16622; Ø 29 mm Ref. 169622.

OYSTER PERPETUAL DAY-DATE   REF. 118206

Movement: mechanical, automatic winding, caliber Rolex 3155. Officially certified "chronometer" (C.O.S.C.).
Functions: hour, minute, second, day and date.
Case: platinum three-piece case (Ø 36 mm, thickness 12.4 mm); sapphire crystal with "Cyclope" magnifying glass on the date; polished bombé bezel; white-gold screw-down crown with double gasket; screwed-on back. Water-resistant to 10 atm.

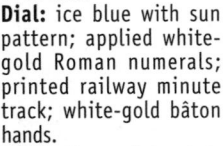

Dial: ice blue with sun pattern; applied white-gold Roman numerals; printed railway minute track; white-gold bâton hands.
Indications: date at 3, day at 12.
Bracelet: Superpresident platinum, polished and brushed finish; recessed fold-over clasp with embossed logo.
Also available: with brilliant markers; in yellow gold with champagne dial and brilliant markers; in pink gold with pink dial and brilliant markers; in white gold with silvered or coppered dial and brilliant markers. Oyster bracelet: in yellow gold with brilliant markers; in pink gold with brilliant markers; in white gold with brilliant markers.

OYSTER PERPETUAL DAY-DATE   REF. 118209

Movement: mechanical, automatic winding, 3155 Rolex caliber. Officially certified "chronometer" (C.O.S.C.).
Functions: hour, minute, second, day and date.
Case: 18 kt white gold, three-piece case (Ø 36 mm, thickness 12.4 mm); sapphire crystal with "Cyclope" magnifying glass on the date; polished white-gold bombé bezel; white-gold screw-down crown with double gasket; screwed-on back. Water-resistant to 10 atm.

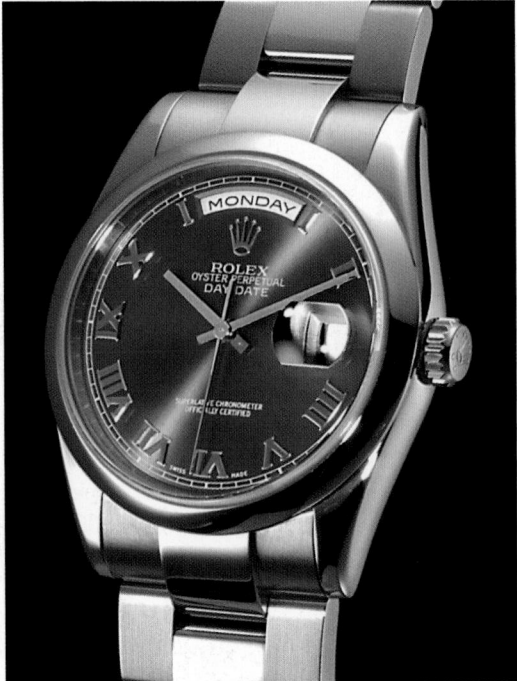

Dial: copper with sun pattern; applied white-gold Roman numerals; white printed railway minute track; white-gold bâton hands.
Indications: date at 3, day at 12.
Bracelet: Oyster white gold with polished and brushed finish; fold-over clasp.

OYSTER PERPETUAL LADY DATEJUST — REF. 79165

Movement: mechanical, automatic winding, 2235 Rolex caliber. Officially certified "chronometer" (C.O.S.C.).
Functions: hour, minute, second, date.
Case: 18 kt pink gold, three-piece case (Ø 26 mm, thickness 10.5 mm); sapphire crystal with "Cyclope" magnifying glass on the date; bombé bezel; pink-gold screw-down crown with double gasket; screwed-on back. Water-resistant to 10 atm.
Dial: black; applied pink-gold Arabic numerals; printed railway minute track; pink-gold bâton hands.
Indications: date at 3.
Bracelet: Oyster pink gold with polished and brushed finish; fold-over clasp.
Also available: in yellow gold with Oyster bracelet; in stainless steel and yellow gold with Oyster bracelet; Jubilé.

OYSTER PERPETUAL LADY DATEJUST — REF. 79239

Movement: mechanical, automatic winding, 2235 Rolex caliber. Officially certified "chronometer" (C.O.S.C.).
Functions: hour, minute, second, date.
Case: 18 kt white gold, three-piece case (Ø 26 mm, thickness 10.5 mm); sapphire crystal with "Cyclope" magnifying glass on the date; knurled bezel; lugs with set diamonds; white-gold screw-down crown with double gasket; screwed-on back. Water-resistant to 10 atm.
Dial: beige mother-of-pearl; applied white-gold Roman numerals; white-gold bâton hands.
Indications: date at 3.
Bracelet: Superpresident white gold with polished and brushed finish; recessed fold-over clasp with embossed logo.
Also available: in yellow gold; other jewel versions.

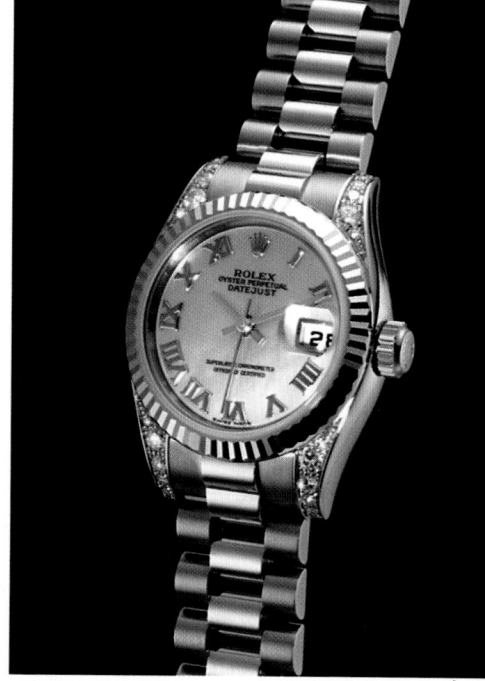

OYSTER PERPETUAL DATEJUST — REF. 78248

The Rolex 2235 caliber is used for the Datejust family with its 30 millimeter diameter. This automatic movement, provided with 29 jewels, is characterized by the "Microstar" balance in Glucydur (a copper-beryllium alloy) with an adjustment device acted by the screws positioned on the external perimeter, ensuring a micrometer precision rate. Other outstanding features are: the Parechoc shock absorber, a Breguet balance spring; its frequency is equal to 28,800 vibrations per hour. The photograph shows a precious piece realized entirely in 18 kt yellow gold with a gold tone mother-of-pearl dial; engine-turned (guilloché) peripheral ring with hours in Roman numerals, at 12 a five-pointed crown. The President bracelet is characterized by numerous small-sized links that make the whole seem particularly smooth.
Also available: with Oyster or Jubilé bracelet; in steel with pink dial, Oyster bracelet.

CELLINI BASKET — REF. 5320/9

Movement: mechanical, manual winding. Rolex 1602 caliber.
Functions: hour, minute.
Case: 18 kt white gold, three-piece case, in square curved shape (size 34x31.5 mm; thickness 6.5 mm); jointed lugs; white-gold crown; snap-on back.
Dial: mother-of-pearl; applied white-gold square markers with set brilliants; white-gold Régate hands.
Strap: ostrich skin; white-gold clasp.
Also available: other versions on request.

SCATOLA DEL TEMPO

winding wonders

For centuries, Italy has been known for its sumptuous fashions and fabrics and for its prestigious lead in leather. It is only fitting, then, that Scatola del Tempo—creators of one of the most elite and luxurious accessories in the world—is based in Italy.

With its home on Lake Como in Barzanò, Italy, Scatola del Tempo finely hand crafts the most exquisite watch and jewelry boxes for men and women using only the finest Italian leathers and silks. But it is the company's superb automatic winding watch boxes that wins it international acclaim.

Founded nearly a dozen years ago by Sandro Colarieti, Scatola del Tempo's winding cases are designed precisely for complicated watches with automatic-winding mechanical movements.

Research in the watch industry indicates that automatic mechanical watches are designed to run all the time. If the watch winds down, its parts are not lubricated as frequently (because the watch is not running), resulting in internal wear and tear, possible accuracy loss and probably more frequent servicing. Scatola del Tempo takes all of this into account with its series of functional yet incredibly elegant cases. For the person who owns even one automatic mechanical watch, a Scatola del Tempo winding watch box is a necessity.

Each box—whether it holds one watch or a dozen or more watches—houses a Swiss-made rotating mechanism that substitutes the natural movement of the wrist, keeping each watch properly wound. The result of extensive research and development into technology and electronics, the multi-unit boxes house a computer chip that can be programmed for use according to the owner. The computer chip allows for easy setting, so the box will operate for as many hours as needed each day (typically six hours is satisfactory), shutting itself off, and restarting regularly as per the memory setting. The boxes can also be programmed to run clockwise or counter clockwise depending on the needs of the rotor in a particular watch.

In addition to their technical prowess, Scatola del Tempo cases are exquisite in their beauty. Each case is entirely made by hand, crafted in the oldest and finest traditions of Italy. Only the best leathers and the most precious briar woods are used for the exteriors

TOP

2RT

This model allows two watches to be wound at the same time. In the upper section there is a tray where watches, jewelry and other accessories can be placed. Natural leather and black.

BOTTOM

7RTA

This very luxurious briar-wood model with two little doors is divided in two parts. The upper part holds and can wind three watches; the lower hold four watches that do not need winding or it can hold other accessories.

The latest offers have a new bidirectional winding system with microprocessor electronic control of the action. These are thoroughly tested mechanisms made in Switzerland, identical to the new Pendulette's mechanism (facing page).

of the cases. The interiors are lined in silk created by Scatola del Tempo, whose other silk creations are made exclusively for the most preeminent designers on today's fashion runways.

Scatola del Tempo offers a complete range of rotating watch boxes, from a single-watch design to multi-unit winding boxes that accommodate the needs of its customers both at home and when traveling. The company also offers an entire line of artfully designed cases for men and women for writing instruments, accessories and jewelry.

IRT PENDULETTE

The IRT Pendulette is the newest creation from Scatola del Tempo. Slightly smaller than the original IRT, the Pendulette possesses several important innovations. The first of these innovations is a completely new electronic system, which controls the rotation. After it is turned ON, the Pendulette will rotate for exactly 1,300 revolution per day, stopping in exactly the same position it was when it began. (If the unit is turned OFF before the 1.300 revolution cycle is complete, it will still stop in exactly the same position as when it was first started.) Another innovation is the cylinder housing, with a precisely engineered groove which holds the spring-loaded watch holder. The spring-loading mechanism makes it easy to put virtually any size watch on the holder. It is powered by standard LR-20 alkaline batteries, which last at least one year under normal use.

The IRT Pendulette is available in two models: gold-colored brass with tan leather or silver-colored brass with black leather.

THE "SdT" WATCH

The name of this chronograph refers to the name of this Italian company, a leader in the production of precious leather cases for watches, considering taste and quality that are particularly modern as well as formal and functional choices of definite class.

Chronograph with automatic movement (Valjoux cal. 7750) with three counters and date. Steel case with screw-down crown and screwed-on caseback, water resistant to 10 atm. Dial with Arabic numerals and sword-style hands with red/sky-blue "SdT" logo, counters and flange with tachymeter scale contrasting the black background. Calfskin strap and case with electronic rotational winding system programmed at 1,200 revolutions in 24 hours, the basic piece of Scatola del Tempo in Barzanò, an old hamlet in the Province of Lecco in Northwest Italy.

Scatola del Tempo

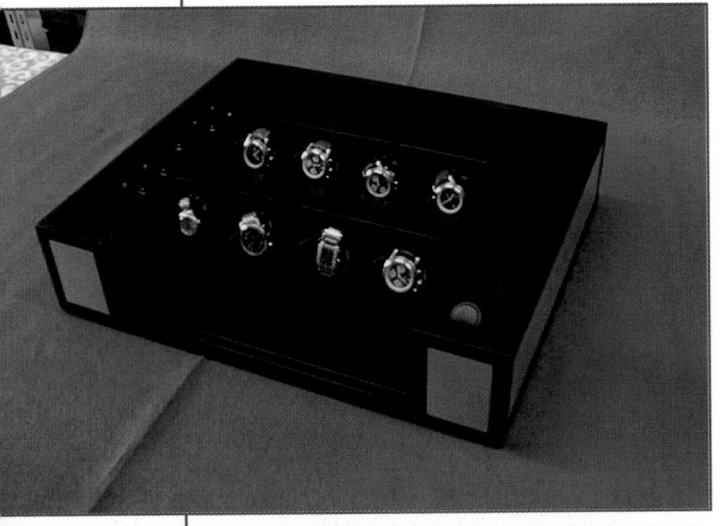

WATCH-WINDING CASE

After the presentation of mechanical watch cases, there is one that could, perhaps, be called a watch-winder drawer, that is a device that will keep watches wound and that can be placed in any ordinary drawer.

It uses a normal battery with a year's autonomy and whose charge state can be visualized. It is made according to the client's specifications that he has described to S.C.S. & Co. informing them of the amount of space available (the internal dimensions of the space he means to use; the number of rotating groups can go from one to four each of which can have two (or multiples of two) or three (or multiples of three rotating elements). Each group functions independently of the others, operated by the same electronic card. It is possible to insert leds that permit checking when the rotating elements turn on or are in pause.

The watch is placed on its support inside a small rotating container; and this operation of inserting or removing the watch from its container—simplified by raising or lowering the rotating groups by using a small lever—can be performed only when the appliance is turned off. The watch is wound on a 1300-revolutions rotation cycle. Clockwise or counter clockwise movements can be selected manually or automatically to accommodate any kind of watch, whether its oscillating mass is bi- or unidirectional.

PRESENTOIR

The most prestigious automatic wristwatches deserve exhibit cases that emphasize their beauty and at the same time keep the watches wound, particularly if the watches have a perpetual calendar. Thus we have Presentoir, designed for shops but easily adapted to display one's favorite timepiece in his or her home.

Composed of a lacquered wood base and a polished brass watch support, the mechanism includes two cog wheels that work together, it can rotate in clockwise or counter-clockwise directions (set by using a switch on the back) and is powered by two common alkaline batteries. There are four switches on the bottom (hidden beneath a small, screw-on brass plaque) to be used to set the rotation cycles of the turning element (switches 1 and 2) and to set the seconds of pause to be made between every two rotations (switches 3 and 4), choosing the most suitable program for one's needs. This selection should be made before inserting the batteries to avoid damaging the appliance.

THE BOXES WITH ROTORY MECHANISM

These devices, designed for automatic movement wristwatches (particularly useful for perpetual calendars) substitute the wrist's movement to keep the watches wound regularly. The S.C.S. & C. Scatola del Tempo has, for several years, produced special containers with one or more rotating supports run by an electronic micro-motor that supplies the movement with ideal winding. The traditional models offer ten different re-winding programs, making it possible to simulate one's own activity level through a program selector placed inside the battery holder. Each program specifies a set schedule (considering the natural habits of people who wear the watches by day and set them down at night) of so many hours of rotations in both directions. Starting from the setting "0" there is a gradual lessening in the number of running hours but an increase in the number of rotations. The indications show, besides on-off, the state of the batteries (both automatic LED signal on the exterior, and a dial indicator on the back activated by a button) and the stand-by power. By using a 6-volt transformer in the jack, one may eliminate the batteries. However, rotors using alkaline batteries will work for about one year for all models.

SCATOLA DEL TEMPO

Trousse

Tool box with utensils produced by Bergeon, a Swiss company, for the care of one's watches.

1RT

Box for keeping one automatic watch wound. Black, natural leather, red. In the one-watch box the selection of the rotation direction (clockwise, suitable for almost all automatics, or counter clockwise as some need) can be made by using a selection-slide on the front of the rotor.

CENTER LEFT

7RT

Box for keeping three automatic watches wound plus four places for watches with leather straps or rigid bracelets. Black, natural leather, red.

CENTER RIGHT

1RTSL

Box for keeping one automatic watch wound, in black. Made of nylon and black leather with an opening with a gold-colored metal ring making the watch visible, this article has a very good price.

BOTTOM

3RT

Box for keeping three automatic watches wound, in black, leather, red. It is available in the Squelette version with briar-wood base and the motor gears visible in black polished brass.

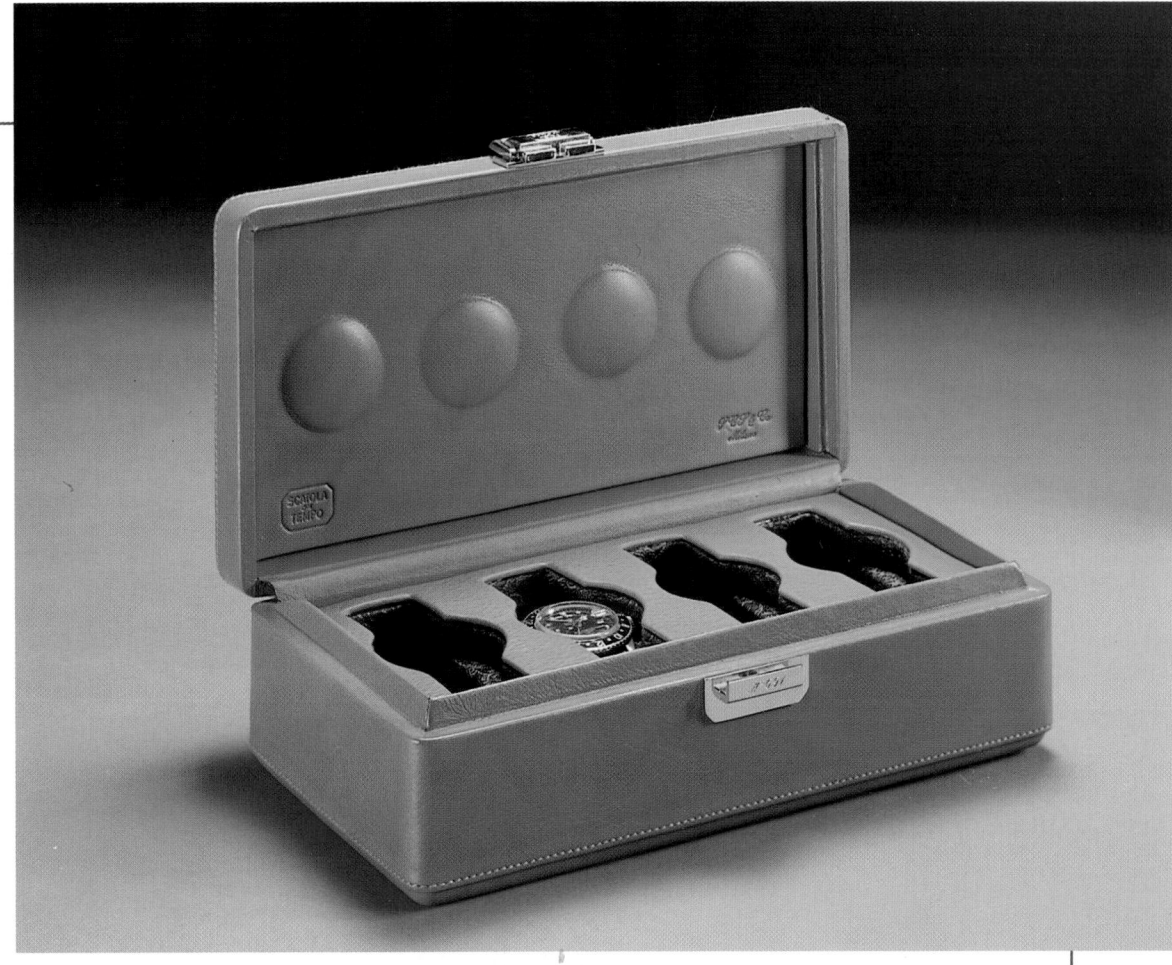

TOP

4B
Box for four watches with leather strap or flexible bracelet. Black, natural leather.

BOTTOM

2A
Box for two watches with leather straps or flexible bracelets. Black, natural leather, red.

1P
Men's jewelry box for travel, black with space for one watch and accessories (cuff links, rings, lighters, pens, etc.)

1A
Box for one watch with leather strap or flexible bracelet. Black, natural leather.

SCATOLA DEL TEMPO

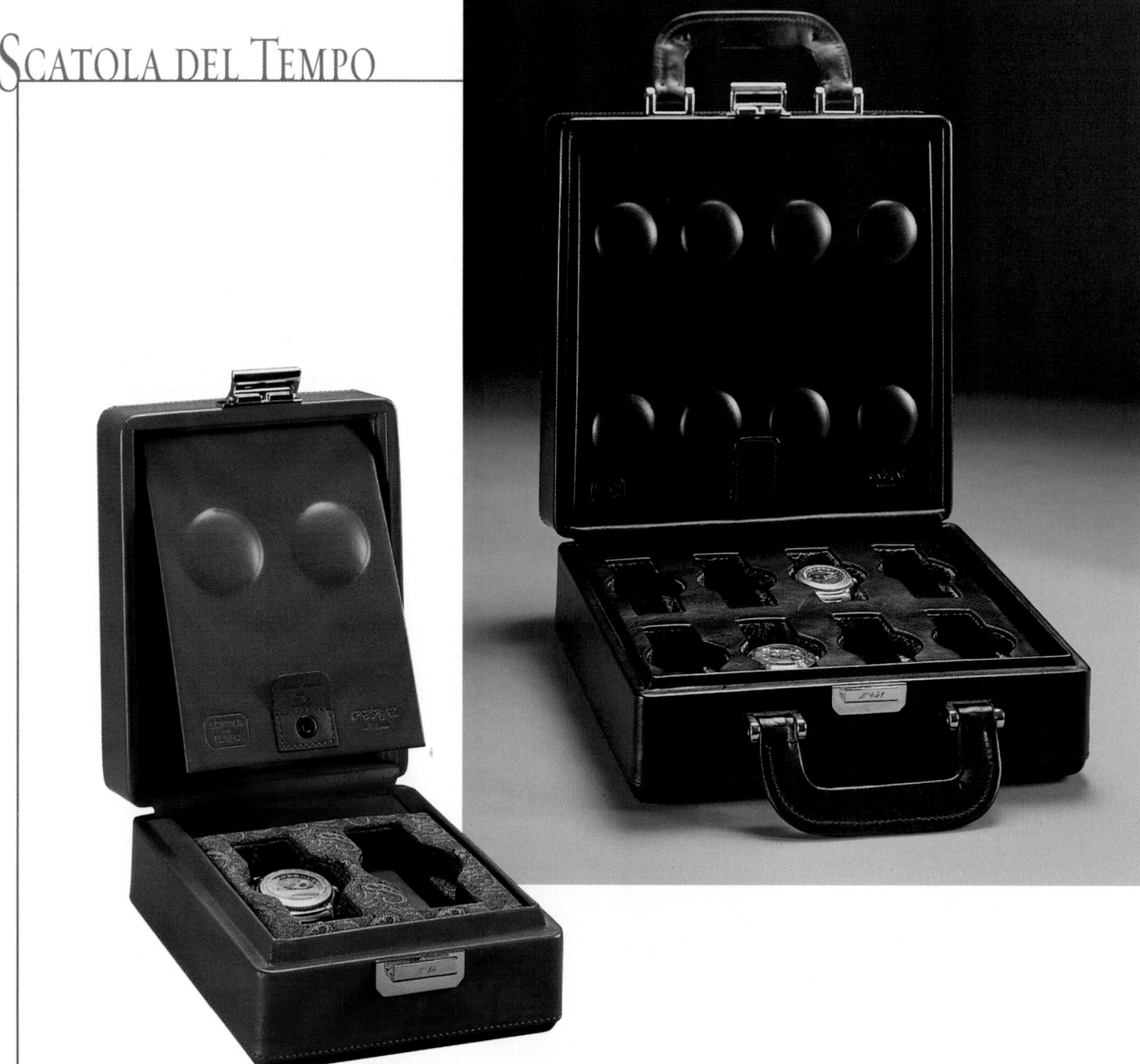

TECHNICAL SPECIFICATIONS

Exterior structure: Evaporated beech wood covered in natural organic tanned leather.

Interior: flexible polyurethane resin, differentiated density, covered in jacquard silk in paisley design or in leather. The internal structure can hold perfectly the specified number and size of watches. Each place provides the necessary space for the winding crown and any possible push-pieces for other functions.

Clasp: in gilded brass, marked and numbered by hand.

Each piece is entirely handmade by craftsmen; the hardware has received anti-magnetic treatment.

TOP LEFT

2+2
Box for two watches with leather strap and two watches with rigid bracelet. Black, natural, red.

TOP RIGHT

16B
Travelling case with places for sixteen watches with leather strap or rigid bracelet. Black, natural leather.

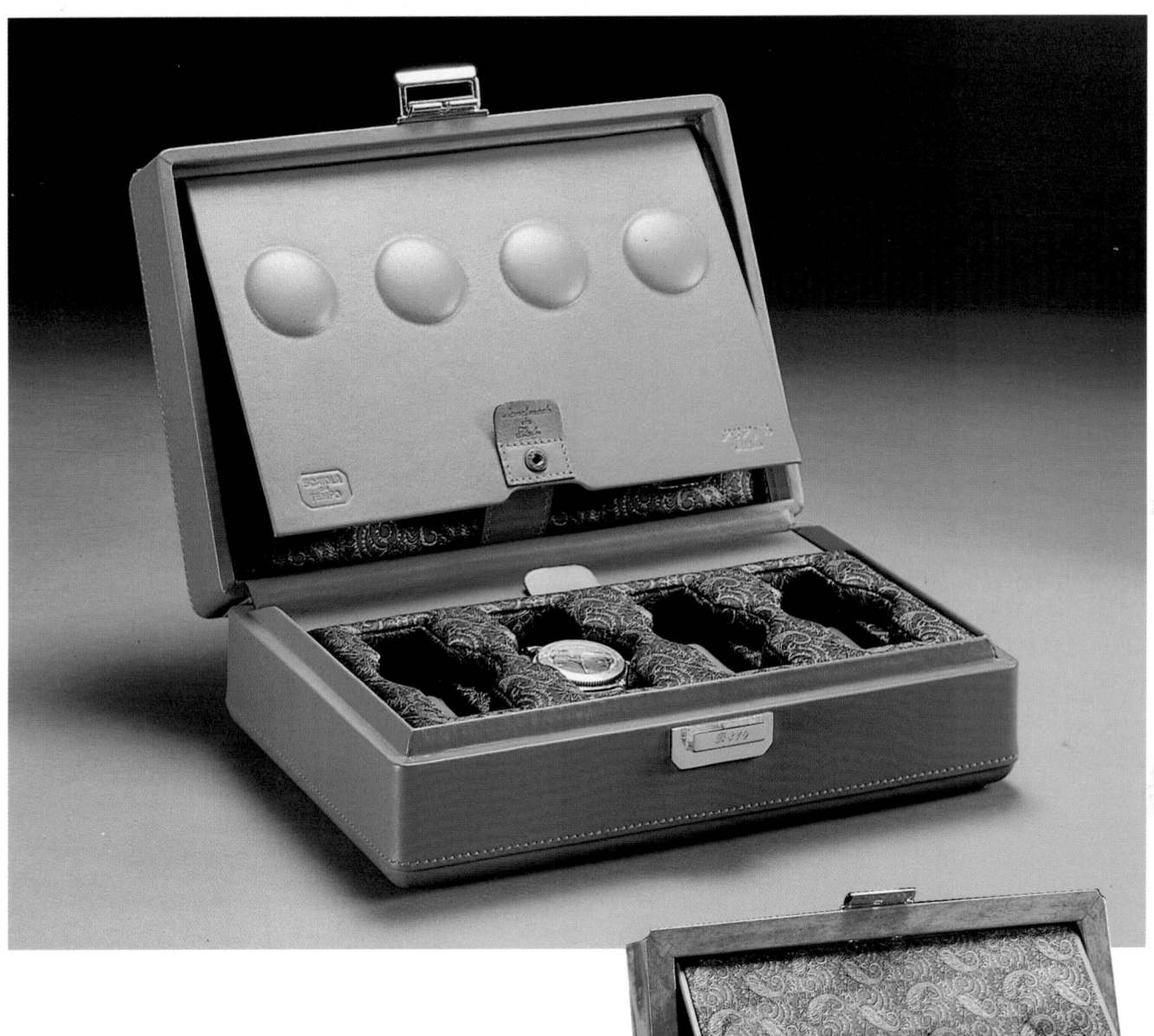

SCATOLA DEL TEMPO

Treasure Box C
Large jewelry box for
women. Red, blue, green.
Medium size available
in green.

CENTER

3P
Men's accessories case in
travel version for three
watches and various
accessories (cuff links,
rings, lighters, pens, etc.).
Black, natural leather, red.

BOTTOM

4P
Men's accessories case for
four watches with leather
strap and accessories
(cuff links, rings, lighters,
pens, etc.).
Black, natural leather.

TOP LEFT

Treasure Box D
Travel jewelry box for women. Red, blue, green.

TOP RIGHT

Small pen case
Holds six pens and comes in black, natural leather and red.

4A
Travel box for four watches with leather strap or flexible bracelet. Black, natural leather, red.

CENTER

Pen case
The medium size model carries 12 pens and comes in black, natural leather, red.

BOTTOM

Pen case
The large size holds 24 pens and is available in red.

TAG HEUER

The History of TAG Heuer began in 1860 in the small town of St-Imier, high up in the Swiss Jura mountains. It was there that Edouard Heuer founded his first workshop. From the beginning Heuer had in mind to offer his contemporaries the most precise and reliable timepieces. Over the years, Heuer's signature became a reference in watchmaking. With numerous patents and innovations, the company contributed to the development of various domains: science, industry, medecine... and above all sport. Heuer made a name for himself in top level competitions. And his name grew.

By 1880, Edouard Heuer was the first to enter series production of chronographs. By doing so, he laid the bedrock for his philosophy and his technical know-how. In 1916, the company launched its high precision «Micrograph», capable of measuring time within an accuracy of 1/100th of a second, a turning point that marked the birth of modern sports timekeeping. Thus, in the 1920's, the brand became the timekeeper of the Olympic Games in Antwerp, Paris and Amsterdam.

As time went by, Heuer's collection boasted some exceptional names: the Solunar, the Carrera and the Monaco chronograph, worn by Steve McQueen in the film «Le Mans». At the same time, Heuer's name was closely associated with Formula One drivers (Jo Siffert, Jackie Ickx, Clay Regazzoni and Nicki Lauda), and the Scuderia Ferrari.

In 1985, Heuer joined forces with TAG group (Techniques d'Avant-Garde) to form TAG Heuer. This was followed by the launch of successful new series: 2000, 6000, Kirium, Link and Alter Ego. A commitment to sport remained a core value. In 1985, TAG Heuer became partner of the McLaren Formula One team with Ayrton Senna a few year later becoming one of its most prominent ambassadors. 17 years later, the partnership with McLaren continues. Since 1992, TAG Heuer has been the Official Timekeeper of the FIA Formula One World Championship. Other key associations have been made with world renowned events such as World Championship skiing and the America's Cup sailing competition.

In 1999, TAG Heuer became part of LVMH (Louis Vuitton Moët-Hennessy), the world's leading luxury goods group. With more than 142 years of know-how and tradition, TAG Heuer is one of the world's largest luxury watch and the leading name in prestigious sportswatches.

In 1999, TAG Heuer paid tribute to women by offering them «their» very own watch: the Alter Ego. Created exclusively with women in mind, this watch has become a language in its own right, a philosophy of life and a token of belief in certain values cherished by the TAG Heuer brand.

TAG Heuer is now reiterating its determination to offer women the best by launching even more precious, congenial and daring models.

In its new 18-carat gold version, the Alter Ego reveals a new facet of its distinctive design. Exuding light and warmth, luxury and style, the Alter Ego is truly subliminal... and in turn sublimates the woman wearing it. Gently encircling a feminine wrist, it brilliantly underscores each gesture. The subtle vibrations of the power of seduction...

TAG Heuer women are all different and the brand therefore provides them with a choice of five exclusive versions of the Alter Ego, each crafted from the most luxurious and refined materials: lizard skin, glossy leather or satin for the straps, natural mother-of-pearl or lacquer on the dials.

The Alter Ego «River of Diamonds» model

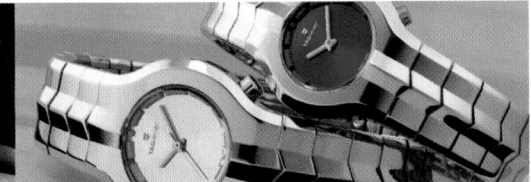

is even more precious and sophisticated... the ultimate tribute to women. With its sophisticated yet casual design, this jewelry watch is set with 346 diamonds running along the bracelet and case, while twelve diamonds subtly mark the hours on the white mother-of-pearl dial. The Alter Ego «River of Diamonds» is inspired by and made for women, right down to the slightest details.

In light of the success already achieved by Alter Ego, three women now embody TAG Heuer's exclusive feminine line: Mysterious and luminous, carefree and determined, strong and vulnerable... Inès Sastre, Marion Jones and Zhang Ziyi.

TAG HEUER

Epitomizing the avant-garde spirit of TAG Heuer, the Kirium line launched in 1997 made its mark on the history of watch design.

In four years, Kirium has become one of the brand's flagship lines.

TAG Heuer now presents the Kirium Formula I Chronograph, an advanced technology timepiece combining the unique design of the series with an extraordinary set of functions.

The only TAG Heuer chronograph capable of measuring time to within 1/100th of a second, the Kirium Formula I Chronograph is packed with technological feats: it offers no less than seven specific functions.

One of the prime features of this digital chronograph is to provide a double time display: analog version, the hour, minute and seconds hands glide smoothly over an understated black dial; digital mode, the otherwise invisible chronograph functions appear. A chronograph with two faces for a radically innovative time read-off.

Fitted with a countdown mechanism, the Kirium Formula I is also endowed with alarm and diary appointment functions: it displays the time in a second time-zone and features a perpetual calendar. The dial is lit up by pressing the crown.

Made from extremely high-performance materials, hitherto used exclusively in cutting-edge industries such as aviation, microsurgery... and particularly in the construction of Formula I racing cars, the Kirium Ti5 chronograph shares the quest for the most rigorous standards with this fiercely competitive sport. Perfect lines; powerful, rugged materials; extreme precision.

This model features a titanium case, carbon fiber dial and vulcanized rubber strap, in a resolutely high-tech spirit bearing direct reference to the extraordinary world of motor-racing. While titanium is not used for the most obvious parts of a FI car, it is nonetheless at the heart of its mechanisms, which require a high level of resistance, such as the clutch or components for suspension or transmission systems. TAG Heuer has opted for a specific version of this avant-garde metal, Grade 5 titanium, that combines the purity and lightness of titanium with exceptional hardness.

The Kirium Ti5 chronograph is fitted with a carbon fiber dial, another material representative of the new technologies employed in high-level competition sports.

High-tech all the way around the wrist, TAG Heuer has fashioned the strap of the Kirium Ti5 chronograph from vulcanized rubber. Like the tires on FI cars, it features exceptional resistance and suppleness. Ergonomic, this vulcanized rubber strap is perfectly integrated into the flowing lines of the Kirium case and offers unparalleled wearer comfort and a perfect fit on the wrist.

With the Kirium Formula I and the chronograph Ti5, TAG Heuer takes sports chronographs into another time sphere, in which an ultra-precise mechanism merges with the power of an incredibly avant-garde design...

TOP LEFT

Chronograph Kirium Formula One
Switched off LCD: the utmost elegant sports watch
Switched on LCD: high-tech multifunctional chronograph.

BOTTOM RIGHT

Chronograph Kirium Ti5 made of high performance materials: case in Grade 5 titanium, carbon fiber dial and vulcanized rubber strap.

TAG Heuer has always been involved in sports as a player, not merely a spectator. This implication has now led the Brand to develop the exclusive *Regatta* movement for its *Searacer* model. TAG Heuer has taken part in the most legendary regatta of all times: the America's Cup. During the 70's TAG Heuer was appointed Official Timekeeper, and participated with Chris Dickson and his splendid «TAG Heuer Challenge» boat. Today, TAG Heuer is the official sponsor of the 2003 America's Cup Challenger, Oracle Racing. The sponsorship will feature the «Link Searacer» watch developed by TAG Heuer to allow racing helmsmen to accurately judge their approach to the start line, something that the Oracle Racing boats will do countless times in training and more than fifty times in competition.

In terms of products, the TAG Heuer Brand has also played a pioneering role: first in 1949 with the launch of the «Maréographe», the world's first and only instrument to indicate the time of tides.

The Link Searacer has been developed by TAG Heuer in conjunction with such great names in sailing as Chris Dickson and Pierre Fehlmann. This cooperation has resulted in a truly accomplished product comprising all the essential functions that will help skippers to get off to the best possible start, thereby maximizing their chances of victory.

The Link Searacer provides the traditional signals at 10, 6 and 5 minutes and the possibility of recalibrating the countdown 1 minute before departure that allows the skipper to readjust the watch once more in line with the official procedure announced by the committee boat.

TAG HEUER

RIGHT

Monza Calibre 36 - 1/10th of a second accuracy. No other automatic chronograph can offer a greater level of precision.

BOTTOM RIGHT

Detail of the TAG Heuer Calibre 36 movement, relying on a pendulum oscillating at a frequency of 36,000 vibrations per hour.

With the «Classics» series, TAG Heuer gives new life to the racing legends of the twentieth century in a tribute to both the drivers and the race tracks. With Monza, Targa Florio and Monaco, TAG Heuer commemorates golden moments in an era of shared passion...

Monza Calibre 36, ultimate precision

When the chequered flag came down on the 1971 Formula I Italian Grand Prix in Monza, just 1/100th of a second separated the winner, Peter Gethin, from his closest rival, Ronnie Peterson.

In honour of the legendary Milanese track, and the closest finish ever in the history of FI racing, TAG Heuer is proud to announce Monza Calibre 36, a chronograph designed to measure short times in tenths of a second. It relies on a pendulum oscillating at a frequency of 36,000 vibrations per hour. No automatic chronograph can offer a greater level of precision.

Inspired by the design of a 1930s model, the chronograph features a sapphire back that shows the movement, finely decorated by hand. The same quest for perfection can be seen in the shape of the cushion case, with its scratch resistant, double-sided anti-reflection treated sapphire crystal. Available in silver or black, the flinqué dial features guilloché engraving with manually applied Arabic figures.

Fitted with a hand sewn strap in black or brown crocodile skin with a folding steel buckle, the Monza Calibre 36 chronometer is certified by the Contrôle Officiel Suisse des Chronomètres, Switzerland's official chronometer inspection body. So TAG Heuer has joined the exclusive circle of watchmakers with expertise in high-precision automatic movements. With this chronograph, stamped with the seal of a motoring legend, TAG Heuer builds a bridge between two ages marked by the same passion.

TOP RIGHT

Monaco automatic
chronograph with silvered
dial and brown alligator
strap.
Fourth re-edition of an
Heuer chronograph: the
Targa Florio automatic
chronograph.

LEFT

Steve McQueen during the
shooting of the film «Le
Mans», wearing the
Monaco chronograph.

CENTER

The Steve McQueen's
edition of the Monaco
chronograph, faithfull to
the original model chosen
for the shooting of «Le
Mans».

RIGHT

Juan Manuel Fangio during
the Targa Florio in 1955.

Targa Florio, a tribute to Fangio

The Targa Florio was one of the first road races, fought out on the pebbly asphalt of Sicily. Created in 1906, this race played host to the world's most sophisticated cars and greatest racing legends, before taking its final bow in 1973.

Many racing heroes gained glory here, without actually winning the event. Five times Formula 1 world champion Juan-Manuel Fangio attempted the challenge in 1953 and 1955 with Mercedes. On his wrist was the Targa Florio chronograph, which TAG Heuer has brought out once more.

Faithful to the original model created in the 1950s, the Targa Florio chronograph features a circular steel case with a fluted bezel. The dial is black with round figures. Two easy-to-read counters - permanent seconds and minutes - give it a fluid, contemporary air. It is available in a sports-style version with a black or brown leather strap, or in a more sophisticated version with an alligator strap.

Steve McQueen's Monaco

In 1969, TAG Heuer invented the Monaco, the world's first automatic chronograph fitted with a square watertight case and equipped with the famous «Chronomatic» calibre. It was an immediate success. The following year, during the shooting of the film «Le Mans», Steve McQueen made it his lucky watch. Enthusiasts of mechanical watches and fans of the actor rushed out to buy this avant-garde chronograph, which became a real collector's item.

This is the exceptional model that TAG Heuer has brought out once more, in its original colours: a metallic blue dial, orange-red chronograph hands and a blue alligator strap. Presented in a number of new versions, with a silver dial, 18-carat gold case, brown or black alligator strap, the Monaco chronograph is also available in the existing model, which features a black dial and calfskin strap. Attractive to look at and powerful in use, this mythical watch is still way ahead of its time.

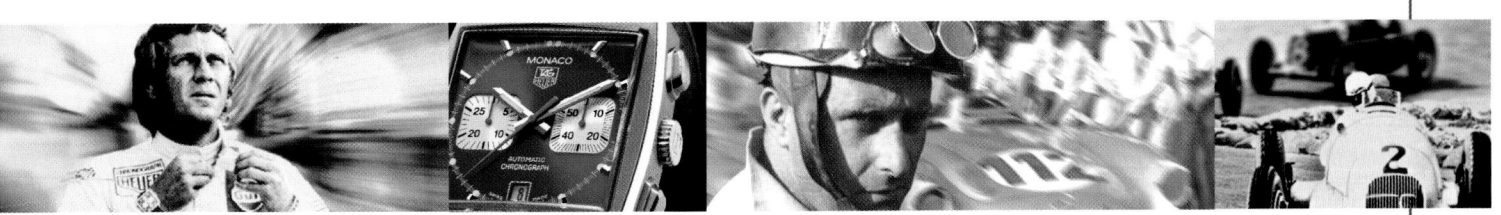

TAG Heuer's «Classics» series commemorates legendary moments in racing history. Looking beyond their time-keeping function, these watches and chronographs express the passion brought by the watch-maker to the quest for perfection and beauty.

TAG HEUER

KIRIUM CHRONOGRAPH   REF. CL2112.BA0701

Movement: mechanical, automatic winding, Tag Heuer Calibre 17.
Functions: hour, minute, second, date, chronograph with 3 counters.
Case: stainless steel, three-piece polished and fine-brushed case (Ø 43.5 mm, thickness 13.2 mm); curved sapphire crystal; polished counter clockwise turning bezel, with luminescent marker and engraved minute track, for the calculation of diving times; screw-down crown with case protection, with micro

gasket preventing water and dust infiltration; screwed-on case back. Water-resistant to 20 atm.
Dial: silvered; luminescent applied round steel markers; printed minute track on the flange; skeletonized rhodium-plated hands with luminescent tips.
Indications: small second at 3, hour counter and date at 6, minute counter at 9.
Bracelet: brushed steel, with polished central link; fold-over clasp with double safety device.
Also available: with rubber strap; in brushed steel, black dial. Man's size with quartz movement, steel with polished and/or fine-brushed finish, silvered, blue and black dial, rubber strap or bracelet.

KIRIUM FORMULA ONE   REF. CL111A.FT6000

Movement: quartz, digital and analog, based on ETA E20 caliber. **Functions:** analog hour, minute and second; LCD numeric display hour, minute, second and date, chronograph 1/100th, countdown, daily and calendar alarm, second time zone, perpetual date, back dial light. **Case:** stainless steel, three-piece brushed case (Ø 43.3 mm, thickness 14.3 mm); curved sapphire crystal with antireflection treatment; fine-brushed counter clockwise turning bezel, with luminescent marker and

engraved minute track, for the calculation of diving times; helicoydal polished crown providing access to the 7 functions, with case protection, with micro gasket preventing water and dust infiltration; screwed-on case back. Water-resistant to 20 atm. **Dial:** LCD numeric display, specifically developed by TAG Heuer, black dial with back light, luminescent painted hour markers, skeletonized rhodium-plated hands with luminescent tips. **Bracelet:** vulcanised rubber bracelet, with folding buckle, perfectly integrated into the case. The insertion of polyamide, reinforced with glass fibre, guarantees excellent quality for the integration of the bracelet into the head. **Also available:** with fine-brushed steel; fold-over clasp with double safety device.

KIRIUM CHRONOGRAPH TI5   CL1181.FT6000

Movement: quartz, ETA 251.262. **Functions:** hour, minute, second, date, chronograph with 3 counters. **Case:** titanium grade 5, three-piece polished case (Ø 42.85 mm, thickness 12.7 mm); curved sapphire crystal with antireflection treatment; polished counter clockwise turning bezel, with luminescent marker and engraved minute track, for the calculation of diving times; screw-down crown with case protection, with micro gasket preventing water and dust infil-

tration; screwed-on case back. Water-resistant to 20 atm. **Dial:** carbon fiber dial; luminescent round markers; printed minute track on the flange; skeletonized rhodium-plated hands with luminescent tips. **Indications:** 1/10th of a second counter at 2, small second at 6, hour counter at 10. **Bracelet:** vulcanised rubber bracelet, with titanium grade 5 polished folding buckle, perfectly integrated into the case. The insertion of polyamide, reinforced with glass fibre, guarantees excellent quality for the integration of the bracelet into the head. **Also available:** in fine-brushed titanium grade 5. Man's size watch with quartz movement, case in titanium with polished finish.

KIRIUM   WL131H.BA0709

Movement: quartz, ETA 956.112.
Functions: hour, minute, second, date.
Case: stainless steel, three-piece polished and fine-brushed case (Ø 32.3 mm, thickness 9.9 mm); curved sapphire crystal; polished counter clockwise turning bezel, with luminescent marker and engraved minute track, for the calculation of diving times; screw-down crown with case protection, with micro gasket

preventing water and dust infiltration; screwed-on case back. Water-resistant to 20 atm.
Dial: blue/grey mother of pearl; luminescent applied round steel markers and Arabic numerals at 6 and 12; printed minute track on the flange; skeletonized rhodium-plated hands with luminescent tips.
Indications: date at 3.
Bracelet: brushed steel, with polished central link; fold-over clasp with double safety device.
Also available: with silvered dial; in brushed steel, black dial; in polished steel, blue translucent dial. Man's size with quartz movement, brushed steel with black or silvered dial or metallic blue or grey with polished/fine-brushed finish, rubber strap or bracelet.

LINK CHRONOGRAPH   REF. CT2111.BA0550

Movement: mechanical, automatic winding, Tag Heuer Calibre 16.
Functions: hour, minute, second, date, chronograph with 3 counters.
Case: stainless steel, three-piece brushed case (Ø 45.75 mm, thickness 15.4 mm); curved sapphire crystal; fine-brushed counter clockwise turning bezel, with luminescent marker and engraved minute track, for the calculation of diving times; screw-down crown with case protection, with micro-gasket preventing water and dust infiltration; screwed-on case back. Water-resistant to 20 atm.

Dial: black; counters decorated with circular beads pattern; applied bâton markers with luminescent dots; tachometer scale printed on the flange; luminescent rhodium-plated bâton hands.
Indications: date at 3, hour counter at 6, small second at 9, minute counter at 12,
Bracelet: brushed steel; fold-over clasp with double safety device.
Also available: with blue or silvered dial; in polished/fine-brushed steel, white dial. Man's size with quartz movement, steel with polished and/or fine-brushed finish, silvered, blue, white and black dial.

LINK SEARACER   REF. CT1113.BA0550

Movement: quartz, exclusive Tag Heuer Regatta movement
Functions: hour, minute, second, date, chronograph with 2 counters, 10, 6 and 5 minutes countdown
Case: stainless steel, three-piece brushed case (Ø 45.75 mm, thickness 13 mm); curved sapphire crystal; polished counter clockwise turning bezel, with luminescent marker and engraved minute track, for the calculation of diving times; screw-down crown with case protection, with micro-gasket preventing water and dust infiltration; screwed-on case back. Water-resistant to 20 atm.

Dial: black; counters emphasized by rhodium applied circle; applied bâton markers with luminescent dots; 10 minutes countdown scale printed on the flange; luminescent rhodium-plated bâton hands. red hand for countdown
Indications: 1/10th of a second counter at 2, date at 6, hour counter at 10, center second counter, center minute counter.
Bracelet: brushed steel; fold-over clasp with double safety device.
Also available: with blue translucent or silvered dial, in polished/fine-brushed steel.

LINK   REF. WT141J.BA0561

Movement: quartz, ETA 956.112.
Functions: hour, minute, second, date.
Case: stainless steel, three-piece polished case (Ø 29.8 mm, thickness 9.55 mm); curved sapphire crystal; polished counter clockwise turning bezel, set with 53 Top Wesselton (VVS) for a total of about 0.25 carat; screw-down crown with case protection, with micro-gasket preventing water and dust infiltration; screwed-on case back. Water-resistant to 20 atm.

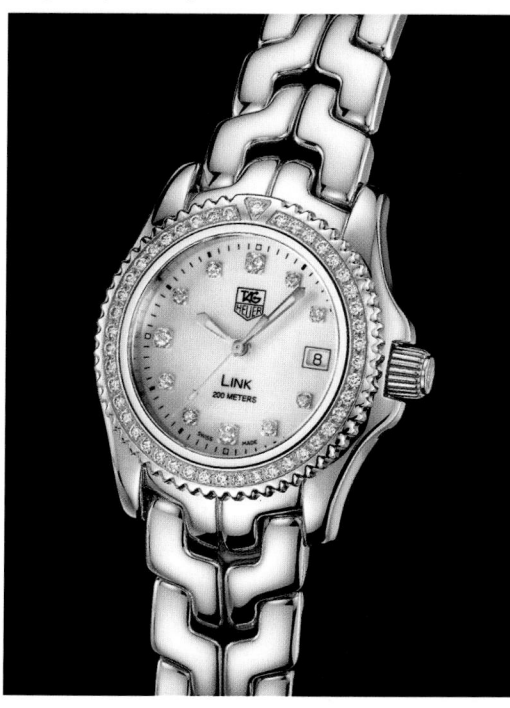

Dial: white mother of pearl set with 11 Top Wesselton (VVS) diamonds for a total of about 0.06 carat; luminescent rhodium-plated bâton hands.
Indications: date at 3.
Bracelet: polished stainless steel; fold-over clasp with double safety device.
Also available: with blue/grey mother of pearl dial; in polished/fine-brushed steel, white or blue/grey mother of pearl dial; in polished steel, blue or silvered dial; in fine-brushed steel with black and silvered dial.

2000 EXCLUSIVE CHRONOGRAPH   REF. CN2111.BA0339

Movement: mechanical, automatic winding, Tag Heuer Calibre 16.
Functions: hour, minute, second, date, chronograph with 3 counters.
Case: stainless steel, three-piece case (Ø 44 mm, thickness 14.6 mm), brushed and polished finish; flat sapphire crystal; counter clockwise turning dodecagonal bezel, with 6 polished hold riders, luminescent marker and engraved minute track, for the calculation of diving times; screw-down crown with case protection; screwed-on case back. Water-resistant to 20 atm.

Dial: black with Clous de Paris pattern; applied faceted bâton markers with luminescent dots, counters decorated with circular beads pattern; tachometer scale printed on the flange; luminescent rhodium-plated bâton hands. **Indications:** date at 3, hour counter at 6, small second at 9, minute counter at 12,
Bracelet: stainless steel, brushed finish with polished and brushed central links; fold-over clasp with double safety device.
Also available: with metallic blue or silvered dial. Man's size with quartz movement, steel with polished and fine-brushed finish, black, silvered and blue dial.

TAG HEUER

2000 EXCLUSIVE   REF. WN 2111.BA0332

Movement: Mechanical, automatic winding, Tag Heuer Calibre 5.
Functions: hour, minute, second, date.
Case: stainless steel, three-piece case (Ø 41.7 mm, thickness 11.2 mm), brushed and polished finish; flat sapphire crystal; counter clockwise turning dodecagonal bezel, with 6 polished hold riders, luminescent marker and engraved minute track, for the calculation of diving times; screw-down crown with case protection; screwed-on case back. Water-resistant to 20 atm.
Dial: silvered with Clous de Paris pattern; applied faceted bâton markers with luminescent dots; applied Arabic numerals; printed railway minute track with luminescent dots at quarters; luminescent steel bâton hands.
Indications: date at 3.
Bracelet: stainless steel, brushed finish with polished and brushed central link; fold-over clasp with double safety device.
Also available: with metallic blue and black dial. Man's size with quartz movement, black, white and translucent blue dial.

2000 CLASSIC   REF. WK2117.BA0311

Movement: mechanical, automatic winding, Tag Heuer Calibre 5.
Functions: hour, minute, second, date.
Case: stainless steel, three-piece brushed case (Ø 41.7 mm, thickness 11.2 mm); flat sapphire crystal; counter clockwise turning dodecagonal bezel, with 6 polished hold riders, luminescent marker and engraved minute track, for the calculation of diving times; screw-down crown with case protection; screwd-on back. Water-resistant to 20 atm.

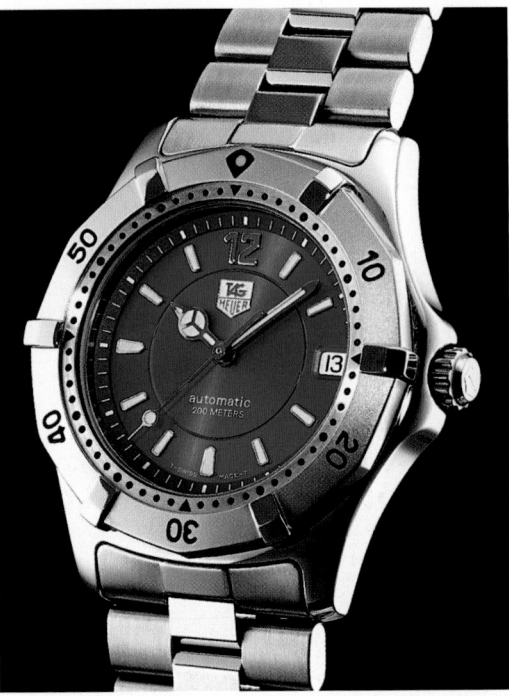

Dial: blue with sun pattern; luminescent applied rhodium plated bâton markers (Arabic numeral 12); printed minute track with luminescent steel Mercedes hands.
Indications: date at 3.
Bracelet: stainless steel brushed finish with polished central link; fold-over clasp with double safety device and extension system for diving suits.
Also available: with silvered dial. Man's size with quartz movement, black, white, silvered and blue dial.

ALTER EGO   REF WP1313.BA0751

Movement: quartz, ETA 956.112
Functions: hour, minute, second.
Case: stainless steel, two-piece polished case (Ø 29 mm, thickness 7.7 mm); convex sapphire crystal; off-centered crown at 4 o'clock with case protection; back fixed with 6 screws. Water-resistant to 10 atm.
Dial: blue translucent; specific architecture with raised flange between the hour markers; thin and elegant rhodium plated hands.
Indications: none.
Bracelet: stainless steel polished finish with massive folding buckle; butterfly opening with a push-button feature.
Also available: with white mother of pearl, mother of pearl, black or rhodium dial. Silvered, black or blue/grey mother of pearl dial with brushed finish.

ALTER EGO   REF WP131G.FC8125

Movement: quartz, ETA 956.112
Functions: hour, minute, second.
Case: stainless steel, two-piece polished case (Ø 29 mm, thickness 7.7 mm) set with 54 Top Wesselton (VVS) diamonds 1.6 mm in diameter for a total of about 0.83 carat; convex sapphire crystal; off-centered crown at 4 o'clock with case protection; back fixed with 6 screws. Water-resistant to 10 atm.

Dial: black; specific architecture with raised flange between the hour markers; thin and elegant rhodium plated hands.
Indications: none.
Bracelet: black varnished calfskin leather strap with standard buckle.
Also available: with white mother of pearl set with 12 diamond dots and steel polished bracelet.

MONZA CALIBRE 36   REF. CR 5111.FC6175

Movement: mechanical, automatic winding, Tag Heuer Calibre 36; 1/10th of a second rating precision guaranteed by high frequency of movement: 36,000 vph; the oscillating weight is decorated with a Côtes de Genève (Geneva Waves) vertically striped pattern; power reserve of minimum 50 hours, Chronometer certified by the Swiss Official Chronometer Testing Institute (C.O.S.C). **Functions:** hour, minute, second, date, chronograph with 3 counters. **Case:** stainless steel, 3-piece polished

and fine brushed case (Ø 41.2, thickness 13.4 mm), scratch-resistant sapphire crystal, glareproofed both sides, large and fluted pull-motion polished crown; transparent caseback in scratch-resistant sapphire crystal, fixed with 4 screws. Water-resistant to 3 atm. **Dial:** silvered base intricately engraved with sectors of guilloché; 9 hand-applied Arabic numerals, luminescent hour-markers and luminescent rhodium-plated bâton hands, printed minute track. **Indications:** date at 6, hour counter at 6, small second at 9, minute counter at 3. **Bracelet:** full-grain hand-sewn genuine crocodile leather strap with polished steel folding clasp with safety push buttons. **Also available:** with black dial and/or brown crocodile strap.

MONACO   REF. CW2113.FC6183

Movement: mechanical, automatic winding, Tag Heuer Calibre 17. **Functions:** hour, minute, second, date, chronograph with 2 counters. **Case:** stainless steel, three-piece polished and fine brushed case (size 40.4 x 38.5 mm, thickness 13 mm), curved plexiglas, semi-recessed crown; protected elliptical pushers with 8 facets; caseback fixed with 4 screws. Water-resistant to 3 atm.

Dial: metallic blue dial with sun pattern, applied faceted rhodium plated bâton markers, with luminescent dots; 2 square silvered registers; printed minute track; luminescent rhodium-plated bâton hour and minute hands, red chronograph's hands.

Indications: small second at 3, date at 6, minute register at 9. **Bracelet:** blue genuine crocodile leather strap with polished steel folding clasp with safety push buttons. **Also available:** with black and silvered dial and/or black or brown crocodile strap or black or brown calfskin leather strap.

TARGA FLORIO   REF. CX2110.FC6177

Movement: mechanical, automatic winding, Tag Heuer Calibre 17. **Functions:** hour, minute, second, date, chronograph with 2 counters. **Case:** stainless steel three-piece polished case (Ø 44 mm, thickness 13.6 mm), curved plexiglas, double fluted bezel; oversized fluted and conical crown; smooth rectangular pushers; polished caseback fixed with 6 screws. Water-resistant to 3 atm.

Dial: black with white luminescent numerals; two easy-to-read counters; printed minute track; white and luminescent skeleton bâton hour and minute hands, white register's hands.

Indications: small second at 3, date at 6, minute register at 9. **Bracelet:** black genuine crocodile leather strap with polished steel folding clasp with safety push buttons. **Also available:** with brown crocodile strap and black or brown calfskin leather strap.

CARRERA   REF. WV2112.FC6169

Movement: mechanical, automatic winding, Tag Heuer Calibre 5. **Functions:** hour, minute, second, date. **Case:** stainless steel, two-piece polished and fine brushed case (Ø 38.2 mm, thickness 11 m), curved plexiglas, fluted crown; screwed-on case back. Water-resistant to 3 atm.

Dial: silvered with sun pattern; 6 hand-applied rhodium plated Arabic numerals and 5 facetted rhodium plated indexes; luminescent hour-markers and luminescent rhodium-plated bâton hands, printed railway minute track and printed second track on the white flange.

Indications: date at 3. **Bracelet:** full-grain brown genuine crocodile leather strap with polished steel folding clasp with safety push buttons. **Also available:** with black crocodile strap or black calskin with perforations leather strap.

TechnoMarine

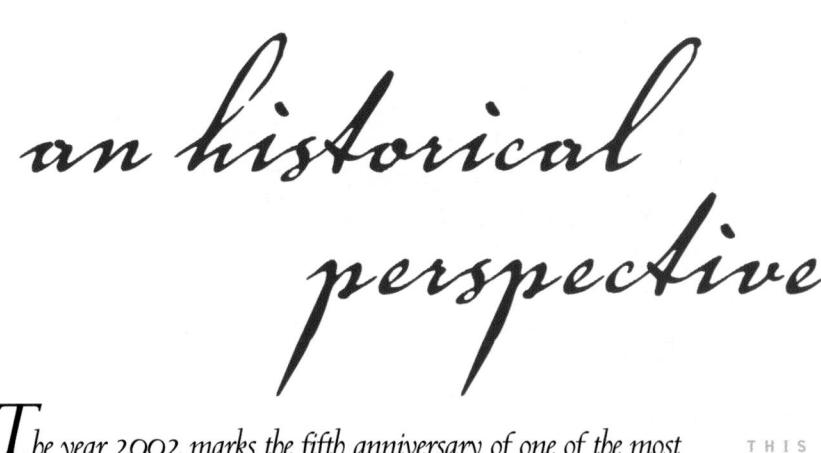

an historical perspective

The year 2002 marks the fifth anniversary of one of the most cutting-edge, trend-setting timepiece companies to date. Founded in 1997 on principles of design and lifestyle, TechnoMarine is a brand that has set new standards in the use of high-tech materials and diamonds.

THIS PAGE
TOP

Founder and creator of TechnoMarine, Franck Dubarry.

BOTTOM

The TechnoLady Pavé is shown here with black pavé diamond dial and unidirectional rotating bezel set with a total of 157 full-cut diamonds(1.33 carat).

FACING PAGE

The Diva in 18-karat yellow gold features an all-diamond dial, case and bezel. The total diamond weight is 3.15 carats.

Founded by Franck Dubarry, a sportsman with a love of the sea and a taste for adventure, TechnoMarine was borne on a combination of creativity and practicality. It was Dubarry's dream to create a lifestyle watch that catered to sports enthusiasts and adventurers, and to position it as a luxury design item. Going beyond the normal expectations of a watchmaker, TechnoMarine has become one of the most successful lifestyle brands of our time.

The first TechnoMarine watches unveiled to the world were anything but typical. They were a mix of brilliant colors and innovative materials. Dubarry deftly combined diamonds and gel in an unusual case treatment that caused an immediate stir of excitement: the steel case was sheathed in a translucent plastic covering that extended as the watchstrap. Called the TechnoMarine Raft, this first chronograph model was so different and enticing that it drew a strong following and soon spawned a full collection of striking dive watches. The combination of French styling and Swiss technology yielded cutting-edge designs and top-quality craftsmanship that gained international attention.

Today, just five years since its inception, TechnoMarine retains its trend-setting position. The collection has grown to include more than 110 distinct styles. In fact, the brand has become so successful that it found it necessary to create two separate divisions in order to cater more closely to the two diverse consumer categories that comprise its followers. In October of 2001, the brand established the two divisions as TechnoMarine and TechnoSport.

The TechnoMarine division will include watches priced at more than $500 retail and will consist of high-end timepieces in luxurious designs. The TechnoSport divisions will include watches priced at less than $500 retail and will feature more trendy, fashion-forward designs for younger consumers.

While the focus and demographics of the two divisions will differ, both will continue to uphold the innovative vision of the TechnoMarine brand. Neither will lose the sporty, adventurous edge that has become synonymous with the brand's name.

TechnoMarine®

TechnoMarine

cutting-edge styling

One of the strongest focal points of the newest TechnoMarine timepieces is diamonds. The collection unveiled in 2001 utilized both white and black diamonds for ultra appeal. The pinnacle of the diamond collection is the new Diva series.

Conceptualized by Dubarry, the Diva comprises the company's highest-priced timepiece in the luxury jewelry category. The sleek, chic look of the round-on-squared timepiece makes it a strong yet sexy statement for women. Housing an ETA movement, the Diva chronographs feature mother-of-pearl subdials set on a diamond pavé dial. The watches are then offset by an all-diamond case and either a diamond or sapphire bezel. Models include white or black diamonds and pink or blue sapphires. The watches are crafted in either 18-karat white, yellow or rose gold. In keeping with TechnoMarine's sporty philosophy, the watches are water resistant up to 50 meters.

Complementing the Diva is the Technolady Pavé watch. This 100-meter water-resistant timepiece features a full pavé dial of black or white diamonds that is offset by a diamond bezel.

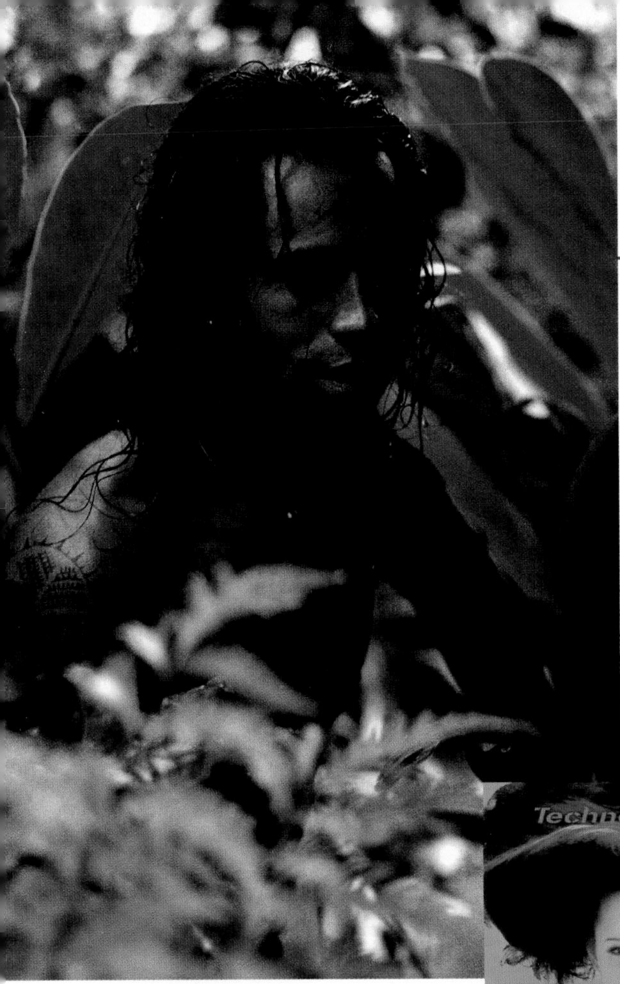

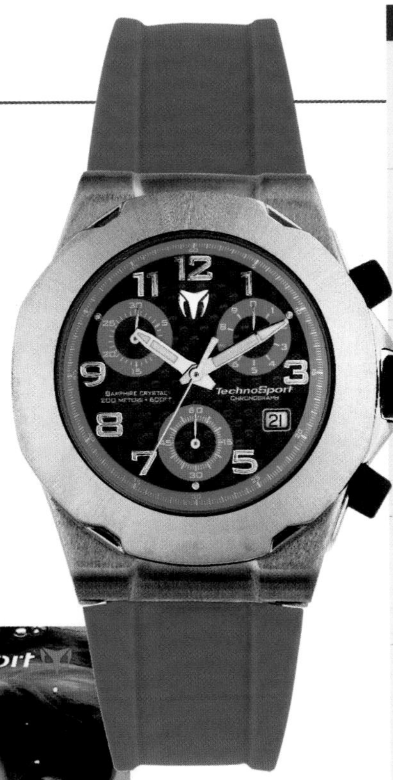

CHRONOLOGY

1997 Earmarked for success with TechnoMarine's company launch in St. Tropez, France, the Raft makes a remarkable statement in the watch industry selling over 50,000 pieces its first year.

1998 The Cruise, Apnea and the Y watch collections are the perfect combination of French design with Swiss technology; TechnoMarine's collections become known for bright hues and interchangeable gel bands that afford each watch many different looks.

1999 TechnoMarine's breakthrough design—TechnoDiamond—earns accolades as one of the most innovative products at the Basel show. The TechnoDiamond chronograph is an international success with its unique and innovative concept of a fully functional diving watch with full-cut diamonds set in stainless steel and with colorful, interchangeable gel bands.

2000 TechnoDiamond-TM is introduced by brand founder Franck Dubarry as "the new watch of the millennium."
The Technolady collection is the brand's most unique introduction this year.

2001 The Diva watch is launched in Basel.
An exquisite 18-karat gold pavé, Diva is TechnoMarine's step into the jewelry timepiece collection.
Technolady Pavé by TechnoMarine is an exquisite 3-hand pavé rendition with 116 full-cut diamonds.
TechnoDiamond-TM Sport collection of twelve elegant, vividly colored mother-of-pearl dials is introduced with color-coordinated leather and gel straps, and 136 full-cut diamonds.
The TechnoSquare Chrono collection is introduced at the JCK show in Las Vegas, setting another unbelievable mark in TechnoMarine's history with its superior craftsmanship and cutting-edge design.
The TechnoSport Alpha Sport collection is designed with fashionable yet adventurous men in mind. An innovative, customized, high-end chronograph, the Alpha Sport possesses the highest level of technological precision and design.
In October, TechnoMarine and TechnoSport introduce a division in the company that will help focus on the individual consumer.

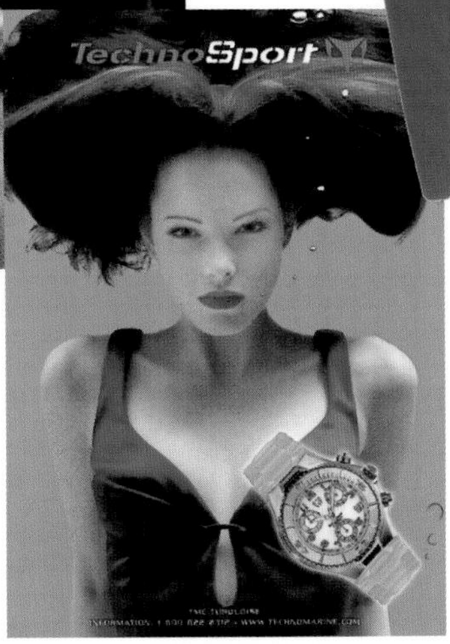

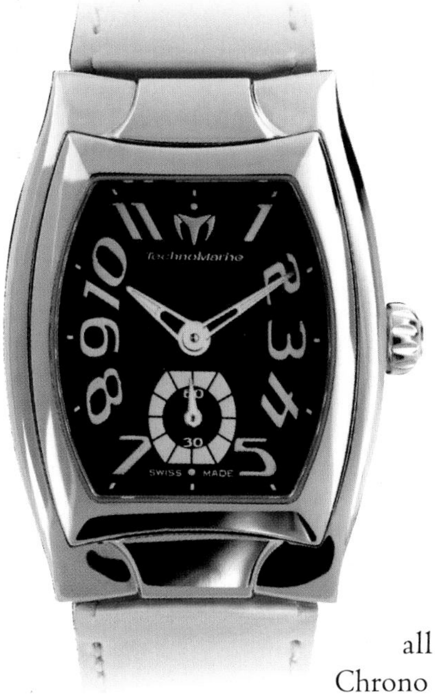

Also unveiled this past year was the brand's first square chronograph collection. Called the TechnoSquare Chrono collection, the watchcases are actually rectangular with tonneau effect. Case sides are concave and convex and the corresponding bezel design emulates the case—all for a truly stylish appeal. The TechnoSquare Chrono collection is water resistant to 100 meters and houses an ETA movement for superior performance. The TechnoSquare Chrono is available in two styles: diamond and non-diamond bezels. They feature steel cases, a variety of striking dial colors, including purple and bright blue, and interchangeable leather or gel straps.

Of course, the brand continues to create cutting-edge styles in the TechnoSport realm, as well, with the Alpha Sport watch stealing the limelight. This new rendition features a steel chronograph with a carbon fiber dial and different colored rubber straps. Water-resistant to 200 meters, the Alpha Sport epitomizes the brand's dedication to underwater adventure.

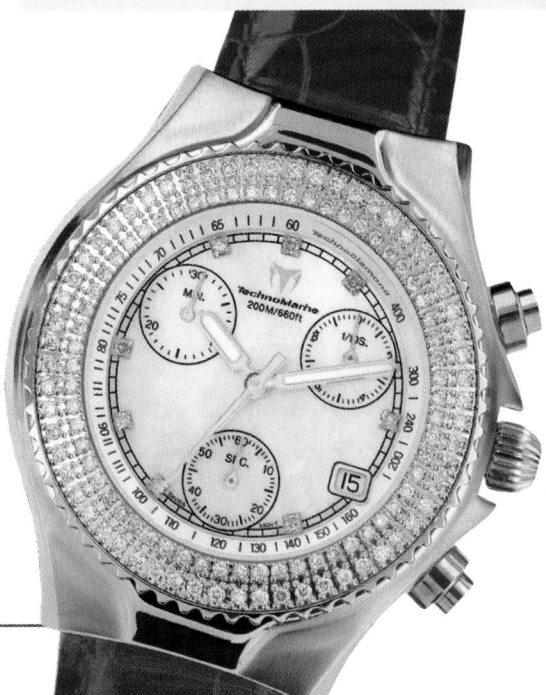

TECHNOMARINE

DIVA   REF: DTWW

Water Resistant: 5 ATM/50 m.
Movement: Swiss ETA 251.272.
Functions: chronograph 1/10 sec. Date indicator, Swiss made.
Case: 18K gold with 256 full-cut white diamonds (or white and black), 3.15 carats (case and dial).
Size: 40mm.

Dial: full-paved diamonds with mother-of-pearl sub-dials.
Crystal: sapphire / 1mm.
Straps: crocodile band and one gel strap.
Fastener: butterfly buckle.
Warranty: 1 year.
Price: Available upon request.

DIVA FULL PAVE   REF: DTRG

Water Resistant: 5 ATM/50 m.
Movement: Swiss ETA 251.272.
Functions: chronograph 1/10 sec. Date indicator, Swiss made.
Case: 18K rose gold with 445 full-cut white diamonds, 3.30 carats (case and dial).
Size: 40mm.
Dial: full-paved diamonds with mother-of-pearl subdials.

Crystal: sapphire / 1mm.
Straps: crocodile band and one gel strap.
Fastener: butterfly buckle.
Warranty: 1 year.
Price: Available upon request.

TECHNOLADY PAVE BLACK DIAMOND   REF: TLSB

Water Resistant: 330 ft/100 m.
Movement: Swiss ETA 902.002.
Case: stainless steel 316 L resistant to water and air pressure, thermal heights or chemical treatment.
Size: 28mm.
Bezel: unidirectional-rotating bezel with 41 full-cut white and black diamonds arranged in a bead setting.

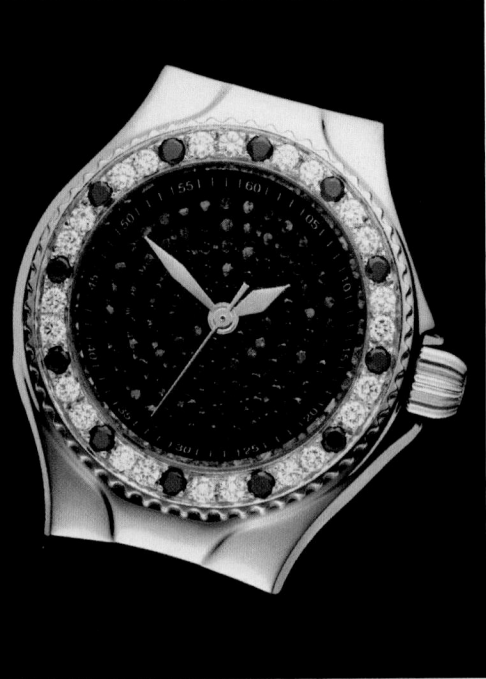

Dial: full-paved diamond face, 116 full-cut diamonds.
Crystal: mineral / 2.6mm.
Straps: black satin band and crocodile band.
Fastener: butterfly buckle.
Warranty: 1 year.
Price: Available upon request.

TECHNOSQUARE CHRONO DIAMOND   REF: DTSC14

Water Resistant: 330 ft/100 m.
Movement: Swiss ETA 251.471.
Functions: chronograph 1/10 sec. Date indicator.
Case: stainless steel 316 L resistant to water and air pressure, thermal heights or chemical treatment, 56 full-cut white diamonds on top and bottom parts and 68 full-cut white diamonds around the face.

Size: 32x43mm.
Dial: lacquer colors or mother of pearl.
Crystal: curved sapphire crystal/ 1.12mm on the edges, 1.95mm on the center.
Straps: one leather band and one gel strap.
Fastener: buckle.
Warranty: 1 year.
Price: Available upon request.

TECHNOSQUARE 3 HANDS   REF:TS3H01

Water Resistant: 330 ft/100 m.
Movement: Swiss ETA 980.163.
Case: stainless steel 316 L resistant to water and air pressure, thermal heights or chemical treatment.
Size: 32x43mm.
Dial: lacquer colors.
Crystal: curved sapphire crystal/ 1.12mm on the edges, 1.95mm on the center.
Straps: one leather band and one gel strap.
Fastener: buckle.
Warranty: 1 year.
Price: Available upon request.

ALPHA SPORT   REF: AQ01

Water Resistant: 660 ft/200 m.
Movement: Swiss ETA G10-71.
Functions: chronograph 1/10 sec. Date Indicator.
Case: stainless steel 316 L resistant to water and air pressure, thermal heights or chemical treatment, sateened.
Size: 40mm.
Crystal: sapphire.
Dial: carbon fiber with colored counters.
Straps: 2 different colored rubber straps.
Fastener: buckle.
Warranty: 1 year.
Price: Available upon request.

ALPHA ROMAN   REF: AR10

Water Resistant: 660 ft/200 m.
Movement: Swiss ETA G10-71.
Functions: chronograph 1/10 sec. Date Indicator.
Case: stainless steel 316 L resistant to water and air pressure, thermal heights or chemical treatment, sateened.
Size: 40mm.
Crystal: sapphire.
Dial: carbon fiber with Roman numerals.
Straps: one crocodile band and one rubber band.
Fastener: buckle.
Warranty: 1 year.
Price: Available upon request.

TECHNODIAMOND-TM   REF: DTMWW

Water Resistant: 660 ft/200 m.
Movement: Swiss ETA G10.
Functions: chronograph 1/10 sec. Date indicator.
Case: stainless steel 316 L resistant to water and air pressure, thermal heights or chemical treatment.
Size: 37.5mm.
Bezel: unidirectional-rotating bezel with 136 full-cut diamonds arranged in a bead setting.
Dial: white mother of pearl with 8 diamond hour-indexes.
Crystal: mineral / 2.6mm.
Straps: one crocodile band and one gel strap.
Fastener: buckle.
Warranty: 1 year.
Price: Available upon request.

ULYSSE NARDIN

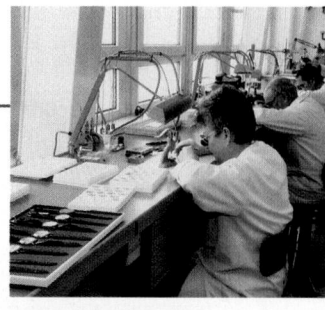

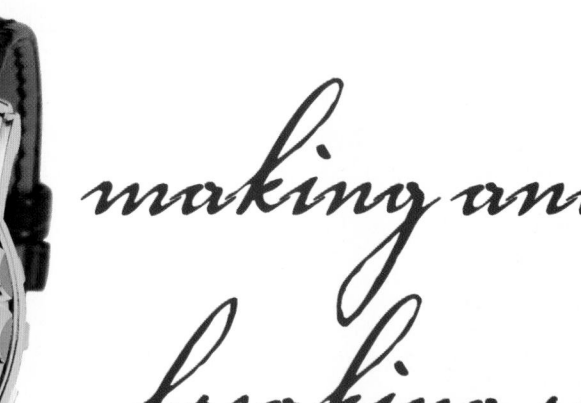

making and breaking records

Since its inception in 1846, this venerable company has laid claim to more than 4,000 awards, including 18 highly coveted gold medals. Building its reputation by perfecting watchmaking technology, Ulysse Nardin fast became a leader in the creation of complicated watches and chronometers. Decade after decade, the brand turned out precision timepieces—many of which broke all previous performance records.

TOP LEFT
Called The Freak, this transparent Tourbillon Carrousel (patent pending) watch has no hands, no dial and no crown.

LEFT CENTER
When the barrel rotates, the fixed rack transmits its power to The Freak movement.

BOTTOM
The case of The Freak watch has no crown. The watch is set by turning the bezel.

In 1983, a group of investors led by Rolf Schnyder purchased Ulysse Nardin. Schnyder was determined that the brand would live up to the glories of its illustrious past. In the two decades since, Schnyder has regularly turned to scientist, inventor and master watchmaker Dr. Ludwig Oechslin to execute his ideas of watchmaking. Among the famed creations fathered by Oechslin: Astrolabium Galileo Galilei, Planetarium Copernicus, Tellurium Johannes Kepler.

Today, Ulysse Nardin's respected status in the watchmaking industry is a direct result of Schnyder's foresight and creativity, Dr. Oechslin's dedication and uncanny knack for invention, and the outstanding skills of the entire Ulysse Nardin watchmaking team. In this past decade alone, Ulysse Nardin has created and produced some of the most complex watches of our time, including the multi-patented, highly acclaimed GMT Perpetual watch which was unveiled two years ago.

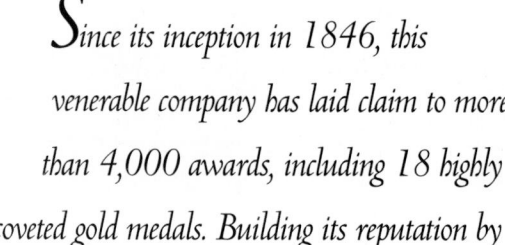

In 2001, Ulysse Nardin once again made timekeeping history with a watch it calls The Freak. A tribute to Oechslin's inventive thinking and to Ulysse Nardin's ability to convert his concepts into extraordinary timepieces, The Freak has several patents pending for its technology. It is an 8-day Tourbillon Carrousel—with no hands, no dial, no crown, and an amazingly simple, novel escapement that needs no lubrication.

To create this concept, the movement and the case had to be radically redesigned. All parts pivot and move in total transparency. Beneath the sapphire crystal of this watch, the entire rotating movement is visible. As the movement rotates from the center, the two bridges indicate the time. The lower bridge indicates the hour, while the upper bridge—fitted with the balance wheel assembly and its patent-pending Dual Direct Escapement—indicates the minutes. Whereas in other tourbillons, the balance wheel assembly moves once every minute in a cage, in the Freak, the whole movement including the balance wheel assembly rotates once an hour inside the watch case.

Oechslin's Dual Direct Escapement invention disposes of the major elements of a traditional anchor escapement. It does not need rubies to reduce friction and it does not require oiling. The mainspring is located underneath the movement and spans across the entire case diameter (much like a dial). Its extra-large size provides The Freak with eight-plus days of power reserve. Turning the caseback winds the main spring. Each full turn is equivalent to a wind-up time of 12 hours. A masterpiece of art, technology and invention, The Freak is set by turning the bezel (including the sapphire crystal) either clockwise or counter clockwise.

Of course, Ulysse Nardin unveiled several other creations in 2001, as well. Among them: The Marine Diver Chronometer 1846 and the Michelangelo UTC. The Marine Diver 1846 is a COSC-certified self-winding chronometer. It is equipped with 48 hours of power reserve, is fitted with a unidirectional bezel with diving scale and is water resistant to 300 meters. The Michelangelo UTC is a world timer watch with a unique time-zone setting system and Ulysse Nardin's patented Big Date double window display. The Michelangelo UTC is crafted either in 18-karat rose gold or in steel.

VACHERON CONSTANTIN

legendary watchmaking

Vacheron Constantin—the very name can conjure images of luxury, tradition and valor. Indeed, this is one of the most revered brands in the history of Swiss watchmaking. Established in the heart of Geneva in 1755, Vacheron Constantin has carried on the art of luxury watchmaking, uninterrupted, for more than 250 years.

LEFT

The Malte Grande Classique is equipped with Vacheron's own Caliber 1400 hand-wound movement.

BELOW LEFT

Vacheron Constantin's Caliber 1400 is designed and built in the company's own workshops.

BELOW RIGHT

The Grande Classique features a transparent caseback to reveal the movement's exceptional finish.

Since its inception, Vacheron Constantin has been a brand driven by perfection. Its founders, Jean-Marc Vacheron and François Constantin, vowed that the watches they produced would reflect the strictest codes of technical excellence and aesthetic beauty. These standards, century after century, have not waned.

Now, attesting to its fine Swiss watchmaking heritage and its venerable reputation, Vacheron Constantin has come full-circle to unveil its own proprietary movement. Designed and developed in its Geneva workshops under the vigilant eyes of Vacheron Constantin's finest engineers and watchmakers, the Caliber 1400 was unveiled in 2001. With this introduction, the brand joins the ranks of the esteemed integrated Manufactures.

The Caliber 1400 is a 20-jeweled hand-wound movement that meets such exacting standards that it has earned the right to carry the coveted Côtes de Genève stamp of excellence. The movement beats at a rate of 28,800 vibrations per hour and provides 40 hours of power reserve. Adjusted in the five classic positions, the movement is an accomplishment in both the technical and artistic venues. Every step in the construction and finishing of the movement must pass a battery of tests and inspections—all designed to ensure the exceptional quality of each proprietary Vacheron Constantin movement.

To unveil its technological advancement, Vacheron Constantin selected the classically elegant Malte case.

The new Malte Grande Classique offers striking elegance and bold personality. Crafted in 18-karat yellow or white gold, the case frames an engine-turned dial with decorative wave pattern and sword-shaped hands. The hours and minutes are read traditionally, while there is a subdial at 6:00 to indicate the seconds.

In addition to this technical feat, Vacheron Constantin continues to unveil masterpieces. One such timepiece is the Openworked Malte Tourbillon. Utilizing the distinctive, curved tonneau-shaped case, Vacheron Constantin has created a skeletonized caliber 1790 with tourbillon. Every component has been painstakingly beveled, pierced and finished with a rare "peacock tail" decorative pattern. The watch is created in either 18-karat pink gold or platinum.

Retaining the bold character of the tonneau case, but finishing it with a slightly sleeker styling, Vacheron Constantin has also unveiled its Royal Eagle watch with a classic, self-winding mechanical movement. The Royal Eagle offers strength of character thanks to its highly polished finish and crisp dial designs. There is a Royal Eagle COSC-certified Chronometer model with Day and Date Calendar and a Royal Eagle Large-Date Chronograph version.

Always true to its clientele, Vacheron Constantin also caters to women of discerning tastes. Striking diamond-adorned watches join the "1972" collection. Based on a concept of the asymmetrical looks of the early 1970s, this watch is available in a variety of mother-of-pearl dial colors, with coordinated straps and features a case set with 46 full-cut Top Wesselton diamonds. As with all Vacheron Constantin watches, the newest 1972 timepieces are clear statements of balance, harmony and individualism.

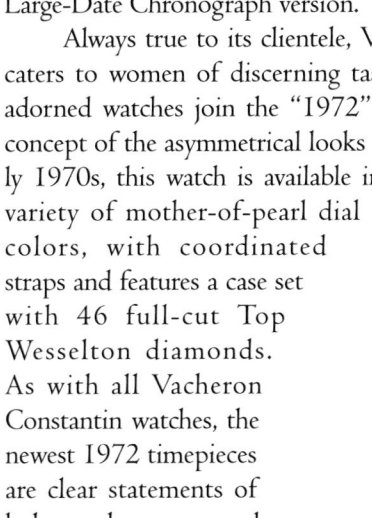

VERSACE

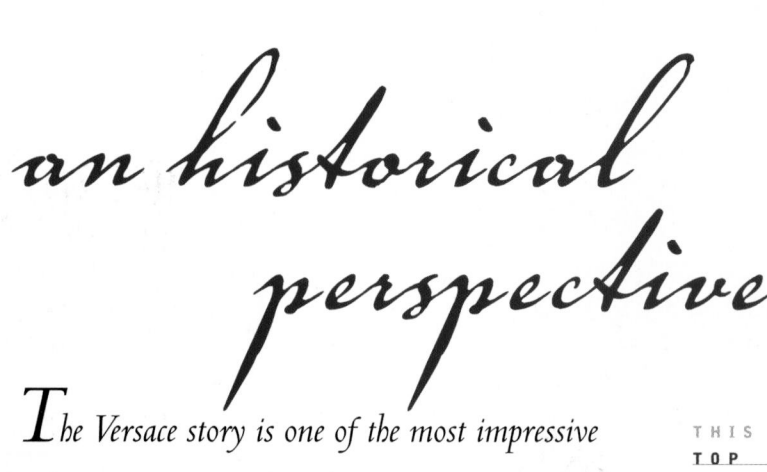

an historical perspective

The Versace story is one of the most impressive legends of our time. Italian-born Gianni Versace started his business with the help of his brother Santo in 1978. Already a prolific freelance designer for top European houses, the then 32-year-old Versace had a flair for defining "different." The first creations unveiled under his own name drew international acclaim and within a decade he had soared to success —winning a multitude of awards and a mass of faithful followers.

THIS PAGE

TOP

Donatella Versace.

CENTER

Versace gold rings depict a flair for shape and contour.

BOTTOM

Versace writing instruments are luxurious renditions indicative of the brand's styling.

FACING PAGE

These Character watches are bold statements of individuality. They feature a python strap in brilliant hues with color-coordinated mother-of-pearl dials.

Versace was known and respected for his ability to bring art and culture into the world of fashion. His bold and creative genius consistently challenged the boundaries of the fashion industry. His designs offered plunging cuts, vibrant prints and subversive accents—but they always embodied the spirit of elegance. Versace's incredible success in luxury clothing led him to delve into the world of accessories, fragrances, makeup, home furnishings and timepieces. Versace originals appeared on stage—outfitting the finest actors on Broadway and the international equivalent.

Year after year, Versace gained international recognition for his designs and the brand quickly became an icon in the global world of top fashion houses. After Gianni's untimely and tragic death in 1997, his sister, Donatella—who had been intimately involved since the brand's inception and had been instrumental in developing the brand's signature advertising style—took over the helm of the Versace global business.

Under the vigilant eye of Donatella, the great house of Versace continued to soar to new heights. Each Versace product line has deftly melded heritage and innovation. Elegance reigns supreme in all collections, as does a decided mark of difference. Couture and accessories alike are bold and beautiful—uniting color and texture, depth and dimension for looks that are definitively Versace.

VERSACE

style

Under Donatella's guidance, the Versace watch line has also climbed to unprecedented heights. Just about three years ago, Donatella targeted the timepiece division as one that needed revamping to more closely reflect the overall Versace image. It was her goal to incorporate bold and brazen color, sharp contours and geometric influences. The new look had to be a distinctive, artful blend of originality that embodied all that the house of Versace stood for.

Donatella brilliantly incorporated her innate sense of style, color and daring spirit into the watches—making each one a true Versace statement. The key to each line is individuality and style. And, in typical Versace tradition, the new watch collections have been soaring successes.

The Versace timepiece collection is built around four main models. The Greca is a rectangular-faced watch with architectural inspiration. The Sapho is a contemporary watch that combines several geometric patterns (including ovals, rectangles and "L" shapes) with mixed finishes for unusual depth and dimension. The Madison series is the brand's resolutely round line with distinctive case-to-bracelet attachments. The Character collection is built around a striking square case that is boldly angled and contoured to perfect dimensions that offer striking style for men and women.

Diamonds and gemstones adorn the collections to varying degrees depending upon Donatella's wishes and the

THIS PAGE

This Character by Versace features luminous hours and markers and is striking in pink python.

FACING PAGE

Elegance and flow are key in Versace jewelry collections.

latest couture unveilings. Certainly, Versace is not afraid to bedeck an entire watch with pale green peridot or bright green emerald if those are the colors of the season. After all, this is a brand built upon brazen leadership and cutting-edge decisions.

Similarly, Versace is ever ready to move into the world of technical timepieces, as long as function follows form. The timepiece collection includes date models, automatics and chronographs. In fact, every Versace timepiece is made in Switzerland according to the strictest standards of watchmaking heritage and Versace quality.

VERSACE

The newest collections from Versace are perhaps best described as bold and colorful. In fact, Versace entered the new millennium with a glamorous look by coordinating dial and strap colors, and adding gemstones and diamonds for maximum sight appeal. Stones such as tourmalines, tsavorites and sapphires offset striking mother-of-pearl dials in bright blue, sparkling pink and dashing green.

Texture came into play in 2001 in a big way, as well, as straps donned geometrical patterns and even nature-inspired designs such as python. In the new Character collection, Versace's two key design directions are incorporated: color and texture. In fact, Versace aptly dubs the Character watches as "chic but shocking."

LEFT

The strength of Character comes into play when set with 32 sapphires and 24 diamonds. The watch is accented with a blue mother-of-pearl dial and blue python strap.

character

Thanks to the bold lines of the square watch, the timepiece is at once sophisticated and stylish. For women, it is a thoroughly modern statement of individuality
and sensuality. The newest Characters blend python straps of royal blue, brilliant pink
and grass green with coordinated gemstones on the bezel and mother-of-pearl dials.

For men, the Character is a rugged watch designed to be worn with bravado.
One particularly striking watch is the new Chrono on Character. A Versace combination of power, technology and elegance, the watch is a thoroughbred of proportions
and volume. The domed sapphire crystal and the oval pushpieces of the chronograph
are enough to emphasize the lines and angles of the watch.

The Chrono on Character houses a quartz chronograph movement endowed with
1/10th of a second, 60-second and 30-minute counters. It also features a date readout at
4:00. The screwed-in crown guarantees water resistance to 30 meters, while its luminous
hands and markers offer maximum readability under any circumstances. The strap of the
Chrono on Character is an unusual microfiber that is tough and resilient. Indeed, Donatella
Versace saw to it that each detail of this watch was carefully planned and executed to ensure
a distinctively elegant setting with a thoroughly Versace twist.

masterpieces

The Versace on Fifth and an all-new Greca were also unveiled in 2001. The Versace on Fifth is an elegant rendition that combines the Versace Grecian frieze with a contemporary, curved rectangular case. The watch features a T-shaped case-to-bracelet attachment that brims with ingenuity in design. The sides of the case are engraved with the Grecian frieze design. The steel version is set with 22 diamonds on the bezel to add a luxurious twist.

The Greca by Versace, a watch that features a Greek architecturally inspired bracelet, has—like the rest of the Versace collection—donned color. The new model includes a striking case-to-bracelet attachment that elegantly displays six gemstones at the top and bottom of the case. The pink mother-of-pearl dial version is set with a total of 12 tourmalines, while the green mother-of-pearl dial version is set with 12 tsavorites.

Of course, Versace carries its color and luxurious design directions through to its other accessories. The striking new Versace on Madison writing instruments, for instance, are sheathed in pink, green or blue python to match the watch collection. The Greca motif is engraved on the pen body and the watch cap carries the Versace logo and head of the Medusa.

TOP LEFT

This steel Versace on Fifth is set with 22 diamonds.

ABOVE

Versace on Madison pen with python sheathing.

BELOW

The Greca by Versace dons color with these striking dials and gemstones.

Similarly, the Vaso collection of jewelry is based on both color and a geometrical interpretation of the Greek symbol. Transformed into a simple square ring, the new Vaso is set with black and white diamonds totaling nearly one carat. Other pieces in the Versace jewelry collection naturally play on geometrics, form, color and the ultimate feel against the body—like every piece of clothing and accessory this design house produces.

Season to season, haute couture pervades each of the brand's collections. From fashions to accessories, Versace remains golden.

ZANNETTI

handmade watches

There is an old saying, "Time is what you make it." Zannetti makes time glamorous, artful and real. This fine watchmaking house located in Rome has been handcrafting watches for three generations, spreading the Italian tradition of fine watchmaking throughout the world.

Beauty. Art. Originality. These are the words that define the Zannetti collection of timepieces. A brand built on passion, Zannetti continues in the footsteps of its founding father, Carmine Zannetti. A master goldsmith enamored with the world of fine mechanics, Zannetti ventured into the world of watchmaking at the turn of the century. His goal was to create a collection of exclusive luxury timepieces that adhered to the strictest standards of perfection.

By paying keen attention to details and adding his own artful touch, Zannetti succeeded beyond his dreams. Carmine Zannetti's son, Mario, also took an avid interest in the world of watches. A famed artist, Mario lent his talent to the Zannetti Maison—introducing great mechanical complications to the stylistically inspired line.

Today, Mario's son, Riccardo, is at the helm of this century-old, full-fledged independent watchmaking company. A man with inherent artistic inclinations, Zannetti is dedicated to preserving the image, style and technical prowess that has built the brand's international success.

Riccardo Zannetti's timepieces bring together realism and fantasy, past and present. The creation of each watch begins as a simple hand drawing. This drawing evolves into a colorful picture that is then redefined and perfected until it is ready for actual production. According to Zannetti, designing a watch is a

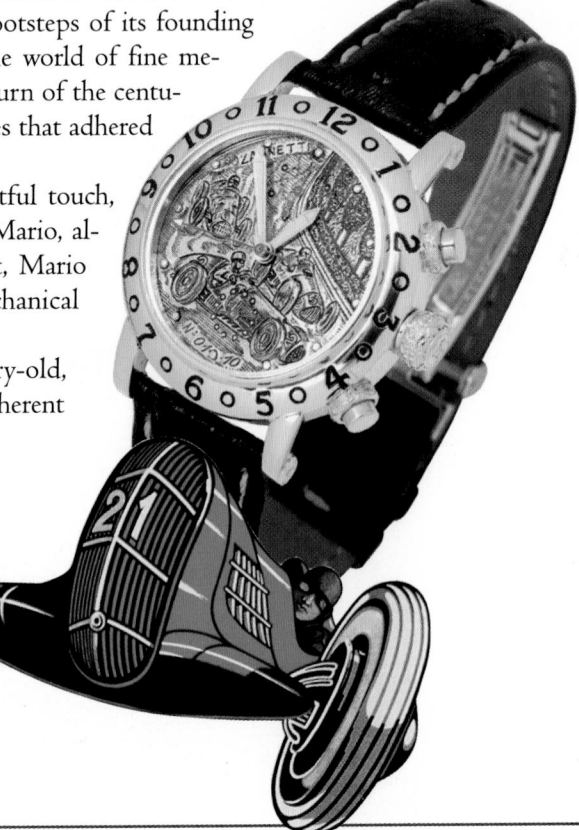

TOP

From the Impero Chronograph Collection, these three watches feature gold or palladium cases, striking mother-of-pearl dials, and enamel accents.

great fascination. It requires time, patience, experience and lots of hard work to bring ideas on paper to fruition.

Zannetti insists on paying the closest attention to every detail. Every Zannetti watch features a case that is hand engraved, finished and polished. All movements are carefully refined and elaborated upon in Zannetti's workshops. Dials are engraved or enameled by hand in procedures that are often incredibly intricate and time consuming. The result is unique watches that offer an individual sense of style and spirit. Among the complications that Zannetti offers are an exquisite minute repeater and elaborate chronographs.

The Impero Chronograph Collection features colorful gold, palladium, enamel and engraved cases with color-coordinated mother-of-pearl dials further brightened by subdial accents in contrasting tones.

In addition to complex watches, Zannetti is a master at bejeweled beauties. Perhaps the most recognizable sign of the Zannetti collection is the Rana Scrigno series. Created in the likeness of a frog and dedicated to women, the Rana (frog) is interpreted through a wide variety of innovative and gorgeous renditions. Some Rana timepieces feature diamonds, rubies, sapphires and other gemstones that adorn the frog and bring it to life. Others are lusciously engraved or embellished otherwise, and often some are strung on silk cords to be worn as pendants rather than wristwatches. Indeed, Zannetti's Rana has become a true symbol of distinction for the brand—one that will serve well into the new millennium.

BOTTOM LEFT

The Rana watch has become a symbol for the brand. The frog opens to reveal the timepiece beneath.

BOTTOM RIGHT

The Rana can also be worn as a pendant.

ZENITH

an historical perspective

Established at the height of prestige watchmaking, the Zenith Manufacture produces measuring instruments and their casings among those most appreciated by connoisseurs.

The Zenith Manufacture was founded in the Swiss Jura, by Georges Favre-Jacot, a visionary of only 22. He believed in changes and in the perfect chord of man to his times. Never renouncing watchmanufacturing tradition, a quality at the beginning of every beautiful movement, he sought to increase productivity while keeping in mind the goal of reaching perfect precision. He understood that the success of his enterprise would depend on total expertise and rationalization of manufacturing operations. Led by an unceasing thirst for innovation, he perfected machine tools and revolutionized the watchmaking habits of Neuchâtel valley.

Success was quick. In 1875, the Manufacture was already employing a third of the population of Le Locle! In 1896, it was rewarded with a gold medal at the Swiss National Fair in Geneva. In 1900, the World Fair in Paris honored it. This wealth of awards and distinctions, recognizing the quality and precision of his watches, would only increase over the years. In 1911, Georges Favre-Jacot renamed the firm: Zenith. According to the legend, this mythical name was chosen after a night-time stroll where the founder discovered a particular resonance between mechanical time and cosmic time. In the second half of the 20th century, Zenith returned to the essentials, and strengthened by its maturity, decided to develop what it was best at. True to its inventive spirit and its faith in progress, Zenith launched the perfect movement: El Primero, the first integrated automatic chronograph, beating at 36,000 alternations per hour. In the late 1960s, new opportunities were opened with quartz. Zenith plunged into this adventure while preciously conserving its tools. In the 1980s, mechanical watches were once again on a roll, Zenith gave a new life to the El Primero movement. And driven by its irrepressible dynamism, the extra-flat Elite movement was introduced in 1994.

THIS PAGE
TOP LEFT

Founding father
Georges Favre-Jacot.

LEFT

Zenith Manufacture
at Le Locle, Switzerland.

FACING PAGE

The ChronoMaster
El Primero watch in
18-Karat rose gold
elegantly houses the
brand's integrated
automatic chronograph
movement.

the perfect movement

THIS PAGE

TOP LEFT

Stamping of a plate.

TOP RIGHT

The Zenith Manufacture
won 1,565 first prizes from
the chronometric Observatory.

RIGHT

The Class Elite HW,
houses the Elite hand-wound
movement with power-
reserve indicator.

Upheld by its remarkable savoir-
faire in traditional watchmaking, it's with
serenity that the Zenith Manufacture,
more avid than ever for innovation and
modernity, makes its entry in the third
millennium. As beautiful outside as it is on
the inside, the watches from the Zenith Manufacture need no artifice to seduce. Beholder
of a unique and prodigious savoir-faire, Zenith
itself conceives, manufactures and assembles its
movements in its workshops in Le Locle. Thus, the
legitimacy of priding itself on the name "Manufacture,"
a term and a guarantee of excellence today.

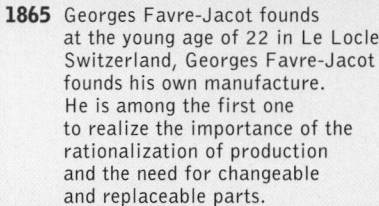

1865 Georges Favre-Jacot founds at the young age of 22 in Le Locle, Switzerland, Georges Favre-Jacot founds his own manufacture. He is among the first one to realize the importance of the rationalization of production and the need for changeable and replaceable parts.

1875 The company already counts several assembly shops and employs a third of the labor force in Le Locle.

1896 Favre-Jacot wins Gold Medal at the Swiss National Fair in Geneva.

1900 The brand wins First Prize at the Grand Prix of Paris.

1903 First Prize in chronometric competition at the Observatory of Neuchâtel.

1907 A series of 6 pockets and bord chronometers are rewarded for their precision.

1911 The firm is officially named "Fabrique des Montres Zenith S.A."; Zenith has accumulated at least 1,565 awards.

1920 The company has already produced more than 2 million watches and has opened in several international markets including Moscow, New York, London, Vienna, Paris...

1954 Zenith beats the record in the category of "wrist-chronometers" at the Observatory of Neuchâtel.

1960 The mechanical movement 5011k appears as the new record holder of absolute precision in its category.

1969 The first integrated automatic chronometer, Zenith's El Primero movement, debuts.

1994 The extra-flat automatic movement, Elite, is voted the Best Mechanical Movement by the International Professional Press.

1999 Zenith joins LVMH, worldwide leader of luxury.

Zenith produces three of the most important mechanical movements of the luxury watch industry – the automatic integrated movement El Primero, the mechanical extra-flat Elite movement, and the hand wound 22-line 5011k movement. Optimizing the integration of the necessary parts of functioning, they are far from cumbersome and come with various complications (moonphase, Fly-Back, Dual-time), enabling Zenith to offer an extended and complete range of watches. Simple to use, extremely reliable, they are evidence of a search for perfection in the smallest details – just as much in the latest advanced micro-mechanics, as in high-tech lubrication, as in aesthetics.

THIS PAGE

TOP

Symbol of excellence, El Primero was the first automatic integrated chronograph movement.

CENTER

The ChronoMaster El Primero watch.

BOTTOM

The extra-flat automatic Elite movement. A thickness of 3.28mm, a real technical achievement.

509

ZENITH

Wearing a Zenith on one's wrist is to identify with a lineage of pioneers – of all those who, following the example of Georges Favre-Jacot, father and founder of the brand, affirm with passion their unshakable will to build and create. Endowed with a tranquil strength, on the fringe of fleeting trends, Zenith expresses an art of living where love for a job well done comes close to the thirst for authenticity: true luxury.

THIS PAGE

TOP LEFT

Class Elite HW

TOP RIGHT

A "Fino" Panama by Montecristi being woven

BOTTOM RIGHT

Class El Primero HW

511

ZENITH

Movement: mechanical, automatic winding, Zenith El Primero caliber 410. Officially certified "chronometer" (C.O.S.C).
Functions: hour, minute, small second, full calendar (date, day, month, moon phase), 3 counters chronograph with a precision rate of 1/10 of a second.
Case: 18 kt rose gold, three-piece case (Ø 40 mm, thickness 12.90 mm), cambered sapphire crystal, anti-reflective coating on both sides, 18 kt rose

gold shaped push-buttons and crown; flat transparent sapphire case back. Water-resistant to 30 meters.
Dial: silvered, guilloché center, 7 polished applied 18 kt rose gold Roman numerals.
Indications: month at 2, minute counter at 3, date between 4 and 5, hour counter and moon phase at 6, small second at 9, day at 10, center second counter, tachometric scale, minute track with divisions for 1/5 of a second.
Bracelet: solid 18 kt rose gold links with double folding clasp.
Also available: platinum, 18 kt yellow gold or stainless steel case; 18 kt yellow gold or stainless steel bracelet; black or brown padded Louisiana alligator strap.

Movement: mechanical, automatic winding, Zenith El Primero caliber 410. Officially certified "chronometer" (C.O.S.C).
Functions: hour, minute, small second, full calendar (date, day, month, moon phase), 3 counters chronograph with a precision rate of 1/10 of a second.
Case: 18 kt yellow gold, three-piece case (Ø 40 mm, thickness 12.90 mm), cambered sapphire crystal, anti-reflective coating on both sides, 18 kt yellow

gold shaped push-buttons and crown; flat transparent sapphire case back. Water-resistant to 30 meters.
Dial: soft white polished, 7 polished applied 18 kt yellow gold Roman numerals.
Indications: month at 2, minute counter at 3, date between 4 and 5, hour counter and moon phase at 6, small second at 9, day at 10, center second counter, tachometric scale, minute track with divisions for 1/5 of a second.
Bracelet: solid 18 kt yellow gold links with double folding clasp.
Also available: platinum, 18 kt rose gold or stainless steel case; 18 kt rose gold or stainless steel bracelet; black or brown padded Louisiana alligator strap.

Movement: mechanical, automatic winding, Zenith El Primero caliber 410. Officially certified "chronometer" (C.O.S.C).
Functions: hour, minute, small second, full calendar (date, day, month, moon phase), 3 counters chronograph with a precision rate of 1/10 of a second.
Case: platinum 950, three-piece case (Ø 40 mm, thickness 12.90 mm), cambered sapphire crystal, anti-reflective coating on both sides, shaped push-but-

tons and crown in platinum. A solid platinum case back. Water-resistant to 30 meters.
Dial: silvered, guilloché center, 7 polished applied white gold Breguet numerals.
Indications: month at 2, minute counter at 3, date between 4 and 5, hour counter and moon phase at 6, small second at 9, day at 10, center second counter, tachometric scale, minute track with divisions for 1/5 of a second.
Strap: deep blue Louisiana alligator with platinum buckle and tongue.
Also available: stainless steel, 18 kt yellow or rose gold case; stainless steel, 18 kt yellow or rose gold bracelet or black or brown padded Louisiana alligator strap.

Movement: mechanical, automatic winding, Zenith El Primero caliber 410. Officially certified "chronometer" (C.O.S.C).
Functions: hour, minute, small second, full calendar (date, day, month, moon phase), 3 counters chronograph with a precision rate of 1/10 of a second.
Case: 18 kt rose gold, three-piece case (Ø 40 mm, thickness 12.90 mm), cambered sapphire crystal, anti-reflective coating on both sides, 18 kt rose gold

shaped push-buttons and crown; flat transparent sapphire case back. Water-resistant to 30 meters.
Dial: silvered, guilloché center, 7 polished applied 18 kt rose gold Roman numerals.
Indications: month at 2, minute counter at 3, date between 4 and 5, hour counter and moon phase at 6, small second at 9, day at 10, center second counter, tachometric scale, minute track with divisions for 1/5 of a second.
Strap: brown Louisiana alligator with 18 kt rose gold buckle and tongue.
Also available: platinum, 18 kt yellow gold or stainless steel case; 18 kt yellow gold or stainless steel bracelet; black or brown padded Louisiana alligator strap.

CHRONOMASTER EL PRIMERO MOON PHASE   REF. 02.0240.410/01

Movement: mechanical, automatic winding, Zenith El Primero caliber 410. Officially certified "chronometer". (C.O.S.C).
Functions: hour, minute, small second, full calendar (date, day, month, moon phase), 3 counters chronograph with a precision rate of 1/10 of a second.
Case: stainless steel, three-piece case (Ø 40 mm, thickness 12.90 mm), cambered sapphire crystal, anti-reflective coating on both sides, shaped push-buttons and crown in solid stainless steel ; flat transparent sapphire case back. Water-resistant to 30 meters.
Dial: silvered, 7 polished applied steel Roman numerals.
Indications: month at 2, minute counter at 3, date between 4 and 5, hour counter and moon phase at 6, small second at 9, day at 10, center second counter, tachometric scale, minute track with divisions for 1/5 of a second.
Bracelet: solid stainless steel links with double folding clasp with push-pieces.
Also available: platinum, 18-karat yellow or rose gold case ; stainless steel, 18-karat yellow or rose gold bracelet ; black or brown padded Louisiana alligator strap.

CHRONOMASTER EL PRIMERO MOON PHASE   REF. 01.0240.410

Movement: mechanical, automatic winding, Zenith El Primero caliber 410. Officially certified "chronometer" (C.O.S.C).
Functions: hour, minute, small second, full calendar (date, day, month, moon phase), 3 counters chronograph with a precision rate of 1/10 of a second.
Case: stainless steel, three-piece case (Ø 40 mm, thickness 12.90 mm), cambered sapphire crystal, anti-reflective coating on both sides, shaped push-buttons and crown in solid stainless steel ; flat transparent sapphire case back. Water-resistant to 30 meters.
Dial: silvered, satin-finished, 7 polished applied steel Roman numerals.
Indications: month at 2, minute counter at 3, date between 4 and 5, hour counter and moon phase at 6, small second at 9, day at 10, center second counter, tachometric scale, minute track with divisions for 1/5 of a second.
Strap: padded black Louisiana alligator with solid steel buckle and tongue.
Also available: platinum, 18-karat yellow or rose gold case ; stainless steel, 18-karat yellow or rose gold bracelet .

CHRONOMASTER EL PRIMERO MOON PHASE   REF. 02.0240.410/21

Movement: mechanical, automatic winding, Zenith El Primero caliber 410. Officially certified "chronometer" (C.O.S.C).
Functions: hour, minute, small second, full calendar (date, day, month, moon phase), 3 counters chronograph with a precision rate of 1/10 of a second.
Case: stainless steel, three-piece case (Ø 40 mm, thickness 12.90 mm), cambered sapphire crystal, anti-reflective coating on both sides, shaped push-buttons and crown in solid stainless steel; flat transparent sapphire case back. Water-resistant to 30 meters.
Dial: black, satin-finished, 7 polished applied steel Roman numerals.
Indications: month at 2, minute counter at 3, date between 4 and 5, hour counter and moon phase at 6, small second at 9, day at 10, center second counter, tachometric scale, minute track with divisions for 1/5 of a second.
Bracelet: solid stainless steel links with double folding clasp with push-pieces.
Also available: platinum, 18-karat yellow or rose gold case; stainless steel, 18-karat yellow or rose gold bracelet; black or brown padded Louisiana alligator strap.

CHRONOMASTER EL PRIMERO MOON PHASE   REF. 01.0240.410/21

Movement: mechanical, automatic winding, Zenith El Primero caliber 410. Officially certified "chronometer" (C.O.S.C).
Functions: hour, minute, small second, full calendar (date, day, month, moon phase), 3 counters chronograph with a precision rate of 1/10 of a second.
Case: stainless steel, three-piece case (Ø 40 mm, thickness 12.90 mm), cambered sapphire crystal, anti-reflective coating on both sides, shaped push-buttons and crown in solid stainless steel; flat transparent sapphire case back. Water-resistant to 30 meters.
Dial: black, satin-finished, 7 polished applied steel Roman numerals
Indications: month at 2, minute counter at 3, date between 4 and 5, hour counter and moon phase at 6, small second at 9, day at 10, center second counter, tachometric scale, minute track with divisions for 1/5 of a second.
Strap: brown padded with solid stainless steel buckle and tongue.
Also available: platinum, 18-karat yellow or rose gold case; stainless steel, 18-karat yellow or rose gold bracelet.

ZENITH

CLASS EL PRIMERO "HW"   REF. 02.0500.420/04

Movement: mechanical, manual winding, Zenith El Primero caliber 420.
Functions: hour, minute, small second, date, 3 counters chronograph with a precision rate of 1/10 of a second.
Case: stainless steel, three-piece case (Ø 40 mm, thickness 11.20 mm) cambered sapphire crystal, anti-reflective coating on both sides, flat transparent sapphire case back, shaped push-buttons and crown in solid stainless steel.

Water-resistant to 100 meters.
Dial: silvered, counters decorated with circular bead patterns, luminescent Arabic numerals and luminescent hands.
Indications: minute counter at 3, date between 4 and 5, hour counter at 6, small second at 9, center second counter, minute track with divisions for 1/5 of a second, tachometric scale.
Bracelet: solid stainless steel links.
Also available: black dial; brown Louisiana alligator strap.

CLASS EL PRIMERO "HW"   REF. 02.0500.420/24

Movement: mechanical, manual winding, Zenith El Primero caliber 420.
Functions: hour, minute, small second, date, 3 counters chronograph with a precision rate of 1/10 of a second.
Case: stainless steel, three-piece case (Ø 40 mm, thickness 11.20 mm) cambered sapphire crystal, anti-reflective coating on both sides, flat transparent sapphire case back, shaped push-buttons and crown in solid stainless steel.

Water-resistant to 100 meters.
Dial: black, counters decorated with circular bead patterns, luminescent Arabic numerals and luminescent hands.
Indications: minute counter at 3, date between 4 and 5, hour counter at 6, small second at 9, center second counter, minute track with divisions for 1/5 of a second, tachometric scale.
Bracelet: solid stainless steel links.
Also available: silvered dial; brown Louisiana alligator strap.

CLASS EL PRIMERO "HW"   REF. 01.0500.420/04

Movement: mechanical, manual winding, ZENITH El Primero caliber 420.
Functions: hour, minute, small second, date, 3 counters chronograph with a precision rate of 1/10 of a second.
Case: stainless steel, three-piece case (Ø 40 mm, thickness 11.20 mm) cambered sapphire crystal, anti-reflective coating on both sides, flat transparent sapphire case back, shaped push-buttons and crown in solid stainless steel.

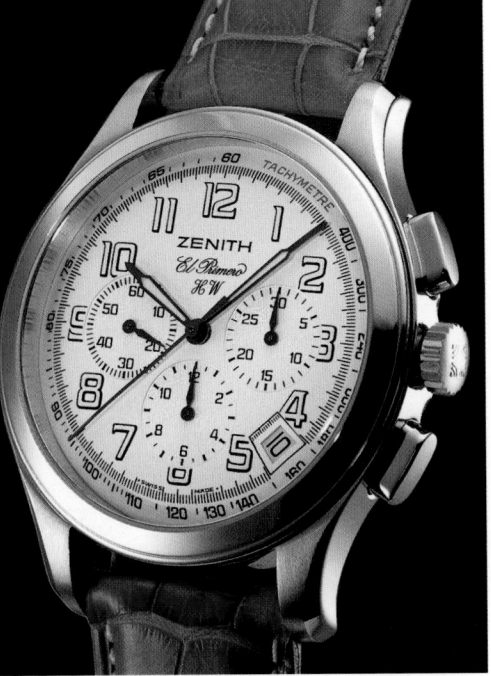

Water-resistant to 100 meters.
Dial: silvered, counters decorated with circular beads patterns, luminescent Arabic numerals and luminescent hands.
Indications: minute counter at 3, date between 4 and 5, hour counter at 6, small second at 9, center second counter, minute track with divisions for 1/5 of a second, tachometric scale.
Strap: brown Louisiana alligator and solid stainless steel buckle and tongue.
Also available: black dial; stainless steel bracelet.

CLASS EL PRIMERO "HW"   REF. 01.0500.420/24

Movement: mechanical, manual winding, ZENITH El Primero caliber 420.
Functions: hour, minute, small second, date, 3 counters chronograph with a precision rate of 1/10 of a second.
Case: stainless steel, three-piece case (Ø 40 mm, thickness 11.20 mm) cambered sapphire crystal, anti-reflective coating on both sides, flat transparent sapphire case back, shaped push-buttons and crown in solid stainless steel.

Water-resistant to 100 meters.
Dial: black, luminescent Arabic numerals and luminescent hands.
Indications: minute counter at 3, date between 4 and 5, hour counter at 6, small second at 9, center second counter, minute track with divisions for 1/5 of a second, tachometric scale.
Strap: brown Louisiana alligator and solid stainless steel buckle and tongue.
Also available: silvered dial; stainless steel bracelet.

CLASS ELITE POWER RESERVE "HW"   REF. 17.1125.655/01

Movement: mechanical, manual winding, extra-flat, Zenith Elite caliber 655.
Functions: hour, minute, small second, date, power reserve.
Case: 18 kt rose gold, three-piece case (Ø 37 mm, thickness 8.00 mm); cambered sapphire crystal, anti-reflective coating on both sides. Water-resistant to 3 ATM.
Dial: silvered, guilloché center, 7 polished applied triangular hour markers, 5 polished applied Arabic numerals.
Indications: power reserve between 12 and 3, date between 4 and 5, small-second (with stopping device) at 9.
Strap: black Louisiana alligator with 18 kt rose gold buckle and tongue.
Also available: stainless steel or 18 kt yellow gold case.

CLASS ELITE "HW"   REF. 17.1125.650/02

Movement: mechanical, manual winding, extra-flat, Zenith Elite caliber 650.
Functions: hour, minute, small second, date.
Case: 18 kt rose gold, three-piece case (Ø 37 mm, thickness 6.80 mm); cambered sapphire crystal, anti-reflective coating on both sides. Water-resistant to 3 ATM.
Dial: silvered, guilloché center, 6 polished applied triangular hour markers, 6 polished applied Arabic numerals.
Indications: date at 3, small second (with stopping device) at 9.
Strap: black Louisiana alligator with 18 kt rose gold buckle and tongue.
Also available: stainless steel or 18 kt yellow gold case.

CLASS ELITE AUTOMATIC   REF. 62.1125.680/21

Movement: mechanical, automatic winding, extra-flat, Zenith Elite caliber 680.
Functions: hour, minute, small second, date.
Case: 18 kt rose gold, three-piece case (Ø 37 mm, thickness 7.80 mm); cambered sapphire crystal, anti-reflective coating on both sides; flat transparent sapphire case back. Water-resistant to 3 ATM.
Dial: black, 6 polished applied triangular hour markers, 6 polished applied Arabic numerals.
Indications: date at 3, small second (with stopping device) at 9.
Bracelet: 18 kt rose gold with a double folding clasp.
Also available: stainless steel or yellow gold case and bracelet / black or brown padded Chesnut alligator strap.

CLASS ELITE AUTOMATIC   REF. 17.1125.680/01

Movement: mechanical, automatic winding, extra-flat, Zenith Elite caliber 680.
Functions: hour, minute, small second, date.
Case: 18 kt rose gold, three-piece case (Ø 37 mm, thickness 7.80 mm); cambered sapphire crystal, anti-reflective coating on both sides; flat transparent sapphire case back. Water-resistant to 3 ATM.
Dial: silvered, 6 polished applied triangular hour markers, 6 polished applied Arabic numerals.
Indications: date at 3, small second (with stopping device) at 9.
Strap: black Louisiana alligator, 18 kt rose gold buckle and tongue.
Also available: stainless steel or yellow gold case and bracelet / brown padded Chesnut alligator strap. All versions are available with silvered or black dial.

ZENITH

CLASS ELITE AUTOMATIC   REF. 60.1125.680/01

Movement: mechanical, automatic winding, extra-flat, Zenith Elite caliber 680.
Functions: hour, minute, small second, date.
Case: 18 kt yellow gold, three-piece case (Ø 37 mm, thickness 7.80 mm); cambered sapphire crystal, anti-reflective coating on both sides; flat transparent sapphire case back. Water-resistant to 3 ATM.

Dial: silvered, 6 polished applied triangular hour markers, 6 polished applied Arabic numerals.
Indications: date at 3, small second (with stopping device) at 9.
Bracelet: 18 kt yellow gold with a double folding clasp.
Also available: stainless steel or rose gold case and bracelet / black or brown alligator strap.

CLASS ELITE "HW"   REF. 30.1125.650/02

Movement: mechanical, manual winding, extra-flat, Zenith Elite caliber 650.
Functions: hour, minute, small second, date.
Case: 18 kt yellow gold, three-piece case (Ø 37 mm, thickness 6.80 mm); cambered sapphire crystal, anti-reflective coating on both sides. Water-resistant to 3 ATM.
Dial: silvered, guilloché center, 6 polished applied triangular hour markers, 6 polished applied Arabic numerals.
Indications: date at 3, small second (with stopping device) at 9.
Strap: brown Chesnut Louisiana alligator with 18 kt gold buckle and tongue.
Also available: stainless steel or 18 kt rose gold case.

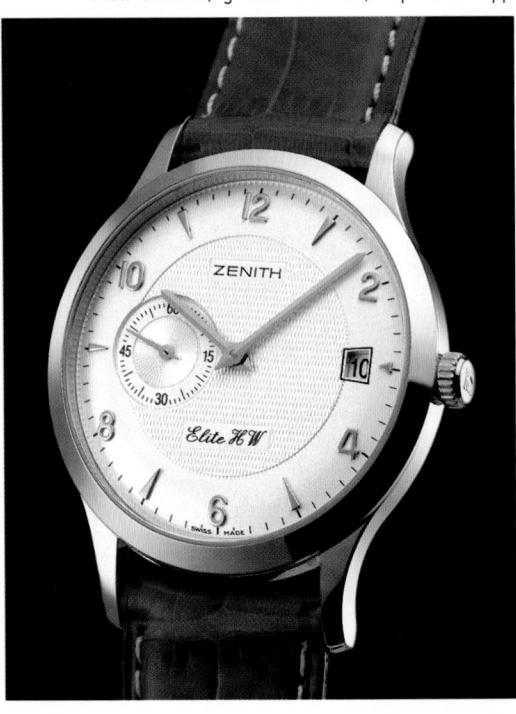

CLASS ELITE POWER RESERVE "HW"   REF. 30.1125.655/01

Movement: mechanical, manual winding, extra-flat, Zenith Elite caliber 655.
Functions: hour, minute, small second, date, power reserve.
Case: 18 kt yellow gold, three-piece case (Ø 37 mm, thickness 8.00 mm); cambered sapphire crystal, anti-reflective coating on both sides. Water-resistant to 3 ATM.
Dial: silvered, guilloché center, 7 polished applied triangular hour markers, 5 polished applied Arabic numerals.

Indications: power reserve between 12 and 3, between 4 and 5, small-second (with stopping device) at 9.
Strap: brown Chesnut Louisiana alligator with 18 kt gold buckle and tongue.
Also available: stainless steel or 18 kt or rose gold case.

CLASS ELITE AUTOMATIC   REF. 30.1125.680/01

Movement: mechanical, automatic winding, extra-flat, Zenith Elite caliber 680.
Functions: hour, minute, small second, date.
Case: 18 kt yellow gold, three-piece case (Ø 37 mm, thickness 7.80 mm); cambered sapphire crystal, anti-reflective coating on both sides; flat transparent sapphire case back. Water-resistant to 3 ATM.

Dial: silvered, 6 polished applied triangular hour markers, 6 polished applied Arabic numerals.
Indications: date at 3, small second (with stopping device) at 9.
Strap: brown Chesnut Louisiana alligator with 18 kt gold buckle and tongue.
Also available: stainless steel or rose gold case and bracelet / and black alligator strap.

CLASS ELITE "HW" — REF. 01.1125.650/02

Movement: mechanical, manual winding, extra-flat, Zenith Elite caliber 650.
Functions: hour, minute, small second, date.
Case: stainless steel, three-piece case (Ø 37 mm, thickness 6.80 mm); cambered sapphire crystal, anti-reflective coating on both sides. Water-resistant to 3 ATM.
Dial: silvered, guilloché center, 6 polished applied triangular hour markers, 6 polished applied Arabic numerals.
Indications: date at 3, small second (with stopping device) at 9.
Strap: black Louisiana alligator with solid stainless steel buckle and tongue.
Also available: 18 kt yellow or rose gold case.

CLASS ELITE AUTOMATIC — REF. 02.1125.680/01

Movement: mechanical, automatic winding, extra-flat, Zenith Elite caliber 680.
Functions: hour, minute, small second, date.
Case: stainless steel, three-piece case (Ø 37 mm, thickness 7.80 mm); cambered sapphire crystal, anti-reflective coating on both sides; flat transparent sapphire case back. Water-resistant to 3 ATM.
Dial: silvered, 6 polished applied triangular hour markers, 6 polished applied Arabic numerals.
Indications: date at 3, small second (with stopping device) at 9.
Bracelet: stainless steel links with a double folding clasp.
Also available: 18 kt yellow or rose gold case and bracelet; black Louisiana alligator strap. All versions are available with silvered or black dial.

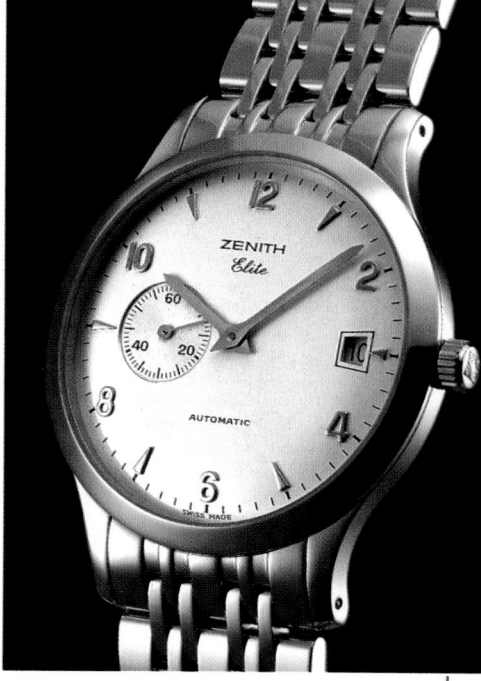

CLASS ELITE POWER RESERVE "HW" — REF. 01.1125.655/01

Movement: mechanical, manual winding, extra-flat, Zenith Elite caliber 655.
Functions: hour, minute, small second, date, power reserve.
Case: stainless steel, three-piece case (Ø 37 mm, thickness 8.00 mm); cambered sapphire crystal, anti-reflective coating on both sides. Water-resistant to 3 ATM.
Dial: silvered, guilloché center, 7 polished applied triangular hour markers, 5 polished applied Arabic numerals.
Indications: power reserve between 12 and 3, date between 4 and 5, small-second (with stopping device) at 9.
Strap: black Louisiana alligator with solid stainless steel buckle and tongue.
Also available: 18 kt yellow or rose gold case.

CLASS ELITE AUTOMATIC — REF. 02.1125.680/21

Movement: mechanical, automatic winding, extra-flat, Zenith Elite caliber 680.
Functions: hour, minute, small second, date.
Case: stainless steel, three-piece case (Ø 37 mm, thickness 7.80 mm); cambered sapphire crystal, anti-reflective coating on both sides; flat transparent sapphire case back. Water-resistant to 3 ATM.
Dial: black, 6 polished applied triangular hour markers, 6 polished applied Arabic numerals.
Indications: date at 3, small second (with stopping device) at 9.
Bracelet: stainless steel links with a double folding clasp.
Also available: 18 kt yellow or rose gold case and bracelet; black Louisiana alligator strap. All versions are available with silvered or black dial.

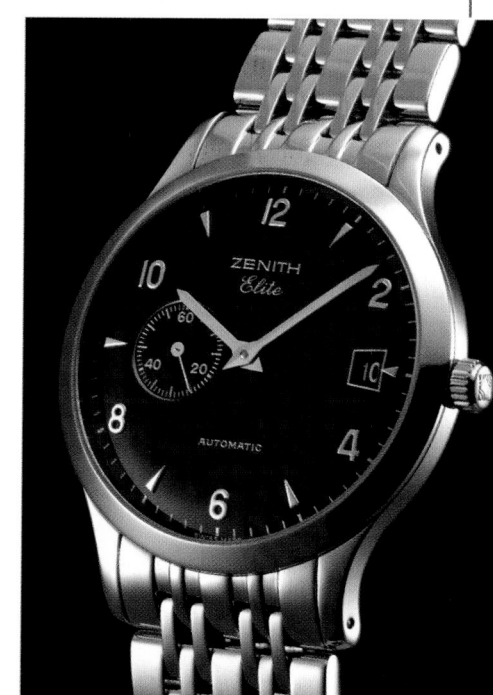

ZENITH

PORT ROYAL EL PRIMERO — REF. 02.0451.400/21

Movement: mechanical, automatic winding, Zenith El Primero caliber 400.
Functions: hour, minute, small second, date, 3 counters chronograph with a precision rate of 1/10 of a second.
Case: stainless steel, three-piece case (Ø 40 mm, thickness 13.00 mm) cambered sapphire crystal, anti-reflective coating on both sides, flat transparent sapphire case back, shaped push-buttons and crown in solid stainless steel. Water-resistant to 50 meters.
Dial: black, counters decorated with circular bead patterns, 4/4 applied rhodium-plated markers and 8/8 painted Arabic numerals.
Indications: minute counter at 3, date between 4 and 5, hour counter at 6, small second at 9, center second counter, minute track with divisions for 1/5 of a second.
Bracelet: solid stainless steel links.
Also available: silvered dial; brown Louisiana alligator strap.

PORT ROYAL ELITE — REF. 02.0451.680/21

Movement: mechanical, automatic winding, Zenith Elite caliber 680.
Functions: hour, minute, small second, date.
Case: stainless steel, three-piece case (Ø 37mm, thickness 8.50 mm) cambered sapphire crystal, anti-reflective coating on both sides, flat transparent sapphire case back. Water-resistant to 50 meters.
Dial: black with 3 applied triangular rhodium-plated hour markers and 8/8 painted Arabic numerals.
Indications: date at 3, small second at 9.
Bracelet: solid stainless steel links with double folding clasp with push-pieces.
Also available: silvered dial; brown Louisiana alligator strap.

PORT ROYAL EL PRIMERO — REF. 01.0451.400/01

Movement: mechanical, automatic winding, Zenith El Primero caliber 400.
Functions: hour, minute, small second, date, 3 counters chronograph with a precision rate of 1/10 of a second.
Case: stainless steel, three-piece case (Ø 40 mm, thickness 13.00 mm) cambered sapphire crystal, anti-reflective coating on both sides, flat transparent sapphire case back, shaped push-buttons and crown in solid stainless steel. Water-resistant to 50 meters.
Dial: silvered, counters decorated with circular bead patterns, 4/4 applied rhodium-plated markers and 8/8 painted Arabic numerals.
Indications: minute counter at 3, date between 4 and 5, hour counter at 6, small second at 9, center second counter, minute track with divisions for 1/5 of a second.
Strap: brown Louisiana alligator with solid stainless steel buckle and tongue.
Also available: black dial; stainless steel bracelet.

PORT ROYAL DUAL TIME — REF. 01.0451.682/01

Movement: mechanical, automatic winding, Zenith Elite caliber 682.
Functions: hour, minute, small second, second time zone, 24-hour indication.
Case: stainless steel, three-piece case (Ø 38.5mm, thickness 9.80 mm) cambered sapphire crystal, anti-reflective coating on both sides, flat transparent sapphire case back. Water-resistant to 50 meters.
Dial: silvered with 12 applied triangular rhodium-plated hour markers and 12 painted Arabic numerals.
Indications: date at 3, small second at 9, second time zone 24-hour display with arrow-point center hand.
Strap: brown Louisiana alligator with solid stainless steel buckle and tongue.
Also available: black dial; stainless steel bracelet.

PORT ROYAL ELITE RECTANGLE
REF. 02.0251.684/01

Movement: mechanical, automatic winding, Zenith Elite Caliber 684.
Functions: hour, minute, small seconds, date.
Case: stainless steel, two-piece rectangular case (height 44 mm, width 31 mm, thickness 7.90 mm), curvilinear sapphire crystal, anti-reflective coating on both sides. Water-resistant to 50 meters.
Dial: silvered, 3 applied triangular rhodium-plated hour markers and 8/8 painted Arabic numerals.
Indications: date at 6, small seconds at 9.
Bracelet: solid stainless steel links, double folding clasp with push-pieces.
Also available: black dial; brown Louisiana alligator strap.

RAINBOW EL PRIMERO "FLY-BACK"
REF. 02.0480.405/24

Movement: mechanical, automatic winding, Zenith El Primero 405 caliber, with Fly-back feature (allowing immediate restarting of the chronograph second hand after a zero setting)
Functions: hour, minute, small second, date, fly-back 3 counters chronograph with a precision rate of 1/10 second.
Case: stainless steel, three-piece brushed case (Ø 40 mm, thickness 12.40 mm); flat sapphire crystal with antireflective treatment on both sides; a bi-directional rotating bezel (60 clicks), with luminescent dot with complete minute track as additional minute counter (with both traditional and count down functions); crown with case protection; screwed-on back. Water-resistant to 10 ATM.
Dial: mat black, with colored minute counter, 9 luminescent Arabic numerals.
Indications: oversized minute counter at 3, date between 4 and 5, hour counter at 6, small second at 9, center fly-back second counter, minute track with divisions for 1/5 of a second, telemetric scale on the flange.
Bracelet: solid steel links with folding clasp with push-pieces.
Also available: shark leather strap; black dial with colored minute counter, stainless steel bracelet.

PORT ROYAL DUAL TIME
REF. 02.0451.682/21

Movement: mechanical, automatic winding, Zenith Elite caliber 682.
Functions: hour, minute, small second, second time zone, 24-hour indication.
Case: stainless steel, three-piece case (Ø 38.5 mm, thickness 9.84 mm) cambered sapphire crystal, anti-reflective coating on both sides, flat transparent sapphire back. Water-resistant to 50 meters.
Dial: black with 12 applied triangular rhodium-plated hour markers and 12 painted Arabic numerals.
Indications: date at 3, small second at 9, second time zone 24-hour display with arrow-point center hand.
Bracelet: solid stainless steel links with double folding clasp with push-pieces.
Also available: silvered dial; brown Louisiana alligator strap.

RAINBOW EL PRIMERO "FLY-BACK"
REF. 02.0470.405/25

Movement: mechanical, automatic winding, Zenith El Primero 405 caliber, with Fly-back feature (allowing immediate restarting of the chronograph second hand after a zero setting)
Functions: hour, minute, small second, date, fly-back 3 counters chronograph with a precision rate of 1/10 second.
Case: stainless steel, three-piece brushed case (Ø 40 mm, thickness 12.40 mm); flat sapphire crystal with antireflective treatment on both sides; bi-directional rotating bezel (60 clicks), black enamelled with complete minute track as additional minute counter (with both traditional and count down functions) and marker with a luminescent dot; crown with case protection; screwed-on back. Water-resistant to 10 ATM.
Dial: mat black, 9 luminescent Arabic numerals.
Indications: oversized minute counter at 3, date between 4 and 5, hour counter at 6, small second at 9, center fly-back second counter, minute track with divisions for 1/5 of a second, telemetric scale on the flange.
Bracelet: solid stainless steel links with folding clasp with push-pieces
Also available: shark leather strap; black dial with colored minute counter, stainless steel bracelet.

Company Addresses

A. LANGE & SÖHNE
Altenberger Strasse 15
D-01768 Glashütte in Sachsen,
Germany
Tel: +49 (35053) 485 41

AUDEMARS PIGUET
1348 Le Brassus, Switzerland
Tel: +41 (21) 845 14 00

BAUME & MERCIER
61, Route de Chêne
1211 Geneva 29, Switzerland
Tel: +41 (22) 707 31 31

BEDAT & C°
45, Rue Agasse
1211 Geneva 29, Switzerland
Tel: +41 (22) 718 01 88

BERTOLUCCI
16, B Champs-Montants
2074 Marin, Switzerland
Tel: +41 (32) 756 75 00

BLANCPAIN
6, Chemin de l'Etang
1094 Paudex, Switzerland
Tel: +41 (21) 796 36 36

BOUCHERON
2, Rue de Monruz
2002 Neuchâtel, Switzerland
Tel: +41 (32) 729 60 20

BREGUET
1344 L'Abbaye, Switzerland
Tel: +41 (21) 841 90 90

BREITLING
Case Postale 1132
2540 Grenchen, Switzerland
Tel: +41 (32) 654 54 54

CARTIER INTERNATIONAL
51, Rue Pierre Charron
75008 Paris, France
Tel: +33 (1) 40 74 62 07

CÉDRIC JOHNER
28, Route de Pressy
1253 Vandoeuvres
Switzerland
Tel: +41 (22) 750 82 13

CHARLES OUDIN
8, Place Vendôme
75001 Paris, France
Tel: +33 (1) 40 15 99 00

CHARRIOL
1227 Prospect Street
La Jolla, CA 92037, USA
Tel: +1 (858) 454 0011

CHAUMET
12, Place Vendôme
75001 Paris, France
Tel: +33 (1) 44 77 24 00

CHOPARD
8, Rue de Veyrot
1217 Meyrin-Geneva 2
Switzerland
Tel: +41 (22) 719 31 31

CHRONOSWISS
Elly Staegmeyr Strasse 12
D-80999 München, Germany
Tel: +49 (089) 892 60 70

CLERC
2, Rue Charles Bonnet
1206 Geneva, Switzerland
Tel: +41 (22) 731 79 31
Tel USA: +1 (800) 840 1447

CONCORD
35, Rue de Nidau
2501 Bienne, Switzerland
Tel: +41 (32) 329 34 00

DANIEL JEANRICHARD
14, Cernil-Antoine
2301 La Chaux-de-Fonds
Switzerland
Tel: +41 (32) 925 70 50

DANIEL MINK
37, Bahnhofstrasse
8001 Zurich, Switzerland
Tel: +41 (01) 211 35 55
Tel USA: +1 (800) 221 6465

DAVID YURMAN
501 Madison Avenue
New York, NY 10022
Tel: +1 (212) 593 11 22

de GRISOGONO
176 bis, Route de St. Julien
1228 Plan-les-Ouates, Switzerland
Tel: +41 (22) 317 10 80

DeLANEAU
29/31, Route de l'Aéroport
1215 Geneva 15, Switzerland
Tel: +41 (22) 799 53 53

DUBEY & SCHALDENBRAND
7, Industries
2316 Les Ponts-de-Martel
Switzerland
Tel: +41 (32) 937 14 30

EBEL
113, Rue de la Paix
2301 La Chaux-de-Fonds
Switzerland
Tel: +41 (32) 912 31 23

FRANCK MULLER
22, Rue de Malagny
1294 Genthod, Switzerland
Tel: +41 (22) 959 88 88

FRANÇOIS-PAUL JOURNE
17, Rue de l'Arquebuse
1204, Geneva, Switzerland
Tel: +41 (22) 322 09 09

FRÉDÉRIQUE CONSTANT S.A.
39, Rue Peillonnex, Chene-Bourg,
1225 Geneva, Switzerland
T: +41 (22) 860 04 40

GEORGES V
4, Rue de Grand-Chêne
1002 Lausanne, Switzerland
Tel: +41 (21) 351 26 26

GEVRIL
23 Dover Terrace
Monsey, NY 10952, USA
Tel: +1 (845) 425 9882

GIRARD-PERREGAUX
1, Place Girardet
2301 La Chaux-de-Fonds
Switzerland
Tel: +41 (32) 911 33 33

GLASHÜTTE ORIGINAL
Altenberger Strasse 1
D-01768 Glashütte in Sachsen
Germany
Tel: +49 (35053) 462 31

**LUXURY TIMEPIECES
INTERNATIONAL S.A.
(GUCCI TIMEPIECES)**
2, Rue de Monruz
2002 Neuchâtel, Switzerland
Tel: +41 (32) 723 06 06

HERMÈS
31a, Erlenstrasse
2555 Brügg, Switzerland
Tel: +41 (32) 366 70 50

HUBLOT
44, Route de Divonne
1260 Nyon 2, Switzerland
Tel: +41 (22) 362 19 70

IKEPOD
38, Rue Saint Hubert
2859 Bassecourt
Switzerland
Tel: +41 (32) 426 80 40

**IWC
(INTERNATIONAL WATCH CO.)**
Baumgarten Strasse 15
8201 Schaffhausen
Switzerland
Tel: +41 (52) 635 65 65

JAEGER-LECOULTRE
8, Rue de la Golisse
1347 Le Sentier, Switzerland
Tel: +41 (21) 845 02 02

JEAN-MAIRET & GILLMAN
11, Chemin du Petray
1222 Vesenaz, Switzerland
Tel: +41 (22) 855 07 60

LEONARD
41a, Route de Chêne
1208 Geneva, Switzerland
Tel: +41 (22) 700 73 53

LOCMAN
Piazza G. da Verrazzano, 7
57034 Marina di Campo, Italy
Tel: +39 (0565) 97 90 02

LONGINES
2610 Saint Imier
Switzerland
Tel: +41 (32) 942 45 25

OFFICINE PANERAI
Via Ludovico di Breme, 44/45
20156 Milano, Italy
Tel: +39 (02) 302 61

OMEGA
96, Rue Stampfli
2500 Bienne 4, Switzerland
Tel: +41 (32) 343 95 80

PARMIGIANI FLEURIER
33, Rue du l'Hopital
2114 Fleurier, Switzerland
Tel: +41 (32) 862 66 30

PATEK PHILIPPE
141, Chemin du Pont du Centenaire
1211 Geneva 2, Switzerland
Tel: +41 (22) 884 20 20

PAUL PICOT
6, Rue du Doubs
2340 Le Noirmont, Switzerland
Tel: +41 (32) 953 15 31

PIAGET
61, Route de Chêne
1208 Geneva, Switzerland
Tel: +41 (22) 707 32 32

POIRAY
4, Rue de la Paix
75002 Paris, France
Tel: +33 (1) 4297 99 00

QUINTING
15, Rue du Tunnel
1227 Carouge-Geneva, Switzerland
Tel: +41 (22) 307 95 45

REPOSSI
6, Place Vendôme
75001 Paris, France
Tel: +33 (1) 4296 42 34

**RICHARD MILLE
HOROMETRIE S.A.**
11, Rue du Jura
2345 les Breuleux, Switzerland
Tel: +41 (32) 954 42 53

ROGER DUBUIS
2, Rue André-de-Garrini
1227 Meyrin, Switzerland
Tel: +41 (22) 783 28 28

ROLEX
3/7, Rue François Dussaud
1211 Geneva, Switzerland
Tel: +41 (22) 308 22 00

SCATOLA DEL TEMPO
Via dei Mille, 17
23891 Barzanò, Italy
Tel: +39 (039) 921 1481

TAG HEUER
14a, Avenue des Champs-Montants
2074 Marin, Switzerland
Tel: +41 (32) 755 60 00

TECHNOMARINE
2915 Biscayne Boulevard
Miami, FL 33137, USA
Tel: +1 (305) 438 0880

ULYSSE NARDIN
3, Rue du Jardin
2400 Le Locle, Switzerland
Tel: +41 (32) 931 56 77

VACHERON CONSTANTIN
1, Rue des Moulins
1204 Geneva, Switzerland
Tel: +41 (22) 310 32 27

VERSACE PRECIOUS ITEMS
645 Fifth Avenue, 12 Floor
New York, NY 10022, USA
Tel: +1 (212) 813 0190

ZANNETTI
Via Monte d'Oro, 18
00186 Roma, Italy
Tel: +39 (06) 687 6651

ZENITH
34, Rue des Billodes
2400 Le Locle, Switzerland
Tel: +41 (32) 930 62 62